Rehabilitation Psychology Desk Reference

CONTRIBUTORS

Laurence M. Binder, Ph.D.
Neuropsychologist, Portland VA Medical Center
Assistant Professor of Medical Psychology
Oregon Health Sciences University
Portland, OR

Grady P. Bray, Ph.D.
Private Practice
Rochester, NY

Bruce Caplan, Ph.D.
Associate Professor
Department of Rehabilitation Medicine
Thomas Jefferson University Hospital
Philadelphia, PA

Bruce M. Coull, M.D.
Chief, Neurology Service, Portland VA Medical Center
Associate Professor of Neurology
Oregon Health Sciences University
Portland, OR

Nancy M. Crewe, Ph.D.
Associate Professor
Department of Rehabilitation Medicine
University of Minnesota
Minneapolis, MN

Jack R. Crisler, Ed.D.
Professor, Rehabilitation Counselor Training Program
University of Georgia
Athens, GA

Stanley Ducharme, Ph.D.
Director of Rehabilitation Psychology
Associate Professor, Department of Rehabilitation Medicine
Boston University School of Medicine
Boston, MA

Michael Dunn, Ph.D.
Spinal Cord Injury Service
Palo Alto VA Medical Center
Palo Alto, CA

Arthur Eberstein, Ph.D.
Institute of Rehabilitation Medicine
New York, NY

Steven G. Fey, Ph.D.
Co-Director, Pain Managment Program
Section of Physical Medicine and Rehabilitation
Virginia Mason Medical Center
Seattle, WA
Clinical Assistant Professor of Rehabilitation Medicine
University of Washington School of Medicine
Seattle, WA

David J. Fordyce, Ph.D.
Co-Director, Neuropsychological Rehabilitation Program
Section of Neuropsychology
Department of Neurosurgery
Presbyterian Hospital
Oklahoma City, OK

Jerome S. Gans, M.D.
Instructor in Psychiatry
Harvard Medical School
Cambridge, MA

John G. Gianutsos, Ph.D.
Institute of Rehabilitation Medicine
New York University Medical Center
New York, NY

Rosamond Gianutsos, Ph.D.
Cognitive Rehabilitation Services
Sunnyside, NY

Meyer S. Gunther, M.D.
Clinical Associate Professor
Departments of Rehabilitation Medicine and Psychiatry
Northwestern University Medical School
Attending Physician (Psychiatrist)
Rehabilitation Institute of Chicago
Chicago, IL

Diane Howieson, Ph.D.
Head, Neuropsychology Section
Portland VA Medical Center
Assistant Professor of Medical Psychology
Oregon Health Sciences University
Portland, OR

James S. Krause
Doctoral Candidate
Department of Rehabilitation Medicine
University of Minnesota
Minneapolis, MN

Jeffrey Levenkron, Ph.D.
Assistant Professor
Department of Psychiatry
University of Rochester School of Medicine
Rochester, NY

William J. Lynch, Ph.D.
Director, Brain Injury Rehabilitation Unit
Palo Alto VA Medical Center
Palo Alto, CA

Jean Muller-Rohland, M.D.
Director, Rehabilitation Unit
Monroe Community Hospital
Rochester, NY

Patrick K. Murray, M.D.
Interim Director
Department of Physical Medicine and Rehabilitation
Cleveland Metropolitan General Hospital
Cleveland, OH

George P. Prigatano, Ph.D.
Clinical Director, Neurological Rehabilitation
Barrow Neurological Institute
Phoenix, AR

Mitchell Rosenthal, Ph.D.
Director of Psychology
Marianjoy Rehabilitation Center
Wheaton, IL

Robert J. Sbordone, Ph.D.
Orange County Neuropsychology Group
Fountain Valley, CA

Judith Shechter, Ph.D.
Department of Rehabilitation Medicine
Thomas Jefferson University Hospital
Philadelphia, PA

Thomas E. Williamson-Kirkland, M.D.
Co-Director, Pain Management Program
Virginia Mason Medical Center
Clinical Assistant Professor of Rehabilitation Medicine
University of Washington School of Medicine
Seattle, WA

Mary Ellen Young, Ph.D.
Assistant Professor
Department of Rehabilitation Counseling
University of Florida
Gainesville, FL

FOR JOAN

Rehabilitation Psychology Desk Reference

Edited by

Bruce Caplan, Ph.D.

Chief Psychologist and Associate Professor
Department of Rehabilitation Medicine
Thomas Jefferson University Hospital
Philadelphia, Pennsylvania

AN ASPEN PUBLICATION®
Apsen Publishers, Inc.

1987

Rockville, Maryland
Royal Tunbridge Wells

Library of Congress Cataloging-in-Publication Data

Rehabilitation psychology desk reference.

"An Aspen publication."
Includes bibliographies and index.
1. Physically handicapped—Rehabilitation—Psychologi-
cal aspects. 2. Physically handicapped—Psychology.
I. Caplan, Bruce. [DNLM: 1. Handicapped—psychology.
2. Rehabilitation—psychology. WB 320 R34623]
RD798.R44   1987   617   86-28834
ISBN: 0-87189-620-6

Editorial Services: Carolyn Ormes

Library of Congress Catalog Card Number: 86-28834
ISBN: 0-87189-620-6

Printed in the United States of America

2 3 4 5

Contents

Preface xiii

Acknowledgments xvii

PART I— PRINCIPAL DIAGNOSTIC CATEGORIES 1

Chapter 1— Spinal Cord Injury: Psychological Aspects 3
*Nancy M. Crewe, Ph.D., and James S. Krause, Ph.D.
Candidate*

Psychophysiologic Consequences of Spinal Cord
Injury 4
Psychological Adjustment to Spinal Cord Injury 8
Emotional Problems Following Spinal Cord Injury 12
Social and Interpersonal Factors 17
Behavioral Changes Resulting from Spinal Cord
Injury 21
Vocational Impact of Spinal Cord Injury 22
Psychological Services to Individuals with Spinal Cord
Injury 23
Special Problems 27

Chapter 2— Traumatic Head Injury: Neurobehavioral
Consequences 37
Mitchell Rosenthal, Ph.D.

Spheres of Disability 38
Course of Recovery 39
Neuropsychological Deficits 43

Mental Competence 47
Cognitive Remediation 48
Behavioral Deficits: Contributing Factors 49
Specific Behavioral Deficits 51
Behavioral Intervention Strategies 53
Social and Family Consequences 55
Vocational Rehabilitation 56
Minor Brain Injury 57
Conclusion 58

Chapter 3— Stroke: Causes, Consequences, and Treatment   65
Laurence M. Binder, Ph.D., Diane Howieson, Ph.D.,
and Bruce M. Coull, M.D.

Types of Stroke 66
Regional Syndromes 69
Factors Related to the Expression of Neuropsychological
    and Neurological Deficits 71
Description of Behavioral Deficits 72
Psychosocial Consequences 81
Treatment of Psychological Consequences 85
Stroke Outcome 91

Chapter 4— Chronic Pain: Psychology and Rehabilitation   101
Steven G. Fey, Ph.D., and Thomas E. Williamson-
Kirkland, M.D.

Characteristics of the Chronic Pain Syndrome 102
Concept of Operant Pain 106
Modern Concept of Multidisciplinary Pain Treatment ... 109
Treatment Outcome Studies 115
What Are the Effective Components of Pain
    Treatment? 120
New Directions in Pain Treatment 123

PART II—   PSYCHOSOCIAL MATRIX: PATIENT,
           FAMILY, AND STAFF   131

Chapter 5— Denial and Depression in Disabling Illness   133
Bruce Caplan, Ph.D., and Judith Shechter, Ph.D.

Denial 135
Depression 144
Conclusion 160

Chapter 6— Family Adaptation to Chronic Illness **171**
Grady P. Bray, Ph.D.

Fear 174
Denial 176
Bargaining 177
Depression 178
Mourning 179
Rapprochement 180
Conclusion 180

**Chapter 7— Facilitating Staff/Patient Interaction in
              Rehabilitation** **185**
Jerome S. Gans, M.D.

Sources of Staff/Patient Conflict 185
Locus of Psychological Intervention 187
Team Attended Psychological Interview 188
Recurring Staff/Patient Difficulties 192
Major Teaching Concepts 210
Summary 216

**Chapter 8— Catastrophic Illness and the Caregivers: Real Burdens
              and Solutions with Respect to the
              Role of the Behavioral Sciences** **219**
Meyer S. Gunther, M.D.

The Staff and Its Distress 221
Suggested Solutions 233
Knowledge Applied: Some Unique Problems
   for the Behavioral Scientist 236

PART III—   REHABILITATION NEUROPSYCHOLOGY **245**

Chapter 9— Neuropsychological Assessment in Rehabilitation **247**
Bruce Caplan, Ph.D.

Issues in Assessment and Interpretation 247
Approaches to Assessment 249
Nonstandard Procedures 250
Interpretation of Test Scores 252
Indications for Reassessment 253
Neuropsychological Tests 254
Conclusion 271

Chapter 10— **Neuropsychological Rehabilitation Program: Presbyterian Hospital, Oklahoma City, Oklahoma** **281**
George P. Prigatano, Ph.D., and David J. Fordyce, Ph.D.

Program Philosophy and Treatment Rationale 282
Patient Selection 284
Methods of Intervention: The Program 286
Medical Consultants 293
Staff Development 293
Clinical Impressions and Ideas Concerning Outcome
  Measures 294

Chapter 11— **Neuropsychological Rehabilitation: Description of an Established Program** **299**
William J. Lynch, Ph.D.

Historical Background 299
Staffing 300
Patient Population 301
Principal Elements of the Program 301
Special Additional Procedures 305
Stages in the Treatment Process 312
Review of Treatment Outcome Data 317
The Emerging Role of Microcomputers 317
Concluding Comments 319

Chapter 12— **A Neuropsychological Approach to Cognitive Rehabilitation within a Private Practice Setting** ... **323**
Robert J. Sbordone, Ph.D.

Private Practice Environment 324
Neuropsychological Assessment Process 325
Cognitive Rehabilitation 335
Summary 340

PART IV— **SELECTED TREATMENT TECHNIQUES** **343**

Chapter 13— **Social Skills and Rehabilitation** **345**
Michael Dunn, Ph.D.

Social Consequences of Motor and Sensory
  Disability 345
Evaluation of Social Skills with
  Rehabilitation Clients 350

Social Skills Training in Rehabilitation 352
Instituting and Conducting a Social Skills Program 355
Conclusions and Suggestions for Future Work 359

**Chapter 14— Computer-Augmented Feedback Displays: Treatment
of Hemiplegic Motor Deficits as a Paradigm 365**
John G. Gianutsos, Ph.D., and Arthur Eberstein, Ph.D.

Role of Feedback in Biological Activities 366
Therapeutic Video Games 372
Combining Feedback with Other Modalities 375
Visual Displays in Equilibrium and Weight Shift
Training 376
Summary 378

**Chapter 15— Behavior Modification in Rehabilitation: Principles
and Clinical Strategies 383**
Jeffrey C. Levenkron, Ph.D.

Medical Applications 385
Conceptual Orientation 386
Principles 387
Clinical Strategies 397
Conclusion 415

PART V— SPECIAL TOPICS 417

Chapter 16— Sexuality and Physical Disability 419
Stanley Ducharme, Ph.D.

Traumatic Head Injury 420
Stroke 423
Spinal Cord Injury 425
Staff Considerations 430
Sexual Attitude Reassessment Programs 432
Conclusion 432
Appendix 16-A 436

**Chapter 17— A New Perspective on Paraprofessionals in
Rehabilitation Counseling 437**
Jack R. Crisler, Ed.D., and Mary Ellen Young, Ph.D.

Dimensions of Professionals and Paraprofessionals 437
Historical Overview of Paraprofessionals in
Counseling 439

Status of Paraprofessionals in Rehabilitation 441
Research on Paraprofessionals 443
Ethical and Professional Issues 445
Recommendations 446

Chapter 18— **Single-Case Experimental Approaches to the
Assessment of Interventions in Rehabilitation 453**
Rosamond Gianutsos, Ph.D., and John Gianutsos, Ph.D.

Specific Design Strategies 456
Detailed Examples 459
Advantages of Single-Case Experimental Designs 467
Conclusion 468

PART VI— **MEDICAL ASPECTS** 471

Chapter 19— **The Medical Aspects of Disabling Conditions:
An Overview** 473
Jean Muller-Rohland, M.D.

Spinal Cord Injury 473
Management of Spinal Injury 477
Cerebrovascular Accident 481
Amputation 488
Head Injury 490
Multiple Sclerosis 494
Guillain-Barré Syndrome 495
Arthritis 496

Chapter 20— **Clinical Pharmacology in Rehabilitation** 501
Patrick K. Murray, M.D.

Pharmacological Principles 501
Central Nervous System Drugs 507
Respiratory Medications 514
Cardiovascular Medications 515
Antirheumatic Drugs 517
Anticoagulants 519
Spinal Cord Injury 520
Gastrointestinal Drugs 520
Conclusion 524

Index 527

Preface

The psychological consequences of physical disability are varied, profound, and far reaching. Patients with disabling conditions of recent onset almost invariably exhibit significant emotional responses. Furthermore, disorders that affect brain function, such as stroke and traumatic head injury, create cognitive, perceptual, memory, and/or language deficits that have additional psychological impact. Members of all therapeutic disciplines are called upon to address these psychosocial and neurobehavioral deficits exhibited by rehabilitation patients. Depression, denial, deficient judgment and insight, impaired memory, loss of language (aphasia)—all of these phenomena are commonly encountered obstacles to successful rehabilitation. Furthermore, research has shown that the barriers to social and vocational reintegration of the disabled person are as likely to derive from emotional or intellectual deficits as from physical limitations. Accurate assessment and effective management of these problems are constant, monumental challenges to rehabilitation clinicians.

The *Rehabilitation Psychology Desk Reference* is a single-source reference for the spectrum of psychological problems encountered in clinical rehabilitation settings. Its particular focus is on the psychological consequences of the conditions that comprise the vast majority of admissions to rehabilitation medicine services—spinal cord injury, head trauma, stroke, and chronic pain. Topics pertaining to the rehabilitation of psychiatric patients are not covered in this book, nor is there material dealing specifically with congenital disabilities, deafness, cancer, or a host of other conditions that traditionally fall within the purview of rehabilitation psychological practice. Containing both descriptive material and guidelines for interventions, the *Desk Reference* offers state-of-the-art summaries of theories and practice in the major domains of contemporary rehabilitation psychology.

Part I presents comprehensive discussions of four conditions commonly encountered in rehabilitation—spinal cord injury, head trauma, stroke, and chronic pain. Crewe and Krause address the psychological consequences of spinal cord injury (SCI). They discuss a number of variables affecting adjustment to the trauma, describe some common emotional reactions, consider the social and vocational impact of SCI, and propose guidelines for psychological intervention. In his review of the sequelae of head injury, Rosenthal describes its epidemiology, emotional and neuropsychological consequences, measures of injury severity and ultimate outcome, and psychosocial and vocational implications. Similarly, most of these areas are covered by Binder, Howieson, and Coull with regard to stroke. They also provide a detailed discussion of the causes of stroke and a description of the various regional arterial syndromes. Fey and Williamson-Kirkland synthesize a wealth of data on the treatment of chronic pain. They discuss the common characteristics of the chronic pain patient, review the concept of operant pain behavior and its treatment by the modern multidisciplinary pain center, critique the outcome research literature, and summarize the effective components of treatment of chronic pain.

The psychological reactions and interactions among patients, families, and staff members are addressed in Part II. Caplan and Shechter discuss the problems of denial and depression, integrating a number of pertinent concepts and findings from fields outside rehabilitation psychology. They analyze the complexities of these two reactions and offer some possible interventions. Bray outlines a scheme of family adaptation, describes common problem behaviors, and suggests management tactics. Gans reports on his provocative technique, the Team Attended Psychological Interview, describing its clinical application and potential for educating rehabilitation staff about patients' psychological states. Gunther details a multitude of burdens that afflict rehabilitation staff, interpreting them in a rich psychiatric framework. He also suggests strategies for avoiding staff burnout.

Part III describes principles and practices in the rehabilitation of brain injured patients. Caplan outlines the role of neuropsychological assessment in the rehabilitation setting and reviews some of the most useful measures. The remaining chapters in this section offer a sampling of approaches to brain injury rehabilitation—two hospital-based programs (Prigatano and Fordyce, and Lynch) and a third developing from private practice (Sbordone). Each chapter discusses staffing issues, patient selection, assessment techniques, and specific remedial interventions.

In Part IV, three treatment techniques with broad applicability to a range of rehabilitation patient population are described. Dunn reviews the literature on the social consequences of physical handicap and describes procedures for developing a social skills training program in rehabilitation. The chapter by Gianutsos and Eberstein addresses the role of biofeedback, with special emphasis on the authors' recent innovative work in enhancing motor function of hemiplegic patients. Levenkron discusses concepts and applications of behavior modification in the rehabilitation setting. He corrects some common misconceptions and provides specific suggestions on the vital components of a behavior modification program.

Part V offers (1) a concise review of the effects of disability on the physiologic and social-emotional aspects of sexual function; (2) an overview of the history and role of peer counseling in rehabilitation; and (3) a description of single-case experimental methodology by which busy clinicians, lacking sufficient time to engage in large-scale research, can contribute to the scientific base required by any clinical enterprise.

Part VI is composed of two chapters concerning medical perspectives of disability. Muller-Rohland provides an overview of the medical aspects of common disabling conditions—head injury, stroke, spinal cord injury, amputation, arthritis, multiple sclerosis, and Guillain-Barré syndrome—with an emphasis on their functional and behavioral implications. Murray offers a primer of clinical pharmacology, describing basic terminology, modes of drug action, and factors affecting patient compliance. He considers the various categories of drugs used with rehabilitation patients.

In recent years, as the field of rehabilitation medicine has continued to develop and grow, there has been an increasing acknowledgment of the salience of psychological factors in the comprehensive rehabilitation of the disabled. I hope that rehabilitation specialists, seeking guidance in their daily confrontations with the emotional, behavioral, and intellectual disturbances of the physically disabled, will find the *Rehabilitation Psychology Desk Reference* a useful tool.

Acknowledgments

I would like to express my gratitute to the many people who have, in one way or another, helped this book come to pass.

First, considerable thanks to each of the contributors to this volume for their diligence, cooperation, and patience.

Laurence Binder, Laura Cushman, Mitchell Rosenthal, and Judith Shechter made helpful suggestions on individual chapters. Grady Bray participated in the initial planning of the book. Charles Gibson, Gary Clark, and other colleagues at the University of Rochester School of Medicine contributed to the stimulating atmosphere in which much of the early work on this book was completed. Jeannette Hassett and Linda Glaser were tireless typists.

Special thanks are due to Mitchell Rosenthal for recommending Aspen Publishers and me to each other.

My association with Aspen Publishers has been a constant source of delight. Margaret Quinlin and Martha Sasser offered endless encouragement, guidance, and wisdom. Gail Chalew's outstanding copy editing skills strengthened most paragraphs. Carolyn Ormes and Betty Bruner made major contributions to production.

Finally, my deepest gratitude goes to my wife, Joan, whose love and good humor have helped to sustain me throughout this lengthy project.

Part I

Principal Diagnostic Categories

Chapter 1

Spinal Cord Injury: Psychological Aspects

Nancy M. Crewe, Ph.D.
James S. Krause, Ph.D. Candidate

The onset of any disability requires psychological as well as physical adaptation. Spinal cord injury (SCI), occurring as it usually does suddenly, unexpectedly, and with dramatic impact, seems to exemplify that fact with particular clarity. Therefore psychological services are an integral part of the process of contemporary SCI rehabilitation. The clinical psychologist may take the lead in this area, but all members of the treating team contribute to the emotional rehabilitation of the SCI patient.

During the initial hospitalization, the patient is likely to be receiving rehabilitation services from an interdisciplinary team of professionals made up of physicians, nurses, therapists, a social worker, a psychologist, and a vocational counselor. The team members may look to the behavioral science personnel for insight into the patient's personality and for guidance regarding effective approaches to treatment. They may also want help with identifying potentially serious emotional problems or reactions.

The role of the mental health professional in treatment of SCI is usually multifaceted. It begins with the provision of counseling to the patient and family members who may need emotional support and help with making decisions and plans. Counseling may address problems created by the injury in any area of life, including self-concept, sexuality, relationships, vocation, and independent living. In addition, other problems, such as chemical dependency, may need attention.

The mental health professional may also serve as an advocate for the patient, mediating disagreements with the staff members and encouraging the patient's active participation in treatment planning. Consultation with staff members is equally important; the psychologist can support other staff members and, using behavioral management skills, increase their effectiveness.

The role of the psychologist in SCI does not end with providing services to the individual patient. Within the hospital, knowledge of psychological principles can help create a treatment environment that encourages positive patient behaviors.

Increasingly, psychologists are participating in efforts to improve social conditions for individuals with disabilities through legislation and community action. They have also frequently participated in research related to SCI.

More than 40 years of research regarding psychological aspects of SCI—literally hundreds of books and articles—have provided a valuable scientific foundation for clinical treatment, but many questions remain unanswered. Trieschmann (1980a and 1980b) undertook a comprehensive review of this literature in the late 1970s, and the reader is referred to her publications for an excellent summary. She noted that, despite all the work that has been done, significant gaps remain in our understanding of the psychological consequences of SCI. One critical problem with published research is the large proportion of cross-sectional studies based on relatively small samples, which makes generalization exceedingly difficult. For example, estimates of the percentage of paraplegics obtaining paid employment in the years following rehabilitation vary from 10 percent (Hardy, 1964) to 88 percent (Hallin, 1968) in the industrialized Western world alone. An equally serious problem is that cross-sectional studies provide little basis for understanding the changes that people experience as they live with SCI. Coping and adaptation must be studied longitudinally. According to Trieschmann, another major shortcoming of published research has been its focus on the individuals with SCI and neglect of the social context in which they live.

A review of literature published since 1980 indicates that the shortcomings identified by Trieschmann still exist. A major longitudinal study of national scope was undertaken in 1977 to provide more definitive information about the psychological, social, and vocational consequences of SCI. Unfortunately, funding for the project was prematurely terminated, not only bringing an end to data collection but also precluding the analysis of most of the data that had already been collected. As a result, rehabilitation specialists must still draw upon a somewhat fragmented body of research findings in addition to their clinical experience in providing psychological services to the person with SCI.

PSYCHOPHYSIOLOGIC CONSEQUENCES OF SPINAL CORD INJURY

The majority of spinal cord injuries affect young, physically active men (Young, Burns, Bowen, & McCutchen, 1982). In most cases they were healthy and strong and had encountered few physical problems before the injury. Then, in a moment's time virtually all aspects of their physical systems were altered. Some of the obvious consequences of the injury include changes in sensation and voluntary motor control, sexual functioning, regulation of internal temperature, blood pressure, and other autonomic functions; impairment of bowel and bladder processes; and possibly the onset of pain, spasticity, and such complications as pressure sores. With survival itself at stake, physical problems receive the "lion's share" of attention during the phase of acute medical treatment. Priority is given to such needs as stabilizing the fracture site, ensuring adequate respiration, and preventing shock. Emotional considerations are likely to be relegated to the background, not only because of the need for urgent medical treatment but also because the injury itself or necessary medication may drastically reduce somatosensory input and cloud the patient's thinking processes, rendering psychological intervention difficult. These effects may help account for the "emotional shock" reaction that is often said to be the first phase of adjustment to disability.

SCI does not directly affect cognitive abilities, but head injury may result from the same accident that produces SCI. Young (1979) reported that 16 percent of paraplegics and 7 percent of quadriplegics in his sample also had major head injuries. Less severe brain injuries may occur even more frequently, but may go unrecognized. Wilmot, Cope, Hall, and Acker (1985) administered a battery of neuropsychological tests to 67 patients in the Northern California Regional SCI Center who met one of the following criteria: (1) quadriplegic with high-energy deceleration accident; (2) documented loss of consciousness at time of injury; (3) significant brainstem or cortical neurologic indicators; and (4) respiratory support required at time of accident. They found that 64 percent of those tested scored mildly to profoundly impaired on the battery. Adjusting for the fact that some subjects had shown evidence of poor academic performance premorbidly, they concluded that 56 percent of those showing impairment had presumably acquired these deficits at the time of injury. The problem of occult brain injury in persons with SCI clearly warrants further attention.

Effects of Sensory Changes

Researchers have suspected that sensory changes resulting directly from the SCI could detract from a person's attention span and intensity of emotional experiences, even if there was no concomitant brain injury. Sensory deprivation results both from impairment of sensory receptors and from prolonged hospitalization and immobilization. It continues beyond the acute phase of injury, especially for those patients with higher and more complete lesions. Some researchers have hypothesized that such reduction in input to the central nervous system (CNS) results in reduced cortical arousal, which, in turn, is believed to detract from task performance and emotional arousal. However, two studies (Hester, 1971; Richards, Hirt, & Melamed, 1982) failed to find a difference in task efficiency between spinal cord injured persons and able-bodied controls.

Schachter and Singer (1962) suggested that emotional responses are determined by two factors: (1) perceived physiologic arousal and (2) interpretation of that arousal. Arousal is interpreted and labeled with reference to the situational context in which it occurs. From this perspective, SCI that leads to reduced awareness of physiologic arousal should produce a correlated degree of diminished emotional response.

Some support for this hypothesis can be found in the literature. Hohmann's (1966) 25 male spinal cord injured subjects reported significant decreases in feelings of anger, fear, and sexual excitement after injury. Men with cervical lesions showed the greatest reduction in emotional feelings. There was no clear pattern of change in grief reactions, possibly because most subjects had difficulty finding comparable situations before injury with which to compare their feelings. The only domain of increased emotional response was sentimentality, e.g., crying while watching sad movies. This finding led Hohmann to conclude that even persons showing sound long-term adjustment may experience some chronic depression after SCI.

Jasnos and Hakmiller (1975) showed slides with varying emotional content to SCI patients with lesions in the cervical, thoracic, or lumbar region. Men with lower lesions showed greater arousal to slides of nude women than to slides of clothed women. No such differences were noted for men with cervical lesions. Men with cervical lesions also reported less intense arousal. Although these results are in line with Hohmann's findings, it must be noted that all subjects with cervical lesions were tested in the hospital, whereas most of the subjects with lumbar injuries were outpatients. The institutional environment alone could have been a factor in decreasing their arousal level, so the results of this study must be interpreted with caution.

Body Image

What happens to an individual's awareness of body structure and bodily functions after SCI? How does the injury influence conception of body size, sensations, perceptions of posture, and movement? Such questions fall under the general topic of body image, which has intrigued researchers for years.

Bors (1951), one of the first researchers to study changes in body image among persons with SCI, examined the phenomenon of phantom sensations that patients describe as feelings of burning, tingling, vibrating, numbness, or tightness. All of Bors' subjects, regardless of age or level of injury, reported such sensations, with the lower limbs generally perceived to be in characteristic positions (flexed or crossed) or enlarged. In a later study, Conomy (1973) identified three general types of body image disturbance: disordered perception of the body in space, inaccurate perceptions of posture and movement, and distorted sensations of size and continuity of the limbs. Evidence from experimental research (Arnhoff & Mehl, 1963) has suggested that there are also distorted body boundaries in space after SCI.

Ettlin, Seiler, and Kaeser (1980) studied 37 paraplegic and quadriplegic patients, 18 of whom sustained brain concussions with loss of consciousness at the time of injury. All patients without concussion had phantom sensations of both shape and position of paralyzed limbs. For many of these subjects, the feelings reflected the position of the limbs at injury, and this phenomenon persisted over time. The authors also concluded that the presence of sensations was unrelated to personality strength or past experience. None of the persons with concussion—they were unconscious following injury—had any phantom sensations; instead, they felt as though paralyzed body parts had been amputated.

These perceptual distortions are significant because they are likely to influence a person's ability to learn new physical skills and to function in the environment. Fink and Shontz (1960) noted that rehabilitation requires awareness of one's body and its positions relative to the wheelchair, crutches, parallel bars, and other objects. Distortion of body image makes those tasks more difficult.

Pain

The presence of pain may impede rehabilitation efforts, and the prevalence of pain in persons with SCI is quite high. One survey (Nepomuceno et al., 1979), found that 80 percent of 200 respondents reported abdominal sensations, and 48 percent labeled this discomfort as pain. In 25 percent of the cases the pain was severe and had become progressively worse for 41 percent of the patients. Furthermore, 44 percent stated that pain interfered with their ability to carry out activities of daily living (ADL).

Burke (1973) described three types of chronic pain that may be a complication of SCI: (1) localized or somatic root pain; (2) visceral pain (cramping, diffuse, and vague), and (3) diffuse pain in areas of sensory loss (the generalized burning and tingling pain associated with phantom sensations).

Richards and associates (1980) carefully measured a large number of medical-descriptive (5), demographic (6), psychosocial (9), and familial-social (11) variables in an effort to predict four pain-related outcome variables. Surprisingly, few significant results emerged. Stepwise multiple regression procedures were used to predict presence or absence of pain, severity, onset, and interference with ADL. The independent variables showed a moderate degree of predictive power, accounting for 15 percent, 43 percent, 19 percent, and 44 percent of the variance of these four outcome measures. The best predictors of the different outcome measures were age, verbal IQ, and clinical ratings of distress. With the exception of age, the best predictors of pain were generally psychosocial variables. Physical variables, including injury level, laminectomy, and spinal fusion, failed to predict any of the outcome measures.

Sexual Functioning

Until the 1970s relatively little attention was given to the sexual sequelae of SCI, but since then this area has been an important focus of treatment and research.

Genital functioning is only one aspect of human sexuality, a broad domain that also includes self-concept and intimacy. The ability to participate in sexual relationships and to give and receive satisfaction and pleasure are not necessarily limited by SCI. However, for most individuals changes in physical functioning require certain adaptations in the sphere of sexuality.

Genital sensation requires that the second, third, and fourth sacral nerves be intact; therefore people with SCI cannot perceive touch in this area. In most males with complete lesions, the capacity for responding to psychological arousal with an erection is lost, although reflex erections are usually possible for those with lesions at about T12 and above. Ejaculation does not occur with complete lesions at any level (Donovan, 1981), so the fertility rate for men is extremely low. Women also experience changes in sexual functioning, including reduction in vaginal lubrication and loss of orgasmic capacity; usually, there is a temporary cessation of menses (see Chapter 16). Fertility in women, however, is unaffected by SCI.

Some early reports indicated that the loss of sexual functioning was more distressing to SCI patients than other losses, including bowel and bladder control or the ability to walk (Bloom, 1974; Cole, Chilgren, & Rosenberg, 1973). This conclusion was challenged by Hanson and Franklin (1976), who found that loss of sexual functioning ranked behind those other losses in a study of 54 paraplegic men. They emphasized that individual differences in priorities should be recognized and that sexual concerns should be placed in appropriate perspective.

PSYCHOLOGICAL ADJUSTMENT TO SPINAL CORD INJURY

Premorbid Personality Characteristics

Several authors have sought to define the "modal personality characteristics" of the individual with SCI. Mueller (1962) wrote of uncontrolled emotionality, potential explosiveness, and hostility. Athelstan and Crewe (1979) noted that caregivers often describe these patients as impulsive, rebellious, nonconforming, and difficult to treat. Noting the consistency of premorbid case histories with this behavior, they concluded that these characteristics predate the injury, rather than follow from it. Pertinent empirical data, however, are scarce. Fordyce (1964) compared the circumstances of the accidents of two groups of 12 patients, one characterized as being "imprudent" and the other "nonimprudent." He found that six out of seven Minnesota Multiphasic Personality Inventory (MMPI) measures showed more impulse-dominated behavior among the "imprudent" group.

Based upon her extensive review of the literature, however, Trieschmann (1980a) concluded that people with very heterogeneous personality characteristics become spinal cord injured. Wright (1983, p. 241) also affirmed that "there is no clear evidence of an association between type of physical disability and particular personality characteristics.'' Even if it is possible to describe accurately some modal characteristics, that knowledge should be used only to raise awareness of potential treatment-related concerns, rather than to formulate treatments for individuals. Only an unprejudiced, personalized assessment can serve as an adequate basis for determining an individual patient's needs and concerns.

Certain characteristics, such as suddenness of onset, distinguish SCI from some other disabling conditions, but the process of psychological adjustment is remarkably consistent in many respects across all disabilities. In fact, adjustment to disability resembles the process by which people generally come to terms with changes and loss throughout life. Similarly, the major criteria that have been put forward to describe people who have made a positive adjustment to disability are appropriate yardsticks for people in general: self-esteem, the ability to maintain satisfying relationships, and productivity.

Stage Theories

Probably the most widely known theories of adjustment to SCI are the ''stage'' theories that posit that the onset of a SCI precipitates a given sequence of psychological reactions. Several such theories have been proposed, all based upon clinical impressions (Eisenberg & Gilbert, 1978; Fink, 1967; Gunther, 1969; Hohmann, 1975; Kerr & Thompson, 1972; Shontz, 1965). In actuality, these theories are very similar, each postulating progression through some variant of shock, denial, depression, and adaptation. The basic premise is that the individual moves from the initial impact of injury through defensive reaction to recognition of and accommodation to the disability. Depression is viewed as a consequence of the individual's acknowledgment of the implications of injury and is believed to be a positive step toward adjustment. Some type of resolution is generally included in the final stage.

Vash (1981) proposed a model that involves three stages:

1. recognition of the facts, wherein the individual admits the extent and implications of the disability, but detests it
2. acceptance of the implications, when the changes caused by the disability are integrated into the lifestyle and viewed simply as an inconvenience
3. embracing of the experience, wherein disability is viewed, along with all other life experiences, as an opportunity for learning or a gift that is positively valued

This last stage, transcendence, is a unique aspect of Vash's theory. Only a few individuals reach the point of embracing disability as a catalyst for psychological and spiritual growth, but this small number reflects the small proportion of individuals in the general population who achieve high levels of spiritual development. Trieschmann (1980) has emphasized the paucity of empirical evidence in support of stage theories. Nevertheless, many professionals, as well as patients and families, find them helpful because they suggest a somewhat orderly and predictable process. Furthermore, they offer the promise of change from the early distressing phases. However, a danger lies in the rigid application of these theories; that is, in attempting to make the person and treatment fit the theory, rather than using the theory as an aid in interpreting observed reactions (see Chapter 5).

Wright (1983) has described some characteristic behaviors of individuals who have adapted successfully to disability. These include the ability to subordinate the importance of physique to other values and to transform comparative-status values into asset values; that is, seeing intrinsic value in what one is able to do, not necessarily measuring it against the performance of others.

Dew, Lynch, Ernst, Rosenthal, and Judd (1985) reported a causal analysis of factors predicting self-perceived adjustment to SCI. They found that a physical variable, level of injury, best predicted their most physical criteria, perception of health and perception of activity. On the other hand, perception of pain, which has a strong psychological component, was best predicted by level of education and degree of responsibility for one's accident.

Trieschmann (1980a, p. 309) reviewed many other predictive studies and summarized her findings as follows:

> The research into the factors associated with adjustment to spinal injury reveals that youth, a warm and loving family background, financial resources, a history of accepting responsibility for educational and vocational plans, an internal locus of control, the presence of interpersonal support, creativity in problem solving, having many goals, and having goals in the accomplishment versus physical function area are associated with success in rehabilitation.

Several of these factors deserve special attention and are discussed below.

Self-Esteem

Beliefs related to self-concept or self-esteem are particularly pertinent in discussing response to SCI. Safilios-Rothschild (1970) and Wright (1983) are among the many authors who have asserted that people with physical disabilities have a devalued status in society; to the extent that the SCI individual accepts society's judgment, feelings of inadequacy will follow. However, the findings of Mayer and Eisenberg (1982), as well as of Green, Pratt, and Grigsby (1984), suggest that lowered self-esteem may not be a typical consequence of SCI, at least in the long term. Both projects used the Tennessee Self-Concept Inventory. The 45 men in Mayer and Eisenberg's study produced overall self-concept scores that were not significantly different from the nondisabled standardization group, although their scores on Physical Self-Concept *were* reliably lower. On the latter measure, no significant associations were found with level of lesion or length of injury, but lower scores were obtained for those patients who were older and who reported a larger number of physical symptoms.

The other sample of 71 persons, who were at least 4 years postinjury (Green et al., 1984), produced even more positive results. Although the Physical Self-Concept scores were again below average, the Personal Self, Moral-Ethical Self, and Social Self indices were significantly above scale norms. The authors identified several factors that related to a positive self-concept: perceived independence, provision of one's own transportation, need for more personal assistance, and more independent living arrangements. Impressed by the generally positive self-concepts of subjects, the authors speculated that persons with SCI are compelled to reassess and rebuild their identity and in doing so may actually develop a more positive view of self than the norm. This description of "growth through adversity" resembles Vash's concept of transcendence.

Goals

Goals have also been identified as instrumental in shaping response to disability. Relevant questions on this subject include: To what extent are individuals able to describe what they are working to achieve? Are the goals confined to a single area, such as physical recovery, or are they diverse? Are they likely to be achieved, or do they seem unreachable? Kemp and Vash (1971) found a strong relationship between goals and productivity in their sample of 50 persons with SCI. Younger individuals with many goals were the most productive, followed by older subjects with many goals. Those without goals, regardless of age, were least productive. The more productive subjects also reported more new (postinjury) goals, regardless of level of injury or the length of time since onset of disability.

Cook (1981) studied the relation between goals and motivational patterns in 110 individuals with SCI. He identified four homogeneous groups on the basis of motivational variables and found differences among them in type of goal chosen and its perceived importance.

Locus of Control

Another valuable concept in the study of SCI adjustment is locus of control—the amount of perceived control over life events (Rotter, 1966). Persons with an internal locus of control see themselves as the primary directors of their lives, whereas those with an external locus believe in the dominance of luck, fate, or chance. Studies of able-bodied persons have linked internal locus of control to a variety of positive psychological characteristics.

This construct is relevant to the study of SCI in two ways. First, the circumstances of injury may affect a person's beliefs about locus of control. Athelstan and Crewe (1979) found that persons who bore some direct responsibility for their SCI were better adjusted years later than were individuals who were innocent victims of a chance accident. Given the drastic consequences of SCI, perhaps the latter individuals were unable to maintain a conviction that their own actions would really govern their lives. A shift to a belief that control is external (or reinforcement of a previously held belief to that effect) would likely sap the person's motivation to struggle toward difficult goals, producing instead a compliant surrender to fate.

Locus of control has also been hypothesized to affect adjustment to disability. The research evidence is mixed, but most of it suggests that any such effect manifests itself in long-term adjustment, rather than in early adjustment patterns. Bulman and Wortman (1977) failed to find any consistent relation between locus of control and other adjustment measures among 29 subjects who were less than 1 year postinjury. Bracken and Bernstein (1980) also found statistically nonsignificant relations between locus of control and 13 of 14 adjustment measures at 1 year postinjury. In a later report using a larger sample (Bracken, Shepard, & Webb, 1981), internal control was significantly correlated with seven adjustment measures, although the magnitude of the correlations was modest (.15 to .27).

In another large study (Shadish, Hickman, & Arrick, 1981) utilizing subjects who were from a few weeks to 38 years after injury, external locus of control and time since onset of injury predicted anxiety and psychological distress. However, the authors report that persons high on internal control were equally or more distressed than other patients during the time shortly after injury. This finding suggests that the beneficial effects of internal locus of control are only observed some time after injury.

EMOTIONAL PROBLEMS FOLLOWING SPINAL CORD INJURY

Depression

Depression, which has probably received more attention than any other problem related to SCI, was formerly viewed as an inevitable sequel to this injury. Siller (1969) stated:

Clinically, the reactions of anxiety and depression are the foremost reactions to traumatization and are usually observed readily. On occasion these affects are displaced, delayed, or otherwise disguised so that the superficial clinical picture suggests their absence. . . . A person should be depressed because something significant has happened, and not to respond as such is denial.

In other words, Siller held that depression is always present and is either apparent or is being denied.

Over the years depression has been measured in several different ways: clinical impressions, rehabilitation staff ratings, behavioral measures, biological measures, and self-report. The prevalence rates for depression have varied depending on which procedure was used.

Follow-up studies conducted in the 1950s were based exclusively on impressions from clinical interviews. Although the prevalence of depression varied somewhat between studies, the findings tended to support the view that depression is a universal or near-universal reaction following SCI. Wittkower and associates (Wittkower, Gingras, Mergler, Wigdor & Lepine, 1954), although observing differences in immediate reactions following injury, found that all 50 persons in their sample showed deep depression. Other researchers have not found such high levels. Although suggesting that some immediate depression is observed in all cases, Nagler (1950) rarely found prolonged reactive depression following a cord injury. Thom, Von Salzen, and Fromm (1946) found that 45 percent of their 109 subjects showed some degree of episodic or prolonged depression. Clearly, the amount of depression reported related to the investigator's definition of depression.

Later investigations, based more on standardized self-report measures, found much lower levels of depression than had previous studies. Using the MMPI, Bourestom and Howard (1965) found levels of depression and general distress to be much lower among spinal cord injured patients than patients with rheumatoid arthritis or multiple sclerosis. Scale level, rather than profile configuration, differentiated cord injured patients from other disability types. Similarly, Taylor (1967) found only mild elevation in levels of depression in subjects less than 1 month postinjury. An interesting aspect of Taylor's study was the inclusion of a group of rehabilitation personnel who completed MMPIs on the basis of their estimation of the reaction of individuals after a cord injury. Persons with injuries showed considerably less distress than was predicted by the rehabilitation personnel. This finding suggests that inaccurate expectancies may account for some of the discrepancies between estimates of depression based upon clinical impressions and those based on objective tests.

Taylor (1970) later identified 11 MMPI items that had questionable validity for persons with SCIs. These items reflected aspects of the injury itself—inability to control bladder function, for example—and tended to elevate scores on the first three scales (Hy, D, and Hs). Before correcting for these items, significant differences were present between the SCI group and a control sample of college men. After correction, only scales 4 and 5 (Pd and M-F) remained significantly deviant, reflecting primarily impulsivity and masculinity. Scales 2 and 3, generally taken as evidence for depression and denial, were no longer significantly elevated. This is particularly notable in light of Taylor's (1967) earlier report that the level of measured depression was less than previous clinical judgments had indicated. Kendall, Edinger, and Eberly (1978) later confirmed the need for correction of physically descriptive items when the MMPI is used with individuals who have SCI.

Lawson (1976, 1978) completed what is probably the most detailed research on depression and SCI found in the literature. He followed ten quadriplegic patients for 5 days a week during their entire rehabilitation period, which averaged 119 days. Patients recorded their daily activities to pinpoint significant events in their experience. These events were then studied in relation to depression as measured by four different methods, including self-report, a behavioral measure (spoken words per minute), ratings by hospital personnel, and an endocrine measure (urinary tryptamine). No well-defined periods of depressive affect were noted across patients, and there was a tendency for the level of depression to decrease during the rehabilitation period. Negative personal events, such as being told one's prognosis and unfavorable doctors' verdicts, were related to the greatest depression. Lawson's study was also significant in that it provided the first data to substantiate the position that the rehabilitation team should work actively to combat depression during initial hospitalization, not simply accept or even encourage it as a normal part of the adjustment process. He found that the patients who were less depressed did better not only during rehabilitation but also after return home.

The use of multiple criteria in assessing depression is very important because there is increasing evidence that simple observation by a hospital staff member is often inaccurate. Gans (1981) reviewed 100 consecutive psychiatric consultations in a physical rehabilitation hospital. Patients varied both in terms of physical condition and reason for referral, but Gans found that normal situational reactions were often mistaken for depression. In 16 of 35 cases where depression was suspected by the referring staff, it was not confirmed by the psychiatrist. In contrast, it was diagnosed in nine cases where it had not been suspected. Half of the 28 patients who were diagnosed as depressed had histories of clinical depression that predated their disability. Reactive depression was the most frequent type, especially among people who had relied upon constant physical activity to deal with problems in the past. He pointed out two serious repercussions that can occur from misdiagnosis: (1) Inappropriate medication can cause serious side effects, such as hypotension, cardiac arrhythmias, and confusion; and (2) counterproductive staff-patient interaction can occur as the staff focuses on the patient's hopelessness, rather than on positive qualities.

Fullerton, Harvey, Klein, and Howell (1981) reported on a group of 30 individuals undergoing initial hospitalization for SCI. Nine met Research Diagnostic Criteria for depression, higher than the rate in the general population (5.7 percent), but considerably lower than the universal incidence that some have expected. The authors suggest that the discrepancy may be due to rehabilitation staff members confusing depression with despondency, the latter being a common, generally brief, reaction to serious illness.

MacDonald, Nielson, and Cameron (1984) examined the relationship between degree of measured depression and activity patterns of 53 SCI persons living in the community. They found that mildly depressed individuals were less active socially and in overall frequency than were nondepressed subjects. Nondepressed paraplegic patients were more involved in work, personal, and travel activities than were their depressed counterparts or quadriplegic patients with or without depression.

Suicide and Indirect Self-Destructive Behavior

Given the relatively high incidence of depression among individuals with recent SCI, one would expect to find an elevated rate of suicide as well. Sakinofsky (1980) reviewed the subject with reference to a wide range of disabling conditions including SCI; he concluded that suicide does occur more often than among the general public, but it is nevertheless relatively infrequent. Hackler (1977) conducted a long-term—more than 20 year—study of men who sustained SCI during World War II or the Korean War. He reported that 4 percent of 137 deaths were due to suicide. Geisler, Jouse, and Wynne-Jones (1977) reported a very similar figure of 4.2 percent in a group of Canadians who sustained SCI during World War II and were studied 29 years later. Nyquist and Bors (1967) followed 2,011 SCI patients from the Long Beach Veterans Administration Hospital. Over a period of 19 years, there were 258 deaths, and direct suicide was responsible for 21 (8.1 percent) of that number. That translates into a suicide rate of 1.3 percent for the whole sample. In addition, 28 persons died of undetermined causes, some of which may have been related to neglect or self-destructive behavior.

Nehemkis and Groot (1980) presented an important investigation of the problem of indirect self-destructive behavior (ISDB) among individuals with SCI. They used a multiple-strategy approach, first examining the incidence of ISDB among 200 patients, only 8 (4 percent) of whom had demonstrated direct self-destructive behavior. They asked staff members of a major Spinal Cord Injury Center to indicate whether or not each of these individuals had exhibited ISDB by abusing drugs or alcohol, refusing essential treatment, sitting for prolonged periods of time, or engaging in other potentially harmful forms of neglect. Sixty-eight of the patients were so identified, and among that number 18 had expressed suicidal ideation and 6 had a history of suicide attempts. Nehemkis and Groot studied the autopsy reports of all SCI patients (N = 52) who had died while on the rolls of the Long Beach Veterans Administration Hospital between 1971 and 1976. They expanded the standard NASH taxonomy for classifying deaths (natural, accidental, suicidal, or homicidal), adding first-, second- and third-degree suicide (Lettieri & Nehemkis, 1974). Judgments were based upon four basic dimensions: (1) lifestyle, (2) agents of death, (3) anticipation of lethal consequences, and (4) positively reinforcing aspects of predeath behavior. A number of cases that had previously been classified as death by natural causes were reclassified as second-degree suicide using this system. One example was a C2 level quadriplegic patient who refused treatment for a massive sacral decubitus ulcer, ate improperly, and continued lying in a supine position, causing osteomyelitis and eventually fatal meningitis. They pointed out that it is easier for a person with SCI to engage in ISDB than to avoid it, because health maintenance requires discipline and constant vigilance. They also noted that society is reluctant to intervene in such behavior patterns, especially if the effects of individual actions are small but cumulative. Such behavior may even be condoned, they suggest, because of a commonly held belief that life with a severe disability is of little value.

Missel (1978) provided guidance on management of suicidal behavior in the rehabilitation setting. He reported that 22 of 150 requests for psychiatric consultation were related to suicide risk. He recommended that several steps be taken by the staff; the first step is to examine carefully the psychosocial impact of the disability. What kinds of losses has the patient suffered, and have they undermined self-esteem? What other reality problems face the individual and family? The next step calls for evaluation of the suicidal situation, including the crisis situation, ambivalence that the patient demonstrates, and communication that may shed light on underlying motives and feelings. An evaluation of the suicide risk is the next step, and it hinges on several questions: (1) What has changed in the person's life? (2) how seriously has suicide been considered or intended? and (3) what is the internal emotional message or meaning behind the threats? A careful history is needed, which includes identification of the individual's past strategies for coping with stress and detailed information about current psychosocial circumstances. Clues to the degree of risk come not only from what the patient reports but also from behavioral observation and from the interviewer's subjective reactions to the person. Missel's final step involves management of the suicidal situation. In the case of a transient or first-time episode, the first task is to devise with the patient a specific plan of action that can be taken if suicidal thoughts recur or intensify. In addition, staff members must be informed and the patient's support system, including family, clergy, and friends, should be mobilized.

The patient with chronic or recurrent episodes often has a psychiatric history that predates the disability. Constant demands and accusations may set this individual at odds with the staff and form the basis of a dangerous situation. Missel recommends a well-structured therapy program with explicit limits that are presented in a firm, consistent, and concerned manner by the staff. Patients need assistance in improving their communication and interpersonal skills at the same time that individual responsibility for behavior is emphasized.

Alcohol and Drug Abuse

Until recently, little was written about the common problem of chemical abuse among individuals with SCI. O'Donnell and his colleagues (O'Donnell, Cooper, Gessner, Shehan, & Ashley, 1981/82) reported that a 10-year review of the literature yielded no studies linking alcoholism or drug abuse to SCI. Yet, their investigation of 47 traumatically injured SCI patients treated during a 6-month period at Montebello Center Spinal Cord Unit in Baltimore revealed that 62 percent had alcohol or drug-related injuries. Khella and Stoner (1977) also reported that 60 percent of 101 individuals with SCI admitted to Philadelphia General Hospital reported a history of heavy drinking, and 30 percent had a history of drug addiction.

Seixas (1980) agreed that chemical dependency has been a serious but neglected issue for the rehabilitation professions. He noted that addiction can interact with physical dependency in three important ways: (1) Disability may result from actions or behavior that are the consequences of chemical use; (2) depression, pain, boredom, sleep disturbances, or other psychosocial consequences of disability may cause the individual to turn to alcohol or drugs for relief; and (3) health professionals may actually support addiction because they feel sorry for the individual. O'Donnell and colleagues (1981/82) outlined the hazards of alcohol and recreational drug usage for the person with SCI, including dangerous interaction with prescribed medications and sabotage of an intermittent catheterization program. Despite those dangers, they found that most patients who had a history of abuse before injury resumed use in the later part of the rehabilitation period or within a few months after discharge (32 of of 41 patients). They recommended intensive alcohol education and intervention programs for patients and families.

SOCIAL AND INTERPERSONAL FACTORS

Marital and Family Relationships

There is no doubt that SCI affects the entire family system, but the data on long-term consequences are equivocal. Abrams (1981) summarized three decades of literature relating to marital stability, sexual interaction, and marital satisfaction among paraplegics (see Chapter 16). He concluded that paraplegia does not seriously impair marital functioning.

El Ghatit and Hanson (1976) reported marriage and divorce rates for approximately 700 SCI veterans. They found that 24.4 percent of the marriages that predated the injury and 23.1 percent of those that took place after injury ended in divorce. There is no significant difference between these two figures and the divorce rate for the general population in the United States (27 percent in 1965 and 33 percent in 1970). Several other studies have also found that divorce rates among preinjury marriages approximate those in the general population, but those in postinjury marriages are lower (Comarr, 1962; Crewe, Athelstan, & Krumberger, 1979; Guttman, 1964/65).

Crewe, Athelstan, and Krumberger (1979) identified some differences in emotional tone between pre- and postinjury marriages. As a whole, the latter group seemed to involve less physical dependency even when severity of disability was comparable and were also judged by the participants and the investigators to be happier. It seems that when SCI intervened in an existing relationship the partners often felt that something had been lost or changed in their relationship, and a feeling of sadness or regret seemed to endure. In contrast, those in postinjury marriages had entered the relationship knowing that one of the partners had a disability, so loss was not an issue. It also appeared that individuals who needed personal care assistance had worked out a way of obtaining it before marriage and continued those arrangements thereafter. This minimized the extent to which the person with SCI relied on the spouse for physical care, thus allowing emotional aspects of the relationship to develop.

For years there was speculation about the probable adverse effects on children of being raised by a disabled parent, and this thinking affected custody decisions. Buck and Hohmann (1981, 1982) examined the effect on children of having a spinal cord injured father. They compared 45 children reared from an early age by fathers with SCI with a matched control group of 36 children who had able-bodied fathers. They found that children of disabled fathers were well-adjusted, emotionally stable persons and that they had attained normal sex role identities. No adverse effects were found with regard to health patterns, body image, interpersonal or family relationships, or recreational interests. They found few relationships between severity of disability and more than 150 variables of child personality, attitudes, and behavior.

Cleveland (1976) conducted an intensive study of the impact on families of the SCI incurred by an adolescent son or daughter. She examined changes in roles, communication patterns, and feelings of affection among family members over a 1-year period following the injury. She found that families initially drew together, but this feeling of increased closeness did not last after the disabled youngster had been home for several months. There were few changes in the communication or work patterns of the family immediately following the crisis. By the time a year had passed, however, the families usually recognized the need for outside services. They were most likely to feel satisfied with the assistance they received if the services were being coordinated by a single individual, sparing them the frustrations of dealing with a fragmented delivery system.

Medical and Rehabilitation Services

The system of Regional Model Spinal Cord Injury treatment centers was established to provide more efficient and effective care to SCI patients. The founders of the system argued that this complex disability could not be properly managed by small hospitals that had infrequent experience with SCI. Lack of expertise would lead to such preventable complications as decubitus ulcers and urinary tract infections and to unnecessarily long hospital stays. Presumably, poor initial rehabilitation could lead to incomplete realization of potential over the individual's life-span.

Even among specialized rehabilitation centers, the treatment provided may vary in its effectiveness. Goldiamond (1976) has written a behaviorist view of the reinforcers that he observed as an SCI patient. If, in the interests of efficiency and convenience, a rehabilitation program rewards primarily compliance and dependent behavior, the newly injured person will be poorly prepared to cope with the struggles involved in living with a disability in the community. Unfortunately, there is considerable evidence that hospitals typically provide very little opportunity for patients to exercise independence or decision-making skills, even though these are essential goals of rehabilitation (Trieschmann, 1980a). Mikulic (1971) found that patients are often rewarded for dependent, nonassertive behaviors, but receive punishment when they try to be independent. Trieschmann therefore called for a careful examination of the effects of rehabilitation programs and either to bring them into line with the proclaimed goals of independence or else develop independent living centers where the postmedical rehabilitation process can take place.

Cultural Context

It stands to reason that the medical and economic resources and the cultural heritage of an area will affect the adjustment of persons with SCI (as well as those with other disabilities). A few recent articles from various countries support that point. Jenik (1982) reported on the socioeconomic impact of SCI on 90 patients from the Swiss Paraplegic Centre in Basle. He noted that 77.8 percent of them either were working or had definite plans to do so, 67.8 percent were driving a car, 25 percent had improved their education since the injury, and that, in general, the socioeconomic conditions of the patients were satisfactory. In contrast, Nwuga (1979), reporting a follow-up study of Nigerian paraplegics and quadriplegics, found that most patients had died within 1 year of hospital discharge and that only one of the subjects was employed. A number of other studies describing the situation of persons with SCI in various countries (Gerner, Rauda, & Witterstatter, 1979; Nicklas, 1980; Rosman, Ohry & Rozin 1982; Sutton et al., 1982) further demonstrate the important effect of environment on adjustment to SCI.

Independent Living

The independent living movement has had a significant impact on persons with SCI in the United States and other Western countries. DeJong (1983) traced many of the forces that contributed to the mobilization of disabled citizens, and Varela (1983) has documented the legislative milestones. The results of the movement include heightened visibility among the general population of persons with disability, removal of some architectural barriers, and the development of a variety of services, such as peer counseling and attendant referral and training, particularly in metropolitan areas. Only a decade ago it was common for quadriplegic individuals to be forced into nursing homes because there was no other place for them to get the personal care they needed. Now a number of states provide reimbursement for personal care and homemaking services rendered in the person's own residence. Transitional and cooperative residences have also helped broaden the spectrum of alternatives available to those with SCI.

Societal Attitudes

Other environmental characteristics that influence quality of life for persons with SCI include prevailing societal attitudes toward persons with disabilities. Siller and his colleagues (Siller, Chipman, Ferguson, & Vann, 1967) conducted some significant research on this subject, analyzing the thematic content of the responses of able-bodied people to those with a variety of disabilities. Although they did not specifically investigate SCI, many of their conclusions are pertinent. They found that the vast majority of responses were negative in tone. Seven stable factors were identified:

1. *interaction strain*, stress resulting from uncertainty about what to say or how to behave in the presence of a disabled individual
2. *rejection of intimacy*, unwillingness to be involved in close, personal relationships, particularly marriage, with a person who has a disability
3. *generalized rejection*, reflecting the belief that people with severe disabilities should be segregated from the rest of society
4. *authoritarian virtuousness*, a sort of patronizing benevolence

5. *inferred emotional consequences*, the assumption that a person who has a physical disability is likely to have been emotionally warped by the experience as well
6. *distressed identification*, sadness and pity for the person with a disability
7. *imputed functional limitations*, assumptions that there are many things a person is unable to do because of the disability

Such attitudes are manifested in a variety of ways, both overt and subtle. Able-bodied persons who are inexperienced with disability often feel strain and discomfort that leads them to avoid interaction with people who use wheelchairs (see Chapter 13). They may feel sympathy or pity, rather than plain aversion, but not wanting to risk saying or doing the "wrong thing," they keep their distance. Superficially they may be friendly, but they avoid the extended interaction necessary to remove these attitudinal problems. Poor employment opportunities, apathy regarding architectural accessibility, and social isolation of persons with disabilities are tangible evidence of these barriers.

BEHAVIORAL CHANGES RESULTING FROM SPINAL CORD INJURY

Before the occurrence of SCI, many affected individuals were absorbed by athletics, physically taxing jobs, and active recreation—all pursuits that are drastically changed by SCI. Immediately after the injury, the person is hospitalized and enrolled in a regimen of medical treatment and rehabilitation. This regimen could include confinement to a circle bed and/or encasement in a halo cast with head tongs, as well as considerable social isolation. Ordinary responsibilities and pleasures are suspended, and activity is focused on medical care.

At a later stage of recovery, the behavioral changes brought about by injury depend on the severity of the lesion. For a quadriplegic patient, virtually all physical behavior may be affected to some degree. Performance of such daily personal care routines as dressing and eating may require the assistance of another person. Some activities, such as driving, may require special training and equipment, whereas others, such as running or ice skating, are impossible.

One way of understanding a spinal cord injured person behaviorally is through "functional assessment" of capacities and limitations. Such an examination can be conducted informally or with one of several specially designed instruments (West Virginia Research and Training Center, 1983).

To study the behavioral patterns of persons with SCI, Gordon, Lehman, and Brown (1982) used the Activity Pattern Indicators. They measured participation in ten categories: general activity level, work, education, family role, outside activity, rehabilitation, independent activities, quiet recreation, inactivity, and social activity. Both quadriplegics and paraplegics differed considerably from nondisabled individuals on these measures. The nondisabled persons were significantly more active than paraplegics in five areas—general activity level, work, family role, independent activities, and outside activity—whereas the paraplegics were more involved in school. There was no difference between the two groups on measures of social activities, quiet recreation, inactivity, or rehabilitation. Quadriplegics were also on a par with the nondisabled persons in the area of social activity, and they spent more time in school, quiet recreation, and rehabilitation activities. Conversely, the nondisabled persons were generally more active and spent more time in work, family role, independent activities, outside activities, and inactivity. These data not only confirm the obvious fact that SCI changes a person's activities but they also expand our understanding of the areas in which change does and does not take place.

Cogswell (1968) described a pattern of behavioral change that she observed over 5 years in 36 young adult paraplegics. Upon returning home after rehabilitation they showed marked reductions in social contacts, number of community settings they entered, and social roles they played. Initially they seemed to endure a self-imposed home bound moratorium on socialization, gradually re-entering the community according to a predictable pattern. They tended to phase out relationships with old friends, at first choosing companions of lower social status. If they experienced success in these relationships, they eventually formed new friendships with people of equal status. Similarly they first entered places that presented the fewest architectural or perceived social barriers. Cogswell noted that these individuals left the hospital with only a vague idea of how to go about resuming their lives in the community. She argued that the transition might be facilitated by the development of an explicit plan that included a series of activities to follow. Feelings of distress and confusion might thus be reduced and the process of re-entry expedited.

VOCATIONAL IMPACT OF SPINAL CORD INJURY

Employment is the most visible component of the broader concept, productivity, that includes study, homemaking, volunteer activity, and sheltered work. The definition of what constitutes work is therefore critical in interpreting studies on the impact of SCI. Siegel (1969), for example, reported that 34 percent of the quadriplegics in his follow-up study were competitively employed, but 83 percent were engaged in productive activity.

The employment rates reported for persons with SCI have varied a good deal from one study to another, reflecting differences in definitions, use of small and possibly unrepresentative samples, and variability in geographic and economic conditions. In general, employment rates for quadriplegics have been lower, ranging from 8 percent (Bors, 1956) to 48 percent (Felton & Litman, 1965) than those for paraplegics, which have been reported to be as high as 60 percent (Felton & Litman, 1965) to 85 percent (Guttman, 1962).

Obviously, many factors in addition to severity of injury are likely to influence employability. Some identified factors include younger age (Dvonch, Kaplan, Grynbaum, & Rusk, 1965), better education (Felton & Litman, 1965), positive psychological adjustment (Kemp & Vash, 1971), and the ability to drive (Dvonch et al., 1965). Trieschmann (1980a) pointed out that environmental factors, such as economic disincentives, which have been largely overlooked by researchers, undoubtedly also play a significant role.

Vocational interests of individuals with SCI were investigated by Rohe and Athelstan (1982). The Strong Vocational Interest Inventory, administered to 134 men and 22 women an average of 82 days after the occurrence of SCI, revealed that these individuals tend to be introverted and to prefer working with things, rather than data or people. The "Realistic" theme was the highest of the six vocational areas for 63 percent of the men. This theme is associated with many occupations that require physical abilities that are impossible for a person with SCI. Rohe and Athelstan note that counselors need extra ingenuity to identify suitable vocational alternatives for these individuals.

Despite these complications, people with SCI have successfully entered a wide range of occupations, as demonstrated by more than 100 case histories recorded in a handbook for counselors (Crewe, Athelstan, & Bower, 1978). For the most part, they reported minimal difficulty and substantial job satisfaction. Accommodations made by the employer tended to be modest, including occasional modifications in working hours, adaptive equipment, personal assistance, or job definition, and more than half of the subjects indicated that no modification had been necessary. Work histories in this sample were quite stable, 36 subjects having been in their current positions for 5 years or longer, 40 for 18 months to 5 years, and 15 for less than 18 months.

PSYCHOLOGICAL SERVICES TO INDIVIDUALS WITH SPINAL CORD INJURY

Based upon the research summarized above and the authors' clinical experience, the staff (especially the psychologist) can contribute to the emotional rehabilitation of an individual with SCI in a number of ways.

Emotional Adjustment

During the initial hospitalization following onset of injury, the patient's current emotional state and prospects for long-term adaptation are of concern. Appraisal of the patient's psychological state in the immediate aftermath may be complicated by such factors as physiologic trauma, pain medications, and sensory deprivation. Some early apparent problems may therefore recede as the medical crisis passes.

Assessment

A complete and sensitive assessment is indicated to identify the person's strengths and weaknesses, potential problem areas, and environmental facilitators or barriers to adaptation. A great many facets of a person's life will be affected by SCI, and an even larger number of variables, both personal and environmental, may affect adjustment.

Premorbid personality and behavior patterns deserve special attention in the assessment process. Obviously, the onset of disability causes a massive disruption of the person's physical and behavioral capacities. Nevertheless, after the initial period of trauma has passed, previous emotional and behavior patterns increasingly reassert themselves. Newly disabled individuals are essentially the same people as they were before, with the same strengths and shortcomings that they possessed before the injury. That is why it is important for health professionals to know how the person dealt with problems in the past. Did they withdraw, blame, become depressed, escape, or tackle them directly? Is there a history of chemical use or abuse? What kinds of achievements can they claim? Of course, disability and its consequences may provide the stimulus for changes and new learning, but these will occur gradually and not as a radical transformation. The challenge for the rehabilitation team is somewhat different if the person needs to learn a new set of adaptive behaviors as opposed to reactivating ones that are already available.

Age at the time of onset is related to the specific problems created by the disability and also determines, in part, the person's coping resources. An individual's roles and responsibilities evolve over the years, and those that are most salient at the time of injury are likely to need special attention in the adjustment process. Zager and Marquette (1981), in treating children and young adolescents, found it important to examine the ways in which developmental issues interact with the process of adapting to disability. Even with adults, awareness of developmental factors may provide the key to understanding puzzling responses. At each developmental stage a person fills a variety of overlapping social roles with respect to school or work, family, and community relationships. The rehabilitation specialist might profitably explore the individual's roles at the time of injury and the extent to which each has been disrupted by the event. Perhaps older adults have somewhat more difficulty with adjustment than do younger people, not because they are less flexible emotionally, but because they have entered into a larger number of social roles and so the injury imposes more pervasive changes. Furthermore, these roles are likely to involve high degrees of responsibility and nurturance, such as parent and breadwinner, that conflict with any dependency imposed by the injury.

The related questions of available resources and practical problems created by the onset of disability must also be considered. The individual who lacks adequate financial resources, family support, education, intelligence, and vocational skills is likely to encounter greater difficulties in adjustment.

Adjustment Process

Many rehabilitation professionals have found some variant of the stage theory of adjustment to disability to be a useful model for understanding patient responses. It is essential to recognize, however, that wide variations in individual patterns are common; it is more important for the clinician to be sensitive to the person's actual experience than to fit that experience into a mold.

Depression, which was once considered an essential part of the adjustment process, has been shown to be a common, but not necessarily helpful, response. Depression drains a person's energy and motivation, interfering with performance in a rehabilitation program. In addition, it seems that those who are less depressed during initial rehabilitation also fare best emotionally over the long term. Rather than simply accepting depression as inevitable, the staff members should support the patient in battling against it.

Seligman's (1975) research suggests that the roots of depression can be found in "learned helplessness," the belief that one is powerless to control life's rewards and punishments. To avoid unnecessarily exacerbating depression, hospitals and rehabilitation centers should endeavor to give the patient maximum autonomy over everyday personal decisions. Traditionally, efficiency and staff convenience have been given priority in such matters as scheduling, and "good" patients have been the compliant ones. In contrast, those patients who try to set their own priorities, even for good reason, may be considered troublemakers. For example, a businessman who sustained a T10 SCI in an automobile accident requested a private room with a telephone in the rehabilitation center and insisted that his therapies be scheduled very early in the morning and late in the afternoon so that he could use the midday to conduct business. One indignant staff member exclaimed in team rounds, "Why does he think he's here—to hold sales meetings?" In fact, he *was* there in an effort to hold his life together, and his anxiety and depression would have been intolerable had he been required to forfeit his work for the sake of staff convenience. If it falls to the psychologist or other clinician to take the role of patient advocate in such matters, it is a service well rendered.

Denial or "defensive retreat" is another of the proposed stages of adjustment. Because this reaction has been implicated in the development of such complications as pressure ulcers (Silverman, 1981), rehabilitation specialists have sometimes been encouraged to break through this defense and help patients become more realistic. As a general rule, however, such a tactic is far too simplistic. Most importantly, a wide continuum of responses have been labeled as denial—from appropriate hope to adamant rejection of the implications of disability. The critical guideline for any helping professional is the effect that the presumed denial is having on the individual's well-being. Is the patient lying in bed, refusing treatment and waiting for a miracle, or perhaps neglecting necessary precautions and thereby developing complications? If so, the defense must be confronted and modified so that it no longer supports self-destructive behavior. In the absence of such problems, however, there seems to be scant justification for attacking denial on principle; for example, demanding that patients with complete SCI acknowledge that they will never walk again. This is not to suggest that staff members should cultivate false hopes, but the psychological responses of patients should be respected at the same time that ethical treatment and education are provided.

Counseling

Counseling services are not always welcomed by individuals with recent SCI, perhaps because of their preoccupation with physical recovery. Medical treatment and physical therapy are linked with "getting better," whereas counseling often implies making plans for a future that includes permanent disability. Rohe and Athelstan (1982, p. 290) also attribute some reluctance to the personality characteristics of many such patients:

> They are likely to feel threatened and bewildered by a process that asks them to express innermost thoughts, concerns, and feelings. . . . Psychological intervention that minimizes cognitive and affective treatment and instead emphasizes behavioral techniques seems more likely to be understood and accepted by the majority of persons with SCI.

For individuals who are receptive to counseling, however, a cognitive-behavioral approach has much to offer. This theory holds that a person's feelings and behaviors are not the direct result of events—that is, the onset of disability—but rather ensue from the person's beliefs or attitudes about the events. This hypothesis helps explain why two individuals who experience the same kind of injury may react in very different ways. One might respond with deep depression, ruminating about the losses of function and opportunity engendered by the injury. Further exploration might reveal that the individual feared being a terrible burden on the family, thought all the pleasures of life were past, and believed that the injury was a punishment for past wrongdoing. Alternatively, another person might focus on the miracle of surviving such an accident, believing that life now held special meaning and purpose. A cognitive-behavioral approach to counseling seeks to identify the individual's beliefs and to help the person understand how they shape feelings and behaviors. The perspective that people need not be the helpless victims of events, but instead can work to shape their own adjustment, offers great freedom.

Locus of control, noted above as a significant correlate of adjustment, consists of beliefs about the degree to which people can direct their own lives. Those who conclude that things happen because of luck or chance or powerful outsiders have little incentive to make plans or sacrifice to achieve goals. Yet, planning assumes increased importance following SCI. Counseling might help an individual recognize that belief in an external locus of control is not necessarily grounded in fact, but is instead an assumption, a choice, that has profound consequences. With this understanding, the person might be able to modify that belief, at least to some extent, in the direction of increased internal control.

In addition to dealing with general adjustment issues, counseling for the person with SCI should include attention to sexuality. At the very least, the topic should be raised openly and permission provided for the individual to express feelings and ask questions about it. It is not uncommon for a person with a new SCI to question whether sexuality has been obliterated, and affirmation of one's continued identity as a sexual being is important. In addition, specific information about the effects of injury on physical functioning and education about alternative techniques for giving and receiving sexual pleasure should be provided. A variety of excellent resources is available (e.g., Mooney, Cole & Chilgren, 1975) and should be available in all SCI rehabilitation centers (see Chapter 16).

At times, one of the greatest services that can be provided by an able-bodied rehabilitation specialist is to call upon a person with SCI to serve as a peer counselor. The self-help movement has grown enormously during the past two decades in tribute to the fact that people often learn best from someone else who has "been there." Professional counselors can help ensure that peers are prepared for such responsibility by providing training and consultation (see Chapter 17).

SPECIAL PROBLEMS

Self-Destructive Behavior

Research cited above suggests that indirect self-destructive behavior is more common than suicide and can have the same result. Mental health professionals have a responsibility to be aware of such behavior and to confront it in cooperation with the rehabilitation team. Missel's (1978) suggestions for managing suicidal gestures within the rehabilitation setting are outlined above.

Personality Disorders

Significant psychopathology is rare following SCI, except among individuals with a preinjury history of hospitalization for depression, attempted suicide, or some other severe psychological maladjustment (Hohmann, 1975). A psychiatric consultation is appropriate for the occasional SCI patient who displays psychotic symptoms, and psychotropic medication may be helpful in those cases.

Silverman (1981) outlined management strategies for a number of personality disorders, including the dependent, overdemanding personality (provide attentive, reassuring care to reduce fear of abandonment); the orderly, controlled personality (share medical information, ensure cleanliness and timeliness of treatment, and allow the patient to share in decision making); the dramatic emotionally involved personality (provide personal attention, including recognition by name and encourage grooming to help the individual feel attractive); the long-suffering, self-sacrificing personality (recognize their pain and sacrifices and present the treatment plan as an additional task or burden for the patient); the guarded personality (be friendly without intimacy and avoid personal defensiveness or arguments); the superior personality (acknowledge strengths and minimize staff defensiveness); and the aloof, uninvolved, or schizoid personality (be friendly without attempting intimacy until the patient indicates readiness).

Among other resources are works relating to the management of anxiety (Taylor & Taylor, 1980), aggressive behavior (Gallagher, 1980), difficult behavior (Crewe, 1980), and sleep problems (Moldofsky & Cleghorn, 1980).

Pain

Pain treatment has become an important and specialized area within rehabilitation. Fordyce (1976) pioneered in the behavioral analysis and treatment of pain, and his efforts spurred the creation of comprehensive programs throughout the country. For individuals with SCI, as for those with other disabling conditions whose chronic pain has caused drastic restriction of activity and prolonged reliance on medications, such programs may be appropriate. For pain that is more acute or has less pervasive effects, other approaches, such as relaxation or self-hypnosis, may prove effective (see Chapter 4).

Chemical Dependency

Evidence has been accumulating that a substantial proportion of individuals who sustain SCI have a history of substance abuse, but the problem has been given little attention until recently. Immediately following injury, the focus is on acute medical treatment, and throughout the period of hospitalization access to alcohol is usually limited. Therefore, the rehabilitation team may seldom confront direct evidence of abuse. However, research suggests that individuals who have used alcohol excessively before injury tend to resume that pattern shortly after discharge (O'Donnell et al., 1981/82). Furthermore, some other individuals may begin or increase their use following SCI as a result of boredom or depression.

Rehabilitation team members should help ensure that patients and their families know about the special problems posed by alcohol. Another staff responsibility may be to evaluate patterns of use and to refer patients to specialized treatment programs when appropriate. Furthermore, the rehabilitation environment might inadvertently encourage problem drinking. For example, the staff members in one center developed an informal pattern of taking SCI patients to a local tavern on Friday evenings as a way to build friendships and reward them for the week's work. Following consideration of this issue, however, they turned to other alternatives, including going to outdoor concerts and restaurants.

Brain Injury

Occult head injury is another problem for some individuals with SCI that has only recently received attention (Wilmot et al., 1985). The team psychologist can assist in this area by being attuned to the possibility that such injury may coexist with SCI and testing for it when appropriate. For those with combined SCI and brain injury, the treatment program may need to be specially structured and goals modified to suit the patient's abilities. Cognitive retraining may be added to the usual therapy schedule.

Education and Support for Family Members

Family members of the SCI person experience serious stresses and emotional reactions; they often need counseling and support from the social worker or psychologist on the rehabilitation team (see Chapter 6). Their responses reflect not only their relationship and concern for the injured person but also the new responsibilities that the accident forces them personally to accept. Sometimes family members will keep an almost continuous vigil during acute treatment but may retreat when the individual reaches rehabilitation in order to recover themselves and handle deferred responsibilities. Providing them with services at this time may therefore be difficult. Their need for support is likely to continue and even grow, however, once the SCI member returns home. The rehabilitation specialist should anticipate these needs and help to arrange for follow-up services in the community, including a coordinator of services when possible.

Structure of the SCI Treatment Program

A maximally therapeutic rehabilitation should provide optimal communication between patients and staff and should allow maximum opportunity for patient control over everyday decisions. In the course of responding to problem behaviors, the rehabilitation team members need to be continually aware of the reinforcement structure of the treatment program and the role it may be playing in creating those problems. At the same time, skills in behavioral management should aid the mental health professionals in either modifying the program or developing a protocol for changing the individual's behaviors (see Chapter 15). As specialists on the subject of individual differences, these professionals can also assist staff in avoiding stereotyping of patients and recognizing the uniqueness of each individual.

Community Re-entry

Recognizing the special challenges that individuals with new SCI will face as they return to the community, rehabilitation specialists have designed social skills training programs that help patients become more assertive and otherwise skillful at interacting with others (see Chapter 13). Additionally, they may assume responsibility for linking the patient to community resources for aid with independent living and vocational rehabilitation.

REFERENCES

Abrams, K. (1981). The impact on marriages of adult-onset paraplegia. *Paraplegia, 19*, 253–259.

Arnhoff, F., & Mehl, M. (1963). Body image deterioration in paraplegia. *Journal of Nervous and Mental Diseases, 137*, 88–92.

Athelstan, G., & Crewe, N. (1979). Psychological adjustment to spinal cord injury as related to manner of onset of disability. *Rehabilitation Counseling Bulletin, 22*, 311–319.

Bloom, D. (1974). Sexual aspects of physical disability (spinal cord injured person would rather be sexually active than walk). *American Archives of Rehabilitation Therapy, 22*, 32–39.

Bors, E. (1951). Phantom limbs of patients with spinal cord injury. *Archives of Neurology and Psychiatry, 66*, 610–631.

Bors, E. (1956). The challenge of quadriplegia: Some personal observations in a series of 233 cases. *Bulletin of the Los Angeles Neurological Society, 21*, 105–123.

Bourestom, N., & Howard, M. (1965). Personality characteristics of three disability groups. *Archives of Physical Medicine and Rehabilitation, 46*, 626–632.

Bracken, M., & Bernstein, M. (1980). Adaption to and coping with disability one year after spinal cord injury: An epidemiological study. *Social Psychiatry, 15*, 33–41.

Bracken, M., Shepard, M., & Webb, S. (1981). Psychological response to acute spinal cord injury; An epidemiological study. *Paraplegia, 19*, 271–283.

Buck, F., & Hohmann, G. (1981). Personality, behavior, values, and family relations of children of fathers with spinal cord injury. *Archives of Physical Medicine and Rehabilitation, 62*, 432–438.

Buck, F., & Hohmann, G. (1982). Child adjustment as related to severity of paternal disability. *Archives of Physical Medicine and Rehabilitation, 63*, 249–253.

Bulman, R., & Wortman, C. (1977). Attributions of blame and coping in the "real world": Severe accident victims react to their lot. *Journal of Personality and Social Psychology, 35*, 351–363.

Burke, D. (1973). Pain in paraplegia. *International Journal of Paraplegia, 10*, 297–313.

Cleveland, M. (1976). *Family adaptation to the permanent disablement of a son or daughter.* Unpublished doctoral dissertation. University of Minnesota.

Cogswell, B. (1968). Self-socialization: Readjustment of paraplegics in the community. *Journal of Rehabilitation, 34*, 11–13, 35.

Cole, T., Chilgren, R., & Rosenberg, P. (1973). A new programme of sex education and counseling for spinal cord injured adults and health care professionals. *International Journal of Paraplegia, 11*, 111–124.

Comarr, A. (1962). Marriage and divorce among patients with spinal cord injury. *Journal of the Indian Medical Profession, 9*, 4353–4359.

Conomy, J. (1973). Disorders of body image after spinal cord injury. *Neurology, 23*, 841–850.

Cook, D. (1981). A multivariate analysis of motivational attributes among spinal cord injured rehabilitation clients. *International Journal of Rehabilitation Research, 4*, 5–15.

Crewe, N. (1980). The difficult patient. In D. Bishop (Ed.), *Behavioral problems and the disabled: Assessment and management*. Baltimore: Williams & Wilkins, pp. 98–119.

Crewe, N., Athelstan, G., & Bower, A. (1978). *Employment after spinal cord injury: A handbook for counselors*. Minneapolis: University of Minnesota, Department of Physical Medicine & Rehabilitation.

Crewe, N., Athelstan, G., & Krumberger, J. (1979). Spinal cord injury: A comparison of preinjury and postinjury marriages. *Archives of Physical Medicine and Rehabilitation, 60*, 252–256.

DeJong, G. (1983). Defining and implementing the independent living concept. In N. Crewe & I. Zola (Eds.), *Independent living for physically disabled people*. San Francisco: Jossey-Bass.

Dew, M., Lynch, K., Ernst, J., Rosenthal, R., & Judd, C. (1985). A causal analysis of factors affecting adjustment to spinal cord injury. *Rehabilitation Psychology, 30*, 39–46.

Donovan, W. (1981). Spinal cord injury. In W. Stolov & M. Clowers (Eds.), *Handbook of severe disability*. Washington, DC: U.S. Department of Education, pp. 65–82.

Dvonch, P., Kaplan, L., Grynbaum, B., & Rusk, H. (1965). Vocational findings in post disability employment of patients with spinal cord dysfunction. *Archives of Physical Medicine and Rehabilitation, 46*, 761–766.

Eisenberg, M., & Gilbert, B. (1978). Individual and family reactions to spinal cord injury: Some guidelines for treatment. In M. Eisenberg & J. Falconer (Eds.), *Treatment of the spinal cord injured*. Springfield, IL: Charles C Thomas, pp. 3–18.

El Ghatit, A., & Hanson, R. (1976). Marriage and divorce after spinal cord injury. *Archives of Physical Medicine and Rehabilitation, 57*, 470–472.

Ettlin, T., Seiler, W., & Kaeser, H. (1980). Phantom and amputation illusions in paraplegic patients. *European Neurology, 19*, 12–19.

Felton, J., & Litman, M. (1965). Study of employment of 222 men with spinal cord injury. *Archives of Physical Medicine and Rehabilitation, 46*, 809–814.

Fink, S. (1967). Crisis and motivation: A theoretical model. *Archives of Physical Medicine and Rehabilitation, 48*, 592–597.

Fink, S., & Shontz, F. (1960). Body image disturbances in chronically ill individuals. *Journal of Nervous and Mental Diseases, 131*, 234–240.

Fordyce, W. (1964). Personality characteristics in men with spinal cord injury as related to manner of onset of disability. *Archives of Physical Medicine and Rehabilitation, 45*, 321–325.

Fordyce, W. (1976). *Behavior methods for chronic pain and illness*. St. Louis: CV Mosby Company.

Fullerton, D., Harvey, R., Klein, M., & Howell, T. (1981). Psychiatric disorders in patients with spinal cord injuries. *Archives of General Psychiatry, 38*, 1369–1371.

Gallagher, R. (1980). Aggressive behavior in the disabled. In D. Bishop (Ed.), *Behavioral problems and the disabled: Assessment and management*. Baltimore: Williams & Wilkins, pp. 71–97.

Gans, J. (1981). Depression diagnosis in a rehabilitation hospital. *Archives of Physical Medicine and Rehabilitation, 62*, 386–389.

Geisler, W., Jouse, A., & Wynne-Jones, M. (1977). Survival in traumatic transverse myelitis. *Paraplegia, 14*, 262.

Gerner, H., Rauda, D., & Witterstatter, K. (1979). The social situation of spinal cord injured persons—an empirical study. *International Journal of Rehabilitation Research, 2*, 517–519.

Goldiamond, I. (1976). Coping and adaptive behaviors of the disabled. In G. Albrecht (Ed.), *The sociology of physical disability and rehabilitation*. Pittsburgh: University of Pittsburgh Press.

Gordon, W., Lehman, L., & Brown, M. (1982). *Psychological adjustment and characteristics in recent spinal cord injuries*. (Final report of NIHR Grant 13-P-59127). New York: New York University Medical Center.

Green, B., Pratt, C., & Grigsby, T. (1984). Self-concept among persons with long-term spinal cord injury. *Archives of Physical Medicine and Rehabilitation, 65*, 751–754.

Gunther, (1969). Emotional aspects. In D. Reuge (Ed.), *Spinal Cord Injuries*, Springfield, IL: Charles C Thomas.

Guttman, L. (1962). Our paralyzed fellowmen at work. *Rehabilitation, 43*, 9–17.

Guttman, L. (1964/65). Married life of paraplegics and tetraplegics. *Paraplegia, 2*, 182–188.

Hackler, R. (1977). A 25-year prospective mortality study in the spinal cord injured patients: Comparison with the long-term living paraplegic. *Journal of Urology, 117*, 486–488.

Hallin, R. (1968). Follow-up of paraplegics and tetraplegics after comprehensive rehabilitation. *Paraplegia, 6*, 128.

Hanson, R., & Franklin, M. (1976). Sexual loss in relation to other functional losses for spinal cord injured males. *Archives of Physical Medicine and Rehabilitation, 57*, 291–293.

Hardy, A. (1964). Resettlement problems of paraplegic mineworkers. *Paraplegia, 2*, 157–163.

Hester, G. (1971). Effects of functional transection of the spinal cord on task performance under varied motivation conditions. *Psychophysiology, 8*, 451–461.

Hohmann, G. (1966). Some effects of spinal cord lesions on experienced emotional feelings. *Psychophysiology, 3*, 143–156.

Hohmann, G. (1975). Psychological aspects of treatment and rehabilitation of the spinal injured person. *Clinical Orthopedics, 112*, 81–88.

Jasnos, T., & Hakmiller, K. (1975). Some effects of lesion level and emotional cues on affective expression in spinal cord patients. *Psychological Reports, 37*, 859–870.

Jenik, F. (1982). Social and vocational reintegration of paraplegic and tetraplegic patients in Switzerland. *Paraplegia, 20*, 65–70.

Kemp, B., & Vash, C. (1971). Productivity after injury in a sample of spinal cord injured persons: A pilot study. *Journal of Chronic Disease, 24*, 259–275.

Kendall, P., Edinger, J., & Eberly, C. (1978). Taylor's MMPI correction factor for spinal cord injury: Empirical endorsement. *Journal of Consulting and Clinical Psychology, 46*, 370–371.

Kerr, W., & Thompson, M. (1972). Acceptance of disability of sudden onset in paraplegia. *Paraplegia, 10*, 94–102.

Khella, L., & Stoner, E. (1977). 101 cases of spinal cord injury. *American Journal of Physical Medicine, 56*, 21–32.

Lawson, N. (1976). *Depression after spinal cord injury: A multi-measure longitudinal study*. Unpublished doctoral dissertation, University of Houston, Houston.

Lawson, N. (1978). Significant events in the rehabilitation process: The spinal cord patient's point of view. *Archives of Physical Medicine and Rehabilitation, 59*, 573–579.

Lettieri, D., & Nehemkis, A. (1974). A socio-clinical scale for certifying mode of death. In A.T. Beck, et al. (Eds.), *The prediction of suicide*, New York: Charles Press.

MacDonald, M., Nielson, W., & Cameron, M. (1984). *Depression and activity patterns following spinal cord injury*. Paper presented to the American Psychological Association, Toronto.

Malec, J., & Neimeyer, R. (1983). Psychological prediction of duration of inpatient spinal cord injury rehabilitation and performance of self-care. *Archives of Physical Medicine and Rehabilitation, 64*, 359–363.

Mayer, J., & Eisenberg, M. (1982). Self-concept and the spinal-cord injured: An investigation using the Tennessee Self-Concept Scale. *Journal of Consulting and Clinical Psychology, 50*, 604–605.

Mikulic, M. (1971). Reinforcement of independent and dependent patient behaviors by nursing personnel. *Nursing Research, 20*, 162–164.

Missel, J. (1978). Suicide risk in the medical rehabilitation setting. *Archives of Physical Medicine and Rehabilitation, 59*, 371.

Moldofsky, H., & Cleghorn, J. (1980). Sleep problems in the disabled. In D. Bishop (Ed.), *Behavioral problems and the disabled: Assessment and management*. Baltimore: Williams & Wilkins, pp. 212–236.

Mooney, T., Cole, T., & Chilgren, R. (1975). *Sexual options for paraplegics and quadriplegics*. Boston: Little, Brown & Co.

Mueller, A. (1962). Psychologic factors in rehabilitation of paraplegic patients. *Archives of Physical Medicine and Rehabilitation, 43*, 151–159.

Nagler, B. (1950). Psychiatric aspects of cord injury. *American Journal of Psychiatry, 107*, 49–56.

Nehemkis, A., & Groot, H. (1980). Indirect self-destructive behavior in spinal cord injury. In N. Farberow (Ed.), *The many faces of suicide*. New York: McGraw-Hill, pp. 99–115.

Nepomuceno, C., Fine, P., Richards, J., Gowens, Stover, S., Rantanuabol, U., & Houston, R. (1979). Pain in patients with spinal cord injury. *Archives of Physical Medicine and Rehabilitation, 60*, 605–609.

Nicklas, K. (1980). The life situation of spinal cord injured persons in a medical facility and in everyday life—A socio-medical study of 246 spinal cord injured persons. *International Journal of Rehabilitation Research, 3*, 541–543.

Nwuga, V. (1979). A follow-up study of paraplegics and tetraplegics discharged from a hospital. *Journal of Tropical Medicine and Hygiene, 82*, 30–33.

Nyquist, R., & Bors, E. (1967). Mortality and survival in traumatic myelopathy during nineteen years, from 1946 to 1965. *Paraplegia, 51*, 22–48.

O'Donnell, J., Cooper, J., Gessner, J., Shehan, I., & Ashley, J. (1981/82). Alcohol, drugs, and spinal cord injury. *Alcohol Health and Research World*, 27–29.

Richards, J., Hirt, M., & Melamed, L. (1982). Spinal cord injury: A sensory restriction perspective. *Archives of Physical Medicine and Rehabilitation, 63*, 195–199.

Richards, J., Meredith, R., Nepomuceno, P., & Bennett, G. (1980) Psycho-social aspects of chronic pain in spinal cord injury. *Pain, 8*, 355–366.

Rohe, D., & Athelstan, G. (1982). Vocational Interests of persons with spinal cord injury. *Journal of Counseling Psychology, 29*, 283–291.

Rosman, N., Ohry, A., & Rozin, R. (1982). The social aspects of the treatment of spinal cord injured patients in Israel. *Paraplegia, 20*, 80–84.

Rotter, J. (1966). Generalized expectancies for internal versus external control of reinforcement. *Psychological Monographs, 80* (Whole No. 609).

Safilios-Rothschild, C. (1970). *The sociology and social psychology of disability and rehabilitation.* New York: Random House.

Sakinofsky, I. (1980). Depression and suicide in the disabled. In D. Bishop (Ed.), *Behavioral problems and the disabled: Assessment and management.* Baltimore: Williams & Wilkins, pp. 17–51.

Schachter, S., & Singer, J. (1962). Cognitive, social and physiological determinants of emotional state. *Psychological Review, 69,* 379–390.

Seixas, E. (1980). The relationship of alcohol and drug abuse to physical medicine and rehabilitation. In D. Bishop (Ed.), *Behavioral problems and the disabled: Assessment and management.* Baltimore: Williams & Wilkins, pp. 165–172.

Seligman, M. (1975). *Helplessness: On depression, development and death.* San Francisco: WH Freeman Co.

Shadish, W., Hickman, D., & Arrick, M. (1981). Psychological problems of spinal cord injury patients: Emotional distress as a function of time and locus of control. *Journal of Consulting and Clinical Psychology, 49,* 297.

Shontz, F. (1965). Reactions to crisis. *Volta Review, 67,* 364–370.

Siegel, M. (1969). The vocational potential of the quadriplegic. *Medical Clinics of North America, 53,* 713–718.

Siller, J. (1969). Psychological situation of the disabled with spinal cord injuries. *Rehabilitation Literature, 30,* 290–296.

Siller, J., Chipman, A., Ferguson, L., & Vann, D. (1967). Attitudes of the nondisabled toward the physically disabled. *Studies in reaction to disability XI.* New York: School of Education, New York University.

Silverman, J. (1981). Emotional care of the cord-injured and chronically ill patient. In M. Constantian (Ed.), *Pressure ulcers: Principles and techniques of management,* Boston: Little, Brown, and Co.

Sutton, R., Bentley, M., Castree, B., Mattinson, R., Pattinson, J., & Smith, R. (1982). Review of the social situation of paraplegic and tetraplegic patients rehabilitated in the Hexham Regional Spinal Injury Unit in the north of England over the past four years. *Paraplegia, 20,* 71–79.

Taylor, G. (1967). *Predicted versus actual response to spinal cord injury: A psychological study.* Unpublished doctoral dissertation, University of Minnesota, Minneapolis.

Taylor, G. (1970). Moderator-variable effect on personality test item endorsements of physically disabled patients. *Journal of Consulting and Clinical Psychology, 35,* 183–188.

Taylor, M., & Taylor, D. (1980). Disability, fear, and anxiety. In D. Bishop (Ed.), *Behavioral problems and the disabled: Assessment and management.* Baltimore: Williams & Wilkins, pp. 52–70.

Thom, D., Von Salzen, C., & Fromme, A. (1946). Psychological aspects of the paraplegic patient. *Medical Clinics of North America, 30,* 473–480.

Trieschmann, R. (1980a). *Spinal cord injuries: The psychological, social, and vocational adjustment.* Elmsford, NY: Pergamon Press.

Trieschmann, R. (1980b). The adjustment to spinal cord injury. In E. Pan, T. Backer, & C. Vash (Eds.), *Annual review of rehabilitation* (Vol. 1). New York: Springer.

Varela, R. (1983). Changing social attitudes and legislation regarding disability. In N. Crewe & I. Zola (Eds.), *Independent living for physically disabled people.* San Francisco: Jossey-Bass.

Vash, C. (1981). *The psychology of disability.* New York: Springer.

West Virginia Research and Training Center. (1983). *Tenth institute on rehabilitation issues: Functional assessment.* Dunbar, WVA: Author.

Wilmot, C., Cope, D., Hall, K., & Acker, M. (1985). Occult head injury: Its incidence in spinal cord injury. *Archives of Physical Medicine and Rehabilitation, 66*, 227–231.

Wittkower, E., Gingras, G., Mergler, L., Wigdor, B., & Lepine, A. (1954). A combined psychosocial study of spinal cord lesions. *Canadian Medical Association Journal, 71*, 109–115.

Wright, B. (1983). *Physical disability—A psychosocial approach.* New York: Harper and Row.

Young, J. (1979). Hospital study report. *Model Systems' SCI Digest, 1*, 11–32.

Young, J., Burns, P., Bowen, A., & McCutchen, R. (1982). *Spinal cord injury statistics.* Phoenix: Good Samaritan Medical Center.

Zager, R., & Marquette, C. (1981). Developmental considerations in children and early adolescents with spinal cord injury. *Archives of Physical Medicine and Rehabilitation, 62*, 427–431.

Chapter 2

Traumatic Head Injury: Neurobehavioral Consequences

Mitchell Rosenthal, Ph.D.

Traumatic head injury is not a new diagnostic entity or clinical phenomenon, yet it is only within the past decade that the professional rehabilitation community has aggressively addressed the rehabilitation of this population. This effort has coincided with the reduction in mortality rates from 50 percent to 32 percent that has resulted from improved acute neurosurgical management techniques (Clifton, 1985). The magnitude of the problem is well illustrated by demographic and epidemiologic data that show that approximately 500,000 persons per year are hospitalized following a head injury; of this number, at least 30,000–50,000 have physical and, more commonly, neurobehavioral dysfunctions that preclude return to preinjury levels of function (U.S. Department of Education, 1981). The vast majority of head injury victims are between the ages of 15–24 (Rimel & Jane, 1983); these individuals are often unable to be economically self-sufficient and must depend on government or other financial resources for basic survival. The associated economic costs are staggering; in 1980 alone, the estimate was 3.9 billion dollars (Lynch, 1983).

There are two major types of head injury: (1) penetrating or open injury and (2) closed head injury. In a penetrating injury, which is usually caused by gunshot wounds, the scalp is lacerated, and brain damage is created by the path of the missile through the brain tissue. Because brain dysfunction is correlated with the specific locus of the path of the missile, the result is usually categorized as "focal" brain injury. The nature of neurobehavioral consequences is dependent upon which brain structures are directly affected. In closed head injury, which usually results from blunt trauma to the head (often in an automobile accident), acceleration/deceleration forces create rotation of the brain within the skull. These forces exert maximal pressure on the frontal and temporal regions and result in diffuse axonal shearing and extensive white matter damage (Teasdale & Mendelow, 1984). Thus, in closed head injury, widespread or diffuse brain damage often results in a tremendous variety of neurobehavioral deficits that generally include loss of consciousness, problems in attention and memory, and alterations in social behavior.

A fundamental premise in head injury rehabilitation is that, although traumatic head injury may be viewed as a single disability category, rehabilitation efforts must be directed toward "a multiplicity of medical, surgical, sensorimotor, cognitive, behavioral, and social problems (Glenn & Rosenthal, 1985, p. 233)." From a functional perspective, sequelae of traumatic head injury encompass impairments in mobility, activities of daily living, strength, coordination, sensation, communication, judgment, memory, reasoning, learning, social interaction, and behavior (Griffith, 1983). Both research and clinical experience confirm, however, that the neurobehavioral sequelae of head injury—that is, diminished cognitive and behavioral capacities—pose the greatest obstacle to the successful restoration of the head injured individual to a productive status within the family and community (Bond, 1975; Jennett & Teasdale, 1981). This chapter therefore examines the cognitive, behavioral, and social consequences of head injury. (See Chapter 19 for a discussion of medical and epidemiologic aspects.)

SPHERES OF DISABILITY

Appreciating the effects of head injury requires more than simply understanding each of the individual and varied neurobehavioral disorders that may result; one must recognize the dynamic interaction among dysfunctions within the several spheres of disability: physical, cognitive, behavioral, and social.

Within the physical sphere, mobility, motor control, sensorimotor skills, and sensation are often impaired. Although many head injured persons recover the physical capacity to walk, dress, and care for basic needs within 6 months after injury, such problems as poor balance, incoordination, weakness, field cuts, pain syndromes, seizures, and heterotopic bone formation may be enduring sequelae of the head injury (Glenn & Rosenthal, 1985; Griffith, 1983).

Among the many problems within the cognitive sphere are disorders of attention and arousal, communication and language, memory, learning, visual and auditory perception, information processing, reasoning, judgment, and problem solving (Ben-Yishay & Diller, 1983; Brooks, 1984b). Because many head injured persons recover the capacity to communicate and interact, these deficits are often hidden from the casual observer. It is only when detailed neuropsychological studies are completed or careful observations made in the home or rehabilitation setting that these dysfunctions and their disabling consequences become apparent.

The behavioral sphere encompasses a wide variety of alterations in personality and emotional expression; these are very often the most devastating for family members to accept and for rehabilitation staff to treat. Problems in initiating and executing simple and complex behavior, expressing emotions, engaging in goal-directed behavior, interacting appropriately with peers and family members, and awareness and acceptance of disability are but a few of these disorders (Benton, 1979).

The interaction of these spheres of disability frequently results in social maladjustment. The young head injured adult has difficulty re-establishing social relationships, returning to educational or vocational activity, establishing financial security, and assuming a meaningful role within the family and community (Brooks, 1984a).

It is important for the clinician to remember that neurobehavioral sequelae of head injury are determined by a number of factors, including (1) premorbid history—preinjury behavior patterns, past education and work experiences, prior substance abuse, family interaction patterns; (2) site of lesion—brainstem, frontal, temporal, or diffuse; (3) course of recovery—medical complications, associated injuries, such as spinal cord injury, duration of posttraumatic amnesia, etc.; and (4) environmental factors—family support system, acceptance by peers, adequacy of community resources, and finances. Successful rehabilitation must therefore begin with an appreciation of the levels and types of impairment that exist for a given patient.

COURSE OF RECOVERY

Although each individual's recovery from head injury is different, it is useful to understand the general progression ''from coma to community'' in order to plan a suitable rehabilitation program. The most widely researched, clinically useful scale to measure depth of unconsciousness is the Glasgow Coma Scale (Teasdale & Jennett, 1974) (Table 2–1).

This scale is based on the arithmetic sum of the patient's responses along three dimensions: eye opening, best motor response, and verbal response. It has been validated in large-scale studies involving thousands of patients in major trauma centers in several countries (Jennett et al., 1977). It can be completed readily by trained paramedical and medical staff in a highly reliable fashion and can be used serially to track the state of patients as they progress or fail to progress over time. In essence, a score of 8 or less reflects unconsciousness, with 9 to 11 denoting injuries of moderate severity and 12 to 15 indicating mild injuries.

Many rehabilitation centers utilize the Levels of Cognitive Functioning Scale (Hagen, Malkmus, & Durham, 1977) developed at Rancho Los Amigos Hospital to track the progress of individual patients. This scale lists eight stages:

1. no response
2. generalized response to stimuli
3. localized response to stimuli

Table 2–1 Glasgow Coma Scale

Examiner's Test		Patient's Response	Assigned Score
Eye opening (E)	Spontaneous	Opens eyes on own	E 4
	Speech	Opens eyes when asked in loud voice	3
	Pain	Opens eyes when pinched	2
	Pain	Does not open eyes	1
Best motor response (M)	Commands	Follows simple commands	M 6
	Pain	Pulls examiner's hand away when pinched	5
	Pain	Pulls a part of body away when pinched	4
	Pain	Flexes body inappropriately to pain	3
	Pain	Body becomes rigid in an extended position	2
	Pain	Has no motor response to pinch	1
Verbal (V)	Speech	Carries on a conversation correctly and tells examiner where he or she is, month, and year	V 5
	Speech	Seems confused or disoriented	4
	Speech	Talks so examiner can understand him or her, but makes no sense	3
	Speech	Makes sounds that examiner can't understand	2
	Speech	Makes no noise	1

Coma Score (E + M + V) = 3 to 15

Source: From "Assessment of Coma and Impaired Consciousness" by G. Teasdale and B. Jennett, 1974, *Lancet, 2*, p. 81. Copyright 1974 by The Lancet. Adapted by permission.

---

4. confused and agitated behavior
5. confused, with inappropriate behavior (nonagitated)
6. confused but appropriate behavior
7. automatic and appropriate behavior
8. purposeful and appropriate behavior

During the initial period of diminished consciousness, the patient is considered to be at levels 1, 2 or 3 on the Rancho scale. At level 1, the patient fails to make any response to stimulation or to verbalize or interact meaningfully with the environment. At level 2, when the patient is given stimulation—tactile, auditory, gustatory—reactions are inconsistent and nonpurposeful. The earliest response may be to pain; it may be a physiologic change, gross body movement, and/or vocalization. At level 3, the patient responds specifically but inconsistently. For example, there may be head turning toward a sound or focusing on an object when it is presented. Simple commands may be followed in an inconsistent, delayed manner, such as by closing eyes, squeezing a hand, or extending an extremity.

On emerging from unconsciousness, the patient is often disoriented, confused, quite agitated, and potentially violent. Sleep-wakefulness cycles are often confused, and the patient's ability to maintain a continuous arousal level is diminished; the upper limit of attention to a given task is usually only a few minutes. Episodes of delirium or hallucinations may occur (Stern, 1978). Reality orientation is impaired, i.e., the patient is usually unable to identify the date, time, place, or the reason for his or her hospitalization. The patient may recognize familiar faces, such as family members, but is unable to learn or remember new information—posttraumatic or anterograde amnesia (Russell, 1971). During this period, the patient's behavior is likely to be viewed as unpredictable, bizarre, impulsive, and generally disinhibited. Physical restraints or psychopharmacologic controls may be required. This behavior corresponds roughly to level 4 on the Rancho scale.

As the period of posttraumatic amnesia ends, the patient displays better orientation to the environment and a limited awareness of the consequences of the injury. This phase of recovery, level 5, is marked by frustration, occasional temper outbursts, impaired communication skills, and short-term memory deficits. The patient is not typically agitated, but will show irritability in response to minor frustrations. Perseverative responses and the inability to switch "set" from one learning situation to another are evident. The patient displays a child-like emotional dependency on parents and caregivers. Confused and impulsive, the patient is still unsafe and thus requires continual monitoring and supervision. Inappropriate social behavior and poor judgment create obstacles to effective therapeutic intervention.

During the latter phases of inpatient rehabilitation, the patient's behavior becomes more manageable. The patient may understand the reason for the hospitalization, but may not yet be fully oriented to time. Questions about the etiology of the injury are often raised. Cognitive and language functions start to recover. The patient's memory improves, and there are usually great gains in therapy due to increased day-to-day carryover. Social interaction becomes more appropriate. The patient starts to recover physical skills and strength and makes the assumption that "if I can walk, I will be back to my old self." Unfortunately, this is not often the case. This phase of recovery corresponds to level 6.

Finally, the patient is fully oriented to surroundings, alert, and able to tolerate extended days of therapy, although the attention span may be limited by distractibility to both internal and external stimuli. The patient may go through the daily routine automatically in a robot-like fashion. Judgment remains impaired, and recall for past events is shallow. New learning can occur, but at a decreased rate. Although gross motor skills have improved, the patient often has difficulty in fine-motor activities due to incoordination, weakness, and/or perceptual-motor dys-function. The patient engages in purposeful behavior and may be upset about restrictions placed on behavior by caregivers. Although unable to return to work or school, the patient is ready to be discharged to the care of family members or significant others (levels 7–8).

To assess the level of disability resulting from head injury, Jennett and Bond (1975) devised the Glasgow Outcome Scale, which consists of the following basic categories:

- good recovery
- moderate disability
- severe disability
- vegetative state
- death

Patients in the "good recovery" category are able to resume some type of gainful occupational and/or social activities, despite the presence of minor mental or physical deficits. Those in the "moderate disability" category are independent in activities of daily living, can use public transportation, but cannot resume previous activities. The patient in the "severely disabled" category requires assistance in the performance of daily activities, due to a combination of mental and/or physical deficits. Such individuals cannot be left alone and are unable to return to work or social activities. Patients in the "vegetative state" cannot obey simple commands or interact meaningfully with the environment (Jennett & Plum, 1972). The outcome of several large studies of head injured patients is shown in Table 2–2.

The Glasgow Outcome Scale (GOS) is a useful tool for analyzing outcomes in large patient populations, but is not a sensitive index of progress of individuals. Furthermore, the global GOS categories do not incorporate sufficient information about cognitive and behavioral dysfunctions. To redress these deficiencies, Rappaport and co-workers (1982) devised the Disability Rating Scale (DRS), a 30-point instrument measuring four categories: (1) arousal and awareness, (2) psychosocial adaptability ("employability") for work, (3) cognitive ability for self-care functions, and (4) degree of physical dependence on others. Eight disability categories may be derived from the DRS: mild, partial, moderate, moderately severe, severe, extremely severe, vegetative state, extreme vegetative state. Hall et al. (1985) reported that, as compared to the GOS, the DRS provides more specific and clinically useful information about patient functioning and is indeed more sensitive to change during the first 24 months postinjury. Further-more, DRS scores correlate well with early multimodality-evoked potentials in terms of prediction of outcome (Rappaport, 1986).

Long-term follow-up studies of head injured patients suggest that neurobe-havioral deficits remain and pose significant barriers to total restoration of func-

Table 2–2 Comparison of Outcome in Survivors of Severe Head Injury at Different Centers[a]

Series	No. of Cases	Good Recovery n	%	Moderate Disability n	%	Severe Disability n	%	Persistent Vegetative State n	%
Galveston	27	10	37	12	44	5	19	0	0
Glasgow	207	94	45	71	34	34	16	8	5
Los Angeles	51	14	28	14	28	18	35	5	9
Netherlands[b]	83	47	57	26	31	9	11	1	1
Richmond	112	57	51	39	35	12	10	4	4
San Diego	128	84	66	20	16	16	12	8	6

[a]Patients who died are excluded.
[b]Groningen, Rotterdam

Source: From *Neurobehavioral Consequences of Closed Head Injury* (p. 68) by H.S. Levin, A.L. Benton, and R.G. Grossman (Eds.), 1982, New York: Oxford University Press. Copyright 1982 by Oxford University Press. Reprinted by permission.

tion. Levin, Grossman, Rose, and Teasdale (1979) studied 27 patients with severe closed head injury—median follow-up interval was 1 year—and found that the major residual sequelae included memory dysfunction, impaired retrieval of names, poor perceptual-motor skills, and behavioral changes (depressed mood, social withdrawal, and motor retardation). Tabbador, Mattis, and Zazula (1984) studied 48 moderate and severely head injured patients up to 12 months post injury; their findings suggest a marked recovery in all aspects of linguistic and cognitive function, but there was still residual impairment in most patients at 12 months. Consistent with the findings of Levin et al. (1979), the primary domains of deficit were memory, naming, and fine motor skills. Bond (1985a) followed a group of head injured patients up to 5 years post injury and found no change on the Raven Progressive Matrices and Mill Hill Vocabulary Test—two frequently used measures of cognitive function in head injured patients—after the first year. In sum, these studies suggest that, despite the improvement in many areas of cognitive function, residual deficits often become permanent sequelae. Long-term social and vocational outcomes are discussed later in this chapter.

NEUROPSYCHOLOGICAL DEFICITS

General Intellectual Function

Although generalized intellectual impairment is commonly found in acutely injured patients, various studies have documented rapid improvement on formal intelligence tests. Mandelberg and Brooks (1975) compared WAIS results of 40 severely head injured patients with those of a matched control group. The WAIS results of the head injury group were obtained at 0–3 months, 4–6 months, 7–12 months and over 13 months post injury. Major findings included lesser initial deterioration of verbal IQ as opposed to performance IQ; more rapid recovery for verbal subtests, especially within the initial 6 months after injury; and an eventual return of IQ to the normal range. Bond and Brooks (1976) assessed 40 closed head injured adults (posttraumatic amnesia greater than 24 hours, on the WAIS) and produced similar findings as the aforementioned study. An additional finding was that the ultimate level of recovery of intellectual function is achieved earlier for verbal than for performance abilities.

That intellectual function often returns to the average range by 6–12 months post injury has often been cited as evidence of a lack of long-term cognitive impairment after head injury. Unfortunately, this is not the case. The resilience of IQ scores may be due to the frequency of frontal lobe dysfunction as the major site of injury in these patients. Formal intellect is often not affected by frontal injuries. Instead, as described by Stuss and Benson (1984), problems in attention, planning, monitoring performance, and initiating and executing behavior are more commonly observed in the head injured patient with frontal impairment.

Speech and Language Disorders

Although classic aphasic syndromes are sometimes observed after head injury, they usually resolve within 6 months (Groher, 1983; Jennett, 1975). Rather, the difficulties in expression are often in word-finding problems and in the pragmatics of communication, i.e., verbal perseveration, disorganized structure of verbal or written communication, circumlocution, reduced capacity for abstract reasoning, and incomplete expression of thoughts. Comprehension and repetition are comparatively well preserved (Heilman, Safran, & Geschwind, 1971). It is sometimes difficult to distinguish true language disturbance from other concomitant cognitive deficits, such as impaired attention or memory.

Some clinicians have concluded that persistent speech and language problems are not found in the head injured patient because many head injured individuals recover basic conversational skills within 6 months of trauma. This notion has been effectively countered by two studies reported by Sarno (1980, 1984). In these studies she analyzed the speech and language function of two series of consecutive admissions to the NYU Institute of Rehabilitation Medicine. She concluded that all patients who experience some duration of coma have persistent verbal impairment, however mild, at 1 year postinjury. Across the two studies, 35 percent of patients demonstrated "subclinical aphasia"—that is, linguistic processing deficits—35 percent evidenced dysarthria and subclinical aphasia, and 30 percent were clinically aphasic.

Attention Deficits

A variety of attentional deficits may be present after head injury, but these can be obscured by memory disorders or behavioral disturbances of various kinds. Initially, a head injured person may be unable to focus attention for more than a few seconds. Such patients derive little benefit from therapy and often cannot be meaningfully evaluated. As recovery proceeds, the attention span increases and the patient can stay on a task for several minutes, but extended vigilance is still not present.

Attentional skills are affected by the complexity of a given task; for example, van Zomeren and Deelman (1976) found a choice-reaction time task to be more sensitive to the effects of head injury than a simple-reaction time task. The psychomotor retardation that is frequently noted probably has an attentional component. Situational factors also affect attention. In an isolated, one-to-one therapy or testing session (with minimal noise), attention may be maintained, but if the same head injured person is presented with a similar task in a group environment, performance may deteriorate. An excellent review of attentional deficits following head injury may be found in the work of van Zomeren, Brouwer, and Deelman (1984).

Memory Disorders

Impaired memory has been viewed by many clinicians as the most enduring and disabling consequence of head injury (Benton, 1979); indeed, most patients report memory problems at some time after injury (Brooks & Aughton, 1979; Oddy et al., 1978b). The nature of the observed impairment varies with the type and complexity of the task.

Failure to recall events before the injury is termed "*retrograde amnesia*" (RA), and although the period of RA is usually brief—less than 30 minutes—several hours or days before the accident occurred may "disappear." In rare cases, there may be a failure to recall a period of several years preceding the injury. There may be "shrinkage" of RA, so that ultimately there is amnesia only for the few minutes or even seconds before injury (Russell & Nathan, 1946).

In the more disabling form of amnesia—*anterograde or posttraumatic amnesia* (PTA)—the ability to learn or remember new information is impaired. The period of PTA begins with emergence from coma and ends with the return of continuous memory. The importance of *continuous* memory must be stressed, for there is evidence (Gronwall & Wrightson, 1980) that patients in PTA have "islands" of preserved memory, retention of scattered events followed by additional periods of amnesia (see Artiola y Fortuna et al., 1980, for procedures to measure PTA; also Levin, Benton, & Grossman, 1982). Duration of PTA is often used as an index of severity of injury (Brooks, 1984b) and has been shown to be correlated with long-term outcome (Jennett, 1983); that is, the longer the PTA (especially when it lasts more than 24 hours), the poorer the outcome.

Once the patient emerges from PTA, other memory disorders become evident. Patients who are relatively good historians in an interview, demonstrating an intact remote memory function, may lack the capacity to recall events within the past few minutes. Head injured individuals can often repeat small bits of information, such as on the Digit Span test, immediately, but seem to lack the ability to store and retrieve information for more extended periods of time (Brooks, 1983; Schachter & Crovitz, 1977). In addition, a distinction can be drawn between *episodic* and *semantic* memory. A patient may be able to recall information about objects, properties, and relationships (semantic memory), but may have great difficulty recalling personal experiences and temporal relations (episodic memory, Newcombe, 1983).

As is true of many other neurobehavioral deficits, memory function often shows a progressive improvement as time passes. However, despite many research efforts, the pattern and time course of memory recovery are difficult to predict (Brooks, 1983). In general, memory function does not improve as quickly as verbal IQ or other cognitive functions, and clinical observation and research suggest that some form of memory deficit is often found in head injured patients for several years after injury (Lezak, 1979; Tabbador et al., 1984).

Visuospatial and Perceptuomotor Dysfunction

As with stroke syndromes, head injured patients who sustain a lesion in the right temporal, parietal, or temporoparietal regions display a variety of visuospatial deficits. In addition to dysfunction secondary to neurologic impairment, visual impairments may be due to direct opthalmologic injury, e.g., retinal and globe injuries, intraocular hemorrhage, etc. In rare instances, cortical blindness can result from an insult to the occipital cortex.

Visual field deficits—a loss of vision in a part (25–75 percent) of the visual field—is often observed. In effect, the patient fails to respond to visual stimuli in the affected field.

Visual neglect is a similar but distinct problem in which the patient tends to ignore visual stimuli coming from the involved side. Visual neglect, or inattention of hemispace, is commonly observed when treating a head injured patient. This deficit is often present without visual field impairment and may be revealed by perimetry (Anderson, 1982). This disability can be demonstrated in the performance of various psychometric tasks, such as Letter Cancellation or WAIS-R Digit Symbol subtest, or in such daily activities as reading, writing, drawing, eating, dressing, and grooming. The patient may also show a reduced awareness of one side of the body, particularly the left side with right-hemisphere lesions, and may actually deny the presence of the left arm.

Impaired understanding of spatial relations can be seen on design-copying tasks, such as the Bender-Gestalt or Benton Visual Retention Test, or puzzles, e.g., Block Design subtest of the WAIS-R. Other problems that have a visual-perceptual basis include constructional apraxia, impaired facial recognition, defective perception of detail, and impaired figure-ground discrimination.

All of the aforementioned visuospatial deficits are compounded by the presence of a variety of motor or sensorimotor problems, such as motor weakness, incoordination, poor manual dexterity, ataxia, or tremors. Due to the complex integration of various cognitive, sensory, and motor systems needed to execute perceptual-motor tasks, the recovery of such skills lags behind that of verbal and general intellectual skills. Unfortunately, it is often the inability to execute both simple and complex motor tasks that precludes a return to self-sufficiency in daily activity and resumption of vocational productivity.

Problem-Solving Skills

The frontal lobes have been described as the seat of "executive functions" (Lezak, 1983). Because of the frequent involvement of the frontal lobes in head injury, deficient problem-solving ability is a common consequence. Problem-solving activities include formulating a plan, selecting a strategy, prioritizing activities, monitoring performance, and verifying the suitability of a given solution. Various neuropsychological tests, such as the Category Test (Dikman, Reitan, & Temkin, 1983) and the Wisconsin Card Sorting Test (Heaton, 1981; Wolfe, 1984), are frequently used to assess problem-solving skills in head injured patients. Problem-solving deficits have been implicated as a major cause of poor long-term adjustment in the head injured individual (Boll, 1981; Eson, 1979).

Examples of daily life tasks that challenge the problem-solving skills of head injured patients are simple tasks, such as self-care and household chores; basic adaptive behaviors, such as shopping and using public transportation; or more complex tasks involving convergent and/or divergent thinking (Ben-Yishay & Diller, 1983). Many head-injured individuals tend to be concrete in thinking and therefore fail to generalize a solution from one problem situation to another. Because problem solving requires a high level of integration and synthesis of ideas and actions, its recovery is dependent upon the re-establishment of more basic cognitive skills. Yet, the reacquisition of problem-solving skills is crucial to the head injured person's ability to function effectively in a less structured, less restrictive environment outside the hospital.

MENTAL COMPETENCE

The cognitive sequelae of traumatic brain injury often affect the head injured patient's capacity to manage adequately daily living activities, financial affairs, and jobs. Attorneys often request rehabilitation psychologists and clinical neuropsy-chologists to render opinions on their client's "competence" in performing the aforementioned tasks. However, the decision is ultimately a legal, not a psycho-metric, one.

The establishment of mental competence or incompetence may have a signifi-cant effect upon the settlement of a civil negligence suit and may thereby determine whether the client will receive financial compensation. This, in turn, may influence the client's access to rehabilitation programming. The determina-tion of competence may establish whether clients can testify on their own behalf. Commonly occurring memory deficits after head injury often make the client his or her own worst witness (Rosenthal & Kolpan, 1986).

To address adequately the problem of competence, the rehabilitation specialist must be familiar with the effects of brain lesions on adaptive abilities; collect sufficient data to establish approximate levels of premorbid mental function; and administer neuropsychological tests, conduct interviews and perform behavioral observations in order to provide comprehensive information on a broad range of neuropsychological functions (McMahon & Satz, 1981).

COGNITIVE REMEDIATION

Perhaps the most novel aspect of the recent growth of interest in head injury rehabilitation is the advent of cognitive remediation. *Cognitive remediation* or cognitive rehabilitation is a generic term for a collection of therapeutic techniques designed to improve mental function. Specific methodologies attempt to reteach lost skills or assist patients in developing compensatory strategies. For example, in cases of memory disorders such techniques as bizarre mental imagery (Glasgow, Zeiss, Barrera & Lewinsohn, 1977; Lewinsohn, Danaher, & Kikel, 1977), elab-orative rehearsal (Gianutsos & Gianutsos, 1979), or prosthetic memory aids and devices (Fowler, Hart, & Sheehan, 1972; Harris, 1984) have been utilized. An early rationale for cognitive retraining was Luria's notion that, by bypassing damaged brain tissue, new functional systems can be established in the brain that allow the patient to execute old skills in new ways (Luria, Nayden, Tsvetkova, & Vinarskaya, 1969).

The proliferation of cognitive remediation treatment techniques can be traced largely to the pioneering efforts of Diller, Ben-Yishay, and their colleagues at the New York University Institute of Rehabilitation Medicine (Diller & Gordon, 1981). Their early programs were designed to remediate perceptual disorders in stroke patients with right-hemisphere damage (Diller, 1980) by teaching them to scan, search, and track effectively in the left visual field. Subsequently, disorders of the head injured patient were addressed.

Currently, the head injury program at NYU consists of 20 weeks of daily training (4 days/week) with five modules (Ben-Yishay & Diller, 1983):

1. ORM—orientation module, which aims to enhance attentional skills
2. DEX—dexterity module, which is directed toward improving eye-hand coordination skills through training on finger dexterity tasks
3. CON—perceptual-cognitive module, which focuses on improving visuo-constructive ability
4. VIP—visual information processing module, designed to improve visual memory, motor planning, and tactile-kinesthetic integration
5. LOG—verbal and logical reasoning, focusing on complex problem-solving tasks

Technological advances have led to the adoption of microcomputers in many rehabilitation programs. Gianutsos (1980) and Bracey (1983), among others (see Chapter 12), have developed special software designed to treat deficits in attention, memory, problem-solving, visuospatial abilities, and abstract thinking. Desirable features of computer-based interventions include a programmed learning approach, immediate and effective delivery of reinforcement, easy storage and retrieval of cumulative data, and portability for use in the home environment. The computer is not used as a replacement for the therapist; instead, it allows the therapist to structure the sessions with specific software, closely monitor the patient's performance, provide social reinforcement, and adjust the levels of task difficulty as needed.

At present, the effects of cognitive remediation techniques on the adaptive abilities of the head injured patient are not well documented. An increasing number of case reports are appearing in the literature, but few systematic experimental studies have been conducted. Recently, however, Prigatano and his colleagues (1984) found that 18 closed head-injury patients who participated in an intensive neuropsychological rehabilitation program showed greater productivity, less emotional distress, and greater improvements on selected neuropsychological measures than did 17 untreated controls (see Chapter 10). More such studies are needed to evaluate the efficacy of cognitive remediation techniques.

BEHAVIORAL DEFICITS: CONTRIBUTING FACTORS

Alterations in behavior and mood are common among individuals who sustain a head injury. The specific expression of changes is a function of several factors: (1) preinjury patterns of behavior; (2) locus of the brain lesion(s) and its effects on specific types of behavior; (3) associated injuries and medical complications; (4) response of the family and significant others to the head injured individual; and (5) capacity of the individual to accept and accommodate to the many changes in physical and mental function caused by the injury. In any individual case, the clinician must carefully analyze each factor to determine its relative contribution to the presenting problems. In the following section, these factors are described in more detail, and illustrative examples are provided.

The premorbid history of a head injured patient is critical to an understanding of postinjury patterns of adaptation. Educational and work history, patterns of peer and family relationships, history of antisocial or maladaptive behavior, past alcohol and/or drug abuse, pre-existing emotional disturbance, preinjury goals and aspirations, and ability to respond to stressful life events and frustration all provide important clues for the clinician. Consider the following case history.

> J.B. was a 21-year-old male who sustained a severe closed head injury 2 years ago with resultant blindness and minimal physical or cognitive impairment. He was referred by a rehabilitation counselor for a neuro-psychological assessment to assist in vocational planning. The present-ing problems were a lack of initiative, apathy, poor motivation, inability to plan for the future, and emotional indifference. This pattern closely resembled a type of frontal lobe syndrome that is often seen after closed head injury; the suspicion of an organic deficit was thus raised. Careful interviews with the patient and his father, however, revealed that J.B. had behaved in an identical fashion before the accident.

Lesions in the frontal and temporal regions of the brain, for which head injuries have a predilection, are known to produce significant alterations in behavior. The frontal lobe syndrome has been described as a cluster of behaviors including aspontaneity, apathy, lethargy, social disinhibition, childish or egocentric behav-ior, poor judgment, dull or flat affect, and inappropriate sexual and aggressive be-havior (Blumer & Benson, 1975; Stuss & Benson, 1984). Periodic violent out-bursts have been associated with damage to the medial temporal lobe (Sweet, Ervin, & Mark, 1968). Fluctuations in mood, sluggishness, sleep disturbances, and appetitive cravings have been associated with hypothalamic and basilar branch injuries (Kretschmer, 1949).

Associated injuries and medical complications are rarely discussed in relation to the behavioral dysfunction of the head injured patient. However, it is not uncom-mon to observe a variety of very serious associated injuries, such as spinal cord damage resulting in quadriplegia, traumatic amputation of an extremity, or frac-tures. Any of these problems can greatly complicate and prolong the rehabilitation process. The process of emotional adaptation to these injuries may greatly inten-sify behavioral deficits associated with the head injury.

The response of the social milieu—family, friends, the community—can have a significant impact on the behavior of the patient. If the patient cannot resume educational, vocational, or leisure activities and must spend most days at home, family stress increases and friends may be lost. Lezak and colleagues (1975) studied the long-term (up to 5 years postinjury) psychosocial consequences of head injury in 39 patients and reported that the most persistent difficulties, as measured by the Portland Adaptability Inventory, were in the areas of social contact, work/school, and leisure. This kind of social dislocation produces anxiety, depression, decreased self-esteem, and social withdrawal.

Finally, the degree of insight into the nature of the injury and its consequences can also affect behavior. The persistence of denial, which serves an adaptive function in the early stages, may create conflict between the patient and health care providers or family members. Conversely, complete acceptance of the reality of head injury often results in a state of depression that creates additional problems. Ideally, the patient recognizes the losses that have occurred, but maintains hope for future improvement.

SPECIFIC BEHAVIORAL DEFICITS

Altered Expression of Emotion

A variety of changes in emotional expression can be seen after head injury. Patients with prefrontal injuries often exhibit flattened or dull affect. The patient appears to be wearing a mask and is unable to respond appropriately to social situations. Frequently, this blunted affect is accompanied by a monotonous, ''robotic'' quality of speech. Patients with right-hemisphere lesions often display an inability to perceive the emotional qualities of a situation, recognize facial expressions, or identify the emotional tone in another person's speech. They often demonstrate emotional lability or loss of control over their emotions. A classic example is the patient who bursts into tears without any provoking antecedent stimulus and without feelings of sadness or depression.

Decreased Initiative and Goal-Directed Behavior

As mentioned earlier, decreased initiative and impairment of goal-directed behavior are classic features of patients with frontal lobe injuries. Although their formal intellectual and communication skills may be intact, their behavior lacks purpose, and they exhibit a poor sense of identity. They respond to questions and perform a task when told to do so; however, they rarely initiate conversation or show intrinsic ''motivation'' to accomplish a task, as illustrated below.

B.S. was a 24-year-old woman who sustained bifrontal contusions as a result of a gunshot wound. She emerged from coma after approximately 3 weeks, but exhibited little volitional verbal or motor behavior. Affect was flat. She responded to simple commands, but did not initiate any conversation, despite preserved language skills. She tended to sit in her wheelchair, staring off into space until someone interacted with her. When the dinner plate was placed in front of her, she did not respond. The nurse would prompt her to eat with a verbal command, but this had no effect. Only when the fork was placed in her hand was she able to feed herself.

Impulsivity and Disinhibition

Individuals with diffuse brain damage often exhibit impulsivity, a tendency to engage in an act without thinking of its potential consequences. An illustrative example is the motorically impaired patient in the wheelchair who suddenly decides to get out of the wheelchair without checking the brakes and falls as a result. Impulsivity in speech is also observed, as in the case of a head injured person who continually interrupts a conversation, being unable to allow the other person to finish. The social consequences of this behavior are apparent.

Head injured patients' inability to monitor or regulate adequately their own behavior is often seen in disinhibited verbal or motor acts that violate social norms and in a tendency to make tactless and discourteous remarks. Patients may be ruled by the need to satisfy primary drives, such as eating, drinking, or sexual gratification. Inappropriate sexual behavior can be either an exaggeration of premorbid tendencies, a direct effect of focal temporal or frontal lobe injury, or a "learned reaction to stress" after head injury (Lishman, 1968; Wood, 1984).

Denial

In a patient with traumatic head injury, denial is occasionally shown by a failure to acknowledge the injury itself. More frequently, however, there is a tendency to disavow or minimize the consequences of the injury, especially neurobehavioral deficits. The permanence of the impairments may be denied, rather than their presence; deficits are seen as transient (see Chapter 5). Denial may be of organic origin—that is, anosognosia (see Weinstein & Kahn, 1955)—or of psychological etiology. Denial may be unwittingly reinforced by family members who, through their interactions with their injured loved one, also exhibit a form of denial (Romano, 1974). Often, denial is maintained during the initial hospitalization, but dissipates after discharge when the long-term realities of living with a head injury must be confronted.

Denial becomes particularly problematic when it is used by the patient to avoid engaging in specific therapeutic activities. For example, a head injured patient who denies memory problems may refuse to participate in a cognitive remediation program focused on the amelioration of memory deficits. Peer group pressure may be used effectively to counteract denial. In the NYU cognitive remediation program, one goal of daily group therapy or "therapeutic community" sessions is to enable each head injured participant to acknowledge residual deficits (Ben-Yishay, 1985).

Depression

Depression is a common and appropriate reaction to any catastrophic acquired disability, either mental or physical. It may be manifested by sadness, decreased activity, tearfulness, and low self-esteem. This reaction can be contrasted with a clinical depression, in which vegetative signs, such as sleep and appetitive disturbances, social withdrawal, and suicidal ideation, are central components. In the early stages of rehabilitation, depression is viewed by staff as an indication of the patient's awareness of disability. It is usually time-limited and is followed by a period of heightened activity and motivation to regain as much function as possible. The clinician, however, should be alert for a form of masked depression characterized by restlessness, agitation, and overreaction to minor frustration.

Unfortunately, depression tends to recur after discharge from the rehabilitation hospital and re-entry into the community. At this point, the head injured person gains a fuller awareness of mental deficits, experiences rejection by friends, and often senses that any further recovery will be slow and difficult. It is at this point that suicidal ideation is sometimes reported by families. Prompt professional intervention is often necessary. Bond (1985b) recently reported that 5 percent of a group of patients with severe head injury reported suicidal ideation. After 5 years, however, 17 percent of these patients reported suicidal ideation. Similarly, suicide attempts increased from 2 percent after 1 year to 15 percent after 5 years.

A few studies have examined the frequency of suicide after head injury. Hilbom (1960) studied 3552 war veterans and found that 1.4 percent (37) of the total sample had committed suicide. Similarly, Vauhkonen (1959) followed 3700 World War II veterans and noted a 1 percent suicide rate by 1957. Achte, Hilbom, and Aalberg (1967) reported that the suicide rate rises as time elapses since injury, reaching a peak at 15–19 years. Contemporary studies of suicide following civilian head injury are needed.

BEHAVIORAL INTERVENTION STRATEGIES

Alterations in mood, behavior, and personality are viewed by both families and staff alike as the greatest obstacle to the complete rehabilitation of the head injured patient. Whether the maladaptive behavior arises directly from primary neurologic damage, an inability to accept or cope with brain injury, or some combination of the two factors, such problems can sabotage successful rehabilitation efforts and preclude the individual's return to educational or vocational pursuits. Some persistent behavioral dysfunctions include disinhibited behavior, impulsivity, apathy, lethargy, lack of emotional control, hyperactive behavior, and low frustration tolerance (Lishman, 1973).

Behavioral management techniques based on operant conditioning theory have become common in the treatment of maladaptive behavior. The token economy system, initially described by Ayllon and Azrin (1968) to modify the behavior of mentally retarded individuals, has been employed with the head injured population. In this method, behaviors are operationalized into their component parts, expectations for appropriate performance are specified, and tokens are awarded that can be exchanged for concrete items, such as food or cigarettes, or special social privileges, e.g., weekend passes, trips to movies, shopping, or recreational events.

A variant on the token economy approach, behavioral contracting, was described by Rosenthal (1984) in modifying the behavior of a 17-year-old head injured youth who displayed passivity, lack of initiation, and a paucity of goal-directed behavior. The family was concerned because the patient exhibited little desire to venture outside the home to engage in any meaningful pursuit. In particular, the family was trying to encourage the patient to seek employment. A written contract was established between the patient and parents that specified the components of job-seeking behavior and the contingencies (rewards) that would follow such behavior. Within a week of the agreement the patient had initiated contact with several prospective employers, completed job applications, and secured part-time employment. Clearly, the success of this technique depends on at least a minimal level of cooperation and motivation from the patient.

Wood and colleagues (1984) have described a behavioral management system in an inpatient setting at the Kemsley Unit in Northampton, England. In this approach, staff members employ behavioral techniques—behavior shaping, token economy, negative reinforcement—to modify, suppress, or extinguish maladaptive behaviors and to increase simultaneously the frequency of desirable social behaviors. In certain cases, positive reinforcement techniques are not effective, and negative reinforcement strategies must be employed. Wood (1984) described the application of negative reinforcement with a head injured patient who refused to walk to therapies or to the dining room to obtain his meals, despite the fact that he was physically able to do so. In this program, the patient was denied his meals unless he walked to the dining room. After a brief period, he came regularly to the dining room, and this behavior generalized to other areas of treatment. Due to the concreteness of many head injured individuals, generalization of treatment effects is difficult to achieve. Thus, behavioral management needs to be continuously administered in different situations to maximize behavior change.

When behavioral management techniques are ineffective in altering maladaptive behavior, psychopharmacologic approaches may be employed. To date, however, there have been few controlled studies of the effects of pharmacologic agents on behavior of the head injured individual. As there may be deleterious side effects on cognition, the clinician is cautioned against the use of medications unless other techniques have been attempted.

Apathy and lethargy have been treated effectively in some cases by the use of psychostimulants, such as amphetamine (Stern, 1978). Tricyclic antidepressants have been reported to control some agitated, restless behavior (Glenn & Rosenthal, 1985), as has propranalol (Elliott, 1977). Major tranquilizers, such as the phenothiazines, have been employed to reduce aggressive behavior. Rosenbaum and Barry (1975) reported that lithium helped control the hypomanic behavior often seen in the head injured patient.

The area of behavioral management of the head injured individual has not been extensively examined in controlled research to date. However, it may be speculated that the combination of behavioral and pharmacologic methods would prove to be the most powerful and efficient treatment approach in altering maladaptive behavior after head injury.

SOCIAL AND FAMILY CONSEQUENCES

It is an unfortunate fact that, despite the availability of integrated, multidisciplinary head injury rehabilitation programs, many of these patients remain "unrehabilitated," i.e., they are unable to resume a productive and satisfying role in society.

Reintegration into the family and community at large can be a painful, enduring struggle. Head injured individuals often find themselves displaced from premorbid roles within the family and must strive to fit into a new structure. The difficulty of this process is compounded by the inability of both patient and family to cope with the neurobehavioral changes that have occurred; physical care requirements are not usually found to be as burdensome (Bond, 1985b; Panting & Merry, 1972; Thomsen, 1974). Spouses may feel as though they are living with strangers; relatives may reject the injured member because they do not recognize and/or understand how to deal with subtle neurobehavioral disturbances. Friends may vanish due to the head injured patient's personality change, physical or mental limitations, impaired social skills, or inability to "fit in" with the group.

Because a return to a competitive or sheltered work environment, if it occurs, may take years, head injured adults may have a drastically reduced number of social contacts. If unable to drive or use public transportation, they must depend on others to venture out. Socially maladroit behavior often necessitates supervision in community activities. Inability to work creates financial hardships and may cause an unwanted change in living arrangements, such as returning to live with parents or other relatives.

Unfortunately, many severely head injured adults cannot even return to leisure activities (Oddy, 1984). Without either vocational or avocational outlets, they lead (and often recognize that they lead) rather empty, unfulfilling lives. Alcohol or drugs may be used to escape feelings of depression and worthlessness and can lead to antisocial behavior and legal entanglements (Hackler & Tobis, 1983). The magnitude of this problem remains inadequately studied.

Intervention Strategies

Family intervention has become increasingly common in rehabilitation programs because of the growing recognition of the important role that the family plays in long-term adaptation to head injury (see Chapter 6). Rosenthal (1984) has described a four-part approach to intervention with families of head injured individuals that consists of (1) patient-family education, (2) family counseling, (3) family therapy, and (4) family support groups.

Families often feel dissatisfied with the level, amount, and kind of information they receive from staff members (Oddy, Humphrey, & Uttley, 1978a). The complex nature of head injury and its sequelae, prognosis, and management strategies must be explained to the family in meaningful terms. This type of education can be provided through individual family meetings or in group teaching sessions as described by Diehl (1983).

Family counseling sessions with a psychologist or social worker can provide needed emotional support and allow discussion of various aspects of the rehabilitation and discharge planning process, and community resources.

For families with a history of maladaptive interaction or with severe postinjury adjustment problems, family therapy sessions—including the patient, if he or she is cognitively able and willing—may be indicated. These sessions aim to improve communication and interaction patterns within the family system by problem solving, role-playing, and other therapeutic techniques. Homework assignments are sometimes provided to help foster generalization of skills learned in the sessions.

The efforts of the National Head Injury Foundation (Framingham, Massachusetts) have stimulated the growth of family support groups. Often organized and conducted by relatives of the head injured patient, these groups offer opportunities to share common experiences, problems, and solutions; vent frustrations and anger; and provide emotional support. Often, family members obtain specific information about community-based resources that can aid their relative. Other services, such as advocacy, hot-line counseling, and referral services, are offered by the National Head Injury Foundation.

VOCATIONAL REHABILITATION

In one sense, vocational rehabilitation represents the "final frontier" in the rehabilitation of the head injured adult; it is the ultimate goal of comprehensive rehabilitation, but the one that may be the hardest to achieve. As Bolger (1983) stated:

> Vocational rehabilitation of the head injured adult is in its infancy. Little is known about the relative efficacy of various techniques of cognitive remediation and their eventual outcome in terms of job placement.

Only recently have researchers addressed vocational outcome in their studies of head injury rehabilitation. The published data are quite variable. Prigatano and colleagues (1984) note that traditional rehabilitative care results in a 33–40 percent return to gainful employment. Other studies cite rates from 30 percent (Gjone, Kristiansen & Sponheim, 1972) to 80–90 percent (Oddy, 1984). In his cogent review of the literature, however, Oddy points out the difficulty of comparing studies due to variations in period of follow-up since the injury, different levels of severity of injury, small samples, and other methodological problems.

The unique neurobehavioral sequelae of head injury have caused many vocational rehabilitation specialists to rethink the process of vocational rehabilitation for this population. Traditional methods of vocational evaluation and sheltered workshop placement have met with little success or enthusiasm from head injured adults and their families. Patients with cognitive impairments or behavioral dysfunctions require specialized vocational training programs in association with cognitive remediation and behavioral management. Vocational specialists must become familiar with the nature of head injury and its consequences in order to serve this population effectively.

MINOR BRAIN INJURY

Minor brain injury may be defined as a blow to the head resulting in unconsciousness for 20 minutes or less, a Glasgow Coma Score of 13–15, and hospitalization not exceeding 48 hours (Rimel, Giordani, Barth, Boll & Jane, 1981). The resultant effects of minor brain injury are often characterized as a "postconcussion syndrome," in which headache, giddiness, irritability, intolerance to light and noise, reduced tolerance to alcohol, difficulty with memory and concentration, and diminished spontaneity are often observed (Freedman, Kaplan & Saddock, 1975). A recent epidemiologic study by Kraus et al. (1984) estimated an incidence of 131 cases per 100,000 population or 294,750 cases per year admitted to hospitals in the United States.

Rimel and colleagues (1981) studied 538 individuals who sustained minor head injury and found that disability persisted up to 3 months postinjury. Specifically, 79 percent of the group complained of headaches, 59 percent reported memory difficulties, and 34 percent were unemployed. Neurologic examination was judged to be normal in virtually all the patients; however, neuropsychological examination did reveal defects in attention, concentration, memory, and judgment. Wrightson and Gronwall (1980) found that such symptoms as memory impairment, difficulties in concentration, easy fatigability, and excessive irritability characterized many of their patients with minor brain injury. Merskey and Woodforde (1972) followed up 27 cases of psychiatric disturbance after minor brain injury and found that mental symptoms persisted for a median period of 4 years after the accident. Pending litigation and financial compensation did not appear to have a significant bearing on the persistence of cognitive and behavioral disorders.

Until long-term, well-controlled prospective studies of minor brain injury are conducted, it will be difficult to determine the extent to which neurobehavioral sequelae of minor brain injury result from actual brain tissue damage, psychogenic stress, premorbid personality disposition, or the likelihood of financial compensation. However, in view of recent studies, it would appear prudent to monitor closely the recovery of patients with minor brain injury by conducting detailed neuropsychological examinations for at least 1 year following injury. (For a thorough review of the neurobehavioral consequences of minor head injury, see *Journal of Head Trauma Rehabilitation, 1986, 1* (2), entire issue.)

CONCLUSION

Advances in clinical care and research during the past decade have produced a better understanding of the neurobehavioral sequelae of head injury and a greater recognition of the complexities involved in remediating these impairments. Growing awareness of the problems of the head injured adult has spurred the development of rehabilitation facilities—both hospital and community based—offering intensive therapeutic programs. However, long-term social and vocational dysfunction are still common problems. Early and continuing intervention by rehabilitation professionals is required to modify primary neurobehavioral deficits and minimize secondary psychosocial disturbances.

REFERENCES

Achte, K.A., Hillbom, E., & Aalberg, V. (1967). *Post-traumatic psychoses following war brain injuries* (Vol. 1). Helsinki: Rehabilitation Institute for Brain Injured Veterans.

Anderson, T.P. (1982). Rehabilitation of patients with completed stroke. In F. Kottke, G.K. Stillwell, & J. Lehmann (Eds.), *Krusen's handbook of physical medicine and rehabilitation* (3rd ed.). Philadelphia: W.B. Saunders Co., pp. 583–603.

Artiola y Fortuna, L., Briggs, M., Newcombe, F., Ratcliff, G., & Thomas, C. (1980). Measuring the duration of post-traumatic amnesia. *Journal of Neurology, Neurosurgery, and Psychiatry, 43,* 377–379.

Ayllon, T., & Azrin, N.H. (1968). *The token economy: A motivational system for therapy and rehabilitation.* New York: Appleton-Century-Crofts.

Benton, A. (1979). Behavioral consequences of closed head injury. In G.L. Odom (Ed.), *Central nervous system trauma research status report.* Washington, DC: National Institute of Neurological, Communicative Disorders and Stroke, pp. 220–231.

Ben-Yishay, Y. (1985). *Improving rehabilitation outcomes in persons who have experienced stroke or traumatic brain damage.* Paper presented at the Annual Meeting of the National Association of Rehabilitation Research and Training Centers, Washington, DC.

Ben-Yishay, Y., & Diller, L. (1983). Cognitive deficits. In M. Rosenthal, E.R. Griffith, M.R. Bond, & J.D. Miller (Eds.), *Rehabilitation of the head injured adult.* Philadelphia: F.A. Davis, pp. 167–183.

Blumer, D., & Benson, D.F. (1975). Personality changes with frontal and temporal lobe lesions. In D. Blumer & D.F. Benson (Eds.), *Psychiatric aspects of neurologic disease.* New York: Grune and Stratton, pp. 151–170.

Bolger, J. (1983). Educational and vocational deficits. In M. Rosenthal, E.R. Griffith, M.R. Bond, & J.D. Miller (Eds.), *Rehabilitation of the head injured adult.* Philadelphia: F.A. Davis, pp. 219–225.

Boll, T. (1981). Assessment of neuropsychological disorders. In D.H. Barlow (Ed.), *Behavioral assessment of adult disorders.* New York: Guilford Press, pp. 45–86.

Bond, M.R. (1975). Assessment of the psychosocial outcome after severe head injury. In R. Porter & D.W. Fitzsimmons (Eds.), *Outcome of severe damage to the central nervous system.* CIBA Foundation Symposium. Amsterdam: Elsevier, pp. 141–157.

Bond, M.R. (1985a). *Long-term cognitive consequences.* Paper presented at the 9th Annual Post-Graduate Course on the Rehabilitation of the Brain Injured Adult and Child, Williamsburg, VA.

Bond, M.R. (1985b). *Treatment of psychiatric syndromes in adult victims of severe brain injury.* Paper presented at the 9th Annual Post-Graduate Course on the Rehabilitation of the Brain Injured Adult and Child, Williamsburg, VA.

Bond, M.R., & Brooks, D.N. (1976). Understanding the process of recovery as a basis for the investigation of rehabilitation for the brain injured. *Scandinavian Journal of Rehabilitation Medicine, 8,* 127–133.

Bracey, O.L. (1983). Computer-based cognitive rehabilitation. *Cognitive Rehabilitation, 1,* 7–8.

Brooks, N. (1983). Disorders of memory. In M. Rosenthal, E.R. Griffith, M.R. Bond, & J.D. Miller (Eds.), *Rehabilitation of the head injured adult.* Philadelphia: F.A. Davis, pp. 185–196.

Brooks, N. (1984a). Head injury and the family. In N. Brooks (Ed.), *Closed head injury: Psychological, social and family consequences.* London: Oxford University Press, pp. 123–147.

Brooks, N. (1984b). Cognitive deficits. In N. Brooks (Ed.), *Closed head injury: Psychological, social and family consequences.* London: Oxford University Press, pp. 44–74.

Brooks, N., & Aughton, M. (1979). Psychological consequences of blunt head injury. *International Rehabilitation Medicine, 1,* 120–125.

Clifton, G. (1985). *The acute management of head injuries.* Paper presented at the 9th Annual Post-Graduate Course on the Rehabilitation of the Brain Injured Adult and Child, Williamsburg, VA.

Diehl, L. (1983). Patient-family education. In M. Rosenthal, E.R. Griffith, M.R. Bond, & J.D. Miller (Eds.), *Rehabilitation of the head injured adult.* Philadelphia: F.A. Davis, pp. 395–401.

Dikman, S., Reitan, R.M., & Temkin, N. (1983). Neuropsychological recovery in head injury. *Archives of Neurology, 40,* 333–338.

Diller, L. (1980). *Methods for evaluation and treatment of visual perceptual difficulties of right brain damaged individuals.* New York: New York University Medical Center Rehabilitation Monograph (Supplement to Eighth Annual Workshop).

Diller, L., & Gordon, W.A. (1981). Interventions for cognitive deficits in brain-injured adults. *Journal of Consulting and Clinical Psychology, 49*, 822–834.

Elliott, F.A. (1977). Propranalol for the control of belligerent behavior following acute brain damage. *Annals of Neurology, 1*, 489–491.

Eson, M.E. (1979). *Neuropsychological approach to assessment of brain injury.* Paper presented at the International Symposium on the Rehabilitation of the Brain Injured Adult, Toronto, Canada.

Fowler, R.S., Hart, J., & Sheehan, M. (1972). A prosthetic memory: An application of the prosthetic environment concept. *Rehabilitation Counseling Bulletin, 15*, 80–85.

Freedman, A.M., Kaplan, H.I., & Saddock, B.J. (1975). *Comprehensive textbook of psychiatry* (3rd ed.). Baltimore: Williams & Wilkins, pp. 1103ff.

Gianutsos, R. (1980). What is cognitive rehabilitation? *Journal of Rehabilitation, 5*, 36–40.

Gianutsos, R., & Gianutsos, J. (1979). Rehabilitating the verbal recall of brain injured patients by mnemonic training: An experimental demonstration using single case methodology. *Journal of Clinical Neuropsychology, 1*, 117–135.

Gjone, R., Kristiansen, K., & Sponheim, N. (1972). Rehabilitation in severe head injuries. *Scandinavian Journal of Rehabilitation Medicine, 4*, 2–4.

Glasgow, R.E., Zeiss, R.A., Barrera, M., & Lewinsohn, P. (1977). Case studies on remediating deficits in brain-damaged individuals. *Journal of Consulting and Clinical Psychology, 33*, 1049–1054.

Glenn, M., & Rosenthal, M. (1985). Rehabilitation following severe traumatic brain injury. *Seminars in Neurology, 6*, 80–90.

Griffith, E.R. (1983). Types of disability. In M. Rosenthal, E.R. Griffith, M.R. Bond, & J.D. Miller (Eds.), *Rehabilitation of the head injured adult.* Philadelphia: F.A. Davis, pp. 23–32.

Groher, M. (1983). Communication disorders. In M. Rosenthal, E.R. Griffith, M.R. Bond, & J.D. Miller (Eds.), *Rehabilitation of the head injured adult.* Philadelphia: F.A. Davis, pp. 155–165.

Gronwall, D., & Wrightson, P. (1980). Duration of post-traumatic amnesia after mild head injury. *Journal of Clinical Neuropsychology, 2*, 51–60.

Hackler, E., & Tobis, J.S. (1983). Re-integration into the community. In M. Rosenthal, E.R. Griffith, M.R. Bond, & J.D. Miller (Eds.), *Rehabilitation of the head injured adult.* Philadelphia: F.A. Davis, pp. 421–434.

Hagen, C., Malkmus, D., & Durham, P. (1977). *Levels of cognitive functioning.* Downey, CA: Rancho Los Amigos Professional Staff Association.

Hall, K., Cope, D.N., & Rappaport, M. (1985). Glasgow Outcome Scale and Disability Rating Scale: Comparative usefulness in following recovery in traumatic brain injury. *Archives Physical Medicine Rehabilitation 66*, 35–37.

Harris, J. (1984). Methods of improving memory. In B.A. Wilson & N. Moffatt (Eds.), *Clinical management of memory problems.* Rockville, MD: Aspen Publishers, Inc., pp. 46–62.

Heaton, R. (1981). *Wisconsin card sorting test: Manual.* Odessa, FL: Psychological Assessment Resources.

Heilman, K.M., Safran, A., & Geschwind, N. (1971). Closed head trauma and aphasia. *Journal of Neurology, Neurosurgery, and Psychiatry, 34*, 265–269.

Hilbom, E. (1960). After effects of brain injuries. *Acta Psychiatrica et Neurologica Scandinavica* (Suppl. 60), 36–47.

Jennett, B. (1975). Scale, scope and philosophy of the clinical problem. In R. Porter, & D. Fitzsimmons (Eds.), *Outcome of severe damage to the central nervous system.* CIBA Foundation Symposium. Amsterdam: Elsevier, pp. 3–9.

Jennett, B. (1983). Scale and scope of the problem. In M. Rosenthal, E.R. Griffith, M.R. Bond, & J.D. Miller (Eds.), *Rehabilitation of the head injured adult*. Philadelphia: F.A. Davis, pp. 3–8.

Jennett, B., & Bond, M. (1975). Assessment of outcome after severe brain damage. *Lancet, 1*, 480–484.

Jennett, B., & Plum, F. (1972). Persistent vegetative state after brain damage. *Lancet, 1*, 734–737.

Jennett, B., & Teasdale, G. (1981). *Management of head injuries*. Philadelphia: F.A. Davis.

Jennett, B., Teasdale, G., Galbraith, S., Pickard, J., Grant, H., Braakman, R., Avezaat, C., Maas, A., Minderhoud, J., Vecht, C.J., Heiden, J., Small, R., Caton, W., & Kurze, T. (1977). Severe head injuries in three countries. *Journal of Neurology, Neurosurgery and Psychiatry, 40*, 291–298.

Kraus, J.F., Black, M.A., Hessol, N., Ley, P., Rokaw, W., Sullivan, C., Bowers, S., Knowlton, S., & Marshall, L. (1984). The incidence of acute brain injury and serious impairment in a defined population, *American Journal of Epidemiology, 119*, 186–201.

Kretschmer, E. (1949). Cerebral orbit and diencephalic syndromes following fractures of the brain and skull. *Archives of Psychiatry, 182*, 452.

Levin, H.S., Benton, A.L., & Grossman, R.G. (Eds.) (1982). *Neurobehavioral consequences of closed head injury*. New York: Oxford University Press.

Levin, H.S., Grossman, R.G., Rose, J.E., & Teasdale, G. (1979). Long term neuropsychological outcome of closed head injury. *Journal of Neurosurgery, 50*, 412–422.

Lewinsohn, P.M., Danaher, B.G., & Kikel, S. (1977). Visual imagery as a mnemonic aid for brain injured persons. *Journal of Consulting and Clinical Psychology, 45*, 717–723.

Lezak, M. (1975). *Relationships between personality disorders, social disturbances and physical disability following traumatic head injury*. Paper presented at the International Neuropsychological Society Meeting, San Francisco.

Lezak, M. (1979). Recovery of learning and memory functions following traumatic brain injury. *Cortex, 15*, 63–72.

Lezak, M. (1983). *Neuropsychological assessment* (2nd ed.). New York: Oxford University Press.

Lishman, W.A. (1968). Brain damage in relation to psychiatric disability after head injury. *British Journal of Psychiatry, 114*, 373–410.

Lishman, W.A. (1973). The psychiatric sequelae of head injury: A review. *Psychological Medicine, 3*, 304–318.

Luria, A.R., Nayden, V.L., Tsvetkova, L.S., & Vinarskaya, E.N. (1969). Restoration of higher cortical function following local brain damage. In P.J. Vinken, G.W. Bruyn, M. Critchley, & J.A.M. Frederiks (Eds.), *Handbook of clinical neurology*. New York: Wiley, pp. 368–433.

Lynch, R.T. (1983). Traumatic head injury: Implications for rehabilitation counseling. *Journal of Applied Rehabilitation Counseling, 3*, 32–35.

McMahon, E., & Satz, P. (1981). Clinical neuropsychology: Some forensic applications. In S. Filskov & T. Boll (Eds.), *Handbook of clinical neuropsychology*. New York: Wiley, pp. 686–701.

Mandelberg, I.A., & Brooks, D.N. (1975). Cognitive recovery after severe head injury. I. Serial testing on the WAIS. *Journal of Neurology, Neurosurgery and Psychiatry, 38*, 1121–1126.

Merskey, H., & Woodforde, J.M. (1972). Psychiatric sequelae of minor head injury. *Brain, 95*, 521–528.

Newcome, F. (1983). The psychological consequences of closed head injury: Assessment and rehabilitation. *Injury, 14*, 111–136.

Oddy, M. (1984). Head injury and social adjustment. In N. Brooks (Ed.), *Closed head injury: Psychological, social and family consequences*. London: Oxford University Press, pp. 108–122.

Oddy, M., Humphrey, M., & Uttley, D. (1978a). Stresses upon the relatives of head injured patients. *British Journal of Psychiatry, 133*, 507–513.

Oddy, M., Humphrey, M., & Uttley, D. (1978b). Subjective impairment and social recovery after closed head injury. *Journal of Neurology, Neurosurgery and Psychiatry, 41*, 611–616.

Panting, A., & Merry, P. (1972). The long-term rehabilitation of severe head injuries with particular reference to the need for social and medical support for the patient's family. *Rehabilitation, 38*, 33–37.

Prigatano, G.P., Fordyce, D.J., Zeiner, H.K., Roueche, J.R., Peping, M., & Wood, B.C. (1984). Neuropsychological rehabilitation after closed head injury. *Journal of Neurology, Neurosurgery and Psychiatry, 47*, 505–513.

Rappaport, M. (1986). Evoked potentials and head injury in a rehabilitation setting. In M. Miner & K. Wagner. *Neurotrauma: Treatment, rehabilitation and related issues*. Boston: Butterworth, pp. 189–194.

Rappaport, M., Hall, K.M., Hopkins, K., & Belleza, T. (1982). Disability rating scale for severe head trauma: Coma to community. *Archives Physical Medicine Rehabilitation 63*, 118–123.

Rimel, R., Giordani, B., Barth, J.T., Boll, T.J., & Jane, J.A. (1981). Disability caused by minor head injury. *Neurosurgery, 9*, 221–228.

Rimel, R., & Jane, J.A. (1983). Characteristics of the head-injured patient. In M. Rosenthal, E.R. Griffiths, M.R. Bond, & J.D. Miller (Eds.), *Rehabilitation of the head injured adult*. Philadelphia: F.A. Davis, pp. 9–21.

Romano, M.D. (1974). Family response to traumatic head injury. *Scandinavian Journal of Rehabilitation Medicine, 6*, 1–4.

Rosenbaum, A.H., & Barry, M.J. (1975). Positive therapeutic response to lithium in hypomania secondary to organic brain syndrome. *American Journal of Psychiatry, 132*, 1072.

Rosenthal, M. (1984). Strategies for family intervention. In B. Edelstein, & E. Couture (Eds.), *Behavioral approaches to the traumatically brain injured*. New York: Plenum Press, pp. 227–246.

Rosenthal, M., & Kolpan, K.I. (1986). Head injury rehabilitation: Psycholegal issues and roles for the rehabilitation psychologist. *Rehabilitation Psychology, 31*, 37–46.

Rosenthal, M., & Muir, C. (1983). Methods of family intervention. In M. Rosenthal, E.R. Griffith, M.R. Bond, & J.D. Miller (Eds.), *Rehabilitation of the head injured adult*. Philadelphia: F.A. Davis, pp. 407–419.

Russell, W.R. (1971). *The traumatic amnesias*. London: Oxford University Press.

Russell, W.R., & Nathan, P.W. (1946). Traumatic amnesia. *Brain, 69*, 183–187.

Sarno, M.T. (1980). The nature of verbal impairment after closed head injury. *Journal of Nervous and Mental Diseases, 168*, 685–692.

Sarno, M.T. (1984). Verbal impairment after closed head injury: Report of a replication study. *Journal of Nervous and Mental Diseases, 172*, 475–479.

Schachter, D., & Crovitz, H. (1977). Memory function after closed head injury: A review of the quantitative research. *Cortex, 13*, 150.

Stern, J. (1978). Cranio-cerebral injured patients: A psychiatric clinical description. *Scandinavian Journal of Rehabilitation Medicine, 10*, 7–10.

Stuss, D.T., & Benson, D.F. (1984). Neuropsychological studies of the frontal lobes. *Psychological Bulletin, 95*, 3–28.

Sweet, W.H., Ervin, F., Mark, V.H. (1968). The relationship of violent behavior to focal cerebral disease. In S. Garuttini & E.B. Sigg (Eds.), *Aggressive behavior*. Proceedings of International Symposium on the Biology of Aggressive Behavior, Milan, Italy, May 1968.

Tabbador, K., Mattis, S., & Zazula, M.A. (1984). Cognitive sequelae and recovery course after moderate and severe head injury. *Neurosurgery, 14*, 701–707.

Teasdale, G., & Jennett, B. (1974). Assessment of coma and impaired consciousness. *Lancet, ii*, 81–84.

Teasdale, G., & Mendelow, D. (1984). Pathophysiology of head injuries. In N. Brooks (Ed.), *Closed head injury: Psychological, social and family consequences*. London: Oxford University Press, pp. 4–36.

Thomsen, I.V. (1974). The patient with severe head injury and his family. *Scandinavian Journal of Rehabilitation Medicine, 6*, 180–183.

U.S. Department of Education Office of Special Education and Rehabilitation Services. (1981). Head injury: The problem, the need. *Programs for the Handicapped, 6*, 1–3.

van Zomeren, A.H., Brouwer, W.H., & Deelman, B.G. (1984). Attentional deficits: The riddles of selectivity, speed and alertness. In N. Brooks (Ed.), *Closed head injury: Psychological, social and family consequences*. Oxford: Oxford University Press, pp. 74–107.

van Zomeren, A.H. & Deelman, B.G. (1976). Differential effects of simple and choice reaction time after closed head injury. *Clinical Neurological Neurosurgery, 79*, 81–90.

Vauhkonen V. (1959). Suicide among the male disabled with war injuries to the brain. *Acta Psychiatrica et Neurologica Scandinavica* (Suppl. 137), 90–91.

Weinstein, E.A., & Kahn, R.L. (1955). *Denial of illness*. Springfield, IL: Charles C Thomas.

Wolfe, S. (1984). *The role of problem solving in the long term readjustment of closed head injured adults*. Unpublished doctoral dissertation, University of Alberta, Edmonton, Alberta.

Wood, R.L. (1984). Behavior disorders following severe brain injury: Their presentation and management. In N. Brooks (Ed.), *Closed head injury: Psychological, social and family consequences*. London: Oxford University Press, pp. 195–219.

Wrightson, P., & Gronwall, D. (1980). Time off work and symptoms after minor head injury. *Injury, 12*, 445–454.

Chapter 3

Stroke: Causes, Consequences, and Treatment

Laurence M. Binder, Ph.D.
Diane Howieson, Ph.D.
Bruce M. Coull, M.D.

Stroke is a major cause of death and disability in the United States (Kurtzke, 1985). Although it is primarily a disease of the elderly, no age group is spared. In a survey of over 4,000 cases the average age of the acute stroke patient was 72 years, with affected women being slightly older than men (Becker et al., 1986; Yatsu et al., 1986). Yet 20 percent of the patients were under 65, and almost 25 percent were employed at the time of the stroke.

Epidemiologic studies have confirmed that the incidence of stroke has been declining for approximately three decades. Statistics from the Mayo Clinic (Garraway et al., 1979; Garraway, Whisnant, & Drury, 1983) indicate roughly a 25 percent decline in the overall incidence of stroke since 1945. This important advance in stroke prevention is ascribed primarily to earlier and better recognition and treatment of risk factors, especially hypertension (Hypertension Detection and Follow-up Program Cooperative Group, 1982). Stroke incidence declined in all age groups studied, but persons over 70 years derived the greatest benefit. Nonetheless, stroke remains a common condition with functional consequences that are often serious. Furthermore, the overall prevalence of stroke may increase during the next decade as the number of elderly in the population rises. Hence, stroke will remain an important health care problem well into the 21st century.

The term "stroke" implies the sudden onset of focal neurologic dysfunction due to an interruption of blood flow supplying a region of brain. The concept of a *regional* disturbance in cerebral blood flow that causes focal brain ischemia separates stroke from the more global insults to brain that occur in cardiac arrest, anoxic encephalopathy, or prolonged severe hypoglycemia. Yet, although the mechanisms of the brain injury may differ, a distinction between focal and global cerebral insults is, in part, arbitrary because cerebral infarctions resulting from large arterial occlusions may cause massive brain damage, whereas relatively small lesions can follow cardiac arrest or anoxic-metabolic encephalopathy. Furthermore, although it is axiomatic that stroke causes a focal injury, it can induce diffuse disruption of brain regions far removed from the lesion site (Reivich et al., 1978). Finally, it is important to recognize that many pathophysiologic mechanisms cause multiple or recurrent strokes, insidiously producing global impairment of brain function (Hachinski, Lassen, & Marshall, 1974).

This chapter discusses the pathogenesis of stroke, outlines the major stroke syndromes, considers the primary behavioral and cognitive deficits resulting from stroke, and describes methods of neuropsychological assessment and psychological treatment.

TYPES OF STROKE

Stroke is a syndrome—that is, a set of symptoms—and is not diagnostic of a particular disease process. The major etiologies of stroke include (1) cerebral infarction resulting from thrombosis secondary to atherosclerotic cerebrovascular disease or embolism, which is usually of cardiac origin, (2) intracerebral hemorrhage usually secondary to hypertensive rupture of a blood vessel, (3) subarachnoid hemorrhage secondary to rupture of an aneurysm, and (4) a miscellaneous group that includes infarction due to cerebral vasculitis, venous thrombosis, and changes in blood coagulability, such as hyperviscosity or hypercoagulable states. In select populations, stroke is associated with certain malignancies, drug use, migraine headache, oral contraceptive use, and trauma.

Cerebral Thrombosis

Cerebral thrombosis, the most common cause of stroke in aged adults, occurs following acute occlusion of an atherosclerosed (narrowed) cerebral artery or arteriole. Infarction also can follow the occlusion of a cerebral vein, but this is rare. In the elderly, most cerebral infarctions are related to underlying disseminated atherosclerosis. Within the atherosclerotic plaque of the arterial wall, degenerative injury may cause the formation of a thrombus, which is composed of platelet-fibrin and red blood cell aggregates. Portions of this clot or the plaque itself can break off and enter the cerebral circulation, causing vascular occlusions and resultant cerebral infarction. Because the brain has a rich collateral blood supply, a slow, progressive occlusion of the internal carotid artery may produce no symptoms. However, if occlusion occurs suddenly or if collateral supply to brain is poor, massive infarction in the territory of the middle or anterior cerebral artery ensues. Brainstem strokes are caused by thrombosis within the vertebral or basilar arteries themselves or from propagation into these large arteries of a clot that formed within one of their small penetrating brainstem arterioles (Kubik & Adams, 1946). Infarctions are fatal during the initial hospitalization in 15–20 per-

cent of cases, whereas 35–50 percent of victims die from intracerebral hemorrhage (Becker et al., 1986).

Lacunar Infarction

From the French word for "small hole" the term "lacune" connotes small
infarctions that are usually 2–15 mm in diameter within the basal ganglia, internal
capsule, thalamus, and pons (Fisher, 1965). They are frequently multiple and may
not be entirely confined to any single vascular territory or to subcortical structures.
Most lacunar infarctions result from disease of the small, deep, penetrating
arterioles located at the base of the brain and along the basilar artery within the
pons and midbrain. Lacunar infarction accounts for up to 20 percent of all cerebral
infarctions, and there is also a high prevalence of clinically silent lacunar events
(Fisher, 1965). Many patients suffer undiagnosed strokes before the stroke that
brings them to the hospital. The nature of the vascular injury that gives rise to
lacunar infarction remains controversial. Fisher (1969) has proposed that
arteriolar damage results from poorly controlled hypertension.

The lacunar syndromes are readily recognized and have important implications
for outcome and rehabilitation efforts. Over 20 clinical syndromes have been
described, of which the most important are listed in Table 3–1. Pure motor stroke
is the most common syndrome, with complete or partial paralysis affecting the
face, arm, hand, and leg. Several other lacunar syndromes are variations of this
syndrome, such as dysarthria and a clumsy hand or leg paresis with ataxia of the
arm. Because lacunar infarctions are small, patients with the acute onset pure
motor syndrome are fully conscious and have no sensory deficits, visual disturbances, or difficulties with language. Although the neurologic deficit may be
profound during the acute stages, many patients make an excellent recovery.
Fisher and Curry (1965) found that over 50 percent of patients were fully
recovered within 6 months.

Table 3–1 Common Lacunar Syndromes

Syndrome	Symptoms	Location of Lacune
Pure motor stroke basis	Paresis of face, arm, and leg	Internal capsule, pontis
Pure sensory stroke	Paresthesias of face, arm, and leg	Ventral posterior thalamus
Ataxic hemiparesis, internal	Appendicular weakness and ataxia, especially leg	Basis pontis, capsule
Dysarthria, clumsy hand, internal	Slurred speech, hemiataxia	Basis pontis, capsule

A uniformly good prognosis is not ensured, however, and a severe long-term deficit may remain in 20 percent of patients (Richter, Brust, Bruun et al., 1977). Recurrent lacunar infarctions can produce multi-infarct dementia, often called the "lacunar state" (Hachinski et al. 1974). Patients with this form of dementia classically have a spastic quadraparesis, dysarthria, dysphagia, incontinence of bladder, small-stepped gait (marché à petit pas) and a pseudobulbar affect with loss of control over emotional expression.

Cerebral Embolism

Embolism to brain of thrombus or other material arising from within the heart is an increasingly common cause of stroke (Hart & Miller, 1983; Mohr et al., 1978). Onset is usually abrupt, but sometimes symptoms evolve slowly or in stuttering fashion. Most emboli lodge within the territory of the middle cerebral artery, but no vascular distribution is spared. Pathologic studies suggest that embolic infarctions often have a hemorrhagic component (Fisher & Adams, 1951), but a recent clinical series using CT scanning has not confirmed this observation (Hart, Coull, & Hart, 1983). This issue needs to be resolved because persons with embolic stroke are frequently given anticoagulant medication to prevent recurrence of emboli. The diagnosis of embolic infarction can be difficult because the resulting neurologic deficits do not differ from cerebral thrombosis. Clinical evidence suggesting multiple systemic or cerebral emboli in the presence of a recognized cardiac source for emboli aids in establishing the diagnosis. Rheumatic and atherosclerotic heart disease are the underlying causes in most cases of cerebral embolism (Easton & Sherman, 1980).

Hemorrhagic Stroke

The two main types of hemorrhagic stroke are subarachnoid hemorrhage (SAH) and intracerebral hemorrhage (ICH).

Subarachnoid Hemorrhage

The principal cause of bleeding into the subarachnoid space on the surface of the brain is a ruptured berry aneurysm. An aneurysm is a weakening and ballooning of an arterial wall; a berry aneurysm is caused by a congenital anomaly. Other sources of hemorrhage include bleeding from an arteriovenous malformation or rupture of an aneurysm because of infection. The aneurysms may be single or multiple and can vary in size from a few millimeters to giant aneurysms of 1–2 cm diameter (Wiebers, Whisnant, & O'Fallon, 1981).

Giant aneurysms produce symptoms by exerting pressure on brain structures, a phenomenon known as mass effect. Rupture per se is infrequent. Symptoms of aneurysmal rupture include severe, sudden headache, which is often described as explosive, accompanied by collapse. Loss of consciousness may be brief, but deep coma leading to death can develop rapidly. Focal neurologic signs are often absent in mild cases. Most aneurysms are asymptomatic before rupture, but they occasionally give rise to distal emboli producing transient or completed infarctions. In addition to headache, alterations in consciousness, and focal neurologic signs, bleeding into the subarachnoid space produces meningeal irritation manifested by rigidity in the neck, which is usually accompanied by severe headache and mild confusion. When the bleeding is excessive, there may be profound encephalopathy.

Roughly 50 percent of those who suffer SAH will die of the initial or repeat hemorrhage or the consequences thereof, about 15 percent will be disabled, and the remainder will recover sufficiently to return to work (Adams & Victor, 1981).

Intracerebral Hemorrhage

Intracerebral hemorrhage (ICH), as stated earlier, is one of the more lethal forms of stroke. Most often, ICH occurs in individuals with poorly controlled hypertension; the improved treatment of hypertension has therefore led to a declining incidence of ICH. In persons under 40, arteriovenous malformations cause a substantial portion of brain hemorrhages, whereas in the very elderly, amyloid deposits within brain arterioles have recently been recognized as an important cause (Ozazaki, Reagan, & Campbell, 1979). In ICH associated with hypertension, the distribution of hematomas is similar to that of most lacunar infarctions: the basal ganglia, deep white matter, thalamus, pons, and cerebellum. Hypertensive ICH and the lacunar infarction may represent two ends of a spectrum of one disease, possibly arteriolosclerosis.

Hemorrhages vary in size, but those sufficiently large to produce mass effect or rupture of blood into the ventricular system are often life threatening if not promptly treated. As with cerebellar infarction, cerebellar hemorrhages can produce irreversible coma because of compression of vital structures within the pons. If they are massive, hemorrhages may produce headache, alterations in consciousness, and elevated intracranial pressure that sometimes leads to death. Patients who survive hemorrhages may recover more rapidly than nonhemorrhagic stroke patients (Hier, Mondlock, & Caplan, 1983).

REGIONAL SYNDROMES

Border-zone Infarction

Certain brain regions are more susceptible than others to ischemic injury. The reason for this selectivity is not entirely clear, but the available evidence suggests several mechanisms. A common form of selective ischemic injury is the border-zone or watershed infarction that occurs in the brain regions that receive overlapping terminal branches of the major intracranial arteries. Border-zone infarctions usually are bilateral and are often hemorrhagic. The ischemic insult is presumed to result from prolonged regional hypoperfusion caused by cardiac arrest, severe hemorrhage, or other causes of profound hypotension; however, focal micro-emboli have been reported to produce the border-zone syndrome. In contrast to the syndromes described above, the clinical signature of border-zone infarction is one of global or multicentric impairment of brain function.

Middle Cerebral Artery Occlusion

The acute clinical syndrome after complete occlusion of the middle cerebral artery (MCA) is characterized by contralateral hemiplegia of face, arm, and leg, which is usually less profound in the leg, and corresponding sensory loss. Homonymous hemianopsia, described below, is common. During the first 2 to 4 days after onset, patients are frequently stuporous or comatose and may exhibit signs of brainstem dysfunction, such as disorders of bulbar and respiratory control. Frequently the eyes deviate toward the side of the hemispheric lesion; when the infarction occurs within the dominant hemisphere, a global aphasia often is produced. Mortality during the acute stage approaches 40 percent, and those who survive are frequently severely impaired.

The two main branches of the MCA are the superior branch, which supplies the primary motor and sensory cortex, and the inferior branch, which feeds portions of the superior temporal and angular gyri and the parietal cortex. Infarction in the distribution of the superior branch can produce motor and sensory impairment in the face, arm, and hand, often sparing the leg. If the inferior branch is affected, then cognitive, perceptual, or language deficits may occur, depending upon the site of the lesion. Small branch infarctions sometimes resolve, leaving only sensory or motor deficits.

Anterior Cerebral Artery Occlusion

Strokes that occur in the distribution of the anterior cerebral artery produce several syndromes. Infarction in the territory of supply to the motor and sensory cortex over the superior medial region produces contralateral paresis of the leg with accompanying sensory loss. When both anterior cerebral arteries are involved, spastic paraplegia, accompanied by bladder and bowel incontinence, may occur. If the infarction extends to more anterior regions, aberrant behavior and labile affect often are produced. Lesions in other portions of the distribution of this artery can produce greater sensory and motor involvement of the shoulder than of the hand and arm.

Vertebrobasilar Stroke

A full discussion of the many types of brainstem strokes is beyond the scope of this chapter, but certain aspects bear emphasis. The blood supply to the brainstem—medulla, pons, and midbrain—and cerebellum derives largely from the vertebrobasilar arteries, often referred to as the posterior circulation. Small perforating and large circumferential branches arise from the vertebral and basilar arteries and supply the vital centers for arousal and respiratory control within the brainstem and cerebellum; strokes affecting these regions are often fatal. Conversely, vital centers may be spared in brainstem strokes that produce apparent coma because of disruption of descending corticospinal tracts. The patient may be fully awake, but is unable to respond because of the loss of motor control. This is termed the "locked in" syndrome and should be ruled out in all patients with apparent coma after brainstem strokes. Furthermore, it is important to remember that, with brainstem infarction, severe impairment of bulbar or motor control of the limbs may result without any major alteration in cognitive function. The prognosis of a functional recovery generally is better for those patients with strokes in the territory of the vertebrobasilar arteries than for those with carotid distribution strokes (Caplan, 1979). This better prognosis may, in part, be attributable to relative sparing of the intellect in the former.

FACTORS RELATED TO THE EXPRESSION OF NEUROPSYCHOLOGICAL AND NEUROLOGICAL DEFICITS

The sensory, motor, and cognitive abnormalities that appear in the acute and chronic stages of stroke are the result of a complex interaction of several variables. The location of the lesion is only one important factor. At first glance it might appear that a detailed knowledge of the brain's vascular system and the neuroanatomic structures it supplies would allow an accurate prediction of the neurologic consequences of occlusion of any given artery. However, such correspondence has often proved to have more theoretical than practical importance, primarily because the brain is endowed with a rich collateral circulation. Thus, the arterial supply to the brain often is shared between the carotid and vertebral arteries at the base of the brain via the Circle of Willis. Also, the cerebral cortex can be fed by leptomeninges, the covering of the brain. Thus, in the event of vascular occlusion, regional cerebral circulation may be maintained through auxiliary channels. In part, cerebral infarction is a reflection of the failure of these auxiliary channels. The importance of the collateral circulation is illustrated by the consequences of complete occlusion of the internal carotid artery. Although this occurrence may be asymptomatic, it can produce massive infarction in the distribution of the middle cerebral artery, with sparing of the anterior and posterior cerebral territories because of the collateral supply available through the anterior communicating and vertebrobasilar systems, respectively.

Age is among the most critical variables affecting the extent and persistence of neurologic deficits. With advancing age there is increased prevalence of systemic and orthopedic diseases and injuries that affect the patient's endurance, mobility, and neurologic functioning. Broken hips, arthritis, chronic obstructive pulmonary disease, heart disease, and dementia are all associated with advancing age and all retard progress in rehabilitation. The impact of focal lesions at distant sites— *diaschisis*—is also directly related to age.

The manifestations of diaschisis have recently been studied. Stroke in one cerebral hemisphere frequently results in bilateral dysfunction as reflected in both blood flow and behavioral measures. The greatest reduction in blood flow occurs 1 week after the stroke (Reivich et al., 1978). In young patients flow in the noninfarcted hemisphere normalizes over the first few weeks after stroke, but reduced flow persists in the elderly (Meyer, Kanda, Fukuuchi, Shimazu, Dennis, & Ericsson, 1971). Electroencephalographic studies have suggested that abnormalities recorded from the "intact" hemisphere predict poor progress in language for aphasic patients (Jabbari, Maulsby, Holtzapple, & Marshall, 1979; Tikofsky, Kooi, & Thomas, 1960). Aphasic patients with motor deficits in the left hand have a worse prognosis than do those with intact left hand function (Ghannam, Javornisky, & Smith, 1980).

DESCRIPTION OF BEHAVIORAL DEFICITS

In stroke rehabilitation settings where patients routinely receive neuropsychological evaluations, the referral question may simply be a request for a description of the patient's cognitive and psychosocial strengths and weaknesses. In some cases, however, more specific diagnostic questions may arise, such as competence for independent living, employment, or driving. This section discusses some cognitive, perceptual, and motor consequences of stroke and describes some methods of assessment of those sequelae (see Chapter 9).

Insight, Decision Making, and Judgment

Subtle deficits may be noted in the areas of insight, decision making, and judgment. Some right-brain-damaged (RBD) stroke patients appear to lack self-evaluative abilities (Weinstein & Kahn, 1955). In fact, they may be completely unaware of a left hemiplegia, left visual field cut, or other obvious problems in the first few days after stroke. This unawareness or minimization of deficits, known as *anosognosia*, is less common in left-brain-damaged (LBD) patients. RBD patients often cannot integrate complex information, draw proper inferences, or detect subtle humor (Wapner, Hamby, & Gardner, 1981). Business and family decisions may be ill-founded because of the patient's incomplete appreciation of situations. Social interactions are awkward, and interpersonal problems emerge, as the insensitivity of RBD patients prevents them from understanding the nature of the interpersonal problems and modifying their behavior accordingly. Interpersonal problems may occur in LBD stroke patients as well because of aphasia or rigidity (Lezak, 1978).

Spectacular and impulsive confabulations can be observed after stroke. These are products of defective judgment and memory; they usually suggest a frontal lobe lesion (Stuss, Alexander, Lieberman, & Levine, 1978). For example, some of the authors' patients have watched dramas on television and believed not only that the events really happened but also that they themselves had observed or participated in them.

In this culture independent mobility is highly valued and, in fact, is often assumed to be a necessity. One of the most important consequences of stroke for many patients is the inability to resume driving. Hemiplegia alone need not be a barrier to driving. The major contraindications for driving are single or recurrent episodes of loss of consciousness; motor weakness, diminished vision or hearing, impaired memory, perception, or judgment (Waller, 1973); and changes in personality. RBD patients may have a number of deficits that interfere with driving ability: persistent neglect of part of their visual field, impaired visual perception, impulsivity, and poor judgment. The latter may be difficult to establish objectively and yet may be the most important factor. Waller (1973) pointed out that problems in judgment that interfere with driving may be subtle and erratic. LBD patients also may have impaired visual perception and are unusually slow in making decisions (Riege, Klane, Metter, & Hanson, 1982), which would impede the quick responses required for driving.

Given the salience of the issue, it is surprising that little information exists about the ability of stroke patients to resume driving. The few studies available (Jones, Giddens, & Croft, 1983; Sivak, Olson, Kewman, Won, & Henson, 1981; Wilson & Smith, 1983) suggest that as a group, brain-damaged subjects have poorer overall driving skills than do non-brain-damaged controls. Interestingly, one study (Sivak et al., 1981) found that those subjects who scored well on tests involving visual scanning, reasoning, and social judgment tended to show good driving performance. Further studies using larger samples and measures of other pertinent functions, such as insight and reaction time, are needed to assess the driving competence of stroke patients.

Often patients resume driving with no professional advice. Golper, Rau, and Marshall (1980) analyzed the accuracy with which aphasic stroke patients judged themselves competent to drive; they found that patient self-judgments agreed significantly with those made by an interdisciplinary rehabilitation team. A comparable investigation is needed for RBD patients who, because of the above-noted tendencies to minimize their deficits, often make unwise decisions to resume driving.

Rehabilitation personnel should provide assessments and advice about driving to patients and their families. A two-stage evaluation, using both driving simulators and actual vehicles, is available in some rehabilitation centers. Mental status or neuropsychological examinations may reveal prohibitive deficits in some patients; others with milder deficits should be referred for a driving simulator evaluation. Patients whose driving is impaired because of visual-perceptual deficiencies might improve their driving skills through perceptual training (Sivak et al., 1984).

Initiation

Some behavioral consequences of stroke may not be detected while the patient is in a structured hospital setting and may become apparent only when the patient returns home or to work. One subtle deficit is an organically based lack of initiative, which the authors define as an inability to plan or begin a series of goal-directed responses. Assessment of initiative depends more upon observation than on test results (Lezak, 1982).

Lack of initiative is exemplified by patients who do not shift from uncomfortable postures in bed, as seen in the case example below; who never complain of hunger or a need to change their bedclothes, or who seem to idle away their time contentedly doing nothing. Some of these patients show little cognitive impairment on standardized measures because the testing situation provides the structure for initiation that they themselves cannot impose. Decreased initiative is particularly evident in patients with bilateral lesions of the frontal lobes (Luria, 1966). Tests that are sensitive to frontal lobe dysfunction, such as the Wisconsin Card Sorting Test (Heaton, 1981), or to planning disorders, such as the Complex Figure Copy Test (Binder, 1982), may provide correlative evidence of the cognitive impairment that often accompanies initiation deficits.

Loss of initiative is distinguishable from poor motivation (Lezak, 1979). A patient may be motivated, but lack the ability to plan and carry out each step of an activity. In contrast, a patient may have the ability to initiate activities, but lack the motivation to do so. Failure to distinguish between these two deficits can lead to inappropriate treatment recommendations and inaccurate prognosis. Therefore, evidence of apathy or inertia must be carefully assessed so as to differentiate between organic lack of initiative and a more psychogenic loss of motivation.

Dementia

The existence of cognitive deficits that are more serious and pervasive than expected on the basis of stroke severity alone suggests the contribution of an additional neurologic process. The incidence of dementia in those persons over the age of 65 living at home is about 10 percent (Kay, Beamish, & Roth, 1964). Therefore, many elderly patients are demented before suffering a stroke. A history of mental decline suggests the presence of a premorbid dementia. Information from the history sometimes shows the ''stepwise'' pattern of decline characteristic of multi-infarct dementia or the progressive global loss of function found in Alzheimer's Disease. Consider the following case example.

> A 76-year-old right-handed man suffered a left CVA that resulted in a moderate right hemiparesis. Although he was not aphasic, the patient exhibited a great deal of trouble following commands to perform motor tasks. He showed marked limb apraxia (see below) in his left arm, was disoriented to time and place, and responded extremely slowly to some questions. His physical therapist also observed marked apraxia in transfer training. In bed he frequently became positioned in uncomfortable ''scissors'' postures, acknowledged that he was uncomfortable, but made no apparent effort to move himself (organic initiation deficit). Cognitive testing revealed global dysfunction. A son reported that the patient's ability to handle his affairs had declined markedly before the stroke. A CT scan revealed a moderate degree of cerebral atrophy. Alterations in medications did not improve his behavior, and he made no progress in rehabilitation.

Global dementias generally guarantee a poor rehabilitation outcome. Reports from informants of decline in adaptive skills before the stroke are helpful diagnostically, although informants may rationalize or minimize the significance of behavior that is clearly impaired. Even in the absence of a clear history, the cognitive evaluation can suggest a prestroke dementia. Right-handed RBD stroke patients generally do not have severe deficits in verbal recent memory or verbal intellectual tasks and do not demonstrate ideational apraxia. LBD patients, unless aphasic, should not be severely impaired on visual perceptual and visual constructional tasks. If these anomalous findings appear, the possibility of generalized intellectual loss should be entertained. In patients with aphasia, who frequently suffer a loss of both language and other intellectual abilities on formal testing, the question of coexisting dementia may only be resolved by observing whether they respond to rehabilitation.

Unilateral Neglect

A patient with unilateral neglect fails to notice or respond to stimuli to the body or from extrapersonal space on the side opposite the lesioned hemisphere, despite adequate sensation and comprehension of the task. Current theories of the underlying mechanisms of neglect are discussed by Heilman (1979). Posterior (usually parietal) cortical lesions predominate. Symptoms occur more frequently, are more severe, and are more persistent with lesions of the right than the left hemisphere. Neglect also can occur with subcortical lesions (Damasio, Damasio, & Chui, 1980; Ferro & Kertesz, 1984; Healton, Navarro, Bressman, & Brust, 1982). Neglect should be distinguished from such deficits in primary sensation as visual field defects or loss of tactile sensation, although it often occurs in combination with a primary sensory loss. Neglect can affect any or all modalities.

The clinical manifestations are variable. In severely affected RBD patients, responses are absent to stimulation in the left visual field or to left-sided bodily sensations. Food on the left side of the plate may not be eaten. These patients have difficulty conversing with someone who is standing on their left side and, in fact, may ignore them. They also may fail to groom or dress the affected side of their body. In truly extreme cases, patients might fail to recognize their own disabled limbs, saying that their left leg belongs to someone else or that their left arm is something they picked up in physical therapy! When patients are asked to produce drawings from memory, such as a clock, they might draw only one-half of the figure.

In less severe cases, neglect may be reflected only in reading or ambulation. The patient may be unable to refixate to the left-hand margin of the page, causing word omissions and impaired comprehension. Especially when there is coexisting tactile sensory loss, problems with ambulation arise, such as colliding with objects on the affected side. The persistence of neglect is associated with failure to regain independence in activities of daily living (Denes, Semenza, Stoppa, & Lis, 1982).

Assessment of neglect is complicated by its inconsistent expression in many patients (Ogden, 1985). Consequently, it is not accurate to rule out neglect on the basis of one brief evaluation. Clinical observation suggests that neglect of one's limbs during ambulation can occur without any sign of neglect on tests that require visual scanning, such as reading, letter cancellation, or line bisection tasks. Such patients may have more of a problem with tactile sensory or motor neglect than with visual neglect.

Aphasia

Language impairment is one of the most salient symptoms of stroke, occurring most often as a result of a left-hemisphere lesion. A minority of left-handed patients develop aphasia following right-hemisphere stroke. Even more infrequently, right-handed patients with right-hemisphere involvement exhibit aphasic symptoms (Hecaen & Albert, 1978).

Aphasia may take many forms, depending largely on the site and size of the lesion within the language regions of the brain. Most aphasic persons have some difficulty with all language tasks: speech, auditory comprehension, reading, and writing.

Anterior lesions tend to produce a prominent defect in expressive language, both oral and written. This disorder, often referred to as *nonfluent aphasia*, is characterized by effortful speech production with errors of grammar, syntax, and omission of words that are meaningful to the sentence structure, e.g., prepositions and articles. Output consists of a few words, usually nouns—telegraphic speech. The pattern of deficits in writing resembles that of speech. Auditory comprehension and reading are relatively well preserved, although comprehension of syntactic structures, such as prepositions, is disrupted. This comprehension disturbance is observed if linguistically complex auditory commands are given.

Fluent aphasics, whose lesions generally lie in the posterior temporal and parietal lobes (Benson, 1979), have difficulty comprehending both oral and written material. They may be unable to follow the simplest verbal instructions. Their speech is effortless, grammatically, and syntactically intact, although there may be word-finding hesitation or naming difficulty (*anomia*). Substitutions of incorrect sounds or syllables—*literal paraphasia*—or incorrect words—*verbal or semantic paraphasia*—are common. For example, a male patient may refer to his wife as his "wofe" or his "mother." When both expressive and receptive functions are severely compromised, the disorder is called *global aphasia*. For a more complete description of the major aphasic syndromes, see Goodglass and Kaplan (1976) and Benson (1979).

Some patients have a disorder of speech articulation but no symbolic language disorder. This condition, known as *dysarthria*, is characterized by distorted speech sounds and results from poor control of the muscles of articulation: the vocal cords, tongue, palate, and lips. Dysarthria may occur with lesions in a variety of sites, including cortical and subcortical areas and the cerebellum. Patients with aphasia may also be dysarthric. They may have motor weakness on the affected side and/or an impairment in fine motor programming needed for speech—*apraxia of speech*.

Spontaneous improvement in aphasia occurs to some degree in most stroke patients. The greatest change occurs during the first 3 months, and further spontaneous improvement, if any, is slight after the first year (Kertesz & McCabe, 1977). A study of prognostic factors showed that initial severity of aphasia and age correlate negatively with improvement, and auditory comprehension ability, speech fluency, and good general health correlate positively (Marshall & Phillips, 1983). Educational and occupational background appear to have scant relation to outcome (Sarno, 1981).

There is evidence that aphasia therapy assists patients in achieving maximum recovery (Basso, Capitani, & Vignolo, 1979; Sarno, 1981). Although many approaches to speech therapy exist, the treatment methods generally involve stimulation with oral language, encouragement of the patient's use of language, and repetitive practice and imitation. Other techniques teach patients to communicate through nonspeech processes, such as drawing, using a communication board, sign language, and using a variety of information-carrying gestures. Aphasia therapy also provides additional emotional support that many stroke patients need in order to adapt to their condition. Those patients who respond most favorably to therapy tend to be younger, in good general health, and to begin therapy soon after onset (Marshall, Tompkins, & Phillips, 1982).

Memory

Few patients who suffer from strokes escape memory problems. Remote memory and recall of experiences before the stroke are usually well preserved. However, new learning, retention, and the ability to keep track of daily events often are compromised (Lezak, 1983). The degree of memory impairment depends on the severity of the stroke, location of the lesion, and the presence of any pre-existing brain pathology. Patients with multiple infarctions often have severe memory deficits, and those with hemorrhages of the anterior communicating artery may develop a severe memory impairment accompanied by confabulation (Volpe & Hirst, 1983). The more common middle cerebral artery strokes produce mild to moderate memory difficulties. Infarctions of the posterior cerebral artery compromise temporal lobe functioning, sometimes bilaterally, and often cause prominent memory deficits.

The type of memory problem is partly determined by the site of the lesion. Nonaphasic patients with LBD have pronounced verbal memory difficulties, whereas RBD patients have more difficulty with nonverbal memory, such as memory for spatial relations (Milner, 1968). Because of their language deficits, aphasic patients may have great difficulty with any verbal tasks, and therefore no pure measure of their verbal memory is possible. Similarly, the visual memory deficits of right-hemisphere stroke patients are compounded by their visual processing and organizing difficulties, but may be less severe than the visual memory deficits of LBD aphasic patients (Boller & DeRenzi, 1967; Gainotti, Caltagirone, & Miceli, 1978).

As with most symptoms of stroke, impaired memory functioning sometimes improves slowly with time following stroke. A few studies (Gasparrini & Satz, 1979; Gianutsos & Gianutsos, 1979) have evaluated memory retraining techniques, such as the use of imagery or verbal associations. As yet, controlled studies have not established that such training carries over to daily tasks.

Visual-Perceptual and Visual Constructional Deficits

Visual-perceptual disorders are quite common after stroke, particularly when the right hemisphere is affected. Some patients have a loss of vision in a portion of their visual field. Visual field defects can include the entire side of space contralateral to the lesion—*hemianopsia*—or either the upper or lower sections—

quadrantanopsia. Compensation for visual field defects, if not accompanied by neglect, can be achieved by head turning. Other common perceptual deficits include impairments in visual synthesis (perception of the whole) and analysis (perception of detail) and in spatial orientation. Less common are visual recognition deficits (visual agnosia), cortical blindness, Balint's syndrome (defective orienting to a visual stimulus), and Anton's syndrome (cortical blindness with denial). These disorders are described in some detail by Hecaen and Albert (1978). Severe visual perceptual deficits greatly limit functional capacity for dressing, ambulation, driving, and other daily activities.

Visual-perceptual impairment also contributes to decreased performance in visual constructional tests. Constructional impairment occurring in the absence of a perceptual disorder can be caused by deficits in abstract thinking, problem solving, or limb praxis. Testing of these abilities has been thoroughly described by Lezak (1983).

What is the significance of a visual constructional deficit for the patient's life? Perhaps because such disorders are not observed directly in everyday activites, and their predictive significance for activities of daily living (ADL) functioning is not well understood, this deficit has been called the "apraxia of the psychologist." Although the authors recognize the paucity of studies relating neuropsychological deficits of any kind to problems in daily living, both the limited available literature (Heaton & Pendleton, 1981) and clinical observation suggest the importance of identifying such problems. Constructional tasks, whether they involve drawings or assembly of objects, elicit data on visual-perceptual abilities, planning, error monitoring and self-corrective behavior, impulsivity, and problem solving. Because they are unfamiliar tasks, tests of constructional ability are generally more sensitive to the effects of cerebral dysfunction than are the measures of over-learned, well-practiced verbal skills included in routine mental status examinations or verbal IQ tests. The authors have observed that moderate or severe constructional deficits are associated with limited ADL skill, low probability of return to work, difficulties with financial record keeping and decision making, and impaired driving. The significance of mild constructional difficulties depends upon such variables as the preservation of other mental abilities and the everyday demands placed upon the individual's intellect. In general, a finding of constructional impairment raises questions about the patient's problem-solving abilities.

Strokes in either cerebral hemisphere can cause visual constructional and visual-perceptual impairment. Although visual constructional disability was first described after right-hemisphere injury (Jackson, 1932) it is now abundantly clear that left-sided strokes also produce comparable deficits (Binder, 1982). Abnormal scores on a three-dimensional block design test were obtained by two-thirds of the LBD aphasics with severe comprehension deficits and one-third of aphasics with moderate deficits. The latter group had only a slightly lower incidence of abnormality than the RBD group (Benton, 1973). In another study RBD patients were similar to LBD patients on Block Design and Object Assembly, whereas the difference between the aphasic and nonaphasic LBD patients was significant (Zubrick & Smith, 1978). Studies employing visual-perceptual tests have also shown that both RBD and aphasic patients are impaired (Arena & Gainotti, 1978; Russo & Vignolo, 1967). Comparison of posterior and anterior lesions suggests that posterior lesions more often affect constructional (Zubrick & Smith, 1978) and perceptual performance (Arrigoni & DeRenzi, 1964) than do anterior lesions.

Disorders of Skilled Movement—Limb Apraxia

The normal execution of such activities as dressing, walking, and eating can be accomplished without much conscious monitoring of the individual components. Nevertheless, their execution requires the participation of many different parts of the brain. Deficits in the execution of learned skilled movements, known as the *apraxias,* are common in hemiplegic patients and have significant implications for rehabilitation progress. Apraxia cannot be explained by sensory loss, weakness, lack of comprehension, inattention, or basal ganglia disorder (Watson & Heilman, 1983).

Two types of apraxia—ideational and ideomotor apraxia—are frequently described in the literature. Unfortunately, there is no consensus on the distinctive features of the two forms. The simplest and most useful distinction is based upon whether the movement involves the demonstration of use of an object or a gesture (DeRenzi, Faglioni, & Sorgato, 1982). In this scheme ideational apraxia is operationally defined as a deficit in the actual use or pantomime of use of objects. Stroke patients with ideational apraxia may be unable to pantomime on command the use of a hammer, comb, or toothbrush or even to perform such actions spontaneously with real objects (DeRenzi, Pieczuro, & Vignolo, 1968). Ideational apraxia is strongly associated with impaired verbal comprehension (Dee, Benton, & Van Allen, 1970; DeRenzi et al., 1968), and may be related to a specific conceptual disorder frequently found in aphasia, although it can occur in the absence of pronounced comprehension deficits (DeRenzi et al., 1968).

Perhaps of more direct significance for rehabilitation is ideomotor apraxia, operationalized as a deficit in the performance of novel motor sequences. A deficit in acquiring sequential movements or imitating postures will retard the learning of new skills, such as transfers and walking with the aid of a brace. Useful examinations that employ both movements on command and imitation have been described in the literature (Brown, 1974; Lehmkuhl, Poeck, & Willmes, 1983; Luria, 1966).

Ideomotor apraxia is a common problem in both RBD and LBD patients. In one study, 20 percent of RBD patients and 50 percent of LBD patients were classified as apraxic (DeRenzi, Motti, & Nichelli, 1980). In LBD patients apraxia was usually associated with the presence of aphasia, but neither the severity of the language deficit (DeRenzi et al., 1980) nor the type of aphasia (DeRenzi et al., 1980; Lehmkuhl, et al., 1983) seems to be strongly related to the severity of the apraxia. There are multiple causes of motor programming deficits of RBD patients. Visual constructional deficits (Dee et al., 1970; Haaland & Delaney, 1981), unilateral neglect, impulsivity, and motor impersistence seem to be pertinent factors. In one study RBD patients were faster than LBD patients at a paced, repetitive tapping task, but made more errors at slower speeds (Carmon, 1971). Impulsivity and unilateral neglect probably account for the fact that RBD patients are more prone to multiple accidents in the rehabilitation setting than are LBD patients (Diller & Weinberg, 1970). Motor impersistence can be observed in repetitive tasks or fixed postures, such as eyes closed with tongue protruding. Using a standardized test, Benton, Hamsher, and Varney (1983) found motor impersistence to be more common in RBD than LBD patients. The authors have found it to be related to poor progress in rehabilitation.

Assessment of Behavioral Deficits

The authors endorse the use of an individualized, hypothesis-testing approach to assessment (Lezak, 1983; Chapter 9). Hypotheses regarding deficits are first generated from knowledge of the lesion location. For example, in a RBD patient, one would be especially alert for the presence of visual and motor sequencing deficit, left-sided inattention, perceptual and constructional problems, and impaired insight. These hypotheses are tested and modified in light of the initial neuropsychological data and/or behavioral observations. For example, if drawing of geometric designs is impaired, the deficit could be explained by one or more abnormalities, including limb apraxia, unilateral inattention or other visual perceptual problems, or a planning/organizing defect. Were the latter domain pinpointed as the causal deficiency, then one might test for deficits in such cognitively or neuroanatomically associated domains as problem solving, concept formation, and initiation.

How much testing is enough? The answer depends upon many variables, including the skill of the neuropsychologist, tolerance (physical and psychological) of the patient, the referral questions, and the severity of the deficits. Given the limited endurance of most stroke patients, the severity of many of their deficits, and the cost of rehabilitation, routinely testing patients for many hours is not justifiable unless the data are translated into suggestions that have an impact on the methods of rehabilitation and counseling.

PSYCHOSOCIAL CONSEQUENCES

Common emotional reactions to stroke have been eloquently described by Goodstein (1983). They include feelings of loss of control and independence; fears of disability, recurrence, and death; the feeling that the stroke is a form of punishment; and fear of loss of affection. Depression is certainly a frequent response and one with important implications for rehabilitation.

Depression

Estimates of the prevalence of clinically significant poststroke depression range from 26 to 60 percent (Binder, 1983). Robinson and Price (1982) found that the prevalence of depression was significantly elevated 6–24 months poststroke. Although depression may be somewhat more common after LBD than RBD (Robinson & Price, 1982), RBD patients are frequently affected (Gordon & Diller, 1983). The severity of depression in RBD patients has been reported to be higher with posterior as opposed to anterior lesions, whereas the reverse was found for LBD patients (Robinson, Kubos, Starr, Rao, & Price, 1984). Clearly, depression after stroke is associated with numerous losses: income, hobbies, work, mobility, independence, and social activities. Frequently, vigorous older persons may believe that, as a result of the stroke, they have become ''old'' overnight, and the resulting feelings of frailty, vulnerability, and incompetence can result in depressed mood.

The assessment of depression in stroke patients is complicated by a number of features. First, patients' reports of their mood are often unreliable because of denial, lack of awareness, or aphasia. A related problem is the dissociation between mood (verbal self-report) and affect (observable facial expression, gestures, tone of voice) that one finds frequently after stroke. Some patients cry in response to mildly sentimental stimuli, for example, remembering that someone had visited them at the hospital. Yet, they deny feeling sad and blame their tears on fatigue. These and other forms of depressed affect are usually signs of depression, the verbal denial notwithstanding.

Several guidelines can aid one in establishing the diagnosis of depression in stroke patients (Ross & Rush, 1981). Important signals include unexpectedly poor recovery or deterioration, poor cooperation, and angry outbursts. Any of those symptoms indicates that depression may be present.

Assessment of depression is also facilitated by quantification with a self-report device with a dichotomous response format, such as the Depression Adjective Checklist (Lubin, 1965). If reading ability is impaired, the adjective checklist can be read aloud to the patient. More cognitively complex self-report scales, such as the Beck Depression Inventory (Beck, Ward, Mendelson, Mock, & Erbaugh, 1961), are often invalid because many stroke patients cannot make subtle distinctions among the available multiple choices. Observations of mood and affect are situation- and observer-dependent. For example, the anger and anxiety exhibited by a patient during frustrating occupational therapy tasks may be incongruent with their self-report during psychological assessment (Caplan, 1983).

The validity of the dexamethasone suppression test as an indicator of depression after stroke has been tentatively documented (Finkelstein et al., 1982), but contradictory evidence exists (Bauer, Gans, Harley, & Cobb, 1983). Whether this test has utility for individual patients remains to be seen.

Other Emotional Consequences

Another common disorder is emotional lability, i.e., abrupt changes in mood. Displays of irritability and anger can be particularly unsettling. A less common consequence of stroke is the unfortunately-named pseudobulbar affect. This misleading term refers to the loss of affective control without corresponding mood changes. The authors prefer to call this behavior ''affective disinhibition'' because most patients do not have pseudobulbar palsy. The clinician must consider both mood and affect in assessing affective disturbance.

The prevalence of other common emotional problems after stroke is unknown. They include excessive irritability, denial and diminished awareness of problems, social insensitivity, paranoia and anxiety, and suicidal ideation or behavior. Suicide, as can depression, may occur when the patient's psychological defenses falter and awareness of the permanence of the disability is gained. In the authors' experience suicidal behavior is most likely after discharge from rehabilitation, probably because inpatients retain a good deal of hope for improvement.

Social Consequences

Reduction in both quantity and quality of leisure activities occurs in a majority of patients with stroke (Sjögren, 1982). In Sjögren's study the major factors contributing to decreased activity during the first year poststroke were physical limitations, such as hemiplegia; feelings of being devalued by others; and reactive depression. In this study patients who were between 3 months and 5.5 years poststroke had not managed to develop new leisure interests within a year after stroke.

Many stroke patients experience a decrease in social contacts following stroke, particularly if depression persists (Feibel & Springer, 1982). In fact, some become housebound with little, if any, contact with anyone other than their caregiver. The Framingham Study (Labi, Phillips, & Gresham, 1980) found that stroke patients experience more difficulty resuming social contacts with friends than with relatives. In addition, this study found social reintegration to be more problematic for women, who may feel considerable shame over their altered appearance, and for those with more education. Family members are often overprotective of patients and may allow or actually encourage this retreat. Friends may not call in order to avoid embarrassment on either side. Friendly visitors may hesitate to maintain contact because of the many unknowns about the consequences of the stroke, the extent of the impairments, and appropriate social behavior for dealing with the awkwardness of the situation.

Some patients show characterological defects, such as impaired capacity for self-control leading to irritability and impulsivity; poor initiative, especially for self-care activities; rigidity or inflexible thinking; emotional alterations, such as silliness, lability, and apathy; and impaired social perception with resultant self-centered behavior (Cicone, Wapner, & Gardner, 1980; Lezak, 1978). The latter problem is more common in RBD than LBD stroke patients as they may have an impairment in their ability to perceive emotional and social cues (Lezak, 1979). The patient may, for example, leave the room without explanation while a friend is visiting. Family members and friends should be advised that this behavior is a consequence of the stroke and is not intended as a personal affront.

Sexuality

Sexual activity ceases in roughly half of all stroke patients who were sexually active premorbidly (Bray, DeFrank, & Wolfe, 1981; Goddess, Wagner, & Silverman, 1979). Premenopausal women may suffer a temporary or permanent interruption of menstruation (Bray et al., 1981). During rehabilitation sexual activity is of limited importance to most patients (Bray et al., 1981), perhaps because they are more concerned with regaining their competence in essential activities of daily living. In the authors' experience sexual concerns become more prominent once such activities are mastered. Thereafter, sexual adjustment is often critical to the well-being of the stroke patient. Factors that have been reported to be related to frequency of sexual activity following stroke are the quality of the interpersonal relationship with the spouse (Sjögren & Fugl-Meyer, 1982), level of prestroke sexual activity (Goddess et al., 1979), dependency in activities of daily living (Sjögren & Fugl-Meyer, 1982) and impaired sensation for touch (Fugl-Meyer & Jääskö, 1980; Sjögren & Fugl-Meyer, 1982). Peripheral vascular disease and certain antihypertensive medications may affect erectile function. Little is known about the effects of these medications on female sexual function.

Factors that do not predict poststroke sexual activity are gender (Sjögren & Fugl-Meyer, 1982), time of follow-up (Fugl-Meyer & Jääskö, 1980; Sjögren & Fugl-Meyer, 1982), degree of motor deficit (Fugl-Meyer & Jääskö, 1980; Sjögren & Fugl-Meyer, 1982) and presence of aphasia (Humphrey & Kinsella, 1980; Sjögren & Fugl-Meyer, 1982). Although the frequency of sexual activity may decline following stroke, sexual drive is usually unaffected (Bray et al., 1981; Goddess et al., 1979); when decrease in drive does occur, it is more likely to affect LBD than RBD patients (Goddess et al., 1979; Kalliomaki, Markkaren, & Mustonens, 1961).

A number of psychological reactions hinder the expression of sexuality after stroke. Patients may feel that their disability has rendered them unattractive

(Allsup-Jackson, 1981); fearing rejection, they may therefore be hesitant about approaching their partner. Thus, they appear uninterested in sexual activity to their partner, who cautiously follows the cue of avoidance and, in so doing, validates the patient's worst fears. In some cases changes in the stroke patient's appearance or personality may cause the spouse to lose interest in him or her as a sexual partner. Finally, the patient or spouse may fear that sexual activity will cause another stroke, although this rarely occurs (Binder, 1983; Muckleroy, 1977; Chapter 16).

TREATMENT OF PSYCHOLOGICAL CONSEQUENCES

Personal injury or illness is one of life's most stressful events (Holmes & Rahe, 1967). The physical illness and chronic limitations produced by stroke almost invariably create considerable emotional trauma. The degree of emotional stress varies among individuals, depending on such factors as the severity of the disability, the patient's attitude and insight, family support, financial resources, and premorbid personality characteristics. Certain deficits, such as aphasia or emotional lability, may cause stroke patients to conclude that they are "going crazy." They usually respond to reassurance that their experience is a common one following stroke. A variety of mental health services, ranging from individual psychotherapy to family counseling, may be useful for stroke victims. The type of psychological intervention planned must derive from the needs of the individual.

Educational Counseling

Patients and families benefit from brief educational counseling regarding stroke and its consequences. The goals of counseling are to help the patient and family understand what a stroke is, establish realistic expectations, and plan for the future. The American Heart Association pamphlet entitled "Strokes: A Guide for the Family" (1969) is a useful introduction. Some families may prefer a full-length book, such as *Stroke* (Sarno & Sarno, 1979) or *A Stroke Family Guide and Resource* (Bray & Clark, 1984). Many hospitals have audiovisual materials on stroke in their patient libraries. The Encyclopaedia Britannica Educational Corporation has produced two videocassettes for educational purposes: "Learning About Stroke" and "Coming Back from Stroke" (1982).

Clinicians have an obligation to answer questions honestly; less clear-cut is the amount of detailed information that one should volunteer to families and patients. Certainly, one should not convey unwarranted optimism. A grimly realistic prediction, however, may not be constructive and may be needlessly upsetting to some persons. It is helpful to inquire about the expectations a family member has before describing the difficulties that may lie ahead. If the family projects an unrealistically optimistic attitude, they should be educated about the range of problems that may arise. The clinician can convey hope for future improvement tempered by cautions about likely limitations and the probability of some residual deficits. If too much information is imparted, then the critical facts may not be retained. Information may need to be repeated on several occasions, because no matter how carefully phrased, the message may be incompletely comprehended or may be distorted by family and friends who are hoping for full recovery and cannot hear suggestions to the contrary.

The counselor can provide helpful information about community resources. Many larger communities have stroke clubs, and senior citizens organizations may offer programs that benefit stroke patients. When the family needs assistance in providing care for the patient, arrangements can be made with Visiting Nurse Associations and other home-based health care services.

Family education begins with assisting the patient and family in coping with their new situation. The information to be covered in an educational session varies. Some family members harbor the fear that something they did caused the stroke. Simply stating that strokes are not precipitated by any single event, such as an argument the day before, corrects this misconception.

Both families and patients should be warned to expect emotional "ups and downs" with the passage of time. They can be advised that the patient may fatigue readily and that symptoms of the stroke, such as weakness, dysphasia, impaired decision making, or memory difficulties, are worse when the patient is tired. Some stroke patients exhibit increased irritability, particularly in the presence of excessive extraneous noises. Their temper threshold may be lowered, and they may find themselves arguing over minor matters that premorbidly would have been ignored. These incidents may be followed by shame and discouragement. The informed family can take steps to avoid circumstances that are likely to prove upsetting.

Perhaps the greatest potential for misunderstanding the patient's limitations is in the area of cognitive abilities. Family members should be informed how best to deal with specific deficits. If the patient is aphasic, verbal messages should be short, simple, and spoken with usual volume and inflections. Nonverbal communication, such as gestures and pointing, can augment the patient's understanding. In the case of right-hemisphere strokes, it may be helpful for the family members to articulate messages that were previously given nonverbally with facial expressions or body language. For example, it may be necessary to state directly, "I'm tired" or "I'm angry," rather than sighing or frowning. It is also helpful if family members simplify complex messages by saying "The major point is . . ." Families of stroke patients with visual neglect may want to arrange the home environment accordingly, e.g., placing the patient's night table on their "good" side. In cases of extreme neglect, families should be encouraged to talk to patients while standing on the intact "good" side. The home environment should be cleared of throw rugs, low furniture, and other hazards to the ambulatory patient.

Family members, especially the primary caregiver, benefit from support and advice regarding their needs. The caregiving burden often falls on one family member, usually the spouse or a child. Those individuals must be made to recognize the danger of becoming so emotionally and physically exhausted that they cannot provide good care (Lezak, 1978). Specific recommendations include: (1) take time to rest and do special things for yourself, including occasional indulgences; (2) avoid social isolation; (3) ask friends and family members for help, and find additional help if needed; (4) recognize that anger and frustration are "rational" emotions in the situation, and don't chastise yourself for feeling them; and (5) trust your decisions, because you are the one who must bear the consequences (Lezak, 1978; Mace & Rabins, 1981).

Sexual counseling is indicated for patients who were sexually active before their stroke, although many patients do not receive it. Because patients and families may be reluctant to raise their questions and concerns, the clinician should routinely inquire about this domain. Recommendations for improving sexual satisfaction range from methods of compensating for sensory and motor limitations to ways of maintaining intimacy without intercourse (Conine & Evans, 1982; Muckleroy, 1977).

Individual Treatment

The primary aim of individual psychotherapy with stroke patients is to assist them to adjust to and compensate for problems arising from the illness. Specific goals include ventilation of feelings and enhancement of self-esteem through emphasis on those abilities and qualities that have not been affected by the stroke. Rehabilitation specialists who understand the behavioral effects of brain damage are better able to assist the patient in establishing realistic goals.

The most common indication for psychotherapy in stroke patients is depression. Disabled stroke patients suffer so many losses that all poststroke depression could be considered reactive in nature, or even "normal." Nonetheless, depression must not be permitted to subvert the patient's motivation for rehabilitation, for progress in therapy often has a marked positive effect on mood.

The stroke patient's mood may be quite variable, particularly during the subacute phase. Patients who appear superficially to have adjusted well may eventually become depressed. This late depression, occurring a few weeks to a few months after onset, often affects patients who have unrealistic expectations about recovery or those with impaired psychosocial skills whose support systems begin to disintegrate.

Persistent depression should be treated with psychotherapy, pharmacotherapy, family counseling or a combination of these modalities. Clinical experience and recent research (Lipsey, Robinson, Pearlson, Rao, & Price, 1984) suggest that antidepressant medication can be effective for poststroke depression. The use of tricyclic antidepressants has been recommended (e.g., Robinson and Szetela, 1981), but they are contraindicated for elderly patients receiving certain antihypertensive drugs and should be used with great caution if there is coexisting cardiovascular disease (Salzman, 1982).

Many psychotherapeutic interventions are quite simple, as seen in the following case example.

> A 71-year-old woman with a right CVA made minimal gains in rehabilitation and was placed in a nursing home. She received another trial of rehabilitation 4 months after her stroke. Although her score on the Depression Adjective Checklist (DACL) (Lubin, 1965) was not in the "depressed" range, she did not admit to many positive feelings on the checklist, and she was frequently tearful. Her nurses observed that dressing and bathing skills fluctuated markedly. When the psychologist suggested that she must be experiencing some losses, she became tearful and asked to describe her feelings in writing. In this way, she described feeling useless and helpless. The ensuing discussion revealed the importance of her homemaking skills to her family. Later, in OT, she assisted in baking, which showed her that she could be useful at home. No further episodes of tearfulness were observed by the staff during her hospitalization. She was discharged to a nursing home, but spent weekends in her home.

Operant treatment of depression has been described (Jain, 1982) for a 53-year-old left hemiplegic woman who exhibited noncompliance in rehabilitation. This approach, which also included psychotherapy, targeted improved ADLs, increased eating, and more consistent attendance in therapy. For each treated behavior separate rewards, such as ice in her fluids, more time in bed, more time in physical therapy (which she enjoyed and attended regularly), and points for a weekend pass, were instituted. The patient's response to treatment was dramatic. For a description of behavioral approaches to rehabilitation patients, see Greif and Matarazzo (1982).

A combination of haloperidol and psychotherapy is often beneficial in the treatment of irritability and angry outbursts. The psychotherapy may consist of relaxation training, coupled with practice in identifying problematic situations and developing coping strategies.

Anxiety, which has multiple causes and symptoms, may improve with medication or psychological intervention.

A 60-year-old man was anxious, agitated, and depressed; slept most of the day at home; and was excessively dependent on his wife. He was psychologically dependent on phenytoin and thioridazine. (He had no seizures and had never been psychotic.) Therapy was conducted with his wife present because his memory deficit rendered him unable to provide a reliable report of his recent problems. After a therapeutic alliance was established, placebos were substituted for the phenytoin and thioridazine in order to demonstrate to him that his positive response to medications was psychological. Because a history of noncompliance suggested that he would be resistant in therapy, the therapist paradoxically bet him that he could not give up the medications. His wife was taught to give him instructions for hypnosis. Initially, he was dependent on her for help with relaxation, but soon learned to respond to an audiotape of the therapist's voice. He won his "bet" by tapering off the thioridazine and phenytoin by using hypnosis as a substitute. He greatly increased his activity level, winning another "bet" with the therapist, after angrily denying the therapist's suggestion that he enjoyed being sick. Although he maintained his activity level, discontinued all psychotropic medications, and ceased cigarette smoking with the aid of hypnosis, he continued to be easily upset by stressful events.

Although normal cognitive functioning is not required for individual psychotherapy, cognitive deficits may impose limits on its goals or content. Relaxation therapies and problem-oriented psychotherapy, for example, can prove impossible with intellectually impaired patients. Furthermore, primary neuropsychological impairments, such as deficits in recent memory, problem-solving ability, language, mental flexibility, reasoning, and judgment, cloud the expression of reactions and may limit the patient's psychological adaptability. However, therapy is not invariably precluded. Leftoff (1983) described the successful treatment of a case of paranoia and confabulation that were related to deficits in memory, conceptual ability, and self-referential orientation.

Given the prevalence of stroke and resulting emotional disorders, the paucity of research on the effects of psychological and pharmacologic treatments constitutes a critical gap in our knowledge. The lack of controlled studies of treatment outcome stems from several obstacles, particularly uncertainty about how much poststroke depression should be considered a "normal" response and the surprising dissociation between intensity of depression and the degree of neurologic handicap (Gordon & Diller, 1983; Robinson & Price, 1982). However, recent controlled studies have suggested that both psychotherapy (Latow, 1983) and antidepressant medication (Lipsey et al., 1984) can be effective.

Family Therapy

In some cases psychotherapy directed toward the patient's family may be more helpful than therapy with the afflicted person, especially when the patient has problems with insight or reasoning. This mode of therapy may help the family members express grief over their loss, identify specifically what is being grieved, determine their own needs, establish realistic expectations and goals, and develop adaptive means of dealing with the behavioral problems of the patient. It is useful to determine the premorbid quality of interpersonal relationships in order to establish the context for interpreting subsequent attitudes and reactions.

Except in cases of minor strokes, the patient is permanently altered. Changes in functional abilities, cognition, or character make the individual different in important ways. Thus, spouses, family members, and friends all mourn the loss of the person they knew. Some family members may primarily grieve for the companionship that existed before the stroke. Others may react to a sense of entrapment caused by the burden of the patient's dependence, whereas some have difficulty adjusting to a change of roles within the family. For example, the wife of a stroke patient may have difficulty assuming the role of decision maker or wage earner. The particular reactions of family members are influenced by their individual needs. One study (Buxbaum, 1967) found that wives with a high need to be nurturant adjusted best to their husband's aphasia. Once the needs and precipitants of grieving are identified, the rehabilitation specialist can assist the family in accepting the loss and making adaptive adjustments. At the same time, the therapist can help the individual identify ways in which the stroke patient has not changed.

Some family members overreact to the stroke patient's disability and develop maladaptive patterns of interaction, such as adopting a custodial attitude that fosters excessive dependence. In fact, in one study (Overs & Healy, 1973), disabled husbands reported that they were willing to take over some household tasks, but their wives did not want this intrusion into their sphere of responsibility. Custodial attitudes usually produce anger and marital dissatisfaction for both partners. A case of family therapy for this problem has been described (Watzlawick & Coyne, 1980).

Custodial behavior by family members eventually may convince the stroke patient of his or her dependence or helplessness. This feeling clearly can impede rehabilitation if it causes the patient to stop striving for self-sufficiency. Furthermore, patients may question their self-worth and become depressed. Family members should be advised to refrain from providing assistance with ADL, regardless of the speed or quality of the patient's efforts, for practice with these activities will eventually pay off. For example, the wife of a hemiplegic patient encouraged her husband to take responsibility for folding clean clothes. It took him most of one day to complete the job because he could not use his preferred right hand. However, he appeared to enjoy it and felt he was making a worthwhile contribution to the household chores.

In some instances family members withdraw from interaction with their disabled relative. If strained interpersonal relationships existed before a stroke, they are likely to deteriorate further after it. In these cases a family member might feel trapped and angry. Even when family relationships have been comparatively good, relatives may gradually come to resent the burden of responsibility they bear and the limitations on their own lives imposed thereby. Resentment may erupt into hostility toward the patient, who may even be blamed, justifiably or not, for having caused the stroke ("He shouldn't have worked so hard").

Family members' embarrassment at the stroke patient's disability may create social isolation. For example, a man who is ashamed of his wife's drooling or aphasia may avoid taking her on outings or even inviting friends into the home. Therapeutic intervention directed at understanding the avoidance and its consequences can assist families in making the choices that are best for them.

Treatment After Discharge

As stroke patients and their families reach a new equilibrium after hospital discharge, psychological counseling should be available. In fact, before this point many patients dismiss the need for counseling because of their usually unrealistic expectation that essentially full recovery will occur. Some patients, particularly those with RBD, sustain the fiction that their disabilities will disappear when they return home. Only after discharge do they realize that the condition is chronic, and this realization may trigger psychological reactions that warrant intervention. Ideally, counseling and follow-up should be available for at least 2 years.

STROKE OUTCOME

Mortality

The survival rate following stroke is a function of several well-defined factors. However, the quality of survival is more difficult to ascertain. As shown in Table 3–2, roughly one-fifth to one-quarter of stroke patients admitted to hospital die during the initial hospitalization, about one-half are discharged to home, and 25–30 percent require longer-term rehabilitation or nursing home care (Becker et al., 1986). Persons with intracranial hemorrhage (ICH and SAH) are up to three times more likely to die during initial hospitalization than those with cerebral infarction (thrombotic or cardioembolic). Other negative prognostic factors include advanced age, impaired level of consciousness at admission to hospital, and the presence of cardiac disease (Matthews & Oxbury, 1974; Sacco, Wolf,

Table 3–2 Outcome of Acute Stroke Hospitalization by Specific Stroke
Diagnosis*

	Home %	Institution %	Died %	Number of Patients
Thrombotic	60	27	13	(1249)
Embolic	50	27	24	(409)
ICH	40	15	45	(180)
SAH	48	12	40	(81)
TOTAL				(1964)

*Infarctions are thrombotic or cardioembolic. Hemorrhages are intracerebral hemorrhage
(ICH) and subarachnoid hemorrhage (SAH).

Source: Data from the community hospital-based stroke programs.

Kannel, & McNamara, 1982). Furthermore, a history of previous stroke portends
a poor outcome (Sacco et al., 1982).

Rehabilitation Outcome

Stroke rehabilitation has proven effective in increasing independent function
(Anderson, 1982; Feigenson, 1981; Lehman et al., 1975; Lind, 1982), but has
only a negligible effect on neurologic function, which generally improves spontaneously during rehabilitation (Lind, 1982). Rehabilitation patients rarely regain
full use of their limbs, but they learn modified means of ambulation, dressing, and
eating. The stroke patient generally need not enter a nursing home, despite
permanent deficits. Nursing home placements are most likely for patients who
cannot walk, are incontinent, or cannot be left unattended because of confusion
(Feigenson, 1981). Other factors predictive of poor outcome include a combination of hemiplegia and hemisensory deficits (Stern, McDowell, Miller, & Robinson, 1971), unconsciousness in the acute stage (Matthews & Oxbury, 1975), and
advanced age.

Family members frequently provide the assistance and supervision that patients
need in order to remain at home. Occasionally, friends fill the caregiver role.
Often, the family can only care for the patient at home with the assistance of a paid
aide. Unfortunately, in many states public assistance is not available to pay for an
aide, but can be secured for the more costly alternative of a nursing home.

Those who will care for the stroke patient after discharge must observe the
patient in all therapies to become fully aware of the level of assistance that is

actually required. This education may prevent functional regression after discharge from the rehabilitation setting (Andrews & Stewart, 1979).

Discussion of cognitive and language therapy is beyond the scope of this chapter (see Chapters 10, 11, and 12). A few highlights must suffice. The New York University Institute of Rehabilitation Medicine's highly structured and lengthy program has produced significant improvement of unilateral neglect in stroke patients (Diller and Weinberg, 1977; Weinberg et al., 1979). A RBD patient with severe cognitive deficits was taught to use verbal cues and written reminders to improve her transfers (Stanton et al., 1983). Such approaches, in which abilities referrable to the intact hemisphere are engaged, appear to hold some promise (Caplan, 1982). Speech and language therapy should be offered to the aphasic patient (Basso et al., 1979; Sarno, 1981). Prognostic factors and treatment techniques were discussed briefly above.

Rehabilitation specialists, especially those with neuropsychological expertise, fill a crucial role in stroke rehabilitation (Caplan, 1982). They assist in answering assessment questions regarding a patient's competence for driving, living independently, financial decisions, employment, and ability to benefit from intensive rehabilitation. After specifying the nature of cognitive impairment they design useful behavior management and therapeutic strategies and serve as a consultant to the rehabilitation team. Through their knowledge of behavior change and family dynamics, they can counsel patients and families effectively.

REFERENCES

Adams, R.D. & Victor, M. (1981). *Principles of Neurology,* 2nd ed. New York: McGraw-Hill.

Allsup-Jackson, G. (1981). Sexual dysfunction of stroke patients. *Sexuality and Disability, 4,* 161–168.

American Heart Association. (1969). *Strokes: A Guide for the Family.* Dallas: Author.

Anderson, T.P. (1982). Rehabilitation of patients with completed stroke. In F.J. Kottke, G.K. Stillwell, & J.F. Lehmann (Eds.), *Krusen's Handbook of Physical Medicine and Rehabilitation* (3rd ed.) (pp. 583–603). Philadelphia: W.B. Saunders.

Andrews, K., & Stewart, J. (1979). Stroke recovery: He can but does he. *Rheumatology and Rehabilitaton, 18,* 43–48.

Arena, R., & Gainotti, G. (1978). Constructional apraxia and visuo-perceptive disabilities in relation to laterality of cerebral lesions. *Cortex, 17,* 463–473.

Arrigoni, G., & DeRenzi, E. (1964). Constructional apraxia and hemispheric locus of lesion. *Cortex, 1,* 170–197.

Baron, J.C., Bousser, M.G., Commar, D., & Castaizne, P. (1980). "Crossed cerebellar diaschisis" in human supratentorial brain infarction. *Transactions of the American Neurological Association, 105,* 459–461.

Basso, A., Capitani, E., & Vignolo, L.A. (1979). Influence of rehabilitation on language skills in aphasic patients: A controlled study. *Archives of Neurology, 36,* 190–196.

Bauer, M., Gans, J.S., Harley, P., & Cobb, W. (1983). Dexamethasone suppression test and depression in a rehabilitation setting. *Archives of Physical Medicine and Rehabilitation, 64,* 421–422.

Beal, M.F., Williams, R.S., Richardson, E.P., Jr., & Fisher, C.M. (1981). Cholesterol embolism as a cause of transient ischemic attacks and cerebral infarction. *Neurology, 31,* 860–865.

Beck, A.T., Ward, C.H., Mendelson, M., Mock, J., & Erbaugh, J.K. (1961). An inventory for measuring depression. *Archives of General Psychology, 4,* 561–571.

Becker, C., Yatsu, F.M., Howard, G., McLeroy, K.R., Toole, J.F., Coull, B., Feibel, J., Springer, C., & Walker, M.N. (1986). Three comprehensive stroke center programs: Demographic description of hospitalized stroke patients in North Carolina, Oregon, and New York. *Stroke, 17,* 285–293.

Benson, D.F. (1979). *Aphasia, alexia, and agraphia.* New York: Churchill Livingstone.

Benton, A.L. (1973). Visuoconstructive disability in patients with cerebral disease: Its relationship to side of lesion and aphasic disorder. *Documented Ophthalmologia, 34,* 67–71.

Benton, A.L., Hamsher, K., & Varney, N.R. (1983). *Contributions to neuropsychological assessment and clinical manual.* New York: Oxford University Press.

Binder, L.M. (1982). Constructional strategies on complex figure drawings after unilateral brain damage. *Journal of Clinical Neuropsychology, 4,* 51–58.

Binder, L.M. (1983). Emotional problems after stroke. *Stroke, 18,* 17–21.

Boller, F., & DeRenzi, E. (1967). Relationship between visual memory defects and hemispheric locus of lesion. *Neurology, 17,* 1052–1058.

Bray, G.P., & Clark, G.S. (1984). *A stroke family guide and resource.* Springfield, IL: Charles C Thomas.

Bray, G.P., DeFrank, R.S., & Wolfe, T.L. (1981). Sexual functioning in stroke survivors. *Archives of Physical Medicine and Rehabilitation, 62,* 286–288.

Brierley, J.B. (1973). Pathology of cerebral ischemia. In F.H. McDowell & R.W. Brennan (Eds.), *Cerebral vascular diseases, eighth conference* (pp. 59–75). New York: Grune & Stratton.

Brown, J.W. (1974). *Aphasia, apraxia, and agnosia* (2nd ed.). Springfield, IL: Charles C Thomas.

Buxbaum, J. (1967). Effect of nurturance on wives' appraisals of their marital satisfaction and the degree of their husband's aphasia. *Journal of Consulting Psychology, 31,* 240–243.

Caplan, B. (1982). Neuropsychology in rehabilitation: Its role in evaluation and intervention. *Archives of Physical Medicine and Rehabilitation, 63,* 362–366.

Caplan, B. (1983). Staff and patient perception of patient mood. *Rehabilitation Psychology, 28,* 67–77.

Caplan, L.R. (1979). Occlusion of the vertebral or basilar artery. Follow-up analysis of some patients with benign outcome. *Stroke, 10,* 277–282.

Carmon, A. (1971). Sequenced motor performance in patients with unilateral cerebral lesions. *Neuropsychologia, 9,* 445–449.

Cicone, M., Wapner, W., & Gardner, H. (1980). Sensitivity to emotional expressions and situations in organic patients. *Cortex, 16,* 145–158.

Conine, T.A., & Evans, J.H. (1982). Sexual reactivation of chronically ill and disabled adults. *Journal of Allied Health, 11,* 261–270.

Damasio, A., Damasio, H., & Chui, H.C. (1980). Neglect following damage to frontal lobe or basal ganglia. *Neuropsychologia, 18,* 123–132.

Dee, H.L., Benton, A.L., & Van Allen, M.W. (1970). Apraxia in relation to hemisphere locus of lesion and aphasia. *Transactions of the American Neurological Association, 95,* 147–150.

Denes, G., Semenza, C., Stoppa, E., & Lis, A. (1982). Unilateral spatial neglect and recovery from hemiplegia: A follow-up study. *Brain, 105,* 543–552.

DeRenzi, E., Faglioni, P., & Sorgato, P. (1982). Modality-specific and supramodal mechanisms of apraxia. *Brain, 105,* 301–312.

DeRenzi, E., Motti, E., & Nichelli, P. (1980). Imitating gestures: A quantitative approach to ideomotor apraxia. *Archives of Neurology, 37,* 66–10.

DeRenzi, E., Pieczuro, A., & Vignolo, L.A. (1968). Ideational apraxia: A quantitative study. *Neuropsychologia, 6,* 41–52.

Diller, L., & Weinberg, J. (1970). Evidence for accident-prone behavior in hemiplegic patients. *Archives of Physical Medicine and Rehabilitation, 51,* 358–363.

Diller, L., & Weinberg, J. (1977). Hemi-inattention in rehabilitation: The evolution of a rational remediation program. In E.A. Weinstein & R.P. Friedland (Eds.), *Advances in neurology, Vol. 18.* New York: Raven Press, pp. 63–72.

Easton, J.D., & Sherman, D.G. (1980). Management of cerebral embolism of cardiac origin. *Stroke, 11,* 433–442.

Encyclopaedia Britannica Educational Corporation. (1982). *Coming back from stroke.* Chicago: Author.

Encyclopaedia Britannica Educational Corporation. (1982). *Learning about stroke.* Chicago: Author.

Feibel, J., & Springer, C. (1982). Depression and failure to resume social activities after stroke. *Archives of Physical Medicine and Rehabilitation, 63,* 276–278.

Feigenson, J.S. (1981). Stroke rehabilitation: Outcome studies and guidelines for alternate levels of care. *Stroke, 12,* 372–375.

Ferro, J.M. & Kertesz, A. (1984). Posterior internal capsule infarction associated with neglect. *Archives of Neurology, 41,* 422–424.

Finkelstein, S., Benowitz, L.I., Baldessarini, R.J., Arana, G.W., Levine, D., Woo, E., Bear, D., Moya, K., & Stoll, A.L. (1982). Mood, vegetative disturbance, and dexamethasone suppression test after stroke. *Annals of Neurology, 12,* 463–468.

Fisher, C.M. (1965). Lacunes: Small, deep cerebral infarcts. *Neurology, 15,* 774–784.

Fisher, C.M. (1969). The arterial lesions underlying lacunes. *Acta Neuropathologica, 12,* 1–15.

Fisher, C.M., & Adams, R.D. (1951). Observations on brain embolism with special reference to the mechanism of hemorrhagic infarction. *Journal of Neuropathology and Experimental Neurology, 10,* 92–93.

Fisher, C.M., & Curry, H.B. (1965). Pure motor hemiplegia of vascular origin. *Archives of Neurology, 13,* 30–44.

Fugl-Meyer, A.R., & Jääskö, L. (1980). Post-stroke hemiplegia and sexual intercourse. *Scandinavian Journal of Rehabilitation Medicine, 7* (Suppl.), 158–166.

Gainotti, G. (1972). Emotional behavior and hemispheric side of the lesion. *Cortex, 8,* 41–55.

Gainotti, G., Caltagirone, C., & Miceli, G. (1978). Immediate visual-spatial memory in hemisphere-damaged patients: Impairment of verbal coding and perceptual processing. *Neuropsychologia, 16,* 501–507.

Garraway, W.M., Whisnant, J.P., & Drury, I. (1983). The continuing decline in the incidence of stroke. *Mayo Clinic Proceedings, 58,* 520–523.

Garraway, W.M., Whisnant, J.P., Furlan, A.J., Phillips, L.H., II, Kurland, L.T., & O'Fallon, W.M. (1979). The declining incidence of stroke. *New England Journal of Medicine, 300,* 449–452.

Gasparrini, B., & Satz, P. (1979). A treatment for memory problems in left-hemisphere CVA patients. *Journal of Clinical Neuropsychology, 1,* 137–150.

Ghannam, J.H., Javornisky, G., & Smith, A. (1980). *Diaschisis in chronic aphasics with left hemisphere infarction.* Paper presented at the eighth International Neuropsychological Society Meeting, San Francisco.

Gianutsos, R., & Gianutsos, J. (1979). Rehabilitating the verbal recall of brain-injured patients by mnemonic training: An experimental demonstration using single-case methodology. *Journal of Clinical Neuropsychology, 1,* 117–135.

Goddess, E.D., Wagner, N.N., & Silverman, D.R. (1979). Post-stroke sexual activity of CVA patients. *Medical Aspects of Human Sexuality, 13,* 16–30.

Golper, L.A.C., Rau, M.T., & Marshall, R.C. (1980). Aphasic adults and their decisions on driving: An evaluation. *Archives of Physical and Medical Rehabilitation, 61,* 34–40.

Goodglass, H., & Kaplan, E. (1976). *The assessment of aphasia and related disorders.* Philadelphia: Lea and Febiger.

Goodstein, R.K. (1983). Overview: Cerebrovascular accident and the hospitalized elderly—a multidimensional clinical problem. *American Journal of Psychiatry, 140,* 141–147.

Gordon, W.A., & Diller, L. (1983). Stroke: Coping with a cognitive deficit. In T.G. Burish & L.A. Bradley (Eds.), *Coping with chronic disease: Research and applications.* New York: Academic Press, pp. 113–135.

Greif, E., & Matarazzo, R.G. (1982). *Behavioral approaches to rehabilitation.* New York: Springer.

Haaland, K.Y., & Delaney, H.D. (1981). Motor deficits after left or right hemisphere damage due to stroke or tumor. *Neuropsychologia, 19,* 17–27.

Hachinski, V.C., Lassen, N.A., & Marshall, J. (1974). Multi-infarct dementia: A cause of mental deterioration in the elderly. *Lancet, 2,* 207–210.

Hart, R.G., Coull, B.M., & Hart, P.D. (1983). Early recurrent emboli associated with nonvalvular atrial fibrillation: A retrospective study. *Stroke, 14,* 688–693.

Hart, R.G., & Miller, V.T. (1983). Cerebral infarction in young adults: A practical approach. *Stroke, 14,* 110–114.

Hecaen, H., & Albert, M.S. (1978). *Human neuropsychology.* New York: Wiley.

Healton, E.B., Navarro, C., Bressman, S. & Brust, J.C.M. (1982). Subcortical neglect. *Neurology, 32,* 773–778.

Heaton, R. (1981). Wisconsin card sorting test: Manual. Odessa, Florida: Psychological Assessment Resources.

Heaton, R.K., & Pendleton, M.G. (1981). Use of neuropsychological tests to predict adult patients' everyday functioning. *Journal of Consulting and Clinical Psychology, 49,* 807–821.

Heilman, K.M. (1979). Neglect and related disorders. In K.M. Heilman & E. Valenstein (Eds.), *Clinical Neuropsychology* (pp. 268–307). New York: Oxford University Press.

Hier, D.B., Mondlock, J., & Caplan, L.R. (1983). Recovery of behavioral abnormalities after right hemisphere stroke. *Neurology, 33,* 345–350.

Holmes, T.H., & Rahe, R.H. (1967). The social readjustment rating scale. *Journal of Psychosomatic Research, 11,* 213–218.

Humphrey, M., & Kinsella, G. (1980). Sexual life after stroke. *Sexuality and Disability, 3,* 150–153.

Hypertension Detection and Follow-up Program Cooperative Group. (1982). Five-year findings of the Hypertension Detection and Follow-up Program. III. Reduction in stroke incidence among persons with high blood pressure. *Journal of the American Medical Association, 247,* 633–638.

Jabbari, B., Maulsby, R.L., Holtzapple, P.A., & Marshall, N.K. (1979). Prognostic value of EEG in acute vascular aphasia: Long-term clinical EEG study of 53 patients. *Clinical Electroencephalography, 10,* 190–197.

Jackson, J.H. (1932). *Selected Writings of John Hughlings Jackson* (J. Taylor, Ed.). London: Hodder and Stoughton.

Jain, S. (1982). Operant conditioning for management of a noncompliant rehabilitation care after stroke. *Archives of Physical Medicine and Rehabilitation, 63,* 374–376.

Jones, R., Giddens, H., & Croft, D. (1983). Assessment and training of brain-damaged drivers. *The American Journal of Occupational Therapy, 37,* 754–760.

Kalliomaki, J.L., Markkaren, T.K., & Mustonens, V.A. (1961). Sexual behavior after cerebral vascular accident. *Fertility and Sterility, 12,* 156–158.

Kanaya, H., Endo, H., Sugiyama, T., & Kinoda, K. (1983). "Crossed cerebellar diaschisis" in patients with putaminal hemorrhage. *Journal of Cerebral Blood Flow & Metabolism, 3* (Suppl. 1), S27–28.

Kay, D.W., Beamish, V., & Roth, M. (1964). Old age mental disorders in Newcastle upon Tyne. Part I: A study of prevalence. *British Journal of Psychiatry, 110,* 146–158.

Kertesz, A., & McCabe, P. (1977). Recovery patterns and prognosis in aphasia. *Brain, 100,* 1–18.

Kubik, C.S., & Adams, R.D. (1946). Occlusion of the basilar artery—a clinical and pathological study. *Brain, 69,* 6–121.

Kurtzke, J.F. (1985). Epidemiology of cerebrovascular disease. In F. McDowell & L.R. Caplan (Eds.) *Cerebrovascular Survey Report.* Washington, DC: National Institutes of Health, pp. 1–34.

Labi, M., Phillips, T.F., & Gresham, G.E. (1980). Psychosocial disability in physically restored long-term stroke survivors. *Archives of Physical Medicine and Rehabilitation, 61,* 561–565.

Latow, J.F. (1983). *Effectiveness of psychotherapy for stroke victims during rehabilitation.* Paper presented at the American Psychological Association Convention, Los Angeles.

Leftoff, S. (1983). Psychopathology in the light of brain injury: A case study. *Journal of Clinical Neuropsychology, 5,* 51–63.

Lehmann, J., De Lateur, B., Fowler, R. et al. (1975). Stroke: Does rehabilitation affect outcome? *Archives of Physical Medicine and Rehabilitation, 56,* 375–383.

Lehmkuhl, G., Poeck, K., & Willmes, K. (1983). Ideomotor apraxia and aphasia: An examination of types and manifestations of apraxic symptoms. *Neuropsychologia, 21,* 199–212.

Lezak, M.D. (1978). Living with the characterologically altered brain injured patient. *Journal of Clinical Neuropsychology, 39,* 592–598.

Lezak, M.D. (1979). *Behavioral concomitants of configurational disorganization in right hemisphere.* Paper presented at the seventh annual meeting of the International Neuropsychological Society, New York City.

Lezak, M.D. (1982). The problem of assessing executive functions. *International Journal of Psychology, 17,* 281–297.

Lezak, M.D. (1983). *Neuropsychological assessment* (2nd ed.). New York: Oxford University Press.

Lind, L. (1982). A synthesis of studies on stroke rehabilitation. *Journal of Chronic Diseases, 35,* 133–149.

Lipsey, J.R., Robinson, R.G., Pearlson, G.D., Rao, K., & Price, T.R. (1984). Nortriptyline treatment of post-stroke depression: A double-blind study. *The Lancet, 11,* 297–300.

Lubin, B. (1965). Adjective checklists for measurement of depression. *Archives of General Psychiatry, 12,* 57–62.

Luria, A.L. (1966). *Higher cortical function in man*. New York: Basic Books.

Mace, N.L., & Rabins, P.V. (1981). *The 36-hour day*. Baltimore: Johns Hopkins University Press.

Marshall, R.C., & Phillips, D.S. (1983). Prognosis for improved verbal communication in aphasic stroke patients. *Archives of Physical Medicine and Rehabilitation, 64*, 597–600.

Marshall, R.C., Tompkins, C.A., & Phillips, D.S. (1982). Improvement in treated aphasia: Examination of selected prognostic factors. *Folia Phoniatrica, 34*, 305–315.

Matthews, W.B., & Oxbury, J.M. (1974). Prognostic factors in stroke. In *Outcome of Severe Damage to the Nervous System*. Ciba Foundation Symposium 34. Amsterdam: Elsevier, pp. 279–289.

Meyer, J.S., Kanda, T., Fukuuchi, Y., Shimazu, K., Dennis, E.W., & Ericsson, A.D. (1971). Clinical prognosis correlated with hemispheric blood flow in cerebral infarction. *Stroke, 2*, 383–394.

Milner, B. (1968). Disorders of memory after brain lesions in man: Material-specific and generalized memory loss. *Neuropsychologia, 6*, 175–179.

Mohr, J.P., Caplan, L.R., Melski, J.W., Goldstein, R.J., Duncan, G.W., Kistler, J.P., Pessin, M.S., & Bleich, H.L. (1978). The Harvard Cooperative Stroke Registry: A prospective registry. *Neurology, 28*, 754–762.

Muckleroy, R.N. (1977). Sex counselling after stroke. *Medical Aspects of Human Sexuality, 11*, 115–116.

Ogden, J.A. (1985). Anterior-posterior interhemispheric differences in the loci of lesions producing visual hemineglect. *Brain and Cognition, 4*, 59–75.

Overs, R.P., & Healy, J.F. (1973). Stroke patients: Their spouses, families and the community. In A.B. Cobb (Ed.), *Medical and Psychological Aspects of Disability* (pp. 87–117). Springfield, IL: Charles C Thomas.

Ozazaki, I.H., Reagan, T.J., & Campbell, R.J. (1979). Clinicopathologic studies of primary central amyloid angiopathy. *Mayo Clinic Proceedings, 54*, 22–31.

Plum, F., & Posner, J.B. (1980). *The Diagnosis of Stupor and Coma* (3rd ed.). Philadelphia: F.A. Davis.

Poeck, K. (1969). Pathophysiology of emotional disorders. In P.J. Vinken & G.W. Bruyn (Eds.), *Handbook of Clinical Neurology, 3*. Amsterdam: North-Holland Publishing Co., pp. 343–367.

Reivich, M., Ginsberg, M., Slater, R., Jones, S., Kovack, A., Greenberg, J., & Goldbergh, H. (1978). Alterations in regional cerebral hemodynamics and metabolism produced by focal cerebral ischemia. *European Neurology, 17* (Suppl), 9–16.

Richter, R.W., Brust, J.C.M., Bruun, B. et al. (1977). Frequency and course of pure motor hemiparesis: A clinical study. *Stroke, 8*(1), 58–60.

Riege, W.H., Klane, L.T., Metter, E.J., & Hanson, W.R. (1982). Decision speed and bias after unilateral stroke. *Cortex, 18*, 345–355.

Robinson, R.G., Kubos, K.L., Starr, L.B., Rao, K., & Price, T.R. (1984). Mood disorders in stroke patients. *Brain, 107*, 81–93.

Robinson, R.G., & Price, T.R. (1982). Post-stroke depressive disorders: A follow-up study of 103 patients. *Stroke, 13*, 635–641.

Robinson, R.G., & Szetela, B. (1981). Mood change following left-hemisphere brain injury. *Annals of Neurology, 9*, 447–453.

Ross, E.D., & Rush, A.J. (1981). Diagnosis and neuroanatomical correlates of depression in brain-damaged patients. *Archives of General Psychiatry, 38*, 1344–1354.

Russo, M., & Vignolo, L.A. (1967). Visual figure-ground discrimination in patients with unilateral cerebral disease. *Cortex, 3*, 113–127.

Sacco, R.L., Wolf, P.A., Kannel, W.B., & McNamara, P.M. (1982). Survival and recurrence following stroke. *Stroke, 13,* 292–295.

Salzman, C. (1982). A primer on geriatric psychopharmacology. *American Journal of Psychiatry, 139,* 67–74.

Sarno, M.T. (1981). *Acquired aphasia.* New York: Academic Press.

Sarno, M.T., & Levita, E. (1979). Recovery in treated aphasia in the first year post-stroke. *Stroke, 10,* 663–670.

Sarno, J.E., & Sarno, M.T. (1979). *Stroke: A guide for patients and their families* (rev. ed.). New York: McGraw Hill.

Sivak, M., Hill, C.S., Henson, D.L., Butler, B.P., Silber S.H., & Olson, P.L. (1984). Improved driving performance following perceptual training in persons with brain damage. *Archives of Physical Medicine and Rehabilitation, 65,* 163–167.

Sivak, M., Olson, P.L., Kewman, D.G., Won, H., & Henson, D.L. (1981). Driving and perceptual/cognitive skills: Behavioral consequences of brain damage. *Archives of Physical and Medical Rehabilitation, 62,* 476–483.

Sjögren, K. (1982). Leisure after stroke. *International Rehabilitation Medicine, 4,* 80–87.

Sjögren, K., & Fugl-Meyer, A.R. (1982). Adjustment to life after stroke with special reference to sexual intercourse and leisure. *Journal of Psychosomatic Research, 26,* 409–417.

Stanton, K.M., Pepping, M., Brockaway, J.A., Bliss, L., Frankel, D., & Waggener, S. (1983). Wheelchair transfer training for right cerebral dysfunctions: An interdisciplinary approach. *Archives of Physical Medicine and Rehabilitation, 64,* 276–280.

Stern, P.H, McDowell, F., Miller, J.M., & Robinson, M. (1971). Factors influencing stroke rehabilitation. *Stroke, 2,* 213–218.

Stuss, D.T., Alexander, M.P., Lieberman, A., & Levine, H. (1978). An extraordinary form of confabulation. *Neurology, 28,* 1166–1172.

Tikofsky, R.S., Kooi, K.A., & Thomas, M.H. (1960). Electroencephalographic findings and recovery from aphasia. *Neurology, 10,* 154–156.

Volpe, B.T., & Hirst, W. (1983). Amnesia following rupture and repair of an anterior communicating artery aneurysm. *Journal of Neurology, Neurosurgery and Psychiatry, 46,* 704–709.

Waller, J.A. (1973). *Medical impairment to driving.* Springfield, IL: Charles C Thomas.

Walsh, K.W. (1978). *Neuropsychology. A clinical approach.* Edinburgh: Livingstone Churchill.

Wapner, W., Hamby, S., & Gardner, H. (1981). The role of the right hemisphere in the apprehension of complex linguistic materials. *Brain and Language, 14,* 15–33.

Watson, R.T., & Heilman, K.M. (1983). Callosal apraxia. *Brain, 106,* 391–403.

Watzlawick, P., & Coyne, J.C. (1980). Depression following stroke: Brief, problem-focused family treatment. *Family Process, 19,* 13–18.

Weinberg, J., Diller, L., Gordon, W.A., Gerstman, L.J., Lieberman, A., Lakin, P., Hodges, G., & Ezrachi, O. (1979). Training sensory awareness and spatial organization in people with right brain damage. *Archives of Physical Medicine and Rehabilitation, 60,* 491–496.

Weinstein, E.A., & Kahn, R.L. (1955). *Denial of illness.* Springfield, IL: Charles C Thomas.

Wiebers, D.O., Whisnant, J.P., & O'Fallon, W.M. (1981). The natural history of unruptured intracranial aneurysms. *New England Journal of Medicine, 304,* 696–698.

Wilson, T., & Smith, T. (1983). Driving after stroke. *International Rehabilitation Medicine, 5,* 170–177.

Yatsu, F.M., Becker, C., McLeroy, K.R., Coull, B.M., Feibel, J., Howard, G., Toole, J.F., & Walker, M.D. (1986). Community hospital-based stroke programs: North Carolina, Oregon, and New York. I. Goals, objectives and data collection procedures. *Stroke, 17,* 276–284.

Zubrick, S., & Smith, A. (1978). *Factors affecting BVRT performances in adults with acute focal cerebral lesions.* Presented at the meeting of the International Neuropsychological Society, Minneapolis.

Chapter 4

Chronic Pain: Psychology and Rehabilitation

Steven G. Fey, Ph.D.
Thomas E. Williamson-Kirkland, M.D.

This chapter examines the history and recent developments in the application of behavioral psychology and rehabilitation strategies to the treatment of chronic pain. The complexity of long-standing pain problems is discussed, the effectiveness of the behaviorally based rehabilitation programs that have been designed to treat pain patients is reviewed, and the effective ingredients of treatment methods currently in use are highlighted. The chapter ends with the authors' speculations on the future development of the field.

Chronic pain is defined as pain that persists beyond the expected healing time for a particular injury or illness (Fordyce, 1976; Sternbach, 1974). To be considered chronic, pain must have existed for longer than 6 months; it is frequently associated with functional disability. Chronic pain patients typically show pain symptoms and disability in excess of that which can be explained entirely by physical pathology. Their pain and disability are stable or show a worsening trend, rather than the expected slow steady path toward improvement. Acute pain, in contrast, usually has an explainable and well-defined etiology, produces a course of disability congruent with the level of discomfort, and shows a steady path of resolution as the pathology is accurately identified and treated. There are exceptions to this chronic-acute distinction—such as the pain and disability associated with malignant neoplasms, rheumatoid arthritis, and similar disease conditions—that can be thought of as *recurring acute illnesses*, even though they produce chronic dysfunction. Nonetheless, it is clear that cancer and arthritis victims can develop many of the same behavioral, social, and psychological features as the chronic pain patient who lacks any evidence of physical disease.

Approximately 75 million Americans suffer from chronic pain of some kind (Bonica, 1979). A report from the National Institute of Neurological and Communicative Disorders and Stroke (NINCDS) found that 40 million Americans may suffer from recurrent headaches, 15 million from low back pain, hundreds of thousands from cancer-related pain (350,000 cancer deaths per year), 20 million from arthritis, and countless others from the more unusual pain syndromes affecting every anatomic site. The number of disabled beneficiaries of the Social Security Administration has grown from 2 million in 1971 to 5 million in 1980, a rate that is approximately 10 times faster than the growth of the general population.

The NINCDS report estimated the total cost of managing chronic pain in this country to be approximately $60 billion annually, a truly staggering figure that reflects costs associated with hospitalization, treatment, medications, and income loss, as well as the expenses of the disability system. Disability payments made by the Social Security Administration amounted to $11.6 billion in 1977, with less than 2 percent of the beneficiaries recovering sufficiently to return to work (Hirsch, 1977). Back injuries alone cost more than $1 billion annually in disability funds and account for 20 percent of annual compensation payments. Brena and Chapman (1983) of the Emory University Pain Control Center report that the disability costs of a single pain patient may run from $15,000 to $24,000 per year.

Interestingly, these expenditures rarely serve to reverse the disability or treat the pain problem, seeming merely to maintain the status quo. A Washington State study (Johnson, 1978) of all industrial injury back pain claimants found 78.3 percent to have *objective* physical findings consistent with their continuing reports of pain. When the documented disk cases were excluded, 93.1 percent of the remaining patients lacked any supportive physical findings. Yet 100 percent of these cases continued to have open workers' compensation claims and were certified by physicians as needing continued medical care and wage replacement (time loss) funding. At the Virginia Mason Medical Center Pain Program, patients with industrial injury have a mean time of 27 months since date of injury. The authors found that 38 percent of the patients lacked objective physical findings; in 23 of the remaining subjects, the only objective finding was a history of lumbar laminectomy and/or fusion (Fey, Williamson-Kirkland, & Frangione, 1984). Yet, again, all the patients had generated health care expenses for their pain problems that had not improved.

The chronic pain problem then is a medical, economic, human, and political problem of great magnitude. The number of afflicted patients is sizable, the utilization of health care services is excessive, and exorbitant sums are often spent unproductively. The staggering number of patients who circulate aimlessly within the health care system attests to the difficulty they present to traditional medical treatment. Despite the proliferation of pain control centers, the problem of chronic pain persists in epidemic proportions.

CHARACTERISTICS OF THE CHRONIC PAIN SYNDROME

Pain is the product of thermal, mechanical, or chemical stimuli that threaten or damage tissue (collectively called nociception). Merskey (1980) defines pain as an "unpleasant experience which we primarily associate with tissue damage or describe in terms of tissue damage or both." It is commonly associated with disease or injury and serves to warn the individual of the need for protective action. In acute medicine, pain is a critical diagnostic tool. In most individuals, there is a clear relationship between pain and disease; good medical care serves to eliminate the noxious suffering associated with pain. On a more complex level, however, the experience of pain is mediated by large components of the nervous system, is strongly influenced by the patient's social and cultural learning history, is intensely sensitive to the social environment, and is affected by a wide range of emotional states. Chronic pain embodies all these characteristics and may be better conceived as a syndrome, rather than simply a continued complaint of discomfort.

Central to the chronic pain syndrome is the *verbal and nonverbal demonstration of discomfort, frequently in widely distributed areas, rather than in a discrete site*, as is the case in an acute injury. The symptoms often defy known anatomic pathways of pain and may occur anywhere, although the musculoskeletal system is often involved, particularly the lumbar area. Low back pain accounts for 50–70 percent of the admissions seen in the authors' pain treatment center (Fey et al., 1984). No part of the anatomy is immune, and very bizarre presentations can be seen involving genital, pelvic, extremity, oral, facial, and rectal areas, as well as total body discomfort.

The physical examination of chronic pain patients reveals several characteristics specific to the chronic pain syndrome. First, their pain tends to be global, affecting multiple unrelated areas that do not correspond to any anatomic or physiologic pathology. Second, the patients are hypersensitive to touch and movement. This hypersensitivity usually is seen in fairly large areas, over bony prominences as well as muscle and fat, and may even occur in response to very light stroking. Their sensitivity to movement tends to be indiscriminate, instead of in response to specific movements that might affect injuries to ligaments, muscles, or joints. Third, on muscle testing, many of these patients show weakness that tends to be "ratchety" or rapidly giving way, which can fairly easily be discriminated from the slow overpowering of weak muscles caused by the true lack of motor neurons or muscle fibers. Finally, there is a tremendous inconsistency in pain presentation, both in the examination itself and from one visit to the next. In the "formal" evaluation patients frequently appear less flexible than they do when they are walking into the examining room, changing clothes, or walking out of the office. It is always somewhat surprising to see someone who cannot flex more than 20 or 30 degrees during an examination, yet can bend over easily to put on shoes afterward. Specific maneuvers, such as straight-leg raising, may elicit significantly different performances in different positions. It is not at all unusual for a standing patient to refuse, because of pain, to bend over more than 30 degrees, yet from a sitting position reach down and touch his or her toes bilaterally. Health care professionals involved with chronic pain patients need to observe them over several examinations to appreciate that findings vary considerably, with no association with identified pathology.

Another major component of the chronic pain syndrome is a *markedly decreased level of activity*. Most of these patients have been treated with long periods of bedrest or immobilization—traction, casting, or splinting—or have voluntarily stopped many of their activities. They therefore show such pathologic signs of disuse as loss of strength and flexibility, muscle atrophy, weight gain, and decrease in cardiovascular fitness. In those patients whose jobs demand physical activity, the bedrest itself can become more disabling in terms of return to work than the original injury (Corcoran, 1981).

Chronic pain patients frequently exhibit what is called "selective inactivity," claiming that certain activities—usually unpleasant ones—are too painful to perform, yet equally demanding enjoyable endeavors elicit no such complaint. It is common to see low back pain patients who are unable to vacuum, but can bowl or play golf without discomfort. Although one might view this as an exaggeration of a normal human phenomenon, it is characteristic of chronic pain patients to compile a list of "chores" that induce intolerable pain.

A third major feature of the chronic pain syndrome is the *abuse of medications*, which is estimated to occur in 90 percent of this population (Black, 1975; Fordyce, 1976; Sternbach, 1974; Ziesat, Angle, Gentry, & Ellinwood, 1979). Although the chemically habituating drugs of the narcotic, sedative, and minor tranquilizer classes are most often abused, virtually any sort of pharmacologic substance may be involved. These drugs almost invariably increase the patient's dysfunction, resulting in thinking and memory problems, decreased activity, increased bedrest, and inconsistent sleep patterns; yet they produce little pain relief (Hendler, Cimini, Terence, & Long, 1980; Maruta, Swanson, & Finlayson, 1979). Thinking and memory disorders are especially prominent in elderly patients who have less tolerance for these drugs and who may show a florid organic brain syndrome before withdrawal of the medication. Chemically dependent patients medicate themselves regularly at 3–4 hour intervals and show a classic pattern of awakening in the middle of the night when they have overslept their narcotic supply and go into low-level withdrawal. They then become aroused and must ingest more medication to go back to sleep. Although narcotics and sedatives are helpful in the acute pain setting, daily consumption for more than 2–4 weeks encourages tolerance and dependence and begins to potentiate the pain problem. Interestingly, alcohol is infrequently abused in this population, as it is a strong sedative but a relatively poor analgesic. In the authors' experience, alcohol-abusing patients are often long-standing alcoholics who use their pain as an excuse to continue drinking.

A fourth common characteristic of the chronic pain syndrome is the *excessive and counterproductive overutilization of health care resources*. The typical patient admitted to a pain center has already visited many physicians, in most cases for years. Under the acute care disease model, these patients frequently receive multiple work ups, invasive testing, and unnecessary surgery. The surgeries are frequently done solely because of pain, without other indications, or for exploratory diagnostic purposes. The Virginia Mason pain patient population averages 1.6 surgeries per patient for 50 percent of the cases, with females being higher surgical consumers (Fey et al., 1984). This copious medical activity communicates to chronic pain patients that there is indeed something physically wrong with them and that only further medical intervention can provide a solution. This perception reinforces the patient's "illness conviction" and sometimes leads patients to be as aggressive in pursuit of surgery as are their physicians.

A fifth trait of the pain patient pertains to *mental status and psychological changes*. Depression, estimated to occur in up to 70 percent of the population, is exacerbated by prolonged inactivity and by the overuse of narcotics and sedatives. (For a complete review of pain and depression, see Roy, Thomas & Matas, 1984). Many pain patients have primary depression that is masked by their pain complaints. The overuse of narcotics and sedatives can produce cognitive and memory impairments that serve to confuse these patients, increase their anxiety, and render them less able to cope with their pain (McNairy, Maruta, Invik, Swanson & Ilstrup, 1984). Some patients become toxic and stuporous on narcotics. In addition, many patients show severe and long-standing predisposing personality problems that lead to exaggerated pain responses. Descriptive studies with the Minnesota Multiphasic Personality Inventory (MMPI) show that chronic pain patients are likely to have elevated scores on the "neurotic triad": the hypochondriasis (HS), hysteria (HY), and depression (D) scales (Sternbach, Wolf, Murphy, & Akeson, 1973). Although MMPI responses are inconsistent in describing the chronic pain patient, research suggests that clinical scale elevations in general and specific elevations on the neurotic scales tend to be associated with exaggerated pain behavior and greater disruption of normal activities. (For a complete review, see Bradley, Prokop, Gentry, Hopson, & Prieto, 1981; Bradley & Van der Heide, 1984; Crown, 1980.)

A final critical characteristic is the presence of *work disability and vocational maladjustment*. A large proportion of pain center referrals—70 percent at the authors' facility—are workers' compensation cases that stem from a poorly resolved on-the-job injury. Although it has not been well documented in the literature, there is a consensus among clinicians that these people have preinjury histories of work difficulty and may exaggerate their pain and disability in order to escape an unpleasant work situation or to avoid possible unemployment. The Virginia Mason Pain Center sees a high proportion of contested disability cases with a low re-employment rate with their prior employer even after successful treatment (Fey et al., 1984). Exploitation of the disability system, with abuse of due process to prolong the life of the claim, is not uncommon. Fey et al. (1984)

found that the simple presence of an attorney in workers' compensation cases was associated with failure to return to work after pain treatment.

CONCEPT OF OPERANT PAIN

It is clear that the disease model of illness, although helpful in understanding acute pain, does not adequately explain or provide a basis for treating the chronic pain syndrome. Rather, it encourages unnecessary medical investigation, surgery, and drug use and reinforces the patient's illness conviction. It rationalizes the search for physical pathology that may not exist and ignores the psychological, social, and legal factors that perpetuate the chronic pain syndrome. A major conceptual advance was achieved by Fordyce and his colleagues (Fordyce, Fowler, Lehmann, & deLateur, 1968) in their paper describing the analysis and treatment of chronic pain in behavioral terms. In the same year, Sternbach wrote that "in order to describe pain, it is necessary for the patient to do something in order for us to determine that he is experiencing pain" (1968, p. 13). In other words, clinicians assess the intensity, frequency, and location of pain by observing *pain behaviors*. Pain behavior can be dramatic, such as screaming, crying, grimacing, limping, or bracing, or subtle, e.g. a stiff posture or furrowed brow.

The complex interaction of social learning factors, emotional state, and situational circumstances produces considerable variability of pain behavior. Schoolchildren being immunized by injection, for example, show a wide range of pain behaviors in response to an identical nociceptive source, mediated in part by their emotional state (fear, anxiety), their history with such injections, and current social or peer pressure, e.g., daring each other to be brave. Verbal self-reports of pain are subject to all of the well-known problems of response bias (Orne, 1962; Rosenthal, 1966). Thus, the true meaning of pain behavior is often unclear to the observer, particularly when there is no visible evidence of physical pathology. In chronic pain patients, it is the rule rather than the exception that there is a less-than-perfect linkage between the magnitude and intensity of the expressed pain and the degree of physiologic nociceptive input (Fey & Fordyce, 1983; Fordyce, 1976). Quite simply, this means that a dramatic display of pain behavior does not necessarily mean that massive tissue pathology is present.

Pain behavior is as subject to the laws of learning and conditioning as is any other behavior. Behaviors are principally respondent or operant (Skinner, 1953). *Respondent behaviors* occur automatically when an adequate triggering stimulus is present. They are reliable reflexive phenomena, such as the knee jerk, and, in the case of acute pain, follow directly from some explicit physical insult. Thus, when a child touches a hot radiator, the resultant pain behavior—withdrawal—would be respondent. Generally, there is a direct association between the extent of tissue pathology and the intensity of respondent pain behavior.

Operant behaviors can also be produced by specific stimuli, but unlike respondent behaviors, they are conditioned by factors present during and after the presentation of the stimulus. Operant behaviors are modified by their consequences; subsequent reward or punishment increases or decreases the likelihood of recurrence. Thus, children who burn their hands on radiators will emit pain behaviors. How loud or dramatic is the cry may depend on the amount of tissue damage caused by the burn (respondent pain) or, regardless of the amount of tissue destruction, on how strongly the child has been reinforced by attention for pain behavior in the past (operant pain). Fordyce (1976) argues that any respondent pain can evolve into operant pain if the pain behaviors are consistently rewarded.

Pain behaviors are perhaps the most compelling and attention-getting of all human communications; in our society, they permit the previously ''well'' person to adopt the ''sick'' role. Sick persons in pain command sympathy and attention and are quickly relieved of their usual responsibilities. Thus, sick children stay home from school, and sick adults do not function as workers or parents. Sick persons are typically insulated from stressful circumstances and, most important, are not held responsible for their illness unless it is apparent that it was self-inflicted. The major responsibility of the sick individual is to pursue health care and to cooperate with treatment. In a marital relationship, pain behavior by one partner typically brings about a subtle but powerful change in the behavior of the other. The sick spouse is treated with sympathetic deference, uncomfortable discussions (arguments) are avoided, oversolicitous behavior occurs, and unpleasant tasks are assumed by others. In a previously troubled marriage, pain behavior frequently serves to deflect attention from the real problem areas and can serve as a device by which the sick partner avoids certain aspects of the relationship, e.g., sexual contact, child management.

The majority of acute or respondent pain problems resolve quickly because the reinforcers for pain behavior are not persistent or compelling enough to prevent the person from resuming a normal life dominated by well behaviors. In the development of chronic pain, however, the psychological atmosphere is such that pain behavior is repeatedly reinforced while well behaviors are ignored or extinguished. The environment makes it more rewarding for the patient to remain sick than to pursue the path to recovery. Pain behaviors slowly become operantly conditioned, wax and wane in response to the positive and negative consequences that they produce, and eventually become *independent* of whatever nociceptive stimuli may be present. Thus, operant pain may become a predictable behavior pattern in which pain behaviors derive from the *social* environment, rather than from the internal physical environment. An understanding of this phenomenon requires the use of the behavioral analysis described by Fordyce (1976) that examines the social contingencies that support and encourage chronic pain behavior. A medically oriented perspective focusing on the presumed underlying pathology is less helpful.

Positive Reinforcement

A good behavioral analysis in chronic pain reveals many reinforcers for pain behavior. The most obvious is *direct positive reinforcement*, which may take the form of attentive, solicitous, affectionate, or comforting behavior from a spouse or significant other when that response is pain-contingent. The problem arises when these reinforcing behaviors are dispensed only in response to displays of pain behavior and are virtually nonexistent in their absence. Physicians provide direct solicitous reinforcement through expressions of professional concern and attempts to treat these patients. Frequent physician visits become common, and chronic pain patients often circulate among several physicians in their community, ensuring themselves of careful attention to their problems by each new practitioner they see. This professional attention further validates the pain problem.

Direct positive reinforcement is also supplied by the prescription of narcotics and sedatives. These drugs typically are given in response to displays of pain behavior, with more medications in stronger doses given to the patients with the most dramatic displays. Because pain behavior can include complaints of discomfort, tension, anxiety, muscle spasm, mood dysphoria, and lack of sleep, these patients receive analgesics, hypnotics, minor tranquilizers, muscle relaxants, and antidepressants, often on an as needed (PRN) self-administered basis. For some patients, these drugs are potently reinforcing, and when tolerance and addiction occur, pain behavior markedly increases in order to obtain more medication. These individuals exhibit the most dramatic, devious, aggressive, and compelling behaviors in order to obtain further prescriptions. Many physicians have little training in the psychology of addiction and underestimate the power of this acquired drive.

A third source of direct reinforcement for pain behavior comes from the monetary compensation for disability, which may equal or exceed what a person was making while employed, thereby providing a substantial disincentive for getting well. Disabled workers with the least interesting jobs, the fewest job options, and the poorest personal and occupational skills are most likely to resist returning to work, thus prolonging their disability claim (Block, Kremer, & Gaylor, 1980a; Peck, Fordyce, & Black, 1978).

An additional source of direct positive reinforcement for continued pain behavior is rest. Chronic pain patients, if not supervised, may exercise until it becomes uncomfortably painful and then rest, thereby making rest and immobility reinforcing. They learn to avoid pain by not moving and ultimately condition themselves into a disabled state.

Avoidance Conditioning

Other more subtle *indirect* forms of reinforcement for pain behavior involve the principles of avoidance conditioning. For example, the public display of pain behavior permits the patient to avoid a difficult, unpleasant, or stressful situation, e.g. work, an unrewarding marriage. Instead of trying to solve these problems, pain patients come to rely on their pain as a convenient excuse to avoid problems without confronting them directly. Chronic pain patients can easily learn to use pain as an "escape hatch" if their preinjury life was fraught with behavioral and situational difficulties.

Other avoidance responses consist of the unusual compensatory body positions and ambulation aids—canes, crutches, etc.—that are seen in the chronic pain population. Patients may initially ambulate with a limp to avoid pain, but the distorted gait becomes habitual over time. Frequently the abnormal gait produces physical pathology in another part of the musculoskeletal system, thereby creating a secondary pain problem. Gait distortion can become extreme and quite bizarre in this population, occasionally precluding normal walking, sitting, and standing (Williamson-Kirkland & Fey, 1984).

Modeling of Pain Behavior

Finally, pain behavior can be learned and reinforced by modeling or imitation, starting in early childhood with children imitating the pain responses that they see in parents, siblings, and friends. Craig (1975) has shown that modeling can influence "pain tolerance," a phenomenon seen often in real life, e.g., in schoolchildren receiving immunizations. Violon and Giurgea (1984) report that chronic pain patients were more likely to have relatives with chronic pain than were nonpain patients.

MODERN CONCEPT OF MULTIDISCIPLINARY PAIN TREATMENT

The development of pain treatment centers has been spurred within the past 20 years by recognition of the complex determinants of chronic pain and by the need for more cost-effective health care delivery. Pain treatment has developed as a multidisciplinary specialty because of the many medical, psychological, vocational, and legal ramifications of chronic pain. The understanding of pain behavior as an operant behavior has led to a behavioral model to treat the syndrome, and this model prevails at most of the major pain treatment centers. Pain control centers now exist at more than 100 medical centers within the United States.

The pain control model is typically rehabilitative, and most pain centers function within a major rehabilitation facility. The typical multidisciplinary team includes physicians, psychologists, physical and occupational therapists, rehabilitation nurses, and vocational rehabilitation specialists. Noninvasive techniques are used to treat the various operant aspects of the chronic pain syndrome, including the vocational disability. *Operant* pain treatment implies the use of behavior modification technology in the rehabilitation setting to provide an environment where pain behavior can be extinguished and well behavior can be learned, practiced, and reinforced. The rehabilitation setting is important because it offers a context that encourages increased activity and independence.

Although there is some variability of approach and procedure among pain centers, the major successful programs share many features in common. The typical operant-based rehabilitation program has been described in detail by Fordyce and his colleagues (Fey & Fordyce, 1983; Fordyce, 1976; Fordyce & Steger, 1978). The evaluation, treatment, and follow-up phases of these programs are reviewed briefly below. (For comprehensive reviews, see Keefe, 1982; Turner & Chapman, 1982; Ziesat, 1981.)

Evaluation Phase

In the evaluation phase the nature and extent of the pain problem are established, and the goals of treatment are defined. Evaluation is conducted on an inpatient basis for extremely disabled or drug-addicted patients, but the more mobile individual who does not use medications can be evaluated as an outpatient. The key element of the evaluation is an intensive review of the problem by a physician and psychologist. The physician commonly is a physiatrist, but consultations from an orthopedist, neurologist, or other specialist may be sought. Careful medical review ensures that all medically treatable conditions are addressed and also allows evaluation of the patient's musculoskeletal condition before treatment. Because of prolonged bedrest, inactivity, and abnormal postures, patients frequently have secondary pain problems, including tendinitis, contracted joints, muscle tension states, and moderate-to-severe levels of overall weakness. It is especially important for chronic pain patients to feel that all their pain problems have received proper medical attention. All previous diagnostic tests must be reviewed, additional testing performed as needed, and multiple examinations carried out, especially in patients with bizarre or unusual pain behaviors.

The psychological and behavioral analysis is conducted by a psychologist and usually involves the examination of pain diaries, observations of the patient's behavior, interviews with patient and spouse, and formal standard psychological testing—the MMPI and in some cases neuropsychological testing. The psychological evaluation seeks to identify mood and personality characteristics that relate to the pain and disability and to analyze the patient's pain behaviors and their environmental determinants.

The behavior analysis can identify specific clues to operant pain behaviors. It is relatively easy to detect the ''selectively inactive'' pain patient by careful examination of the diary and movement patterns during the evaluation. Interviewing the spouse may uncover inconsistent patterns at home, as in the case of patients who consistently avoid unpleasant house chores, yet seem capable of more enjoyable, but equally strenuous activities. Sleep patterns often are informative here as well. Patients with operant pain who are in great "pain" during the day often sleep quite comfortably at night when there is little available social reinforcement. The pain patient who shows a disturbed sleep pattern typically is depressed or narcotic- or sedative-addicted.

The behavioral analysis should identify the patient's range of pain behaviors, particularly those manifestations that elicit reinforcement from the spouse. As mentioned previously, many of these behavioral signals are subtle and are only detected by careful observation. Episodes of extreme and dramatic pain at home are usually operant and occur when pain behavior will be most potently reinforced. Drug-dependent pain patients typically have "crises" at night when their doctors are unavailable, and they are likely to obtain injectable narcotics at the local emergency department. Spouses can be extremely helpful in determining these patterns; they should be asked to describe or demonstrate how they respond to the patient's pain behaviors.

Another area of behavioral inquiry involves *pain activators*, activities or situations that bring on pain behavior. It is important to have the patient specify explicitly the motion or activity that produces pain; the limitations that follow, such as rest, time out, or medications; and the measures taken to diminish pain once it has occurred. Some behavior patterns that are thought by the patient to reduce discomfort are little more than superstitions and bear little relationship to the pain problem at all. The authors evaluated a patient with chronic headache who believed that inhaling cold air exacerbated the headache; she engaged in a complex ritual to avoid breathing cold air, which included wrapping her head with a heating pad in an effort to preheat the air surrounding her face.

Other pertinent issues concern the history of behavioral and psychological difficulties preceding the pain problem, e.g., pre-existing depression, job stress. For married patients, the behavioral analysis reviews the couple's pattern of social, leisure, and work activities before the injury. The less the spouse's activity has been changed by the patient's pain problem, the less likely it is that the spouse is reinforcing pain behaviors. Spouses who change or postpone their own goals because of the patient's pain may be collaborators in the pain problem and may have an investment in the patient remaining sick.

A critical part of any pain evaluation is the assessment of medication use. If excessive narcotic or sedative intake is suspected, it should be evaluated in a hospital setting. To evaluate discrepancies between *actual* and *reported* narcotic and sedative use, newly admitted patients may be given medications on request to control their pain for 2–3 days in order to establish a baseline. Their intake is monitored carefully with upper limits set to prevent cardiac and respiratory distress. This baseline procedure defines the level of drug habituation more accurately than the patient's self-report. It has been observed that reported drug use is significantly lower than actual drug use as defined by this drug profile procedure (Ready, Sarkis, & Turner, 1982). Some pain programs require patients to sign releases to allow staff members to search their belongings and confiscate drugs that they have brought with them.

Several specialists participate in the typical pain evaluation. Physical and occupational therapists measure exercise and work tolerance in activities that can affect the pain behavior. Patients are instructed to exercise until they reach their pain, weakness, or fatigue tolerance, and their performance is carefully quantified. Vocational assessment includes a work history, aptitude testing, and some investigation into the details of the patient's past job, e.g. relations with supervisors and colleagues, physical requirements.

Many pain programs include an assessment of possible contributing legal factors. Chronic pain patients are often involved in litigation related to personal injury claims, disability compensation, or malpractice claims. Many pain patients and their spouses believe that their cases will be weakened if they report less pain and disability, and they thus view the pain treatment program as an adversarial procedure. Frank exploration of these perceptions, along with direct contact with the patient's legal counsel, is becoming a standard part of evaluation procedure.

Treatment Phase

The treatment phase of the operant pain and rehabilitation program typically begins after 1 week of evaluation. Programs have differing entry criteria, but most proceed with treatment if it is determined that no further medical treatment or diagnostic tests are necessary, that the pain behavior has strong operant characteristics, and that there are no other significant vocational or legal barriers to rehabilitation. The basic components of treatment are medication detoxification, physical reactivation, reinforcement of well behavior, reduction of attention and social reinforcement for pain and disability behavior, vocational counseling, psychological treatment, and, in most cases, some form of stress reduction treatment.

Medication detoxification and deconditioning involve changing administration of pain killers from a pain-contingent schedule to a time-contingent schedule. That is, instead of providing (reinforcing) pain medication when the patient complains of pain, medication is given on a regularly scheduled basis, usually every 6 hours. Short-acting narcotics and sedatives used during the initial drug profile are replaced in equivalent doses by long-acting substances, such as methadone and phenobarbital. These are administered in a "pain cocktail," a color- and taste-masking vehicle that conceals the size of the doses (Fordyce et al., 1973; Halpern, 1974). The narcotic and sedative ingredients are gradually reduced during the first 2–3 weeks of treatment until they are eliminated altogether. The slow fading schedule minimizes the risk of withdrawal symptoms and also allows the pain-contingent narcotic habit to be deconditioned gradually while other pain control behaviors are acquired.

The physical reconditioning and reactivation part of treatment is extremely important and yet frequently very difficult to accomplish. Most of these patients have lost confidence in their physical abilities, have deep-seated fears of activity, and fear reinjury. The physical restoration program is designed to help restore confidence and prepare patients to return to active lifestyles and their specific jobs. Physical and occupational therapy sessions typically are intensive, last from 4 to 6 weeks, and involve gradual daily increases in activity. Physical therapy exercises aim to increase cardiovascular endurance, muscular strength, and flexibility. Occupational therapy focuses on return to work and work-related activities, with the teaching of good biomechanics during exercise and at the eventual work site. Exercise quotas or specified time limits are initially set below the pain threshold, and compliance is carefully monitored; patients are not allowed to do too little or to overexercise and thus cause pain (Fordyce, 1976). This system of gradually increasing quotas is critical to physical reactivation because it neutralizes the reinforcing value of rest, allows physical strength to build gradually, desensitizes patients to movement, and teaches them to pace their physical output.

The operant part of the pain program consists of the systematic reduction of social attention and reinforcement for displays of pain behavior. The entire treatment staff is consistently nonresponsive to displays of pain while they praise and reinforce well behavior, such as increased physical activity, tolerance, social activity, and the like. In a medical setting, pain behavior cannot be entirely ignored, but it is restricted to discussion between the patient and physician during regularly scheduled visits. From a theoretical perspective, pain behaviors should not be prohibited by fiat; in order to be extinguished, the pain behavior must occur, but must elicit responses that will diminish the frequency of that behavior. Most pain programs involve the spouse and family, teaching them to inhibit their natural tendency to provide social attention to pain behaviors. Frequently the family needs as much therapeutic intervention as does the spouse.

Vocational counseling is another critical rehabilitation tool. Vocational counselors assess work abilities during treatment, observe behavior in structured work-like situations, and assist patients in finding employment after discharge. The University of Washington pain program uses a unique system of "job stations," where, as part of treatment, patients perform in real work settings on the medical center campus, gradually increasing their hours of work as the program progresses (Fey & Fordyce, 1983). This work simulation program increases tolerance for work-related demands—both physical and psychological—and orients patients to a work environment while they are still under supervision.

Most multidisciplinary pain programs now employ a variety of adjunctive stress- and tension-reducing treatments. Muscle relaxation and biofeedback treatments are used with headaches, orofacial pain, and musculoskeletal pain of the back, neck, and shoulders. Electromyographic (EMG) feedback is used in conjunction with muscle relaxation therapies to help patients learn to relax unusually tight muscles. Hypnosis, an older form of pain control, is currently used with a variety of pain syndromes, although the understanding of its mechanism of action remains vague. Some researchers maintain that hypnosis produces symptom-specific physiologic changes (Crasilneck & Hall, 1975); others suggest that hypnosis alters the patient's awareness of pain (Hilgard, 1975; McGlashan, Evans, & Orne, 1969). Barber has consistently argued against the existence of a unique hypnotic state, suggesting that hypnotized patients are simply engaging in a sophisticated form of role-playing (Barber, 1963; Barber & Hahn, 1962).

A recent addition to the pain control arsenal derives from cognitive-behavioral theory, a central tenet of which holds that individuals cognitively label and evaluate situations in ways that later influence their emotional reactions (Goldfried, 1977). In the case of chronic pain, cognitive-behavioral interventions attempt to increase the patient's awareness of situations and events that lead to pain responses so that these may be avoided or managed more effectively. Meichenbaum and Turk (1976) describe an approach called *stress inoculation*, which consists of education about the nature of pain and practice in the use of behavioral and cognitive coping strategies.

Cognitive behavior therapies have been found to be of benefit in the treatment of mixed pain syndromes (Gottlieb et al., 1977; Rybstein-Blinchik, 1979), abdominal pain (Levendusky & Pankratz, 1975), myofascial pain (Stenn, Mothersill, & Brooke, 1979), tension headache (Holroyd, Andrasik, & Westbrook, 1977; Reeves, 1976), and migraine headaches (Mitchell & Mitchell, 1971; Mitchell & White, 1977).

Adjunctive therapies, such as muscle relaxation and biofeedback, have been shown to be effective supplements to the treatment of particular conditions, especially headache; neck, shoulder, and orofacial pain; and other syndromes where abnormal muscle tension is a central factor. (For reviews, see Adams, Feuerstein, & Fowler, 1980; Beaty & Haynes, 1979; Jessup, Neufeld, & Merskey, 1979; Nuechterlein & Holroyd, 1980; Silver & Blanchard, 1978; and Turk, Meichenbaum, & Berman, 1979). A few studies have reported the use of EMG biofeedback with other chronic pain syndromes. Hendler, Derogatis, Avella, and Long (1977) reported significant pain reduction with biofeedback in 6 of 13 patients with chronic generalized pain. Keefe, Schapira, Brown, Williams, and Surwit (1982) utilized EMG biofeedback-assisted relaxation training with chronic low back pain patients and found that 15 of 18 patients reported improvement at the end of treatment, with 9 of 13 maintaining these gains for 1 year. EMG biofeedback has also been reported to reduce temporomandibular joint pain in some cases (Carlsson & Gale, 1976; Carlsson, Gale, & Ohman, 1975; Gessel, 1975).

Follow-Up Phase

There is great variability in the follow-up procedures used by the multidisciplinary pain centers. Although there is a consensus that long-term follow-up—6 months to 2 years—is needed, this is difficult to achieve in many cases. Generally it is reported that the posttreatment relapse rate is higher than desirable, and many programs now employ face-to-face follow-up interviews and booster sessions to prevent relapses (Keefe & Bradley, 1984; Turner & Chapman, 1982; Ziesat, 1981). In the absence of direct contact with patients, some studies use questionnaires to gather data. The following discussion of treatment effectiveness highlights the difficulties of longitudinal evaluation of the effectiveness of operant pain treatment.

TREATMENT OUTCOME STUDIES

The behavioral treatment of chronic pain is well suited to outcome evaluation because of the many pertinent behaviors that can be observed, recorded, and quantified. Such variables as time spent standing and walking (up time), distance walked, exercise repetitions, weights lifted, levels of muscle tension as measured by surface electromyography, amounts of medication, sitting tolerances, and aerobic fitness can all be documented at baseline, during treatment, and in follow-up. These are objective measures that are not subject to the distorting effects of memory or self-report. Additionally, one can study economic outcome variables, including whether the patient returns to gainful employment, the utilization of disability services, and the patient's subsequent use of health care services.

Fordyce et al. (1973) reported on 56 patients who underwent 4- to 6-week inpatient operant pain treatment. They found significant posttreatment increases in time spent out of bed and general activity level and significant decreases in medication intake. These patients were followed by questionnaire for an average of 22 months after discharge and were found to have maintained these treatment gains. However, the use of a questionnaire to obtain follow-up data and the absence of a control group limit the usefulness of these results.

Data from the University of Minnesota rehabilitation medicine program were reported by Anderson, Cole, Gullickson, Hudgens, and Roberts (1977). Thirty-four chronic pain patients were studied after completing a 6- to 8-week treatment program. By a variety of criteria related to activity level, drug use, and exercise tolerance, 25 of these patients were found to be leading normal lives without the use of analgesics at 2- to 4-week follow-up. The authors report good maintenance of these gains in most patients 1 to 8 years after treatment.

In a study from the Minnesota program, Roberts and Reinhardt (1980) compared 26 graduates of their inpatient operant pain program to 20 patients who had been rejected for treatment and to 12 patients who had refused treatment. Criteria for success were (1) male subjects either employed or retired; (2) retired males able to function to their own and their families' satisfaction in other roles, such as husband, father, or maintenance person around the house, and be physically active at least 8 hours per day; (3) women employed, if necessary, for their own or their children's support; (4) unemployed married women able to function in their chosen roles, such as homemaker, mother, or volunteer, to their own and their families' satisfaction and to be physically active at least 8 hours per day; (5) no receipt of any compensation for pain problems; (6) no pain-related hospitalization or surgery since treatment; and (7) no use of any prescription analgesics, sedatives, muscle relaxants, or tranquilizers.

Of the 26 treated patients, 20 (77 percent) met all these criteria, whereas only 5 percent of the patients rejected for treatment and none of those refusing treatment did so. The authors compared the pretreatment data of the 20 successfully treated patients and the 6 failures. It was found that the former had lower baseline levels of analgesic usage and pain problems that were less chronic, whereas the failures more frequently reported job-related exacerbations of their pain. The successful patients had lower scores on MMPI scale 6 (paranoia) and higher scores on the ego strength scales. Roberts and Reinhardt report the interesting finding that the spouses of the successful patients had lower scores on the hypochondriasis (scale 1) and hysteria (scale 3) scales of the MMPI than did spouses of the unsuccessful patients.

This study represents a major advance in two ways: (1) the delineation of outcome criteria and (2) the use of pertinent control groups in an effort to evaluate treatment success more clearly. Yet, as with the earlier study by Fordyce et al. (1973), the Roberts and Reinhardt investigation (1980) did not separate the many ingredients of the operant pain treatment program, and thus assessment of the relative contributions of the various therapies to the successful outcome was not possible.

Seres, Newman, Yospe, and Garlington (1977, 1978) reported outcome data for low back pain patients who underwent a multidisciplinary pain treatment program at the Northwest Pain Center in Portland, Oregon. Follow-up interviews were conducted 80 weeks after the completion of treatment. They found significant reduction in medication use and improvement in four measures of physical functioning. Despite these positive findings the patients' subjective reports of pain did not diminish significantly from the start of treatment to follow-up.

Painter, Seres, and Newman (1980) conducted a mail survey of 500 former pain clinic patients. Of the 145 respondents, 77 percent reported improvement as a result of treatment, with an average reduction in subjective pain of 35 percent. Further improvement after discharge was reported by 27 percent of the sample, with a further decrease in subjective pain of 21 percent. However, 27 percent reported a deterioration in their condition, with an average increase in posttreatment pain of 23 percent. On the basis of their parameters of treatment gains, Painter et al. identified "success" and "failure" groups of 25 patients each. The "failure" group had less economic incentive for maintaining treatment gains, as most patients in this group continued to receive monetary compensation for their pain and disability. This group also seemed to have a more dependent and passive attitude toward their pain problem, as a considerable number were still seeking medical treatment or using narcotics, whereas 75 percent of the successful patients had stopped visiting physicians altogether. Depression was more prevalent in the failure group and may have contributed to the deterioration of its members' conditions. These subjects continued to receive positive reinforcement from their families for pain behavior, thereby undercutting whatever gains had been achieved. By contrast, successful patients reported substantial changes in lifestyle after treatment. These results underscore the importance of extending intervention to family members, as well as patients.

Several studies have explored the issue of vocational restoration as a goal of pain treatment. Malec, Cayner, Harvey, and Timming (1981) followed 40 subjects by questionnaires for 6 months to 3 years after an inpatient pain treatment program. They found increased activity levels and decreased medication usage, as well as dramatic changes in employment status, compared to admission. At admission, none of their patients were employed full-time or part-time, whereas at follow-up these figures had climbed to 25 percent and 11 percent, respectively. Eleven percent of their patients were in some type of vocational training program, and 25 percent were running a household. Thus, only 25 percent were unemployed as compared to a pretreatment figure of 86 percent.

Tyre and Anderson (1981) reported follow-up on 13 former inpatients up to 1 year after treatment. Five patients were in vocational training programs or had returned to work; the remainder either had retired or were still disabled.

Catchlove and Cohen (1982) reported return-to-work outcome in two groups of workers' compensation patients; group I received a directive return-to-work emphasis during treatment, whereas group II did not. Both outpatient groups received similar multimodal pain treatment programs. Sixty percent of the group I patients returned to work within 16 months after treatment as compared to only 25 percent of the group II patients. The return-to-work orientation consisted of telling patients that return to work was an "expected" goal of treatment and providing strong psychological support to seek employment.

Fey, Williamson-Kirkland, and Frangione (1984) reported return-to-work data for 92 workers' compensation cases in a pain program specifically designed to produce re-employment. Twenty-five percent of these patients had returned to work within 1 month after treatment, and an additional 31 percent returned within 3 to 16 months. When the 23 percent of patients who failed to complete treatment were excluded, the total return-to-work figure climbed to 65 percent. Men became employed at a significantly greater rate than women, although there were no medical or demographic differences to account for this fact. These return-to-work statistics were verified directly with the patients' insurance carriers.

Limitations of Pain Outcome Research

The preceding selective review of pain treatment outcome literature shows positive results in virtually all studies reported. It is important to note, however, that negative findings tend not be published. Graduates of pain programs tend to demonstrate reduced intensity of pain behavior, increased activity level, and decreased medication usage, and some are able to return to work. Despite the variability in reported success rates, it is widely accepted that the multidisciplinary model approach to pain treatment is superior to the traditional disease model approach.

The beneficial effects of behaviorally based multidisciplinary treatment support the conceptualization of chronic pain behavior as an operant phenomenon that is largely independent of ongoing nociception. Patients in most of these treatment programs receive no active medical treatment to reduce nociception; in fact, patients are encouraged to maintain activity levels that would be expected to increase pain, yet to reduce their use of analgesics. Nonetheless, pain reports and observable pain behavior tend to decrease while general activity level, stamina, and endurance increase.

Because of the overwhelmingly positive findings, it is of special concern that the majority of outcome research studies suffer from serious flaws in experimental design, rendering many of these results questionable. A crucial difficulty is the consistent absence of adequate control groups, such as untreated patients (waiting list), those who receive traditional therapeutic modalities (drugs and/or surgery), and those whose pain is clearly respondent in nature. The Roberts and Reinhardt study (1980), which used two control groups—patients rejected for treatment by the staff and patients who were accepted by the staff but refused to join the program—is an important exception. Nonetheless, the size of these groups was small—20 and 12 patients, respectively—and they may not have been comparable to the treatment group. In one case, they were deemed unfit for treatment, and in the second, the patients refused to participate for reasons that were not clearly specified.

Although the design and implementation of research with adequate control groups are beset with clinical and ethical problems, such studies must be conducted so that valid conclusions may be drawn about the effects of pain treatment programs. Perhaps pain programs with long waiting lists could monitor their patients before admission and later compare their pretreatment responses to active treatment, thus using patients as their own controls. Because the pain population is so widely variable, the use of comparable patient selection criteria across studies would enable meaningful comparisons of data to be carried out.

Another problem with these studies is the difficulty of assessing the independent contributions of the various treatment elements to the ultimate outcome of multidisciplinary programs. A typical program consists of physical and occupational therapy, medical intervention, drug detoxification, psychological treatment, and vocational therapy, as well as various adjunctive stress-reducing procedures. There is no clear evidence that any one of these procedures is more effective than the others, nor is there any consensus on the value of targeting particular combinations of techniques at certain diagnostic categories. This is particularly true for the adjunctive treatments. For example, progressive muscle relaxation is frequently used in conjunction with biofeedback; if successful results are achieved, one does not know whether the effectiveness of the treatment lies in one or the other component or in their interaction. Blanchard, Theobald, Williamson, Silver, and Brown (1978) compared finger temperature feedback with relaxation training for migraine headaches and found that relaxation alone was as effective as biofeedback. Cox, Freundlich, and Meyer (1975) found that frontalis EMG biofeedback and relaxation were equally effective in reducing headache pain and medication use. Haynes, Griffin, Mooney, and Parise (1975) and Chesney and Shelton (1976) reported similar results. Although there are exceptions to these findings (Hutchings & Reinking, 1976), it may be that simple relaxation treatments are as potent in cases of muscle tension disorders as are the more complex and esoteric biofeedback methods.

Studies of the effect of hypnosis on pain have tended to use small subject samples (case reports are common), to lack control groups, and to confound experimental procedures with general relaxation (Sternbach, 1974). Although Hilgard (1975) has argued that hypnotic pain control is qualitatively different from the placebo effect, relaxation, or simple anxiety reduction, there are few well-controlled pertinent studies to support that hypothesis.

The cognitive behavioral therapies also suffer from this confounding of multiple components, as they are essentially packages of several techniques. For example, some authors (Khatami & Rush, 1978; Levendusky & Pankratz, 1975; Stenn et al., 1979) combined multiple elements—relaxation, visual imagery, cognitive relabeling, biofeedback, stress inoculation, etc.—in an uncontrolled fashion and were unable to specify the relative effectiveness of any one constituent. Other research (Holroyd et al., 1977; Mitchell & Mitchell, 1971; Mitchell & White, 1977; Reeves, 1976) compared selected procedures in randomly assigned groups, but the results are difficult to synthesize. For example, Holroyd et al. (1977) showed that "stress coping" training was a more effective treatment for headache pain than either EMG biofeedback or being placed on a waiting list. Mitchell and Mitchell (1971) showed "combined desensitization"—applied relaxation, desensitization, and assertion training—to be more effective in the relief of migraine headache pain than either relaxation or desensitization alone. Mitchell and White (1977) reported that self-recording and monitoring of stressful life situations alone did not reduce the frequency of migraine headaches, but they became effective when progressive relaxation and assertion training were added. These studies certainly illustrate the value of carefully designed research that assesses the varying contributions of different techniques for pain relief in well-defined pain syndromes.

A major difficulty with the pain outcome research is the vagueness and lack of consistency in the criteria used to gauge treatment outcome. Although most studies use quantifiable measures, the variables and methods differ from one study to another, e.g., observational data, patient self-report, electromechanical devices, questionnaires, and face-to-face interviews. The Roberts and Reinhardt study (1980) is exemplary in that very clear criteria are defined, including vocational and avocational pursuits, as well as medical and health care utilization. Here again it would be desirable to develop standardized outcome criteria, especially in the vocational domain. For workers' compensation cases, it should be possible to develop clear criteria regarding employment status that could be independently verified through the disability insurance carriers, as done by Fey et al. (1984).

Another major problem with pain outcome research concerns follow-up. Many studies report follow-up data collected less than 1 year after treatment; given the characteristic chronicity of pain problems, the period of follow-up should be at least of the same duration as the history of the pain. Furthermore, a considerable number of studies are based on questionnaires that require patients to make retrospective judgments about their pain and activity at varying intervals. Face-to-face evaluation of patients is preferable to mailed questionnaire responses, and objective measures of physical abilities, psychological state, and vocational and avocational activities should be used. A vital but neglected area is the analysis of treatment failure. Careful examination of those patients who either do not improve or who failed to maintain treatment gains might assist pain programs in developing better admission criteria and would help clarify the most effective treatment "package" for the particularly chronic and recalcitrant patient.

WHAT ARE THE EFFECTIVE COMPONENTS OF PAIN TREATMENT?

As is clear from the above discussion of the flaws and ambiguities of the existing literature, there exists no well-validated "cookbook" for the treatment of specific chronic pain conditions. Nonetheless, certain ingredients seem essential to good outcomes. The following discussion outlines what the authors consider to be the core characteristics of effective treatment for pain problems and provides suggestions about the directions of future research.

First, chronic pain treatment is *rehabilitative* and is most profitably conducted within a major multidisciplinary rehabilitation center. Chronic pain problems are almost always multifactorial, starting with an injury and tissue damage, but compounded by functional disability, depression, drug dependence, operantly learned behavior, and severe deconditioning. Using isolated treatment procedures, such as nerve blocks, drugs, psychotherapeutic techniques, physical therapy, and the like, and ignoring other facets of the problem leads to a less successful outcome than if all components of the problem are addressed *simultaneously*. This process of rehabilitation can only be carried out through a coordinated team approach that involves many professionals who provide a consistent message to the patient. The physician who leads this team should not only have specific expertise in musculoskeletal medicine, pathophysiology of pain, exercise physiology, and treatment of addiction but also should be somewhat of a generalist to deal with the many medical problems that arise during treatment. The physician and other members of the rehabilitation team also must be adept at working together and at establishing patient relationships that can induce effective change without alienating the sensitive patient.

A critical target symptom of the chronic pain syndrome is the excessive use of drugs. The narcotic-and/or sedative-dependent patient has a pharmacologic addiction, a powerful acquired drive, that will subvert every other avenue of treatment. Thus, pain programs must initiate detoxification as the first treatment step. It also must be understood that the relapse rate for narcotic addiction is quite high, particularly in the first year, and follow-up procedures for the addicted patient must therefore be extremely vigorous. Pain patients are notoriously unreliable informants regarding their drug intake habits, frequently underreporting their usage (Ready et al., 1982). Taylor, Zlutnick, Corley, and Flora (1980) obtained urine toxicology screens during follow-up and verified that 50 percent of their patients misreported their drug usage. If one wishes to have accurate information about a patient's drug use, urine and blood toxicology screens must be used during and after treatment.

Another important target symptom is depression, a common finding in the pain treatment population, that results from depressant drug abuse, inactivity, loss of work, and diminished self-esteem (Blumer, 1982; Roy, Thomas, & Matas, 1984; Swanson, 1984). Depressed pain patients display more pain behavior and more dramatic suffering than their nondepressed counterparts. Painter et al. (1980) found that patients who regressed following treatment tended to be those whose mood disorders persisted during treatment and follow-up. The tricyclic antidepressants, such as amitriptyline and doxepin, have an active place in pain treatment, as they contribute to better sleep patterns, improved daytime mood, increased activity level, and a reduced preoccupation with symptoms (Kocher, 1976; Spiegel, Kalb, & Pasternak, 1983; Ward, Bloom, & Friedel, 1979). Psychotherapy may also be useful. It is critical to incorporate antidepressant care directly into the pain treatment program to help break the mutually exacerbating cycle of pain, depression, and loss of physical function.

Physical reconditioning is an important factor in pain treatment for several reasons. It helps the patient become desensitized to previously painful movement; reduces joint stiffness, muscle atrophy, and hamstring tightness; and enhances cardiovascular fitness, which permits greater work tolerance. In addition, physical and occupational therapies can teach appropriate body mechanics to patients who are aggravating their condition, e.g., the low back pain patient who is obese, weak in the legs, and tight in the hamstrings who persists in bending from the waist while doing daily activities. Although most pain programs utilize physical and occupational therapists, the degree and intensity of these treatments vary greatly. The authors contend that chronic pain patients need *aggressive* physical reconditioning to allow them to function normally in the home and at work. Patients who intend to return to heavy industrial jobs need physical therapy and occupational therapy programs that are carefully tailored to their individual job requirements. Many on-the-job injuries result from musculoskeletal strains and sprains that can be prevented by proper physical conditioning and good body mechanics.

Another important task of pain treatment is to address what Fordyce (1976) calls the patient's "illness conviction," the belief that one's pain reflects the presence of illness or the operation of some destructive process. This illness conviction is often powerfully reinforced by multiple medical examinations and diagnostic tests. It is the authors' experience that pain treatment will fail as long as this disabling belief persists. Patients must come to accept that their pain symptoms are benign and that discomfort is probably caused by deconditioning, not further injury. The actions of the treating staff are critical in changing these beliefs, as patients may require extensive teaching and frequent authoritative reassurance about their medical condition.

An additional concern is the identification of coexisting cognitive deficits; for example the cognitive impairment that results from chronic opiate and sedative abuse (McNairy et al., 1984). Many toxic pain patients show memory and intellectual disturbances that persist even after detoxification (Grant, Mohns, Miller, & Reitan, 1976; Judd, Grant, Bickford, & Lee, 1978). Confused patients cope poorly with their pain problems and are unable to participate fully in therapeutic activities. Such patients often use their pain as a socially acceptable excuse to avoid responsibilities that are cognitively difficult. In patients with cognitive deficits resulting from Alzheimer's disease, stroke, and head injury, chronic pain problems may appear later, thereby providing an escape route from demands that can no longer be met. Pain programs, therefore, should have the ability to provide neuropsychological evaluation, especially for elderly patients.

A critical requirement of effective treatment pertains to the patient's family and home environment. Pain problems develop within environmental and social circumstances that reinforce and sustain pain behavior and disability (Block,

1982; Block, Kremer, & Gaylor, 1980b; Roy, 1982). Simply removing patients to a rehabilitation setting does not affect those factors that are likely to invite a relapse once the patient returns home. Pain treatment is a *family* treatment in which the habit and pattern of family reinforcement must be changed. Doing so may involve merely encouraging the spouse and relatives to reward well behaviors. Alternatively, in instances where the spouse has some pathologic need to promote the patient's illness, extensive psychotherapy might be required.

Another major issue concerns the patient's vocational history and plans for re-employment. Workers' compensation cases, which comprise the majority of the average pain treatment center clientele, typically involve a complex constellation of disability issues. Rarely is the original physical injury severe; most cases involve relatively minor lifting and twisting accidents (Fey et al., 1984). Often, claimants have poor work records and histories of multiple jobs with little longevity on any one of them, and some even have prior workers' compensation claims. Often the individual may view the pain problem as a preferable alternative to certain unemployment or unemployability. Pain programs need to investigate their patients' vocational backgrounds if they expect to have a successful outcome that involves return to work. Aggressive vocational rehabilitation in all of its aspects—assessment, counseling, placement—is essential to long-term success. Tenacious follow-up is required, as the first 6 to 12 months after discharge are most critical in determining whether adaptive work habits and attitudes have been established.

A final issue that the authors view as important is the notion of the "bottom line"—why does pain behavior persist in the absence of an adequate physical explanation? What benefits accrue to this patient as a result of pain and disability? There are usually several answers to these questions, many of which have been outlined above. Sometimes the answer is quite simple, such as cognitive loss, depression, an arduous job, or marital problems, but often one finds a complex set of factors that have gradually developed since the onset of the pain problem. Failure to gain a thorough understanding of the development of the pain problem will render treatment efforts useless and will cause frustrating relapses.

NEW DIRECTIONS IN PAIN TREATMENT

Our sophistication and effectiveness in the management of chronic pain have increased significantly over the past 15 years. Nonetheless, we still operate under a tertiary care model, in which many patients are allowed to lapse into chronicity and severe disability before being referred to a pain treatment facility. The pain treatment program then, by necessity, is extensive, complex, and expensive with a relatively low success rate to date. There is a consensus that efforts should be directed toward preventing acute pain episodes from becoming chronic pain disorders. Doing so requires careful review and modification of the acute health care process, as well as the various disability and entitlement systems that currently support disabled persons.

A significant step toward prevention would be early referral to a multidisciplinary pain treatment center of patients whose pain problems have persisted for 6 months after the time of the injury. Such a referral would require considerable sensitivity and awareness on the part of the primary care or consultant physician, disability carriers, and work site supervisiors. For industrial injury cases there could be a mandatory pain center referral at 6 months following injury for evaluation and determination of the future course of care.

Another tactic is to educate physicians about the proper role of narcotics and sedatives in the treatment of pain patients. In part, prescribing appropriate medication depends on an accurate understanding of the normal course of recovery in musculoskeletal injuries. Although rest, analgesics, and sedation are indicated initially, these injuries heal in 12 weeks, and that healing should be accompanied by a gradual *reduction* in analgesia and sedation and a gradual *increase* in physical activity. Narcotic and sedative addiction problems begin from a single prescribing source and can be prevented. Physicians may not recognize the signs of a building addiction or see through the techniques used by their drug-abusing patients to obtain drugs, becoming "duped docs."

A third step toward chronic pain prevention involves direct prophylactic measures at the industrial work site. Low back pain is quite widespread within the working population, especially when heavy lifting is required by the job. Employers could provide instruction for their employees in proper lifting mechanics and ensure compliance through safety inspections. Insurance carriers could promote these safer work practices and strive for early recognition of the disabled worker who is abusing the disability system.

Finally, major steps could be taken to reform the disability law system so that it prevents rather than promotes chronic pain. For example, there could be mandatory review of disability cases at 6-month intervals, with a legal requirement that patients participate in active rehabilitation in order to remain eligible for continued payments. Additionally, monetary incentives could be provided to patients for rehabilitating rapidly and to employers for rehiring injured workers. Washington state, for example, now has a "preferred workers program," which is a waiver of industrial insurance premium for an employer that hires a worker leaving the disability system. Finally, disability settlements could be based on *objective* findings of disease, defect, and disability, rather than on subjective pain complaints. Monetary settlements can be linked to good rehabilitation efforts, with payments only for ultimate residual disability. In contrast, the current system frequently awards permanent partial disability payments to patients who never have been involved in any active rehabilitation program.

The solution to the fiscal nightmare of pain problems requires recognition by all participants in the system—physicians, rehabilitation specialists, insurance carriers, employers, labor unions, legislators, plaintiff's attorneys, etc.—that their own interests must be subordinate to the long-term interests of the patient. Thus, physicians who hold on to patients who are not improving in their care serve only to reinforce illness behavior and promote disability. Similarly, labor unions that aggressively promote the right to compensation for injured workers can prevent and defeat rehabilitation efforts. So can insurance companies that seek to cut costs by refusing to pay for a potentially restorative pain treatment or rehabilitation program. Employers who refuse to rehire rehabilitated pain patients because they fear liability for a subsequent injury also defeat rehabilitation efforts. This serves only to route injured workers to another job site and perhaps an even greater probability that they will repeat their injury and disability.

Despite the great strides in pain management made by multidisciplinary pain centers, chronic pain and disability is a costly and complex social, economic, medical, and psychological problem. Efforts aimed at prevention—that is, early identification of at-risk patients—education of physicians in contemporary principles of treatment, and reform of the compensation and entitlement programs would have considerable impact on health care costs, industrial productivity, and the lives of those afflicted by the chronic pain syndrome.

REFERENCES

Adams, H.E., Feuerstein, M., & Fowler, J.L. (1980). Migraine headache: Review of parameters, etiology and intervention. *Psychological Bulletin, 87*, 217–237.

Anderson, T., Cole, T., Gullickson, G., Hudgens, A., & Roberts, A. (1977). Behavior modification of chronic pain: A treatment program by a multidisciplinary team. *Clinical Orthopaedics and Related Research, 129*, 96–100.

Barber, T.X. (1963). The effects of "hypnosis" on pain: A critical review of experimental and clinical findings. *Psychosomatic Medicine, 24*, 303–333.

Barber, T.X., & Hahn, K. (1962). Physiological and subjective response to pain producing stimulation under hypnotically-suggested and waking-imagined "analgesia." *Journal of Abnormal and Social Psychology, 65*, 411–418.

Beaty, E.T., & Haynes, S.N. (1979). Behavioral intervention with muscle constriction headache: A review. *Psychosomatic Medicine, 41*, 165–180.

Black, R.G. (1975). The chronic pain syndrome. *Clinical Medicine, 82*, 17–20.

Blanchard, E., Theobald, D., Williamson, D., Silver, B., & Brown, B. (1978). Temperature biofeedback in the treatment of migraine headaches. *Archives of General Psychiatry, 35*, 581–588.

Block, A.R. (1982). A multidisciplinary treatment of chronic low back pain: A review. *Rehabilitation Psychology, 27*, 51–63.

Block, A.R. (in press). Marital interaction and chronic pain: A trimodal assessment of spousal response to chronic pain behavior. *Psychosomatic Medicine*.

Block, A.R., Kremer, E.F., & Gaylor, M. (1980a). Behavioral treatment of chronic pain: Variables affecting treatment efficacy. *Pain, 8*, 367–375.

Block, A.R., Kremer, E.F., & Gaylor, M. (1980b). Behavioral treatment of chronic pain: The spouse as a discriminative cue for pain behavior. *Pain, 9*, 243–252.

Blumer, D. (1982). Chronic pain as a psychobiologic phenomenon: The pain-prone disorder. In D. Benson & D. Blumer (Eds.), *Psychiatric aspects of neurologic disease*, Vol 2. New York: Grune & Stratton, pp. 289–302.

Bonica, J.J. (1979). *Pain: A serious national health and economic problem*. Paper presented at the National Conference on Pain, Discomfort and Humanitarian Care. Bethesda, MD.

Bradley, L.A., Prokop, C.K., Gentry, W.D., Hopson, L.A., & Prieto, E.J. (1981). Assessment of chronic pain. In C.K. Prokop & L.A. Bradley (Eds.), *Medical psychology: Contributions to behavioral medicine*. New York: Academic Press, pp. 102–126.

Bradley, L.A. & Van der Heide, L.H. (1984). Pain related correlates of MMPI profile subgroups among back pain patients. *Health Psychology, 3*, 157–175.

Brena, S., & Chapman, S.L. (1983). *Management of patients with chronic pain*. New York: S.P. Medical and Scientific.

Carlsson, S.G., & Gale, E.N. (1976). Biofeedback for muscle pain associated with the temporomandibular joint. *Journal of Behavior Therapy and Experimental Psychiatry, 7*, 383–385.

Carlsson, S.G., Gale, E.N., & Ohman, A. (1975). Treatment of temporomandibular joint syndrome with biofeedback training. *Journal of the American Dental Association, 9*, 602–605.

Catchlove, R., & Cohen, K. (1982). Effects of a directive return to work approach in the treatment of Workman's Compensation patients with chronic pain. *Pain, 14*, 181–191.

Chesney, M.A., & Shelton, J.L. (1976). A comparison of muscle relaxation and EMG biofeedback treatments for muscle contraction headache. *Journal of Behavior Therapy and Experimental Psychiatry*, 221–225.

Corcoran, P.J. (1981). Disability consequences of bed rest. In W. Stolov & M. Clowers (Eds.), *Handbook of severe disability*. Washington DC: US Department of Education, Rehabilitation Services Administration, pp. 68–79.

Cox, D.J., Freundlich, A., & Meyer, R.G. (1975). Differential effectiveness of electromyographic feedback, verbal relaxation instruction, and medication placebo with tension headaches. *Journal of Consulting and Clinical Psychology, 43*, 892–898.

Craig, K. (1975). Social modeling determinants of pain processes. *Pain, 1*, 375–378.

Crasilneck, H.B., & Hall, J.A. (1975). *Clinical hypnosis: Principles and applications*. New York: Grune & Stratton.

Crown, S. (1980). Psychological aspects of low back pain. *Rheumatology and Rehabilitation, 17*, 114–124.

Fey, S.G., & Fordyce, W.E. (1983). Behavioral rehabilitation of the chronic pain patient. In E. Pan, T. Backer & C. Vash (Eds.), *Annual review of rehabilitation*, Vol. 3. New York: Springer, pp. 32–63.

Fey, S.G., Williamson-Kirkland, T.E., & Frangione, R.M. (1984). *Return to work of injured workers following comprehensive pain management*. Paper presented at the IV World Congress on Pain, Seattle, WA.

Fordyce, W.E. (1976). *Behavioral methods for chronic pain and illness*. St. Louis: C.V. Mosby.

Fordyce, W.E., Brena, S., deLateur, B., Holcombe, S., & Loeser, J. (1978). Relationship of patient semantic pain descriptors to physician diagnostic judgments, activity level measures and MMPI. *Pain, 5*, 293–303.

Fordyce, W.E., Fowler, R.S., & deLateur, B. (1968). An application of behavior modification technique to a problem of chronic pain. *Behaviour Research and Therapy, 6*, 105–107.

Fordyce, W.E., Fowler, R., Lehmann, J., & deLateur, B. (1968). Some implications of learning in problems of chronic pain. *Journal of Chronic Disease, 21*, 179–190.

Fordyce, W.E., Fowler, R., Lehmann, J., deLateur, B., Sand, P., & Treischmann, R. (1973). Operant conditioning in the treatment of chronic pain. *Archives of Physical Medicine and Rehabilitation, 54*, 399–408.

Fordyce, W.E., & Steger, J.C. (1978). Behavioral management of chronic pain. In J. Brady & O. Pomerleau (Eds.), *Behavioral medicine: Theory and practice*. Baltimore: Williams & Wilkins, pp. 298–331.

Gessel, A.H. (1975). Electromyographic feedback and tricyclic antidepressants in myofascial pain-dysfunction syndrome: Psychological predictors of outcome. *Journal of the American Dental Association, 91*, 1048–1052.

Goldfried, M.R. (1977). The use of relaxation and cognitive relabeling as coping skills. In R.B. Stuart (Ed.), *Behavioral self-management: Strategies, techniques and outcomes*. New York: Brunner/ Mazel.

Gottlieb, A., Strite, L., Koller, R., Madorsky, A., Hockersmith, V., Kleeman, M., & Wagner, J. (1977). Comprehensive rehabilitation of patients having chronic low back pain. *Archives of Physical Medicine and Rehabilitation, 58*, 101–108.

Grant, I., Mohns, L., Miller, M., & Reitan, R. (1976). A neuropsychological study of polydrug users. *Archives of General Psychiatry, 33*, 973–978.

Halpern, L. (1974). Psychotropic drugs and the management of chronic pain. In J.J. Bonica (Ed.), *Advances in neurology: International symposium on pain*. New York: Raven Press.

Haynes, S., Griffin, P., Mooney, D., & Parise, M. (1975). EMG biofeedback and relaxation instructions in the treatment of muscle contraction headache. *Behavior Therapy, 6*, 672–678.

Hendler, N., Cimini, C., Terence, M., & Long, D. (1980). A comparison of cognitive impairment due to benzodiazepines and to narcotics. *American Journal of Psychiatry, 137*, 827–830.

Hendler, N., Derogatis, L., Avella, J., & Long, D. (1977). EMG feedback in patients with chronic pain. *Diseases of the Nervous System, 38*, 505–514.

Hilgard, E.R. (1975). The alleviation of pain by hypnosis. *Pain, 1*, 213–231.

Hilgard, E.R. (1978). Hypnosis and pain. In R.A. Sternbach (Ed.), *The psychology of pain*. New York: Raven Press, pp. 102–119.

Hirsch, T. (1977). Billion dollar headache. *National Safety News, 116*, 51–54.

Holroyd, K.A., Andrasik, F., & Westbrook, T. (1977). Cognitive control of tension headache. *Cognitive Therapy and Research, 1*, 121–134.

Hutchings, D.G., & Reinking, R.H. (1976). Tension headaches: What form of therapy is most effective? *Biofeedback and Self-Regulation, 1*, 183–190.

Jessup, B.A., Neufeld, R.W., & Merskey, H.J. (1979). Biofeedback therapy for headache and other pain: An evaluative review. *Pain, 7*, 225–270.

Johnson, A.D. (1978). *The problem claim: An approach to early identification. A synopsis*. (Available from The Department of Labor and Industries, State of Washington, Olympia, WA.)

Judd, L.L., Grant, I., Bickford, R.G., & Lee, W.G. (1978). Comparison of results from serially collected neuropsychological and EEG data. In D.R. Wesson, A.S. Carlin, K.M. Adams, & G. Beschner (Eds.), *Polydrug abuse. The results of a national collaborative study*. New York: Academic Press, pp. 238–249.

Keefe, F.J. (1982). Behavioral assessment and treatment of chronic pain: Current status and future directions. *Journal of Consulting and Clinical Psychology, 50*, 896–911.

Keefe, F.J., & Bradley, L.A. (1984). Behavioral and psychological approaches to the assessment and treatment of chronic pain. *General Hospital Psychiatry, 6,* 49–54.

Keefe, F.J., Schapira, B., Brown, C., Williams, R., & Surwit, R. (In press). Relaxation training in the management of chronic low back pain. *Journal of Behavioral Medicine.*

Khatami, M., & Rush, A.J. (1978). A pilot study of the treatment of outpatients with chronic pain: Symptom control, stimulus control and social system intervention. *Pain, 5,* 163–172.

Kocher, R. (1976). Use of psychotropic drugs for the treatment of chronic severe pain. In J.J. Bonica & D. Albe-Fessard (Eds.), *Advances in pain research and therapy* Vol. 5. New York: Raven Press, pp. 312–322.

Levendusky, P., & Pankratz, L. (1975). Self-control techniques as an alternative to pain medication. *Journal of Abnormal Psychology, 85,* 165–168.

Malec, J., Cayner, J., Harvey, R., & Timming, R. (1981). Pain management: Long-term follow-up of an inpatient program. *Archives of Physical Medicine and Rehabilitation, 62,* 369–372.

Maruta, T., Swanson, D.W., & Finlayson, R.E. (1979). Drug abuse and dependency in patients with chronic pain. *Mayo Clinic Proceedings, 54,* 241–244.

McGlashan, T.H., Evans, F.J., & Orne, M.T. (1969). The nature of hypnotic analgesia and placebo response in experimental pain. *Psychosomatic Medicine, 31,* 227–246.

McNairy, S.L., Maruta, T., Invik, R.J., Swanson, D.W., & Ilstrup, D.M. (1984). Prescription medication dependence and neuropsychological function. *Pain, 18,* 169–179.

Meichenbaum, D., & Turk, D. (1976). The cognitive-behavioral management of anxiety, anger, and pain. In P.O. Davidson (Ed.), *The behavioral management of anxiety, depression and pain.* New York: Brunner/Mazel, pp. 110–126.

Merskey H. (1980). The role of the psychiatrist in the investigation and treatment of pain. In J.J. Bonica (Ed.), *Pain.* New York: Raven Press, pp. 182–196.

Mitchell, D.R., & Mitchell, D.M. (1971). Migraine: An explanatory treatment application of programmed behavior therapy techniques. *Journal of Psychosomatic Research, 15,* 137–157.

Mitchell, K.R., & White, R.G. (1977). Behavioral self-management: An application to the problem of migraine headache. *Behavior Therapy, 8,* 213–221.

Neuchterlein, K., & Holroyd, F. (1980). Biofeedback in the treatment of tension headache: Current status. *Archives of General Psychiatry, 37,* 866–873.

Orne, M. (1962). On the social psychology of the psychological experiment: With particular reference to demand characteristics and their implications. *American Psychologist, 17,* 776–783.

Painter, J.R., Seres, J.L., & Newman, R.I. (1980). Assessing the benefits of the pain center: Why some patients regress. *Pain, 8,* 101–114.

Peck, C.J., Fordyce, W.E., & Black, R.G. (1978). The effect of the pendency of claims for compensation upon behavior indicative of pain. *Washington Law Review, 53,* 251–278.

Ready, L.B., Sarkis, E., & Turner, J.A. (1982). Self-reported vs. actual use of medications in chronic pain patients. *Pain, 12,* 285–294.

Reeves, J.L. (1976). EMG biofeedback reduction of tension headache: A cognitive skills training approach. *Biofeedback and Self-Regulation, 1,* 217–225.

Roberts, A.H., & Reinhardt, L. (1980). The behavioral management of chronic pain: Long-term followup with comparison groups. *Pain, 8,* 151–162.

Rosenthal, R.(1966). *Experimenter effects in behavioral research.* New York: Appleton-Century-Crofts.

Roy, R. (1982). Marital and family issues in patients with chronic pain. *Psychotherapy and Psychosomatics, 37,* 1–12.

Roy, R., Thomas, M., & Matas, M. (1984). Chronic pain and depression: A review. *Comprehensive Psychiatry, 25,* 96–105.

Rybstein-Blinchik, E. (1979). Effects of different cognitive strategies on chronic pain experience. *Journal of Behavioral Medicine, 9,* 110–116.

Seres, J., Newman, R., Yospe, L., & Garlington, B.E. (1977). Evaluation and management of chronic pain by non-surgical means. In L.J. Fletcher (Ed.), *Pain management: Symposium on the neurological treatment of pain.* Baltimore: Williams & Wilkins, pp. 269–281.

Seres, J., Newman, R.I., Yospe, L.P., & Garlington, B.E. (1978). Multidisciplinary treatment of chronic pain: A long-term follow-up of low back pain patients. *Pain, 4,* 283–292.

Silver, B., & Blanchard, E. (1978). Biofeedback and relaxation training in the treatment of psychophysiological disorders: Or are the machines really necessary? *Journal of Behavioral Medicine, 1,* 217–239.

Skinner, B.F. (1953). *Science and human behavior.* New York: Macmillan.

Speigel, K., Kalb, R., & Pasternak, G.W. (1983). Analgesic activity of tricyclic antidepressants. *Annals of Neurology, 13,* 462–465.

Stenn, P.G., Mothersill, K.J., & Brooke, R.J. (1979). Biofeedback and a cognitive behavioral approach to treatment of myofascial pain dysfunction syndrome. *Behavior Therapy, 10,* 29–36.

Sternbach, R.A. (1968). *Pain: A psychophysiological analysis.* New York: Academic Press.

Sternbach, R.A. (1974). *Pain patients: Traits and treatments.* New York: Academic Press.

Sternbach, R.A., Murphy, R., Akeson, W., & Wolfe, S.(1973). Chronic low back pain: Characteristics of the "low back loser." *Postgraduate Medicine, 53,* 135–138.

Sternbach, R.A., Wolfe, S.R., Murphy, R.W.,& Akeson, W.H. (1973). Traits of pain patients: "The low back loser." *Psychosomatics, 14,* 226–229.

Swanson, D.W. (1984). Chronic pain as a third pathologic emotion. *American Journal of Psychiatry, 141,* 211–214.

Taylor, C.B., Zlutnick, S.I., Corley, M., & Flora, J. (1980). The effects of detoxification, relaxation, and brief supportive therapy on chronic pain. *Pain, 8,* 319–330.

Turk, D.C., Meichenbaum, D., & Berman, W.H. (1979). Application of biofeedback for the regulation of pain: A critical review. *Psychological Bulletin, 86,* 1322–1338.

Turner, J.A., & Chapman, R. (1982). Psychological interventions for chronic pain: A critical review. II. Operant conditioning, hypnosis, and cognitive behavioral therapy. *Pain, 12,* 23–46.

Tyre, T., & Anderson, D. (1981). Inpatient management of the chronic pain patient: A one-year follow-up study. *Journal of Family Practice, 12,* 819–827.

Violon, A., & Giurgea, D. (1984). Familial models for chronic pain. *Pain, 18,* 199–205.

Ward, N., Bloom, U., & Friedel, R. (1979). The effectiveness of tricyclic antidepressants in the treatment of coexisting pain and depression. *Pain, 7,* 331–341.

Williamson-Kirkland, T.E., & Fey, S.G. (1984). *The rehabilitation of learned gait disturbances in chronic pain patients.* Paper presented at the IV World Congress on Pain. Seattle, WA.

Ziesat, H.A. (1981). Behavioral approaches to the treatment of chronic pain. In L. Bradley & C. Prokop (Eds.), *Medical psychology: Contributions to behavioral medicine.* New York: Academic Press, pp. 142–171.

Ziesat, H.A., Angle, H.V., Gentry, D., & Ellinwood, E.H. (1979). Drug use and misuse in operant pain patients. *Addictive Behavior, 4,* 263–266.

Part II

Psychosocial Matrix: Patient, Family, and Staff

Chapter 5

Denial and Depression in Disabling Illness

Bruce Caplan, Ph.D.
Judith Shechter, Ph.D.

The onset of a disabling condition almost invariably produces a profound psychological reaction on the part of the afflicted individual. The range of possible responses is sizeable and may include confusion, emotional numbing, depression, grief, anxiety, paranoia, and denial. Some authors (e.g., Herman, 1983) have argued that illness or disability may actually elicit positive feelings in individuals for whom the condition fulfills needs for attention, dependence, or perhaps even punishment. Coping techniques are equally varied and may be employed in numerous combinations (see Cohen & Lazarus, 1979; Lazarus & Folkman, 1984; Moos & Schaefer, 1986). Despite this diversity of potential reactions, a number of authors (e.g., Burton, 1985; Fink, 1967; Green, 1985; Hohmann, 1975; Krupp, 1976; Ravenscroft, 1982) have proposed that response to disability takes the form of a limited series of identifiable stages that occur in a predictable sequence.

Intended by most advocates as a description of general patterns of adjustment in large populations, the stage conceptualization of the adjustment process has often been needlessly reified, becoming thereby a destructive force in clinical settings. Health care professionals frequently apply the concept in a facile manner, designating particular patients as being, for example, "in Denial," without adequate regard for the vast individual differences on the many parameters that affect both the course of adjustment to disability and the extent to which a particular patient openly displays his or her emotional state. As Sprock and Blashfield (1984) note, "Use of a diagnostic label creates an illusion of understanding, which distracts the clinician . . . from dealing with the serious issues of living that confront a patient" (p. 291). Gans (1983) wrote that "painful psychologic states appropriate to the circumstances still can be treated without assigning a clinical, that is, pathologic, designation" (p. 203).

The notion that stages occur in a set sequence poses additional hazards. Staff members may be tempted to prod patients through the disruptive initial phases by aggressively confronting denial or by attempting to talk patients out of depression under the mistaken assumption that they are facilitating adjustment. Horowitz (1985) argues that people tend to underestimate the amount of time required to recover from disaster or trauma. Thus, attempts to expedite accommodation generally fail and may be destructive if patients perceive that staff members are unwilling to hear their true feelings (Davidson, 1963). Goldiamond (1976) observes that staff members who view the postulated reactions as developmental stages are relieved of the responsibility of questioning whether and how their own behavior might be contributing to the patient's emotional state, thereby foreclosing the possibility of staff serving as agents of therapeutic change.

Yet, stage theories do have some merit. They may be clinically useful, implying as they do the notion of change and progress beyond an unpleasant early state (Russell, 1981) and providing a comforting sense of predictability during a time of chaos and turmoil. Furthermore, the emotional states for which stages are named are commonly observed in rehabilitation; newly disabled individuals do exhibit anger, denial, depression, and so on. However, the most helpful sort of stage theory may be the one that postulates the fewest stages—for example, Prugh and Eckhardt's (1980) sequence of impact, recoil, and restitution—allowing the maximum explanatory power of individual differences. As LeBaron, Currie, and Zeltzer (1984) state:

> Passage through the stages, the order in which they are experienced and the duration of each stage vary widely among different individuals. . . . Indeed, these stages should not be viewed as a sequence to which patients need necessarily conform (but) . . . as a hypothetical construct that may help the clinician organize continuing observations of a given patient. . . . The actual progression of psychological adjustment is unpredictable and unique in each patient. (p. 281)

Bracken and Shepard (1980) and Geller and Greydanus (1979) share this stance. Regrettably, these caveats are often disregarded by busy clinicians. This misapplication of stage theories is especially unfortunate in view of much recent literature that has emphasized the multiple determining factors that contribute to the emotional state of an individual patient.

Concluding a recent study of psychosocial status in chronic illness, Cassileth et al. (1984) stated:

> Individual psychic resources and capacity to adapt are substantial, as variably successful in response to chronic illness as to ordinary events, and specific for personality rather than for situation. . . . We suggest that the psychological status of chronically ill patients . . . reflects that of the population at large because adaptation represents not the demands of particular stress, such as specific diagnosis, but rather the manifesta-

tions of enduring personality constructs and personality capacities. (p. 506)

Shontz (1977) argues that psychological responses to physical disability "are not uniformly disturbing or distressing and do not necessarily result in maladjustment." More recently, he wrote that "reactions to illness and disability are not responses to physical conditions, but to the meanings of those conditions to the individual" (Shontz, 1984, p. 77). Trieschmann (1980) reviewed the literature on stages of adjustment following spinal cord injury and concluded that there was scant empirical evidence in support of stage theory. Thus, many recent authors have cast doubt upon the alleged inevitability and predictability (Goldberg, 1982; Jochheim, 1983; Kerr & Thompson, 1972; Krupp, 1976; Siller, 1969) of stages of adjustment to disability.

Nevertheless, the stage theory monolith has tended to dominate rehabilitation specialists' thinking about the emotional status of disabled individuals. The rich and relevant theoretical and experimental literature of related fields has, therefore, been largely ignored. This chapter considers the applicability of a number of concepts and findings from other disciplines, such as neuropsychology, neurophysiology, behavioral medicine, psychiatry, and cognitive-behavioral theory, to the troublesome and commonly observed psychological problems of denial and depression. The accumulated findings suggest that these emotional states are best viewed as multidimensional concepts with a variety of associated causes, meanings, and implications for treatment. The traditional view of these two responses as components of a natural, invariable, and inevitable series of stages of adjustment is an untenable oversimplification that provides a poor basis for assessment and treatment of rehabilitation patients.

DENIAL

Numerous authors have discussed the phenomenon of denial following onset of disabling illness (Baretz & Stephenson, 1976; Binder, 1983; Bracken & Shepard, 1980; Bradley & Burish, 1983; Breznitz, 1983a & 1983b; Chodoff, 1959; Cook, 1979; Cutting, 1978; Diller, 1959; Gainotti, 1969; Gordon & Diller, 1983; Hackett & Cassem, 1974; Lazarus, 1983; Lazarus & Golden, 1981; Levine & Ziegler, 1975; Nathanson, Bergman, & Gordon, 1952; Nemiah, 1957; Prigatano, in press; Reden & Jackson, 1979; Trieschmann, 1980; Weinstein & Kahn, 1955; Weisman, 1972). Denial is observed in patients with stroke, traumatic head injury, myocardial infarction, spinal cord injury (SCI)—indeed, the gamut of conditions encountered in physical rehabilitation settings. Bracken and Shepard (1980) call denial the most commonly discussed defensive reaction to SCI, but note that the term is defined in quite dissimilar ways by different investigators. The relative contributions of neurologic and psychologic factors are variably emphasized.

Definitions and Determinants

As typically interpreted by professional staff, denial refers to a disavowal of aspects of reality affected by the patient's condition. It is generally thought to be a willful, even oppositional act that is indicative of a regressed psychological state. As shall be seen, however, this oversimplified definition has many distorting effects on clinical practice with potentially disastrous consequences for the patient.

Lazarus and Golden (1981) point out that denial is often confused with related concepts, e.g., illusion, repression, and avoidance. Dimsdale (1984) asserts that the term "denial" is meaningless without a subsequent predicate and that it is the common failure to specify the object of denial that has produced disagreement about whether denial is a primitive defense or a healthy coping response. He also notes other factors that must be assessed, including the behavioral setting of denial, its duration, the magnitude of the actual threat, and the degree of the individual's control over the situation; that is, whether there is any real possibility for effective action.

In a report describing the development of a quantitative rating scale for the assessment of denial, Hackett and Cassem (1974) challenge the psychoanalytic view of denial as a sign of serious psychopathology, observing that this conception offers little of value to those working in a medical setting. The nonpathologic view of denial is articulated most poignantly by Aadalen and Strobel-Kahn (1981) in a personal memoir on coping with quadriplegia: "Denial is one of the ways we get through hell" (p. 1475). Indeed, several authors, such as Krantz and Deckel (1983) and Viney and Westbrook (1984) have suggested that medically ill patients are well aware of the instrumental coping strategies, including denial, that they choose to adopt.

Lazarus and Golden (1981) describe denial as an "emotion-focused" method of coping; that is, an internal and psychically oriented process. By contrast, one may characterize participation in rehabilitation therapy as "problem-focused coping," an active and externally oriented tactic. It is important for rehabilitation clinicians to remember that the two forms are not mutually exclusive. Lazarus and Golden state, "When denial is partial, tentative or minimal in scope, it does not necessarily preclude the simultaneous use of problem-focused forms of coping" (p. 303). Indeed, Folkman and Lazarus (1980) found that complex stressful situations prompt subjects to use both types of coping.

Several authors have suggested useful typologies of denial and associated concepts. For example, Lazarus (1983) distinguishes between *denial of fact* ("I do not have a spinal cord injury") and *denial of implication* ("I will walk again"), noting the rarity of the former response. That is, although patients rarely deny being sick, they often deny the meaning of their illness. One should add Chodoff's (1959) *denial of affect arising from the fact* ("I am not upset about what has happened to me").

Both Gainotti (1972) and Diller (1959) differentiate between explicit and implicit denial. Discussing the patient with brain damage, Gainotti equates explicit denial with anosognosia, minimization, and confabulation, all verbal expressions of denial; he views indifference and euphoria as evidence of implicit nonverbal denial. Diller interprets reports by amputees and quadriplegics of phantom sensation as instances of implicit denial. He argues that anosognosia is rarely observed in rehabilitation because it tends to occur in the context of confused mental state (a notion later confirmed by Cutting, 1978), and confused patients are not typically admitted to rehabilitation.

Janis (1983) discusses "pathogenic denial," a notion with clear relevance to rehabilitation patients. According to Janis, pathogenic denial occurs in somewhat ambiguous circumstances in which the probability of threat is high, but is difficult to ascertain until further developments have occurred. The salient psychological tactic in such situations is minimization. Janis views pathogenic denial as a component of the process of defensive avoidance; it involves suppression of upsetting thoughts and selective inattention to certain (threatening) aspects of a situation, coupled with equally selective acceptance of more encouraging facets. This discussion calls to mind Waller, Todress, Cassem, and Anderten's (1979) description of the tactic of "partializing," by which patients and families focus on one aspect (often trivial) of the patient's medical condition or treatment in an effort to find hopeful signs. This selective gating accounts for the fact that there is often a considerable discrepancy between what patient and families have been *told* and what they *know*.

Weinstein and Kahn (1955) list five major manifestations of denial: (1) complete denial, (2) denial of major disability (significant incapacities are denied), (3) minimization, (4) projection of ownership of illness, and (5) temporal displacement (the patient admits illness or disability in the past, not the present).

Breznitz (1983b) postulates seven levels of denial, each involving a progressively greater distortion of reality: (1) denial of personal relevance of threatening information, (2) denial of urgency, (3) denial of vulnerability (or responsibility), (4) denial of affect (that is, of anxiety produced by threat), (5) denial of affect relevance (attribution of cause of perceived anxiety to a source other than primary threat), (6) denial of threatening information (that is, distortion of perception of threat), and (7) denial of information in its totality.

Breznitz avows that the process of denial must begin with the appraisal of the stress-inducing information, which clearly requires some level of awareness. The greater the perceived threat, the more profound the initial level of denial. Breznitz (1983b) argues that, although many individuals do not pass through the entire sequence, in no case do people regress. He (1983a) notes that "denial is a dynamic

phenomenon, ever-changing, always elusive to the simple tools of the researcher''
(p. 297). This sentiment is echoed by Lazarus (1981), who decried the fact that the

> trait-centered static research paradigm leads us to treat denial as an
> established fact, a coping achievement, in which case we tend to speak
> of "deniers" rather than "denying." This is misleading because rarely
> does a process like denial become so fully consolidated as a mode of
> coping that it is no longer subject to uncertainty, challenge or even
> dissolution in the face of the evidence. (p. 204)

Lazarus and Golden (1981) write that "most denials are probably fluctuating
constructions, responsive to this or that bit of information, mood or whatever" (p.
290); indeed, deniers may merely be "shading things a bit in the face of ambiguous input" (p. 289).

Several investigators have called attention to the variability of manifest denial.
Lazarus (1981) stresses that the clinician must consider the patient's coping
pattern(s) at diverse moments in different kinds of encounters with a variety of
people—professional staff, relatives, other patients, and friends. Breznitz (1983b)
notes the importance of individual differences in tolerance for ambiguity; more
tolerant individuals are better able to focus on potentially promising aspects of the
distressing situation and by manifesting optimism may acquire the label of
"denier." Lazarus (1983) observes that there are individual differences in
whether people are threatened or challenged by a troubling event; one might
expect those who are threatened to adopt a posture of denial more readily, whereas
those who are challenged would aggressively confront the situation.

Weisman and Hackett (1966) call denial "a social act," subject to the impact of
context. An illustrative example is provided by Waller, Todress, Cassem, and
Anderten (1979) who describe how parents of children in a pediatric intensive care
unit sustained a hopeful, positive (denying) attitude during conversations with
physicians, but exhibited profound grieving (acknowledgment) during sessions
with social workers. One parent expressed the fear that, if she did not project hope
while in the presence of the physician, his treatment of the child would falter. This
same dynamic may well contribute to the inconsistent expression of denial in
many rehabilitation patients and in their families.

Whatever the relative contributions to denial of neurologic and psychological
factors, one could argue that interpreting denial as an "organic" symptom assists
the patient's family in coping with the crisis. Attribution of denial to psychological
factors tends to be pejorative and causes the patient to be tagged with such labels as
"malingering," "unrealistic," (Baretz & Stephenson, 1976), or "uncooperative." As Baretz and Stephenson point out, the problem lies in the disparity
between staff and patient assessments of the extent and probable duration of
disability. The passage of time and the persistence of illness ultimately make

denial untenable. As long as the denial is limited to verbal disavowal and does not subvert the patient's effort in rehabilitation therapies, one may wonder what purpose is served by belittling what may well be the patient's best efforts to cope with disaster. Gans (1983) stated:

> A person responds strongly to his disability because irreversible loss disrupts a person's entire sense of self. These reactions are frequently unreasonable and upsetting to others, but they are not bad and must be respected. They are attempted solutions for overwhelming problems and fears. (p. 202)

Denial in Defined Populations

There is little doubt that both neurologic and psychological factors, independently or in combination, may play a role in denial (Binder, 1983; Prigatano, in press). The contributions of both sets of factors are evident in the patient with head injury or stroke. LaBaw (1969) discusses the ambivalence he felt toward some of his post-head-injury symptoms and his wish that they were attributable to conversion reaction, rather than neurologic causes: "I thus had some mixed emotions about whether I desired neurological or psychological defects" (p. 180). He notes rather poignantly, "At thirty months after my accident I suddenly realized that surviving the wreck was one thing and that surviving the subsequent denial was another" (p. 184). Fordyce, Roueche, and Prigatano (1983) have also described the problem of denial in head trauma patients. They found greater emotional distress—anxiety and depression—among chronic head trauma patients as opposed to a more acute group, presumably due to the progressive disintegration of denial.

A number of studies have examined denial in stroke populations. Cutting (1978) studied 100 cases of acute hemiplegia and found that 58 percent of those with right-hemisphere involvement denied muscle weakness, whereas only 14 percent of testable left-hemisphere damaged patients did so. Gainotti (1968) studied the evolution of denial in ten patients with right cerebral lesions. He found frank anosognosia only in the acute period; in the subacute stage patients admitted the fact of hemiplegia, but minimized its importance. Gainotti (1969) subsequently reported data that suggested a link between unilateral neglect and denial, minimization, and indifference. Nathanson et al. (1952) reported denial in 28 of 76 stroke patients and noted that its severity was related to the degree of disorientation. Ullman, Ashenhurst, Hurwitz, and Gruen (1960) found that approximately half of their stroke patients exhibited denial, but in contrast to the results of other studies, these authors observed a higher incidence of denial among those with left-hemisphere involvement.

Levine and Ziegler (1975) studied denial in patients with stroke, lung cancer, or heart disease. They examined disparities between real and ideal selves on the assumption that denial in the seriously ill patient is reflected in a real-ideal self difference that is no greater than those of normal controls. Although all three patient groups employed denial, the stroke patients seemed to do so to the greatest degree. The interpretation of these results is complicated by Levine and Ziegler's statement that the denial they observed had less to do with the patients' appraisal of their own functional ability than with their limited level of aspiration. This attenuated striving, if it stems from awareness of functional impairment, may simply be an effective method of achieving emotional stability and not denial at all, as it is commonly construed. However, commenting on this study, Krantz and Deckel (1983) note that stroke threatens one's sense of self and competence to a greater extent than does cancer of heart disease. Therefore, they argue that stroke patients may have a greater need for denial (in the usual sense of the word) in order to preserve their psychological integrity.

Some evidence suggests that denial is associated with decreased activation. Heilman, Schwartz, and Watson (1978) note that patients with neglect and the indifference syndrome showed hypoarousal on galvanic skin response measures. In a provocative article, Bear (1983) proposes that damage to the right hemisphere produces a fundamental deficit of which denial is a special case; namely, impaired emotional surveillance. The patient fails to detect threat and therefore does not sustain attention, exhibit stress, or undertake adaptive action. Bear hypothesizes that pharmacologic intervention to heighten arousal may be the most effective means of remediating this deficit. He further advises that the clinician "repeatedly tell the verbal hemisphere about the tendency to neglect, minimize and socially misperceive; . . . steps in emotional perception and communication may have to be explicitly rehearsed" (p. 201). This last suggestion is based on the notion that control of the social uses of language resides primarily in the right hemisphere (Weintraub, Mesulam, & Kramer, 1981) and that right-hemisphere dysfunction tends to produce the constellation of diminished emotional surveillance, denial, and neglect.

Bear's position is difficult to reconcile with that of Breznitz (1983a & 1983b), who believes that denial is precipitated by perception of an anxiety-producing threat. Even at the level of most profound denial—disavowal of information in its totality, akin to denial of *fact*—Breznitz believes that perception of the *existence* of the disturbing fact does occur. One's position on this issue has certain clinical implications, for it may be tantamount to deciding whether the patient's behavior is a comprehensible reaction to extreme stress or a psychotic break with reality.

Denial has often been reported to be common in other groups of rehabilitation patients. Cook (1979), operationalizing denial as a difference between the Minnesota Multiphasic Personality Inventory (MMPI) F and K scales of minus 12 or less, found evidence of denial in approximately one-third of 118 spinal cord injured patients who had been referred for vocational rehabilitation. As Cook himself notes, however, denial as defined in this study reflects denial of emotional problems, rather than outright denial of disability.

Baretz and Stephenson (1981) examined emotional reactions in multiple sclerosis patients. They reported that overt denial was a common manifestation of masked depression. At this point, it is important to note the common "catch 22" situation in which patients and families often find themselves. As Turk, Kerns, and Rudy (1984) point out, research suggests that newly disabled patients and relatives are offered an implicit choice between denial and depression; if they appear to be coping in a satisfactory manner, staff conclude that this is because they are employing denial and true pathology lies concealed. Turk et al. (1984) note that mental health professionals are prepared by their training to uncover maladjustment and spend most of their professional time with individuals who are coping poorly. As a consequence, they may be ill-equipped to recognize healthy coping under extreme stress.

Cost and Benefits of Denial

Many authors have taken the position that denial in the early aftermath of a disabling event is an adaptive response, preventing psychic disintegration and allowing the individual time to marshall needed coping resources (Bracken and Shepard, 1980; Bradley & Burish, 1983; Hamburg & Adams, 1967; Jackson & Redden, 1978; Krantz & Deckel, 1983; Lazarus & Golden, 1981). In most instances, newly disabled patients are initially unable to undertake direct action to change their situations. Thus, denial at that point is irrelevant to functional adaptation, but serves to reduce stress and allow gradual acknowledgment of aspects of the disaster. At such times, denial may be viewed as tentative, just one component of the dynamic process of coping. As Bradley and Burish (1983) write, "Denial, therefore, may be adaptative to the degree that it allows patients to process slowly information concerning the nature of their illness as well as the potential consequences of their illness and associated treatments" (p. 476).

Clinicians should recognize that the concept of chronicity is initially foreign to many newly disabled patients, especially those in the younger age ranges. Their experience of illness is generally limited to those that are acute in nature. Therefore, some time is required before they are able to understand that, for example, an injured spinal cord will not "heal up" like a broken leg. During this period, patients may express sentiments that are interpreted as evidence of denial but that may, in fact, more accurately indicate incomplete awareness of the permanence of the condition. Clinicians must learn to distinguish between willful disbelief and ignorance; the therapeutic responses are quite different.

Bracken and Shepard (1980) found considerable agreement among researchers that early denial plays a positive role in long-term adjustment, whereas persistence of denial inhibits rehabilitation. Jackson and Redden (1978) suggest that the key issue is whether denial facilitates or interferes with the acquisition of disability-appropriate behaviors. It is their belief that some patients in a state of adaptive denial consider their disability to be temporary, view therapy as a means to the end of full recovery, and therefore participate fully and willingly. From another perspective, the behavior of these patients may be viewed as illustrating the common phenomenon of a discrepancy between verbally stated beliefs and behavior. In the rehabilitation context, behavioral denial—that is, denial that inhibits rehabilitation training—should indeed provoke professional intervention; verbal denial perhaps ought to be indulged as long as there is no concomitant behavioral denial.

The benefits of denial may not be entirely without cost. One study found lower levels of corticosteroid secretion among subjects exhibiting denial-like processes than in those who were poorly defended (Wolff et al., 1964). Thus, there is physiologic evidence that denial reduces stress level. Follow-up of these patients, however, found a rebound effect; that is, much higher corticosteroid levels among early deniers (Hofer, Wolff, Friedman, & Mason, 1972). This finding suggests that, although grieving can be delayed, it cannot be avoided altogether. Such findings highlight the importance of evaluating adaptational processes in a serial fashion (Moos & Tsu, 1977).

Management of Denial

The ultimate question for the rehabilitation team confronted with a patient or family exhibiting denial or the associated phenomena of indifference, minimizaton, or avoidance is the proper management of such behavior. There is a common misconception that denial subverts the rehabilitation process, deters adjustment, and permits the patient and family to wallow in unrealistic expectations. These beliefs compel the conclusion that staff members must confront the patient with ''the reality of his situation and force him into a period of depression while he works out his acceptance of his loss'' (Nemiah, 1957, p. 146). Proponents of this action may argue that it is better for patients to experience major affective responses while they are hospitalized and the support of experienced professionals is available. Whatever merit inheres in this position must be weighed against myriad counterproductive effects that confrontation of denial can produce (Barth & Boll, 1981; Pakaslahti & Achte, 1983), foremost among which is the destruction of hope.

In fact, Prugh and Eckhardt (1980) argue that some degree of denial is probably necessary in order for the patient to maintain hope. Staff members are often upset by a patient's expression of unrealistic hopes, viewing this as an indication of failure to adjust. In so doing, they confuse *hope* with *expectation*. Although few would argue that unrealistic expectations should be encouraged, there seems little justification for shattering hope. Certainly, all involved—patient, family, staff—*hope* for recovery. Furthermore, hope may serve as a major motivating force, sustaining the patient in the arduous task of rehabilitation. More than 35 years ago Wepman (1951) observed that patients who are not hopeful often reject therapy.

Breznitz (1983a) points out that hope implies awareness of disability; one cannot hope without a specific target, e.g., to walk, to use a hemiparetic limb, etc. A review of the existing literature led Heinemann, Geist, and Magiearo-Plansy (1983) to the conclusion that moderate levels of hope are most conducive to positive outcome among spinal cord injured patients. Clinicians can thus perform a valuable educational and supportive service by helping patients and families understand the distinction between hope and expectation. Heinemann, Geist, and Magiearo-Plansy (1983) suggest that establishing therapy goals in collaboration with the patient serves as a way of gauging the patient's hope; this tactic also helps develop an alliance between patient and staff.

Many of the following management suggestions are distilled from articles by Baretz and Stephenson (1976) and Weisman and Hackett (1966):

- When possible, provide information regarding the patient's condition and its implications at the optimal time—when it is requested.

- If such information is not requested, but staff members feel that it must be provided, convey it with tact and sensitivity and with the promise of therapeutic commitment. Hohmann (1975) suggests that the information provided should be truthful, but perhaps ambiguous so that patients can interpret it in ways consistent with their current needs.

- Before providing information, first ask the patient and family to describe what they have been told by other professionals.

- Acknowledge and reflect, but do not reinforce or counter feelings of disbelief or denial expressed by the patient and family. Countering the denial may prompt immediate antagonism and withdrawal; Prigatano (in press) warns that confrontation of denial in the head injured patient often produces a catastrophic reaction. Reinforcing denial may instill false expectations and set the stage for later feelings of resentment by a patient and family who feel deceived.

- Solicit input from all team members regarding the patient's adjustment.

- Permit some degree of hope. Recognize the multilevel character of denial, and remember that verbal statements of denial may merely be expressions of hope. Denial that is circumscribed in this way and does not inhibit participation in rehabilitation therapy often does not merit concern.

- Allow patients to test their fantasied capacity. It is imperative that patients not feel they are being impeded in their progress by staff caprice.

- Be aware of possible staff biases or unspoken reasons for confronting or encouraging denial. Kubler-Ross (1975) suggests that staff members sometimes encourage a patient's denial in order to ease their own burdens. In contrast, Waller et al. (1979) argue that staff members may develop a personal stake in securing the patient's acceptance of the negative prognosis. Failure to do so may be regarded as a personal affront, a repudiation of their professional expertise. Waller et al. (1979) also suggest that prevailing upon the patient to abandon hope is a defensive maneuver on the part of the professional, for it frees one from responsibility for the patient's improvement or recovery.
- Provide continuing emotional support.
- Use the term "denial" conservatively, with full awareness of its pejorative implications and effects on staff thinking and behavior.

Taylor (1983) proposes a novel conceptualization of the process of adjustment to threatening events, with special reference to the role of denial or illusion. She argues that adjustment focuses on three elements:

1. a search for meaning in the experience
2. an attempt to regain mastery over both the event and one's life
3. an effort to enhance self-esteem

Taylor asserts that such efforts require the development and maintenance of illusions, the ability to look at known facts in a particular light because "a different slant would yield a less positive picture, or the beliefs have yet to yield any factual basis of support" (p. 1161). She states that specific cognitions (beliefs) are not robust elements, but may change their meaning from situation to situation, are functionally overlapping, and may serve several functions simultaneously. Given this flexibility, disconfirmation of a particular belief does not sabotage the utility of illusions. "The effective individual in the face of threat, then, seems to be one who permits the development of illusions, nurtures those illusions and is ultimately restored by those illusions" (p. 1168). Rehabilitation specialists might profitably reflect on such potentially anarchic notions as a useful counterbalance to the traditional insistence on confrontation with reality.

DEPRESSION

Depression has been reported to be a common emotional accompaniment of medical illness (e.g., Katon, 1984; Klerman, 1981; Lloyd, 1977; Magni, DeLeo, & Schifano, 1985). Rodin and Voshart (1986) conclude from their review that roughly one out of three medical inpatients exhibits mild or moderate depressive symptomatology and that up to 25 percent have a depressive syndrome. Cavanaugh (1984) asserts that the somatic manifestations of depression are found in 50–80 percent of medical patients. Lloyd (1977) calls depression the most common psychiatric disorder accompanying physical illness. It seems reasonable to expect that this formulation would apply as well to individuals with physically disabling conditions. However, the clinical presentation of depression in rehabilitation patients is often unclear and inconsistent, and the complexities of assessment rival those involved in the evaluation of denial. Consequently, the true incidence of depression among rehabilitation patients remains unknown.

Depression is frequently cited as a major psychological response in patients with a variety of conditions encountered in rehabilitation, including stroke (Charatan & Fisk, 1978), SCI (Orbaan, 1986), amputation (Langer, Hibbard, Egelko, & Gordon, 1984), multiple sclerosis (Baretz & Stephenson, 1981), and head injury (Rosenthal, 1983). In contrast to the above reports, Trieschmann (1980) reviewed a number of studies suggesting that rehabilitation staff tend to overestimate the magnitude of emotional distress in the newly disabled. Furthermore, several recent studies (Fullerton, Harvey, Klein, & Howell, 1981; Gans, 1981; Howell, Fullerton, Harvey, & Klein, 1981) conclude that depression among rehabilitation patients is surprisingly rare. Why these vastly different opinions among experienced clinicians/investigators?

A considerable portion of the disagreement on the incidence of depression in rehabilitation patients is attributable to the lack of a consensus regarding the factors that constitute reliable and valid indices of depression in this population. For instance, Caplan (1983) found significant interdisciplinary variability in the behavioral data bases that determined staff judgments of depression. Some (e.g., Cella, 1985; Gans, 1983) have argued that the criteria for depression employed by psychiatrists are not suitable parameters in medical or rehabilitation contexts. Behavioral symptoms that are the hallmarks of depressive illness in other populations—loss of appetite, sleep disturbance, psychomotor retardation—often do not signify depression in rehabilitation patients; they may be concrete consequences of the acquired physical disability or concurrent medical conditions, or they may derive from the stress of illness and hospitalization. Kathol and Petty (1981) detail the significant frequency of such symptoms among the nondepressed medically ill.

Gans (1983) further argues that "extreme emotional reactions are appropriate to devastating physical illness and usually are not pathologic" (p. 201). He calls attention to the hazards of evaluating emotional problems of the disabled using conventional psychiatric nomenclature. "It is diagnostically risky, if not reckless, and inequitable to the patient to take psychologic diagnostic criteria evolved from physically healthy patients and indiscriminately transpose these to patients who have just undergone irreversible change and loss" (p. 203). For example, diminished self-esteem, a common feature of depression, if limited to the present and not a distortion of the past, is a normal, nonpathologic response to newly acquired functional limitations. He further distinguishes "depression" from "demoralization," applying the latter term to those patients who become sad when they are asked to do things that they would like to do but cannot. Klerman (1981) has proposed the term "secondary affective disorder" for those emotional disturbances that accompany medical illnesses.

In a similar vein, several authors have observed that what is often labeled "depression" among medical patients may more properly be called "grieving," brought on by the stresses and losses that accompany hospitalization. Lipowski (1983) argued that there is no clear boundary between normal grief and depressive disorder following physical illness: The symptoms overlap considerably. As Turk, Kerns, and Rudy (1984) note:

> All chronic illnesses represent assaults on multiple areas of functioning, not just the body. Patients with various chronic illnesses may face separation from family, friends, and other sources of gratification, loss of key roles, disruption of plans for their future, assaults on self image and self esteem, uncertain and unpredictable future, as well as such illness-related factors as permanent changes in physical appearance or in bodily function. (p. 2)

All of these losses and changes constitute "deprivation of reinforcers," which, according to Fordyce (1982), precipitates grieving or depression. Of course, as Billings and Moos (1982) suggest, individual differences in magnitude of manifest depression result from the operation of such factors as the individuals' personal and social resources, their appraisal of the impact of the illness, and idiosyncratic coping responses. It follows that the clinician must strive to determine the operative factors contributing to the emotional state of each individual patient. As Horowitz (1985) observes, the point at which a given affective state, such as depression, becomes pathologic must be judged clinically in each case.

Weiner and Lovitt (1979) propose that the concept of "conservation-withdrawal" could profitably be applied to the emotional state of the medically ill. This response is described as a "self-limited biologic reaction pattern of withdrawal and inactivity that protects the organism against overstimulation or excessive deprivation" (p. 347). Behavioral signs resemble those of depression and include diminished energy, apathy, and feelings of being overwhelmed and unable to exercise control. These features connote the concept of "learned helplessness" (Miller & Norman, 1979; Seligman, 1975), which is often implicated in the genesis of depression and which is a notion with much explanatory power in rehabilitation. Weiner and Lovitt state that the re-emergence of hope and the restoration of some degree of personal efficacy produce remission of the symptoms. In support of this claim, Albrecht and Higgins (1977) found evidence of an association between a sense of control and success in rehabilitation; this finding suggests that achievement of progress produces a restored sense of confidence and consequent alleviation of depression. The tactic of "conservation-withdrawal" seems to have some of the same self-preserving features as "adaptive denial." Thus, behavior interpreted by staff members as evidence of depression may represent strenuous efforts by the patient to attain some level of adaptive coping.

Recognizing the terminological, interpretive, and phenomenological obstacles to appraisal of depression among the physically disabled, the literature on depression in some major handicapping conditions is now considered.

Depression Following Brain Injury

It has long been recognized that depression is a frequent consequence of brain injury. The causal and contributing factors, however, remain a matter of some disagreement. Ravenscroft (1982) contends that "every significant injury affects brain functioning to some degree, ranging from direct head trauma to systemic pathophysiologic effects" (p. 450). He notes the contribution to distorted cognition in the acute phase of physical trauma of such factors as toxic-metabolic imbalance, febrile and drug effects, emotional stress, sleep disruption, and sensory deprivation. Furthermore, conflicting reports abound regarding the characteristics, incidence, time course, and treatment of depression following traumatic head injury, stroke, or brain tumor, perhaps because, as Kinsbourne and Bemporad (1984) note, "All reports of depression may not be equal." Depression may be an emotional response to the recognition of physical and/or neuropsychological deficit. Alternatively, as recent work by Robinson and his colleagues has suggested, depression may be a direct consequence of the cortical lesion (e.g., Robinson & Price, 1982; Robinson, Starr, Lipsey, Rao, & Price, 1984; 1985).

Describing some common emotional consequences of stroke, Binder (1983) points out that the assessment of poststroke depression may be confounded by the presence of medications, the psychomotor effects of which mimic the behavioral slowing that often accompanies depression. He also observes that the interpretation of the traditional vegetative signs of depression is complicated because strokes cause reduced appetite, easy fatigability, and loss of libido.

Recent research has demonstrated the existence of impairments in affective communication (aprosodias) following brain damage (Ross, 1981; Ruckdeschel-Hibbard, Gordon, & Diller, 1986). These deficits in emotional comprehension and expression further complicate the diagnosis of depression following brain injury. Patients who, by virtue of a cortical lesion, are impaired in the expression of affective responses may be judged to be depressed on the basis of manifest flat affect, regardless of their actual mood. Patients with motor aprosodia (Ross, Harney, deLacoste-Utamsing, & Purdy, 1981) may describe feelings of profound depression, but these statements are discounted by caregivers because they are delivered with little emotional intonation.

Acknowledging its elusive nature, Ross and Rush (1981) refer to "the protean manifestations of depression in brain damaged patients." They report their experience that

> the neurological lesion may either obliterate or distort criterion signs and symptoms or may prevent collection of adequate historical information because of propositional and affective language disturbances. Furthermore, the depressive disorder can modify the clinical course usually associated with the neurological lesion, and changes in affective behavior resulting from a brain lesion may be misconstrued as being etiologically related to a depressive syndrome. (p. 1344)

Depression following head trauma

Rosenthal (1983) suggested that a mild form of reactive depression is quite common following traumatic head injury and may be viewed positively as it represents increasing awareness and acknowledgment of disability (also see Bond, 1984). A related factor that may contribute to the development and maintenance of depression after brain injury is described by Davidson (1963) in a discussion of the psychological aspects of stroke. He noted the negative impact on a patient's self-image of the knowledge that he or she has had a stroke and the stereotypic association of brain damage with insanity, epilepsy, and other undesirable characteristics. Kwentus, Hart, Peck, and Kornstein (1985) list other reactive components—feelings of frustration and discouragement, loss, and demoralization—that might also contribute to posttraumatic depression.

Strub and Black (1981) state unequivocally that depression is the most common emotional response among the head injured. However, depressive psychosis seems to be relatively rare (Levin, Grossman, Rose, & Teasdale, 1979).

Glenn and Rosenthal (1985) write that reactive depression is most common months or years after the injury. According to these authors, depressed head injured patients may not exhibit vegetative signs, such as sleep disruption or loss of appetite; furthermore, their cognitive deficits may hinder the expression of sadness or grief, compelling the clinician to employ atypical diagnostic criteria, such as those suggested by Ross and Rush (1981, see below). Kwentus et al. (1985) assert that some head injured patients develop a nonreactive, endogenous, biologically based depression, but provide no supporting data for that conclusion.

Robinson and Szetela (1981), using the Hamilton Rating Scale, found an 18 percent incidence of depression in a head injured group studied approximately 9 months after onset. Mikula and Rudin (1983) obtained responses to a mail questionnaire from 131 head trauma patients who were at least 6 months postinjury. Fifty-five percent of all patients reported being depressed. Cartlidge and Shaw (1981) found that the incidence of depression in their series doubled between the time of discharge and 6 month follow-up and remained remarkably stable at 1- and 2-year evaluations. Based on retrospective evaluation, they asserted that most of the patients who were depressed at the time of discharge had been premorbidly depressed as well.

The association between emotional state and cognitive function in head trauma has been examined by several groups of investigators with conflicting results. Fordyce, Roueche, and Prigatano (1983) studied head trauma patients in the acute (less than 6 months since injury) and chronic (greater than 6 months since injury) phase. The latter group displayed a clinically significant level of depression on the MMPI, whereas the more recently injured subjects did not. No group differences were found on neuropsychological measures. This finding accords with the assertions of Lishman (1978) and Prigatano (in press) that the degree of depression after head injury is unrelated to injury severity or degree of cognitive deficit. However, Dikman and Reitan (1977) found a higher level of depression shortly after injury in patients who exhibited moderate to marked neuropsychological deficits compared to subjects with more mild injuries. They reported that the difference between the groups increased at both 12- and 18-month follow-up.

Another view is offered by Wood, Novack, and Long (1984). They argue that, by virtue of brain injury, the individual is less well equipped to cope with environmental stress, even the mundane demands of everyday life; a series of failures—in relationships, work, leisure activities—is likely to produce depressed mood. They maintain that the emotional impact may be greatest with mild injuries because of the expectation of full recovery and the discrepancy between comparatively good physical restoration and persistent cognitive impairment.

Reports from close relatives further support the contention that depression is a common consequence of head injury. McKinlay, Brooks, Bond, Martinage, and Marshall (1981) interviewed relatives of severely injured patients at 3, 6, and 12 months after injury. At each assessment, between 52 and 57 percent of patients were reported to exhibit depressed mood. In a 5-year follow-up to the McKinlay et al. (1981) study, Brooks et al. (1986) discovered an incidence of depression (relative's report) among severely impaired patients that was actually slightly higher than had been found in the earlier investigation.

It has been reported that depression may persist for extended periods. One long-term (25–30 years) follow-up study of brain-damaged war veterans found an 85 percent incidence of depression; roughly half suffered from "relatively deep depression" (Lonnqvist & Achte, 1983).

Persistent depression may be accompanied by suicidal ideation. Vauhkonen (1959) reported that 1 percent of a series of brain injured soldiers had committed suicide by 10-year follow-up. (It should be noted that many of Vauhkonen's patients had sustained penetrating injuries; the features and etiology of affective disorders in this group may well differ from those that characterize individuals with closed head injuries.) Bond (1985) studied severely injured patients 1 and 5 years after onset and found substantial increases in both thoughts of suicide (5 percent versus 17 percent) and suicide attempts (2 percent versus 15 percent). Informative contemporary data are lacking concerning the incidence of successful suicide following head injury in both civilian and military populations (see Chapter 2 for further discussion).

The features, frequency, intensity, associated findings, and natural history of depression following head injury have not yet been definitively documented, especially for the period during which patients are participating in inpatient rehabilitation. At this stage, it is perhaps best to assume, as Prigatano (in press) contends, that postmorbid emotional disturbances result from an interaction of pre-existing personality characteristics and neuropathologically based alterations of cognition and affect, yielding highly variable clinical presentations. Therefore, it is imperative that each case be evaluated on its own merits, with consideration given to all possible contributing factors and signs. Possible treatment strategies, including individual and/or group therapy, physical and vocational rehabilitation, and drug therapy, would follow from this analysis (see Grimm & Bleiberg, 1986; Chapter 10; Bond, 1984).

Depression following stroke

A review of the published studies and opinions regarding depression following stroke reveals a variety of conflicting statements regarding incidence, severity, correlates, course, and effective treatment methods. Although some authors (Charatan & Fisk, 1978; Fisher, 1961; Herman, 1983; Magni & Schifano, 1984) have claimed that depression is the most common emotional response to stroke, others (Espmark, 1973; Krantz & Deckel, 1983) have argued that depression occurs no more frequently than other reactions such as anxiety or irritability.

Incidence, Etiology, and Characteristics

Binder (1983) found that the reported incidence of poststroke depression ranged from 26-60 percent. Based on their series of studies, Lipsey, Robinson, Pearlson, Rao, and Price (1985) note that "between 30% and 60% of both acute and chronic stroke patients had clinically significant depressions, that the high risk period extends for two years after stroke, and that the untreated course of these depressions is at least six months" (p. 318). Similarly, Finklestein et al. (1982) identified 48 percent of their group of stroke patients as moderately to severely depressed. Shinar et al. (1986) reported substantially lower incidences of 26 percent and 15 percent for minor and severe depression, respectively, in their group of non-aphasic stroke patients.

However, Krantz and Deckel (1983) maintain, "Of the studies that have been performed, few demonstrate that the incidence of depression is statistically greater for stroke patients than for either healthy control groups or patients with other disorders matched for extent of functional disability'' (p. 104). Some support for this assertion is found in the study of Robins (1976), who compared a group of stroke patients to a group equally disabled by orthopedic or neuromuscular causes (SCI, arthritis, amputation). Although stroke patients had a higher average score on the Hamilton Rating Scale, the difference was not statistically significant. It is important to point out that both groups were chronically disabled, all having been stricken at least 1 year prior to study and most with a disability history greater than 5 years.

In contrast, Folstein, Maiburger, and McHugh (1977), studying a more acute sample, found a much higher incidence (45 percent versus 10 percent) of depression among stroke patients than among equally disabled orthopedic patients. On the basis of their data, they argue that depression may be a specific sequel of stroke, not merely a reaction to functional impairment. In a group of stroke patients studied an average of 2 months after onset, Sinyor et al. (1986) found nonsignificant correlations among several measures of depression (both patient self-report and staff observation) and indices of functional impairment completed by physical and occupational therapists. Robinson, Starr et al. (1985) posit that the relation between depression and functional ability is a dynamic one. Thus, poststroke depression in the acute period may have a neurophysiologic basis and therefore be independent of physical function; later-developing mood disturbance, however, is more likely to derive from frustration over functional limitations. This suggestion is consistent with their finding of a steadily increasing correlation between depression and functional ability from 2 weeks to 6 months postonset (Robinson, Starr, Lipsey, Rao, and Price, 1984).

Accepting that some variation regarding incidence is inevitable in view of the various measurement tools and sample characteristics of the different studies, it is clear that poststroke depression is extremely common. Typical features include hopelessness, decreased appetite and libido, social withdrawal, anxiety, irritability, and cognitive deficit (Feibel & Springer, 1982; Labi, Phillips, & Gresham, 1980; Robinson & Price, 1982; Robinson, Bolla-Wilson, Kaplan, Lipsey, & Price, 1986). Functional regression following hospital discharge (Andrews & Stewart, 1979) may be another sign of depression.

As Robinson, Lipsey, and Price (1985) observe, depression following stroke probably consists of a ''mixed bag'' of mood disorders, the presentation of each modified to varying extents by numerous factors—time since onset of illness and of depression, age, functional limitations, cognitive deficit, social supports, finances, etc. Lateralization and localization of lesion have also been found to be important determinants of poststroke depression; data relating to this issue are discussed in the next section.

Interhemispheric Differences

A number of authors have discovered differences in frequency of poststroke depression between groups with left- or right- hemisphere involvement. Finklestein et al. (1982) reported depression to be more common (69 percent versus 25 percent) among patients with left-hemisphere damage. Robinson and his colleagues (Robinson & Price, 1982; Robinson & Szetela, 1981; Robinson et al., 1985) have consistently reported that patients with left anterior infarcts exhibit the most intense depression, but they do find depression (usually of a less severe nature) in some right-hemisphere patients, especially those with more posterior lesions (Robinson, Kubos, Starr, Rao, & Price, 1983). By contrast, Folstein et al. (1977) and Raymond and Susset (1984) describe depression as more common and more intense following right-hemisphere stroke. Gainotti (1972), Kerns (1980), Langer et al. (1984), Ruckdeschel-Hibbard (1984), and Sinyor et al. (1986) report no significant differences between their respective unilaterally lesioned groups.

The above-cited caveat of Kinsbourne and Bemporad (1984) about the nonequivalence of various reports of depression has special application to poststroke mood disturbance, especially the notion of hemispheric specificity. More precisely, it has been suggested that the depression that accompanies left-hemisphere lesions derives from feelings of anger and frustration about communicative limitations (aphasia). Under demanding conditions, the elevation of distress may eventuate in the "catastrophic reaction" described by Goldstein (1939, 1942). Benson (1973) argues that the catastrophic reaction is more common in nonfluent aphasics whose communicative failures are quite obvious, especially to the patients themselves. In this regard, Robinson's repeated finding (e.g., Robinson & Price, 1982; Robinson & Szetela, 1981) of an association between intensity of depression and proximity of left-hemisphere lesions to the frontal pole (where lesions tend to produce nonfluent aphasia) is pertinent. The clinical presentation of depression in left-hemisphere patients thus seems to be characterized by anxiety and agitation (Gainotti, 1972).

By contrast, right-hemisphere-based depression tends to be typified by "negative" symptoms, such as flat affect, aprosodic speech (Ross, 1981), and decreased emotional arousal with consequent difficulty interpreting and/or expressing emotion (Heilman, Scholes, & Watson, 1975; Ross et al., 1981). Kinsbourne and Bemporad (1984) have proposed a similar typology, specifically indicting the left anterior and right posterior regions.

Whatever the actual incidence of depression in the left- and right-hemisphere subgroups, there is evidence that the rate of detection and referral is higher for patients with right- than left-hemisphere lesions. In their group of depressed stroke patients referred for psychiatric consultation, Rosse and Ciolino (1985–86) found that 62 percent had right-sided lesions, whereas only 9.5 percent had left-sided involvement; the remaining patients had bilateral lesions. As Rosse and Ciolino note, many patients with left-hemisphere lesions and aphasia are not referred for psychiatric consultation on the assumption that linguistic impairment precludes the effectiveness of supportive counseling.

It is of interest that Rosse and Ciolino's chart review revealed that, over a 4-year period, only 6.3 percent of all stroke patients on the neurology service were referred for psychiatric consultation. This finding suggests that inadequate attention may be given to the emotional needs of this group. Feibel and Springer (1982) note that less than one-fourth of stroke patients found to be depressed 6 months after onset had received treatment for this problem. In Robinson and Price's (1982) sample, treatment for depression was almost nonexistent.

Diagnosis

The above discussion provides some indication of the difficulties involved in diagnosing depression in the poststroke individual. Observing that exclusive reliance on standard psychiatric criteria or psychological testing often produces an inaccurate diagnosis, Ross and Rush (1981) suggest some useful (albeit unconventional) guidelines for this endeavor (N.B.—These principles also apply to patients with head injuries). They state that the initial indication of depression may be (1) poor or erratic recovery, (2) failure to cooperate with a rehabilitation program, (3) "management" difficulties, and (4) deterioration from a previously stable state. They further advise interviewing both patient and family, inquiring specifically about vegetative signs. Also, the occurrence of pathologic laughing and crying may signify depression.

Ross and Rush (1981) caution clinicians against discounting the emotional content of statements made by aprosodic patients; even experienced clinicians may overlook a patient's admissions of despair or hopelessness if these are spoken in a way that conveys unconcern; content of speech and tone must be evaluated separately. They suggest that the dexamethasone suppression test (DST) may be useful in the detection of endogenous depression in the brain injured patient, an opinion endorsed with guarded enthusiasm by Lipsey, Robinson, Pearlson, Rao, and Price (1985). Reding et al. (1985) also report the DST to be a valuable diagnostic tool for poststroke depression. Bauer, Gans, Harley, and Cobb (1983), however, found the DST to be insensitive to depression in a small sample of stroke patients undergoing rehabilitation; they attribute this to the "secondary" nature of most poststroke depression.

In some instances, firm diagnosis may only be made retrospectively, as in the case of a patient who demonstrates a positive clinical response to antidepressant medication.

Treatment

Several treatment interventions have been suggested for the depressed stroke patient. Some authors advocate supportive counseling (Charatan & Fisk, 1978;

Fisher, 1961; Latow, 1983), whereas others propose participation in group therapy (Bucher, Smith, & Gillespie, 1984; D'Affliti & Weitz, 1974; Oradei & Waite, 1974; Watzlawizk & Coyne, 1980). A few (Benson, 1973; Goodstein, 1983) suggest that both techniques ought to be used. Charatan and Fisk (1978) note the anti-depressant effects of occupational therapy, but this is probably true primarily for those patients who are able to achieve significant progress on tasks that are meaningful to them.

Griffith (1975) describes a program in which lay volunteers made home visits to stroke patients for the purpose of providing support, encouragement, and stimulation. This program, which focused on aphasic patients, was reported to effect improvements in attitude, morale, and speech.

Few studies of the effects of individual psychotherapeutic interventions in stroke report outcome measures. Latow (1983) found that stroke patients who received brief psychotherapy three times per week showed greater gains than did untreated patients on a measure of physical function and had decreased scores on indices of depression and sick role identification.

Somatic treatment of depression in the elderly stroke patient must proceed cautiously. Nortriptyline has recently been reported to be effective in the alleviation of poststroke depression (Lipsey et al., 1984). However, such tricyclic antidepressants are contraindicated for elderly patients with cardiovascular conditions, or those who are taking medications that may dangerously interact with the antidepressants. Nonetheless, although pharmacologic treatments for poststroke depression have historically been neglected and/or discouraged (e.g. Charatan & Fisk, 1978), reconsideration of this stance seems to be in order. Elevation of mood by the antidepressants might also render some patients more receptive to psychological counseling. Electroconvulsive therapy may alleviate severe depression in a mildly impaired stroke patient with little neurological involvement (Karliner, 1978), but this drastic treatment is only rarely indicated.

Depression and Spinal Cord Injury

As Fraser (1982) succinctly states, "The psychological impact of spinal cord injury is extreme" (p. 246). Although this assertion would meet with little disagreement from rehabilitation staff, there is little consensus about the specific nature of the response, aside from the general assumption that depression is common (e.g., Bracken & Bernstein, 1980; Brucker, 1983; Orbaan, 1986; Stewart, 1977a & 1977b). In fact, some authors have suggested that depression should be regarded as a necessary, albeit painful stage through which all SCI patients must progress if psychological adjustment to the disabling condition is to be attained (Nemiah, 1957; Siller, 1969). It follows that any nondepressed patient should then be perceived as "in denial," a state that staff members frequently feel obliged to confront, often with counterproductive results.

Individual Differences versus Stage Theory

The notion that all spinal cord patients must naturally experience significant depression conflicts with the mounting evidence that psychological reactions are complexly determined (e.g., Bartol, 1978; Dew, Lynch, Ernst, Rosenthal, & Judd, 1985). Some important determinants include premorbid level of emotional and cognitive development (LeBaron, Currie, & Zeltzer, 1984); perceived "locus of control" (Bulman & Wortman, 1977; Shadish, Hickman, & Arrick, 1981); preinjury tendencies toward depression (Katz, Gordon, Iversen, & Myers, 1978–79); socioeconomic status (Kalb, 1971); depth and breadth of social-familial support; and financial resources (Trieschmann, 1980).

Recognizing the role of these and other factors compels the conclusion that the notion of "necessary depression" is a clinical procrustean bed, an oversimplification that distorts and deceives. Rehabilitation staff members must evaluate the idiosyncratic contributions of various intrapsychic and socioeconomic factors to each patient's affective course following SCI. Only then can a rational treatment plan be developed (Brucker, 1983). This need for individualized assessment of emotional response to SCI is further underscored by the repeated failures to identify a modal response pattern, including depression, among spinal cord patients (Chapter 1; Trieschmann, 1980; Wright, 1983).

The rarity of depression as a specific emotional response has been illustrated by a number of studies. For example, Cook (1979) investigated the emotional profiles of 118 SCI patients on the Mini/Mult (abbreviated form of the MMPI) and the State/Trait Anxiety Inventory and found that both depressive and anxiety reactions were almost nonexistent. In fact, a review of individual scores revealed only two persons who met the criteria for reactive depression. Howell and his associates (1981) utilized three measures of depression in their study of 22 patients with recent spinal cord injuries. Each patient was interviewed using the Schedule for Affective Disorders and Schizophrenia (SADS/L) (Endicott & Spitzer, 1978) and diagnosed according to Research Diagnostic Criteria (RDC), a standardized protocol. In addition, each patient completed the Beck Depression Inventory (Beck et al., 1961; Beck, 1967), a self-report measure. Only 22 percent (n = 5) of the patients were identified as depressed according to the RDC criteria. The authors suggested that the discrepancy between their findings and common clinical wisdom might be a function of their reliance on strict diagnostic guidelines in identifying depression versus clinical impressions/expectations about normal reactions. "The assumption that these patients, having suffered a major loss with profound consequences, must or should be depressed may have contributed to an observer bias and led to an overestimation of the incidence of depression" (Howell, Fullerton, Harvey, & Klein, 1981, p. 287).

The validity of this statement has received recent support in the findings of Richards (1986). Thirty-six SCI patients were followed during their first year after discharge from a physical rehabilitation program. In addition, 29 able-bodied control subjects were assessed during the same time interval. Outcome measures included the Beck Depression Inventory, the Wiggins Hostility Scale, and the Handicapped Problems Inventory. The results suggested that, although the SCI group demonstrated somewhat greater depression shortly after discharge (3 weeks), these differences had disappeared as early as 3 months posthospitalization. Moreover, although the initial level of depression in the SCI group was significantly higher than that of the controls by statistical criteria, it was not, according to the author, of clinically meaningful magnitude.

A comprehensive study by Lawson (1978) discovered another individual difference variable that appears to affect patients' emotional response to SCI. Ten spinal cord injured patients were followed throughout their entire rehabilitation hospitalization with repeated administration of four measures of depressive affect: (1) a self-report measure; (2) staff rating; (3) a behavioral measure of spontaneous verbalization, and (4) a physiologic index of depression, i.e., 24-hour output of urinary tryptamine. The data suggested that those patients who could identify options that would allow for the realization of premorbid hopes and plans were the least likely to experience depression. Interestingly, level of injury was not associated with degree of depressed affect, an observation that has been made by others (e.g., Orbaan, 1986). The patient who was most depressed was injured at the C6–7 level. He died within 3 months of discharge. In contrast, the subject who was least depressed during rehabilitation admission (a C4–5 quadriplegic) was working full-time and living independently in his own apartment 1 year after injury.

Treatment Implications

Lawson's (1978) findings led him to conclude: "An extended period of depression or grief . . . appears to be counterproductive to post-hospital adjustment (p. 578)." This does not mean that expressions of sadness, unhappiness, grief, and the like can or should be discouraged but merely that staff members should not approach patients with the presupposition that clinical depression is a necessary or inevitable psychological response.

Similar observations regarding the negative correlation between the degree of depression during rehabilitation and subsequent adaptation/adjustment to SCI have been made by others (e.g., Bracken and Shepard, 1980; Dinardo, 1971; Fraser, 1982). The implications for rehabilitation staff seem clear. Strategies designed to mitigate and/or prevent depression and to enhance the patient's particular premorbid ways of coping should be employed throughout a patient's hospitalization. For example, during the early stages of the patient's recovery, attention could be given to reducing the deleterious effects of sensory deprivation (apart from those directly associated with the SCI itself), with the aim of reducing the regression, withdrawal, and vegetative reactions often associated with severely reduced sensory input. Later, a combination of individualized cognitive-behavioral and social skills training interventions (see Chapter 13) should enable spinal cord injured individuals to participate most fully in rehabilitation and ultimately to return to the community with the least emotional turmoil.

Long-Range Psychological Impact

An emphasis on the central role of individual coping dispositions and problem-solving skills permits a hopeful perspective regarding psychological adaptation to SCI. However, most of the studies cited above have focused on reactions during patients' early—that is, 1 year—postinjury recovery, much of which is spent in the hospital. Certainly, there are important differences between adjustment in the hospital setting and that which occurs at home and in the community. In the words of one quadriplegic patient, "The true meaning of the loss doesn't really hit until you are home for the first time" (Aadalen & Stroebel-Kahn, 1981, p. 1473). Kerr and Thompson (1972) conducted a longitudinal investigation of 181 SCI patients across a 10-year period and concluded that, on the average, it took at least 2 years for a patient to make the necessary adjustments. Similarly, Trieschmann (1980) writes:

> Learning to live with a disability appears to be a lengthy and often frustrating process. No matter how long a person has been injured, he or she never ceases to get irritated, frustrated, and perhaps depressed over the inconveniences that the disability entails—e.g., finding one's clothing is wet with urine when . . . hurrying to get to an appointment . . . (p. 20).

Clearly, if rehabilitation specialists are to better understand and help SCI patients prepare for a lifetime of unique psychological demands, more extended investigations are needed.

Unfortunately, our knowledge of the long-range psychological impact of SCI is not well developed. However, it is helpful to consider the small number of follow-up studies that have retrospectively investigated the incidence of late or persistent depression following SCI. These studies have examined case records for evidence of either direct self-destructive behavior—suicide—or indirect self-injury—failing to take prescribed medicine—as indicators of depressed affect in patients. Some of these studies have found that up to 50 percent of spinal cord injured individuals describe suicidal thoughts/wishes (e.g., Pinkerton & Griffin, 1983).

Yet, although the suicide rate for the disabled is higher than that for the general population (Hopkins, 1971), suicide is reportedly rare among spinal cord patients (Sakinofsky, 1980). For example, Hackler (1977) reviewed 270 spinal cord cases 25 years postinjury and found that, although the mortality rate was 49 percent, the cause of death was listed as suicide in only five patients. Similarly, Nyquist and Bors (1957) identified a 15 percent mortality rate among 2,011 SCI patients during a 19-year period; suicide was the cause of death in only 21 cases. There was no correlation between suicide and level of injury. Nehemkis and Groot (1980) found that out of 200 patients in their study, only 8 (4 percent) had demonstrated direct self-destructive behaviors. However, they argued that the actual number of suicidal patients is "probably considerably greater if we take into account that for some quadriplegics the only feasible way to commit suicide is by indirect means . . . . What at first blush looks like ISDB (indirect self-destructive behavior) is in actuality intended to be self-destructive" (p. 111).

That suicide is only one potential outcome of self-destructive tendencies, albeit the most extreme one (Ducharme & Freed, 1980), is evident. Therefore, to obtain a more valid assessment of the emotional impact of SCI, it is imperative that one examine the frequency of indirect suicide or, as Seymour (1955) termed it, "physiological suicide."

Nehemkis and Groot (1980) found that, in contrast to the small number of spinal cord patients who attempted suicide by direct means, a much higher percentage (34 percent) displayed various forms of indirect self-destructive behaviors, such as refusal to eat; declining necessary weight shift; and failure to follow prescribed treatment for decubiti, leading to chronic infection and death. Comarr (1965) describes a case of self-induced ischiectomy in a spinal cord injured person due to prolonged sitting. Similarly, Price (1973) reports three instances in which self-neglect appeared to be the cause of death in spinal cord patients: renal failure after developing pneumonia, septicemic shock secondary to urinary tract infection, and decubitus ulcers resulting in osteomyelitis and death. Finally, Wilcox and Stauffer (1972) examined the records of 423 patients admitted to the spinal cord center at Rancho Los Amigos Hospital. They concluded that 34 percent of the deaths were probably avoidable. That is, 17 of the 50 known deaths were due to indirect means of self-destruction, such as abuse of alcohol and drugs, multiple pressure sores, and other forms of self-neglect.

Long-Term Adjustment and Individual Differences

Although these studies have closely examined direct and indirect self-destructive behaviors as indicators of postdischarge emotional status—that is, depression—few studies have attempted to identify intraindividual factors that contribute to the occurrence of self-destructive feelings and acts. However, the sparse extant findings suggest the importance of individual differences in understanding these tendencies. For example, Anderson and Andberg (1979) found that two variables—acceptance of responsibility for skin care and satisfaction with the activities of daily life—were associated with a low incidence of decubitus ulcers. In like manner, Gordon, Harasymiw, Bellile, Lehman, and Sherman (1982) studied the relation between psychosocial variables and pressure sores and found that decubiti were more common in patients with diminished social and economic self-esteem. Interestingly, both studies found the level of neurologic impairment to be unrelated to the incidence of pressure sores. These investigations suggest that significant problems in coping with daily social and vocational demands following SCI are associated with the development of depression. Self-injurious behaviors, either direct or indirect, then become the vehicle through which these depressed feelings are expressed.

It is important to note that it is actually easier for the SCI patient to inflict self-harm through indirect neglect than to be a "model" patient and comply with medical regimen. As Farberow (1980) and others have emphasized, an individual with a SCI has to actively "work at it if he is to survive and be comfortable " (p. 7). Thus, as rehabilitation clinicians, it is critical that we strive to determine the differences between those patients who do "work at it" and those who abdicate responsibility for their self-care, either directly or indirectly. The implications for rehabilitation specialists seem clear; intervention strategies should be directed toward teaching each patient how to capitalize on pre-existing coping skills, as well as to learn new techniques for adapting to the physical, social, and psychological changes that result from the disabling condition. Without the skills needed to maintain self-esteem and establish rewarding personal relationships, isolation, withdrawal, and consequent depression will likely follow.

Advantages of Individual Difference Approach

The potential benefits of adopting this perspective are significant. First, rehabilitation staff would more readily recognize that the onset of SCI does not necessarily lead to emotional problems of the psychiatric variety (e.g., Gans, 1981; Trieschmann, 1978–79). Instead, each spinal cord patient could be viewed as an individual whose injury has produced what Trieschmann (1978–79) terms "problems in living . . . reality problems associated with the fact that major changes must be made in how one relates to the world" (p. 214). The rehabilitation process thereby is seen as one of teaching patients to cope with a world designed for able-bodied individuals. Further, because learning to adapt to any set of new circumstances is stressful for anyone—disabled or not—then clearly it is sensible to apply Hohmann's (1975) perspective that most emotional reactions to spinal cord injuries are "normal sequelae to any severe loss . . . normal reactions to an abnormal situation" (p. 81), reactions that must be understood with reference to the various individual difference factors discussed above.

A related benefit to be derived by eschewing the traditional expectation of depression is improvement in patient-staff relations. Gans (1981) emphasizes that, when staff incorrectly assume a patient is (or should be) experiencing depression, patients frequently detect this misperception. Its countertherapeutic impact is reflected in the following statement made by a quadriplegic patient: "Nursing and counseling personnel . . . made assumptions about how I should be feeling and assessments about what I was or was not expressing" (Aadalen & Stroebel-Kahn, 1981, p. 1477). When this occurs, patients report that they feel unjustly accused of having psychological problems and, in turn, respond with feelings of anger, disappointment, and betrayal. Many disabled persons have stated that the most "depressing" aspect of their postinjury rehabilitation experience was staff members telling them that they should be depressed (Lawson, 1977). Such a situation clearly reduces the potential for effective and therapeutic staff-patient interaction (Chapter 7) and stands in direct conflict with the ever-growing data base negating the validity of such expectations by staff and others. (For suggestions on management of depression in SCI, see Chapter 1; Trieschmann, 1980, Chapter 8.)

CONCLUSION

It is the fundamental premise of this chapter that the stage theory approach to understanding the psychological consequences of disabling conditions hinders good clinical practice to a far greater extent than it helps. This view is shared by an increasing number of authors and supported by an ever-growing base of empirical data. However, the popularity of the stage perspective is not difficult to understand. As Gunther (Chapter 8) observes, people strive to make sense out of traumatic and chaotic conditions; in this effort, some sort of organizing and/or explanatory principle is sought for the sake of both cognitive and emotional relief. However, the counterproductive effects of day-to-day clinical application of the stage theory, in the authors' opinion, render it little more than a facile heuristic device that has the unfortunate effect of supporting poor patient care. Rather, the "individual differences" view, discussed in special detail with reference to SCI, provides a more practicable alternative by emphasizing the important contributions to psychological accommodation made by an array of variables that scientific study and common sense have identified.

The literature reviewed in this chapter provides substantial support for the notion that denial and depression following the onset of disability are multidimensional phenomena with various etiologies, features, and treatment implications. Rehabilitation clinicians must labor to understand the meanings of manifest denial or depression on a case-by-case basis. This necessitates awareness of the many factors that, as have been seen, may produce, attenuate, or exacerbate emotional states.

Using the "individual differences" perspective requires significant effort on the part of the clinician; many questions must be asked (and answered) and much information must be integrated. Preconceived notions of sequences of adjustment and their time course must be jettisoned; patients cannot be placed in convenient categories. However, the result is a patient who is better understood, *feels* understood, and is treated more effectively with interventions based on the facts of the individual case, and not speculations.

REFERENCES

Aadalen, S., & Stroebel-Kahn, F. (1981). Coping with paraplegia. *American Journal of Nursing, 81*, 1471–1478.

Albrecht, G., & Higgins, P.C. (1977). Rehabilitation success: The interrelationships of multiple criteria. *Journal of Health and Social Behavior 18*, 36–45.

Anderson, T.P., & Andberg, M.M. (1979). Psychosocial factors associated with incidence of pressure sores in spinal cord injured patients. *Archives of Physical Medicine and Rehabilitation, 60*, 341–345.

Andrews, K., & Stewart, J. (1979). Stroke recovery: He can but does he? *Rheumatology and Rehabilitation, 18*, 43–48.

Baretz, R.M., & Stephenson, G.R. (1976). Unrealistic patient. *New York State Journal of Medicine, 76*, 54–57.

Baretz, R.M., & Stephenson, G.R. (1981). Emotional responses to multiple sclerosis. *Psychosomatics, 22*, 117–127.

Barth, J.T., & Boll, T.J. (1981). Rehabilitation and treatment of central nervous system dysfunction: A behavioral medicine perspective. In C.K. Prokop & L.A. Bradley (Eds.), *Medical psychology: Contributions to behvioral medicine*. New York: Academic Press, pp. 241–266.

Bartol, G. (1978). Psychological needs of the spinal cord injured person. *Journal of Neurosurgical Nursing, 10*, 171–175.

Bauer, M., Gans, J., Harley, J., & Cobb, W. (1983). Dexamethasone suppression test and depression in a rehabilitation setting. *Archives of Physical Medicine and Rehabilitation, 64*, 421–422.

Bear, D.M. (1983). Hemispheric specialization and neurology of emotion. *Archives of Neurology, 40*, 195–202.

Beck, A.T. (1967). *Depression: Causes and treatment*. Philadelphia: University of Pennsylvania Press.

Beck, A.T., Ward, C.H., Mendelson, M., et al. (1961). An inventory for measuring depression. *Archives of General Psychiatry, 4*, 561–571.

Benson, D.F. (1973). Psychiatric aspects of aphasia. *British Journal of Psychiatry, 123*, 555–566.

Billings, A., & Moos, R. (1982). Psychosocial theory and research on depression: An integrated framework. *Clinical Psychology Review, 2*, 213–237.

Binder, L. (1983). Emotional problems after stroke. *Current Concepts of Cerebrovascular Disease [Stroke], XVIII*, 17–20.

Bond, M. (1984). The psychiatry of closed head injury. In N. Brooks (Ed.), *Closed head injury*. New York: Oxford University Press, pp. 148–178.

Bond, M.R. (1985). *Treatment of psychiatric syndromes in adult victims of severe brain injury*. Paper presented at the 9th Annual Post-Graduate Course on the Rehabilitation of the Brain Injured Adult and Child, Williamsburg, VA.

Bracken, M. & Bernstein, M. (1980). Adaption to and coping with disability one year after spinal cord injury: An epidemiological study. *Social Psychiatry, 15*, 33–41.

Bracken, M.B., & Shepard, M.J. (1980). Coping and adaptation following acute spinal cord injury: A theoretical analysis. *Paraplegia, 18*, 74–75.

Bracken, M.B., Shepard, M.J., & Webb, S.B. (1981). Psychological response to acute spinal cord injury: An epidemiological study. *Paraplegia, 19*, 271–283.

Bradley, L.S., & Burish, T.G. (1983). Coping with chronic disease: Current status and future directions. In T. Burish & L. Bradley (Eds.), *Coping with chronic disease: Research and application*. New York: Academic Press.

Breznitz, S. (1983a). Denial versus hope. In S. Breznitz (Ed.), *The denial of stress*. New York: International Universities Press, pp. 297–302.

Breznitz, S. (1983b). Seven kinds of denial. In S. Breznitz (Ed.), *The denial of stress*. New York: International Universities Press, pp. 257–280.

Brooks, N., Campsie L., Symington C., et al. (1986). The five year outcome of severe blunt head injury—a relative's view. *Journal of Neurology, Neurosurgery and Psychiatry. 49*, 764–770.

Brucker, B. (1983). Spinal cord injuries. In T.G. Burish & L.A. Bradley (Eds.), *Coping with chronic disease: Research and applications*. New York: Academic Press, pp. 285–311.

Bucher, J., Smith E., & Gillespie, C. (1984). Short-term group therapy for stroke patients in a rehabilitation center. *British Journal of Medical Psychology, 57*, 283–290.

Bulman, R. & Wortman, C.B. (1977). Attributions of blame & coping in the "real world": Severe accident victims react to their lot. *Journal of Personality & Social Behavior, 35*, 351–363.

Burton, G. (1985). Psychosocial aspects and adjustment during various phases of a neurological disability. In D.A. Umphreid (Ed.), *Neurological rehabilitation*. St. Louis: C.V. Mosby, pp. 118–133.

Caplan, B. (1983). Staff and patient perception of patient mood. *Rehabilitation Psychology, 28*, 68–77.

Cartlidge, N.E.F., & Shaw, D.A. (1981). *Head injury*. Philadelphia: W.B. Saunders.

Cassileth, B.R., Lusk, E.J., Strouse, T.B., Miller, D.S., Brown, L.L., Cross, P.A., & Tenaglia, A.N. (1984). Psychosocial status in chronic illness; A comparative analysis of six diagnostic groups. *The New England Journal of Medicine, 311*, 506–511.

Cavanaugh, S. (1984). Diagnosing depression in the hospitalized patient with chronic medical illness. *Journal of Clinical Psychiatry, 45*, 13–16.

Cavanaugh, S., Clark, D.C., & Gibbons, R.D. (1983). Diagnosing depression in the hospitalized medically ill. *Pyschomatics, 24*, 809–815.

Cella, D.F. (1985). Psychological adjustment and cancer outcome: Levy versus Taylor. *American Psychologist 40*, 1275–1276.

Charatan, F.B., & Fisk, A. (1978). Mental and emotional results of strokes. *New York State Journal of Medicine, 78*, 1403–1405.

Chodoff, P. (1959). Adjustment to disability: Some observations on patients with multiple sclerosis. *Journal of Chronic Disease. 9*, 653–670.

Cohen, F., & Lazarus, R.S. (1979). Coping with the stresses of illness. In G.C. Stone, F. Cohen, N.E. Adler, & Associates (Eds.), *Health psychology–A handbook*. San Francisco: Jossey-Bass, pp. 217–254.

Cook, D.H. (1979). Psychological adjustment to spinal cord injury: Incidence of denial, depression and anxiety. *Rehabilitation Psychology, 26*, 97–104.

Comarr, A. (1965). A self-induced ischiectomy. *Journal of Indian Medical Profession, 12*, 5509.

Cutting, J. (1978). Study of anosognosia. *Journal of Neurology, Neurosurgery and Psychiatry, 41*, 548–555.

D'Afflitti, J.G., & Weitz, G.W. (1974). Rehabilitating the stroke patient through patient-family groups. *International Journal of Group Psychotherapy, 24*, 323–332.

Davidson, R. (1963). The psychologic aspects of stroke. *Geriatrics, 18*, 151–157.

Dew, M., Lynch, K., Ernst, J., Rosenthal, R., & Judd, C. (1985). A causal analysis of factors affecting adjustment to spinal cord injury. *Rehabilitation Psychology, 30*, 39–46.

Dikman, S., & Reitan, R.M. (1977). Emotional sequelae of head injury. *Annals of Neurology, 2*, 492–494.

Diller, L. (1959). The problem of denial. In D. Martin (Ed.), *Whither diagnosis: Evaluation of the atypical*. Boulder, Col: University of Colorado Press, pp. 89–101.

Dimsdale, J. (1984). Untangling the phenomenon of denial. Review of "The Denial of Stress," S. Breznitz (Ed.) *Contemporary Psychiatry, 3*, 120–121.

Dinardo, O.E. (1971). Psychological adjustment to spinal cord injury. *Dissertation Abstracts International, 36*, 4206B–4207B. (University Microfilms No. 71-24, 248)

Ducharme, S.H. & Freed, M.M. (1980). The role of self-destruction in spinal cord injury mortality. *SCI Digest, 2*, 29–38.

Dunn, M.E. (1975). Psychological intervention in a spinal cord injury center: An introduction. *Rehabilitation Psychology, 22*, 179–184.

Endicott, J., & Spitzer, R.L. (1978) A diagnostic interview: The schedule for affective disorders and schizophrenia. *Archives of General Psychiatry, 35*, 837–844.

Espmark, S. (1973). Stroke before 50: A follow-up study of vocational and psychological adjustment. *Scandinavian Journal of Rehabilitation Medicine, 5*, 1–107.

Farberow, N.L. (1980). Introduction. In N. Farberow (ed.), *The many faces of suicide*. New York: McGraw-Hill, Inc., pp.1–12.

Feibel, J. & Springer, C. (1982). Depression and failure to resume social activities after stroke. *Archives of Physical Medicine and Rehabilitation, 63*, 276–278.

Fink, S.L. (1967). Crisis and motivation: A theoretical model. *Archives of Physical Medicine and Rehabilitation, 48*, 592–597.

Finklestein, S., Benowitz, L.I., Baldessarini, R.J., Arana, G., Levine, D., Woo, E., Bear, D., Moya, K., & Stoll, A.L. (1982). Mood, vegetative disturbance and dexamethasone suppression test after stroke. *Annals of Neurology, 12*, 463–468.

Fisher, S.H. (1961). Psychiatric considerations of cerebral vascular disease. *The American Journal of Cardiology, 7*, 379–385.

Folkman, S. & Lazarus, R.S. (1980). An analysis of coping in a middle-aged community sample. *Journal of Health and Social Behavior, 21*, 219–239.

Folstein, M.F., Maiberger, R., & McHugh, P.R. (1977). Mood disorder as a specific complication of stroke. *Journal of Neurology, Neurosurgery, and Psychiatry, 40*, 1018–1020.

Fordyce, W. (1982). Psychological assessment and management. In F.J. Kottko, G.K. Stillwell, & J.F. Lehmann (eds.) *Krusen's handbook of physical medicine and rehabilitation*. Philadelphia: W.B. Saunders, pp. 124–150.

Fordyce, D.J., Roueche, J.R, & Prigatano, G.P. (1983). Enhanced emotional reactions in chronic head trauma patients. *Journal of Neurology, Neurosurgery and Psychiatry, 46*, 620–624.

Fraser, A. (1982). The psychiatrist in the spinal unit. *Australian and New Zealand Journal of Psychiatry, 16*, 246–250.

Fullerton, D.T., Harvey, R.F., Klein, M.H., & Howell, T. (1981). Psychiatric disorders in patients with spinal cord injuries. *Archives of General Psychiatry, 38*, 1369–1371.

Gainotti, G. (1968). Aspetti qualitativi ed evolutivi della sintomatologia conseguente a lesioni dell'a emisfero destro. *Ann. Neurol. Psichiatr., 62*, 1–29.

164   REHABILITATION PSYCHOLOGY DESK REFERENCE

Gainotti, G. (1969). Reactions "catastrophiques" et manifestations d'indifference au cours des atteintes cerebrales. *Neuropsychologia, 7,* 195–204.

Gainotti, G. (1972). Emotional behavior and hemispheric side of the lesion. *Cortex, 8,* 41–55.

Gainotti, G. (1983). Laterality of affect: The emotional behavior of right- and left-brain-damaged patients. In M. Myslobodsky (Ed.), *Hemisyndromes: Psychology, neurology, & psychiatry.* New York: Academic Press, pp. 175–192.

Gans, J.S. (1981). Depression diagnosis in a rehabilitation hospital. *Archives of Physical Medicine and Rehabilitation, 62,* 386–389.

Gans, J.S. (1983). Psychosocial adaptation. *Seminars in Neurology, 3,* 201–211.

Geller, B., & Greydanus, D.E. (1979). Psychological management of acute paraplegia in adolescence. *Pediatrics, 63,* 563–565.

Glenn, M.B., Rosenthal, M. (1985). Rehabilitation following severe traumatic brain injury. *Sesminars in Neurology, 5,* 80–90.

Goldberg, R.L. (1982). Psychologic sequelae of myocardial infarction. *American Family Physician, 25,* 209–213.

Goldiamond, I. (1976). Coping and adaptive behaviors of the disabled. In G. Albrecht (ed.), *The sociology of physical disability.* Pittsburgh: University of Pittsburgh Press.

Goldstein, K. (1939). *The organism: A holistic approach to biology: Derived from pathological data in man.* New York: American Book Co.

Goldstein, K. (1942). *After effects of brain injuries in war.* New York: Grune and Stratton.

Goodstein, R.K. (1983). Overview: Cerebrovascular accident and the hospitalized elderly—A multidimensional clinical problem. *The American Journal of Psychiatry, 140,* 141–147.

Gordon, W.A., & Diller, L. (1983). Stroke: Coping with a cognitive deficit. In T.G. Burish & L.A. Bradley (Eds.), *Coping with chronic disease: Research and applications* (pp. 113–135). New York: Academic Press.

Gordon, W.A., Harasymiw, S., Bellile, S., Lehman, L., & Sherman, B. (1982). Relationship between pressure sores and psychosocial adjustment in persons with spinal cord injury. *Rehabilitation Psychology, 27,* 185–191.

Green, S.A. (1985). *Mind and body: The psychology of physical illness.* Washington, DC: American Psychiatric Press.

Griffith, V.E. (1975). Volunteer scheme for dysphasia and allied problems in stroke patients. *British Medical Journal, 3,* 633–635.

Grimm, W. & Bleiberg, J. (1986). Psychological rehabilitation in traumatic brain injury. In S. Filskov and T. Boll (eds.) *Handbook of Clinical Neuropsychology,* vol. 2, New York: John Wiley, pp. 495–560.

Hackett, T.P., & Cassem, N.H. (1974). Development of a quantitative rating scale to assess denial. *Journal of Psychosomatic Research, 18,* 93–100.

Hackler, R. (1977). A 25-year prospective mortality study in the spinal cord injured patient: Comparison with the long-term living paraplegic. *Journal of Urology, 117,* 486–488.

Hamburg, D. & Adams, J. (1967). A perspective on coping behavior: Seeking and utilizing information in major transitions. *Archives of General Psychiatry, 17,* 277–284.

Heilman, K.M., Scholes, R., & Watson. R.T. (1975). Auditory affective agnosia: Disturbed comprehension of affective speech. *Journal of Neurology, Neurosurgery and Psychiatry, 38,* 69–72.

Heilman, K.M., Schwartz, H.D., & Watson, R.T. (1978). Hypoarousal in patients with the neglect syndrome and emotional indifference. *Neurology, 28,* 229–232.

Heinemann, A., Geist, C.S., & Magiearo-Plansy, R. (1983). *The role of hope in spinal cord injury rehabilitation.* Paper presented at American Psychological Association Convention, Anaheim, CA.

Herman, C.D. (1983). Psychiatric aspects of the stroke patient. In W.E. Kelly (Ed.), *The changing role of rehabilitation medicine in the management of the psychiatric patient.* Springfield, IL: Charles C Thomas, pp. 83–89.

Hirschenfang, M.S., & Benton, J.G. (1966). Rorschach responses of paraplegic and quadriplegic patients. *Paraplegia, 4*, 40–42.

Hofer, M.A., Wolff, C.T., Friedman, S.B., & Mason, J.W. (1972). A psychoendocrine study of bereavement. Part I. 17-Hydroxycorticosteroid excretion rates of parents following death of their children from leukemia. *Psychosomatic Medicine, 34*, pp. 492–504.

Hohmann, G.W. (1975). Psychological aspects of treatment and rehabilitation of the spinal cord injured person. *Clinical Orthopaedics and Related Research, 112*, 81–88.

Holmes, M. (1975). Psychological intervention in a spinal cord injury center: An evaluation. *Rehabilitation Psychology, 22*, 179–184.

Hopkins, G. (1971). Patterns of self-destruction among the orthopedically disabled. *Rehabilitation Research and Practice Review, 3*, 5–16.

Horowitz, M.J. (1985). Disasters and psychological responses to stress. *Psychiatric Annals, 15*, 161–167.

Howell, T., Fullerton, D.T., Harvey, R.F., & Klein, M. (1981). Depression in spinal cord injured patients. *Paraplegia, 19*, 284–288.

Jackson, D.R., & Redden, J. (1978). *Adaptive vs. maladaptive denial: Treatment implications.* Paper presented at the American Congress of Rehabilitation Medicine Convention, New Orleans.

Janis, I. (1983). Preventing pathogenic denial by means of stress inoculation. In S. Breznitz (Ed.), *The denial of stress.* New York: International Universities Press, pp. 35–77.

Jochheim, K.-A. (1983). Psychological aspects of physical disability—an important point in the outcome in rehabilitation. *International Rehabilitation Medicine, 5*, 53–55.

Judd, F.R., & Burrows, G.D. (1986). Liaison psychiatry in a spinal injuries unit. *Paraplegia, 24*, 6–19.

Kalb, M. (1971). *An examination of the relationship between hospital ward behaviors and post-discharge behaviors in spinal cord injury patients.* Unpublished doctoral dissertation, University of Houston, Houston.

Karliner, W. (1978). ECT for patients with CNS disease. *Psychosomatics, 19*, 781–783.

Kathol, R.G., & Petty, F. (1981). Relationship of depression to medical illness. *Journal of Affective Disorders, 3*, 111–121.

Katon, W. (1984). Depression: Relationship to somatization and chronic medical illness. *Journal of Clinical Psychiatry, 45*, 4–17.

Katz, V., Gordon, R., Iversen, D. & Myers, S. (1978–79). Past history & degree of depression in paraplegic individuals. *Paraplegia, 16*, 8–14.

Kerns, R. (1980). *Depression following stroke: Self-evaluation, neuropsychological evaluations and laterality of lesions as predictor variables.* Unpublished doctoral dissertation, Southern Illinois University, Carbondale, IL.

Kerr, W., & Thompson, M. (1972). Acceptance of disability of sudden onset in paraplegia. *Paraplegia, 10*, 94–102.

Kinsbourne, M., & Bemporad, B. (1984). Lateralization of emotion: A model and the evidence. In N. Fox & R. Davidson (Eds.), *The psychobiology of affective development.* Hillsdale, NJ: Lawrence Erlbaum Associates.

Klerman, G.L. (1981). Depression in the medically ill. *Psychiatric Clinics of North America, 4*, 301–316.

Knights, E.B., & Folstein, M.F. (1977). Unsuspected emotional and cognitive disturbance in medical patients. *Annals of Internal Medicine, 87*, 723–724.

Krantz, D.S., & Deckel, A.W. (1983). Coping with coronary heart disease and stroke. In T.G. Burish & L.A. Bradley (Eds.), *Coping with chronic disease*. New York: Academic Press, pp. 85–112.

Krupp, N.E. (1976). Adaptation to chronic illness. *Postgraduate Medicine, 60*, 122–125.

Kubler-Ross, E. (1975). *Death, the final stage of growth*. Englewood Cliffs, NJ: Prentice-Hall, Inc.

Kwentus, J.A., Hart, R.P., Peck, E.T., & Kornstein, S. (1985). Psychiatric complications of closed head trauma. *Psychosomatics, 26*, 8–17.

LaBaw, W.L. (1969). Denial inside out: Subjective experience with anosognosia in closed head injury. *Psychiatry, 32*, 174–188.

Labi, M.L.C., Phillips, T.F., & Gresham, G.E. (1980). Psychosocial disability in physically restored long-term stroke survivors. *Archives of Physical Medicine and Rehabilitation, 61*, 561–565.

Langer, K.G., Hibbard, M.R., Egelko, S.E., & Gordon, W.A. (1984). *Depression in the physically disabled: Amputee and stroke patients*. Paper presented at American Psychological Association Convention, Toronto.

Latow, J.F. (1983). *Effectiveness of psychotherapy for stroke victims during rehabilitation*. Paper presented at the American Psychological Association Convention, Los Angeles.

Lawson, N. (1977). *Significant events in a rehabilitation center: A multilevel longitudinal approach*. Paper presented at the American Congress of Rehabilitation Medicine, Miami Beach.

Lawson, N. (1978). Significant events in the rehabilitation process: The spinal cord patient's point of view. *Archives of Physical Medicine and Rehabilitation, 59*, 573–579.

Lazarus, R.S. (1981). The stress and coping paradigm. In C. Eisdorfer, D. Cohen, A. Kleinman, & P. Maxim (Eds.), *Models for clinical psychopathology*. New York: SP Medical & Scientific Books, pp. 177–214.

Lazarus, R.S. (1983). The costs and benefits of denial. In S. Breznitz (Ed.), *The denial of stress*. New York: International Universities Press, pp. 1–30.

Lazarus, R., & Folkman, S. (1984). *Stress, appraisal and coping*. New York: Springer.

Lazarus, R., & Golden, G. (1981). The function of denial in stress, coping and aging. In J. McGaugh & S. Kiesler (Eds.), *Aging: Biology and behavior*. New York: Academic Press, pp. 283–307.

LeBaron, S., Currie, D., & Zeltzer, L. (1984). Coping with spinal cord injury in adolescence. In R. Blum (Ed.), *Chronic illness and disabilities in childhood and adolescence*. New York: Grune & Stratton, pp. 277–297.

Levin, H.S., Grossman, R.G., Rose, J.E., & Teasdale, G. (1979). Long term neuropsychological outcome of closed head injury. *Journal of Neurosurgery, 50*, 412–422.

Levine, J., & Ziegler, E. (1975). Denial and self-image in stroke, lung cancer, and heart disease patients. *Journal of Consulting and Clinical Psychology, 43*, 751–757.

Lindemann, J.E. (1981). *Psychological and behavioral aspects of physical disability*. New York: Plenum.

Lipowski, Z.J. (1983). Psychosocial reactions to physical illness. *Canadian Medical Association Journal, 128*, 1069–1072.

Lipsey, J.R., Robinson, R.G., Pearlson, G.D., Rao, K., & Price, T.R. (1983). Mood change following bilateral hemisphere brain injury. *British Journal of Psychiatry, 143*, 266–273.

Lipsey, J.R., Robinson, R.G., Pearlson, G.D., Rao, K., & Price, T.R. (1984). Nortriptyline treatment of post-stroke depression: A double blind study. *Lancet, 1*, 297–300.

Lipsey, J., Robinson, R., Pearlson, G., Rao, K., and Price, T. (1985). The dexamethasone suppression test and mood following stroke. *American Journal of Psychiatry, 142*, 318–325.

Lishman, W. (1978). *Organic psychiatry*. Oxford: Blackwell Scientific Publications.

Lloyd, G.G. (1977). Psychological reactions to physical illness. *British Journal of Hospital Medicine*, 352–358.

Lonnqvist, J., & Achte, K. (1983). Psychiatric disability and adaptation in brain-damaged patients. In E. Koranyi (Ed.), *Physical illness in the psychiatric patient*. Springfield, IL: Charles C. Thomas.

Magni, G., DeLeo, D., & Schifano, F. (1985). Depression in geriatric and adult medical inpatients. *Journal of Clinical Psychology, 41*, 337–344.

Magni, G., & Schifano, F. (1984). Psychological distress after stroke. *Journal of Neurology, Neurosurgery, and Psychiatry, 47*, 567–571.

McKinlay, W.W., Brooks, D.N., Bond, M.R., Martinage, D.P., & Marshall, M.M. (1981). The short-term outcome of severe blunt head injury as reported by relatives of the injured persons. *Journal of Neurology, Neurosurgery and Psychiatry, 44*, 527–533.

Mikula, J.A., & Rudin, J. (1983). *Outcome of severe head injury patients after head injury rehabilitation*. Paper presented at the American Congress of Rehabilitation Medicine, Boston.

Miller, I.W., & Norman, W.H. (1979). Learned helplessness in humans: A review and attribution-theory model. *Psychological Bulletin, 86*, 93–118.

Moos, R.H., & Schaefer, J.A. (1986). The crisis of physical illness. In R. Moos (Ed.), *Coping with physical illness, 2*, New York: Plenum Press, pp. 3–25.

Moos, R.H., & Tsu, V.D. (1977). The crisis of physical illness: An overview. In R. Moos (Ed.), *Coping with physical illness*. New York: Plenum Press, pp. 3–21.

Murphy, E. (1985). The impact of depression in old age on close social relationships. *American Journal of Psychiatry, 142*, 323–327.

Nathanson, M., Bergman, P.S., & Gordon, G.G. (1952). Denial of illness: Its occurrence in one hundred consecutive cases of hemiplegia. *Archives of Neurology and Psychiatry, 68*, 380–387.

Nehemkis, A., & Groot, H. (1980). Indirect self-destructive behavior in spinal cord injury. In N. Farberow (Ed.), *The many faces of suicide*. New York: McGraw-Hill Book Co., pp. 99–115.

Nemiah, J.C. (1957). The psychiatrist in rehabilitation. *Archives of Physical Medicine and Rehabilitation, 38*, 143–147.

Newman, S. (1984). The social and emotional consequences of head injury and stroke. *International Review of Applied Psychology, 33*, 427–455.

Nyquist, R. & Bors, E. (1967). Mortality and survival in traumatic myelopathy during 19 years forom 1946–1965. *International Journal of Paraplegia, 5*, 22–48.

Oradei, D.M., & Waite, N.S. (1974). Group psychotherapy with stroke patients during the immediate recovery phase. *American Journal of Orthopsychiatry, 44*, 386–395.

Orbaan, I.J.C. (1986). Psychological adjustment problems in people with traumatic spinal cord lesions. *Acta Neurochirurgica, 79*, 58–61.

Pakaslahti, A., & Achte, K. (1983). Psychiatric complications of chronic physical disease. In E. Koranyi (Ed.), *Physical illness in the psychiatric patient*. Springfield, IL: Charles C. Thomas.

Pinkerton, A.C., & Griffin, M.L. (1983). Rehabilitation outcomes in females with spinal cord injury: A follow-up study. *Paraplegia, 21*, 166–175.

Price, M. (1973). Causes of death in 11 of 227 patients with traumatic spinal cord injury over a period of 9 years. *International Journal of Paraplegia, 11*, 217–220.

Prigatano, G.P. (in press). Personality and psychosocial consequences after brain injury. In M. Meir, L. Diller, & A. Benton (Eds.), *Neuropsychological rehabilitation*. New York: Guilford Press.

Prugh, D.G., & Eckhardt, L.O. (1980). Stages and phases in the response of children and adolescents to illness or injury. *Advances in Behavioral Pediatrics, 1*, 181–194.

Ravenscroft, K. (1982). Psychiatric consultation to the child with acute physical trauma. *American Journal of Orthopsychiatry, 52*, 448–461.

Raymond, P.M., & Susset, V. (1984). *Depression in stroke: Further evidence for an organic etiology*. Paper presented at Annual Assembly of American Academy of Physical Medicine and Rehabilitation, Boston.

Redden, J., & Jackson, D.R. (1979). *Denial in spinal cord injured patients: Cognitive behavioral treatment approaches*. Paper presented at American Psychological Association Convention.

Reding, M., Orto, L., Willensky, P., et al. (1985). The dexamethasone suppression test: An indicator of depression in stroke but not a predictor of rehabilitation outcome. *Archives of Neurology, 42*, 209–212.

Richards, J.S. (1986). Psychologic adjustment to spinal cord injury during first postdischarge year. *Archives of Physical Medicine and Rehabilitation, 67*, 362–365.

Robins, A.H. (1976). Are stroke patients more depressed than other disabled subjects? *Journal of Chronic Disease, 29*, 479–482.

Robinson, R.G., Bolla-Wilson, K., Kaplan, E., Lipsey, J.R., & Price, T.R. (1986). Depression influences intellectual impairment in stroke patients. *British Journal of Psychiatry, 148*, 541–547.

Robinson, R.G., Kubos, K.L., Starr, L.B., Rao, K., & Price, T.R. (1983). Mood changes in stroke patients: Relationship to lesion location. *Comprehensive Psychiatry, 24*, 555–567.

Robinson, R.G., Kubos, K.L., Starr, L.B., Rao, K., & Price, T.R. (1984). Mood disorders in stroke patients: Importance of location of lesion. *Brain, 107*, 81–93.

Robinson, R.G., Lipsey, J.R., Bolla-Wilson, K., Bolduc, P.L., Pearlson, G.D., Rao, K., & Price, T.R. (1985). Mood disorders in left-handed stroke patients. *American Journal of Psychiatry, 142*, 1424–1429.

Robinson, R., Lipsey, J., & Price, T. (1985). Diagnosis and clinical management of post-stroke depression. *Psychosomatics, 26*, 769–778.

Robinson, R.G., & Price, T.R. (1982). Post-stroke depressive disorders: A follow-up study of 103 patients. *Stroke, 13*, 635–641.

Robinson, R.G., Starr, L., Lipsey, J.R., Rao, K., & Price, T.R. (1984). A two-year longitudinal study of post-stroke mood disorders: Dynamic changes in associated variables over the first six months of follow-up. *Stroke, 15*, 510–516.

Robinson, R.G., Starr, L.B., Lipsey, J.R., Rao, K., & Price, T.R. (1985). A two-year longitudinal study of poststroke mood disorders: In-hospital prognostic factors associated with six-month outcome. *The Journal of Nervous and Mental Disease, 173*, 221–226.

Robinson, R.G., Starr, L.B., & Price, T.R. (1984). A two year longitudinal study of mood disorders following stroke: Prevalence and duration at six months follow-up. *British Journal of Psychiatry, 144*, 256–262.

Robinson, R.G., & Szetela, B. (1981). Mood change following left hemispheric brain injury. *Annals of Neurology, 9*, 447–453.

Rodin, G., & Voshart, K. (1986). Depression in the medically ill: an overview. *American Journal of Psychiatry, 143*, 696–705.

Rosenthal, M. (1983). Behavioral sequelae. In M. Rosenthal, E. Griffith, M. Bond, & J. Miller (eds.), *Rehabilitation of the head-injured adult*, Philadelphia: F.A. Davis, pp. 197–208.

Ross, E.D. (1981). The aprosodias: Functional-anatomic organization of the affective components of language in the right hemisphere. *Archives of Neurology, 38*, 561–569.

Ross, E.D., Harney, J.H., deLacoste-Utamsing, C., & Purdy, P.D. (1981). How the brain integrates affective and propositional language into a unified behavioral function: Hypothesis based on clinicoanatomic evidence. *Archives of Neurology, 38*, 745–749.

Ross, E.D., & Rush, A. (1981). Diagnosis and neuroanatomical correlates of depression in brain-damaged patients. *Archives of General Psychiatry, 38*, 1345–1354.

Rosse, R.B., & Ciolino, C.P. (1985–86). Effects of cortical lesion location on psychiatric consultation referral for depressed stroke inpatients. *International Journal of Psychiatry in Medicine, 15*, 311–319.

Ruckdeschel-Hibbard, M. (1984). *Affect communication impairments in brain-damaged individuals.* Unpublished doctoral dissertation. New York University, New York.

Ruckdeschel-Hibbard, M., Gordon, W., & Diller, L. (1986). Affective disturbances associated with brain damage. In S. Filskov & T. Boll (Eds.), *Handbook of clinical neuropsychology, 2,* New York: John Wiley & Sons, pp. 305–337.

Russell, R.A. (1981). Concepts of adjustment to disability: An overview. *Rehabilitation Literature, 42*, 331–339.

Sakinofsky, I. (1980). Depression and suicide in the disabled. In D. Bishop (Ed.), *Behavioral problems and the disabled: Assessment and management.* Baltimore: Williams & Wilkins, pp. 17–51.

Seligman, M.E. (1975). *Helplessness.* San Francisco: W.H. Freeman and Company.

Seymour, C.T. (1955). Personality and paralysis. I. Comparative adjustment of paraplegics and quadriplegics. *Archives of Physical Medicine and Rehabilitation, 36*, 691–694.

Shadish, W.R., Hickman, D. & Arrick, M.C. (1981). Psychological problems of spinal cord injury patients: Emotional distress as a function of time and locus of control. *Journal of Consulting and Clinical Psychology, 49*, 297.

Shinar, D., Gross, C.R., Price, T.R., Banko, M., Bolduc, P.L., & Robinson, R.G. (1986). Screening for depression in stroke patients: The reliability and validity of the Center for Epidemiologic Studies depression scale. *Stroke, 17*, 241–245.

Shontz, F.C. (1977). Six principles relating disability and psychological adjustment. *Rehabilitation Psychology, 24*, 207–210.

Shontz, F.C. (1978). Psychological adjustment to physical disability: Trends in theories. *Archives of Physical Medicine and Rehabilitation, 59*, 251–254.

Shontz, F.C. (1984). Spread in response to imagined loss: An empirical analogue. *Rehabilitation Psychology, 29*, 77.

Siller, J. (1969). Psychological situation of the disabled with spinal cord injuries. *Rehabilitation Literature, 30*, 290–296.

Sinyor, D., Jacques, P., Kaloupek, D., Becker, R., Goldenberg, M., & Coopersmith, H. (1986). Poststroke depression: An attempted replication. *Brain, 109*, 537–546.

Sprock, J., & Blashfield, R. (1984). Classification and nosology. In M. Hersen & A. Bellack (Eds.), *Clinical psychology handbook.* New York: Pergamon Press.

Steger, H.G. (1976). Understanding the psychologic factors in rehabilitation. *Geriatrics, 31*, 68–73.

Stewart, T.D. (1977a). Spinal cord injury: A role for the psychiatrist. *American Journal of Psychiatry, 134*, 538–541.

Stewart, T.D. (1977b). Coping behavior and the moratorium following spinal cord injury. *Paraplegia, 15*, 338–342.

Strub, R.L., & Black, F.W. (1981). *Organic brain syndromes: An introduction to neurobehavioral disorders.* Philadelphia: F.A. Davis.

Taylor, S.E. (1983). Adjustment to threatening events: A theory of cognitive adaptation. *American Psychologist, 38,* 1161–1173.

Thompson, S.C. (1981). Will it hurt less if I can control it?—A complex answer to a simple question. *Psychological Bulletin, 90,* 89–101.

Trieschmann, R.B. (1978–79). The role of the psychologist in the treatment of spinal cord injury. *Paraplegia, 16,* 212–219.

Trieschmann, R.B. (1980). *Spinal cord injuries: Psychological, social, and vocational adjustment.* New York: Pergamon Press.

Turk, D.C., Kerns, R.D., & Rudy, T.E. (1984). *Identifying the links between chronic illness and depression: Cognitive-behavioral mediators.* Paper presented at the American Psychological Association Convention, Toronto.

Ullman, M., Ashenhurst, E.M., Hurwitz, L.J., & Gruen, A. (1960). Motivational and structural factors in the denial of hemiplegia. *Archives of Neurology, 3,* 306–318.

Vauhkonen, V. (1959). Suicide among the male disabled with war injuries to the brain. *Acta Psychiatrica et Neurologica Scandinavica, 137 (suppl.)* 90–91.

Viney, L.L., & Westbrook, M.T. (1981). Psychological reactions to chronic illness-related disability as a function of its severity and type. *Journal of Psychosomatic Research, 25,* 513–523.

Viney, L.L., & Westbrook, M.T. (1982). Patients' psychological reactions to chronic illness: Are they associated with rehabilitation? *Journal of Applied Rehabilitation Counseling, 13,* 38–44.

Viney, L.L., & Westbrook, M.T. (1984). Coping with chronic illness: Strategy preferences, changes in preference and associated emotional reactions. *Journal of Chronic Disease, 37,* 489–502.

Waller, D.A., Todress, I.D., Cassem, N.H., & Anderten, A. (1979). Coping with poor prognosis in the pediatric intensive care unit: The Cassandra prophecy. *American Journal of Diseases of Children, 133,* 212–224.

Watzlawick, P. & Coyne, J. (1980). Depression following stroke: Brief, problem-focused family treatment. *Family Process, 19,* 13–18.

Weiner, M.F., & Lovitt, R. (1979). Conservation-withdrawal versus depression. *General Hospital Psychiatry, 1,* 347–349.

Weinstein, E.A., & Kahn, R.I. (1955). *Denial of illness.* Springfield, IL: Charles C Thomas.

Weintraub, S., Mesulam, M.M., & Kramer, L. (1981). A right-hemisphere contribution to language. *Archives of Neurology, 38,* 742–744.

Weisman, A.D. (1972). *On dying and denying.* New York: Behavioral Publications.

Weisman, A.D., & Hackett, T.P. (1966). Denial as a social act. In S. Levin & R. Kahana (Eds.), *Geriatric psychiatry: Creativity, reminiscing and dying.* New York: International Universities Press, pp. 79–110.

Wepman, J.M. (1951). *Recovery from aphasia.* New York: Ronald Press Co.

Wilcox, N., & Stauffer, E. (1972). Follow-up of 423 consecutive patients admitted to the spinal cord centers, Rancho Los Amigos Hospital, 1 January to 31 December 1967. *Paraplegia, 10,* 115–122.

Wood, F., Novack, T.A., & Long, C.J. (1984). Post-concussion symptoms; Cognitive, emotional, and environmental aspects. *The International Journal of Psychiatry in Medicine, 14,* 277–283.

Wolff, C., Hofer, M., and Mason, J. (1964). Relationship between psychological defenses and mean urinary 170HCS excretion rates. *Psychosomatic Medicine, 26,* 592–609.

Wright, B. (1983). *Physical disability—a psychological approach.* New York: Harper & Row.

Chapter 6

Family Adaptation to Chronic Illness

Grady P. Bray, Ph.D.

It is a truism that the family plays a central role in the rehabilitation and social reintegration of the traumatically disabled individual (Bishop & Epstein, 1980; Mauss-Clum & Ryan, 1981; Turnblom & Myers, 1952; Versluys, 1980). During initial hospitalization, family members provide emotional support and encouragement, helping the patient maintain motivation for the arduous task of rehabilitation. Mechanic (1977, p. 83) states that the family "can become a very effective extension of the clinical team." After discharge, family members may also provide physical care, supervision, and transportation, perhaps for an indefinite period of time. In order to fulfill this supportive role, the family must overcome the turmoil and disequilibrium produced by the disabling event, thereby reconstituting itself in the process. However, family problems are often neglected to the detriment of all concerned (Lewis & Beavers, 1977).

Furthermore, there are consequences of the patient's illness for individual members of the family system (see Turk & Kerns, 1985, for discussion of the pertinent factors). Klein, Dean, and Bogdonoff (1967) and Jaffe (1978) described increased psychosomatic problems in spouses of the chronically ill, and Lezak (1978) noted the high incidence of social isolation, depression, anxiety, and fatigue among partners of brain injured patients. These ailments sabotage the family members' efforts to care for their disabled relative. Turk and Kerns (1985) list several studies that have demonstrated detrimental effects on siblings of ill children (see Fields, 1974). Clearly, it is vital to the successful rehabilitation of disabled patients that the problems of their families be addressed, understood, and managed. Indeed, Gans (1983) proposes that, in rehabilitation, the family unit, not merely the afflicted individual, should be viewed as the "patient."

Power and Dell Orto (1980a) specify four general goals of intervention with families of disabled patients:

1. *Providing the family with a sense of competence:* Family members must feel capable of managing the multiple crises that confront them.

171

2. *Facilitating normalization of family relations, including those involving the patient-member:* Families need to be helped to avoid "over adjusting"; maintenance of some degree of premorbid functioning sustains stability.
3. *Renewing the family's awareness of its strengths and resources:* Doing so provides some balance to the natural tendency to focus on losses and obstacles to adjustment.
4. *Creating a corrective, supportive atmosphere in which family needs and feelings are recognized and acknowledged:* Free expression and acceptance of the various and conflicting feelings foster a sense of mutuality and cohesion within the family.

As Power and Dell Orto note, each intervention may be directed to additional goals, as well, but these four goals form an essential core applicable to all cases.

This chapter presents a conceptual framework for understanding common effects of disabling conditions on the family system. (Specific phenomena associated with particular disabling illnesses are discussed in Chapters 1–4; also see Kerns & Curley, 1985.) Certain therapeutic intervention strategies follow logically from this model. The proposed scheme provides a useful framework for discussing family reactions to chronic illness; however, it is not a description of the necessary or ideal response, a deviation from which signals maladjustment. It is vital that rehabilitation clinicians employ this or any other model with caution, remembering at all times the complexities and idiosyncrasies of individual family constellations.

The model described below has much in common with the formulations of other authors (e.g., Fink, 1967; Horowitz, 1985; Kubler-Ross, 1969, Shontz, 1973) who have examined how individuals react to crisis. The salient common characteristic is the postulation of phases (stages) through which the organism (individual or family) passes in the attempt to re-establish homeostasis after crisis. Unfortunately, many exponents of the stage approach have proposed a linear progression from one phase to another. Although this idea has a simplistic appeal, it lacks empirical verification and can distort clinical judgment (see Chapter 5). As Bugen (1977) among others has noted, stages tend to blend at the boundaries, and the sequence, intensity, and duration of stages are quite variable. Although families may manifest similarities in the adaptation process and comparable critical points frequently appear, some families arrest, regress, skip phases, or become trapped in a repetitive cycle. Thus, in order to describe reality more adequately, a number of loops and regressive routes are included. Again, the model should be viewed as a heuristic device, not a blueprint for adaptation.

Finally, the author must emphasize an important, if obvious, point. Although this chapter discusses "the family" as a unit, families are composed of individuals, each of whom may exhibit a unique course of adjustment (Bicknell, 1983). Indeed, a common cause of intrafamilial stress is a sort of "asynchrony of adaptation'' among its members. However, because families do function as units, particularly in interactions with the health care system, it is valuable to employ this perspective, albeit in a flexible fashion.

Figure 6–1 depicts the course and options for families as they move through the Family Adaptation System (FAS). Critical decision points, represented by a

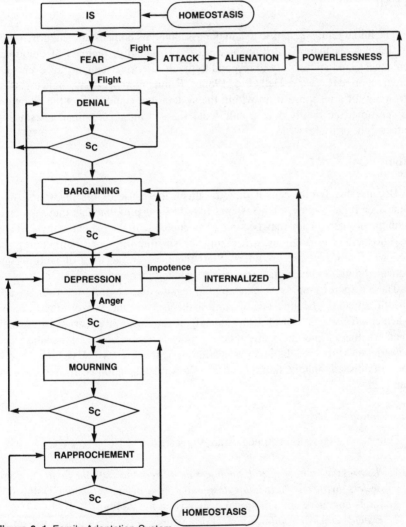

Figure 6–1 Family Adaptation System

Source: From *A Stroke Family Guide and Resource* (p. 125) by G. Bray and G. Clark (Eds.), 1984, Springfield, Ill.: Charles C Thomas Publisher. Copyright 1984 by Charles C Thomas Publisher. Reprinted by permission.

diamond shape, most often result from repeated confrontation (S_C = stimulus confrontation) with effects from the initial stimulus (IS), i.e., stroke, head injury, diagnosis of multiple sclerosis, etc. Directional arrows represent commonly observed options exercised by families at critical decision points.

FEAR

The initial family response to a major assault on its homeostatic integrity—that is, trauma—is fear. Confusion or a sense of unreality, feelings of emotional numbness, and an inability to respond to the disorienting sequence of events are often reported (Power & Dell Orto, 1980b). Family members may come together, grasping for a response from within the system that could correct the situation. Given time, the family does usually coalesce and muster a unified response of either fight or flight.

Fight

Because the family cannot directly attack the cause of the disruption—the illness or injury—they often respond by attacking professionals they associate with the problem. They may become preoccupied with the patient's physical and psychosocial environment, criticizing the surroundings and denouncing the actions of primary care providers. Staff members are accused of ignoring the patient, providing inadequate treatment, or being incompetent.

These responses represent an attempt to regain some control over a strange and chaotic situation. Feeling out of control themselves, the family may question whether *anyone* is in control. Unfortunately, assuming an adversarial posture only alienates them from the staff; this, in turn, fosters a sense of isolation and powerlessness that results in an escalation of aggressiveness. A vicious cycle is thus established, and the family's progress toward adaptation is arrested before it can begin.

Intervention

Four basic intervention strategies are suggested.

1. *Restrict the number of staff members having contact with the family to three or less, with one individual designated as a primary liaison.* Doing this limits cognitive and emotional demands on the family.
2. *Provide consistent information.* For a variety of reasons families often feel that they have received conflicting information about the patient's condition and prognosis (Mechanic, 1977). This perception may result from differences in the disciplinary perspectives or the time at which assessments

were made. Also, persons under stress may not fully comprehend or retain complex, threatening, and unwanted facts; there may be a selective "gating" process, in which only positive, or merely the least negative, statements of staff are heard and believed. Whatever the cause, families that believe they are being given conflicting information quickly lose faith in those caring for their injured relative. Mauss-Clum and Ryan (1981) found that families of brain injured patients almost unanimously rated "receiving a clear explanation" as their top priority at the time of injury. Mathis (1984) reported that the majority of "need statements" endorsed by families of critically ill patients pertained to matters of information. Power and Sax (1978) provide a useful discussion of aspects of communicating information to families of neurologically impaired individuals.

3. *Orient the family to the patient's location in time and space.* The size and maze-like structure of modern hospitals can be intimidating. Family members may be reassured by simply being told precisely where they, as well as the patient, are physically located. Although the family may not initially know where "Room 310A in the X-ray Department" is, it is a name they can use for orientation purposes. It is also helpful, when possible, to inform the family about the amount of time the patient is expected to spend at each location. Temporal perspective is often distorted under stress; brief intervals may seem endless. Relatives may become upset and agitated if tests and procedures seem to be taking unreasonably long periods of time. Providing spatial and temporal anchors can reduce the family's anxiety during the patient's absence.

4. *Provide support and an opportunity for family members to express their feelings.* It is usually helpful for staff members to assist relatives in understanding and managing the intense and volatile emotions they are experiencing. They must be allowed and encouraged to express their apprehensions and explore their fears. They need reassurance that virtually all reactions are understandable and permissible, including anger at the disabled patient (Epperson, 1977). Lezak's (1978) excellent guidelines for dealing with families of the brain injured patient are applicable to families dealing with other disabilities.

A final intervention tactic, not specifically directed at the family but one that works to its benefit, is to assist staff members to maintain perspective and some degree of distance from the family's turmoil. Reminding staff members of the roots of the family's overt hostility can help them avoid personalizing those assaults and responding in kind.

Flight

Although it is rarely the case that a family abandons a patient, many exercise an emotional flight response, withdrawing from the intensity of the accident or illness. This "pulling away" produces increased levels of guilt and anxiety, but also may serve to free certain emotional resources for use in coping.

Some families exhibit a modified flight response that could be characterized as avoidance. These families, if they visit the hospital at all, tend to do so at odd hours and therefore rarely encounter the patient's caregivers. Frequently, these families are suspicious of hospitals, viewing them as places where people go to die or as the lairs of intrusive social workers. They may regard the hospital with awe, superstition, anger, or mistrust. Essential facts, such as the patient's medical history or insurance information, may be withheld.

Intervention

When a family exhibits the flight response, it is advisable to engage the assistance of someone who has worked with the family before the occurrence of the presenting medical problem. This individual can also provide valuable information about how the family has historically reacted to stress.

The fear phase, although frightening and emotionally dislocating, is important to the family because it serves to mobilize and energize it. Although some families use this energy combatively to perpetuate the fight, most exhibit a continuing flight to denial.

DENIAL

As the immediate effects of the traumatic events begin to dissipate, the family adopts a defensive posture characterized by denial. In order to ward off feelings of devastation and to maintain hope for recovery, the family asserts: "In a couple of days we're sure Mom is going to be fine," or "He has hurt his back, but it will heal and he'll walk out of here." Such statements as these reveal a tacit acknowledgment of the fact of the injury or illness. However, it is the significance of the condition that is denied. By exhibiting denial, the family may be expressing uncertainty about whether it can continue to function in the changed circumstances. As Fordyce (1982) has noted, family members do not yet know what lies ahead and have difficulty imagining a future that includes caring for a chronically disabled member.

This type of denial differs from the florid disavowal of symptoms that has been described in brain injured patients (Weinstein & Kahn, 1955); rather, it resembles the tactic of "minimization" noted by Lipowski (1970). Viewed in this way, denial is a temporarily adaptive mechanism that allows the family and patient to avoid disintegration.

Power (1985) reported that positively adjusted families of multiple sclerosis patients felt that early denial facilitated adjustment by "cushioning" the shock of the initial diagnosis. When perpetuated, however, denial becomes destructive.

(See Romano, 1974, for discussion of the consequences of protracted denial in families of head injured patients.)

A particularly difficult management problem occurs when some family members—usually the parents or spouse—cling tenaciously to patently unrealistic expectations after other relatives have relinquished them. Accusations of abandonment, irresponsibility, and lack of faith then become common.

Intervention

Many staff members feel compelled to confront the family with current facts and long-range implications of the patient's disability. This strategy subverts the basic gain that denial affords the family: a temporary sense of control and distance from an overwhelming situation. Many families use this time constructively to reallocate roles and functions—adjustments that are avowed to be minor and temporary. A forced confrontation with grim reality tends to exacerbate the family's defensive retreat, further entrench them in their unrealistic hopes, and increase their isolation.

The most fruitful strategy at this point is one that acknowledges the family's hopes for the patient's ultimate recovery, neither reinforcing nor aggressively contradicting them. Epperson (1977, p. 269) suggests such statements as the following: "John was such a healthy boy. It must be difficult for you to believe that he is now paralyzed." This statement conveys understanding of the enormity of the family's struggle, confusion, and disbelief; however, it also incorporates a reiteration of the central fact of disability. A primary goal at this point is to avoid outright antagonism, thereby maintaining open lines of communication with the family that will be required at a later date.

With the passage of time and the persistence of the disabling condition, denial becomes progressively less tenable, and the family must choose one of two routes: (1) regression to fear or (2) progression to bargaining.

BARGAINING

The bargaining family devises a tacit agreement or contract that specifies what the family will do in order for the patient to recover. A common example is the family whose members come to the hospital every day to assist with the patient's care or rehabilitation therapies. Such families are extremely cooperative, if occasionally overbearing. They often extend their concern to other patients in the unit. The family's compliance and solicitousness are the price they have agreed to pay in return for the patient's recovery. Bargaining represents a major advance over denial by virtue of the family's concrete acknowledgment that a problem of major significance exists. In the absence of this recognition, there is no need for bargains to be developed.

Staff members are generally relieved to see families enter this phase. Few staff-family conflicts occur, and staff members may be seduced into believing that the patient and family have adjusted well. Attention to the needs of the family may therefore be prematurely discontinued.

Intervention

Bargaining is an ideal time for counseling and family education (Bray & Clark, 1984; Diehl, 1983). Families are eminently receptive to advice and teaching about the patient's condition and care, because they believe that by their compliance they are "fulfilling their part of the bargain."

With the passage of time, the family recognizes that the bargain will not be fulfilled by the other party (God, the rehabilitation team); improvement will occur, but not cure. The family may therefore feel cheated or deceived. A critical decision point has been reached. The family's options include (1) complete regression to fear, (2) less severe regression to denial, or (3) entry into depression.

DEPRESSION

As their attempts at bargaining fail, the family's acknowledgment of reality must come to incorporate not only the fact of the patient's disability but also its long-range significance. The recognition that the patient and therefore the family will never be the same has a depressing effect. It is at this point that families and patients are most frequently referred for psychological services.

Depression has been defined as anger turned inward. Families that internalize their anger are usually quiet, withdrawn, and physically passive. Their earlier interest in learning about the patient's disability and how to provide care tends to dissolve. Diminished affect, poor appetite, and sleep disturbance may also be noted. Depressed families usually refuse to join in activities with the families of other patients and spend a great deal of time alone. Family members often have difficulty identifying the problems they are experiencing, lamenting, "I just don't know. It's everything and nothing. There is really no problem except for Dad's stroke."

A few families deal with their depression through open expressions of anger. Occasionally the attack is directed at the injured relative; however, this produces terrible feelings of guilt and escalates conflict within the family system. Therefore, family members must seek alternate targets, often finding them among the very staff members that the family knows are committed to providing care for the patient. One or two especially vulnerable staff members may bear the brunt of the family's attack.

Intervention

At this point the emotion at the core of depression —anger—must be addressed. Family members should be prompted to express themselves on sensitive issues, such as their feelings about the patient, concerns about future burdens, and mistrust of staff members. This direct confrontation of submerged issues is often highly volatile, and considerable affect can be elicited. This approach carries certain risks and must only be undertaken by adequately trained individuals. Periodically the therapist must remind the family that a technique is being employed in order to help them articulate and address their feelings. As in earlier phases, staff members may again need to be told not to take the comments of depressed family members personally. They should also be reminded of the important role they can play at this point by serving as "friendly ears."

It is the author's experience that few families regress further than depression once they have reached this point. Most progress from the nebulous sadness of depression to mourning.

MOURNING

Families now enter a quiescent phase during which they begin to identify specific losses and relinquish unrealistic expectations. They are now fully coming to grips with the long-term implications of disability. A veil of sorrow shrouds the family, and crying is frequently observed. Staff members may misinterpret this behavior as a sign of depression. It is not. The depressed family reports feeling overwhelmed, but is vague about the cause. By contrast, the mourning family can usually name and discuss specific losses, e.g., a husband whose eagerly antici-pated retirement will now be radically different because of the stroke; a son whose promising athletic career has been ended because of a spinal cord injury.

The family now stands on the threshold of reconstruction. Old family beliefs, roles, and myths are no longer tenable, but new ones have not yet been established. In the process of rebuilding the system, it is not uncommon for family members to exclude the injured relative, whose future role is the most uncertain, by failing to offer that individual a role and the challenges that accompany it for fear of causing further pain, embarrassment, and shame. The intent may be simply to relieve the patient of mundane concerns that it is feared may cause stress and relapse (Leventhal, Leventhal, & Nguyen, 1985). This misguided overprotectiveness impedes the patient's recovery and fosters excessive dependence (Kinsella & Duffy, 1980; Turk, Meichenbaum, & Genest, 1983). Many families express surprise and chagrin when confronted with this interpretation. Most, however, can modify their behavior accordingly.

Intervention

Staff members can facilitate the mourning process by encouraging the family to work together to identify problems that significantly affect the family as a whole. They are instructed to develop a hierarchy of problems in terms of significance and to address the most trivial ones first. Team members should merely observe and aid communication within the family, helping them to arrive at their own decisions. In this way, the family develops a sense of its own ability to handle difficult situations.

RAPPROCHEMENT

After the necessary task of mourning, the family completes the work of reconstructing the family system, incorporating the fact and implications of the disabled member's condition. New expectations and functions for each participant are defined as the family comes to crystallize its new conception of itself. In most cases, families striving for rapprochement no longer have much contact with the hospital or rehabilitation setting. Thus, staff members will have scant opportunity to see their interventions come to fruition.

It is not until this phase that the patient/family member is reintegrated into the family system, with new expectations held regarding the contributions they can make. The individual is no longer viewed as a patient, but as a relative who has sustained an illness or injury. This change in the family's perspective enhances the self-esteem of the disabled member, diminishes the burdens on the rest of the family, and permits establishment of a new homeostasis.

Intervention

Rapprochement by definition derives from the efforts of the family itself and as such requires no specific intervention from outside resources, although community support groups, such as the stroke groups organized by the American Heart Association, may be helpful (Gussow & Tracy, 1976). For most families, time alone provides the essential drive for completion of the accommodation process.

CONCLUSION

A number of factors affect the amount of time each family requires to achieve accommodation, including the duration and prognosis of the presenting medical problem, the magnitude of the patient's disability, and the coping strengths and styles of the family as a whole, as well as of its individual members. For example, the author found that most families with a spinal cord injured member required an average of 2 years to achieve a new homeostasis, whereas those coping with a major stroke required approximately half that period of time (Bray, 1977). One of the beneficial by-products of extended follow-up of rehabilitation patients is the possibility it affords for the treating team to gain a more accurate perspective on the lengthy course of adjustment.

Families confronting uncertain diagnoses or prognoses, such as multiple sclerosis or Alzheimer's disease, may arrest at critical points, progressing only when a major change occurs in the patient's medical status (Power, 1985; Ware & Carper, 1982). In such families, worsening of the patient's condition can precipitate what the author has termed "reflux"; that is, regression to an earlier phase, usually depression or mourning, followed by a somewhat more rapid recapitulation of the succeeding stages (Bray, 1978). Reflux may also be precipitated if it becomes necessary for the patient to be institutionalized (Montgomery, 1983).

Chronic disability is a family affair, and its effects are multiple and pervasive. The rehabilitation team can facilitate the disabled individual's immediate and long-term adjustment by careful observation and judicious intervention with the patient's family.

REFERENCES

Bicknell, J. (1983). The psychopathology of handicap. *British Journal of Medical Psychology, 56*, 167-178.

Bishop, D., & Epstein, N. (1980). Family problems and disability. In D. Bishop (Ed.), *Behavioral problems and the disabled*. Baltimore: Williams & Wilkins, pp. 337–364.

Bray, G. (1977). Reactive patterns in families of the severely disabled. *Rehabilitation Counseling Bulletin, 20*, 236–239.

Bray, G. (1978). Rehabilitation of spinal cord-injured: A family approach. *Journal of Applied Rehabilitation Counseling, 9*, 70–78.

Bray, G., & Clark, G. (Eds.) (1984). *A stroke family guide and resource*. Springfield, IL: Charles C Thomas.

Bugen, L. (1977). Human grief: A model for prediction and intervention. *American Journal of Orthopsychiatry, 47*, 196–206.

Diehl, L. (1983). Patient-family education. In M. Rosenthal, E. Griffith, M. Bond, & J. Miller (Eds.), *Rehabilitation of the head injured adult*. Philadelphia: F.A. Davis, pp. 395–406.

Epperson, M. (1977). Families in sudden crisis: Process and intervention in a critical care center. *Social Work in Health Care, 2*, 265–273.

Fields, G. (1974). Social implications of long-term illness in children. In J. Downey & N. Low (Eds.), *The child with disabling illness*. Philadelphia: W.B. Saunders, pp. 541–557.

Fink, S. (1967). Crisis and motivation: A theoretical model. *Archives of Physical Medicine and Rehabilitation, 48*, 592–597.

Fordyce, W. (1982). Psychological assessment and management. In F. Kottke, G. Stillwell, & J. Lehmann (Eds.), *Krusen's handbook of physical medicine and rehabilitation*. Philadelphia: W.B. Saunders.

Gans, J. (1983). Psychosocial adaptation. *Seminars in Neurology, 3*, 201–211.

Gussow, Z., & Tracy, G. (1976). The role of self-help clubs in adaptation to chronic illness and disability. *Social Science and Medicine, 10*, 407–414.

Horowitz, M. (1985). Disaster and psychological response to stress. *Psychiatric Annals, 15*, 161–167.

Jaffe, D. (1978). The role of family therapy in treating physical illness. *Hospital and Community Psychiatry, 29*, 169–174.

Kerns, R., & Curley, A. (1985). A biopsychosocial approach to illness and the family: Neurological diseases across the life span. In D. Turk & R. Kerns (Eds.), *Health, illness and families: A life-span perspective*. New York: John Wiley & Sons, pp. 146–182.

Kinsella, G., & Duffy, F. (1980). Attitudes towards disability expressed by spouses of stroke patients. *Scandinavian Journal of Rehabilitation Medicine, 12*, 73–76.

Klein, R., Dean, A., & Bogdonoff, M. (1967). The impact of illness upon the spouse. *Journal of Chronic Disease, 20*, 241–248.

Kubler-Ross, E. (1969), *On death and dying*. New York: MacMillan & Co.

Leventhal, H., Leventhal, E., & Nguyen, T. (1985). Reactions of families to illness: Theoretical models and perspectives. In D. Turk & R. Kerns (Eds.) *Health, illness and families: A life-span perspective*. New York: John Wiley & Sons, pp. 108–145.

Lewis, J., & Beavers, W. (1977). The family of the patient. In G. Usdin (Ed.), *Psychiatric medicine*. New York: Brunner/Mazel, pp. 401–424.

Lezak, M. (1978). Living with the characterologically altered brain-injured patient. *Journal of Clinical Psychiatry, 9*, 592–598.

Lipowski, Z. (1970). Physical illness, the individual and the coping process. *Psychiatric Medicine, 1*, 91–101.

Mathis, M. (1984). Personal needs of family members of critically ill patients with and without acute brain injury. *Journal of Neurosurgical Nursing, 16*, 37–44.

Mauss-Clum, N., & Ryan, M. (1981). Brain injury and the family. *Journal of Neurosurgical Nursing, 13*, 165–169.

Mechanic, D. (1977). Illness behavior, social adaptation and medical models. *Journal of Nervous and Mental Diseases, 165*, 79–89.

Montgomery, R. (1983). Staff-family relations and institutional care policies. *Journal of Gerontological Social Work, 6*, 25–37.

Power, P. (1985). Family coping behaviors in chronic illness: A rehabilitation perspective. *Rehabilitation Literature, 46*, 78–83.

Power, P., & Dell Orto, A. (1980a). Approaches to family intervention. In P. Power & A. Dell Orto (Eds.), *Role of the family in the rehabilitation of the physically disabled*. Baltimore: University Park Press, pp. 321–330.

Power, P., & Dell Orto, A. (1980b). General impact of adult disability/illness on the family. In P. Power & A. Dell Orto (Eds.), *Role of the family in the rehabilitation of the physically disabled*. Baltimore: University Park Press, pp. 145–151.

Power, P., & Sax, D. (1978). The communication of information to the neurological patient: Some implications for family coping. *Journal of Chronic Disease, 31*, 57–65.

Romano, M. (1974). Family response to traumatic head injury. *Scandinavian Journal of Rehabilitation Medicine, 6*, 1–4.

Shontz, F. (1973). Severe chronic illness. In J. Garrett & E. Levine (Eds.), *Rehabilitation practices with the physically disabled*. New York: Columbia University Press, pp. 410–445.

Turk, D., & Kerns, R. (Eds.) (1985). *Health, illness and families: A life-span perspective*. New York: John Wiley & Sons.

Turk, D., Meichenbaum, D., & Genest, M. (1983). *Pain and behavioral medicine: A cognitive-behavioral perspective*. New York: Guilford Press.

Turnblom, M., & Myers, J. (1952). Group discussion programs with the families of aphasic patients. *Journal of Speech Hearing Disorders, 17,* 393–396.

Versluys, H. (1980). Physical rehabilitation and family dynamics. *Rehabilitation Literature 1,* 58–65,

Ware, L., & Carper, M. (1982). Living with Alzheimer disease patients: Family stresses and coping mechanisms. *Psychotherapy: Theory, Research and Practice 9,* 472–481.

Weinstein, E., & Kahn, R. (1955). *Denial of illness*. Springfield, IL: Charles C Thomas.

Chapter 7

Facilitating Staff/Patient Interaction in Rehabilitation

Jerome S. Gans, M.D.

This chapter describes a novel technique to facilitate staff/patient interaction in an acute physical rehabilitation setting. The technique, a hybrid of consultation and liaison psychiatry, is called the Team Attended Psychological Interview (TAPI). As the name implies, the salient feature is the presence of the treatment team while the patient is being interviewed. This approach is employed in situations of *major* staff/patient conflict; most psychiatric consultations are performed in the traditional patient-oriented model (Hengeveld & Rooymans, 1983). The author has previously described this form of consultation in a cardiac care unit (Gans, 1979).

The acute physical rehabilitation setting has many distinctive features that give rise to staff/patient conflict. After reviewing these components and the importance of making the staff rather than the patient the locus of psychological intervention, this chapter discusses the format, rationale, and content of the TAPI and the reasons why staff request this intervention. The next section addresses three categories of recurrent staff/patient difficulties: non-disability-related, disability-related, and those where a disability is superimposed on pre-existing character pathology. The final section reviews major teaching concepts employed in the TAPI.

SOURCES OF STAFF/PATIENT CONFLICT

Five factors account for the inevitable staff/patient conflicts in a rehabilitation setting: (1) the intrinsic differences between staff members and patients, (2) the nature of the rehabilitation hospital setting, (3) the phenomenology of catastrophe, (4) staff members' insufficient psychological training, and (5) the goal-oriented nature of rehabilitation.

Rehabilitation staff members and patients live in very different worlds. The candidate for rehabilitation is a person who has just suffered an irreversible loss

The author acknowledges the helpful comments of Drs. Anne Alonso, Daniel Asnes, and John Romano and the editorial assistance of Bruce Caplan, Ph.D., with the manuscript.

and will never again be, to self and others, the same person. This profound loss produces a deep narcissistic wound. Cherished beliefs about oneself—physical indestructibility, enduring beauty, and everlasting lovableness—are dealt a harsh blow. The person responds with numbness, disbelief, anger, and a frightening sense of loss of control (Gans, 1983b). Self-esteem declines because patients are deprived of their usual sources of self-esteem: work, health, and feeling loving and lovable.

Team members differ in important ways from the patients for whom they care. They are young, healthy, in control, and goal-oriented and often take these qualities for granted. Bombarded by disasters that have befallen their patients, staff members often retreat from these tragedies and, as a result, underestimate their patients' suffering. Even when they truly wish to understand what the patient is experiencing, they discover the limits of empathy.

A rehabilitation setting is unlike an acute hospital. Accustomed to the dependent care of the acute facility, patients may initially be baffled by the rehabilitation team's goal of maximal patient independence. As a result, they may conclude that staff members are misguided and/or sadistic. With most of their time scheduled for them, patients feel that they are continually being told what to do, and to make matters worse, that they are not measuring up to the task. As with castor oil, these decrees are swallowed reluctantly. In contrast, the choices that rehabilitation patients do have, while monumental, are less visible. Although told when and how much therapy they are to have, patients "decide" how much energy to expend, how they will view their situation, and, ultimately, whether to give up or persevere. Patients are extremely sensitive to the degree to which the decision-making power they retain is acknowledged and respected by their caregivers.

The catastrophe that attends disability can complicate staff/patient interactions in three ways. First, the mesmerizing effect of catastrophic illness can create the illusion that everything that follows the catastrophe results from it. It may seem that the patient and the family did not exist before the disability. Yet, if one examines the history, one finds with surprising frequency family conflict, which often becomes the source of the most intractable postcatastrophe problems. Unfortunately, insufficient attention is often paid to the nature of this pre-existing conflict, and an indispensable aid for dealing with postcatastrophe events is lost. In a similar vein, the history of the patient and family relationships often reveal considerable strengths that can be employed in the rehabilitation process. Second, because the victim ordinarily elicits sympathetic feelings from staff members, those family members who seem inadequately attentive may be viewed in an unfavorable light. If precipitous judgments are made, the opportunity to learn about the family and how it has functioned is sacrificed. Certain that they already "know," some staff members feel they have no further incentive to learn about the patient and family. These premature clinical judgments inhibit the spirit of clinical inquiry. Third, in the midst of catastrophe, usual coping mechanisms are insufficient. For example, families that, under normal circumstances, cope and communicate in the "good" range find they must function at an "excellent" level in order to sustain a precatastrophe level of integration (Bishop, 1983). Families that are unable to adapt appear less competent than usual, even though they are trying hard and doing the best they can. When such efforts are demeaned or not recognized by staff members, family resentment may erupt in staff/patient or staff/family conflict.

Rehabilitation staff members deal with powerful psychological feelings, yet most are not trained to deal conceptually with these forces. Unaware of transference phenomena, they may misjudge their importance or significance to the patient. They may not understand how the patient actually experiences them: as a disappointing daughter, unresponsive son, or benevolent father. Unaware that patients, and people in general, tend to believe their projections, some staff members may earnestly believe, despite massive evidence to the contrary, that if only they try harder or act differently, they can change the patient or the patient's perception of them. Unfortunately, a patient's opinions of staff behavior have more to do with the patient's present regressed condition or past experience than with the staff member's actual behavior. Yet, when staff behaviors actually do provoke, inhibit, or enhance patients' reactions, staff members are often unaware of this fact.

Rehabilitation staff members are extremely goal-oriented and often experience patients' achievements of these goals as evidence of their own competence. In the process they unwittingly assign to patients the task of preserving their self-esteem. More importantly, staff members may overlook what their patients need most: unconditional acceptance of them as people, independent of their performance in therapy. The rehabilitation team members therefore have the difficult clinical task of being invested enough in achievement of goals to teach, motivate, and encourage their patients, but not so much that the focus on performance supersedes the appreciation of individual worth.

LOCUS OF PSYCHOLOGICAL INTERVENTION

The following analysis argues that the most important target of mental health intervention for resolving major staff/patient conflict in a rehabilitation setting is the staff, not the patient. This intervention is primarily educative in nature and serves to enhance the staff members' psychological sophistication, thereby enabling them to interact more therapeutically with their patients.

An important aspect of rehabilitation settings has received insufficient attention: Staff members, especially nonmental health specialists, spend enormous amounts of time just talking with patients and families. This time is not formally conceptualized as part of therapy, although it may be considered to constitute "provision of emotional support,'' a continuing process in rehabilitation. Unfortunately, nonmental health staff rarely have received sufficient psychological training to prepare them to offer their patients something of value from "just talking."

The nonmental health team members are logical candidates to take the lead in providing emotional support, for they have a special relationship with patients. They are the ones who are with the patients as they learn again how to walk, talk, eat, dress, and even urinate and defecate. To patients, these nonmental health members are surrogate family and, as a result, are heir to the powerful feelings that exist between parent and child. Even if it were possible to assign a mental health member to counsel each patient in depth, given the nature of the rehabilitation process, patients would select from the team the members they most trust and wish to confide in. Those team members selected would only infrequently be part of the mental health team. Clearly, it would be valuable to find a mechanism by which the psychological skills of the nonmental health members of the team could be increased sufficiently so that the "talking" component of rehabilitation therapy would have therapeutic value.

This need for psychological training is underscored by comparing the rehabilitation staff's role and the patient population it treats with those in other hospital settings. In acute medical settings the length of stay is short, and becoming shorter; the approach is predominantly biomedical—disease rather than illness-oriented; and the therapy is performed *on* or *for* patients, rather than *with* them. The therapeutic alliance is not so crucial because proper diagnosis and treatment usually lead to improvement and because the relationship between the patient and caregiver is short-lived. In a psychiatric hospital, where psychosocial problems are the focus of treatment, staff are well trained to deal with these problems. In addition, psychiatric staff members have the luxury of treating people who, although disturbed, are usually physically intact. Rehabilitation staff, in contrast, work over extended periods with physically devastated patients who are suffering profound psychological disturbances. These disturbances are either a natural reaction to extreme conditions or unrecognized pre-existing psychopathology or both (Gans, 1981). Maintaining a healthy therapeutic alliance with regressed, sad, disappointed, hateful (Gans, 1983a), humiliated, impatient, indecisive, angry, critical, and sometimes psychotic patients requires psychological understanding and skill that may not be possessed by many rehabilitation staff (Gunther, 1977).

TEAM ATTENDED PSYCHOLOGICAL INTERVIEW

The Team Attended Psychological Interview (TAPI) is a psychiatric consultation-liaison procedure directed at helping staff members deal more effectively with this task while at the same time giving patients needed support and input in their own care. Participation in the TAPI also serves to educate staff members about psychological and psychiatric concepts that are pertinent to their work.

The TAPI involves psychiatric intervention with both the patient and rehabilitation team; it introduces a novel feature to consultation-liaison work in that the rehabilitation team (consultee) is present during the psychiatric interview (McKegney & Beckhardt, 1982).

TAPIs are requested when, through daily clinical activity, the team identifies certain patients with whom it has particular difficulty. Once alerted by the team, the psychiatrist approaches the patient with the following standardized introduction:

> I am Dr. X, a psychiatrist and a consultant to the team. The team—the physical therapist, occupational therapist, nurse, physician, social worker, speech therapist—working with you is planning to hold a meeting about you that you are invited to attend. Your attendance is purely elective. We are holding this meeting for three reasons: (1) to understand better what it is like for you to be a patient in a rehabilitation hospital, (2) to understand you better as a person—not just a stroke (spinal cord injury, amputation, brain injury) patient, and (3) to give me an opportunity to teach members of the team more about talking with patients in helpful ways.

Patients are given a real choice whether they wish to participate in the meeting. Showing respect for the patient's right to choose is in itself a powerful communication to the patient. Further, the way in which the individual makes the decision quite often constitutes important psychological data, either about the patient's premorbid personality, feelings toward the hospital, present mental status, or an idiosyncratic understanding of the meeting's purpose, regardless of what has actually been explained. For the patient who decides to attend, a fuller, more genuine sense of participation in the rehabilitation process results.

The TAPI has three parts. In the preinterview discussion biopsychosocial data are presented by the internist, neurologist, and social worker, and all team members are encouraged to tell what it is like to work with the patient and how the patient makes them feel. They are asked such questions as, "What will you remember most about this patient in 6 months?" Staff members are told that attending a TAPI is a fringe benefit of working at the hospital, because it provides the privilege of learning how an overwhelmed person copes with devastating loss. The notion that the patient has something to teach is stressed; interest in and acceptance of this "gift" are understood as a sign of respect for the patient.

The second part of the TAPI is the patient interview. Patients are initially asked what they understand to be the purpose of the meeting. The psychiatrist facilitates whatever story the patient wishes to tell and provides empathy and support. For example, the patient is encouraged to describe his or her childhood, work, military experience, or marriage. A mental status exam is performed when indicated. If the patient's family attends the TAPI, interactions among family members are facilitated and treated as data. At the end of the 20–30 minute interview, the patient is asked if he or she has any questions for the interviewer; with the patient's permission, any team member may ask questions.

The patient then leaves the room, and the third portion of the TAPI, the postinterview discussion, takes place. Here an attempt is made to identify the psychological data of the interview, to organize them, make formulations, and translate these into suggestions to be incorporated into the treatment plan. Psychological data include the patient's actual idea of the purpose of the meeting compared to what he or she was told; the first and last things the patient said in the interview; the patient's ability to remember important dates; significant omissions; important biographical data; the point in the interview where the patient showed the most feeling; dimensions of the patient previously unknown to the team that surfaced during the interview; feelings stirred up in team members; how the patient related to the group, as well as to the interviewer; an assessment whether the relationship between the interviewer and patient became closer, stayed the same, or grew more distant during the interview.

While observing the patient interview, members of the rehabilitation team may note that the patient presents in a much different manner than they have found the patient to act with them. They may now ask, ''Could our behavior with the patient in some way be preventing certain dimensions of the patient from being expressed and encouraging selective expression of others?'' Increasing staff members' self-consciousness in this manner is important because caregivers may frequently be unaware of how they provoke, enhance, or inhibit what patients reveal about themselves. Participant-observation in the TAPI teaches rehabilitation team members that different ways of interacting with the patient can elicit strikingly different responses.

The TAPI greatly aids the psychiatrist or mental health consultant in several ways. The preinterview discussion provides an extremely rich exchange of clinical vignettes from which emerges a portrait of the patient that the consultant would have been hard pressed to gather alone. A further advantage is the presence of the team during the interview, in contrast to an individual consultation, where the consultants must rely only on their own powers of observation. The presentation of the psychiatrist's interviewing skills to the other team members serves to demystify the process and to diminish the psychiatrist as the object of idealization or denigration. The TAPI also provides an excellent opportunity to teach staff members experientially about the nature of psychological data. So often, team members begin to make formulations about what the psychological data mean— even before agreeing about what they consist of. The aim here is to encourage the team to continue to accumulate data and to avoid premature judgments or conclusions about patients.

TAPI Subjects

Over an 8-year period—1975 through 1983—107 TAPIs were performed. Fifty-five percent of the patients were women, and the mean age was 53 years. Age categories included (1) less than 35 years—18.7 percent, (2) between 35–65 years—55.1 percent, and (3) over 65 years—26.2 percent. Fifty-one percent of the patients were living alone—single, widowed, divorced, or separated—before their disability. Diagnostic categories included left CVA—12.8 percent, right CVA—19 percent, multiple sclerosis—16.8 percent, Guillain-Barré syndrome—5.6 percent, traumatic injury—9.3 percent, and back problems—6.5 percent. Other diseases of the nervous system included cerebral palsy, syringomyelia, extrapyramidal movement disorder, olivopontocerebellar degeneration, transverse myelitis, polyneuropathy, and viral encephalitis. Arthritic diseases included rheumatoid arthritis, scleroderma, and cervical spondylosis. Other diagnoses were amputation, fractured hip, cancer, and massive obesity.

Reasons Why TAPIs Were Requested

The team requested TAPIs for the following 12 reasons.

1. To obtain help in understanding and dealing with patients who are especially controlling, critical, angry, demanding, manipulative, chronically complaining, frustrating, or resistant; patients with whom staff over-identify; and those patients who are physically abusive or sexually provocative. Although the main reason for requesting the TAPI was to talk about the patient, the team members usually wanted the chance to ventilate, share, understand, and deal more effectively with feelings that such patients aroused.
2. To distinguish between organic and functional components of disability; that is, to distinguish between deficit and resistance, character traits, or personal idiosyncrasy.
3. To assess psychological strength and disability.
4. To assist in the management of the "pain patient" who demands excessive medication.
5. To enhance patient care and discharge planning through greater understanding of conflictual marital and family relationships.
6. To improve the management of unrealistic or unmotivated patients.
7. To obtain help in negotiating contracts and setting limits with disruptive or uncooperative patients.
8. To understand and better deal with a patient's past psychiatric history and its effect on the rehabilitation process.

9. To evaluate the potential for suicide or behavior that is a suicidal equivalent.
10. To help with staff conflicts caused by "splitting," an unconscious psychological process whereby a patient assigns good and bad parts of him- or herself to various team members.
11. To distinguish among normal sadness, reactive depression, and pathologic grief.
12. To evaluate a patient's mental status with particular attention to bizarre behavior.

RECURRING STAFF/PATIENT DIFFICULTIES

This discussion of recurring staff/patient difficulties focuses on the staff's contribution to these difficulties. It echoes the sentiments of one patient, who at the end of a TAPI said to the staff, "My job is to accept my disability; your job is to accept me." Rehabilitation team members must assume that patients can be worked with, no matter how offensive, unlikable, ungrateful, or even hateful they may be. Patients deserve competent caregivers. Occasionally, one encounters abusive or highly disturbed patients intent on destroying the system that cares for them. These rare patients are not the focus of this chapter.

A review of the 107 TAPIs was made in an effort to identify basic recurring staff/patient interactional difficulties. These difficulties can be divided into those that are not disability-related, those that are a result of the disability, and those that result when disability is superimposed on pre-existing character pathology.

Non-Disability-Related Difficulties

Non-disability-related staff/patient difficulties stem from two common staff errors: (1) a tendency to ignore the patient's past personal history and (2) a tendency to try to escape patients' projections.

The Patient's Past

There is a pervasive tendency to perceive patients as if they had not existed before one met them. One of the paradoxes of rehabilitation is that the most enduring staff/patient difficulties do not result from the physical disability itself. The origin of these difficulties lies in the troublesome, abrasive aspects of the patients that predate the disability and that characterized their past interpersonal relationships. This inclination to negate the importance of the patient's past has several causes. First, catastrophe has a profound mesmerizing effect on those in its midst; it seems natural to think that everything that follows catastrophe results from it. Second, victims of catastrophe enlist rehabilitation specialists' sympathy and enjoy the benefit of the doubt. Staff members may feel sorry for them, and when they do think analytically, it is about patients' diagnoses, treatments, and prognoses—not about their emotional and interpersonal pasts. Third, rehabilitation patients frequently have such overwhelming, multisystem problems that staff members need an inflated sense of their own healing powers to believe they can help the patients. Minimizing or ignoring the importance of the patient's past serves to enhance the caregivers' sense of their own importance: Because there have been no important events or influences in the patient's life up to this point, everything depends on the caregivers.

Staff/patient conflict frequently arises because staff members lack the necessary conceptual framework to gauge the patient's past level of psychological health. Considerable miscalculations result. Pre-existing psychological disturbance may be unrecognized or underestimated and signs of psychological strength unnoticed. Consider the following case example.

A TAPI was requested for an obese 64-year-old mother of two, grandmother of two, and widow of 4 years who had sustained a right-hemisphere CVA. The request was made because some of the staff members felt the patient lacked the willpower to control her obesity, which greatly interfered with her rehabilitation. As a result, staff members questioned her motivation. Despite her weight of 310 pounds, and her 5 foot, 1 inch frame, Mrs. A said her major problem was neither her weight nor her CVA but her height, "I'm too short." Although she lost 120 pounds after an intestinal bypass operation, she gained it all back beginning only 6 weeks prior to her admission. She blamed the weight gain on inadequate surgery, but her daughter stated the weight gain was a blatant result of massive overeating. The patient seemed oblivious to the threat her obesity posed to her well-being, if not her survival. Her demeanor alternated between superficial pleasantness, self-denigrating humor, and self-pity. She transiently idealized several staff members while denigrating others. She distorted facts; for example, she claimed the nurses left her on a bedpan for 8 hours. She praised her family to the staff, but would gorge herself during their visits, leaving the family impotent with rage. Her family described her as having had a hostile, dependent, guilt-ridden relationship with her parents and an idealized relationship with her husband, whom she allowed to take advantage of her. "If he stepped on her foot, she'd apologize." Her family noted her self-destructive overeating since her husband's death. Devoted to her in the past but now at the end of their rope, the family members began visiting her less often. Over time, staff members came more to judge than to understand this patient. Her massive obesity was seen as a kind of moral weakness. Her behavior toward her family was seen as disgusting and inexcusable.

This case illustrates the extent to which staff members can underestimate the severity of premorbid psychopathology. Such miscalculations result in an enormous drain on staff energy. Unfortunately, giving the patient a psychiatric diagnosis does not remedy the problem. Such labeling in a rehabilitation setting often results in patients receiving less and inferior care. What is of benefit to staff is a conceptual framework that allows the team members to estimate in simple human terms how psychologically sick or healthy a patient has been in the past.

The proposed approach assumes that people are more alike than different and that they are usually doing the best they can under the circumstances. One similarity among people involves basic life tasks, including (1) survival, (2) getting other people to do things for them, and (3) maintaining existing relationships.

Knowledge of an individual's primary task provides some index of his or her location on the spectrum of psychological health. Each enterprise is usually accompanied by certain unconscious ego defense mechanisms or associated pathologic conditions (Valliant, 1977). For example, patients dealing mainly with the task of survival use the most primitive psychological mechanisms of defense: denial, distortion, projection, projective identification, and splitting.

Patients who are primarily trying to get other people to do things for them use the following mechanisms of defense.

- They become very good (perfectionists).
- They become astutely inept so that initially others are impelled to rush in and help.
- They use their body to secure personal relationships (hypochondriacs).
- They become anxious or depressed.

Patients trying to maintain and preserve relationships they already have utilize the following more sophisticated defense mechanisms: intellectualization, repression, reaction formation, displacement, and dissociation.

Consider Mrs. A's behavior in this framework. She blocks out (denies) her life-threatening condition and its self-destructive nature, blames (projects) it on her surgeon, reacts to staff members as either all good or all bad (splits), and alters facts (distorts). Struggling to survive, it is not surprising that her major problems center around food. Mrs. A also uses her body to gain other people's help and attention, but her provocative manner is not calculated to secure involvement on a durable basis. It is clear that Mrs. A is doing little to maintain or preserve relationships that she already has. Thus one sees Mrs. A as someone who uses predominantly primitive defense mechanisms associated with the task of survival.

Her use of the hypochondriacal mode for the task of getting people to do things for her is failing. This assessment enables one to see the depths of Mrs. A's psychological illness. By perceiving such a patient as Mrs. A as very sick psychologically, rather than as disgusting or weak, the team can substitute empathy for judgment. Concern and consideration replace feelings of frustration, annoyance, disappointment, and anger.

The team members must decide who is most likely to change—the patient or themselves. Where the patient has demonstrated psychological strength and coping ability before disability, they can expect the patient to respond to education, encouragement, firmness, support, and the maintenance of hope. By contrast, in managing patients with significant premorbid psychopathology, staff members should try to modify their own perceptions of and reactions to the patient, rather than the patient him- or herself. Of course, in both situations, the natural history of the disease itself is a major determinant of change. It is also true that change in one party changes all others in the system.

Taking into account the patient's level of premorbid emotional functioning allows the staff to decide *where* to direct its therapeutic energies and to set realistic goals. If goals are set too high, staff members become frustrated and angry, and patients feel misunderstood and unfairly treated because their best efforts are viewed as inadequate or manipulative.

When family functioning is understood on the same conceptual framework, staff members can better identify family members who are likely to be responsible and reliable.

Knowledge of a patient's past frequently reveals substantial psychological strength and offers clues as to how to engage these resources.

A TAPI was requested because of the hostile, provocative behavior of a 33-year-old electrician with quadriparesis secondary to cervical laminectomy. Mr. B. let the team know that an army of lawyers was going "to nail the surgeons responsible." Given the facts, his threatened action seemed indicated and his attitude understandable. The patient maintained his determination despite having suffered the following losses in the year-and-a-half prior to surgery: the breakup of his 10-year marriage, his father's suicide by gunshot, and his mother's death from cancer.

During the interview the patient told of being the oldest of five children of alcoholic parents. He realized at an early age that his parents were difficult, that he could not change them, but that it was not his fault. Their home was often without heat, and he would hold his younger siblings to keep them warm. At age 15 he left home to live and work on a farm owned by a Yankee widow. She was very strict with him, but he liked her because he knew she had his best interests at heart. He still keeps in touch with her. By age 17 he joined the Coast Guard and sent money home to support his family. He married at age 23 and went to night school to become an electrician.

When he first came for rehabilitation he welcomed death, and although he does not feel that way now, he still does not know for what he has to live. He said that at times he feels pure hate, does not care what he says to people, and wants to hurt them back. He was especially devastated because the quadriparesis, if it does not improve, would prevent him from working again as an electrician.

Despite his angry provocative behavior, the postinterview discussion revealed that the team liked and admired the patient very much and that he was working hard in therapy.

The patient's relationship with the Yankee widow provided the team with the prescription for treatment. The team realized that "the hard time" Mr. B. gave the therapists did not interfere with his rehabilitation and that, in fact, he seemed disappointed when high expectations were not maintained for him. The TAPI ended with the team members discovering their own feelings of respect and admiration for the patient's ability to express anger at people he also cared about, despite his vulnerable position. The team members were inspired by the honesty, openness, dependability, and courage that the patient had distilled from his painful life experience.

Patients' Projections

The second domain of non-disability-related staff/patient difficulty derives from staff members' attempts to avoid becoming the object of patients' projections.

People overlearn and internalize the patterns of their childhood interpersonal experience and, as adults, anticipate that they will be treated similarly. For example, children who were disappointed and criticized repeatedly when young anticipate similar treatment as adults and project these expectations onto other people. People believe their projections and are not receptive to rational persuasion (Havens, 1973). Individuals employing such projections are quite invested in believing that all defects reside in the world, not in themselves.

A TAPI was requested for a 76-year-old woman with a diagnosis of polyneuropathy because the team felt devastated by the patient's negativity and accusations. In the interview, Mrs. C. described her family, especially her mother, in such idealized terms as to be unbelievable. The patient made a telling slip of the tongue when describing a doctor's comment about her ailing mother's condition: "I think she has cancer, but I can't promise you that.'' The patient then suddenly changed the subject and wanted to know, "Why was I picked on for this meeting? You tell me, you tell me.'' She then asked the occupational therapist, "Why did you put me up against the wall?'' Here, the patient— speaking literally and not metaphorically—was referring to a balance test that had been performed in therapy earlier that day. The patient experienced the test as an attempt to put her on the spot and humiliate her. She also accused the rest of the team of intentionally looking the other way during the test and ignoring her.

Team members who were the objects of Mrs. C.'s projections behaved in a predictable manner. No one likes to be misperceived, and when it does occur the natural reaction is to disprove the projection. Caregivers often go to great lengths to convince the patient that they are really good, competent, and caring. This pattern may hold true even when the caregivers are fully cognizant that the problem lies in the patient's misperception. The reason for this persistence lies in the staff member's wish to be important to, approved of, and liked by the patient.

A therapeutic response that may seldom occur to staff members, because it is not natural, is to welcome these projections. The central unappreciated point here is that people deal with painful feelings by sharing them with others. Projection is a form of sharing. Seen in this way, receptivity to sharing the patient's projections reduces the patient's emotional burden. It is a way of making the denominator larger when the numerator is the patient's pain. But staff members, accustomed to being realistic, may fear that by nurturing these projections they will retard the patient's adjustment, thereby impeding the rehabilitation process.

The usual staff response to projections of a critical nature is rejection: "I am not bad, I am good; it is you who is bad.'' A different approach, based on the above formulation, might be, "It must be hard to work at therapy when you have found your caregivers so disappointing.'' The purpose of such a comment is not to corroborate the patient's contention that the staff is incompetent, but rather to empathize with the patient's feeling. Such a comment is possible only when staff members feel secure and proficient enough not to be threatened by the patient's projection, assuming of course that it is a projection and not reality. Acceptance of the projection circumvents the struggle that results from refuting the projection. Deprived of a fight and provided with compassion, the patient feels more trust in his or her caregivers and, paradoxically, tends to project less.

Disability-Related Staff/Patient Conflict

Certain staff/patient conflicts result from the fact and nature of the disability itself. Devastating loss is frequently accompanied by powerful feelings of sadness, anger, failure, and despair. Sometimes staff members protect themselves from such feelings by unwittingly trivializing or discrediting the patient's and family's heroic efforts to cope.

A TAPI was requested for a 40-year-old, twice-married mother of two sons with severe incapacitating multiple sclerosis. Her second husband had adopted her children, was extremely attentive to her, and was resourceful in working on discharge planning. The team felt the couple's interaction was "too good to be true" and hoped that the "real underlying conflicts" could be unearthed in the TAPI. Instead, the interview revealed two people very much in love, capable of discussing intimate issues openly, yet appropriately grief-stricken over the future that would be denied them. In the postinterview discussion, the staff members expressed sadness over "life's unfairness" and an appreciation for this couple's openness, honesty, and ability to share.

Given this opportunity to acknowledge, bear, and share the couple's pain, the staff found itself better able to work with the patient, support her husband, and minimize its own feelings of stress in the process.

Regression

Regression frequently accompanies disability and, when of limited duration, is a normal reaction. Through regression patients attempt to minimize the painfulness of current reality and to restore lost control. This defense mechanism mobilizes archaic self-concepts of indestructibility, omnipotence, omniscience, everlasting beauty, and lovability. To admit that one has needs, is incomplete, or defective contradicts such grandiose ideas. Preservation of these notions can become more important for a regressed patient than acceptance of needed services. The caregiver who attempts to deal on a rational basis with such patients feels confused and helpless.

A TAPI was requested for a 47-year-old, twice married woman who had sustained her third CVA, because of the patient's unrealistic goal of total independence in activities of daily living, as well as her threat to sign out against medical advice. The therapists reported that upon admission Mrs. E. acted as if she could do everything and that she didn't need therapy. The occupational therapist described how convincing the patient was about her tremendous abilities, which, in reality, were slight. Nurses noted that the patient would never admit her own mistakes and would constantly criticize them instead. The patient convinced the team, against its better judgment, to give her a weekend pass, even though her coumadin levels were very unstable. She called the hospital in a panic because she was hemorrhaging vaginally. She stated that she knew this was going to happen and that the team should have never sent her out.

Staff members have difficulty dealing with regression because it does not yield to rational explanation or punishment and cannot be overcome by motivation, willpower, or positive thinking (Gunther, 1971). It does, however, respond to empathy. Mrs. E. calmed down when staff members empathized with her feelings of helplessness and fear. She was told, "We can't blame you for wanting to believe that everything is fine when your situation is so scary." At the same time, using the patient's language, the team gave her credit "for having the guts to want to fight this thing."

Staff members often need help in making empathic connection with regressed patients. To perceive regressed behavior as "human" rather than "childish," one must be aware and accepting of the infantile, disturbing parts of oneself. Staff members may fear that what begins as an attempt to empathize with a regressed patient will degenerate into a regressed staff (Corradi, 1983).

Particular Diseases

TAPIs were requested for a disproportionately high number of patients with Guillain-Barré syndrome. Certain features of this disease and staff proclivity to identify with its victims combine to produce almost predictable staff/patient conflict. Staff members find it easy to imagine that this condition could happen to them because it begins with a mild viral illness; as a result, they wish to minimize the devastating effects of the disease. Normal but massive patient regression is seen as childish because, after all, this is a disease from which patients frequently fully recover. The patient, still paralyzed or paretic, feels angry at the health care staff, frequently those from the acute hospital, who probably would have given erroneous assurance of "full recovery in a few months." The resulting scenario is a clinical impasse between a patient who feels deceived and misunderstood and a staff that feels stuck with a "big baby who is not trying."

Another diagnostic entity that is disproportionately represented in TAPI requests is multiple sclerosis. The usual staff/patient conflict centers around the patient's motivation: Staff members often feel that the patient is insufficiently motivated, whereas the patient contends that he or she is participating fully or else is not participating because there is no problem. The perplexing quality of the denial seen in multiple sclerosis patients accounts for the team's dilemma. Unsure of the relative contributions to the patient's denial made by organic CNS factors and regression or characterologic immaturity, staff members usually favor the latter factors to maintain hope that the patient's condition is reversible. Unfortunately, the team members may tend to overlook organicity and mistake deficit for resistance or, if psychological factors are suspected, to underestimate premorbid psychopathology.

Another staff/patient conflict occurs when a patient with a degenerative illness that is refractory to all therapeutic intervention does not directly express any negative feeling. The staff members' mounting feelings of ineffectiveness and guilt are intensified by the patient's continued praise, if not idealization, of them. The patient's inevitable angry feelings find indirect expression in manipulative behaviors, usually involving the most basic human processes, such as eating, bowel and bladder functions, sleep, and mobility. Angry over being so controlled but unable to express it because of the patient's coercive praise and their own guilt, staff members feel exhausted and preoccupied with the patient's physical condition. Anxiety results not only from the precariousness of the patient's actual condition but also from the buildup in the team of unacknowledged hostility toward the patient. Unaware that these angry feelings threaten their therapeutic value to the patient, staff members instead perceive the patient to be in greater (physical) danger. The catharsis and disclosure that take place in the TAPI postinterview discussion are frequently sufficient to permit the staff to resume a more therapeutic posture.

Caregivers may be unable to understand or empathize with patients whose diseases produce deficits foreign to the caregivers' own experience. A woman with syringomyelia whose performance fluctuated from day to day was thought to be an unreliable historian and unmotivated for therapy. During the TAPI the patient described how bewildered she was by the daily variability in her strength. She herself was not even sure when she was trying her hardest or what her actual strength was on a given day. It never occurred to her that others would perceive her dilemma in such different and negative terms. Similarly, some patients with right-hemisphere disease have difficulty expressing their feelings or identifying the emotional states of others (Ross, 1981). The patient is unaware of these communication barriers, which alienate family and friends. In both of the above examples, staff/patient interaction is improved through sharing of information and education.

Rehabilitation Philosophy versus Religious Dogma

In certain instances, rehabilitation philosophy can be transformed into religious dogma, which may produce staff/patient conflict. Financially secure patients who refuse to work on some activities of daily living or self-care—"I'll hire someone to help me with that at home"—may evoke strong emotional responses in staff members. Feelings of envy, intimidation, and resentment may be expressed through moral pronouncements about the importance of independence as a rehabilitation goal. Such preaching is rarely well received.

Another important rehabilitation goal—facing and accepting reality—can assume spiritual dimensions with the young spinal cord injured patient.

> A TAPI was requested for Mr. F., a 31-year-old married man who was paraplegic as a result of a motorcycle accident. The therapists were upset that 3 months after the accident the patient was still talking about walking in the near future. Therapists spent much time trying to induce a more realistic perspective, to which manipulation he usually reacted with anger. The staff members were baffled and occasionally hurt by these outbursts because, from their point of view, "We're only telling him this for his own good."

The team's underestimation of the patient's difficulty in accepting the reality of the disability and their insistence that the patient be more realistic than he or she is apparently able to be cause considerable conflict (Baretz & Stephenson, 1976). Staff members may begin implying that ominous things will happen if the patient does not face reality. The fact that they may be right is irrelevant. The central point is that the patient is beyond reason and is overwhelmed with emotional distress. At some level the patient may know the truth, but his or her fantasies are the basis of hope, and that hope may provide the only motivation for rehabilitation (Menninger, 1959). The only helpful interventions at this point are directed at the patient's feelings or fantasies.

However, staff members may fear that, if they allow patients to talk about their fantasies, two undesirable side effects will result: (1) Patients will cling even more firmly to their unrealistic expectations and, as a result, (2) they will be even less interested in doing the work of rehabilitation. Both fears are usually unfounded, because allowing patients to express and share their fantasies helps in two ways. First, staff interest and willingness to listen to such fantasies indicate they view the patient's psychological predicament, as well as his or her performance in therapy, as important. Conversely, when staff members stifle these visions and emphasize reality, patients feel that team members care merely about their performance of ADL, for example. Patients worry that they are merely vehicles through which staff members can demonstrate their competence.

Second, encouraging patients to fantasize provides them, paradoxically, with an unrivaled opportunity to begin to mourn their losses. Patients' elaborations of their fantasies usually center on the wish to be able to resume pleasurable and rewarding past activities. Permitting patients to put these desires into words, rather than forcing them to bury them within, allows the discrepancy between fantasy and reality to emerge in a clear-cut fashion, a result that force-feeding reality does not achieve.

The team members who can temporarily put reality aside and allow the patient access to these fantasies find a responsive patient. If a patient could articulate this gratitude, he or she might say: "I appreciate your allowing me to be unrealistic back when I needed to be; even though you knew I'd never be able to do the things I was hoping I could, you didn't rub my face in reality. You put my well-being in front of your own need to complete your job." It is frequently argued that, because rehabilitation is time-limited, the above approach is an unaffordable luxury. The validity of that argument is highly questionable. It is impossible to blast through denial and make an emotionally devastated person face reality. Attempts to do so waste time, alienate the patient, and have as their true aim relieving the staff's sense of helplessness and frustration.

Taking Sides

When disability results from self-neglect or self-indulgence, staff members tend to take sides when patient/family conflict occurs.

> Mr. F., the 31-year-old paraplegic motorcycle victim mentioned above, demeaned his devoted wife when she visited. He bragged about his many affairs to the nurses, who thought he was offensive. One nurse said she was so upset by the patient's unfaithfulness, male chauvinism, and lack of appreciation of his wife's efforts to keep the household together and care for their four children that these feelings interfered with her ability to work with him.
>
> Mr. G., a 55-year-old father of six with a 20-year history of hypertension and a strong family history of hypertension, did not take his antihypertension medication, despite his family's daily prodding. He developed malignant hypertension with many of its dreaded complications: blindness, chronic renal failure, and stroke. The staff found the patient likable and felt sorry for him. His family was furious with him. His wife refused to take him home and suggested that he be transferred to a veteran's hospital. The team was forced to convey this message to the patient and felt very angry with the wife "for making us do the dirty work for her." A few staff members wanted legal action to be taken against her.

Staff members frequently take the side of the more likable or sympathetic party or the one with whom they identify. Doing so restricts the team's capacity to make useful, objective clinical observations. In the first case example above, further inquiry revealed that, although the staff was upset about Mr. F.'s behavior toward his wife, she was not upset. His wife was an adopted child, brought up by extraordinarily strict and critical parents who disapproved of her marriage. She felt that her husband rescued her from a most unhappy situation and that her life had been immeasurably happy since her marriage. She knew when she married him that he took chances—scuba diving and motorcycles—and that she would have to reconcile herself to it. Mr. F. was the youngest of six. When he was 8 years old, his 25-year-old brother died from a spinal tumor. When he was 12, his 13-year-old sister was discovered to have leukemia and died 3 months later. The patient made a remarkable statement about his motorcycle accident: "I don't blame anybody. When you drive a motorcycle, it's just a matter of time before you get into an accident." This clinical information helped the staff understand, rather than judge. When all available psychological data on Mr. F. were reviewed, he was seen as a guilt-ridden person whose bravado was actually a way of seeking the punishment he felt he deserved for causing his siblings' deaths.

In the second case example, the staff's positive feeling for Mr. G. precluded their understanding that the patient was at least partly responsible for his predicament and that his family's reaction to him was not worthy of censure. Although the patient idealized his family relationships, his wife spoke of long-standing marital conflict and his volatile temper. The children said their father neglected his health, worked long hours, and spent little time at home; instead he owned single season's tickets to four sports teams and regularly attended meetings of various social and civic clubs. Interestingly, a 6-month follow-up revealed that his wife had not left him.

In most cases, the more that staff members know about family members and their pasts, the harder it becomes to take sides. Conversely, the more that staff members initially take sides the harder it becomes to learn about past and current family life. They need to recognize that in marriage there are neither devils nor angels, and that, psychologically, marital partners usually obtain what they want and need in each other.

When the team takes sides, it is detrimental not only to the patient and family members but also to other patients who, aware of staff preferences, are left to wonder what about themselves may evoke staff disfavor.

Disability Superimposed on Pre-Existing Unrecognized Character Pathology

Disability can calcify the inflexibility of premorbid character pathology and, as a result, prevent the usual give-and-take involved in the rehabilitation process. Usually, staff members expect that patients will pay for and accept services that they have been hired to perform and that both parties will work hard on agreed-upon goals. The team assumes that the paycheck and the satisfaction that comes from a job well done are sufficient reward. However, when disability combines with unrecognized, pre-existing psychopathology, the so-called impossible patient results. Such patients are often unwilling to participate in therapy and are unreasonable in their demands and expectations. Their emotional impact on their caregivers is devastating. Team members find their professional image threatened as they discover within themselves previously unacknowledged hostility and punitive sentiments toward their patients. In extreme instances, caregivers may even question their career choice itself.

Narcissistic Patient

Narcissistic patients, who relied on their physical attractiveness for maintenance of their self-esteem, experience rehabilitation very differently than the caregivers who offer it (Lerman, 1979). Although the team tries to restore function, the patient is concerned only about appearance.

> A TAPI was requested on Mrs. H., a 72-year-old widow with a long-standing history of multiple sclerosis and a recent right-hemisphere CVA, because she would not accept the team's treatment recommendations. The therapist noted that Mrs. H. was very resistant to wearing sneakers, slacks, elastic stockings, and orthopedic shoes because "a stylish proper lady wouldn't wear these." The patient refused to move her bedroom to the first floor because "that's no place for a boudoir." As the patient was wheeled into the interview, she referred to her wheelchair as "the royal coach." She became most animated when describing her home: "It was 150 years old and had originally been built for a famous seaman and his family." She described proudly how her husband built her a Japanese garden with a pagoda, a bridge, and a pond, which she can see when she comes down the main staircase. She minimized any difficulties in using her upstairs bedroom. She reminded us that before her admission she would pull herself up the stairs in spite of her intermittently incapacitating multiple sclerosis.

After the TAPI, the team stopped trying to make the patient do things that would adversely affect her appearance. The staff members then found the patient to be more cooperative and likable. The TAPI helped the staff realize that psychological make-up can be as, and sometimes more, unmodifiable than physical disability.

Hyperindependent Patient

Disability threatens hyperindependent people, whose character structure is partially an attempted solution for unacceptable dependent longings. Although disability legitimizes the indulgence of these feelings, these patients frequently need to "fight against them." They often accuse the staff of trying to undermine their independence. This accusation both maintains the patient's self-image as independent and assigns to others the forbidden wish—to remain dependent.

A TAPI was requested on Mr. I., a 61-year-old renowned molecular biologist and a father of two, who was paraplegic as a result of early childhood polio. He walked with crutches and a long leg brace, despite obesity. At age 60 he broke his leg in a car accident and inexplicably spent the next year at home in bed, where he smoked three packs of cigarettes per day, gained 40 pounds, (which brought his weight to 260 pounds), lost considerable muscle strength, and suffered irreversible brachial plexus injury. The rehabilitation team decided the patient would not be able to walk again and directed their efforts toward preparing the patient for a functional, but wheelchair, existence. The patient contended that this was an attempt to make him more dependent than necessary. He saw no need for long-term change in his functional ability. He described his professional accomplishments and took pride in the family he raised, but he could take no responsibility for his behavior prior to admission or in the hospital, which was massively regressed. He described how he had worked while attending school since age 10 because of the early deaths of his parents.

The team spent countless hours trying to break through this patient's denial and demonstrate his limitations. After a while, the team's persistence at this task matched the patient's own irrationality and intransigence. Eventually staff members became very frustrated and angry at "trying to pump up dead weight." Staff recognition of their contribution to the clinical impasse was elicited by the following questions: "How do you understand the fact that you are much more invested in the patient's rehabilitation than he is?," and "Why has it become *so* important for you to get somewhere with the patient?" Discussion of these questions helped staff members distinguish their own needs from those of the patient. As one staff member realized, "Why should I be *angry* at a patient if his failure to make progress ultimately affects him?"

Staff confidence in their ability to rehabilitate such patients as Mr. I. results from the underestimation of psychopathology. Conversely, appreciation of the extent of the patient's *psychological* disability yields more realistic expectations. It is painful, though, for a staff to confront and acknowledge the limits of their restorative powers; mental health professionals can support the mourning of this quest for professional omnipotence by siding with reality while also appreciating the staff members' well-intentioned efforts to change the unchangeable (Sharaf & Levinson, 1964).

The Moral Masochist

Other patients cannot benefit from rehabilitation because they do not feel they deserve it. These moral masochists (Berliner, 1947) have managed to idealize their early lives that were filled with deprivation, rejection, and loss. To them, their situation "isn't that bad at all." They fear change or risk taking because, although it might lead to some better situation, it will be unfamiliar. These patients remain "emotional diabetics," surrounded by the caring of the team but unable to allow any of it into their tissues.

A TAPI was requested for Mrs. J., a 48-year-old, twice-divorced diabetic and hypertensive mother of two with her second CVA. Although the patient was in perpetually good spirits, the team was quite worried about her. The middle of three children, she was obese as a child and shied away from men. She married at age 29, adopted two sons, but was divorced at age 36 because her husband was drinking and beating her and she discovered that he was a homosexual. Her mother died of lupus, which allegedly was diagnosed only 3 days before her death. She described her mother as "reaching out to her, but depressed." Her first CVA occurred at 45. She married for a second time at 46, but was divorced 11 months later because her second husband also beat her. Therapists described her as undermining her own treatment by working so hard in therapy that she actually harmed herself. At the interview the patient stated that her mother was brought up in a home where *her* parents never talked for 45 years. When asked what she thought she'd be doing in 5 years, the patient answered, "I'll be working, I'll have grandchildren; don't worry about me, I'll be all right."

The team is tantalized and seduced by the neediness and apparent initial receptivity of such patients. Rescue fantasies abound. Ultimately, the team is at a loss to understand why, when all the ingredients for successful rehabilitation are present, the patient does not improve and yet remains so friendly toward them. Explanations of the psychodynamics of such patients help the team members appreciate why their therapeutic efforts must fail. Such patients recall their unhappy, deprived early years as pleasurable and, in the process, idealize the important figures in their lives who have disappointed or even been sadistic to them. Unacknowledged hostility is expressed through recurrent failure, sickness, and humiliation that, curiously, are more disturbing to others than to the patient. Masochists can no more tolerate a positive experience in rehabilitation than they can in life. In fact, it is only by ensuring that treatment is unproductive that the masochist can feel positively toward the caregivers.

The Guilty, Obsessional Patient

Staff members frequently feel an unexplainable antagonism toward guilt-ridden, obsessional patients. These patients cause therapists to feel bored, left out, and unneeded. The patient does not use the team's expertise but, in one form or another, tells the team about his or her own past accomplishments. Frequently, such patients make substantial gains in therapy, but never actually acknowledge any real progress. Long after the patient has made it clear that the team's aid is not necessary, the team members still try to give, but gradually the quality of the giving changes. They now must give in order to neutralize their wish to withhold that which they know will not be accepted.

These patients also frustrate and confuse staff by their incessant talking. Staff members assume when talking with such patients that a conversation is taking place. Actually, the staff members are superfluous bystanders witnessing a dialogue between two parts of a guilty patient. One part, a voice that is muted but never silenced, tells the patient how bad he or she is. This part is usually projected and experienced as staff criticism. The other voice speaks in defense of the patient, telling the staff about his or her goodness and accomplishments. If one only listened to the responses given by such patients without hearing the question, one would conclude that the patient had been asked: "Tell me what is wrong with you," rather than "Tell me about yourself." Staff members may feel controlled by such patients and are reluctant to interrupt for fear of being rude, even though such patients actually welcome interruptions of their compulsive talking. Underlying staff complaints about therapy time wasted by incessant chatter is the team's loss of confidence in its ability to provide anything of value.

A TAPI was requested on Mr. K., a 78-year-old single man with a CVA, because the team wished to explore the patient's apparent difficulty understanding the purpose of rehabilitation, as well as his inordinate need to control. When the patient was 24 years old, his immigrant father died and the patient left the Conservatory of Music to help his mother run the family store, which she unexpectedly sold 2 years later. The patient assumed responsibility for his ailing mother over the next 11 years while his younger brother became a successful anesthesiologist. After his mother's death he became a successful tax specialist for the IRS, but was demoted because of an allegedly improper relationship with a state senator. The most striking feature of the interview with Mr. K. was his conviction that the TAPI had been called because he had done something wrong for which he was going to be punished, and perhaps thrown out of the hospital. He could not pinpoint his misbehavior, but alluded to one incident where his paralyzed arm slipped off its resting place and hit a nurse on the buttocks. The patient quickly pointed out that he hadn't meant anything by it, and "Anyway, she had her clothes on." He then cited his generosity toward his family, stating that over the years he had given them $150,000, "all of it legitimate." Other gratuitous disclaimers punctuated his story. The patient also stated that rehabilitation is ''a period of time when you recover naturally.'' In the postinterview discussion the staff members commented on the patient's total lack of awareness of the hostility toward him that he generated in other people.

The Schizoid Patient

Before the onset of their disability, some people were existing, rather than living. During rehabilitation these patients go through the motions, but their hearts are not in it. Like robots, they do what they are told, but they remain remote and detached from their surroundings.

> The patient, Mrs. L., and her husband were invited to the TAPI, the purpose and format of which were fully explained. The interviewer focused his initial questions on how they each decided to attend the meeting. The patient said she had forgotten the purpose of the meeting—her memory was normal on psychological testing—but she asked neither the team member who brought her to the meeting nor her husband where she was being taken or for what reason. Her husband remembered the purpose of the meeting and suspected that his wife had forgotten, but he never asked her if she wanted to know it nor did he volunteer any information. When asked about this lack of interaction, her husband expressed his discouragement and resignation over ever having any impact on his wife's thoughts or feelings. In the postinterview discussion the team noted: ''One thing about the patient never changes; when we come to get her, she is always sitting facing the mirror, combing her hair. Her hair is often stringy and greasy, but she never has requested to have it washed or set. She also has long hairs growing on her chin, which we asked if she wanted trimmed and she said no.''

Mrs. L. made the team feel as if they were torturing her. At the same time her hostile compliance conveyed the message: ''It's okay, do what you have to with me—but we both know it's meaningless.'' Initial staff feelings of enthusiasm yielded to frustration and finally to hopelessness and despair. Excluded from the patient's schizoid world and unable to gain entry into it through encouragement, hard work, or constructive threats, team members began to feel too depleted and hopeless to give any more.

Team members feel emotionally ravaged by such narcissistic, hyperindependent, masochistic, obsessional, and schizoid personality types. The team's altruistic wishes to give may become distorted and find the following expression:

- No matter how much I give and give, you are never satisfied. Unless you become grateful, I don't want to give any more, *or* I've poured so much of myself into you and you're not getting better. I can't afford to give any more unless you improve and relieve my doubts about my own competence.
- The things you want from me are not what you need. I'm determined to make you accept what I think you need.
- Please do me a favor and vanish. I can't stand how impotent your hopeless condition makes me feel.
- Fine, if you don't want to accept, then I don't want to give.
- I feel like I have nothing of value to give you.

The Likable Patient

If wishes to withhold, to obtain something for one's self, or to give with a vengeance are stimulated in staff members by the above-mentioned patients, then the impulse to give excessively or inappropriately can be activated by overidentification with a likable patient.

> A TAPI was requested for Mr. M., a 77-year-old retired college professor who sustained quadriplegia after an accidental fall while at his daughter's home on Christmas Eve. The team wanted an opportunity to discuss its sense of overidentification with the patient.
>
> At 4 months postinjury Mr. M. was essentially totally helpless with little chance of neurologic improvement. The patient and his wife of 51 years, looking forward to enjoying their retirement on their modest savings, were now faced with financial devastation. His wife encountered massive red tape when dealing with an out-of-town skilled nursing home that made an inappropriate decision not to admit the patient. The couple wondered, "Will he be thrown out on the street?" and commented, "We're not going to sue our children," and "We don't want to go on welfare." Near the end of the interview it came out that on the night of the accident an insurance agent came over immediately and had the family sign a settlement for only $1,000. At this point in the interview, the psychiatrist, overinvolved and perhaps speaking for the team as well, suggested some legal action that the family could take against the insurance company's settlement.

Here, the patient was MR. EVERYMAN, and the staff members could easily imagine themselves in the patient's predicament. The psychiatrist's intervention expressed a thinly disguised wish to reassure himself that under similar circumstances he too would be taken care of.

The omission of patients with borderline personality (Stoudemire & Thompson, 1982) from the above discussion warrants explanation. Borderline patients were infrequently addressed in the TAPI format because their disruptive behaviors surfaced so quickly after admission that they required immediate attention, and they were seen in the more customary psychiatric consultation. In fact, nursing and social services notes from the acute hospital frequently prompted psychiatric consultation on the day of admission. In contrast, the less conspicuous quality of the character pathology outlined above may partly explain why staff members, not forewarned, "got in over their heads."

MAJOR TEACHING CONCEPTS

Although the causes of staff/patient conflict are many and variable, the enduring and pervasive tensions originate in the emotional devastation patients feel as a result of irreversible loss. As staff members become enmeshed in the patient's emotional turmoil, three undesirable staff reactions may result.

1. The team, in an unconscious attempt at self-protection and self-preservation, underestimates the patient's pain and suffering and perceives the patient as a disease process or diagnostic category instead of an afflicted human being.
2. The staff members lose sight of the inevitability, even the desirability, of conflict and view it as something to be eliminated.
3. The staff members perceive their inevitable conflicts with patients as caused exclusively by patients and remain unaware of their own contribution to these conflicts.

In addition to the teaching concepts already mentioned in this chapter, a review of the 107 TAPIs shows that a few basic psychiatric methods and concepts repeatedly surfaced as the above staff difficulties were confronted. The first problem was addressed in the patient interview by meticulously keeping the patient's life history in a time framework, emphasizing the obvious, but often overlooked, fact that the patient had a "life before rehab." The second issue was reframed through the use of the concept of projective identification. The third issue was illustrated through the concept of counterprojection.

Use of a Time Framework

The most humanizing event in any clinical setting occurs when the patient's unique personal history is shared with the staff. Compare and contrast the following two accounts of the same patient.

The patient, Mr. N., a 59-year-old married father of seven, is himself the oldest of three boys whose parents divorced when he was seven. His youngest brother died as an infant. The patient's father moved him and his middle brother from Massachusetts to New York shortly thereafter. He kept in touch with his mother who remained in Massachusetts. He finished high school and spent 4 years in the Navy. After working several enjoyable years as a machinist, he married a recently widowed woman who had three children, and they settled in Massachusetts. The patient and his wife had four children of their own. The patient's mother is living, and his father, who had a drinking problem, died 3 months after the patient had relocated him to a Massachusetts nursing home. During the 16 years of marriage before his first stroke, the patient bought 20 automobiles, none of which ever satisfied him.

Mr. N. was born in 1924, the oldest of three boys, to parents who were 18 and 17. In 1928 when he was 4 his middle brother was born, and in 1931 when he was 7 his youngest brother was born. In early 1932 his youngest brother died at the age of 11 months. At this time his parent's marriage was breaking up. They divorced in 1933, and his mother was given custody. In 1934 the patient's father took the patient and his brother and resettled in New York state. The patient kept in touch with his mother who remained in Massachusetts. The patient graduated from high school at age 18 and served in the Navy for the next 4 years, from 1942 through 1946. For the next 17 years, 1946 through 1963, the patient worked as a machinist, had one unhappy love affair, but generally led a carefree life. In 1963 at the age of 39 the patient married a woman recently widowed who had three children ages 9, 8, and 7. Over the next 5 years, 1964 through 1969, the patient and his wife settled in Massachusetts and had four children. In 1976 at the age of 52 the patient brought his 70-year-old father, who had two strokes, from New York to Massachusetts and placed him in a nursing home. His father died 3 months later. The patient's 76-year-old mother is still living. During the patient's first 16 years of marriage, 1963 to 1979, he bought 20 new automobiles, none of which ever satisfied him.

The first description was supplied in the preinterview discussion. The material in the second account was gathered in a 20-minute TAPI interview.

The TAPI was requested because the patient's great disappointment in every staff attempt to help him left the staff members utterly demoralized and uninterested in the patient.

Organizing the patient's story in a time framework highlights relationships among life events that would otherwise be missed. Born to very young parents, ages 18 and 17, the patient's early life during the Depression was traumatic—a sibling's death, parental divorce, and being taken from his mother, all occurring between ages 8 and 10. Nevertheless, the patient managed to graduate from high school in 1942 whereupon he enlisted in the Navy for 4 years (1942 to 1946). For the next 17 years the patient, single and working as a machinist, had fun and little responsibility. Over the next 6 years from ages 39 to 45, the patient went from being carefree and single to married with seven children! At age 52 in 1976, feeling the full brunt of parenthood with stepchildren ages 22, 21, and 20 and his own children ages 12, 11, 9, and 7, he recontacted his now feeble 70-year-old father whom he placed in a Massachusetts nursing home only to have him die 3 months later.

In the post-interview discussion the author helped the team develop the following provisional formulation of psychological issues and conflicts in the patient's life. Disappointed, conflicted, and probably guilty over his parent's divorce and his sibling's death, the patient nevertheless possessed sufficient strength to keep in touch with his mother, graduate from high school, and function well in the military. Hurt and frightened by family life, he had "fun" for 17 years while he avoided dealing with his inner conflicts. He then tried to solve his inner fears about family experience with an external solution: creating the stable home he yearned for but never had. Instead of gaining him the fantasized "perfect family," this faulty solution saddled the patient with massive responsibilities that overwhelmed and drained him. He began to identify with his sickly father who died shortly thereafter. He began to resent having to give to his children all that he never received. Even the compulsive buying of 20 cars in 16 years could give him no pleasure. He ended up feeling like a sibling to his children and the least favored by his wife. In this context, the patient fell ill.

Following this exercise, the staff was able to appreciate the patient's painful life experiences, his valiant but ineffectual attempts to deal with them, and his inability to be satisfied with anything, including, of course, the staff's therapeutic efforts.

Reframing Conflict and Projective Identification

An often unexplored assumption underlies many requests for psychiatric consultation for staff/patient conflict. The assumption is that conflict is bad, and the existence of conflict signifies that something is wrong. Yet, staff/patient conflict is inevitable in a setting where catastrophic illness and irreversible loss are the norm (Nason, 1981). The consultant must modify the team's strong bias against conflict.

Reframing is a psychological technique that assigns a novel interpretation to events previously perceived in a stereotyped way (Minuchin & Fishman, 1981). This tactic provides an opportunity for the participants to view themselves, each other, and the situation in an unaccustomed way, thereby allowing new avenues of analysis and discussion to emerge. For example, a therapist treating a brash, egocentric, decisive husband and his considerate, passive wife because of marital discord over the husband's alleged affair might sympathize with the husband by saying, "Mr. X, it must be difficult for you to have to use such extreme provocation to get a reaction out of your wife." Here the stereotype of the macho husband/victimized wife is reframed, and new possibilities are introduced: Perhaps the husband's behavior is partially a product of his wife's chronic emotional unresponsiveness, despite her virtuous presentation.

The concept of projective identification provides a means of reframing the usual interpretations that staff members ascribe to conflict. The distinction between projection and projective identification is important. Projection involves unconscious ascription of unacceptable parts of the self to other people who are then avoided. Prejudice is an example of projection. Because the target of projection is avoided, projection is considered to have intrapsychic, rather than interpersonal, utility. In contrast, projective identification, which also involves unconscious attribution to external objects of unacceptable aspects of the self, is primarily interpersonally motivated (Horowitz, 1983). It differs from projection in that the object is not only *not* avoided, but is closely attended to. For example, staff members are driven to distraction by the continually critical patient who, paradoxically, seems to hover around them. These are the patients whom staff members describe as follows: "She really gets under my skin," "I can't seem to get him out of my hair," "I seem to take him home with me and dream about him."

It does not occur to the team, who is tormented by a patient's projections, that the patient is trying to solve a problem and needs the staff's help to do it. It is much more natural and understandable for the team members to experience such a patient as someone who does not like them and would like to be rid of them. Sometimes, of course, that is the case. But, in many instances, patients need the staff members to be a temporary "container" for feelings in themselves that they find unacceptable. Despite outward appearances, the patients are not trying to end or destroy their relationship with staff; rather, doing the best they can, they are maladaptively trying to maintain the relationship. They "hope" that the stronger egos of the staff members can contain, metabolize, and evolve ways of dealing with these overwhelming parts that they themselves have been unable to manage. The unwanted elements may be intolerable affects resulting from the present situation or long-standing conflicts unrelated to the disability itself. The object of these projections may be the entire team or a particular team member.

A TAPI was requested for a Mr. O., a 77-year-old man with olivo-pontocerebellar degeneration, because of the patient's insulting provocative behavior toward the staff members and their distress over the nature of the patient's relationship with his wife. He made the therapists feel that what they had to teach him was trivial and silly. He taunted other patients and said that other patients' therapists wanted to kill him. The physical therapist said, "He is the most unpleasant person I've ever met. Nobody ever got me to yell at them before." The patient's wife and daughter attended the TAPI with him. His wife was extremely passive and meek. She said, "Oh, you're going to murder me, John, but the TV broke and I've never had it fixed." On one occasion, the patient began crying over his unhappy early relationship with his strict unappreciative father, and his wife hushed him up immediately. His wife ended what was actually a productive meeting by saying in a pitiful tone, "Oh, what a way to live." Aside from the interviewer, the patient related most to the physical therapist and on several occasions turned to her, acknowledged that he had been difficult and rude, and apologized.

In the postinterview discussion, the physical therapist's behavior was reframed as an achievement, rather than a failure. First, the patient's interaction with his wife was discussed dynamically using the concept of projective identification. It was proposed from evidence in the interview that Mr. O. identified with the passivity in his wife that he found unacceptable in himself. Similarly, his wife identified with the aggression in her husband that she could not express. This relationship, secured by projective identification, prevented each person from dealing with fears and problems. Mr. O., for example, did not have to deal with his passive longings. The physical therapist unwittingly provided Mr. O. with a response he both feared and needed. By fighting with him and putting him in his place, she assumed the role of the aggressor and provided the patient an opportunity to express his profound disappointment in his deceased father. It was clear to all present during the interview that, although the physical therapist was distressed and angry with the patient, he was actually fond of her. The conflict between the physical therapist and patient, in other words, was not a sign that something was wrong; rather, it was evidence that the physical therapist cared enough to "allow" the patient to provoke her and in turn, to provide him with the kind of limit-setting responses he needed and wanted. Staff members may need assistance in recognizing that psychological achievements can be as important in rehabilitation as physical ones.

Use of Counterprojection

When staff/patient difficulty arises, certain traits or behaviors of patients and their families are commonly cited as the causes of these problems. Seldom do staff members acknowledge their own role in shaping the behavior of patients and families. For example, there are pervasive staff expectations that a patient be polite, grateful, and cooperative. It is the "bad" patient who is angry, uncooperative, or resistant. And yet, because the irreversible loss in disability is such an outrageous narcissistic injury, negative feelings exist in every patient.

What is the effect on a patient of having to suppress negative feelings for fear of losing the staff's interest and help? Conversely, if the team possessed ways of facilitating the expression of the patient's negative feelings, would the patient present differently? In other words, would the so-called objective qualities of the patient change as the staff's approach changed? This question is of more than academic interest. Frequently in rehabilitation what can change the most is not the patient's physical condition, but (1) the team's thoughts and feelings about and, consequently, behavior toward the patient and (2) the patient's corresponding changes in thoughts, feelings, and behavior.

The concept of counterprojection provides staff with a means of changing patient behavior by first changing their own (Havens, 1976). As mentioned earlier, patients continually project onto staff and misperceive staff according to these projections. The most common projection is that staff members insist that patients be good, i.e., cooperative, motivated, appreciative, free of doubt about the work of therapy, and not angry. Staff members who are able to convey to patients, by benign self-mockery or mildly denigrating quips about their specialty, that such qualities are not mandatory make it harder for patients to maintain these projections. Such behaviors are therefore called counterprojective. Counterprojective behavior subtly conveys to patients that all is not lost if they fail to maintain adoration of the staff, the institution, and the rehabilitation process. Thus, to patients who tolerate occupational therapy and are deferential when they obviously feel contemptuous, the occupational therapist can say, "Well, I'm here again to do our Mickey Mouse activities." The metacommunication to the patient is, "I understand that you think this is ridiculous and wonder how this will ever help you. I can understand how you might have these doubts. Let's give it a try anyway." Such comments yield patients whose "negative" feelings have been validated and who are more relaxed because they do not have to hide or apologize for such feelings. Paradoxically, therapists' diminished but still substantial valuation of their own product may result in patients who feel less compelled to devalue it—and possibly patients who value it.

A similar situation obtains with the patient who continually complains of pain. A frequent projection of such a patient is that the staff members do not believe there is that much pain. As a result the patient feels impelled to impress the team with increased complaints of pain and requests for medication. A counterprojective response, assuming of course that the facts justify it, in this deteriorating staff/patient scenario is, "You tell us, Mr. X., that you have a lot of pain. From what I can see you have even more pain that you are letting us know about—pain not only in your body but also in your life." The reluctance to make this response comes from the fear that the patient's pain, now validated and reinforced, will increase. In fact, paradoxically, such a comment reduces pain expression for two reasons. If the statement is correct—that is, if the patient has found someone who can be more honest about his or her condition than the patient has felt able to be—the patient will feel safer because of increased trust. This feeling lessens the need for securing staff attention through complaints of pain. If the statement is false, the patient will indicate this fact by talking about positive and heretofore unrevealed aspects of his or her situation. In either event, the pain behaviors are partly determined by the way in which staff interact with the patient (see Chapter 4).

SUMMARY

This chapter describes approaches to facilitating staff/patient interaction in an acute rehabilitation hospital. Staff/patient conflict in rehabilitation is inevitable because of a number of factors: the intrinsic differences between patients and staff, the nature of the rehabilitation setting, the phenomenology of catastrophe, the staff's insufficient psychological training, and the goal-oriented nature of rehabilitation. The more difficult staff/patient conflicts often originate in troublesome dimensions of the patient that predate the disability. The most important and productive locus of psychological intervention for these difficulties is the staff, not the patient.

Staff/patient difficulties are divided into three categories: non-disability-related, disability-related, and those that result when disability is superimposed on pre-existing unrecognized psychopathology. Non-disability-related conflicts result largely from two staff tendencies: (1) to ignore the patient's personal history and (2) to try to escape the patient's projections of anger and disappointment. Disability-related staff/patient conflicts have many sources: the powerful, dysphoric feelings stirred up by irreversible loss; the psychic regression that normally accompanies physical devastation; the nature of certain diseases; the patient's inability to express anger and, instead, the tendency to idealize staff in the face of deteriorating illness; the limits of empathy; certain staff reactions that transform rehabilitation philosophy into religious dogma; and the tendency of staff to take sides in patient/family conflict. When disability combines with pre-existing unrecognized character pathology the result is a highly unreasonable patient who elicits in staff reactions that are sufficiently disturbing to threaten its professional functions.

Staff/patient conflict can cause staff members to insulate themselves from their patients' suffering and view them as disease processes; produce the staff view that staff/patient conflict is bad, rather than inevitable or even desirable; and compel staff members to believe that the patient's behavior, but never their own, is the source of conflict. A few basic psychiatric concepts and methods can help deal with these three unproductive responses: maintaining an awareness of each patient's complex life history, of which the disabling condition is only the most recent part; reframing conflict through the use of projective identification; and teaching staff to use counterprojective techniques to undermine patients' maladaptive projections.

The Team Attended Psychological Interview has proven to be a dramatically effective tool for enhancing the psychological sophistication of nonmental health rehabilitation personnel, enabling them to understand, empathize, and interact better with their physically disabled and emotionally devastated patients.

REFERENCES

Baretz, R.M., & Stephenson, G.R. (1976). Unrealistic patient. *New York State Journal of Medicine, 76,* 54–57.

Berliner, B. (1947). On some psychodynamics of masochism. *Psychoanalytic Quarterly, 16,* 459–471.

Bishop, D. (1983). Disability: A family affair. In D.S. Freeman & B. Trute (Eds.), *Treating families with special needs.* Alberta, Canada: Alberta Association of Social Workers and Canadian Association of Social Workers, pp. 3–14.

Corradi, R.B. (1983). Psychological regression with illness. *Psychosomatics, 24,* 353–362.

Gans, J.S. (1979). Consultee-attended interview: An approach to liaison psychiatry. *General Hospital Psychiatry, 1,* 24–30.

Gans, J.S. (1981). Depression diagnosis in a rehabilitation hospital. *Archives of Physical Medicine and Rehabilitation, 62,* 386–389.

Gans, J.S. (1983a). Hate in the rehabilitation setting. *Archives of Physical Medicine and Rehabilitation, 64,* 176–179.

Gans, J.S. (1983b). Psychosocial adaptation. *Seminars in Neurology, 3,* 201–211.

Gunther, M.S. (1971). Psychiatric consultation in rehabilitation hospital: Regression hypothesis. *Comprehensive Psychiatry, 12,* 572–585.

Gunther, M.S. (1977). Threatened staff: Psychoanalytic contribution to medical psychology. *Comprehensive Psychiatry, 18,* 385–397.

Havens, L.L. (1973). *Approaches to the mind.* Boston: Little, Brown.

Havens, L.L. (1976). *Participant observation.* New York: Jason Aronson.

Hengeveld, M.W., & Rooymans, H.G.M. (1983). The relevance of a staff-oriented approach in consultation psychiatry: A preliminary study. *General Hospital Psychiatry, 5,* 259–264.

Horowitz, L. (1983). Projective identification in dyads and groups. *International Journal of Group Psychotherapy, 33,* 250–279.

Lerman, A. (1979). Narcissism in physical rehabilitation patient. *American Journal of Psychoanalysis, 39,* 265–272.

McKegney, F.P., & Beckhardt, R.M. (1982). Evaluative research in consultation-liaison psychiatry. *General Hospital Psychiatry, 4,* 199–200.

Menninger, K. (1959). Hope. *American Journal of Psychiatry, 116,* 481–491.

Minuchin, S., & Fishman, H.C. (1981). *Family therapy techniques.* Cambridge: Harvard University Press.

Nason, F. (1981). Team tension as a vital sign. *General Hospital Psychiatry, 3,* 32–36.

Ross, E.D. (1981). The aprosodias. *Archives of Neurology, 38,* 561–569.

Sharaf, M.R., & Levinson, D.J. (1964). The quest for omnipotence in professional training. *Psychiatry, 27,* 135–149.

Stoudemire, A., & Thompson, T.L. (1982). The borderline personality in the medical setting. *Annals of Internal Medicine, 96,* 76–79.

Valliant, G.E. (1977). *Adaptation to life.* Boston: Little, Brown.

Chapter 8

Catastrophic Illness and the Caregivers: Real Burdens and Solutions with Respect to the Role of the Behavioral Sciences

Meyer S. Gunther, M.D.

The web of disaster that attends catastrophic illness entraps not only its victims but also the victims' families, caregivers, and the community at large. During its initial life-threatening, life-disrupting phase, catastrophic illness makes maximal physical, psychological, and social demands on all who are immediately involved. The problems of the caregivers necessarily take second place to issues of patient and family. Yet caregivers too are victims—burdened, exhausted, and demoralized over their comparative therapeutic impotence with the desperately damaged human beings who lie behind the overt physical symptomatology.

This chapter explores a basic thesis about the staff's burdens: *The price a dedicated and effective rehabilitation staff pays for significant therapeutic involvement with seriously damaged patients is periodic subjective distress and impaired professional behavior.* A corollary is self-evident. If significant emotional distress never occurs, there has never been significant involvement. Some ways to relieve staff distress are also suggested in this chapter.

Stress takes many forms, some of which are indirect, unnoticed, or inadequately understood. Awareness of the origins of staff distress may be persistently avoided by everyone involved. The uniqueness of the stress and the need to remain ignorant of its origins and meanings are interrelated and involve two broad classes of variables: (1) *context factors*, those burdens arising from the special physical, emotional, and interpersonal circumstances of rehabilitation work with catastrophically damaged patients and (2) *symbolic factors*, specific meanings, both conscious and unconscious, to the caregivers of the patient's illness, of rehabilitation work itself, and of the inevitable limitations of their own therapeutic capabilities. Thus, both classes of variables produce a common, often unrecognized, psychological threat: the arousal of staff members' narcissistic anxieties— that is, fear of exposure of their fantasies about their immortality, their absolute power to control their destinies, and their capability to achieve any aim to which they set their minds (Gunther, 1977, 1979). This discussion focuses primarily on

219

the (depth-psychological) impact of such factors on the psychic integrity and professional behavior of the individual staff member.

It is useful for rehabilitation specialists to note the experience of liaison-consultation psychiatrists who work with other catastrophic illnesses. Among the pertinent findings of such work have been the following generalizations:

- Behavioral scientists' appraisals of serious patient pathology—major ego
  disruptive reactions, posttraumatic stress disorders, severe depression, psychoses, etc.—are significantly higher (numbers and severity) than the estimates made by nonpsychiatrically oriented medical personnel (Blacher,
  1972, 1978; Castelnuovo-Tedesco, 1973; Craig & Van Natta, 1976; Penn
  et al., 1971; Schwab, 1982).

- Staff members often display limited awareness of the extent to which their
  feelings and attitudes influence patient behavior, especially recovery. Similarly, staff views of the impact of their behavior on patients differ dramatically from patients' views of that impact (Campbell, 1980; Caplan, 1983;
  Freedman, 1983; Quinlan, Kimball & Osborne, 1974; Schnaper & Cowley,
  1970).

There is only a modest amount of rehabilitation literature addressing the role of
the staff (Caplan, 1983; Gallagher et al., 1982; Gans, 1983; Gunther, 1977;
Holland & Whalley, 1981; Neff, 1971; Trieschmann, 1980). The small number of
studies is due, in part, to the relative youth of rehabilitation medicine and to the
monumental burden of immediate patient needs that tends to preoccupy available
therapeutic resources. However, two other issues might also be relevant in
explaining this paucity of studies. The first concerns the investigators' assumptions of what constitutes significantly relevant psychological data (Basch, 1977;
Klein, 1976). Or, more specifically, what conceptual patterns shall one utilize to
interpret psychological data derived in the rehabilitation setting (Gans, 1983;
Trieschmann, 1980)? Second, investigators often fail to recognize the existence of
specific factors in rehabilitation that might stiffen unconscious resistance to awareness of stress on the part of both investigator and subject (Gunther, 1972; 1977). If
one seeks evidence of staff members' distress largely through staff self-report or
direct behavioral observation, one is not likely to obtain a significant yield.
Professional staff members, insofar as they have any (preconscious) awareness of
painful emotions, such as guilt, shame, anxiety, humiliation, helplessness, frustration, or disappointment, are likely to be self-protective in the face of formal
investigations while assuming an apparently cooperative stance for the sake of
propriety. Only investigative procedures that address hidden evidence of distress—that is, evidence that eludes conscious personality defenses—are likely to
yield meaningful results.

THE STAFF AND ITS DISTRESS

First-Order Evidence

For 25 years this author has served as staff psychiatrist in a large rehabilitation center treating a range of seriously disabled patients. In addition to providing patient-related psychiatric services, he has assisted staff members in their collective struggles and difficulties arising from everyday work with seriously damaged patients and with their inevitable conflicts with both administration and fellow clinical services. It is clear that copious indirect evidence of staff distress is available to the thoughtful participant-observer.

Four sources of evidence are described in this discussion: (1) staff complaints about patients; (2) staff complaints about other staff members; (3) patients' complaints about staff; and (4) the author's direct observation of the staff. Whatever the source, such evidence becomes available only if one probes below the surface. It is derived from informal small group discussions, from listening to fellow staff members' conversations during mealtime, and in the course of "curbstone consultations" around the nursing station or in the treatment areas. (Occasionally a staff member makes a seemingly innocuous request for advice, which begins with the classic introduction, "Doctor, I have a friend who has the following problem.") Not all observations refer equally to all participants.

Staff complaints about patients may be illustrated by the following comments:

- "Patients complain too much. They complain about the burden of their disability and the burden of our treatment. When they run out of these complaints, they turn to nitpicking issues like rules, procedures, hospital food. There's always something more to complain about."
- "Patients don't have the right attitude about their illness. They don't want to understand what has happened to them or what they can realistically expect. Instead of being logical and mature, they are childish and upset, as if they don't want to grow up."
- "It really appears that all they want is our attention. Continuing to capture our attention by remaining sick and helpless seems more important than getting something out of rehabilitation."
- "At times they seem to be engaged in a secret war to sabotage their recovery. Otherwise, why would they take pleasure in defeating the very help from us that they so badly need?"
- "They delight in defying rules and proving we can't enforce them. They disregard the regulations about passes and visiting hours; they drink and they smoke; they refuse their medication; they stay in bed when they shouldn't;

and they don't go to therapies when they should. If it isn't perversity and negativism that motivates them, perhaps it is attention-getting.''

- ''Why do they swear so much, and why do they talk dirty, especially the men?''

Staff members also complain about other personnel:

- ''The administration doesn't support our work properly. They favor other services over ours, and they don't recognize how uniquely important our work is to ultimate patient recovery.''
- ''*We* don't have any trouble with patients; only other services do. Their troubles must be their own fault. Their difficulties tend to make our work tougher. Why should we have to be burdened by their failures?''
- ''Ours is the crucial work in the entire setting. If patients do well on our service, they will have a successful rehabilitation outcome. If they don't do well, nobody else's work will be worth much.''
- ''They (nursing, medicine, occupational therapy, speech, or physical therapy) really don't understand the patients like we (behavioral science) do. Why don't they understand that patients' disorganized, regressed, dysphoric reactions to the catastrophe overwhelm them, preventing them from lifting themselves up by 'bootstrapping'?''
- ''They (behavioral science services) mollycoddle patients. By catering to their childishness and attention-getting tactics, they make it much more difficult for us (nursing, medicine, occupational therapy, physical therapy, etc.) to do our work properly.''
- ''They (medicine) expect much of us (nursing, occupational, and physical therapy), yet they seldom give us the support that we need. They don't trust our efforts to work more creatively with the patient. We're the ones who spend the most time with patients. We have to deal with their harshness and their unresponsiveness.''
- ''They (the nursing service) try to act like physicians. They don't understand the limits of their own knowledge. We (medicine) have the overall responsibility for the integration of all components of the patient's treatment plan, specifying the designation of basic aims and methods.''

And so on, and so on, and so on.

But staff members are not alone in their complaints about patients and other staff. Patients too complain, but more timidly, perhaps because they fear provoking staff retaliation:

- "The staff members are not interested in us as people; they're interested in our overt performance. That makes them look good. They don't take time to know us because they're not really concerned with how we feel about our illnesses, our rehabilitation, or our damaged lives."

- "Staff members never seem satisfied with what we do, even when we try our best. They are always pushing us. They're so chintzy with admiration for accomplishments. It almost seems as if it hurts them to give a compliment now and then."

- "Staff members avoid us when we're hurting, when we're feeling bad, helpless, hopeless, and especially when we can't tolerate ourselves. It is as if the worse we feel, the less they want to have to do with us."

- "Staff members play favorites. The good patient, the high performer, or the compliant child—these are the people who get the compliments, attention, and concern. Not us, the ordinarily anxious, ordinarily depressed ones who quietly plod along. We're the ones who deserve and need a helping hand."

- "Staff members have little ability to recognize that we are still ordinary human beings whose human needs go on, despite the fact that we've been through a catastrophic illness and have suffered physical damage. O.K., so occasionally we drink or do drugs or have sex—after all, so do most people. Just because we've had a spinal cord injury, a terrible burn, our nerves are degenerating, or our brains are a little addled, does that mean our desires cease? Why do hospital staff members act like parole officers?"

Through a variety of formal and informal contacts with rehabilitation specialists the author has developed the following observations that pertain to persistent staff problems in the rehabilitation setting:

- *Inevitability of staff burnout:* Burnout is a common phenomenon in the helping and teaching professions (Emener, 1979; Gardner & Hall, 1981). It is related to many issues: excessive burdens of work, lack of special support programs, overall inadequacy of institutional policy, poor individual professional preparation, unique stresses in the working situation, peer group or team disorganization, and inappropriate or absent reward by management. The rehabilitation setting is not immune from these problems. When staff members leave the hospital at the end of a shift, they take their exhaustion, anxieties, disappointments, and feelings of self-condemnation home with them—evidence of the toll taken by the grinding effect of the daily struggle with seriously damaged patients. Many speak, privately and with some shame, of the forms of reprieve they adopt—alcohol or drugs, extra sick and vacation days, exploitation of their families, etc.

Two types of crises occur during a staff member's initial years in rehabilitation work. The first crisis comes during the first months of work in the rehabilitation setting when a combination of the newness of the professional demands, lack of self-confidence, and the overwhelming effect of the patients' injuries produces a state of serious anxiety that threatens personal stability. There is a later crisis of commitment that is characterized by fatigue, diminished sensitivity to patients, and chronic doubt about the ultimate value of rehabilitation work, leading to the presence of urgent fantasies about a major career change. This crisis tends to occur between 1 and 1½ years after beginning rehabilitation work. A significant number of rehabilitation specialists leave during this period.

- *Problems with new learning in the personality behavioral areas:* The long-term clinical effectiveness of staff education programs cannot be gauged by responses on a post lecture evaluation form. Repeated contacts with staff members in problematic clinical situations, during which one can observe their capacity to initiate and implement effective patient management procedures, reveal a striking paradox. Most team members are eager to acquire the clinical tools for understanding the meaning of patients' "problem" behavior in order to prevent development of stalemating situations. Yet despite these laudable intentions, many staff members consistently have difficulty internalizing new knowledge in a way that facilitates proper clinical deployment. They may forget important facts and concepts so that they confront recurring crises as if they were occurring for the first time. When they do recall new ideas, they may apply them in an awkward, ineffective manner.

- *The avoidance of empathy:* Empathy may be defined as that process of gathering subjective psychological data through putting oneself imaginatively within the skin of the other (Basch, 1982). Rehabilitation personnel frequently avoid taking an empathic stance with their patients because they find such emotional closeness to be extremely upsetting (Schwaber, 1981). Human beings are often reluctant to establish empathic contact with the innermost feelings and thoughts of individuals whose life experiences have been significantly different from their own. Another barrier to empathy arises when that experience has been so devastatingly traumatic as to induce in the observer the feeling that the observed can no longer be considered "human." A classic case in point is the common tendency to misunderstand or avoid concentration camp survivors and their experiences (see Niederland, 1981; Schwaber, 1978). For similar reasons rehabilitation staff members may exhibit similar distorting and distancing behavior toward their patients.

- *Staff members' repression or avoidance of their distress:* With considerable hesitation, rehabilitation specialists may admit to a trusted colleague some awareness of their own distress. The more introspective members will confess, "Certain patients are simply so demanding or threatening that I cannot maintain my professional equanimity. I become anxious, depressed, and so upset that I have to withdraw to protect myself. When I really get upset, I find myself chastising patients for 'poor performance.' When that happens, I know I'd better withdraw for a while. My inability to meet my own expectations is so humiliating to me that I wonder if I can continue to work in this field." Thus, even those staff members who are aware of the fact of their distress, and even their own possible contributions to that distress, seem unable to find workable solutions—except to withdraw.

Preliminary Inferences

Catastrophic illness is a monumentally evocative experience for all participants—patients, staff members, and families. Feelings, attitudes, expectations, and meanings abound in the material cited above. Some conceptual framework for organizing and interpreting this extensive data is necessary: Uninterpreted data do not speak for themselves.

The author has found helpful three elementary dynamic concepts that are concise, consistent, and at least partially predictable. They are (1) massive psychic trauma, (2) the dynamic unconscious, and (3) the uniquely human need to make sense from experience.

Massive Psychic Trauma

Massive psychic trauma refers to a small group of extreme stresses—natural disasters; catastrophic medical-surgical lesions; and prolonged imprisonment combined with torture, deprivation, and ever-present death, which were the typical experiences of concentration camp survivors, the first group studied. As described by Krystal (1968), Niederland (1981), Winnick (1968), and others, this syndrome involves an array of severely distorting, long-lasting effects on both mind and body. Horrifying in its sudden onset, it quickly leads to a sense of total abandonment by the world, as many previously stable personality functions become disorganized or paralyzed. Long-term constriction or distortion in all major affective, cognitive, and interpersonal spheres is ubiquitous. Persistent physical consequences are analogous and include increased vulnerability to disease, diminished energy, shortened life expectancy, permanent major role changes, and the like. In psychopathologic terms, all the classical psychoneurotic symptoms have been reported, with particular emphasis on anxiety, depression, somatization, and mood disorders. The resemblance between spinal cord injury as the prototypical traumatic/catastrophic illness and the syndrome of massive psychic trauma has been discussed elsewhere (Gunther, 1972).

Two elements of this concept are significant. First, massive psychic trauma can produce severe disorganization and permanent sequelae in its victims, independent of premorbid personality constellation or developmental deficits. Second, this trauma produces a paradoxical response in its victims, its perpetrators, and its caregivers. Some members of all three groups (each for their own reasons) attempt to minimize the profound distress of the victims and the degree of repugnance elicited in the caregivers. For example, many competent professionals expressed the belief that concentration camp survivors who suffered from posttraumatic syndromes were predisposed to them because of premorbid neurotic difficulties (Krystal, 1968), as if the victims themselves were responsible for their own posttraumatic stress reactions! May there be a universal human tendency on the part of victims, victimizers, and observers alike to disavow awareness of such horrifying traumatic experiences that are of a proportion simply too massive to be encompassed, let alone neatly categorized into existing pigeonholes of experience and understanding?

Dynamic Unconscious

The concept of the dynamic unconscious holds that mental processes involving intentionality, predisposition to action, problem-solving activities, the experience of emotions, and the like, exist at different levels of consciousness and in different patterns of organization, order, conflict, and interaction within the mind. Most mental processes and their contents occur autonomously, automatically, and unconsciously; that is, they are inaccessible through simple introspection. Instead, they are revealed through their derivative effects in the form of ordinary behavior and ordinarily conscious thoughts and feelings.

Assigning Meaning

People must assign meaning to their experiences in the world. From the time of Aristotle's attempts to explain thunder as the result of clouds banging against each other to Einstein's anxiety about quantum mechanics, human beings have been compelled to try to make sense out of their world. To be unable to do so is so frightening and disrupting as to be intolerable. To have one's relationship with oneself or with the world lying about in senseless pieces is worse than to have a psychotically distorted but integrated relationship with that world (Monchaux, 1978).

Explanation of First-Order Evidence

These three concepts are useful in examining the descriptive data presented in the first section.

- *Emotional distress:* Anxiety, guilt, depression, disappointment, help-lessness, humiliation, frustration, outrage, surprise—all stand out clearly in the data. But how inconsistent and erratic is the staff members' awareness of such feelings! Both patients and caregivers find it too painful to permit themselves full consciousness of what they are feeling toward one another, toward themselves, toward the work of rehabilitation, or toward the personal meanings of the lesion itself. It is even more difficult to confront the origin of those feelings that are conscious.

- *Resistance to psychological learning:* Allied health professionals' difficulty in absorbing and using psychological knowledge is not necessarily due to poor psychological-mindedness, inadequate intellectual endowment, exces-sive neurotic predisposition, or improper professional training. There is a reasonable two-part explanation: (1) Human beings have an innate, non-specific resistance to certain kinds of emotionally stimulating learning. Issues of human motivation or intentionality often tend to stir one's own feelings in a way that interferes with the comfortable deployment of one's logical capabilities. Considerable self-confidence is required to confront uncertain, uncomfortable, and even irrational new experience for the sake of enhanced professional competence. (2) The institution must provide an environmental context that facilitates such learning. Unfortunately, the culture of many rehabilitation institutions does not place a high value on basic educational activities, nor are such activities supported by funds, time off, or other incentives.

- *Poor defenses:* A good defense is an autonomously deployed, mental attitude that controls one's anxiety, contains a dangerous psychological threat, pre-serves available energy, and thereby keeps one in proper contact with one's inner and outer worlds in the face of danger. See Moore and Fine (1967), pp. 24–25, for a more complete definition of the concept of defense. The above data suggest three common inadequate or ineffective defenses utilized by some staff members: (1) *The avoidance of anxiety at all costs:* By avoiding patients who cause anxiety, its disorganizing effects can be avoided. By avoiding introspection, one can submerge one's awareness of subjective sources of that discomfort. But the costs—loss of contact with parts of one's inner resources and loss of empathic contact with the patient—are significant. (2) *Blaming someone else:* By blaming patients, the administration, or other staff members—that is, through the use of projection or externalization—one can avoid discomfort, although this defense is also ultimately maladaptive. It is a barrier estranging one from involvement with the very patients one is attempting to serve, and it creates great animosity among team members. (3) *Manipulating patient relationships:* By utilizing a combination of moral exhortation, technical intellectualizing, guilt-evoking threats, or shallow promises, rehabilitation personnel can manipulate the needy patient into a compliant posture of dutiful learning and thereby produce apparently stable, commendable patient behavior, at least while the patient is hospitalized. Unfortunately, this third solution produces only shallow, transiently adaptive behavior and also destroys the more mature and trusting aspects of the relationship with the patient.

- *Conflicting aims:* Staff members aspire to more effective therapeutic work to help patients achieve their own authentic, relevant, and permanent goals. At the same time, the team members may be afraid to expose themselves to the uncertainty or failure of such efforts. One way to minimize this danger is to substitute conventional aims that are sanctified by third party payers and institutional management, ones that are clearly measurable in terms of time-honored performance standards. Patients, for good reasons, comply with such expectations. But the conflict between individualized, meaningful, and permanent aims, on the one hand, and conventional, quantifiable, but often functionally trivial aims, on the other, may arise from a more subtle hidden question in the minds of staff workers: How truly meaningful/helpful is the work of rehabilitation to which I have devoted my professional life?

- *Trauma:* So many of the staff members' "problem behaviors"—defenses against empathic involvement in patients' suffering, countertherapeutic approaches to patients, difficulties in new learning—appear to have as their goal the reduction of emotional discomfort that is a common feature of rehabilitation work. Persistent mild threats operate collectively as if they constituted a continuous trauma endangering the basic stability of staff members' personalities, eroding their energies and sensitivities. This factor may explain the "problem behaviors." But the large unknown continues to be this configuration of nebulous chronic, trauma-like threat. What is its nature? What are its sources? In the next section, possible answers to these puzzling questions are considered.

Higher-Order Inferences

If a third step is taken in the process of examining staff experience—that is, abstraction from observed behavior to simple clinical inference to larger clinical generalizations—it becomes possible to sketch answers to the preceding questions.

In the author's opinion, staff members' threatened state arises from two factors: (1) The unique physical, emotional, and interpersonal burdens inherent in rehabilitation work constantly threaten to exhaust the professional resources, personal energies, and sensitivity of staff members, rendering them uncertain about the extent to which they are fulfilling their professional self-expectations.

(2) Certain universal (unconscious) human vulnerabilities—dormant residues of the processes of normal personality development—seem especially available for reawakening by the stimulating experience of catastrophic illness, disability, and rehabilitation. Particularly prominent domains include self-esteem, childhood problems with sexuality and aggression, authority and dependency, and autonomy and integrity of the self. The concept of transference proneness is another way of characterizing this state of affairs (Greenson, 1967).

The Psychological Context of Rehabilitation Work: Special Physical and Mental Burdens

Uncertainty and Anxiety. Rehabilitation deals with complex, multiple-system illnesses that are often inadequately stabilized when patients first come to the rehabilitation hospital. Frequently, outcome is uncertain until near the end of rehabilitation treatment. Trial-and-error decision making is common in both organization of day-to-day rehabilitation activities and formulation of long-term goals. Despite a multiplicity of aims and processes, the product must be a sensible, individualized, coherent rehabilitation plan. In light of the many tasks, the variety of possible ways of organizing them, and the prognostic uncertainty whatever path is taken, anxiety is both universal and inevitable in the rehabilitation situation.

Allied health caregivers have few well-validated models to guide their treatment planning in a predictable and clear manner; there are few models analogous, for instance, to the stages of labor in a normal spontaneous delivery or progression through the healing phases following myocardial infarction. Instead, rehabilitation has an abundance of models and conceptual schemes for organizing treatment and specifying its aims. Discussion of differing aims and activities often carries a defensive edge as if each allied health specialty felt compelled to prove its activities and goals equal, if not superior, in value to the others. This puts rehabilitation specialists under considerable competitive pressure to produce easily measurable, quantifiable results.

Exposure, Self-Esteem, and Performance Anxiety. In few other fields of medicine is one's professional work so subject to searching scrutiny by others. Results are universally measured, often by the simplest common denominators: How closely has the individual been restored to the pre-illness state? How many specific tasks can be performed fully at discharge, compared to admission? Never mind the permanence or relevance of these defined tasks to the individual's life. That anyone can see, evaluate, and judge (however foolishly) the result of one's work throughout the rehabilitation process places specialists under unusual self-esteem pressure measured in terms of patient achievement. The result may be a host of anxieties regarding one's professional worth, because one's work is so perpetually on exhibit.

Patient Transferences. Rehabilitation specialists are subject to a vast range of patient transferences, which are intensified by several factors in the rehabilitation setting: the traumatic disorganization of the patient's personality, the overdetermined psychological regression, the long duration and intensity of day-to-day physical dependency, and the like. Patients' loss of major motor control—limbs, tongue, sphincters, even breathing—produces intolerable feelings of helplessness and hopelessness and necessarily generates intense abandonment anxieties. All these factors disrupt personalities and reawaken latent conflicts and vulnerabilities that belong to earlier developmental experiences. This upheaval is often expressed by patients through a disguised question, "Can you ever *love* me again?" But hidden within is a more important question, "Can you ever *value* me again?" Thus, profound physical impairment causes temporary loss of significant portions of reliable adult psychological structure, which in turn compels patients to make intense interpersonal demands upon the staff.

Patients utilize their ordinary learning relationships, organized around everyday rehabilitation tasks, as the vehicle for their emotional demands on staff. Staff members frequently report feeling that patients are relating to them as if they were somebody else, a configuration perhaps arising from within the patient that has very little to do with the staff member as a real person. They complain that patients view them as if they were nothing but a "genie in a bottle," a set of impersonal powers lacking autonomous existence, motivation, and reactions. Seen through the patient's eyes, the staff member exists only for the sake of the patient, to be utilized at the beck and call of the patient. This experience of being treated by patients as if one had no independent existence constitutes a particularly exhausting emotional burden for staff members. This phenomenon has been summarized by the concept "self-object transferences" (Basch, 1981; Kohut, 1971; Goldberg, 1983; Tolpin, 1978).

Staff Members' Hidden Vulnerabilities

All human beings retain residues of childhood experiences. These "forgotten" memories constitute potential vulnerabilities with the capacity of resonating in intense ways with current crises. Despite staff members' lack of conscious awareness, these issues affect their professional behavior in several ways.

Interrelationships among Developmental Maturity, Age, and Psychological Status. The majority of rehabilitation personnel, especially those with the most patient contact—residents, interns, nurses, occupational and physical therapists, recreation and vocational specialists—are under the age of 30. This places them within 10 years of the average age of two large groups of rehabilitation patients, those with spinal cord injury or head trauma. (Stroke patients are the exception, because the majority are nearer the age of staff members' parents or grandparents.) Many young adults in their early twenties have not yet achieved mature postadolescent personality consolidation and conflict resolution. Capacities and resources needed to meet the burdensome demands of rehabilitation are less available in some staff members because their own conflict-resolving processes, developmental needs, and defensive propensities are still active and preoccupying. As a result, many staff members have trouble maintaining an optimal professional role: being comfortably separate, but empathically involved, with patients; selfless, but realistic, in their approaches; and responsive, but neutral, in their emotional involvement.

Staff Transference Issues. The youth and lack of developmental consolidation in some staff members make them especially susceptible to the possibility of regression. As aspects of their own normal, phasic developmental experiences are awakened under the stimulating effect of intense patient transferences (Erikson, 1959; Gedo, 1979), staff members frequently adapt by developing intense identifications with patients. Because rehabilitation care requires intimate body contact with patients, it is likely that unconscious developmental residues having to do with early childhood—sexuality, toileting—may be reawakened, but not at a high level of awareness. An example of this would be the situation of a 21-year-old nurse who had recently terminated her first serious love affair, who suddenly discovered herself to be the object of considerable intense, provocative sexual interest by a macho 18-year-old high-level spinal cord injured male who was desperately attempting to reassure himself of his attractiveness to women, despite his complete physical dependence.

Most common of all is the difficulty that staff members have in recognizing the origin of their rage, even hatred, toward a patient who consistently frustrates their best therapeutic efforts. It makes little difference what behavioral mechanism of frustration the patient employs: passive resistance, provocative counterassaults on the staff member, self-injury, or refusal to acknowledge the usefulness of any therapeutic activity. Staff helplessness, frustration, rage, and hatred of the patient sometimes leads, not merely to a therapeutic stalemate, but to the team's self-protectively coalescing in order to exclude the patient, pressuring the physician to discharge that patient as "hopeless and unmotivated, a poor rehabilitation candidate." How difficult it is for staff members to attain the objectivity needed to recognize that their distress is the result of the patient's attempts to work free of unbearable feelings of helplessness and hopelessness. By provoking or inducing staff to feel about them what they feel about their own injured bodies, these patients partially succeed in getting rid of their own terrible feelings. These matters have been more extensively explored in articles by Gans (1983; Chapter 7) and Winnicott (1958).

Narcissistic Vulnerability. Inside the privacy of our own minds we think of ourselves as uniquely special (powerful, beautiful, wise, clever, strong), able to influence the world in any way we decide, and able to experience any form of gratification that we desire (Kohut, 1971). *We* will never grow old, have a terrible catastrophe, or suffer a decline in our physical or mental powers. Above all, we will *never* become a patient in a rehabilitation facility! However, when we are unable to achieve our desires or fulfill our personal performance goals, we feel disappointed, frustrated, and possibly mildly depressed. Sometimes we fear there might be something terribly wrong with us. Narcissistic vulnerability—the general term for this state—involves more than a simple potential for experiencing a drop in one's self-esteem. The term also encompasses feelings of intolerable distress, helplessness, weakness, hopelessness, inner disorganization—not simply because one is frustrated, but because one is unworthy—as if one is about to be or has been abandoned by the world, as if something vital but irretrievable has been lost. This is very similar to the feelings of a C3–4 spinal cord injured patient or the victim of a pseudobulbar palsy—and sometimes, what rehabilitation workers feel when a favored patient falls short of their goals!

Massive Counteridentification. When first viewing the victims of catastrophic illnesses, able-bodied persons often experience reactions of anxiety, alienation, or humiliation, as if it were intolerably threatening to be reminded of the universality of their vulnerability as human beings. They may feel, "There but for the grace of God go I, and thank God it's somebody else. How would *I* be able to survive if I felt so different, so damaged, and so worthless? God will see that this will never happen to me." Among the more introspective staff members, efforts to deal with these terrible anxieties may take the form of a basic question—"I really wonder whether these people are human after all. Is someone so damaged, so distorted, so awful-appearing really still a human being?" This issue is portrayed vividly in a recent play and movie, "Elephant Man."

More Complex Ethical Issues. Rehabilitation values tend to be strongly performance-oriented and behavioral in nature. The good patient is thought to be the one who is happy and can perform actively, vigorously, and independently. Creative, contemplative, and spiritual values are minimized. The individuality and complexity of "quality of life" are simply ignored. This perspective has two subtle, but important, consequences: (1) A performance-oriented value system reflects typical young adult (defensive/adaptive) orientations—the solution that many young adults utilize in efforts to integrate their phase-appropriate postadolescent conflicts and tasks. Young staff members typically overgeneralize the applicability of these values for patients. With the passage of time, as they acquire more life and rehabilitation experience and develop capacities for introspection and empathy, allied health members begin to question the universal validity of performance-based values. Slowly they become more accepting of life aims that involve spiritual, moral, or introspective qualities. Many rehabilitation personnel come to believe that participating with the patient in the struggle to transcend adversity and master trauma, whatever individually determined form that struggle may take, is the ultimately worthy goal of rehabilitation. (2) But this realization may bring workers to an awareness of another dilemma regarding the meaning of their work. Under the secure socially sanctioned system of performance-based goals, staff members can avoid thinking about the limitations of their own efforts to accomplish such things as transformation of irreparable lesions, restoration of broken anatomy, or the forestalling of death. However, increasing self-scrutiny and self-doubt may create in the young worker previously unknown conflicts between professional and personal values.

What is the resolution of these conflicts? No single answer can suffice. Continuous personal struggle to make sense out of one's experience with one's patients, sharing of that experience with peers, and comparing one's own views with those of one's mentors and colleagues all help. Sometimes self-scrutiny may be facilitated by individual psychotherapy. For most rehabilitation personnel, this continuous introspective activity leads to realization of the significance of patient care, not only for their professional identity and professional gratification but also for maintaining the basic equilibrium of their adult personalities. Resolution of conflict and achievement of a stable personal balance in these matters may be selectively facilitated by multilevel staff educational programs designed to provide an appropriate combination of support, information, and experience. However, to be effective, any such program must have an ultimate aim: enhancement of capacity for individual professional growth and development.

SUGGESTED SOLUTIONS

A review of the psychiatric liaison-consultation literature, containing a myriad of educational/therapeutic solutions for the staff, is beyond the scope of this chapter. Rather, two specific educational solutions that have evolved from the author's lengthy experience are discussed.

Any educational program should have the following six features:

1. Ideally, any programmatic solution should address the etiology of the underlying problem.
2. The program should improve allied health workers' personal equilibrium and self-esteem, enlarge their capacity for understanding patients, and enhance their ability to deploy their competencies in actions.
3. It should actively involve the participants themselves at all levels of the process, with room for progressively more sophisticated involvement and responsibility.
4. It should utilize resources that are available and acceptable within the culture of the specific institution and whose use will lead to reasonably predictable results.

5. It should be economically justifiable, with results measured by staff members' acquisition of "process and tool" skills, rather than by their absorption of new terminology. Improvement in their capacity to manage complex patient problems, as well as ability to contain their own distress, is the best measure of effectiveness.

6. An educational program should be consistent with the "least wavemaking" principle; to ensure administrative acceptance and support, a program must not disturb other basic institutional activities or circumvent fundamental lines of responsibility and authority.

Component Goals

The ultimate goals of a staff education program may be stated simply: to endow staff members with the capacity to acquire new knowledge about their patients and themselves and to enhance the effectiveness of their therapeutic work with patients while facilitating the maintenance of their personal equilibrium. It is assumed that staff/patient reciprocal interactions are a major variable affecting the outcome of rehabilitation, as well as the self-esteem of the staff members (see Chapter 7). There are three subgoals.

Better Theory

Better concepts are needed, not only to help most allied health personnel understand their experiences with patients, but also to serve as tools to guide their own professional growth. In an earlier section of this chapter, three central organizing constructs for understanding data of staff/patient interaction exchanges were suggested: (1) the dynamic unconscious, (2) massive psychic trauma, and (3) the human need to make sense out of experience. One could supplement those concepts with an unlimited array of other significant ideas derived from the general field of psychiatry, such as regression, self-object transferences, conflict and defense, development, as well as an equivalent array from cognitive psychology, group psychology, sociology, and the like. However, a fundamental issue permeates many areas of staff difficulty—that of helping staff members learn how to talk, comfortably and effectively, to human beings called patients. A particularly useful set of concepts with respect to this task of communication has been developed by Ornstein and Kalthoff (1967) in an article designed to acquaint psychiatry and psychology residents with elementary interview skills. It describes the use of the self (and its subcomponent skills—observation, empathy, introspection, and intuition) as the basic tool for developing a reliable relationship with a patient so that essential diagnostic information can be elicited and then organized in a sensible way.

Self-Knowledge

Socrates is reputed to have answered a question regarding the highest form of human wisdom with two words: "Know thyself." Certainly staff members must strive to understand themselves and their reactions as significant forces influencing their work and their patients. Such self-inquiry inevitably raises the risk of discovering disquieting things about oneself, particularly angry, hateful, and negative feelings towards one's patients (Gans, 1983) or disappointment, humiliation, guilt, or anxiety with respect to one's own expectations (Gunther, 1977). Without encouraging staff members to run this risk, however, efforts to educate will be foreshortened and compromised and restricted to learning something about "the other [patient]." Self-knowledge, even its painful aspects, must be made an acceptable and institutionally supported goal. Otherwise, strivings for self-awareness will simply be resented and avoided.

Better Defenses

If staff members are to become aware of their own attitudes, feelings, and behavior through an educational program, that program must at the same time confront issues of their anxiety and general emotional vulnerability. One's psychological defenses against anxiety are determined by *all* the circumstances of one's past development and current life situation. Nevertheless, certain defenses can be specified as more useful in the rehabilitation setting and others as less useful. Among the less useful defenses are (1) projection and externalization, in which the patient is viewed as either the source of or the solution to one's discomfort; (2) avoiding anxiety by simply avoiding the patient as much as possible; (3) utilizing moral exhortation, rationalization, or intellectual explanations to put distance between oneself and the patient's painful subjective self.

Better defenses begin with the acceptance of an essential generalization: *Some emotional distress for staff members is ubiquitous and recurring—an inevitable outcome of significant involvement with patients.* Such distress is not a sign of individual neurosis, but rather a function of universal vulnerabilities stimulated in able-bodied human beings who must assume therapeutic responsibility for severely damaged people. To make such distress more tolerable, a few basic attitudes are necessary.

- Conscious selective disavowal is essential; that is, the temporary setting aside of some painful realities that have to do either with the patient or with ourselves (Basch, 1977). The ultimate truth of these realities is acknowledged, but is minimized as temporarily unimportant. One says, "A particular thing (e.g., the patient's shortened life-span, visually disgusting deformity, or refusal to acknowledge the need for help) really is true, but I can set it aside because, at the moment, it is not the important part of the patient or the important part of my activity.''

• Responsibility tinged with guilt is a willingness to accept limited personal responsibility for helping patients mitigate the disasters that have befallen them. Above all, one must accept patients' anger and disappointment that staff members cannot restore them to their premorbid condition. One simply must learn to live with patients' reactions to the team's inability to accomplish miracles and the guilt that this may produce; rehabilitation specialists cannot abandon patients who may provoke them by expressing their disappointment in staff.

• Another essential quality is some capacity for ordering and managing different feelings, ideas, and attitudes. This capacity parallels the setting of priorities in the tasks and aims that staff members expect the patient to accomplish. It permits one to deal with emotion-laden issues in the patient's treatment *one at a time*, instead of feeling compelled to "jump into the swamp." Attempting (and failing) to deal with everything at once merely produces a disorganized, overwhelming onslaught of subjective distress that is counterproductive to the rehabilitative process.

• Feelings can be separated from intentionality just as thoughts can be separated from action. Adults do not act on everything they feel, nor do they refuse to act realistically simply because it fails to make them "feel good." Rehabilitation staff must be guided by such principles as "If it is *necessary*, I will do it," rather than "If it feels good, I will do it." Team members must make this distinction for themselves, as well as for their patients.

KNOWLEDGE APPLIED: SOME UNIQUE PROBLEMS FOR THE BEHAVIORAL SCIENTIST

Behavioral scientists find themselves enmeshed in multiple role expectations, multiple activities, and multiple value systems. Empowering behavioral scientists as initiators, planners, and leaders in an educational program often stimulates and heightens latent conflicts in both audience and educators. From what do these conflicts arise and what do they involve?

Behavioral scientists, particularly those sophisticated in depth psychology, are regarded by the laity with many ambivalent attitudes and role expectations—awe, fear, suspicion, and occasionally respect. They are expected to, and frequently do, know more about the meaning of others' motives and behaviors than those others do. Yet, behavioral scientists are expected to use that knowledge with selflessness and discretion, never for personal gain. This is translated into a series of magical expectations with respect to their work with patients: "Change, discipline, or motivate him or her." They are constantly required to make judgments, not merely technical ones, but also ethical, political, and institutional ones. Perhaps the best behavioral scientists can do is offer an optimal compromise among many factors, rather than provide "guaranteed to work" technical answers to a patient's difficulty. The underlying issue, which is usually avoided, is the quest for certainty on everybody's part and the corresponding severe anxiety when that is not forthcoming. Premature decisions and lofty technical jargon may be temporarily reassuring, but they do little to address the origins of patients' or staff's chronic anxiety.

Behavioral scientists have multiple professional roles that come with their inherently contradictory responsibilities and divided loyalties. They are therapists to the patient and consultants to the teams, to the family, and occasionally to the administration. The balancing of multiple aims and roles is inevitably tedious and anxiety-provoking, but it is one of the pressures that behavioral scientists must learn to endure—it comes with the job.

In the usual rehabilitation setting, behavioral science personnel may be the only team members trained in small group dynamics, particularly the psychodynamic processes that are intrinsic to team function along the lines of the "therapeutic community model" (Jones, 1968). The effects of small group processes are, if anything, intensified in rehabilitation settings, especially for the treatment team (Nason, 1981). Splitting, the exclusion and extrusion of members, criminalizing behavior alternating with idealization, love-hate alliances all occur regularly and intensely. At a minimum, behavioral scientists must be aware of these processes. What they can do to mitigate their disruptive effect depends on a myriad of factors, in addition to their own competence.

Methods

How does one go about educating one's colleagues, ambivalent as they might be, about confronting the unknown, even irrational, factors that influence everyone's behavior? Not by the splendor of one's erudition or one's personal charisma, but by establishing a series of individual relationships of mutual trust, confidence, and respect based upon shared aims and activities "on the firing line" of patient care. Initially, it is essential to obtain institutional support and clear-cut, publicly proclaimed, upper-echelon backing for an educational program so as to ensure large-scale participation in it. Nonetheless, some resistance to participation is inevitable. A special problem is the recurring wish of certain groups to exempt themselves from the program. Although recognizing the mandated expectation of participation, they assume that their own need for such a program is not really very great. The alternative excuse offered is the urgent press of clinical responsibility in "our" department.

It is imperative that a psychologically framed educational program be modeled as nearly as possible on typical department or hospital inservice educational programs and be integrated with those programs. Assigning it special status may intimidate and deter staff members from attending. Thus, top management support is vital in order to secure time, location, personnel, and money for that program in the everyday organizational structure and activities of the hospital.

How to develop relationships of mutual trust, respect, and sharing is more difficult to specify. Often, this task is best achieved through individual transactions with key staff members about specific problem patients, especially if one has previously established oneself as an effective advisor or therapist. Naturally, rehabilitation personnel more easily accept as an educator somebody whom they know and respect. Through the support of key individuals, with whom other members in the educational group will identify, such a program can be sustained in its early days until it develops its own momentum generated by interest, value, and motivation. This helps explain why the "specially imported" eminent lecturer from outside so often has minimal long-term impact.

Forms of Educational Activity

No one form of educational activity is universally superior. The best form and content for a particular institution is determined by the specifics of the institution—its values, history, size, relationship to a university or medical school, and overall mission. However, there are several guiding principles. Education in a health care institution is an unending process, not only because of personnel changes but also because staff members go stale in the face of the endless burden of the rehabilitation situation. When properly deployed, education can be stimulating, revitalizing, and renewing of any professional's enthusiasm, confidence, and dedication. A properly integrated program counters the inevitable chronic exhaustion of personal and professional resources.

Typical educational activities may be day-long programs with a lecture followed by small group discussions; special-topic group participation seminars, such as the impossible patient, the uses of hate, or the battered staff; a short-term lecture series by a staff member or someone within the local professional community, usually organized around limited subject areas, such as alternative approaches, community maintenance, etc.; and regular low-key inservice activities, such as rounds, team meetings, and staffings. In addition, two unique kinds of educational activities have, in the author's experience, been significant in producing subtle changes in staff understanding and effectiveness. These are (1) the agendaless "free-for-all" department discussion and (2) the unusual psychiatric staffing.

Small Group Agendaless Free-For-All Discussion

This is a regular meeting with a team or department-based small unit. It is scheduled once or twice a month during the working day at an off-peak hour, typically mid-afternoon. Topics are spontaneously suggested and agreed upon by the group. The author has been accepted as discussion leader in part because his connection to administration is so indirect. Relationships of mutual trust, confidence, and respect have been built through multiple experiences of shared struggle with both staff and patient problems. Nevertheless, from time to time disruptive dynamic features have emerged, leading to crises. When such crises could not be managed effectively, the group process was disrupted, and meetings were temporarily discontinued.

During the many years of meetings, the format and subject matter have evolved and matured. Initially, the group gravitated toward safe topics, such as a "wastebasket" case. Gradually, however, content shifted from insoluble special problems to typical or everyday dilemmas. The more important shift was in the focus of discussion. Instead of a how-to-do-it level of discussion, the deeper understanding of motives, meanings, and consequences became the predominant aim. Consideration of the subjective experiences of both participants and patients gradually assumed prime importance. Among all participants self-awareness came to be a commonly expected basis for their contributions.

What issues became the focus of these meetings? With respect to patients, topics included the differences between provocative, helpless, or avoidant patient behavior and the underlying emotional states that fuel such behavior; how to make contact with withdrawn or traumatized patients; the difference between limit setting and punitive retaliation; the discomfort associated with staff's own helplessness and humiliation in the face of patient "failures" (Menninger, 1984); the difficulties of understanding, let alone managing, patients who "split" their relationship with staff members; and the uses of one's own self as a tool for both understanding and influencing patients. As in all careful educational enterprises, it is the match between subject matter—"the issue"—and the group's temperament, maturity, and integrity that is the crucial determinant of success; the specific subject matter is almost of secondary importance!

Unusual Psychiatric Staffing

Early in the author's work at this hospital routine psychiatric staffings were introduced. These involved members of the team, usually the physiatrist or resident, the psychiatrist, and all the allied health members of the team. The patients discussed were those whom the psychiatrist had seen the preceding week on referral from staff members. As the format relaxed senior team members (nurse, therapist, supervisors, residents, etc.) assumed the responsibility for suggesting patients for staffings. In the early stages, staffings were run in a semiformal manner with each specialist reporting in turn. As a more relaxed atmosphere took hold and greater trust developed, the aim shifted from problem solving toward broader educational goals, i.e., those with wider applicability than the individual cases. Better understanding of the whole person behind the current problem became possible through the free exchange of information and impressions. Not only were more complex objective data and observations presented but, most importantly, the subjective data of individual staff members, which they had previously dismissed as interfering or upsetting, were now searched out and discussed. This evolution required the utilization of special skills, particularly the leader's empathic sensitivity to the nuances of others' experience. Recognizing, softening, and reducing some of the intensely upsetting subjective reactions that staff members were having to particular patients became a broad additional goal. This came about as staff members learned to identify and accept as inevitable the twin phenomena of induced transferences and the experience of their own vulnerabilities, which were particularly manifested by feelings of humiliation and anxiety. Eventually, a third goal emerged, that of discerning previously unrecognized staff strengths that could be engaged in novel (prophylactic) ways with the patient, e.g., the use of each member's everyday rehabilitative activities as a therapeutic vehicle, framed against the team's collective aims and methods.

What was crucial in the development of this educational format? An attitude of mutual enthusiasm, benevolent tolerance, and encouragement and validation of the staff's contributions were all essential. The creation of this atmosphere facilitated maximal free participation by all staff members. Equally important, it led to a subtle shift in staff self-esteem and self-perception as they became more aware of their own diagnostic and therapeutic competence. In this context, Napoleon's saying is relevant: "Every private carries a marshall's baton in his knapsack."

Outcome and Summary

There is little in the way of hard data with which to determine the effectiveness of the program described here. Its usefulness, however, can be demonstrated by several indirect methods. Patients being seen today are more complex, suffer from more multiple insults (physical, psychological, social, and educational-cultural) than those of 25 years ago. Yet, fewer patients are being precipitously discharged as "untreatable." Staff members appear to be more tolerant of rehabilitation patients with nontraditional disabilities—for instance, carcinoma-salvage patients—than they did when the new disease categories began to be admitted for rehabilitation. More consistent and better use is made of both formal and informal psychiatric consultation. More complex kinds of patient difficulties are recognized earlier, and assistance is sought sooner and utilized more effectively. Less time is spent reteaching old lessons. A preventive orientation had taken hold even before recent economic pressures altered the organization of treatment programs. Staff members have adopted a more holistic orientation to patients, understanding them more fully and treating them as whole human beings. This is especially true with respect to the issue of patients' emotional/behavioral response to disability. The common attitude in years past was that only behavioral scientists needed to be concerned about the patient's psychological problems.

Staff distress has diminished, or at least is better managed; patients are less often targets of retaliation and more often recipients of empathy. Hospital administration has become more sophisticated and understanding of the special burdens that their job imposes on staff members working with multiply-damaged high-risk patients.

Measurement of the ultimate success of a staff educational program lies not only in the statistics of patient hospital days or the permanence of rehabilitation gains maintained after patients leave the hospital or even the kinds of patients that staff members are willing to treat. Rather, it lies in less tangible areas, such as staff's willingness to accommodate modest revisions of their own professional value systems to encompass less conventional or quantifiable goals, but ones that may be more meaningful to patients. Such an attitude serves not only to enhance patient understanding and management but also acts as a buffer against the endlessly recurrent stresses and exhaustive burdens of rehabilitation work. Thus, it offers an avenue toward continuous professional revitalization, growth, and development.

REFERENCES

Basch, M.F. (1977). Developmental psychology and explanatory theory in psychoanalysis. *The Annual of Psychoanalysis, 5*, 229–283.

Basch, M.F. (1981). Self-object disorders and psychoanalytic theory: An historical perspective. *Journal of the American Psychoanalytic Association, 29*, 337–351.

Basch, M.F. (1982). Empathic understanding: A review of the concept and some theoretical considerations. *Journal of the American Psychoanalytic Association, 30*, 101–126.

Blacher, R.S. (1972). The hidden psychosis of open heart surgery with a note on the sense of awe. *Journal of the American Medical Association, 222*, 305–308.

Blacher, R.S. (1978). Paradoxical depression after heart surgery: A form of survivor syndrome. *Psychoanalytic Quarterly, 47*, 267–283.

Campbell, T.W. (1980). Death anxiety on a coronary care unit. *Psychosomatics, 21*, 127–136.

Caplan, B. (1983). Staff and patient perception of patient mood. *Rehabilitation Psychology, 28*, 67–77.

Castelnuovo-Tedesco, P. (1973). Organ transplant, body image, psychosis. *Psychoanalytic Quarterly, 42*, 349–363.

Craig, T.M., & Van Natta, P.S. (1976). Recognition of depressed affect in hospitalized psychiatric patients: Staff and patient perceptions. *Diseases of the Nervous System, 38*, 561–566.

Emener, W.G. (1979). Professional burn-out: Rehabilitation's hidden handicap. *Journal of Rehabilitation, 45*, 55–58.

Erikson, E.H. (1959). Identity and the life cycle. *Psychological Issues, 1*, 1–171.

Freedman, A. (1983). Psychoanalysis of a patient who received a kidney transplant. *Journal of the American Psychoanalytic Association, 31*, 917–956.

Gallagher, R.H. et al. (1982). Psychiatric interventions in spinal cord injuries. *Psychosomatics, 23*, 1153–1167.

Gans, J.S. (1983). Hate in the rehabilitation setting. *Archives of Physical Medicine and Rehabilitation*, *64*, 176–179.

Gardner, E.R., & Hall, R.C.W. (1981). The professional stress syndrome. *Psychosomatics, 22*, 673–680.

Gedo, J.E. (1979). *Beyond interpretation*. New York: International Universities Press.

Goldberg, A. (1983). On the scientific status of empathy. *The Annual of Psychoanalysis, 11*, 155–169.

Greenson, R.R. (1967). *The technique and practice of psychoanalysis*. New York: International Universities Press.

Gunther, M.S. (1972). Psychiatric consultation in a general hospital: A regression hypothesis. *Comprehensive Psychiatry, 12*, 572–585.

Gunther, M.S. (1977). The threatened staff: A psychoanalytic contribution to medical psychology. *Comprehensive Psychiatry, 18*, 385–397.

Gunther, M.S. (1979). The psychopathology of psychiatric consultation: A different view. *Comprehensive Psychiatry, 20*, 187–198.

Holland, L.K., & Whalley, M.J. (1981). Work of the psychiatrist in a rehabilitation hospital. *British Journal of Psychiatry, 130*, 22–29.

Jones, M. (1968). *The therapeutic community*. New Haven: Yale University Press.

Klein, G.S. (1976). *Psychoanalytic theory: An explanation of essentials*. New York: International Universities Press.

Kohut, H. (1971). *The analysis of the self*. New York: International Universities Press.

Krystal, H. (1968). *Massive psychic trauma*. New York: International Universities Press.

Lichtenberg, J. (1981). The empathic mode of perception and alternative vantage points for psychoanalytic work. *Psychoanalytic Inquiry, 1*, 329–355.

Menninger, W.W. (1984). Dealing with staff reactions to perceived lack of progress by chronic mental patients. *Hospital and Community Psychiatry, 35*, 805–808.

Moore, B.E., & Fine, B.D. (1967). *A glossary of psychoanalytic terms*. New York: American Psychoanalytic Association.

Monchaux, D.C. (1978). Dreaming and the organizing function of the ego. *International Journal of Psychoanalysis, 59*, 443–453.

Nason, F. (1981). Team tension as a vital sign. *General Hospital Psychiatry, 3*, 32–36.

Neff, W.S. (1971). *Rehabilitation psychology*. Washington: American Psychological Association.

Niederland, W.G. (1981). The survivor syndrome: Further characteristics and dimensions. *Journal of the American Psychoanalytic Association, 29*, 415–426.

Ornstein, P.H., & Kalthoff, R.J. (1967). Toward a conceptual scheme for teaching psychiatric evaluation. *Comprehensive Psychiatry, 8*, 404–426.

Penn, I. et al. (1971). Psychiatric experience with patients receiving renal and hepatic transplants. In P. Castelnuovo-Tedesco (Ed.), *Psychiatric aspects of organ transplants*. New York: Grune & Stratton.

Quinlan, D.M., Kimball, C.P., & Osborne, F. (1974). The experience of open heart surgery. *Archives of General Psychiatry, 31*, 241–253.

Schnaper, N., & Cowley, R.A. (1970). Overview: Psychiatric sequelae to multiple trauma. *American Journal of Psychiatry, 133*, 883–889.

Schwab, J.J. (1982). Psychiatric illness in medical patients: Why it goes undiagnosed. *Psychosomatics, 23*, 225–229.

Schwaber, E. (1978). Reflections in response to "A psychoanalytic overview of children of survivors," by J. Kestenbaum. *The Holocaust: Psychological effects on survivors and their children.* Symposium conducted at Brandeis University, Waltham, MA.

Schwaber, E. (1981). Empathy, a mode of analytic listening. *Psychoanalytic Inquiry, 1,* 357–392.

Tolpin, M. (1978). Self-object and oedipal object: A crucial developmental distinction. *Psychoanalytic Study of the Child, 33,* 167–186.

Trieschmann, R.B. (1980). *Spinal cord injury: Psychological, social and vocational adjustment.* New York: Pergamon Press.

Winnick, H.Z. (1968). Traumatization through social catastrophe: A symposium. *International Journal of Psychoanalysis, 49,* 298–329.

Winnicott, D.W. (1958). Hate in the Countertransference. *Collected papers.* London: Tavistock.

Part III

Rehabilitation Neuropsychology

Chapter 9

Neuropsychological Assessment in Rehabilitation

Bruce Caplan, Ph.D.

ISSUES IN ASSESSMENT AND INTERPRETATION

With the proliferation of programs directed at the remediation of cognitive and perceptual consequences of brain injury (see Chapters 10, 11, and 12), proper neuropsychological assessment has assumed increased importance in rehabilitation settings. Because successful intervention requires accurate diagnosis, a thorough mapping of the brain damaged patient's "intellectual topography" is a necessary prologue to the institution of any remedial program. Furthermore, a report by Garcia, Tweedy, and Blass (1984) suggests that the need for neuropsychological testing in rehabilitation is even greater than has been recognized. They found evidence of cognitive impairment in 25 percent of a series of consecutive admissions to a rehabilitation hospital. An unexpected finding was the discovery of cognitive impairment in 33 percent of patients with peripheral vascular disease and 17 percent of those with ischemic cardiac disease. There is growing recognition that many medical conditions and physical ailments encountered in rehabilitation are accompanied by deficits in certain higher mental abilities (Boll, 1985). The purpose of this chapter is to outline a practical approach to rehabilitation-oriented neuropsychological assessment.

Although patients with a vast array of conditions—dementing processes, brain tumor, multiple sclerosis, anoxia, learning disabilities—may be referred for neuropsychological evaluation, the most likely candidates in a rehabilitation setting are patients with stroke or traumatic head injuries. The patterns of deficits exhibited by these two groups tend to differ; stroke patients typically manifest focal signs, such as aphasia, visual neglect, or hemiplegia, that are primarily a function of the locus of the compromised brain tissue, whereas head injured patients—specifically those who have sustained nonpenetrating injuries—are most likely to display diffuse signs, such as increased response latency, reduced attention span, and global intellectual loss. However, exceptions to this typology are not uncommon.

By the time a patient is ready for rehabilitation, the nature, location, and extent of brain damage will almost certainly have been documented by one or another neuroradiologic technique. Consequently, the traditional diagnostic function (Schreiber, Goldman, Kleinman, Goldfader, & Snow, 1976; Swiercinsky & Leigh, 1979) of the neuropsychologist—which sought to answer the questions, "Is this patient's brain damaged or dysfunctional?" and "If so, what is the likely locus?"—is superfluous in these cases. Furthermore, although the "localizationist" view is widely accepted as the best available model of brain function, it is also acknowledged that there are important individual differences among normal subjects in cerebral organization (Galaburda, Sanides, & Geschwind, 1978; Mateer, Polen, & Ojemann, 1982); when one considers, in addition, the uniqueness of each patient's brain damage, collateral circulation, and compensatory capabilities, it becomes evident that an assessment that merely documents and localizes cerebral dysfunction offers little to the rehabilitation team. The value of contemporary neuropsychological assessment in this setting, therefore, lies in the determination of the individual patient's intellectual strengths and weaknesses and in the translation of that information into suggestions about how best to shape therapeutic practices for that patient (Caplan, 1982a). The most helpful rehabilitation neuropsychological assessment is one that yields statements about skills and processes—for example, "This patient displays good attention/concentration ability, but deficient auditory-verbal comprehension. Instruction in physical therapy should, therefore, take the form of gestures and demonstrations"—rather than summaries of test performance, e.g., "This patient's intellectual functioning is in the 'borderline' range."

In certain cases, neuropsychological testing provides valuable insights into the causes of disparities between a patient's behavioral *potential* and actual *performance* in therapy. It is, for instance, important to know that a patient who has been reported to be unmotivated for occupational therapy—for example, does not work at copying parquetry designs—is suffering from lesion-related distractibility and cannot sustain attention in the noisy chaos of the therapy room long enough to complete the task. Noticeable improvement may occur when this patient is removed to a quiet, uncluttered testing room. In rehabilitation settings, one needs to know what the patient can do under ideal conditions and precisely how those conditions differ from the norm. To this end, the neuropsychologist endeavors to elicit the patient's *best* (not *typical*) performance. Doing so requires special sensitivity to certain factors: the slowing effects of fatigue, inertia, or motor impairment; the patient's comprehension of task demands (instructions may need to be repeated or rephrased); or the patient's need for eyeglasses or a hearing aid, etc. A related point is that, although neuropsychological assessments have traditionally focused on the analysis of deficiencies, it is often vital in rehabilitation settings that areas of strength be as carefully evaluated (Chelune, 1983). This information is of significant value in planning effective treatment.

Observation of patients in occupational therapy can be quite useful in understanding how brain-based deficits interfere with "real-world" activities; equally informative and somewhat sobering is observation of patients with profound test-documented deficits who achieve important functional goals, despite their impairments. This disjunction reflects both the variability of patient performance and the predictive limits of neuropsychological testing (Sunderland, Harris, & Baddeley, 1983).

Neuropsychologists working in rehabilitation settings could perform a valuable service by initiating collaborative studies with therapists and nurses of the activities of daily living (ADL) implications of neuropsychometric impairments (Ben-Yishay, Gerstman, Diller, & Hass, 1970; Heaton & Pendleton, 1981; McSweeney, Grant, Heaton, Prigatano, & Adams, 1985). Despite the assurances of some clinicians (e.g., Long, Gouvier, & Cole, 1984), solid evidence is lacking that neuropsychological test results "provide essential information about an individual's behavioral competence—that is, how well he or she can learn, remember, tolerate stress, and generally function in day-to-day living" (Long et al., p. 43). Extrapolation from test performance to independent living skills cannot yet be performed with great facility or confidence.

APPROACHES TO ASSESSMENT

There are two general perspectives regarding the format of the neuropsychological examination (Lezak, 1984; Russell, 1984). The "fixed battery approach" proposes that the identical set of tests be administered to all patients, whereas the "individualized approach" posits that the specific symptomatology of each patient should dictate a unique combination of measures. In actual practice, the distinction may become artificial. A recent survey of internship training in neuropsychology (McCaffrey, Malloy, & Brief, 1985) found that, although the vast majority of programs taught a standardized battery, 95 percent reported using "an individualized test selection strategy." The composition of a particular assessment is likely to depend on several factors: the presenting complaint(s) and referral question(s), time since onset of the condition, deficits detected prior to and during the course of the examination, biases of the clinician, etc.

Rehabilitation neuropsychologists (Golden,1978), as are their colleagues (e.g., Boll, 1984; Smith, 1975), are likely to find most congenial and useful an approach that incorporates elements of both paradigms. Under this method, a screening battery that taps a variety of functions is routinely administered to all patients. This allows the systematic collection of data for research purposes as well. Particular deficit areas uncovered thereby may then be examined in more detail. For example, preliminary testing may yield evidence suggestive of memory difficulty, e.g., failure to retain three words during a 5-minute interval. Further examination of memory function in different modalities might confirm impairment of verbal memory with relative preservation of visual memory. Alternatively, additional data may suggest that an attentional deficit caused poor performance on the word retention task, i.e., the material was never actually registered; such patients may display adequate memory for material to which they attend. This example illustrates the importance of what has been called syndrome analysis (Luria, Naydin, Tsvetkova, & Vinarskaya, 1969; see McFarland, 1983, for another method of syndrome analysis), qualitative analysis (Boll, O'Leary, & Barth, 1981), and the process approach (Milberg, Hebben, & Kaplan, 1986). In another context, Berg (1984) has described an individualized hypothesis-testing approach to assessment, and Kinsbourne (1971) has discussed the experimental analysis of cognitive deficit. These terms imply an emphasis on careful behavioral observation and analysis of the patient's performance on individual test items, strategy selection, and other process factors, in addition to interpretation of patterns of test scores.

Most neuropsychological tests are multifactorial in nature; the title of a test does not always indicate which functions are required for adequate performance on the test. For instance, the Benton Visual Retention Test (Benton, 1974) requires not only the capacity to remember visually presented material but also the ability to attend, scan, perceive, and draw. Also, because some of the stimuli lend themselves to verbal labeling, the test may tap certain language skills in some subjects. Thus, it is imperative that the examiner go beyond a numerical profile of scores to search for consistent common factorial threads of performance underlying the patient's successes and failures across tests. Kaplan (1983) stresses that test instruments must be viewed as tools by means of which one observes how the patient thinks, learns, selects and employs strategies, self-corrects, and so on. She argues that observation of *process* is more informative than analysis of *achievement* (response). Invaluable rehabilitation-relevant information can be lost if the examiner clings to the "bottom line" of quantitative data.

NONSTANDARD PROCEDURES

It is often revealing to administer tests under nonstandard conditions; that is, to employ procedural modifications in the service of fair and informative assessment (e.g., Sattler & Tozier, 1970). The modifications may involve recasting test instructions (or using gestures for patients with comprehension problems); placing test materials, such as the jigsaw puzzle pieces of the Object Assembly subtest of the Wechsler Adult Intelligence Scale-Revised (Wechsler, 1981), in the portion of the visual field to which a patient with visual neglect preferentially attends; or modifying test materials themselves.

As an example of modifying the test itself, consider the Raven Coloured Progressive Matrices (RCPM), a multiple-choice test that requires the subject to complete a visual display by pattern matching, completion, or analogical reasoning. Patients with unilateral (especially right-sided) cortical lesions often fail to scan the entire multiple-choice display—two rows of three items each—tending instead to choose an item on the side of the page ipsilateral to the lesioned hemisphere (Costa, Vaughan, Horwitz, & Ritter, 1969). Performance on the RCPM thus becomes a function of lateral scanning, not of visual-perceptual or reasoning ability. To restore the validity of the test as a measure of these latter functions, one may realign the response alternatives in a vertical array, thereby eliminating the need for left-to-right scanning (Caplan, 1983; Miceli et al., 1981).

Popkin, Schaie, and Krauss (1983) developed a special version of the Primary Mental Abilities test for use with older adults. Employing test stimuli that were identical to the original, they eliminated the computer-scored response sheet, enlarged the printed materials, and spatially rearranged some stimuli to enhance readability. Bolla-Wilson, Robinson, Price, and Squires (1984) created multiple-choice analogues of the WAIS-R Block Design and Object Assembly in order to study the contribution of perceptual ability to constructional performance, independent of visuomotor skill.

An important aspect of nonstandard assessment is "testing the limits" of the patient's abilities. For example, motorically impaired individuals might be allowed to work on a constructional task until they are finished, even if doing so means exceeding the stated time limits. Although performance may be scored according to both standard and nonstandard guidelines, adherence to the former is likely to yield only the redundant information that this patient has a manual motor deficit. Lezak (1983) suggests that patients who are unable to do mental arithmetic should be allowed to work the problems out with pencil and paper, thereby eliminating the potentially limiting effects of memory overload. In this way, a more accurate appraisal of arithmetic ability per se can be obtained.

Nonstandard methods may be indicated when testing patients with the sorts of special problems frequently encountered in rehabilitiation settings; for example, sensory impairment, tendency to fatigue, and poor motivation. It may be necessary to provide more than the usual amount of encouragement to ensure adequate effort by brain damaged patients who are both sensitive and depressed about the cognitive consequences of their injuries. Indeed, there is considerable evidence (e.g., Cole & Zarit, 1984; Weingartner, Cohen, Murphy, Martello & Gerdt, 1981) that depression disrupts cognitive functioning. Geriatric patients, who often find neuropsychological assessment procedures peculiar or pointless, may also require additional reassurance and reorientation to the task. Rabbitt (1982), noting that elderly patients may initially be anxious and perplexed during testing, suggests discarding data from the first session as unrepresentative. The same point may be well taken with regard to many neuropsychological assessments.

Nonstandard testing is an invaluable tool in the assessment of brain injured patients (see Heaton & Heaton, 1981, for discussion of the vicissitudes inherent in the assessment of impaired patients); it complements, but does not replace, conventional evaluation.

INTERPRETATION OF TEST SCORES

When interpreting the results of the neuropsychological evaluation, one must consider the patient's premorbid level of function. A scaled score of 9 on the WAIS-R Vocabulary subtest might be within normal limits for a taxi driver with a high school diploma, but would signify significant impairment in a professor of literature with an advanced degree. The best comparative standard is premorbid test data but these are rarely available. Several possible solutions exist. Wilson et al. (1978) have attempted to quantify the clinical "seat-of-the-pants" approach; namely, inferring premorbid abilities on the basis of certain demographic informa- tion—educational level, occupation, race, age, and sex—often associated with intellectual performance. They derived regression equations that may be used to estimate premorbid Verbal, Performance, and Full-Scale I.Q. scores by inserting the appropriate values for a given patient. Although this approach appears promis- ing, further substantiation is required.

Some authors have proposed inferring premorbid level of function from the subject's best current test score on the assumption that this reflects the functioning of intact areas. However, this tactic is not useful with diffusely brain damaged patients in whom all scores may be depressed. Furthermore, this method is predicated on the questionable assumption of premorbid equivalence of the various mental functions; a particular test may tap an overlearned and well- practiced skill in a given individual, thus yielding a spuriously inflated estimate of premorbid level. For instance, an otherwise severely impaired watchmaker might perform quite well on a test that assesses manual dexterity and psychomotor speed (e.g., Purdue Pegboard).

Several authors (Nelson & McKenna, 1975; Nelson & O'Connell, 1978; Ruddle & Bradshaw, 1982) have suggested that current reading level provides a reasonable estimate of premorbid intellectual skills. Clearly, however, this method cannot be used with language-impaired subjects.

Another suggested approach relies on the assumption that certain tests are resistant to the effects of brain damage and therefore may be used as indices of premorbid function. This method is embodied in the "hold" versus "don't hold" dichotomization of Wechsler subtests. Wechsler (1955) argued that certain tests (Vocabulary, Information, Object Assembly, and Picture Completion) are rela- tively unaffected by brain damage, whereas others (Digit Span, Similarities, Block Design, and Digit Symbol) are more vulnerable. Comparison of the two subsets of tests should yield a quantified estimate of intellectual loss. However, this technique has not proven successful (Bersoff, 1970). Indeed, neurologic patients have been found to show depressed scores on all WAIS subtests (Russell, 1972). The Shipley-Hartford (Shipley, 1946) test also employs this comparative method. A "conceptual quotient" is derived based on the patient's scores on the vocabulary measure (presumed to be lesion-resistant) and on the abstraction test (presumed to be lesion-susceptible).

The obtained data must be compared with exisitng age- and education-related norms. This is especially difficult in the case of older stroke patients for, as Albert (1981) noted, there is a serious paucity of neuropsychological studies of unimpaired elderly persons. Furthermore, tests need to be restandardized periodically to control for generational changes in educational level, nutrition, and other factors that may affect performance; the clinician must stay abreast of current literature in order to remain informed of contemporary normative performance levels.

In a provocative recent article that addresses issues of concern to rehabilitation specialists, McCauley and Swisher (1984) argued that, for many clinical purposes, such as formulation of treatment plans, monitoring of change, and analysis of patterns of deficit, norm-referenced tests are less useful than other measures.

INDICATIONS FOR REASSESSMENT

It is frequently advisable to conduct serial evaluations of patients during the course of their rehabilitation and afterward. As cerebral edema ebbs, physical and mental stamina increase, and compensatory brain mechanisms commence operation, the patient's neuropsychological profile may be profoundly altered (Bieliauskas, Topel, & Huckman, 1980). Certainly, recommendations regarding return to work or school, resumption of leisure activities, driving, and the like should be made on the basis of up-to-date data, not the results of initial testing. Legal proceedings may require documentation of residual intellectual deficit and course of recovery (Gilandas & Touyz, 1982; McMahon & Satz, 1981). Ideally, for these purposes, one should have available parallel forms of all tests because readministering the same instruments may jeopardize the validity of the assessment. (The interested reader is referred to Eckhardt & Matarazzo, 1981; Matarazzo, Carmody, & Jacobs, 1980; Seidenberg, O'Leary, Giordani, Berent, & Boll, 1981; and Shatz, 1981, for discussion of the test-retest issue with regard to the Wechsler and Halstead-Reitan Battery.) Unfortunately, a flaw in the contemporary neuropsychologist's armamentarium is the virtual absence of such parallel forms for the most common measures. For certain tests, such as word list learning (Hannay & Levin, 1985) or vocabulary, the examiner may develop relatively comparable forms by substituting new words of equal difficulty. In the case of tests that require inferential reasoning, deduction of a principle, certain psychomotor skills, or the like, the effects of prior exposure (learning) create interpretive hazards. Although one may reasonably conclude that a decline in performance over time represents a true loss, one can be less certain that a higher score reflects recovery.

The remainder of this chapter describes a number of neuropsychological tests that are useful in the evaluation of rehabilitation patients. These tests are grouped into several conventional categories—attention, psychomotor functions, language, perception, memory, constructional capacity, and higher cognitive functions. However, because many tests have a complex structure, a test's classification under a particular heading is admittedly debatable. In some cases, a test is mentioned under more than one heading. The order of the sections corresponds to the suggested sequence of assessment.

This review is highly selective and not exhaustive. It discusses conventional standardized tests, as well as instruments drawn from the experimental literature that may have less extensive and well-validated norms. The reader is referred to Benton, Hamsher, Varney, and Spreen (1983), Filskov and Boll (1981, especially Part Four), Smith (1975), and Walsh (1978) for discussions of additional tests. The volume by Lezak (1983) is an indispensable comprehensive sourcebook.

Two final points: It is entirely proper and desirable for clinicians occasionally to devise test procedures on an ad hoc basis. Indeed, it is not uncommon for an examiner to develop a hypothesis about some aspect of a particular patient's deficits, residual skills, or problem-solving style that cannot be addressed by an existing test. In such cases, a bit of creative thinking can produce a novel device that may eventually become an established part of the testing repertoire. Second, certain consequences of brain injury, such as loss of mental stamina, decreased initiative, distractibility, and perplexity (Lezak, 1978; Williams, 1979) that may affect test performance are not in themselves easily measurable. Understanding their contribution to the performance of individual patients depends on careful behavioral observation by the examiner.

NEUROPSYCHOLOGICAL TESTS

Attention/Concentration

The preliminary conversation with the patient, during which one describes the nature and purpose of the assessment, serves several important purposes. In addition to allowing the development of some degree of rapport, it offers the opportunity to make gross observations about the patient's orientation and attention span. Disorientation and inattentiveness are often considered to render a patient unsuitable for rehabilitation; however, one encounters patients with mild to moderate degrees of attentional impairment. The examiner should therefore begin by briefly testing for deficits in these areas. If the patient is not oriented and/or cannot attend to a task, further testing is likely to be unproductive. It is important to note, however, whether the individual can be "engaged," perhaps by a particularly interesting (or in the case of a severely impaired patient, a particularly easy) task or activity, an eye-catching magazine picture, or the like in a way that does not otherwise occur.

"Attention" and "concentration" are vaguely defined concepts that are difficult to quantify. They are variously used to suggest arousal, alertness, and sustained or directed focusing. A common test of attention (and of echoic memory, see below) is digit repetition, in which the patient is requested to repeat progressively lengthening strings of numbers recited by the examiner and to maintain the correct sequence. The Digit Span subtest of the WAIS-R requires the subject to repeat digits in reverse order. A considerable discrepancy is often observed between forward and backward spans, the latter being especially susceptible to the effects of aging and visuospatial deficit. The impact of that deficit becomes clear when one considers the very different strategies elicited by the two varieties of digit repetition. On the forward span portion, subjects tend to parrot the numbers read by the examiner; in order to recite the reverse order, however, many subjects visualize a row of numbers and read them off from right to left. This strategy places at a disadvantage those subjects, usually those with posterior right-hemisphere lesions, who have impaired scanning or visuospatial dysfunction (Costa, 1975; Weinberg, Diller, Gerstman, & Schulman, 1972). Each trial takes only a few seconds, and the entire test is usually completed within 5 minutes.

Benton, VanAllen, and Fogel (1964) have provided a useful test of temporal orientation. The Mini-Mental State examination (Folstein, Folstein, & McHugh, 1975) includes items dealing with orientation in time and space.

The visual cancellation tasks developed by Weinberg et al. (1977; see also Caplan, 1985) require the patient to scan across several typewritten lines of numbers, symbols, or letters and to cross out a particular target each time that it appears. (This task has other uses, as discussed below.) Unimpaired subjects can perform a six-line test in as little as 60 seconds; brain damaged subjects may require 6 minutes or more. Although the accuracy of target detection is of interest, simple observation of the individual's perseverance and effort may provide the most useful information. Another task is to ask patients to sort several decks of playing cards according to suits or simply by color. Here again, observation is most informative.

The Trail-Making Test (Reitan, 1958), which requires the subject to draw a line connecting numbers (and, in the more difficult version, to alternate between numbers and letters) in sequence, and the Symbol Digit Modalities Test (Smith, 1973), a kind of coding task, are other commonly employed measures of concentration. Gronwall (1977) describes the Paced Auditory Serial Addition Test. The subject listens to a tape recording of 60 digits, which are presented at a rate of one every 1–2 seconds and must add the two most recently heard numbers. For example, if the recorded digits are 2-7-3-5-1, the subject's responses should be 9-10-8-6. Clearly, this test cannot be used with patients who have hearing loss or expressive language difficulties.

All these tests of attention/concentration require at most only a few minutes to complete. It may therefore be necessary to administer a series of tasks in order to ascertain the limit of the patient's attention span. For example, some patients may perform well on digit repetition, but that time interval may define the limit of their attentional capacity; they may therefore be found to be distractible in occupational therapy sessions.

Clinicians who have access to microcomputers might be able to develop an automated analog of the continuous performance test described by Rosvold, Mirsky, Sarason, Bransome, and Beck (1956). In this paradigm, subjects monitor a constantly changing display of letters, responding with a button press whenever a designated target appears. In a more difficult version, the subject responds only when a designated pair of letters occurs in a particular sequence.

By the end of this portion of the evaluation, the examiner should know how long the patient can work at a task, and this information should be considered in administering the remaining tests. It is also useful to know whether occasional short breaks serve as adequate refreshers or whether the patient's mental stamina is easily depleted. Throughout the assessment, one should note whether the patient frequently requests repetition of test instructions, for this can signal poor attention span, as well as lack of motivation or comprehension deficit.

Psychomotor Functions

In most rehabilitation settings, the patient's motor abilities—grip strength, manual dexterity, etc.—are appraised by occupational and/or physical therapists. The neuropsychological examiner may, however, wish to obtain measures of certain psychomotor functions. (See Chapter 3 for discussion of assessment of the *apraxias*, disorders of skilled movements.)

One of the simplest motor tasks requires the subject to tap a telegraph key as rapidly as possible. The key is attached to a counter that records the number of taps for a given time interval. When administered as part of the Halstead-Reitan battery under the title "Finger Oscillation Test," five 10-second trials are given using the index finger of the preferred hand, followed by five trials for the index finger of the opposite hand. Normal subjects average about 5 taps per second with the dominant hand and only slightly less with the nondominant hand. Unilateral cerebral lesions often reduce the contralateral tapping rate.

The Purdue Pegboard Test (Tiffin, 1968) requires the subject to insert small metal pegs into one of two parallel vertical lines of holes. Each hand is tested individually for a 30-second trial, followed by one trial with the two hands working together, each placing pegs in a different line. Tiffin (1968) reports normative scores in the range of 15–19 for right hand performance, 14.5–18.0 for the left hand, and 12.0–15.5 for the two hands simultaneously. Costa, Vaughan, Levita, and Farber (1963) found the Purdue Pegboard to be a good screening test for the detection and lateralization of brain damage, although Heaton, Baade, and Johnson (1978) and Lezak (1983) doubt its usefulness for these purposes.

A potentially useful nonstandardized task (mentioned, although not described, by Shankweiler & Studdert-Kennedy, 1975) calls upon the subject to cut out a complex shape with a pair of scissors. Although Shankweiler and Studdert-Kennedy measured elapsed time in a normal population, some measure of accuracy rather than of time would probably be more useful in the assessment of rehabilitation patients.

The Trail-Making Test that was discussed above is also considered an informative measure of psychomotor function.

Language

Evaluation of linguistic impairment (aphasia) in brain damaged patients is traditionally the special province of speech pathologists, and neuropsychologists are well advised to consider the results of these assessments in their analyses and reports. Among the most popular batteries employed by speech pathologists are the Boston Diagnostic Aphasia Examination (Goodglass & Kaplan, 1983), the Porch Index of Communicative Abilities (Porch, 1967), the Neurosensory Center Comprehensive Examination for Aphasia (Spreen & Benton, 1969), and the Western Aphasia Battery (Kertesz, 1979). Many neuropsychologists who do not routinely administer these batteries use particular subtests to assess such skills as repetition, spelling, or writing; others may employ tests of specific functions, such as the Token Test (DeRenzi & Vignolo, 1962; a brief version was developed by Spellacy and Spreen, 1969), a test of receptive language, or the Boston Naming Test (Goodglass & Kaplan, 1983).

Goldstein and Shelley (1984) note that the neuropsychological assessment of language functions differs in significant ways from traditional aphasia testing. First, neuropsychological measures often reflect the effects of age and/or educational level; second, certain patterns of language deficit are at variance with the classic aphasia syndromes, and these are best evaluated by "nontaxonomic" measures.

The findings of recent studies support the contemporary aphasiologist's expansion of the traditional "expressive versus receptive" dichotomy; most theorists propose at least six syndromes. Schwartz (1984) has argued that the "polytypic structure" of the aphasias will frustrate efforts to create comprehensive schemes and that what is needed is the development of a "multivariate space that charts the simultaneous variation in (aphasia) as a function of, for example, site of lesion, age of patient, etiology, time since onset, etc.'' (p. 5).

Significant information regarding the patient's language abilities can be acquired by monitoring spontaneous speech and by observing difficulties with comprehension of test instructions. Paraphasias, reduced output, anomia (word-finding difficulty), and dysarthria (impaired articulation) are some of the expressive deficits that may be noted. Benson (1979) has provided a useful typology of comprehension disturbances.

A brief, but potentially revealing test is the Controlled Word Association test, also known as the "verbal fluency" or "F-A-S" test (Borkowski, Benton, & Spreen, 1967). The patient is allowed 60 seconds to produce as many words as possible that begin with a designated letter or that fit a particular category, such as fruits and vegetables or animals at the zoo. This test provides some gross data on the level of the patient's working vocabulary, presence of articulatory impairment, speed of response, and, particularly relevant to cases of head injury or frontal lobe involvement, difficulty in initiating activity or maintaining task orientation ("cognitive set"). Semantic memory skills are also involved.

Several measures of vocabulary are available. The 35-item Vocabulary subtest of the WAIS-R, administered orally, is traditionally considered to be a measure of well-learned, crystallized information and an excellent index of premorbid ability. In cases of dominant hemisphere involvement, especially when there is expressive deficit, another vocabulary test may be required. The Shipley Institute of Living Scale (Shipley, 1946) contains a multiple-choice vocabulary test that requires the subject to underline the appropriate synonym. Lezak (1983), noting the difficulty of many of the words, points out the comparative insensitivity of the Shipley test in distinguishing brain damaged from normal subjects. Its usefulness in rehabilitation settings is probably limited to relatively high-level patients. Each of the two forms of the revised Peabody Picture Vocabulary Test (Dunn & Dunn, 1981) is comprised of 175 four-picture sets. The subject points to or says the number of the picture that represents the stimulus word spoken by the examiner. Items on the Peabody span a much broader range of difficulty levels—normative data exist for 2½-year-old children—than does the Shipley; it is therefore more useful with neurologically impaired subjects.

Several measures of reading ability are available. The Wide Range Achievement Test-Revised (Jastak & Wilkinson, 1984; a large-print edition is available) and the Reading Recognition subtest of the Peabody Individual Achievement Test (Dunn & Markwardt, 1970) measure reading of single words, whereas the Boston Diagnostic Aphasia Examination contains subtests of sentence and paragraph reading. The Gates-MacGinitie Reading Tests (Gates & MacGinitie, 1965/1969) are suitable for measuring several reading functions in a variety of age and ability groups.

This discussion has been limited to consideration of a few specific language functions. The brevity of this section should not be taken to suggest that assessment of language is an unimportant component of the neuropsychological evaluation. Rather, an adequate treatment of the forms of language disturbance and methods for their evaluation is beyond the scope of this chapter. The interested reader is referred to Benson (1979), Darley (1982), and Kertesz (1979) for particularly readable summaries of this area. Furthermore, language is an integral aspect of domains yet to be discussed.

Perception

The neuropsychological measurement of perceptual abilities in brain damaged rehabilitation patients tends to center on the visual modality. In part, this is due to the comparatively direct implications for rehabilitation of visual-perceptual deficit. Furthermore, intact visual-perceptual ability can serve a compensatory function when perception in another modality is impaired. Finally, there is a wealth of clinical/experimental literature concerning the nature and assessment of defects in visual perception.

Benton (1979) notes that brain injured patients, with the possible exception of those with right posterior involvement, usually perform adequately on tests of simple visual discrimination. Tests employing complex stimuli or demanding sophisticated visual analysis are more likely to reveal deficits, especially in right-hemisphere-damaged patients. Modified administration of the Benton Visual Retention Test-Multiple Choice Version, now called Visual Form Discrimination (Benton et al., 1983), in which both the stimulus (geometric shapes) card and the multiple-choice array are presented simultaneously, is a useful test of a simple visual-analytic (matching) ability. The Matching Familiar Figures Test (Kagan et al., 1964) provides a more intricate analog; there are six response alternatives, in contrast to four on the Benton, and the differences among the figures are far more subtle. Newcombe's (1969) pattern-matching task is of intermediate difficulty.

The Complex Figure Test, developed by Rey (1941) and standardized by Osterrieth (1944), demands intact form perception, adequate motoric ability, and sequencing skills (Binder,1982). The subject must copy a complicated design, using a different color pen for each segment. Points for accuracy of reproduction are assigned according to a precise system. Also of interest is the subject's approach to the task; that is, the cognitive style employed. Osterrieth devised a typology of seven "plans of action," including a well-conceived, systematic approach, exclusive focus on individual details without regard to the total gestalt, drawing of a visually similar object, and an undecipherable drawing. When the subject has finished or after 3 minutes, the examiner removes the model and the subject's copy, provides a clean sheet of paper, and instructs the subject to reproduce the design from memory. Osterrieth (1944) reported larger discrepancies between "copy" and "memory" scores for his brain damaged subjects than for the control group.

Several tests of figure-ground discrimination are available. The original test developed by Gottschaldt (1926, 1929) and modified by Thurstone (1944) and Witkin, Oltman, Raskin, and Karp (1971) has been widely used in neuropsychological research. An easier version was created by Benton and Spreen (1969). The subject is required to detect and trace a simple figure that is embedded in, and obscured by, a more complex pattern. Thurstone and Jeffrey (1956) developed a multiple-choice version that can be used with subjects who have impaired function of the dominant upper extremity. Patients who perform poorly on this task because of defective figure-ground discrimination—impaired concentration or motor deficit are other possible causes of poor performance—may have difficulty with a variety of ADL tasks. For example, such patients might be unable to locate articles of clothing, eating utensils, or grooming implements (figures) in their room (ground).

Another test requiring intact visual-analytic skills is the Picture Completion subtest of the WAIS-R. This test consists of a series of 20 cards depicting a variety of objects, people, and settings, each of which is lacking an important feature. The subject is allowed 20 seconds to find the missing component. This test assesses perception of detail, but also depends to some extent on memory factors, as some items require comparison of the incomplete picture with a stored representation of the intact form, and on reasoning ability. General intellectual level appears to be important (Cohen, 1957). The content of the patient's responses should be evaluated for evidence of concrete thinking (characteristic of brain injured patients), denial (of the existence of missing parts, perhaps reflecting the patient's denial of illness), and psychiatric disorder (extremely idiosyncratic or bizarre responses).

The Hooper Visual Organization Test requires the subject to analyze and synthesize visually presented material (Hooper, 1958). Fragmented drawings of 30 familiar objects are presented for identification. Hooper's suggested cut-off scores, which categorize performance as unimpaired, mildly impaired, moderately impaired, or severely impaired, have been questioned by Boyd (1981), who notes that no simple set of cut-off scores can be universally applicable. Nonetheless, this test can provide important qualitative insights. For example, Hooper (1958) describes a tendency of some patients to provide "isolate responses," that is, answers based primarily on a single fragment of the picture. He suggests that the degree of this inclination, which is also called "stimulus boundedness," is prognostic for schizophrenic patients. It would be interesting to know whether the same holds for brain damaged patients. Tamkin and Jacobsen (1984) give normative data for six age groups and note the significant impact of I.Q.

As the individually administered Hooper requires only a spoken response, it is a useful test for motorically impaired patients. In cases of expressive aphasia, jigsaw puzzle tests, such as the WAIS-R Object Assembly subtest, provide another route to assessment of the same functions. The dextrous examiner might consider creating a jig-saw puzzle version of the Hooper by judicious use of a pair of scissors.

Another visual task requiring both analysis and synthesis is identification of incomplete drawings. The Gestalt Completion Test (Street, 1931) consists of 15 items that have been partially obscured by shading. Because some of the objects are no longer commonly seen, this test is now of primarily historical interest. The incomplete drawings test developed by Gollin (1960) is probably more suitable in clinical practice. Each item is depicted in five versions of graduated degrees of clarity. Thus, one may determine the extent of cuing required by a given subject. Warrington and James (1967) used incomplete silhouettes of common objects and incomplete letters. Two versions of each item were prepared, representing 30 percent and 70 percent of the complete figure. Patients with right-hemispheric (especially parietal) lesions tended to achieve lower scores on these tests than did left-hemispheric patients or controls. Warrington (1982) offers an excellent concise review of measures of several visual-perceptual functions, as well as an interesting neuropsychological model of object recognition.

The standard and colored versions of the Raven Matrices (Raven, 1960, 1965) should be mentioned as tests that require visual-analytic and visual-synthetic skills, in addition to problem-solving and reasoning abilities. The Raven is discussed below.

An intriguing visual-perceptual deficit that often accompanies right posterior damage, but which has been found with lesions in several other locations, is unilateral neglect; that is, failure to attend to or process input from the side of space contralateral to the lesion. Neglect may be observed in the auditory and tactile modalities as well; the associations among the various types of neglect have not been well studied. (See Heilman, 1979 for a discussion of the differentiation among neglect, extinction, and hemianopia.)

The presence and severity of neglect have been assessed with a variety of instruments. When asked to bisect horizontal lines, patients with neglect displace the dividing line toward their "good" side. Schenkenberg, Bradford, and Ajax (1980), however, caution against the diagnostic use of this test in individual cases. Weinberg et al. (1977) employed a series of visual cancellation tasks (discussed above under "attention/concentration") in studies of neglect. Patients with neglect tend to omit targets on one side of the page, and performance often deteriorates markedly on succeeding (lower) lines. Drawings of common objects, whether spontaneous or copies of a model, may be literally one-sided. A drawing of a clock face may have a flattened left side, and the numbers are likely to cluster on the right.

The neglecting patient's ability to read may be seriously compromised by difficulty locating the left-side margin of the column; some patients even omit the leftmost letter(s) of single words, e.g., reading "none" as "one." However, some patients with subtle degrees of neglect can adequately read conventionally printed material; when they are given a specially prepared paragraph that has an irregular left-hand margin (the beginning of each line is indented a variable number of spaces), performance often declines considerably (Caplan, 1987). Refixation to the beginning of each line requires a separate act of controlled scanning; the adoption of a "spatial set" is not possible. This task may also be a useful retraining tool.

A variant of the cancellation task was developed at the Boston Veterans Administration Hospital. In this version letters are scattered in random fashion across the entire page. While the patient crosses out each instance of the designated target, the examiner indicates on a similar sheet (with targets already circled) the order in which the subject detects targets. In this way, one captures the patient's self-imposed scanning style (systematic versus haphazard; one-sided versus all-encompassing); Weinberg and co-workers' method enforces, or at least encourages, linear scanning.

Other tasks dependent upon visual search or scanning have been developed by DeRenzi, Faglioni, and Scotti (1970), Teuber (1964) and Elithorn, Jones, Kerr, and Lee (1964). These instruments are not as readily available as the cancellation test, but clinicians may wish to create their own versions based upon similar principles.

Certain tests, not specifically developed as measures of neglect, may shed light on the degree of lateral attentional bias present in a given patient. The performance of brain damaged patients on the Raven Coloured Progressive Matrices was analyzed by Costa et al. (1969) in an innovative way. The Raven is a visually administered, multiple-choice test of pattern matching, completion, and analogical reasoning with response alternatives arrayed in two rows of three items each. Costa et al. (1969) derived a "position preference index" (PPI) by subtracting the number of times a subject selected an item in one extreme column from the number of selections from the opposite column (ignoring central choices). The PPI thus provides a quantified measure of neglect. Indeed, it could be maintained that the PPI obtained from the Raven is a more useful index of neglect than is cancellation performance, as the former is obtained under conditions of relative complexity that more closely approximate real-world requirements. Specifically, although cancellation requires little more than simple scanning and low-level motor skill, performance on the Raven taps a variety of skills, only incidentally engaging spatial exploration abilities. Because scanning is not so clearly demanded, the patient who is deficient in this area may, in focusing on the higher-level cognitive demands, fail to employ whatever compensatory scanning mechanisms have been developed, thus revealing subtle (but salient) neglect.

The Matching Familiar Figures Test, which has a format similar to that of the Raven, also allows the calculation of a PPI. The author has observed (Caplan, 1982b) that PPIs for these two tests are highly correlated in right-brain-damaged patients (r = .777). Not surprisingly, high PPIs tend to be associated with low test scores. Thus, the neuropsychological examiner must exercise extreme caution when interpreting test data obtained from patients with neglect, because any visually presented test may be performed poorly by virtue of neglect alone.

Memory

From the standpoint of prognosis for rehabilitation, impaired memory is probably the most devastating intellectual consequence of brain damage, for the essence of rehabilitation is relearning (Steger, 1976). The patient who is unable to acquire and retain new information therefore stands little chance of achieving significant functional gains. Yet, despite the obvious importance of clinical assessment of memory, Erickson and Scott (1977, p. 1131) concluded a literature review by calling the area "neglected and in disarray," and Lawrence (1984) claimed that most memory tests were supported only by face validity and clinical inertia. Benson and Blumer (1982) asserted that informal memory testing—asking the patient who visited last night, what activities the patient participated in during the last therapy session—is no worse than formal assessment and is clinically more informative.

A prime cause of this chaos is the multiplicity of factors that contribute to observed performance on memory tests. Furthermore, Ross (1980a & b) has described sensory-specific and fractional disorders of memory in which impairment was limited to a single modality or to one-half of the body. Thus, the clinician is well advised to use multiple tests of memory for different kinds of material (words, digits, shapes, pictures, etc.) employing a variety of paradigms (e.g., free recall, serial recall, recognition, selective reminding, multiple-choice format, paired-associate learning, delayed recall with filled and unfilled intervals). The experimental literature on amnesia, especially on Korsakoff's syndrome, is a source of many useful tests (see Butters & Cermak, 1980; Squire & Butters, 1984; Talland, 1965).

In attempting to demonstrate and characterize memory deficit in a given patient, it is important to understand the several subprocesses involved in learning and remembering (Baddeley, 1976). The subject must attend to the material, process and understand it, encode it for storage, retain it for a certain interval, and retrieve it when needed. Dysfunction at any of these stages may produce poor performance on memory tests. In addition, aphasia may impair verbal memory, and visuoperceptual deficit may affect visual memory. Proper assessment therefore must not only document the existence of the "final common pathway" of poor retention, but also specify the defective phase. The use of different paradigms aids in this effort. For example, if a patient cannot spontaneously recall a list of words, but can recognize them when they are embedded in a longer list and can distinguish between material that was previously presented and that which was not, this pattern of performance suggests adequate attention, comprehension, encoding, and storage, but defective retrieval. The examiner should also investigate the effects of various kinds of cuing—semantic, phonemic, categorical—on recall.

If a patient presents with a very short attention span, it may be impossible to obtain a valid assessment of memory functions. In an attempt to ensure adequate attention to and processing of to-be-remembered material, Fuld (1980) developed an object memory test. The subject is presented with a bag containing ten objects and is asked to identify each item by touch alone. Following each response, the item is removed from the bag, errors are corrected, and a one-word name is agreed upon for the item. After each object has been identified, the subject is distracted for 60 seconds and then asked to recall the items in the bag. Fuld says that the test may be used with patients who have naming difficulty if they can respond via gestures, circumlocutions (describing the use of the object), or consistent paraphasic substitutions. Caution must be exercised if the test is used in this way.

Buschke (1984) describes a related procedure in which to-be-remembered target items are associated with common categories. To guarantee processing of each item, the subject is asked to identify the "animal," "piece of furniture," "tool," etc. contained in the array. After free recall is attempted, the subject is cued with the category name of each item not spontaneously retrieved and is asked to provide the exemplar.

The WAIS-R Digit Span Forward is commonly employed as a test of memory, although, as noted above, it may also be viewed as a measure of attention ("freedom from distractibility"). The subject repeats strings of digits of increasing length. Patients with expressive difficulties may respond by pointing to printed digits. The relation of this type of memory—echoic memory—to the more complex learning required for rehabilitation is tenuous at best. The Serial Digit Learning Test (Benton et al., 1983), in which the subject is allowed up to 12 trials to learn an 8- or 9- digit sequence, has been found to be more sensitive to brain dysfunction than is the conventional Digit Span.

A number of tests of recognition memory are available. Botwinick and Storandt (1974) developed visual and auditory versions of a verbal learning task. In the visual format, the subject examines a list of 8 words for 10 seconds and is then required to find those words in a list of 32 words. In the auditory version, the examiner reads 8 different target words, and the subject must find them in another 32-word display. These two tasks differ not only in modality of stimulus presentation but also with regard to the sequential (auditory)—simultaneous (visual) dimension.

Buschke and Fuld (1974) devised two useful and efficient paradigms—selective reminding and restricted reminding. Both tests begin with the examiner reading a list of words that the patient then attempts to recall. Under the selective reminding condition, before each subsequent attempt at recall, the examiner reads only those items omitted on the immediately preceding recall. Under the restricted reminding condition, the examiner reads only those items that have not yet been recalled on any trial. Measures of several aspects of storage, short- and long-term retention, and retrieval may be derived from the record of the subject's performance.

Lezak (1983) provides a detailed description of the Rey Auditory Verbal Learning Test (Rey, 1964). The subject is given five trials to learn a 15-word list, then a single trial of another 15-word list, and a sixth recall trial of the original list. Lezak suggests assessing retention over intervals ranging from 30 minutes to several days. She also reproduces a word list to be used for testing recognition of the original series. This list contains phonemically and semantically related distractors, as well as words from the interpolated group.

Numerous paired associate learning tests are available, the most commonly used one being the Associate Learning subtest of the Wechsler Memory Scale (see below). Subjects are read a list of word pairs, some of which are logically associated whereas others are not. The examiner then reads the first word of each pair, and the subject must supply the associate. Newton and Brown (1985) describe the development of verbal and figural paired associate tests of equivalent difficulty.

Several investigators have noted the paucity of tests for retention of sentences, a skill that is likely to relate more directly to rehabilitation success than do word learning tests. The Neurosensory Center Comprehensive Examination for Aphasia includes a sentence repetition subtest comprised of 22 sentences ranging in length from 1 to 36 syllables. The subject listens to a tape recording of each sentence and immediately repeats it aloud. The Multilingual Aphasia Examination (Benton & Hamsher, 1978) and Western Aphasia Battery (Kertesz, 1979) contain sentence repetition tests of differing lengths and linguistic complexity. Newcombe and Marshall's (1967) 20-item instrument contains grammatically correct and meaningful sentences, as well as anomalous sentences and random word strings of equivalent length.

Daly, Ostreicher, Jonassen and Darnton (1981) describe two sentence memory tests. One, developed by Bloomer (1970), consists of a series of sentences of increasing length (4 to 28 syllables) that tell a continuous story. The second, devised by Ostreicher (1973), is a series of ten unrelated sentences ranging from 4 to 32 syllables in length. Daly et al. report an average performance of 28 syllables for persons over 16 years of age.

Recall of paragraph or story content can be assessed with subtests from the Wechsler Memory Scale or Randt Memory Battery (see below).

A few tests of memory for important events of the past (Albert, Butters & Levin, 1979; Perlmutter, Metzger, Miller, & Nesworski, 1980; Squire & Slater, 1975) are available. However, the implications for rehabilitation of remote memory skills are not clear. Furthermore, patients with relatively intact historical memory often exhibit defective recent memory.

Of the several available measures of visual memory, probably the most versatile is the Benton Visual Retention Test (BVRT). There are two versions of the BVRT, one which requires the subject to draw sets of geometric figures from memory following a 10- (administration A), or 5-second (administration B) exposure (Benton, 1974); the multiple-choice version (Benton, Hamsher, & Stone, 1977) requires the subject to select from among four response alternatives the one that matches the originally presented standard. This latter version is, of course, well suited for subjects with severe motor impairment; in fact, in extreme cases the examiner can point to each response alternative, and the subject can blink when the examiner arrives at the correct answer.

Because the BVRT uses visually presented material, interpretation of the performance of patients with visual-perceptual impairments can be hazardous, i.e., there is a high rate of false positives. In fact, both versions contain an alternative format against which performance on the memory administration may be compared. Administration C of the drawing version is essentially a copying test that allows the examiner to assess the possible contribution of perceptual and/or motor disturbance to the patient's reproductions from memory (administration A or B). For the multiple-choice version, one may present the standard and the response alternative cards simultaneously, rather than sequentially (Benton et al., 1983). One can then compare performance on this "visual match" test to that on the "visual memory" form. Patients with perceptual deficit perform poorly on both versions, whereas those with selective memory loss improve under "copy" or "match" instructions. The various forms and administrations of the BVRT thus make it a broadly useful instrument.

As noted above, immediate recall is usually requested on the Complex Figure Test, thus yielding one measure of immediate visual memory. Delayed recall may be employed, with suggested intervals ranging from a few minutes to 45 minutes (Taylor, 1979).

Corsi (1972) developed a nonverbal analog of the digit repetition test. Nine blocks are placed in irregular fashion on an 8" × 10" field. The blocks are numbered on the side facing the examiner; the patient sees only a seemingly random array. The examiner taps out progressively lengthening sequences that the subject must reproduce. DeRenzi and Nichelli (1975) reported that patients with posterior lesions of either hemisphere performed poorly on this test relative to patients with anterior lesions and to controls, a finding confirmed by DeRenzi, Faglioni, and Previdi (1977). Smirni, Villardita, and Zappala (1983) found that block tapping performance depended not only on the length of the span but also on the spatial configuration of the particular sequence. They provide three sets of equivalent difficulty for each length from four to nine blocks.

An innovative memory measure, the Misplaced Objects Task, was developed by Crook, Ferris, and McCarthy (1979) for the purpose of studying memory dysfunction in the elderly. The subject is shown a board depicting a seven-room house and representations of ten common objects, e.g., eyeglasses, keys, watch. The subject places the objects in various rooms and, following an interval of 5–30 minutes, must recall the locations of the objects. Crook et al. (1979) demonstrated the reliability and validity of this test for aged subjects with and without documented memory impairment and for a young normal control group. In view of the real-word relevance of this task, further development and application seem warranted.

Of the various memory batteries, the best known is undoubtedly the Wechsler Memory Scale (Wechsler, 1945), the strengths and weaknesses of which were reviewed by Prigatano (1978). The test consists of seven parts: Personal and Current Information, Orientation, Mental Control (timed tests of alphabet recitation, counting backward and counting forward by 3's), Logical Memory (retention of facts in two short passages that the examiner reads aloud), Digit Span, Visual Reproduction (drawing of geometric designs from memory), and Associate Learning (retention of ten word pairs). Russell (1975) proposed repeating the Logical Memory and Visual Reproduction tests after a 30-minute interval in order to obtain measures of delayed verbal and nonverbal memory. A "memory quotient" may be derived from the patient's subtest scores and can be compared to the IQ score for the purpose of inferring the existence of a memory deficit (see Prigatano, 1978 for a critique of this tactic). Margolis and Scialfa (1984) confirm earlier reports of significant age differences on most subtests and provide normative data for a range of age groups.

Randt, Brown, and Osborne (1980) described a memory battery developed at New York University. Some subtests are similar to components of the Wechsler Memory Scale (Digit Span, Associate Learning, Logical Memory), but the scoring is less ambiguous, the content is more contemporary, and several new tasks—list learning, picture recognition, incidental learning—have been added. Furthermore, four subtests are readministered during the initial session, thus providing measures of delayed recall. The same four subtests are again re-administered on the day after initial testing, thus allowing assessment of retention over a 24-hour interval. Given the importance in rehabilitiation settings of a patient's ability to carry over skills from one day to the next, this information is quite useful. A final advantage is the existence of five parallel forms of the test.

A careful delineation of memory deficit is of particular importance in view of the growing use of memory retraining techniques (Crovitz, 1979; Gasparrini & Satz, 1979; Gianutsos & Gianutsos, 1979; Schacter, Rich, & Stampp, 1985).

Because many of these methods are compensatory in nature, it is crucial that areas of deficit and areas of strength be accurately demarcated.

Constructional Ability

Benton (1979) classified constructional tasks into five categories: (1) vertical assembly—building a tower, (2) horizontal assembly—WAIS Block Design subtest, (3) three-dimensional constructions—Benton's test of three-dimensional constructional praxis, (4) copying line drawings—Benton Visual Retention Test, administration C; Complex Figure Test, copy instructions, and (5) drawing to verbal command—clock, flower, three-dimensional cube. Clearly, allowances must be made when assessing the constructional abilities of patients with significant motor impairment. As suggested above, a hemiparetic patient who must use the nondominant hand to perform a speeded task might be permitted extra time; at the very least, the motor impairment would be considered when interpreting the timed score.

The WAIS-R Block Design subtest is probably the most extensively used constructional task. This is a timed test requiring the subject to form geometric designs using red and white blocks. On the first task, a four-block design with a 1-minute time limit, the examiner constructs a model that the subject must reproduce using four other blocks. The remaining patterns—four additional four-block designs followed by four nine-block designs with 2-minute time limits—are displayed on cards. Kaplan's (1981) description of qualitative analysis of Block Design performance addresses the factors of strategy and error type.

The Stick Test, part of the Parietal Lobe Battery developed at the Boston VA Hospital, calls upon the subject to create two-dimensional constructions using wooden sticks with a blackened tip (Borod, Goodglass, & Kaplan, 1980). The examiner first sits beside the subject and constructs models for the subject to copy. The examiner then moves to the opposite side of the table and proceeds to construct the same ten designs. The subject must now adopt the perspective of the examiner, mentally rotating the patterns 180 degrees, and must construct the pattern accordingly.

The WAIS-R Object Assembly subtest requires the subject to put together representations of four items—mannequin, profile, hand, and elephant—that have been cut into pieces. The first two items have a 2-minute time limit, and the last two have a 3-minute limit. Bonus points are given for rapid completion, and partial credit is allowed.

The Test of Three-Dimensional Constructional Praxis (Benton, 1973) consists of two equivalent sets of three items each. The subject must copy models composed of square and rectangular blocks. The number of deviant block placements is subtracted from the maximum possible correct (N = 29) to obtain the subject's score. This test appears to be sensitive to mild defects of constructional ability and is therefore particularly useful as a pre-vocational assessment measure with certain patients.

Strub, Black, and Leventhal (1979) described the usefulness of a 24-item drawing test in the detection of brain dysfunction. They reported the following conclusions: (1) Very simple designs were not sensitive, (2) more complex designs had some utility with patients of average premorbid intelligence, but did not distinguish between brain damaged and low IQ non-brain-damaged subjects, (3) a subset of 11 items effectively differentiated the low IQ brain damaged patients from low IQ controls.

Higher Cognitive Functions

The tests described in this section are quintessential illustrations of the multifactorial character of neuropsychological measures. Many of them presuppose intact attention span, perceptual ability, language, memory function, or the like and have as their primary aim the appraisal of abstract thinking, concept formation, problem solving, or some other term that suggests cognitive synthesis and integration. Before concluding that a patient is impaired in higher cognitive skills, it is vital that the examiner test rival hypotheses that indict lower-level functions. Only after a satisfactory demonstration that these simpler processes are intact, and could not therefore have caused the observed impaired performance, may one infer the existence of a higher cortical deficit.

Certain items on the Raven Matrices require not only the visual-perceptual abilities noted above but also the capacity for inferential reasoning. Costa (1976) and Weinberg, Piasetsky, Diller, and Gordon (1982) suggested a distinction between "perceptual" and "conceptual" items on this test, a typology that may be helpful in clinical interpretation. Because the test requires only a pointing response, it is ideal for use with patients who have expressive difficulties. Good performance, especially on the conceptual items, by such patients suggests that their "internal speech" is intact, because the logical reasoning involved is almost unquestionably a language-mediated skill.

Two verbal subtests of the WAIS-R should be mentioned in this context. The Similarities test demands the ability to discern salient parallels between two items or concepts. Although some points are awarded for accurate concrete responses ("A bear and a pig both have four legs"), higher scores are attained with more abstract categorical answers ("A bear and a pig are both animals"). The Comprehension subtest assesses social judgment, reasoning, and proverb interpretation. Again, more sophisticated answers yield higher scores.

The Abstraction portion of the Shipley Institute of Living Scale (Shipley, 1946) consists of 20 sequences of letters, numbers, or words, each with a missing term. The subject must analyze the principle underlying the sequence and supply the missing bit. Ease of administration and scoring are strong points of this test, but it is comparatively difficult and suitable only for higher-level patients.

The Verbal Concept Attainment Test (VCAT) has been shown to have some utility as a verbal reasoning task (Bornstein, 1982). Each item is composed of a card with several lines of words printed on it. The subject must find the words, one in each line, that are conceptually or functionally related. Bornstein reported significant correlations between the VCAT and several other reasoning and intelligence tests—WAIS-R Similarities and Vocabulary, Wisconsin Card Sorting Test, and Halstead Category Test.

The Wisconsin Card Sorting Test (WCST) requires the subject to form concepts, make use of feedback from the examiner, and exhibit mental flexibility (Heaton, 1981). Sixty-four cards, each containing a display of varying forms (crosses, squares, triangles, circles), colors (red, blue, yellow, green), and numbers (one to four items), are given to the subject. Four stimulus cards—one red triangle, two green stars, three yellow crosses, and four blue circles—are laid out before the subject. The subject sorts the cards into groups under the four stimulus cards according to a principle that the examiner knows and that the subject must discover. After each card placement, the examiner says "right" or "wrong," and the subject must use the feedback in deciding where to put the next card. When the subject has discerned the first rule (sort according to color), the examiner changes the principle (sort according to form) and responds "right" or "wrong" accordingly. The subject must shift from the established "set" to a new one and shift again when the principle changes (to number). Robinson, Heaton, Lehman, and Stilson (1980) found the WCST to be highly effective in detecting frontal lobe involvement, although they argue that it does not discriminate between focal frontal and diffuse damage including the frontal region.

The Category Test, a component of the Halstead-Reitan Battery, has long been touted as a powerful test of "organicity" (Reitan & Davison, 1974; Shaw, 1966). The subject sits in front of a screen upon which is projected a series of 208 slides, each suggesting a number from 1 to 4. A response panel containing four numbered levers is located just below the screen, and the subject responds by operating the lever below the number suggested by the content of the slide, e.g., I, II, III or IV; the oddity item in a group of four. As with the WCST, the subject must deduce the principle on the basis of feedback—a bell for correct answers and a buzzer for incorrect answers—following each response. The Category test requires the ability to form and test hypotheses, develop concepts, and modify performance on the basis of feedback. Low scores may also result from impaired attention, visuospatial deficit, perseveration, or poor memory, as well as deficient conceptual ability. The equipment required to administer the Category test in its conventional format is costly and cumbersome. An inexpensive booklet form of the test, developed by DeFilippis, McCampbell, and Rogers (1979), is available.

Bond and Buchtel (1984) conducted a comparative analysis of the cognitive components of the WCST and the Category Test. They used a "process tracing" method in which subjects were required to think aloud as they worked through the items—a useful nonstandard procedure. Although the two tests demand some of the same skills, Bond and Buchtel found differences with respect to demands on perceptual-abstraction ability, hypothesis generation and hypothesis testing, and cognitive flexibility factors.

In working with relatively intact patients or those with high premorbid intelligence for whom these tests may be insufficiently challenging, the author has found it useful to employ material from Graduate Record Examination preparation booklets. A variety of verbal (vocabulary, sentence completion, analogies, reading) and mathematical (written arithmetic, geometry, word problems) measures can be found in these guides. In addition, insight into the patient's cognitive strategic style and use of feedback can be gained through observation of performance on the game "Mastermind." Other commercially available games, such as "Memory" or "Shape Sorter," are useful adjuncts to nonstandard assessment (Caplan, 1984).

CONCLUSION

The role of neuropsychological assessment in rehabilitation settings is rapidly enlarging as new target populations, such as patients with multiple sclerosis or chronic obstructive pulmonary disease, are identified and neuropsychological rehabilitation programs proliferate (Boll, 1985; Costa, 1983; Diller & Gordon, 1981). Quantified measures of the sort reviewed in this chapter permit precise documentation of the effects of interventions directed at higher cortical deficits. Qualitative analysis of individual patient performances on these instruments can contribute much of value to the design of those rehabilitation programs.

The data base required to function as a neuropsychologist is extensive, encompassing the domains of basic sciences, behavioral neurology, neuroanatomy, and educational methods, as well as conventional clinical psychology (Meier, 1981). Such expertise can only be acquired through intensive specialized training; brief exposure to particular packaged approaches is clearly inadequate. Although educational and training opportunities in neuropsychology are increasing, they are still insufficient to satisfy the demand.

This chapter has dealt almost exclusively with the process of assessment of the intellectual sequelae of brain dysfunction. This does not define the limits of neuropsychological practice. There are profound emotional consequences of neurologic impairment (see Newman, 1984 for a review of the social and emotional sequelae of stroke and head injury; see also Chapters 2 and 3) that neuropsychologists neglect at their and the patient's peril, for these may compromise adaptive functioning as surely as can any cognitive or perceptual deficit.

REFERENCES

Albert, M.S. (1981). Geriatric neuropsychology. *Journal of Consulting and Clinical Psychology, 49*, 835–850.

Albert, M., Butters, N., & Levin, J. (1979). Temporal gradients in the retrograde amnesia of patients with alcoholic Korsakoff's disease. *Archives of Neurology, 36*, 211–216.

Baddeley, A. (1976). *The psychology of memory*. New York: Basic Books.

Ben-Yishay, Y., Gerstman, L., Diller, L., & Haas, A. (1970). Prediction of rehabilitation outcomes from psychometric parameters in left hemiplegics. *Journal of Consulting and Clinical Psychology, 34*, 436–441.

Benson, D.F. (1979). *Aphasia, alexia, and agraphia*. New York: Churchill Livingstone.

Benson, D., & Blumer, D. (1982). Amnesia: A clinical approach to memory. In D. Benson & D. Blumer (Eds.) *Psychiatric aspects of neurologic disease, Volume II*. New York: Grune & Stratton, pp. 251–278.

Benton, A.L. (1973). *Test of Three-Dimensional Constructional Praxis. Manual*. (Neurosensory Center Publication No. 286). Iowa City: University of Iowa.

Benton, A.L. (1974). *The Revised Visual Retention Test* (4th ed.). New York: Psychological Corporation.

Benton, A.L. (1979). Visuoperceptive, visuospatial, and visuo-constructive disorders. In K. Heilman & E. Valenstein (Eds.), *Clinical neuropsychology*. New York: Oxford University Press, pp. 186–232.

Benton, A., & Hamsher, K. (1978). *Multilingual aphasia examination*. Iowa City: University of Iowa.

Benton, A.L., Hamsher, K., & Stone, F. (1977). *Visual Retention Test: Multiple choice form I*. Iowa City: Department of Neurology, University Hospitals, University of Iowa.

Benton, A., Hamsher, K., Varney, N., & Spreen, O. (1983). *Contributions to neuropsychological assessment*. New York: Oxford University Press.

Benton, A.L., & Spreen, O. (1969). *Embedded Figures Test: Manual of instructions and norms*. Neuropsychology Laboratory, University of Victoria, British Columbia.

Benton, A.L., VanAllen, M.W., & Fogel, M.L. (1964). Temporal orientation in cerebral disease. *Journal of Nervous and Mental Disease, 139*, 110–119.

Berg, M. (1984). Expanding the parameters of pyschological testing. *Bulletin of the Menninger Clinic, 48*, 10–24.

Bersoff, D.N. (1970). The revised deterioration formula for the WAIS. *Journal of Clinical Psychology, 26*, 71–73.

Bieliauskas, L., Topel, J., & Huckman, M. (1980). Cognitive, neurologic, and radiologic test data in a changing lesion pattern. *Journal of Clinical Neuropsychology, 2*, 217–230.

Binder, L.M. (1982). Constructional strategies of Complex Figure Drawings after unilateral brain damage. *Journal of Clinical Neuropsychology, 4*, 51–58.

Bloomer, H.H. (1970). Memory test for related sentences. Unpublished research, University of Michigan.

Boll, T.J. (1984). Neuropsychological assessment. In I.B. Weiner (Ed.), *Clinical methods in psychology*. New York: John Wiley & Sons.

Boll, T.J. (1985). Developing issues in clinical neuropsychology. *Journal of Clinical and Experimental Neuropsychology, 7,* 473–485.

Boll, T.J., O'Leary, D.S., & Barth J.T. (1981). Quantitative and qualitative approach to neuropsychological evaluation. In C.K. Prokop & L.A. Bradley (Eds.), *Medical psychology: Contributions to behavioral medicine.* New York: Academic Press, pp. 67–80.

Bolla-Wilson, K., Robinson, R., Price, T., & Squires, N. (1984). *Visuoconstructional assembly difficulty—influence of site of lesion and task.* Paper presented at Annual Meeting of the International Neuropsychological Society, Houston.

Bond, J., & Buchtel, H (1984). Comparison of the Wisconsin Card Sorting test and the Halstead Category test. *Journal of Clinical Psychology, 40,* 1251–1254.

Borkowski, J.G., Benton, A.L., & Spreen, O. (1967). Word fluency and brain damage. *Neuropsychologia, 5,* 135–140.

Bornstein, R.A. (1982). A factor analytic study of the construct validity of the Verbal Concept Attainment Test. *Journal of Clinical Neuropsychology, 4,* 43–50.

Borod, J., Goodglass, H., & Kaplan, E. (1980). Normative data on the Boston Diagnostic Aphasia Examination, Parietal Lobe Battery, and the Boston Naming Test. *Journal of Clinical Neuropsychology, 2,* 209–215.

Botwinick, J., & Storandt, M. (1974). *Memory, related functions and age.* Springfield: Charles C Thomas.

Boyd, J.L. (1981). A validity study of the Hooper Visual Organization Test. *Journal of Consulting and Clinical Psychology, 49,* 15–19.

Buschke, H. (1984). Cued recall in amnesia. *Journal of Clinical Neuropsychology, 6,* 433–440.

Buschke, H., & Fuld, P. (1974). Evaluating storage, retention and retrieval in disordered memory and learning. *Neurology, 11,* 1019–1025.

Butters N., & Cermak L. (1980). *Alchoholic Korsakoff's syndrome: An information-processing approach to amnesia.* New York: Academic Press.

Caplan, B. (1982a). Neuropsychology in rehabilitation: Its role in evaluation and intervention. *Archives of Physical Medicine and Rehabilitation, 63,* 362–366.

Caplan, B. (1982b). *Consistency of visual neglect.* Paper presented at American Congress of Rehabilitation Medicine, Houston.

Caplan, B. (1983). *Nonstandard neuropsychological assessment: An illustration.* Paper presented at American Congress of Rehabilitation Medicine, Los Angeles.

Caplan, B. (1984). *Toys and games in rehabilitation.* Paper presented at American Congress of Rehabilitation Medicine, Boston.

Caplan, B. (1985). Task factors in unilateral neglect. *Cortex, 21,* 69–80.

Caplan, B. (1987). Assessment of unilateral neglect: A new reading test. *Journal of Clinical and Experimental Neuropsychology,* in press.

Chelune, G. (1983). *Neuropsychological assessment: Beyond deficit testing.* Paper presented at Annual Meeting of American Psychological Association, Anaheim, CA.

Cohen, J. (1957). The factorial structure of the WAIS between early adulthood and old age. *Journal of Consulting Psychology, 21,* 283–290.

Cole, K.D., & Zarit, S. H. (1984). Psychological deficits in depressed medical patients. *The Journal of Nervous and Mental Disease, 172,* 150–155.

Corsi, P. (1972). Human memory and the medial temporal region of the brain. Unpublished doctoral dissertation, McGill University, Montreal.

Costa, L. (1975). The relation of visuospatial dysfunction to digit span performance in patients with cerebral lesions. *Cortex, 11*, 31–36.

Costa, L. D. (1976). Interset variability on the Raven Coloured Progressive Matrices as an indicator of specific ability deficit in brain-lesioned patients. *Cortex, 12*, 31–40.

Costa, L. (1983). Clinical neuropsychology: A discipline in evolution. *Journal of Clinical Neuropsychology, 5*, 1–11.

Costa, L.D., Vaughan, H.G., Horwitz, M., & Ritter, W. (1969). Patterns of behavioral deficit associated with visual spatial neglect. *Cortex, 5*, 242–263.

Costa, L.D., Vaughan, H.G., Levita, E., & Farber, N. (1963). Purdue Pegboard as a predictor of the presence and laterality of cerebral lesions. *Journal of Consulting Psychology, 27*, 133–137.

Crook, T., Ferris, S., & McCarthy, M. (1979). The misplaced-objects task: A brief test for memory dysfunction in the aged. *Journal of the American Geriatrics Society, 27*, 284–287.

Crovitz H.F. (1979). Memory retraining in brain-damaged patients: The airplane list. *Cortex, 15*, 131–134.

Daly, D.A., Ostreicher, H.J., Jonassen, S.A., & Darnton, S.W. (1981). *Memory for unrelated sentences: A normative study of 480 children*. Paper presented at the Annual Meeting of the International Neuropsychological Society, Atlanta.

Darley, F.L. (1982). *Aphasia*. Philadelphia: W.B. Saunders Company.

DeFilippis, N.A., McCampbell, E., & Rogers, P. (1979). Development of a booklet form of the Category Test: Normative and validity data. *Journal of Clinical Neuropsychology, 1*, 339–342.

DeRenzi, E., Faglioni, P., & Previdi, P. (1977). Spatial memory and hemispheric locus of lesion. *Cortex, 13*, 424–433.

DeRenzi, E., Faglioni, P., & Scotti, G. (1970). Hemispheric contribution to exploration of space through the visual and tactile modality. *Cortex, 6*, 191–203.

DeRenzi, E., & Nichelli, P. (1975). Verbal and non-verbal short term memory impairment following hemispheric damage. *Cortex, 11*, 341–353.

DeRenzi, E., & Vignolo, L.A. (1962). The Token Test: A sensitive test to detect disturbances in aphasics. *Brain, 85*, 665–678.

Diller, L., & Gordon, W. (1981). Rehabilitation and neuropsychology. In S.B.Filskov & T.H. Boll (Eds.), *Handbook of clinical neuropsychology*. New York: John Wiley & Sons, pp. 702–733.

Dunn, L.M., & Dunn, L.M. (1981). *Manual. Peabody Picture Vocabulary Test - Revised*. Circle Pines, MN: American Guidance Service.

Dunn, L.M., & Markwardt, F.C., Jr. (1970). *Manual. Peabody Individual Achievement Test*. Circle Pines, MN: American Guidance Service.

Eckhardt, M.J., & Matarazzo, J.D. (1981). Test-retest reliability of the Halstead impairment index in hospitalized alcoholic and nonalcoholic males with mild to moderate neuropsychological impairment. *Journal of Clinical Neuropsychology, 3*, 257–269.

Elithorn, A., Jones, D., Kerr., M., & Lee, D. (1964). The effects of the variation of two physical parameters on empirical difficulty in a perceptual maze test. *British Journal of Psychology, 55*, 31–37.

Erickson, R.C., & Scott, M.L. (1977). Clinical memory testing: A review. *Psychological Bulletin, 84*, 1130–1149.

Filskov, S.B., & Boll, T.H. (Eds.) (1981). *Handbook of clinical neuropsychology*. New York: John Wiley & Sons.

Folstein, M.F., Folstein, S.E., & McHugh P.R. (1975). "Mini-Mental state." *Journal of Psychiatric Research, 12*, 189–198.

Fuld, P.A. (1980). Guaranteed stimulus-processing in the evaluation of memory and learning. *Cortex, 16,* 255–271.

Galaburda, A., Sanides, F., & Geschwind, N. (1978). Human brain: Cytoarchitectonic left-right asymmetries in the temporal speech region. *Archives of Neurology, 35,* 812–817.

Garcia, C., Tweedy, J., & Blass, J. (1984). Underdiagnosis of cognitive impairment in a rehabilitation setting. *Journal of the American Geriatrics Society, 32,* 339–342.

Gasparrini, B., Satz, P. (1979). Treatment for memory problems in left hemisphere CVA patient. *Journal of Clinical Neuropsychology, 1,* 137–150.

Gates, A.I., & MacGinitie, W.H. (1965/1969) *Gates-MacGinitie Reading Tests.* New York: Teachers College Press, Teachers College, Columbia University.

Gianutsos, R., & Gianutsos, J. (1979). Rehabilitating the verbal recall of brain-damaged patients by mnemonic training: An experimental demonstration using single-case methodology. *Journal of Clnical Neuropsychology, 1,* 117–135.

Gilandas, A., & Touyz, S. (1982). The neuropsychologist as an expert witness. *Australian Psychologist, 17,* 255–264.

Golden C.J. (1978). *Diagnosis and rehabilitation in clinical neuropsychology.* Springfield: Charles C Thomas.

Goldstein, G., & Shelly, C. (1984). Relationships between language skills as assessed by the Halstead-Reitan battery and the Luria-Nebraska language-related factor scales in a nonaphasic patient population. *Journal of Clinical Neuropsychology, 6,* 143–156.

Gollin, E.S. (1960). Development studies of visual recognition of incomplete objects. *Perceptual and Motor Skills 11,* 289–298.

Goodglass, H., & Kaplan E. (1983). *The assessment of aphasia and related disorders* (2nd ed). Philadelphia: Lea & Febiger.

Gottschaldt, K. (1926). Uber den Einfluss der Erfahrung auf die Wahrnehmung von Figuren. *Psychol. Forsch. 8,* 261–317.

Gottschaldt, K. (1929). Uber den Einfluss der Erfahrung auf die Wahrnehmung von Figuren. *Psychol. Forsch., 12,* 1–87.

Gronwall, D. (1977). Paced auditory serial-addition task: A measure of recovery from concussion. *Perceptual and Motor Skills, 44,* 367–373.

Hannay, H., Levin, H. (1985). The selective reminding test: An examination of the equivalence of four forms. *Journal of Clinical & Experimental Neuropsychology, 7,* 251–269.

Heaton, R. (1981). *Wisconsin Card Sorting Test: Manual.* Odessa, FL: Psychological Assessment Resources, Inc.

Heaton, R.H., Baade, L.E., & Johnson, K.L. (1978). Neuropsychological test results associated with psychiatric disorders in adults. *Psychological Bulletin, 85,* 141–162.

Heaton, S.R., & Heaton, R.K. (1981). Testing the impaired patient. In S.B. Filskov & T. J. Boll (Eds.), *Handbook of clinical neuropsychology.* New York: John Wiley & Sons, pp. 526–544.

Heaton, R.K., & Pendleton, M.G. (1981). Use of neuropsychological tests to predict adult patients' everyday functioning. *Journal of Consulting and Clinical Psychology, 49,* 807–821.

Heilman, K.M. (1979). Neglect and related disorders. In K.M. Heilman & E. Valenstein (Eds.), *Clinical neuropsychology.* New York: Oxford University Press, pp. 268–307.

Hooper, H.E. (1958). *The Hooper Visual Organization Test. Manual.* Los Angeles: Psychological Services.

Jastak, S., Wilkinson, G. (1984) *Wide Range Achievement Test. Manual.* Wilmington, DE: Jastak Associates.

Kagan, J., Rosman, B., Day, D., Albert, J., & Phillips, W. (1964). Information processing in the child: Significance of analytic and reflective attitudes. *Psychological Monographs, 78* (1, Whole no. 578).

Kaplan, E. (1981). Changes in cognitive style with aging. In L.K. Obler & M.L. Albert (Eds.), *Language and communication in the elderly*. Lexington, MA: D.C. Heath and Co.

Kaplan, E. (1983). Process and achievement revisited. In S. Wapner & B. Kaplan (Eds.), *Toward a holistic developmental psychology*. Hillsdale, NJ: Lawrence Erlbaum Associates.

Kertesz, A. (1979). *Aphasia and associated disorders: Taxonomy, localization, and recovery*. New York: Grune & Stratton.

Kinsbourne, M. (1971). Cognitive deficit: Experimental analysis. In J. McGaugh (Ed.), *Psychobiology*. New York: Academic Press, pp. 285–348.

Lawrence, C. (1984). Testing for memory disorder. *Australian and New Zealand Journal of Psychiatry, 18*, 207–210.

Lezak, M.D. (1978). Subtle sequelae of brain damage. *American Journal of Physical Medicine, 57*, 9–15.

Lezak, M.D. (1983). *Neuropsychological assessment* (2nd ed.). New York: Oxford University Press.

Lezak, M. (1984). An individualized approach to neuropsychological assessment. In P. Logue & J. Schear, (Eds.), *Clinical neuropsychology: A multidisciplinary approach*. Springfield, IL: Charles C Thomas, pp. 29–49.

Long, C.J., Gouvier, W.D., & Cole, J.C. (1984). A model of recovery for the total rehabilitation of individuals with head trauma. *Journal of Rehabilitation, 50*, 39–45.

Luria, A.R., Naydin, V.L., Tsvetkova, L.S., & Vinarskaya, E.N. (1969). Restoration of higher cortical function following local brain damage. In P.J.Vinken, G.W. Bruyn, M. Critchley, & J.A.M. Frederiks (Eds.), *Handbook of clinical neurology*. (Vol. 3). New York: John Wiley & Sons, pp. 368–433.

Margolis, R., & Scialfa, C. (1984). Age differences in Wechsler Memory Scale performance. *Journal of Clinical Psychology, 40*, 1442–1449.

Matarazzo, J.D., Carmody, T.P., & Jacobs, L.D. (1980). Test-retest reliability and stability of the WAIS: A literature review with implications for clinical practice. *Journal of Clinical Neuropsychology, 2*, 89–105.

Mateer, C., Polen, S., & Ojemann, G. (1982). Sexual variation in cortical localization of naming as determined by stimulation mapping. *The Behavioral and Brain Sciences, 5*, 310–311.

McCaffrey, R., Malloy, P.F., & Brief, D. (1985). Internship opportunities in clinical neuropsychology emphasizing recent INS training guidelines. *Professional Psychology: Research and Practice, 16*, 236–252.

McCauley, R., & Swisher, L. (1984). Use and misuse of norm-referenced tests in clinical assessment: A hypothetical case. *Journal of Speech and Hearing Disorders, 49*, 338–348.

McFarland, K. (1983). Syndrome analysis in clinical neuropsychology. *British Journal of Clinical Psychology, 22*, 61–74.

McMahon, E., & Satz, P. (1981). Clinical neuropsychology: Some forensic applications. In S. Filskov & T. Boll (Eds.), *Handbook of clinical neuropsychology*. New York: John Wiley & Sons, pp. 686–701.

McSweeney, A.J., Grant, I., Heaton, R., Prigatano, G., & Adams, K. (1985). Relationship of neuropsychological status to everyday functioning in healthy and chronically ill persons. *Journal of Clinical and Experimental Neuropsychology, 7*, 281–291.

Meier, M. (1981). Education for competency assurance in human neuropsychology: Antecedents, models and directions. In S.B. Filskov & T.J.Boll (Eds.), *Handbook of clinical neuropsychology*. New York: John Wiley and Sons, pp. 754–781.

Miceli, G., Caltagirone, C., Gainotti, G., Masullo, C., & Silveri, M.C. (1981). Neuropsychological correlates of localized cerebral lesions in non-aphasic brain-damaged patients. *Journal of Clinical Neuropsychology, 3,* 53–63.

Milberg, W., Hebben, N., & Kaplan, E. (1986). The Boston process approach to neuropsychological assessment. In I. Grant & K.M. Adams (Eds.), *Neuropsychological assessment of neuropsychiatric disorders*. New York: Oxford Unviersity Press, pp. 65–86.

Nelson, H., McKenna, P. (1975). The use of current reading ability in the assessment of dementia. *British Journal of Social and Clinical Psychology, 14,* 259–267.

Nelson, H., & O'Connell, A. (1978). Dementia: The estimation of premorbid intelligence levels using the New Adult Reading Test. *Cortex, 14,* 234–244.

Newcombe, F. (1969). *Missile wounds of the brain*. London: Oxford University Press.

Newcombe, F., & Marshall, J.C. (1967). Immediate recall of "sentences" by subjects with unilateral cerebral lesions. *Neuropsychologia, 5,* 329–334.

Newman, S. (1984). The social and emotional consequences of head injury and stroke. *International Review of Applied Psychology, 33,* 427–455.

Newton, N., & Brown, G. (1985). Construction of matched verbal and design continuous paired associate tests. *Journal of Clinical and Experimental Neuropsychology, 7,* 97–110.

Osterrieth, P.A. (1944). Le test de copie d'une figure complexe. *Archives de Psychologie, 30,* 206–365.

Ostreicher, H. (1973). Investigation of four tasks of auditory retention span in children. Unpublished research, University of Michigan.

Perlmutter, M., Metzger, R., Miller, K., & Nezworski, T. (1980). Memory of historical events. *Experimental Aging Research, 6,* 47–60.

Popkin, S., Schaie, K., & Krauss, I. (1983). Age-fair assessment of psychometric intelligence. *Educational Gerontology, 9,* 47–55.

Porch, B.E. (1967). *Porch Index of Communicative Ability*. Palo Alto: Consulting Psychologists Press.

Prigatano, G.P. (1978). Wechsler Memory Scale: A selective review of the literature. *Journal of Clinical Psychology, 34,* 816–832.

Rabbitt, P. (1982). How to assess the aged? *British Journal of Clinical Psychology, 21,* 55–60.

Randt, C.T., Brown, E.R., & Osborne, D.P. (1980). A memory test for longitudinal measurement of mild to moderate deficits. *Clinical Neuropsychology, 2,* 184–194.

Raven, J.C. (1960). *Guide to the Standard Progressive Matrices*. London: H.K. Lewis & Co.

Raven, J.C. (1965). *Guide to using the Coloured Progressive Matrices*. London: H.K. Lewis & Co.

Reitan, R.M. (1958). Validity of the Trail Making Test as an indicator of organic brain damage. *Perceptual and Motor Skills, 8,* 271–276.

Reitan, R.M., & Davison, L.A. (Eds.) (1974). *Clinical neuropsychology: Current status and applications*. New York: Winston/Wiley, 1974.

Rey, A. (1941). L'examen psychologique dans les cas d'encephalopathie traumatique. *Archives de Psychologie, 28,* 286–340.

Rey, A. (1964). *L'examen clinique en psychologie*. Paris: Presses Universitaires de France.

Robinson, A.L., Heaton, R.K., Lehman, R.A.W., & Stilson, D.W. (1980). The utility of the Wisconsin Card Sorting Test in detecting and localizing frontal lobe lesions. *Journal of Consulting and Clinical Psychology, 48,* 605–614.

Ross, E.D. (1980a). Sensory-specific and fractional disorders of recent memory in man. I. Isolated loss of visual recent memory. *Archives of Neurology, 37,* 193–200.

Ross, E.D. (1980b). Sensory-specific and fractional disorders of recent memory in man. II. Unilateral loss of tactile recent memory. *Archives of Neurology, 37,* 267–272.

Rosvold, H., Mirsky, A., Sarason, I., Bransome, E. & Beck, L. (1956). A continuous performance test of brain damage. *Journal of Consulting Psychology, 20,* 343–350.

Ruddle, H., & Bradshaw, C. (1982). On the estimation of premorbid intellectual functioning: Validation of Nelson & McKenna's formula, and some new normative data. *British Journal of Clinical Psychology, 21,* 159–165.

Russell, E.W. (1972). WAIS factor analysis with brain-damaged subjects using criterion measures. *Journal of Consulting and Clinical Psychology, 39,* 133–139.

Russell, E.W. (1975). A multiple scoring method for the assessment of complex memory functions. *Journal of Consulting and Clinical Psychology, 43,* 800–809.

Russell, E.W. (1984). Theory and development of pattern analysis methods related to the Halstead-Reitan battery. In P. Logue & J. Schear (Eds.), *Clinical neuropsychology: A multidisciplinary approach.* Springfield, IL: Charles C Thomas, pp. 50–98.

Sattler, J., & Tozier, L. (1970). A review of intelligence test modifications used with cerebral palsied and other handicapped groups. *The Journal of Special Education, 4,* 391–398.

Schacter, D., Rich, S., & Stampp, M. (1985). Remediation of memory disorders: Experimental evaluation of the spaced-retrieval technique. *Journal of Clinical and Experimental Neuropsychology, 7,* 79–96.

Schenkenberg, T., Bradford, D.C., & Ajax, E.T. (1980). Line bisection and unilateral visual neglect in patients with neurologic impairment. *Neurology, 30,* 509–517.

Schreiber, D., Goldman, H., Kleinman, K., Goldfader, P., Snow, M. (1976). The relationship between independent neuropsychological and neurological detection and localization of cerebral impairment. *The Journal of Nervous and Mental Disease, 162,* 361–365.

Schwartz, M.F. (1984). What the classical aphasia categories can't do for us, and why. *Brain and Language, 21,* 3–8.

Seidenberg, M., O'Leary, D.S., Giordani, B., Berent, S., & Boll, T.J. (1981). Test-retest IQ changes of epilepsy patients: Assessing the influence of practice effects. *Journal of Clincal Neuropsychology, 3,* 237–255.

Shankweiler, D., & Studdert-Kennedy, M. (1975). A continuum of lateralization for speech perception? *Brain and Language, 2,* 212–225.

Shatz, M.W. (1981). WAIS practice effects in clinical neuropsychology. *Journal of Clinical Neuropsychology, 3,* 171–179.

Shaw, D.J. (1966). The reliability and validity of the Halstead Category Test. *Journal of Clinical Psychology, 22,* 176–180.

Shipley, W.C. (1946). *Institute of Living Scale.* Los Angeles: Western Psychological Services.

Smirni, P., Villardita, C., & Zappala, G. (1983). Influence of different paths on spatial memory performance in the Block-Tapping Test. *Journal of Clinical Neuropsychology, 5,* 355–359.

Smith, A. (1973). *Symbol Digit Modalities Test.* Los Angeles: Western Psychological Services.

Smith, A. (1975). Neuropsychological testing in neurological disorders. In W.J. Friedlander (Ed.), *Advances in neurology* (Vol. 7). New York: Raven Press, pp. 52–109.

Spellacy, F.J., & Spreen, O. (1969). A short form of the Token Test. *Cortex, 5,* 390–397.

Spreen, O., & Benton, A.L. (1969). *Neurosensory Center Comprehensive Examination for Aphasia.* Victoria, British Columbia: Neuropsychology Laboratory, Department of Psychology, University of Victoria.

Squire, L., & Butters, N. (Eds.) (1984). *Neuropsychology of memory*. New York: The Guilford Press.

Squire, L., & Slater, P.C. (1975). Forgetting in very long-term memory as assessed by an improved questionnaire technique. *Journal of Experimental Psychology: Human Learning and Memory, 104,* 50–54.

Steger, H.G. (1976). Understanding the psychologic factors in rehabilitation. *Geriatrics, 31,* 68–73.

Street, R.F. (1931). A Gestalt Completion Test. Contributions to education, #481. New York: Bureau of Publications, Teachers College, Columbia University.

Strub, R.L., Black, F.W., & Leventhal, B. (1979). The clinical utility of reproduction drawing tests with low IQ patients. *Journal of Clinical Psychiatry, 40,* 386–388.

Sunderland, A., Harris, J.E., & Baddeley, A.D. (1983). Do laboratory tests predict everyday memory? A neuropsychological study. *Journal of Verbal Learning and Verbal Behavior, 1922,* 341–356.

Swiercinsky, D., & Leigh, G. (1979). Comparison of neuropsychological data in the diagnosis of brain impairment with computerized tomography and other neurological procedures. *Journal of Clinical Psychology, 35,* 242–246.

Talland, G.A. (1965). *Deranged memory*. New York: Academic Press.

Tamkin, A.S., & Jacobsen, R. (1984). Age-related norms for the Hooper Visual Organization Test. *Journal of Clinical Psychology, 40,* 1459–1463.

Taylor, L. (1979). Psychological assessment of neurosurgical patients. In T. Rasmussen & R. Marino (Eds.), *Functional neurosurgery*. New York: Raven Press, pp. 165–180.

Teuber, H. (1964). The riddle of frontal lobe function in man. In J.M. Warren & K. Akert (Eds.), *The frontal granular cortex and behavior*. New York: McGraw-Hill, pp. 410–444.

Thurstone, L.L. (1944). *A factorial study of perception*. Chicago: University of Chicago Press.

Thurstone, L., & Jeffrey, T. (1965). *Closure Flexibility (Concealed Figures)*. Chicago: Industrial Relations Center, University of Chicago.

Tiffin, J. (1968) *Purdue Pegboard Examiner's Manual*. Chicago: Science Research Associates.

Walsh, K.W. (1978). *Neuropsychology: A clinical approach*. New York: Churchill Livingstone.

Warrington, E. (1982). Neuropsychological studies of object recognition. In D. Broadbent & L. Weiskrantz (Eds.), *The neuropsychology of cognitive function*. London: The Royal Society, pp. 15–33.

Warrington, E.K., & James, M. (1967). Disorders of visual perception in patients with localized cerebral lesions. *Neuropsychologia, 5,* 253–266.

Wechsler, D. (1945). A standardized memory scale for clinical use. *Journal of Psychology, 19,* 87–95.

Wechsler, D. (1955). *Wechsler Adult Intelligence Scale. Manual*. New York: Psychological Corporation.

Wechsler, D. (1981). *Wechsler Adult Intelligence Scale—Revised. Manual*. New York: Psychological Corporation.

Weinberg, J., Diller, L., Gerstman, L., & Schulman, P. (1972). Digit span in right and left hemiplegics. *Journal of Clinical Psychology, 28,* 361.

Weinberg, J., Diller, L., Gordon, W. A., Gerstman, L. J., Lieberman, A., Lakin, P., Hodges, G., & Erachi, O. (1977). Visual scanning training effect on reading-related tasks in acquired right brain damage. *Archives of Physical Medicine and Rehabilitation, 58,* 479–486.

Weinberg, J., Piasetsky, E., Diller, L., & Gordon, W. (1982). Treating perceptual organization deficits in nonneglecting RBD stroke patients. *Journal of Clinical Neuropsychology, 4,* 59–75.

Weingartner, H., Cohen, R.M., Murphy, D.L., Martello, J., & Gerdt, C. (1981). Cognitive processes in depression. *Archives of General Psychiatry, 38,* 42–47.

Williams, M. (1979). *Brain damage, behavior, and the mind.* New York: John Wiley & Sons.

Wilson, R., Rosenbaum, G., Brown, G., Rourke, D., Whitman, D., & Grisell, J. (1978). An index of premorbid intelligence. *Journal of Consulting and Clinical Psychology, 48,* 1554–1555.

Witkin, H.A., Oltman, P.K., Raskin, E., & Karp, S.A. (1971). *A manual for the embedded figures tests.* Palo Alto: Consulting Psychologists Press.

Chapter 10

Neuropsychological Rehabilitation Program: Presbyterian Hospital, Oklahoma City, Oklahoma*

George P. Prigatano, Ph.D. and David J. Fordyce, Ph.D.

Significant brain injury in young adulthood can have devastating long-term personal and social effects (Exhibit 10–1). Even when physical and gross neurologic recovery are relatively good, residual cognitive disturbances, such as impaired concentration and memory deficit, are common (Levin, Benton, & Grossman, 1982). Clearly, absence of findings on a neurologic examination after severe traumatic head injury is no guarantee of normal higher-order functioning. In fact, many individuals with craniocerebral trauma exhibit notable neuropsychological deficits on standardized testing. Often, these deficits implicate brainstem and frontal and/or temporal lobe structures, regions that seem to be particularly at risk in head trauma (Ommaya & Gennarelli, 1974).

Changes in personality are frequently observed (Prigatano, 1987). The patient is impulsive and irritable, and signs of depression, anxiety, or paranoia are often noted. The ultimate consequences are (1) social withdrawal and isolation as pretrauma relationships progressively deteriorate (Fordyce, Roueche, & Prigatano, 1983; Levin & Grossman, 1978), (2) significant stress on the family, and (3) an economic burden on society if the patient remains unemployable (Oddy, Humphrey, & Uttley, 1978; Weddell, Oddy, & Jenkins, 1980).

There has been a growing recognition that traditional rehabilitation methods do not adequately address these cognitive and personality disturbances (Bond, 1975; Bond & Brooks, 1976; Bruckner & Randle, 1972; Fahy, Irving, & Millac, 1967; Najenson et al., 1974; Walker, 1972) and that enabling these individuals to "walk and talk" is only the first phase of intervention.

In response to the needs of brain injured adults who have been unable to return to gainful employment, the Department of Neurosurgery at Presbyterian Hospital,

*From *Neuropsychological Rehabilitation after Brain Injury* (pp. 96–118) by George P. Prigatano et al., 1986, Baltimore, Md.: Johns Hopkins University Press. Copyright 1986 by Johns Hopkins University Press. Adapted by permission.

Exhibit 10–1 Common Persisting Neuropsychological and Psychosocial
Problems of Traumatic Head Injury Patients

1. Decreased motor and psychomotor functioning to the point that gainful employment is often impossible
2. Decreased speed of information-processing and possibly reduced channel capacity depending on the perceptual and cognitive systems involved
3. Variable concentration and attentional skills
4. Impulsivity
5. Irritability and low frustration tolerance
6. Inappropriate social comments
7. Verbal expansiveness and tangential thought, possibly related to faulty feedback mechanisms
8. Misperception of social comments and situations, with associated problems of depression, anger, and paranoia
9. Eventual alienation of friends, relatives, and spouse because of inappropriate behavior, with associated changes in work, marriage, and leisure activities
10. Minimization of residual neuropsychological deficits
11. Impairment in rate and capacity for new learning, with associated problems of "memory" relative to psychometric intelligence
12. Preoccupation with how "life used to be," with associated angry outbursts, thoughts of suicide, and loss of interest and motivation in the present environment
13. Unrealistic expectations of friends, relatives, employers, and medical personnel because the patient frequently "looks so good" on the surface
14. Possible release of underlying psychiatric disturbance that was either not noted or controlled prior to the traumatic head injury

Source: This list was presented to the Traumatic Coma Data Bank Outcome Meeting, July 25, 1980, Bethesda, Maryland by the senior author.

with the support of hospital administrators,[1] decided to develop a neuropsychologically oriented treatment program. The Neuropsychological Rehabilitation Program (NRP) began operation in February, 1980. This chapter describes its program philosophy and treatment rationale, patient selection procedures, and methods of intervention. Clinical impressions about which patients benefit from such intervention are presented. Specific outcome data for the first 18 closed head-injury patients are discussed elsewhere (Prigatano et al., 1984).

PROGRAM PHILOSOPHY AND TREATMENT RATIONALE

Rehabilitation after brain injury has historically been medically oriented during the initial stages of recovery. Following medical stabilization, therapies were instituted to increase the patient's strength, improve ambulation and basic self-care skills, and enhance communication. The NRP approach differs in several fundamental ways from the more traditional rehabilitation setting in attempting to help brain injured individuals resume a productive lifestyle.

First, *neuropsychological deficits are seen as a primary rehabilitation target.* Goldstein (1942) recognized that higher cerebral deficits needed to be addressed in the rehabilitation of brain injured soldiers. He suggested that such patients be given extensive psychological examinations and retrained in a protected work environment. After treating traumatic head injured soldiers during World War II, Zangwill (1947) recognized the need to remediate cognitive deficits, primarily by teaching patients compensatory techniques. Luria (1980) also felt that restoration of higher cerebral function was quite possible, particularly after local brain damage (Luria, Naydin, Tsvetkova, & Vinarskaya, 1969). His conceptualization of brain functions as interlocking functional subsystems has been a central principle of the NRP. The work of these pioneers provided the theoretical rationale and empirical basis for intensive cognitive retraining activities following brain injury. In addition, Luria (Luria et al., 1969) and Ben-Yishay, Diller and their colleagues (Ben-Yishay & Diller, 1983; Ben-Yishay, Diller, Gerstman, & Gordon, 1979; Diller, 1976; Diller & Gordon, 1981a and 1981b) have provided practical approaches to the remediation of specific neuropsychological deficits.

Second, in addition to addressing specific neuropsychological deficits, *the NRP approach places equal emphasis on the personality of the patient and on the emotional/motivational states that accompany cognitive, perceptual, motor, and language deficits* (Gordon & Diller, 1983; Levin & Grossman, 1978). Outcome studies clearly demonstrate that both cognitive and personality disturbances may limit the patient's ability to return to work and have satisfying interpersonal relationships (see Bond, 1975; Bruckner & Randle, 1972; Gilchrist & Wilkinson, 1979; Walker, 1972). Indeed, with the passage of time, personality dysfunction may overshadow cognitive deficits as the major obstacle to adjustment (Fordyce, Roueche, & Prigatano, 1983).

Baker's (1955) emphasis on the importance of understanding the patient's personal or intrapsychic reactions to brain injury, especially the permanence of the consequences, has helped to refine the psychotherapeutic interventions employed in the NRP. Her thoughtful consideration of the common reactions to rehabilitation activities—the shame, depression, and anxiety that invariably affect participation in rehabilitation—has been quite important in the clinical management of these individuals. Goldstein's (1942) work reaffirms that some emotional and motivational disturbances are secondary symptoms stemming from failure to cope, rather than primary results of brain damage. Teaching patients new coping strategies, therefore, may be very therapeutic.

Many clinicians feel that psychotherapy is ineffective with brain injured patients. There is some truth to this notion if psychotherapy is undertaken in isolation from other treatments. However, the authors have found that, when it is integrated with other rehabilitation activities in a consistent and intensive manner, psychotherapy in its group and individual forms provides an important therapeutic tool with brain dysfunctional young adults.

Thus, it is the authors' conviction, reflected in this program, that both cognitive remediation and psychotherapeutic approaches are essential in the rehabilitation of brain injured patients, particularly those with traumatic head injury. Neither intervention in and of itself is sufficient to enable most brain injured patients to return to a productive life.

A third guiding principle of the program follows from the fact that the neuropsychological consequences of head injury are frequently so pervasively disruptive to daily life. *Rehabilitative efforts must be intensive and integrated across therapies.* Short or periodic interventions are usually inadequate. Also, because of memory deficits, patients require daily practice to consolidate improvements in functional living skills. The authors have found that a 6-month period of training is usually needed. Because these patients present with a myriad of problems and are frequently easily confused, rehabilitation themes must be consistently applied across various treatment hours. An aggressive attempt is made to maintain consistency of approach through daily staff meetings where each patient's status is discussed and treatment strategies are formulated. Thus, such problem areas as memory dysfunction, depression, and impaired awareness can be addressed in a similar fashion by all staff members and during all activities. A truly integrated interdisciplinary approach is vital.

Rehabilitation of brain damaged patients must constantly deal with patients' diminished awareness or denial of residual cognitive (Johnston & Diller, 1983; LaBaw, 1969) and personality deficits (Fordyce, 1983). Thus, a fourth guiding principle of the NRP is that *enhanced awareness is an explicit primary rehabilitation target.* This aim is accomplished indirectly at first with didactic educational sessions on the effects of brain injury. Later, patients are asked to record and chart their performances across a variety of behavioral domains. Awareness training then becomes more directive with videotaping, public review, and the generation of individual problem lists. These lists are openly discussed by all program members. Statements reflecting greater self-awareness and acceptance are rigorously reinforced by staff members.

The families of brain injured individuals may be as unrealistic as patients themselves in appraising cognitive and personality functioning (Romano, 1974). Therefore, issues of awareness and acceptance are also addressed in weekly relatives' meetings and in occasional family therapy sessions.

PATIENT SELECTION

The Section of Neuropsychology at Presbyterian Hospital offers two broad services: neuropsychological evaluation of patients with known or suspected brain dysfunction and neuropsychological rehabilitation of brain injured young adults. Patients are initially seen for a standardized neuropsychological examination. All testing is done by psychologists, as opposed to technicians, because information regarding the qualitative neuropsychological responses of the patients and their reaction to testing is vital in determining the suitability of the patient for the intensive NRP. All candidates have suffered serious brain injuries, are well past the stage of rapid spontaneous recovery, and have been unable to resume a productive independent life. In nearly every case, a constellation of cognitive deficits and personality changes forms the foundation of their adjustment problem.

Before a decision is made regarding admission, prospective patients are typically seen for a series of six to eight 1-hour trial sessions. Answers are sought to the following questions: What do the patients understand about their neuropsychological deficits? How do they respond to both positive and negative feedback? How realistic are their goals? Are psychiatric disorders present? How motivated are they and their relatives to attend sessions, keep appointments, and complete homework exercises? How do they respond to the idea of group work? What is their style of interpersonal interaction? What is the nature of their cognitive deficits?

During this time, patients are exposed to various cognitive remediation tasks, and their performance is discussed with them and their family members. Doing so gives the staff, patient, and family practical information about the type of work that would be involved in an intensive rehabilitation program. It also allows all individuals involved to decide whether a 6-month commitment to this intensive program is feasible for a given patient. Neuropsychological test findings that typically (but not always) exclude a patient are:

- IQ levels below 75.
- WAIS or WAIS-R Digit Symbol score below 5. A score of 6 or above is considered favorable as it suggests that patients can learn at a reasonable rate with repeated practice, an important skill for everyday functioning.
- Wechsler Memory Quotient below 75
- Minnesota Multiphasic Personality Inventory (MMPI) profile and/or a psychiatric history suggesting psychotic disorder or severe characterological problems

Patients must demonstrate from their history and behavior, as witnessed in the initial therapy trial, sufficient motivation to engage in rehabilitation activities. Repeated failure to keep appointments is grounds for exclusion, as is an inability to engage in basic cognitive retraining tasks. Finally, a commitment by the family to involve themselves in the rehabilitation program is highly desirable. Without family participation, generalization to home environments of progress made during rehabilitation becomes unlikely.

Most patients involved in the NRP to date have sustained traumatic head injuries, but a number have had localized cerebral anomalies, such as a tumor or ruptured arteriovenous malformation. The degree of neuropsychological impairment has varied from mild to severe as indicated by the Average Impairment Rating (see Prigatano, Parsons, Wright, Levin, & Hawryluk, 1983). Most patients are nonaphasic, but several aphasics have been treated in the program; all these patients had functional comprehension of spoken language. All participants have been able to manage personal hygiene needs and have been ambulatory, with at most the use of a cane. Some patients, however, have been clearly amnestic, but retained other cognitive skills on which to base a retraining program. Most patients have been males between the ages of 18 and 40. Usually at least 1 year has elapsed since the injury occurred.

METHODS OF INTERVENTION: THE PROGRAM

The general format of the NRP is that of a structured outpatient day-treatment program divided into formal treatment modules that each last 50 minutes. The morning sessions occur in group format, whereas the afternoon activities are individualized, with the exception of the final session of each treatment day. Active treatment lasts for approximately 6 hours per day, 4 days per week. Six to eight patients work with five or six therapists—three clinical psychologists and neuropsychologists, one speech and language therapist, one occupational therapist, and one physical therapist.

9:00 A.M. to 9:50 A.M., Cognitive Retraining

Following brain injury, certain neuropsychological deficits are frequently observed. These include attentional deficits, perceptual dysfunction, learning and memory disorders, impaired problem-solving and abstraction skills, and reduced information-processing speed (Bond, 1975; Goldstein, 1942; Gronwall & Sampson, 1974; Levin, Grossman, Rose, & Teasdale, 1979; Mandleberg & Brooks, 1975). Cognitive retraining, occurring during the first hour of each treatment day, addresses these general deficits. Two or three patients work with a single staff member—either a clinical psychologist, occupational therapist, or a speech and language pathologist—on a system of hierarchically arranged paper-and-pencil cognitive tasks. The content is quite basic at first, involving simple fine motor speed and basic orientation. As performance improves, more complex tasks are added. Daily scores and times are recorded for each patient in individual notebooks, and average weekly scores are graphed. Although these activities occur in a group format, patients progress at their own rate. Recent data suggest that intensive practice of these cognitive skills contributes to improvement on subsequent neuropsychological testing (Prigatano et al., 1984).

Several purposes of this early morning cognitive retraining hour have evolved:

- Patients are trained to use problem-solving strategies. The daily graphing of performance, (1) without strategies, (2) with poor and inefficient strategies, and finally (3) with good strategies highlights the practical benefits of their use. As patients discover for themselves the beneficial effects of strategies, resistance to their use lessens. This technique may also be used to illustrate to some patients that, if they cannot generate their own strategies, they must rely on others to provide a "template."
- Patients compile objective evidence of their performance, which enhances their awareness of their own strengths and deficits. The weekly graphing of performance and daily recording of scores serve to quantify certain behaviors. For patients with diminished awareness, scores lower than those of other patients working at the same table illustrate their deficits without casting staff members in the role of "bearer of bad news." Patients who are excessively depressed over the effects of their brain injury are shown their increasing scores as evidence of improvement. Patients are less likely to minimize these objective measures as "just someone else's opinion that I am improving."
- The patient's ability to calculate, graph, and record is determined. These are real-life tasks with benefits that the patient can recognize. Patients frequently exhibit confusion, impaired memory, calculation problems, and psychomotor retardation. Such solutions as using electronic pocket calculators or compensating for memory loss by asking others for information or by referring to a written list of procedures are employed. The patient learns that the use of prosthetic aids is considered an acceptable strategy.
- Information about performance in this hour is used to guide other treatment activities. The integrated daily use of information derived in one hour to guide therapy in a different hour is a major difference between this program and traditional rehabilitation approaches.
- Patients' performance characteristics are assessed. These characteristics are then considered in vocational planning or may be modified with training during the individual cognitive retraining hours. Frequently, patients can be shown, in an immediate and practical manner, the effects of fatigue, rest breaks, and conversational distraction upon the performance of a well-routinized behavior.

10:00 A.M. to 10:50 A.M., Cognitive Group Therapy

This hour has two major treatment goals. The first is to identify and remediate residual cognitive deficits as they are reflected in interpersonal communication difficulties. The second is to facilitate increased self-awareness of both residual deficits and current strengths. Both of these goals are accomplished in a group therapy format led by a clinical neuropsychologist and a speech and language pathologist. All patients participate in this group.

With respect to the remediation of cognitive deficits, initial emphasis is placed on identifying specific problems in thinking and communication that are common following brain injury. A formal simplified system is presented describing traditional aphasic problems, nonaphasic communication disorders, and cognitive deficits that accompany brain injury (Prigatano, Roueche, & Fordyce, 1985). Patients are helped to understand their particular difficulties. Special emphasis is placed on nonaphasic communication problems and related cognitive difficulties, which tend to be subtle and less easily detected or explained. These include the tendency to talk excessively; to become tangential in communication—that is, wandering from one topic to the next; to interrupt ongoing conversation; to forget the topic of conversation; to speak inappropriately with potentially offensive results; and to employ peculiar words and phraseology. Such difficulties are frequently associated with inattention, impulsivity, concrete thinking, and memory dysfunction.

As these concepts are grasped, patients come to understand how their own brain injury has affected their ability to function in social environments. Next, compensation strategies and techniques designed to offset these difficulties are introduced. These are practiced and monitored in highly structured group activities and in specific role-playing exercises. Later, when the patient can tolerate such direct feedback, sessions are videotaped and reviewed. Toward the end of the program, the social situations practiced in cognitive group are made increasingly complex and lifelike. Conflict resolution, dating, explaining the injury to others, interpersonal interaction, job interviews, and other such scenarios are designed and rehearsed to help patients deal effectively with the inevitable stresses encountered in the transition to productive living.

Improved social effectiveness also results from exercises designed to increase self-awareness—the second goal of cognitive group therapy. After a rapport has developed between patients and staff members, exercises are gradually introduced to help inhibit catastrophic reactions, denial, and defensiveness. Initially, problems in awareness are addressed in a nonthreatening fashion through presentation of previous case examples, including the review of videotapes of former patients. Subsequently, a model of the stages of recovery following brain injury is presented and discussed. This model, developed by the NRP staff, emphasizes awareness and acceptance of residual deficits. A large flowchart mounted permanently on the treatment room wall illustrates the course of a typical closed head-injury patient from the time of injury through stages of coma and intensive care, posttraumatic amnesia, acute rehabilitation, medical discharge, and resettlement. It demonstrates that cognitive/communication problems and incomplete awareness or denial can create predictable emotional, interpersonal, and vocational problems at each stage of recovery. Patients attempt to identify their current stage of recovery, and group members provide public feedback regarding the accuracy of each patient's choice. This process of contrasting group and individual opinion frequently provides to patients the first clear evidence of disparity between their perception of themselves and how they are perceived by others. Finally, patients are videotaped in group interaction or in specific communication tasks, and the videotape is reviewed specifically to identify current strengths and weaknesses. Patients initially attempt to critique their own tapes. This is followed by group feedback and formal discussion. The result is a public list of the particular cognitive and personality problems that staff members and patient agree must be addressed if rehabilitation is to be successful. A problem list for each patient is posted on the treatment room wall.

The process of facilitating awareness and acceptance is a delicate one. Therapists must be sensitive to the emotional and motivational state of each patient, particularly his or her ability to tolerate critical feedback. Identification of weaknesses is carefully balanced with the recognition of realistic strengths. Statements of awareness, acceptance, or attempts to compensate for residual problems elicit substantial public reinforcement. Throughout the course of cognitive group therapy, progress in problem areas is repeatedly reviewed, recorded, and graphed. Earlier videotapes are compared to later ones to capture for each patient the improvements or lack thereof accomplished over the course of cognitive group therapy.

11:00 A.M. to 11:50 A.M., Group Psychotherapy

Many clinicians feel that brain injured patients are poor candidates for psychotherapy because of their problems with attention, comprehension, memory, and decreased control over their affective reactions; some workers are therefore concerned that discussing painful topics will aggravate and distress the patient with brain injury. However, the authors argue that brain injury does not destroy one's humanness or the need to have an integrated sense of self and that the function of group psychotherapy is to assist patients in their efforts to re-establish an integrated personality.

Group psychotherapy is conducted by two psychologists who are trained in both clinical psychology and neuropsychology. Sessions focus on the emotional and motivational difficulties frequently associated with brain damage. Catastrophic reactions, neuropsychologically based personality disturbances, and premorbid characteristics that influence rehabilitation activities are discussed.

Each group psychotherapy hour begins with the identification by a group member of the name of the hour, its purpose, and why it is an important part of the rehabilitation program. Patients are taught that the purpose of the hour is to "discuss feelings and emotions." This is important because "how you feel determines how you act, and how you act determines how other people react to you." It is stressed that frequently after brain injury, people experience negative reactions from others that they do not fully understand and that group psychotherapy should help them achieve this understanding.

Early in treatment, patients are asked to answer specific questions concerning their personality functioning as they now perceive it and to identify emotional and motivational problems that they have experienced since injury. Subsequently, they are asked to gauge their relatives' perception of them. This process is facilitated by reviewing a list of affective problems that have been found to be associated with brain injury, a sort of menu from which the patient can pick and choose. The concept of "the catastrophic reaction" is interwoven in this initial discussion.

Group psychotherapy activities then focus on neuropsychologically based personality disturbances. Patients are taught as much as possible about the brain and the consequences of their own injuries. This educational portion of the group psychotherapy hour strays furthest from the traditional format. Yet, it provides valuable insights for patients as they learn to understand the neuropsychological substrate of their behavior problems. A brief and simplified overview of functional neuroanatomy is presented, employing films, slides, videotapes, and models of the brain. Each patient's medical histories, x-rays, and CT scans are discussed in order to help the individual understand how cognitive and affective problems have come about. This discussion also enhances patients' empathy for each other, as they come to recognize that some personality disturbances may be as organically mediated as a hemiparesis or an aphasia. The amount and pace of information provided are dictated by the capabilities of the patients, as well as by the overall tone of the group that exists on a given day. The authors have found that the discussion of this "intellectual" material helps defuse tense situations because it does not focus on specific patients and is therefore not threatening. It conveys to patients the notion that, even though they are brain damaged, they still can learn important information about themselves. This strengthens their self-esteem and adds to their dignity as individuals. It also fosters a true milieu experience.

The next formal section of psychotherapy involves discussion of premorbid personality characteristics or characterological problems, such as impulsivity, risk-taking, and substance abuse, that may predate the injury. The purpose of this discussion is to demonstrate to patients how their brain injury interacts with previous characteristics to determine their current behavior. This particular activity typically meets with the greatest resistance from patients. If these premorbid personality traits are disregarded, however, the patient will later be burdened, often to an exaggerated degree, with many of the same psychosocial problems that existed prior to their injury. The authors have found that the use of humor and reference to published scientific work help create a nonthreatening, but realistic atmosphere in which patients can talk about premorbid difficulties and ways in which unstable personality traits may be affecting their efforts to adapt to their conditions. These are often powerful discussions, and they seem to help patients accept responsibility for the consequences of their actions.

Problems with parents, spouses, children, and friends are also discussed within the context of neuropsychological, behavioral, and psychodynamic perspectives. Patients are encouraged to devise ways to enhance their ability to get along with others and to maintain satisfactory interpersonal relationships.

Finally, toward the end of the 6-month period, the group psychotherapy process assumes a more traditional psychiatric character in which group leaders primarily facilitate discussions among patients. In this way, one can observe whether the group members listen to and interact with each other in socially acceptable fashion. The ability to cope with this type of unstructured activity without losing emotional control is considered a reasonably good sign of effective interpersonal adjustment.

That one of the psychotherapists is also a co-leader of the cognitive group facilitates transfer of emotional and motivational topics generated in the cognitive group to the psychotherapy session. When patients become angry, upset, or depressed during cognitive group, they are told that these feelings can be discussed during group psychotherapy, which will occur shortly; thus, patients learn the importance of emotional control. This tactic also fosters a recognition by therapists from all disciplines of the inevitable emotional and motivational difficulties that must be formally addressed.

1:00 P.M. to 1:50 P.M. and 2:00 P.M. to 2:50 P.M., Individual Therapy

After lunch, each patient receives two sessions of individual therapy. These sessions may include some combination of individual psychotherapy, which every patient receives, speech and language therapy, occupational therapy, cognitive retraining, physical therapy, or vocational counseling and placement activities. The nature of the individual therapies depends on the problems identified during initial evaluations. The content of afternoon activities may change over the course of rehabilitation.

The cognitive retraining tasks given during this individualized time are integrated forms of problem solving and skill remediation. For example, if the patient presents a visuospatial deficit, it may initially be addressed through the use of verbal descriptions of geometric materials to solve visuospatial problems. Later training may include teaching the rules of gestalt—proximity, closure, similarity, continuity—to facilitate visuospatial problem-solving skills. The retraining progressively becomes integrated into vocational planning, e.g., map reading, taking bus routes, manual work with complex materials, operating equipment. Finally, the effects of the patient's deficits are determined in simulated work settings, and ways are found to minimize these effects. Cognitive, language, and motor deficits are approached in a similar manner. The goal is to approximate normal independent life tasks and vocational demands as closely as possible.

3:00 P.M. to 3:45 P.M., Independent Supervised Therapy

The purpose of this module is to foster independence and the capacity to work productively under minimal supervision. Although structure is initially provided in the form of specific assignments, patients are progressively encouraged to function autonomously. It is the authors' impression that patients' capacity to work under these conditions appears to be a good predictor of their ability to undertake employment in the real world.

3:45 P.M. to 4:15 P.M., Milieu

The final treatment session of the day involves a meeting of the entire rehabilitation community, including all patients and staff members. This time provides an opportunity for the discussion of issues of general interest. Important events, both positive and negative, that occurred during the day are reviewed and discussed, as are routine business matters. Thus, the milieu hour helps promote the continuity and consistency that is so important in rehabilitating brain injured patients.

4:30 P.M. to 5:15 P.M., Staff Meetings

Following milieu, the treatment staff has its daily meeting. After documentation and accounting duties are completed, the progress of each patient for that particular day is reviewed, and possible changes in intervention are discussed. When particular critical or sensitive therapeutic issues arise, as is inevitable for each patient, staff members collectively and carefully plan the most productive strategy for dealing with these issues. Doing so ensures consistency and allows the staff to capitalize on the therapeutic strengths of both staff and patients. In addition to these important clinical functions, the daily staff meetings serve another vital purpose—the provision of support, guidance, and a productive outlet for the frustrations that develop when working so closely with disabled patients (see Chapters 7 and 8). The authors have found that such an opportunity contributes immeasurably to the maintenance of staff morale and enthusiasm for this arduous work.

5:00 P.M. to 6:00 P.M., Wednesday Nights, Relatives Group

Once a week, the primary relatives of patients involved in the NRP meet for a 1-hour session. Although the session is usually conducted by two staff psychologists, all rehabilitation staff members occasionally participate in this meeting to provide an opportunity for mutual exchange with relatives. These meetings have two major purposes. First, they provide a forum for exchange of information concerning the patient's behavior at home and in the program. Staff members can give relatives the details of major treatment strategies and progress, relatives can inform staff of the difficulties that are encountered at home, and approaches to management can be jointly developed. Second, Relatives Group provides an important emotional outlet for the pain and frustration that afflict the relatives of brain injured patients (Lezak, 1978). In the authors' experience, the group format provides a powerful means by which relatives can educate and support each other.

In addition to these weekly relatives' meetings, periodic individual family counseling sessions are scheduled as needed, especially in the case of husband-wife dyads who are experiencing marital stress.

MEDICAL CONSULTANTS

The staff meets monthly with an experienced psychiatrist to devise treatment strategies for individual patients who present especially difficult behavioral management problems. In addition, consulting physicians routinely monitor patient medications and are available for medical evaluations as needed.

STAFF DEVELOPMENT

Intensive work with brain injured patients is a difficult task for even the most capable and committed therapists. Brain injury produces a plethora of problems, many of which are permanent or very slow to change. As can patients and their families, staff members can become demoralized, frustrated, and fatigued. They need support and occasional relief from this type of work if they are to remain energetic and dedicated. The authors have found that limiting the rehabilitation program to 4 days per week is helpful in this regard. On Fridays, staff members either see patients who are not in the program or engage in research and educational activities.

Staff members also benefit from continuing education regarding brain-behavior relationships and their disruption after brain damage. Viewing the injured patient as someone from whom one can learn is a valuable attitude that is characteristic of effective staff members.

Staff members need a time to express their frustration and irritation with patients and with one another. When the clinical work does not go well, negative feelings surface (Gans, 1983), and these must be addressed in staff meetings.

Although many decisions regarding patients are truly group decisions, staff members also need a leader. Someone must accept ultimate clinical responsibility for administration and clinic management. Otherwise, the staff lacks the structure and support it needs in carrying out its mission. The group leader should be identified as the most experienced and knowledgeable individual, regardless of professional discipline, in the treatment of these patients.

CLINICAL IMPRESSIONS AND IDEAS CONCERNING OUTCOME MEASURES

The basic questions that have to be answered regarding intensive neuropsychological rehabilitation are: Can the rate or level of neuropsychological functioning of brain injured patients be improved through cognitive remediation? Can personality difficulties be substantially altered by the combination of cognitive retraining and psychotherapy? Can patients be enabled to return to a productive life style? Finally, is such training cost-efficient?

The authors have found that modest improvements in neuropsychological functioning are possible with extensive retraining past the period of spontaneous recovery (see Prigatano et al., 1984). Yet, it appears that the amount of improvement is relatively small. Consequently, a more productive approach may be to enhance patients' awareness of their deficits and teach them compensation strategies. Obviously, one cannot claim to know the ultimate possible level of neuropsychological recovery. At this point, however, the authors concur with Zangwill's (1947) observation that teaching compensation techniques is the most expeditious way of helping brain injured individuals.

Personality disturbances that are part of the catastrophic reaction following brain injury can be substantially modified. They are, in the authors' experience, clearly tied to rehabilitation success, especially the ability of the patient to maintain employment (Prigatano et al., 1984). Given a minimal cognitive level—IQ greater than 75—personality factors are the most potent predictors of eventual recovery in this patient population. The NRP outcome highlights the relationship between persistent belligerence, helplessness, and/or denial and ultimate poor work adjustment. Also, recent data suggest that, without active intervention, behavioral problems may worsen with the passage of time, rather than spontaneously improve (Fordyce et al., 1983).

Some chronic unemployed brain-injured patients certainly can be helped to return to gainful employment, but the process is a difficult one, and the parameters for predicting successful readjustment are ill defined. However, the authors have found that at least low-average IQ and the ability to compensate for memory, perceptual, and motor deficits are vital to success and that the presence of psychosis or severe characterological disturbance is a strong predictor of failure. Patients who can be made aware of their difficulties, accept their limitations, and realistically readjust their goals have the best success.

Although the authors have attempted to correlate locus and type of lesion with recovery, the sample is too small to permit any definitive statements in this regard. However, it is the authors' clinical impression that patients with extensive temporal lobe disturbances are the most difficult to rehabilitate. They tend to be easily angered, paranoid, and unrealistic in their self-appraisal, and their cognitive deficits are substantial. In contrast, patients who have mainly frontal lobe injuries are more amenable to this form of rehabilitation. Their unawareness of their impairments seems organically mediated and, with daily feedback, can be altered. Also, they are less suspicious, and their cognitive deficits are less complex.

Reliable statistics regarding return to work after traumatic head injury are presently not available. From the few studies in the literature, it appears that only about one-third of severely injured patients—that is, in coma for at least 24 hours—achieve gainful employment following traditional rehabilitative efforts. Of the first 18 traumatic head injury patients who have undergone the program, approximately 50–60 percent have been able to obtain and maintain employment. It is expected that, with refined selection criteria, this figure may increase to 75 percent.

Finally, the question of cost efficiency of this and other programs must be seriously considered. Because it is a day treatment program, the NRP requires less staff time and more modest facilities than do inpatient rehabilitation programs. Patient fees range from $15,000 to $20,000 for the 6-month course. Although this is a substantial amount, it is considerably less than the cost of inpatient rehabilitation for a comparable period. Obviously, program fees must reflect the costs of operation (primarily staff salaries), local economic conditions, latitude of third party payers to authorize such treatment, and the like. The authors have found this figure to be acceptable to many of the funding sources that pay for rehabilitation. Ways of streamlining the program to make it more cost-efficient are presently being considered. This is a difficult venture, but one that is necessary in order for neuropsychological rehabilitation programs to negotiate the fiscal realities of life.

One can note with some hope the potential parallel of this program to the economic justification within health maintenance organizations for psychotherapy. Research that has been carried out in these settings has shown that psychotherapy substantially reduces the use of other expensive medical procedures, and consequently, it has been supported within such systems (Cummings, 1977). It may well be that the ultimate effectiveness of neuropsychological rehabilitation programs will be judged on this same criterion. What reduction in other expenditures accrues to insurance companies or government agencies by placing the patient in an intensive neuropsychological rehabilitation program? Does the patient make less frequent visits to neurosurgeons, neurologists, or internists? Do they need less medication, repeat EEGs or CT scans? Do patients and their families require less frequent psychiatric consultation? Is there a lower rate of alcoholism, divorce, or job turnover? These social and economic questions should be addressed in any comprehensive outcome study.

Choice of adequate outcome measures in rehabilitation is always difficult. The authors consider the percentage of patients who return to gainful employment to be the single most important criterion. From society's perspective, these patients will be less of an economic burden with the reduction in disability benefits, and they will themselves become taxpayers, thereby helping support and perpetuate the very system that sponsored their rehabilitation. (See Newman, 1984 for a review of work status following brain injury.)

Another useful outcome measure is the quality of life of patients and their families. Degree of marital satisfaction, capacity to tolerate the normal stresses of life, and the patient's sense of well-being are important indices, albeit difficult to quantify. Although such factors are important from a social and humanitarian point of view, unfortunately they are often minimized by agencies that must pay for these treatments.

NOTE

1. The authors wish to acknowledge the support of Dr. Barton Carl and Mr. Harry Neer in the development and financial support of this program. Without their commitment, it would simply not have been a reality. Also, the guiding administrative support of Mr. Dennis Millirons has been greatly appreciated.

REFERENCES

Baker, G. (1955). Diagnosis of organic brain damage in the adult. In B. Klopfer (Ed.), *Developments in the Rorschach Technique* (Vol. 2). Yonkers-on-Hudson, NY: World Book Company, pp. 318–375.

Ben-Yishay, Y., & Diller, L. (1983). Cognitive remediation. In M. Rosenthal, E. Griffith, M. Bond, & J.D. Miller (Eds.), *Rehabilitation of the head injured adult*, Philadelphia: F.A. Davis Company, pp. 367–380.

Ben-Yishay, Y., Diller, L., Gerstman, L., & Gordon, W. (1979). *Working approaches to remediation of cognitive deficits in brain damage*. Supplement to Seventh Annual Workshop for Rehabilitation Professionals, New York University, Institute of Rehabilitation Medicine.

Bond, M.R. (1975). Assessment of the psychosocial outcome after severe head injury. In *Outcome of severe damage to the central nervous system*, CIBA Foundation Symposium 34, New York: Elsevier, pp. 141–153.

Bond, M.R., & Brooks, D.N. (1976). Understanding the process of recovery as a basis for the investigation of rehabilitation for the brain injured. *Scandinavian Journal of Rehabilitation Medicine, 8,* 127–133.

Bruckner, F.E., & Randle, A.P.H. (1972). Return to work after severe head injuries. *Rheumatology and Physical Medicine, 11,* 344–348.

Cummings, N.A. (1977). The anatomy of psychotherapy under national health insurance. *American Psychologist, 32,* 711–718.

Diller, L. (1976). A model for cognitive retraining in rehabilitation. *The Clinical Psychologist, 29,* 13–15.

Diller, L., & Gordon, W.A. (1981a). Rehabilitation and clinical neuropsychology. In S. Filskov & T. Boll (Eds.), *Handbook of clinical neuropsychology*. New York, John Wiley & Sons, pp. 702–733.

Diller, L., & Gordon, W.A. (1981b). Interventions for cognitive deficits in brain-injured adults. *Journal of Consulting and Clinical Psychology, 49*, 822–834.

Fahy, T.J., Irving, M.H., & Millac, P. (1967). Severe head injuries—a six-year followup. *Lancet, 2*, 475–479.

Fordyce, D.J. (1983). *Underestimates of behavioral dysfunction in brain-injured individuals: Assessment methodology and implications for rehabilitation and psychosocial adjustment*. Paper presented at the Third International Symposium on Models and Techniques of Cognitive Rehabilitation, Indianapolis, IN.

Fordyce, D.J., Roueche, J.R., & Prigatano, G.P. (1983). Enhanced emotional reactions in chronic head trauma patients. *Journal of Neurology, Neurosurgery and Psychiatry, 46*, 620–624.

Gans, J. (1983). Hate in the rehabilitation setting. *Archives of Physical Medicine and Rehabilitation, 64*, 176–179.

Gilchrist, E., & Wilkinson, M. (1979). Some factors determining prognosis in young people with severe head injuries. *Archives of Neurology, 36*, 355–358.

Goldstein, K. (1942). *After effects of brain injury in war*. New York: Grune & Stratton.

Gordon, W.A., & Diller, L. (1983). Stroke: Coping with a cognitive deficit. In T.B. Burish & L.A. Bradley (Eds.), *Coping with chronic disease: Research and applications*. New York: Academic Press, pp. 113–135.

Gronwall, D., & Sampson, H. (1974). *The psychological effects of concussion*. Auckland: Auckland University Press.

Johnston, C.W., & Diller, L. (1983). Error evaluation ability of right-hemisphere brain-lesioned patients who have had perceptual cognitive retraining. *Journal of Clinical Neuropsychology, 5*, 401–402.

LaBaw, W.L. (1969). Denial inside out: Subjective experience with anosognosia in closed head injury. *Psychiatry, 32*, 174–188.

Levin, H.S., Benton, A.L., & Grossman, R.G. (1982). *Neurobehavioral consequences of closed head injury*. New York: Oxford University Press.

Levin, H.S., & Grossman, R.G. (1978). Behavioral sequelae of closed head injury: A quantitative study. *Archives of Neurology, 35*, 720–727.

Levin, H.S., Grossman, R.G., Rose, J.E., & Teasdale, G. (1979). Long-term neuropsychological outcome of closed head injury. *Journal of Neurosurgery, 50*, 412–422.

Lezak, M.D. (1978). Living with the characterologically altered brain-injured patient. *Journal of Clinical Psychiatry, 39*, 592–598.

Luria, A.R. (1980). *Higher cortical functions in man* (2nd ed.). New York: Basic Books.

Luria, A.R., Naydin, V.L., Tsvetkova, L.W., & Vinarskaya, E.N. (1969). Restoration of higher cortical function following local brain damage. In P.J. Vinken & G.W. Bruyn (Eds.), *Handbook of clinical neurology, (vol. 3)*. New York: North Holland Publishing Company, pp. 368–433.

Mandleberg, I.A. & Brooks, D.N. (1975). Cognitive recovery after severe head injury I. Serial testing on the Wechsler Adult Intelligence Scale. *Journal of Neurology, Neurosurgery and Psychiatry, 38*, 1121–1126.

Najenson, T., Mendelson, L., Schechter, I., David, C., Mintz, N., & Groswasser, Z. (1974). Rehabilitation after severe head injury. *Scandinavian Journal of Rehabilitation Medicine, 6*, 5–14.

Newman, S.P. (1984). The social and emotional consequences of head injury and stroke. *International Review of Applied Psychology, 33*, 427–455.

Oddy, M., Humphrey, M., & Uttley, D. (1978). Subjective impairment and social recovery after closed head injury. *Journal of Neurology, Neurosurgery, and Psychiatry, 41*, 611–616.

Ommaya, A.K., & Gennarelli, T.A. (1974). Cerebral concussion and traumatic unconsciousness: Correlation of experimental and clinical observations on blunt head injuries. *Brain, 97*, 633–654.

Prigatano, G.P. (1987). Personality and psychosocial consequences after brain injury. In M. Meier, L. Diller, & A. Benton (Eds.), *Neuropsychological rehabilitation*, New York: Guilford Press.

Prigatano, G.P., Fordyce, D.J., Zeiner, H.K., Roueche, J.R., Pepping, M., & Wood, B.C. (1984). Neuropsychological rehabilitation after closed head injury in young adults. *Journal of Neurology, Neurosurgery and Psychiatry, 47*, 505–513.

Prigatano, G.P., Parsons, O.A., Wright, E., Levin, D.P., & Hawryluk, G. (1983). Neuropsychological test performance in mildly hypoxemic patients with chronic obstructive pulmonary disease. *Journal of Consulting and Clinical Psychology, 41*, 108–116.

Prigatano, G.P., Roueche, J.R., & Fordyce, D.J. (1985). Nonaphasic language disturbances following severe closed head injury. In F.C.C. Peng (Ed.), *Language sciences*, vol. 7 (no. 1), 217–229.

Romano, M.D. (1974). Family response to traumatic head injury. *Scandinavian Journal of Rehabilitation Medicine, 6*, 1–4.

Walker, A.E. (1972). Long-term evaluation of the social and family adjustment to head injuries. *Scandinavian Journal of Rehabilitation Medicine, 4*, 5–8.

Weddell, R., Oddy, M., & Jenkins, D. (1980). Social adjustment after rehabilitation: A two-year follow-up of patients with severe head injury. *Psychological Medicine, 10*, 257–263.

Zangwill, O.L. (1947). Psychological aspects of rehabilitation in cases of brain injury. *British Journal of Psychology, 37*, 60–69.

Chapter 11

Neuropsychological Rehabilitation: Description of an Established Program

William J. Lynch, Ph.D.

HISTORICAL BACKGROUND

Until the last decade, the rehabilitation of brain injured persons consisted of some combination of physical, occupational, and speech therapies. Deficits in the areas of reasoning, abstract thinking, memory, and affective control were considered either insignificant or, more commonly, untreatable. In the early and middle 1970s, a number of rehabilitation programs began to address these higher cortical dysfunctions. The Institute of Rehabilitation Medicine-New York University Medical Center; Brain Injury Rehabilitation Unit-Veterans Administration Medical Center, Palo Alto, CA; Community Hospital of Indianapolis, IN; Braintree Hospital-Braintree, MA; Medical College of Virginia-Richmond, VA; Santa Clara Valley Medical Center-San Jose, CA; Rancho Los Amigos-Downey, CA; Casa Colina-Pomona, CA; and Good Samaritan Hospital-Phoenix, AZ are but a few of the dozens of programs now in existence (see Chapters 10 & 12).

This expansion attests to the importance assigned to cognitive abilities by practicing clinicians (see Levin, Benton, & Grossman, 1982; Trexler, 1982) and reflects the realization that successful rehabilitation must address these complex and significant deficits. In addition to the cognitive sequelae of brain injury, there are frequently severe and lasting emotional or affective disorders, such as depression, apathy, agitation, or paranoia, that seriously impede progress in rehabilitation and create tremendous strains on interpersonal relationships. It is therefore the impairments in the cognitive and affective domains that are the focus of efforts in neuropsychological rehabilitation.

The traditional role of the neuropsychologist in rehabilitation settings has been that of an evaluator or diagnostician; all too often, the neuropsychologist's conclusions were not relevant to treatment planning, tending to obscure rather than illuminate the patient's actual abilities and disabilities. Most neuropsychologists in rehabilitation settings learned through experience that their colleagues cared little that neuropsychological assessment could corroborate findings of neurodiagnostic studies, such as computed tomography or magnetic resonance imaging, or provide esoteric names for disabling deficits. Eventually, the focus of neuropsychological practice in rehabilitation changed, as both Caplan (1982) and Lynch (1983) have discussed. These authors point out that the current emphasis is upon deriving from neuropsychological data those descriptions of assets/liabilities or cognitive/perceptual-motor profiles that are relevant to rehabilitation settings.

This chapter describes a comprehensive outpatient rehabilitation program—the Brain Injury Rehabilitation Unit (BIRU) at the Veterans Administration Medical Center, Menlo Park Division, Palo Alto, California—with both cognitive and traditional components for patients suffering such brain disorders as traumatic head injury or stroke.

STAFFING

Because the BIRU is a 5 day-a-week program, it has staffing needs that differ from those of an inpatient program. The present staffing pattern is as follows:

- *Program director* (Ph.D.): Has both administrative and clinical responsibilities; acts as the overall director of BIRU service and training functions; performs direct clinical services as well
- *Head nurse* (R.N.): Assistant Director of BIRU, in addition to role as direct supervisor of BIRU nursing staff; performs clinical functions, such as group leadership and case management
- *Psychology technicians* (2): Perform assessment and rehabilitation roles, such as leaders of memory, language, and family support groups; each is coordinator (case manager) for as many as four patients
- *Licensed vocational nurse and nursing assistant*: Perform rehabilitation roles, including group leadership, individual treatment, and coordination of BIRU patients; provide some traditional nursing care, but is not a major element of their position
- *Secretary* (½ Time)
- *Trainees in clinical psychology* (1–3): Perform assessments and treatment under supervision of BIRU staff
- *Volunteers:* Perform elementary assessments under supervision; also assist BIRU staff in co-leading groups and/or individual treatments

PATIENT POPULATION

BIRU patients are virtually all males, with a mean age of 43 years. The majority (about 60 percent) are head injured, whereas the remaining 40 percent have suffered either cerebrovascular disease (30 percent) or other conditions (10 percent) such as tumor, anoxia, infections, or early degenerative dementia. Table 11-1 presents a detailed description of a consecutive sample of 50 BIRU patients.

PRINCIPAL ELEMENTS OF THE PROGRAM

Admission Criteria and Process

Rather than employing strict admission criteria, a set of flexible guidelines have been developed for determining the suitability of patients for admission to the BIRU. Such factors as age, time since onset, and type and site of lesion are considered, but are given no more weight than such elements as degree of motivation, areas of deficit, and extent of family involvement. The only strict criteria for admission are that the patient is a veteran who is qualified for Veterans Administration (VA) care and that the veteran has a brain disorder that requires cognitive rehabilitation. Exclusionary criteria include *current* substance abuse, major mental disorder, or clear potential for physical violence.

The process of admission begins with a referral. Once it is determined that the referral is appropriate, the medical record is requested and reviewed. If, after this review, the patient remains a viable candidate for admission, the staff then conducts a comprehensive evaluation of cognitive, affective, and perceptual motor abilities.

Evaluations of the Patient

Routine evaluations are requested from a variety of sources, and therefore it is essential that coordination is maintained throughout the admissions and treatment

---

Table 11-1 Patient Data for an Unselected Sample of 50 BIRU Patients

Variable	Median	Mean	Standard Deviation	Range	Mode(s)
Age (at admission)	43.5	43.2	15.36	19–70	34
Months, onset to admission	20.0	31.4	35.31	1–151	3,4,9,24
Months in treatment	9.5	9.9	5.06	4–15	7,10

period. This is accomplished by assigning a coordinator or case manager to the case who is responsible for generating and following up on all referrals. Further, an attempt is made to include members of any evaluating and/or treating discipline in treatment conferences or patient/family staffings involving the patient. Routine feedback in the form of progress notes and treatment summaries is solicited at least on a monthly basis. All these measures create a sense of therapeutic unity among the various disciplines with regard to the individual patients.

Neuropsychology

A careful neuropsychological evaluation is carried out over several days. The measures employed consist of some or all of the following: parts of the Halstead-Reitan Battery; Wechsler Adult Intelligence Scale-Revised (WAIS-R) (Wechsler, 1981); Wechsler Memory Scale (Wechsler, 1945) in both the standard and modified (Russell, 1975) formats; Wide Range Achievement Test-Revised (WRAT-R) (Jastak & Wilkinson, 1984) or Peabody Individual Achievement Test (PIAT) (Dunn & Markwardt, 1970); Woodcock-Johnson Psychoeducational Battery Parts I–III—Cognitive Abilities, Aptitude, and Achievement (Woodcock & Johnson, 1977); and the Minnesota Multiphasic Personality Inventory (MMPI) (Hathaway & McKinley, 1951). Recently, the staff members have also begun to use a selection of computer-administered cognitive skills measures (Psychological Software Service, 655 Carrollton Avenue, Indianapolis, IN 46220) that assess such abilities as reaction time (visual and auditory; simple and complex), scanning, tracking, maze learning, perceptual organization, and reading. The neuropsychological test data are organized into standard score (T-score) profiles for ease of intertest comparisons and communication of results to staff, patient, and family. The evaluation attempts to move beyond the presentation of test scores, striving to translate these data into more meaningful statements about abilities and deficits and the relevance of the findings for everyday activities. For example, the T-score profile for patients and their families has been modified so that such terms as "memory" or "eye-hand coordination" are substituted for test names, such as the Wechsler Memory Scale or Purdue Pegboard. Problems on neuropsychological tests are discussed as problems in living that pertain to the patient's current situation.

Neurology

Patients referred to the BIRU are typically under the care of a physician, yet the physician is frequently not a neurologist. Thus, all new admissions are evaluated by a neurologist if they have not been so examined for more than 6 months. The importance of a careful neurologic exam cannot be exaggerated, because many of the problems encountered by brain impaired persons, such as seizures, motor control disorders, agitation, and lethargy, can be identified and sometimes treated by a neurologist skilled in assessing behavioral issues. In addition to the management of seizures, the neurologist is expert in the interpretation of neurodiagnostic procedures, such as the EEG.

Psychiatry

Because many brain injured patients experience acute and chronic affective or behavioral disorders, the involvement of psychiatrists with relevant expertise in a rehabilitation program is a valuable addition. Staff members also consult with a psychiatrist on matters of medication, as well as routine medical tests.

Speech/Language and Audiology

Because many patients suffer communicative deficits as a result of brain disorders, there is often a need for a speech/language pathologist (SLP) to evaluate the patient's linguistic skills. Audiologic consultation is sought whenever there is a question of a hearing loss. Subtle hearing losses may mimic or exacerbate an aphasic disorder. In most instances, a series of specialized techniques, such as speech reception thresholds, that evaluate cortical language processing are requested, in addition to the standard measures of hearing acuity. Clearly, it is imperative to identify and treat peripheral sensory impairments before addressing central processing deficits.

Occupational Therapy

Referral to the occupational therapist (OT) is virtually automatic in brain injury programs. The OT evaluates the patient's level of independence in the key areas of self-care, such as dressing, grooming, toileting, and eating, in order to devise an individualized treatment plan. Many OTs have broadened their interests to include remediation of temporal and spatial orientation deficits ("reality orientation"). In a more traditional vein, OTs also provide training in fine motor skills, commonly by means of avocational activities.

Physical Therapy

Most patients are also referred to the physical therapist (PT) for assessment and treatment in the areas of walking, general mobility, transferring, and strengthening of the upper and lower extremities.

Clearly, there needs to be a close and continuing collaboration between the OT and PT in order to coordinate their respective treatments. Indeed, *all* treatments must be coordinated, because few abilities or functions are the exclusive province of one discipline. As an example, the apparently simple act of buttoning a shirt on request requires language in order to hear and analyze the command, perception of the article of clothing, appreciation of the complex sequence of motor acts required, and the ability to move the limbs and fingers in a timely and coordinated fashion. In this example, speech pathology, neuropsychology, OT, and PT are all integral. Neuropsychological rehabilitation, therefore, requires a team approach in order to be effective.

Psychosocial

The information derived from a psychosocial history, as well as that obtained from psychological measures of personality, such as the MMPI, and social adjustment, is indispensable in treatment planning. Staff members attempt to identify such problems as depression, excessive tension or anxiety, delusional thinking, problems with assertion, and/or family conflicts that may impede the patient's progress. The patient's spouse or other family members are often interviewed in order to obtain a more balanced picture of the home situation. Decisions may then be made regarding the need for psychotherapy, pharmacotherapy, and/or family counseling. All spouses and/or significant others are strongly encouraged to attend a biweekly Family Support Group.

Neuroradiology

Patients are referred for computed tomography (CT) scans of the head if they have never had one or if more than 6 months has elapsed since their latest scan and there is reason to expect that there has been some change, e.g., change in ventricular size, reabsorption of blood following cerebral hemorrhage. The CT scan provides a detailed view of brain *structures*, whereas the matter of brain *function* remains largely a matter of clinical inference. Newer procedures, such as positron emission tomographic (PET) scanning (Ter-Pogossian, Raichle, & Sobel 1980), brain electrical activity mapping or BEAM (Morihisa, Duffy, & Wyatt, 1983) and magnetic resonance imaging (MRI) (Pykett, 1982), which yield information regarding regional metabolic activity, electrical activity, and tissue composition of the brain, respectively, have great potential as diagnostic and perhaps prognostic aids in rehabilitation. For example, CT and MRI may reveal areas that have been affected by a brain insult and thus can be used to track structural changes, such as ventricular enlargement, that may occur during recovery. BEAM and PET, in contrast, can be used to document *functional* status and changes in the brain throughout the course of treatment. These procedures allow the clinician to determine the patency of brain systems, such as motor and sensory pathways, that are critical in cognitive and perceptual-motor activity. An area that is not visibly lesioned, but is currently nonfunctional, may be engaged in treatment, whereas one that is clearly damaged may not.

SPECIAL ADDITIONAL PROCEDURES

Rating of Patient's Independence

Additional procedures are routinely employed in the evaluation of a new admission to the BIRU program. One such procedure, the Rating of Patient's Independence or ROPI (Porch & Collins, 1974), consists of three main sections: Self-Care, Socialization, and Communication. Within each section, there are five, eight, and five subsections, respectively. Each of these subsections consists of five individual behavioral measures. Thus, the ROPI consists of 90 elements that represent the major aspects of independent living that are of concern to the rehabilitation clinician. Figure 11–1 illustrates the ROPI profile form designed at the BIRU by the author and Nancy Mauss-Clum (head nurse). This profile was not part of Porch and Collins' original effort.

The ROPI is administered on admission and at discharge. The patient's spouse or parent or "significant other" is required to be present in order to verify and elaborate upon the patient's responses. A unique feature of the ROPI is its 15–point multidimensional scoring system, (Porch, 1971) which contains three general categories:

CATEGORY:	SCORE RANGE:
Independent	8–15
Needs supervision	4– 7
Needs assistance or	2– 3
can't do	1

Ability to perform an activity is evaluated according to four primary criteria:

1. Independence: Does the patient require supervision or direct assistance?
2. Completeness: Does the patient do *all* or only *some* of the task?
3. Consistency: Does the patient perform the task on a regular basis?
4. Efficiency: Does the patient perform the task with normal or with reduced efficiency as compared to before onset?

Each of these criteria contributes to the final numerical score for each of the 90 abilities. The process of assigning a score is quite logical; indeed, it follows the pattern of a decision tree (Fig. 11–2).

Thus, if the patient performs a task independently, incompletely, inconsistently, and with reduced ability, the score for that task would be 8. Likewise, if the patient required supervision, yet carried out the task completely and consistently,

		1	2	3	4	5	6	7	8	9	10	11	12	13	14	15
	Overall Rating			·	·	·	·		·	·	·	·	·	·	·	·
	Self-Care (SC)			·	·	·	·		·	·	·	·	·	·	·	·
	Socialization (SOC)			·	·	·	·		·	·	·	·	·	·	·	·
	Communication (COM)			·	·	·	·		·	·	·	·	·	·	·	·
	CAN'T DO →	DIRECT ASSIST.		SUPERVISION				INDEPENDENT								
SC	A. Dressing			·	·	·	·		·	·	·	·	·	·	·	·
	B. Grooming			·	·	·	·		·	·	·	·	·	·	·	·
	C. Toilet activities			·	·	·	·		·	·	·	·	·	·	·	·
	D. Ambulation			·	·	·	·		·	·	·	·	·	·	·	·
	E. Eating			·	·	·	·		·	·	·	·	·	·	·	·
SOC	A. Health awareness			·	·	·	·		·	·	·	·	·	·	·	·
	B. Memory			·	·	·	·		·	·	·	·	·	·	·	·
	C. Scheduling			·	·	·	·		·	·	·	·	·	·	·	·
	D. Interpersonal activ.			·	·	·	·		·	·	·	·	·	·	·	·
	E. Transportation			·	·	·	·		·	·	·	·	·	·	·	·
	F. Occupation/avocation			·	·	·	·		·	·	·	·	·	·	·	·
	G. Personal business			·	·	·	·		·	·	·	·	·	·	·	·
	H. Housing			·	·	·	·		·	·	·	·	·	·	·	·
COM	A. Speech			·	·	·	·		·	·	·	·	·	·	·	·
	B. Understanding			·	·	·	·		·	·	·	·	·	·	·	·
	C. Reading			·	·	·	·		·	·	·	·	·	·	·	·
	D. Writing			·	·	·	·		·	·	·	·	·	·	·	·
	E. Gestural			·	·	·	·		·	·	·	·	·	·	·	·

Patient: _____   Date(s) Evaluated _____

_____

_____

BRAIN INJURY REHABILITATION UNIT - VAH, PALO ALTO, CA

Figure 11–1 Rating of Patient's Independence Summary Profile

Source: From *The Rating of Patient's Independence* by B. Porch and M. Collins, 1974, unpublished manuscript. Adapted by permission.

the score would be 7. Figure 11–3 illustrates the mean ROPI summary scores obtained by a sample of 12 BIRU patients at admission and discharge.

These data demonstrate that the most deficient domain for BIRU patients is socialization. This follows from the fact that the average BIRU patient is some 1½ to 2 years postonset, by which time the bulk of improvement in the areas of self-

FOR TASKS DONE INDEPENDENTLY, ARE THEY DONE:
COMPLETELY? CONSISTENTLY? WITH NORMAL ABILITY? (SCORE)

YES ⟶	YES ⟶	YES(15)
YES ⟶	YES ⟶	NO(14)
YES ⟶	NO ⟶	YES(13)
YES ⟶	NO ⟶	NO(12)
NO ⟶	YES ⟶	YES(11)
NO ⟶	YES ⟶	NO(10)
NO ⟶	NO ⟶	YES(9)
NO ⟶	NO ⟶	NO(8)

FOR TASKS DONE ONLY WITH SUPERVISION, ARE THEY DONE:
COMPLETELY? CONSISTENTLY? (SCORE)

YES ⟶	YES(7)
YES ⟶	NO(6)
NO ⟶	YES(5)
NO ⟶	NO(4)

FOR TASKS REQUIRING DIRECT ASSISTANCE, ARE THEY DONE:
COMPLETELY? (SCORE)

YES(3)

NO(2)

PATIENT CANNOT DO TASK? (SCORE)

YES(1)

Figure 11–2 Decision Tree used to Arrive at Multidimensional Scores for a ROPI

---

care and communication has occurred. These findings also suggest that the primary problems that persist beyond the period of traditional treatment (6 months) are only indirectly related to physical disability.

The ROPI provides the staff with an objective assessment of a patient's level of independence in a broad range of abilities and is useful as an index of treatment effectiveness or outcome. In addition, the results of the ROPI are used to generate a list of problems that form the foundation of the treatment plan. The following section describes the BIRU Problem List in its current form.

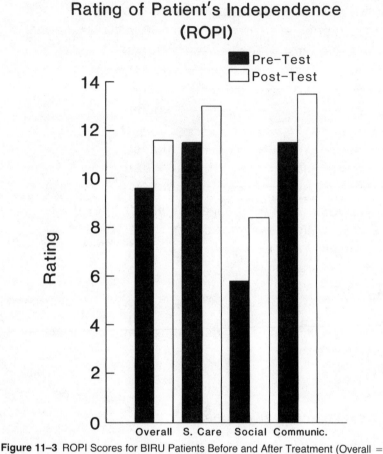

Figure 11-3 ROPI Scores for BIRU Patients Before and After Treatment (Overall = Average of all ROPI items; S. Care = Self-care items; Social = Socialization items; Communic. = Communication items).

BIRU Standard Problem List

In order to standardize the terminology and operational definitions of commonly encountered problems, a Standard Problem List (SPL) was developed (Lynch & Mauss, 1981), which facilitates the creation of better organized and focused treatment plans. Exhibit 11-1 presents the major elements of the list.

Data from neuropsychological testing, the ROPI, and the other consultants involved in the case are integrated, along with observational and historical information, in order to provide a data base for development of an individualized problem list.

Exhibit 11–1 Elements of the BIRU Problem List

BRAIN INJURY REHABILITATION UNIT

Problem List

NAME:

DATE OF STAFFING: COORDINATOR:

TYPE OF STAFFING: INTAKE   1-MONTH   3-MONTH
                  PRE-DISCHARGE   DISCHARGE

PROBLEM: TREATMENT: STAFF:

1. MEMORY DIFFICULTY (GENERAL)
   (Trouble remembering what he has heard/seen; can't
   find way around; confused about day/date/place)
   a. Auditory
   b. Visual
   c. Spatial

2. IMPAIRED LANGUAGE PROCESSING
   GENERAL — SPECIFIC
   (Trouble talking/listening/reading
   writing/using gestures)
   a. Reading Comprehension
   b. Word Recognition
   c. Auditory Comprehension
   d. Writing
   e. Word Finding
   f. Fluency
   g. Spelling

3. MATH DIFFICULTY
   (Trouble with figures/slow or
   inaccurate figuring costs or making
   change/can't do math in head)

4. IMPAIRED SENSORY ANALYSIS
   (Problems with seeing, hearing
   or awareness of body parts)
   a. Visual
      1). Field cut
      2). Low acuity
      3). Inattention
      4). Field cut and inattention
   b. Impaired Hearing
   c. Impaired body awareness

5. IMPAIRED MOTOR FUNCTION: GENERAL
   (Problems with taking things
   apart/putting them back
   together; slow/awkward with
   hands/fingers; problems with

Exhibit 11–1 continued

PROBLEM: *TREATMENT:*   *STAFF:*

walking/uncoordinated; not
in good physical condition/
lacks energy/endurance)
problems swallowing food;
slurred speech
  a. Impaired Constructional Skills
  b. Impaired Fine Motor Coordination
  c. Impaired Gross Coordination
  d. Extremity Weakness
  e. Impaired Physical Conditioning
  f. Impaired Flexibility
  g. Impaired Ambulation
  h. Difficulty Swallowing
  i. Dysarthria

6. PERTINENT MEDICAL CONDITIONS
   (Any illnesses or conditions that
   are being treated or that could
   affect course of treatment)
   (Problems caused by use of either
   alcohol or non-prescribed drugs)
   a. Seizures
   b. Hypertension (High Blood Pressure)
   c. Diabetes
   d. Heart Disease
   e. Chronic Lung Disease
   f. Substance Abuse: Alcohol
   g. Substance Abuse: Other

7. EMOTIONAL PROBLEMS
   (Any problems with feelings or
   behavior, such as sadness, quick
   temper, nervousness, tension, too
   quiet, too loud, low opinion of
   self, can't seem to "get going")
   a. Depression
   b. Anxiety
   c. Low Self-Esteem
   d. Inappropriate/Inconsistent
      Assertion
   e. Aggressive Behavior
   f. Family Stress
   g. Apathy/Inertia

8. SOCIAL PROBLEMS
   (Problems with dressing, grooming,
   getting cleaned up, using toilet;
   doesn't socialize; problems taking
   care of self; not independent in
   buying clothes, managing money,

Exhibit 11–1 continued

```
buying/preparing food; can't live
without supervision; relies on others
to get around; can't/won't drive or
take bus/train; can't/won't work)
a. Impaired Self-Care:
   Dressing
   Grooming
   Toileting
b. Impaired Interpersonal Skills
c. Impaired Independent Living:
   1). Clothing
   2). Finances
   3). Food
   4). Housing
d. Impaired Use of Transportation
e. Job Impairment
```

9. COGNITIVE PROBLEMS (other)
   (Problems with abstract thinking,
   reasoning, figuring out problems,
   knowing what to do in difficult or
   possibly dangerous situations)
   a. Problems with reasoning,
      logic and/or with solving problems
   b. Problems with understanding
      and following directions:

ANY ADDITIONAL PROBLEMS OR CONCERNS:

NOTES ON STAFFING

END OF PROBLEM LIST FOR:

Source: From "Brain Injury Rehabilitation: Standard Problem Lists" by W. Lynch and N. Mauss, 1981, *Archives of Physical Medicine and Rehabilitation, 62,* p. 225. Copyright 1981 by American Congress of Rehabilitation Medicine. Reprinted by permission.

The Goal-Attainment Follow-Up Guide

The next step is to complete a structured statement of treatment objectives called the Goal-Attainment Follow-Up Guide (GAFG) (Kiresuk & Sherman, 1968). For each problem area, possible outcomes are specified that reflect what the patient is expected to achieve, as well as what would represent less-than and greater-than expected levels. The staff members strive to define outcomes in terms of real-life performances, rather than neuropsychological test results. The GAFG encourages a rational and pragmatic approach to the process of goal setting, one that is based upon experience with similar cases. Table 11–2 contains an example of a completed GAFG for 3 problems.

By examining the GAFG for a patient at discharge, the staff can determine its success in resolving the problems initially targeted for treatment. The resulting percentage of successes can be viewed as a treatment "batting average," which can aid in evaluation of the program's effectiveness.

STAGES IN THE TREATMENT PROCESS

The BIRU program has many stages intended to reflect the typical long-term patterns of recovery of many brain-injured patients.

Orientation

In order to evaluate patients more thoroughly, a period of orientation was instituted. This lasts about 4 weeks and consists of evaluations, as well as exposure to many of the treatments. The evaluations are intentionally scheduled for brief periods (1–2 hours) over several days. The rationale for this approach is the belief that lengthy neuropsychological evaluations tend to be exhausting and frustrating for the patient and may produce misleading results. Patients who are evaluated over several days are apt to display a typical level of performance, one that is less influenced by time of day, energy level, and motivation.

During the orientation period, the staff completes a checklist of behavioral observations, as well as a listing of assessments to be completed. Exhibit 11–2 depicts a portion of the four-page BIRU Orientation Checklist.

Table 11–2 Sample Goal-Attainment Follow-Up Guide (GAFG) for Three Problems

	Problem #1: Impaired Dressing	Problem #2: Impaired Driving	Problem #3: Impaired Reading
Much less than expected	Requires direct assistance	Cannot drive	Cannot read
Expected level of outcome	Dresses self, supervised	Drives with supervision	Reads brief messages
Much greater than expected level	Dresses self, unaided	Drives self, unaided	Reads books, articles

BRAIN INJURY REHABILITATION UNIT

VA Medical Center–Menlo Park Divison (205 B1)

Palo Alto, CA 94304

BIRU ORIENTATION CHECKLIST

A. Self Care:	Yes	No	Comments
1. Can Find BTRM:			
2. Is Continent:			
3. Feeds Self:			
4. Grooming:			
5. Hygiene:			
6. Dresses Self:			
7. Makes Coffee:			
8. Gets Lunch:			
9.			
B. Ambulation:			
1. Wheelchair			
2. Self–Propels?			
3. Walks Safely?			
4. Safe/Stairs?			
5.			
C. V.A. Grounds: Finds Way To:			
1. Dining Room:			
2. Back To BIRU:			
3. To Canteen:			
4. Shuttle Bus:			

BIRU ORIENTATION
CHECKLIST FOR: _____

Exhibit 11–2 Brain Injury Rehabilitation Unit Orientation Checklist

Following the orientation period, some patients are discharged, either because they do not appear to be in need of intensive treatment or because they decline to pursue additional rehabilitation. If further treatment is indicated, the patient enters the 3-phase BIRU Treatment Program described below.

The Three-Phase Process

Basic Phase

The basic phase emphasizes individual treatment sessions, with only a few group therapies other than the twice-weekly general rap group. Sessions might focus on individual relaxation, assertiveness, social skills, language, memory, and computer-assisted cognitive retraining.

The rap group is attended by the majority of BIRU patients—up to 12 at a time—and is intended to provide a loosely structured forum for discussing ongoing personal, family, or program-related problems. The group leaders provide guidance and direction as needed and may on occasion present specific topics, such as finances, controlling assaultive behavior, or dealing with social agencies, to the group for discussion. The group plans and arranges bimonthly BIRU outings. Each element of the outing is proposed, discussed, and approved by the group. In addition, group members themselves make the arrangements and determine such matters as admission charges and wheelchair access to the chosen destination.

Relaxation training is conducted by a staff member, a licensed vocational nurse with training and interest in this treatment. He is supervised by the program director. Therapy is provided weekly for 1 hour and typically begins with a period of conversation regarding progress and observations during the previous week. Relaxing tapes are played—"Slow Ocean" from the commercially available Environments Series or "Letting Go of Stress" from The Source Cassette Learning Systems, P.O. Box M, Stanford, CA 94305—and patients are trained to relax themselves. Eventually the instructor provides tapes to the patient for home use. Both self-report and objective measures, such as pulse rate or blood pressure, are used to evaluate the effectiveness of the training. The relaxation group, containing perhaps five or six patients, functions in a similar fashion.

Assertiveness training and communication skills training are offered individually or in a weekly group for 1 hour. The group members, led by a licensed vocational nurse, discuss the role of assertiveness in their daily lives. The group leader proposes situations that call for assertive responses, such as being ignored by a waiter or feeling angry with a spouse, and presents alternative ways of dealing with each situation. The group members offer solutions to the problem and/or engage in role-playing to illustrate the various approaches proposed. A group discussion follows that leads to a consensus about the proper assertive response for a given situation.

Social skills are taught individually or in a weekly group. The group members discuss appropriate appearance, dress, conversation, and response to others when the patient is on the outside. Relationships with family, co-workers, friends, and strangers are the primary focus. The individual or group members are taken on monthly field trips to the VA canteen or other nearby establishments as a way of putting into practice what they have learned (see Chapter 13).

The language group is attended by any patients with communicative disorders—dysphasia or dysarthria—and supplements individual speech/language therapy. The group leader discusses individual problems with verbal expression, comprehension, or writing. Group members participate in various group exercises dealing with effective listening techniques, writing, spelling, or speaking. For example, patients with receptive language deficits may be taught to utilize nonverbal cues to help them understand what others are saying.

All BIRU patients are evaluated thoroughly on admission to determine the presence and extent of memory deficit and the suitable level of retraining required. The measures employed include the Wechsler Memory Scale (with delayed recall), Benton Visual Retention Test, Benton Facial Recognition Test, and the Goldman-Fristoe-Woodcock Auditory Memory Skills Battery. Memory training is provided either individually or in twice-weekly groups. Patients who are overly restless, distractible, or disruptive in a group setting are assigned to individual sessions.

Depending on the extent of the patient's memory impairment he or she is placed in a basic or advanced group. In the basic group there are simple discussions and demonstrations of basic memory enhancement methods, such as verbal rehearsal, visual reminders (the "string around the finger"), or note taking. The advanced group deals with more complex memory improvement techniques, such as complex visualization, mnemonic lists, and the practice of discussing reading material to improve comprehension. The sessions include didactic presentations of and exercises demonstrating effective memorization techniques.

The staff has compiled a guide for memory training that is distributed to all group members (Tercero & Boczkowski, 1983) and serves as a general outline of the material covered during training. The first part of the guide briefly describes memory processes and problems. Common memorization aids—visualization; number chunking; the loci system, which links items to be recalled to familiar locations, such as adjacent areas of one's house; and number imagery, such as the "one = bun, two = shoe, etc. technique (e.g., Cermak, 1975; Higbee, 1977; Lorayne & Lucas, 1974)—are then described. Strategies for remembering names and faces, telephone numbers, addresses, and lists are provided in a step-by-step fashion, complete with illustrative exercises.

Computer-assisted cognitive retraining (CACR) constitutes less than 10 percent (1–2 hours per week) of the typical patient's BIRU schedule. Due to limitations in staff and equipment, the program is able to provide only minimal CACR. Patients receive CACR, using either a microcomputer or a video game system, for treatment of problems with alertness, attention, concentration, fine motor skill, memory, or certain language abilities, such as spelling, reading, and word finding. Sessions last 1 hour, with a clinician present at all times. Results of each session are recorded on a computer file system for later analysis. Progress is illustrated both for staff and patients by transferring CACR data to a graph construction program.

Patients at the basic level are typically in need of fairly close supervision and are felt to be unable to adapt to the demands of group treatment sessions. Patients may remain in the basic phase for several months; indeed, they may be discharged directly from this phase. However, when they demonstrate increased stress tolerance and self-control, they graduate to the next phase. This decision is made slowly after continuous monitoring of the patient's progress. Periodic conferences among the staff members permit exchanges of information and opinions and ultimately lead to a decision by consensus on patient placement.

Advanced Phase

In the advanced phase, there is a greater emphasis upon group treatments, with a corresponding reduction of individual treatments. Patients at this level participate in one or more of the following groups: rap, social skills, assertiveness, relaxation, current events, memory, and language. Patients are also given opportunities for ''independent study,'' which consists of self-directed and self-monitored therapeutic activities. Toward the latter part of this phase, patients begin to seek out opportunities for work or education in preparation for discharge. Although perhaps not completely independent, advanced patients are felt to be capable of maintaining a daily schedule of treatments with minimal supervision. Similarly they should be capable of participating in group sessions that contain as many as eight to ten persons. Those who demonstrate periods of gross confusion, aggressive outbursts, irrelevant verbalizations, or other behaviors that are disruptive in group settings are generally unsuited for the advanced phase.

Transitional Phase

The final element of the BIRU treatment program is the transitional phase, during which the patients prepare for discharge either to another institution, home, or, preferably, to an educational or work setting. Patients who are ready for this stage have largely obtained maximum benefit from the standard course of treatments and are ready to re-enter the community at some level. To impress upon them that they will soon be leaving the comforts and protection of hospital supervision and care, their therapeutic contacts on the Unit are drastically reduced. The only regular session that they attend is the transition group, which meets bi-weekly. Otherwise, they attend classes at a local junior college or work part-time in a competitive or sheltered workshop environment. The emphasis is upon strengthening social and adaptive skills, rather than upon treatment of cognitive or perceptual-motor deficits.

Patients are discharged from the transitional phase after suitable discharge planning has been completed. They are followed either by clinic or home visits, telephone contact, or mail for a period of 1 year after discharge—monthly for 6 months, bimonthly for the final 6 months. Continued contact beyond 1 year is encouraged, and patients are urged to continue in the transitional support group as long as they wish.

The BIRU family support group provides continuous support, advice, and assistance to the families of the patients. The group meets twice each month— once in the evening and once in the morning—in order to permit maximal attendance. The group typically consists of about six members who discuss such issues as finances, emotional problems (theirs as well as the patient's and other family members'), and the need for respite care. Attendance at one of the groups is strongly recommended upon admission and throughout, as well as after, active treatment.

REVIEW OF TREATMENT OUTCOME DATA

As mentioned previously, the system of setting treatment goals and measuring performance permits a fairly straightforward evaluation of each patient's success in the program (Fig. 11–3).

Another way of assessing outcome is to compare initial and final performance on a variety of neuropsychological tests. This can be done by comparing individual test scores or by grouping the tests in some fashion. The program uses two of the latter methods: Average T-Score and Deficit Index.

The Average T-Score method (Kiernan & Matthews, 1976) involves translating raw scores into T-scores—standard scores with a mean of 50 and a standard deviation of 10—based upon appropriate norms. The T-scores are then summed, and an average is calculated. The Deficit Index (Knights & Watson, 1968) is actually the percentage of impaired scores (T-score $\leq$ 30, i.e., 2 or more standard deviations below the mean). Figure 11–4 shows the decision tree that has been developed to arrive at a verbal descriptor for given Average T-Score and Deficit Index values.

THE EMERGING ROLE OF MICROCOMPUTERS

The role of microcomputers in rehabilitation has become a source both of excitement and unease among health care professionals. In the program, home videogames were used as therapeutic techniques beginning in late 1978. An Atari

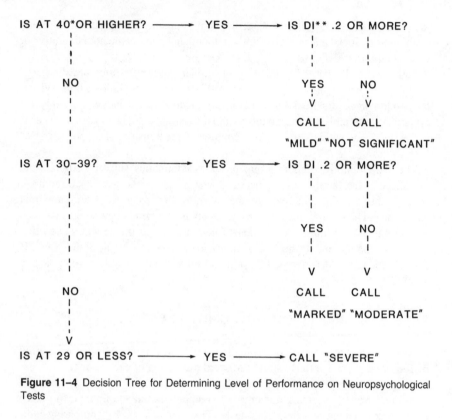

Figure 11-4 Decision Tree for Determining Level of Performance on Neuropsychological Tests

* = Average T-Score   ** = Deficit Index

---

800 microcomputer system was obtained for use in cognitive rehabilitation in October 1981. The reasons for employing videogames and computer programs include:

- *Speed and precision of stimulus presentation:* Computers can present information rapidly, reliably, and repetitively. These features are valuable in working with brain impaired persons, because their treatment often requires numerous repetitions of stimuli or tasks, which can tax even the most dedicated clinician. The precision and uniformity of presentation can be useful in research applications.
- *Variety of programs:* Currently, there are thousands of computer programs available for the major microcomputer models (Atari, Apple, Commodore, and TRS-80), many of which are either specially written for rehabilitation

settings or are useful in rehabilitation due to their educational theme. There are computer versions of all major card or board games as well. The clinician can easily switch from one program/game to another with minimal disruption of the session, thereby helping maintain the patient's interest without excessive delays or distractions. The author has written a guide for selection and use of microcomputers and software in rehabilitation settings (Lynch, 1984).

- *Variety of input devices*: The ways in which the patient interacts with the computer can be modified to suit persons with sensory or motor deficits. Special input devices include customized paddle controllers, joysticks, or keyboards. In addition, many programs have been written for the light pen, which requires the patient simply to touch the device to the desired place on the video screen in order for it to respond. Newer systems, such as the Hewlett-Packard Model HP 150, require only that the user touch the screen with a fingertip.

- *Storage and retrieval of data*: Computers are uniquely capable of storing large amounts of numeric or verbal information for later retrieval and analysis. Data can be routinely gathered with minimal effort by the clinician.

- *Relatively low cost*: Microcomputers now cost as much as a good electronic calculator cost some 10 years ago, thus making them more affordable for many clinics. Similarly, patients' families can now afford to purchase computers and programs for use in the home. An entire system—computer, disk drive, monitor, and printer—can cost as little as $700.

- *Patient acceptance*: This program's experience over the past 6 years has indicated that patients respond favorably to the notion of computer-assisted cognitive retraining. Initial hesitation has been overcome by offering clear explanations regarding the reasons for the program. Training on a computer tends to move fairly quickly and to attract and maintain attention. In addition, the patient with severe motor impairment can sometimes learn to manipulate a controller—a standard or customized joystick, for example—which allows them to exercise a degree of control over their environment.

CONCLUDING COMMENTS

This chapter has presented the essential elements of one cognitive rehabilitation program. Although it shares many features with other rehabilitation programs around the country, there are inevitable differences in approach to the evaluation and treatment of brain disorders. The reader should recognize that no single approach to cognitive rehabilitation has been shown to be superior to the rest. Furthermore, the diversity among rehabilitation programs makes direct comparisons difficult.

With regard to the future role of microcomputers, the clinician should be cautiously optimistic. The author's feeling is, however, that there is inadequate justification at present for putting aside traditional treatments to make way for these machines. They have *potential* as adjuncts, and although they can perform certain routine clinical activities quite well, they require human input and supervision in order to be maximally effective. The future of rehabilitation will be determined by how successfully rehabilitation specialists can integrate the roles of humans and machines in the process of rehabilitation. Ideally, we will be able to effect an interaction that is synergistic, rather then antagonistic.

REFERENCES

Caplan, B. (1982). Neuropsychology in rehabilitation: Its role in evaluation and intervention. *Archives of Physical Medicine and Rehabilitation, 63,* 362–366.

Cermak, L. (1975). *Improving your memory.* New York: McGraw-Hill.

Dunn, L, & Markwardt, F. (1970). *Peabody Individual Achievement Test Manual.* Circle Pines, MN: American Guidance Service.

Hathaway, S., & McKinley, J. (1951). *The Minnesota Multiphasic Personality Inventory Manual* (rev. ed.). New York: Psychological Corporation.

Higbee, K. (1977). *Your memory: How it works and how to improve it.* Englewood Cliffs, NJ: Prentice-Hall.

Jastak, S., & Wilkinson, G. (1984). *The Wide Range Achievement Test* (rev. ed.). Wilmington, DE: Jastak Associates, Inc.

Kiernan, R., & Matthews, C. (1976). Impairment index versus T-score averaging in neuropsychological assessment. *Journal of Consulting and Clinical Psychology, 44,* 951–957.

Kiresuk, T., & Sherman, R. (1968). Goal-attainment scaling: A general method for evaluating comprehensive mental health programs. *Community Mental Health Journal, 4,* 443–453.

Knights, R., & Watson, P. (1968). The use of computerized test profiles in neuropsychological assessment. *Journal of Learning Disabilities, 1,* 696–709.

Levin, H., Benton, A., & Grossman, R. (1982). *Neurobehavioral consequences of closed head injury.* New York: Oxford University Press.

Lorayne, H., & Lucas, J. (1974). *The memory book.* New York: Ballantine.

Lynch, W. (1983). The role of the neuropsychologist in cognitive rehabilitation. *Cognitive Rehabilitation, 1,* 5–6.

Lynch, W. (1984). *A guide to Atari home computer and Apple II + /IIe programs for rehabilitation settings.* Unpublished manuscript.

Lynch, W., & Mauss, N. (1981). Brain injury rehabilitation: Standard problem lists. *Archives of Physical Medicine and Rehabilitation, 62,* 223–227.

Morihisa, J., Duffy, F., & Wyatt, R. (1983). Brain electrical activity mapping. *Archives of General Psychiatry, 40,* 719–728.

Porch, B. (1971). Multidimensional scoring in aphasia testing. *Journal of Speech and Hearing Research, 14,* 776–792.

Porch, B., & Collins, M. (1974). *The rating of patient's independence (ROPI).* Unpublished manuscript.

Pykett, I. (1982). NMR imaging in medicine. *Scientific American, 246,* 75–88.

Russell, E. (1975). A multiple scoring method for the assessment of complex memory functions. *Journal of Consulting and Clinical Psychology, 43,* 800–809.

Tercero, D., & Boczkowski, J. (1983). *A guide for group and individual memory retraining.* Unpublished manuscript.

Ter-Pogossian, M., Raichle, M., & Sobel, B. (1980). Positron emission tomography. *Scientific American, 243,* 170–181.

Trexler, L. (Ed.). (1982). *Cognitive rehabilitation: Conceptualization and intervention.* New York: Plenum Press.

Wechsler, D. (1945). A standardized memory scale for clinical use. *Journal of Psychology, 19,* 87–95.

Wechsler, D. (1981). *WAIS-R manual.* New York: The Psychological Corporation.

Woodcock, R., & Johnson, M. (1977). *Woodcock-Johnson psychoeducational battery.* Hingham, MA: Teaching Resources Corp.

Chapter 12

A Neuropsychological Approach to Cognitive Rehabilitation within a Private Practice Setting

Robert J. Sbordone, Ph.D.

Cognitive deficits, emotional disturbances, and personality change have long been recognized as salient, and sometimes permanent, sequelae of brain damage, especially severe head injuries; recent evidence suggests that less profound, but potentially disabling, consequences follow minor head injuries as well (Rimel, Giordani, Barth, Boll, & Jane, 1981). Among the symptoms of this posttraumatic syndrome are impairments in attention and concentration, easy fatigability, disturbances in memory, emotional instability, lower tolerance for frustration and noise, personality alteration (depression, withdrawal, disinhibition, euphoria), aphasic deficits, and a variety of elementary and complex sensory, perceptual, and cognitive deficits (Benton, 1979; Chapter 2).

A recent study (Cooper, 1982) estimated that 8.8 million people in the United States sustained head injuries in a single year. Approximately one-fourth of these injuries included skull fracture and intracranial injury, characteristic of major head trauma. According to an earlier report, the estimated cost of head injuries during 1976 was $2.24 billion in lost wages and medical expenses (Caveness, 1979).

Historically, rehabilitation programs for these patients were geared toward physical recovery, with relative neglect of the injury's cognitive, emotional, and social consequences. Although physical weakness, spasticity, and dysphasia tend to show eventual improvement, intellectual and psychosocial deficits often cause long-lasting disablement (Bond, 1975), the severity of which may not be appreciated until the patient attempts to return to school or work. Nonetheless, patients are rarely allowed to remain in or be readmitted to the hospital solely for the purpose of cognitive rehabilitation therapy.

Until recently (e.g., Rothi & Horner, 1983), most neuropsychologists viewed their task as solely a diagnostic one and adhered to what is best described as "therapeutic nihilism." This pessimism was based on several factors: (1) the assumption that, because neurons in the central nervous system do not regenerate following injury (Schneider & Tarshis, 1975), the effects of brain damage are permanent and irreversible; (2) the fact that neuropsychological tests or batteries offer little assistance for rehabilitation planning (Luria & Majovski, 1977); (3) the past failure of graduate clinical psychology programs to teach the use of psychotherapeutic or rehabilitation techniques with brain injured patients or their families (Meier, 1981); (4) the invidious dichotomy between psychological and organic causes of behavior (Geschwind, 1975); and (5) the scarcity of neuropsychologists involved in rehabilitation (Hartlage & Telzrow, 1980). As a consequence, the notion, and the presentation of supporting cases, that recovery could be enhanced through cognitive rehabilitation has met with skepticism. Nonetheless, during recent years there have been renewed efforts to develop effective techniques to remediate cognitive and perceptual deficits of brain injured persons.

This chapter presents one approach to the cognitive rehabilitation of patients with traumatic head injuries. Philosophy, assumptions, techniques, and biases based on work with hundreds of patients are discussed.

PRIVATE PRACTICE ENVIRONMENT

The author conducts a clinical neuropsychology private practice with one associate (Dr. Arnold Purisch) and two secretaries. Approximately 90 percent of the patients have some form of brain insult; 80 percent of these patients have sustained severe traumatic head injury. Patients are typically referred by neurologists, neurosurgeons, or attorneys and only rarely by psychiatrists or clinical psychologists. Referrals from attorneys are primarily requests for neuropsychological documentation of deficits or disability. Physicians frequently request neuropsychological assessment for the purpose of planning a cognitive rehabilitation program for the patient. Referrals from other professionals, such as speech pathologists, psychiatrists, or psychologists, generally are for the purpose of obtaining an assessment of the patient's strengths and deficits, as well as recommendations for treatment. It has been the author's experience that these professionals are often unwilling to "let go" of their patient when cognitive rehabilitation is recommended, even though they do not claim expertise in this area. Of those patients for whom cognitive rehabilitation is suggested, the author has found that only 20 percent of the families comply with that recommendation. Some reasons for this low compliance rate include: distrust of professionals based on previous inaccurate predictions of recovery, the emotional burden that the patient's injury has placed upon them, and their depressed mood, physical exhaustion, and feelings of hopelessness.

The majority of head injured patients referred to the author's program are 1–2 years postinjury. Most have had at least one major failure, such as an abortive return to school or work, within the past year and have been causing havoc at home. Many have been unsuccessfully treated by psychiatrists, typically with psychotropic medications, or by dynamically oriented psychologists (the patient's poor memory for recent events makes failure a foregone conclusion). Some have even received extensive and costly treatment by chiropractors who performed "cranial adjustments" to improve their mental abilities. All these factors obviously contribute to the family's pessimism and distrust of professionals offering another treatment.

Funding for cognitive rehabilitation can be a problem, because most insurance companies do not yet recognize this form of treatment and may question its therapeutic effectiveness. Because there are few controlled studies in this field, its objective scientific merit has not been established (one could raise a similar argument for psychotherapy). The author has found it expedient to bill for cognitive rehabilitation as individual or family psychotherapy because the same amount of time is spent with the patient or family; however, this billing may sometimes be disputed by insurance carriers. As a rule, the patient or the insurance company is not billed for time spent in computer-assisted cognitive rehabilitation (CACR) unless the author is physically present. The patient and family are usually seen an average of once every week or two weeks. The usual duration of treatment is 1 year, although in some cases 2 or 3 years may be required.

NEUROPSYCHOLOGICAL ASSESSMENT PROCESS

History

The first step in designing a cognitive rehabilitation program is to collect a detailed history, including developmental, clinical, and social factors. Table 12–1 presents a list of factors that the author has found to be helpful in compiling the history. In order to obtain accurate information, it is essential that the patient be accompanied by a relative and/or significant other. The author has found that at least 2 hours are required for the initial interview. In addition, every effort should be made to review the patient's educational, medical, and rehabilitation records before seeing the patient. These reports should be compared to the accounts of the patient and family. When discrepancies are found, one should clarify or identify the basis for the discrepancy. Families often present inaccurate information for a number of reasons, such as faulty recollections, distorted perceptions of the patient or accident, persistent anxiety that is rekindled whenever they discuss the accident, denial, suggestibility, or the tendency to exaggerate in cases involving litigation. The degree of concordance between the history as obtained from the patient and family and from medical charts can provide a crude index of how the family is coping with the consequences of this traumatic event.

Table 12–1 Patient History

DEVELOPMENTAL
Problems or drugs during pregnancy
Place of birth
Birth order
Birth weight
Problems during delivery
Developmental milestones
Childhood diseases
Emotional problems during childhood and
adolescence
History of learning difficulties
History of health problems
History of hyperactivity
History of physical or emotional trauma

DOMINANCE
Initial preference
Changes in preference
Familial history of sinistrality
Tasks performed with dominant and
nondominant hands

LANGUAGE
First language spoken
Other languages spoken
Preferred language
History of speaking or language
difficulties

EDUCATION
Highest grade completed
Grades obtained
Best/preferred courses
Worst/least preferred courses
Extracurricular activities
Awards and achievements
Courses or grades repeated
History of remedial training
History of conduct disturbances or
expulsions
Reasons for leaving school
Additional schooling or nonacademic
training

MILITARY SERVICE
Branch and dates of service
Highest rank
Jobs held within service
Combat history
Rank at discharge
Type of discharge

OCCUPATIONAL
Present occupation
Job duties
Salary
Last worked
Previous occupations
Longest job held
History of job termination

LEGAL
Arrest history
Types of offenses
Time served in jail
Current legal problems

CULTURAL BACKGROUND
Country of birth
Ethnic background of patient and family
History of discrimination

RELIGIOUS
Religious background
Church attendance
History of religious discrimination

MARITAL HISTORY
Marital status
Number of years married
History of previous marriages
Education and occupation of spouse
Expectations placed on spouse
Expectations placed on patient
Previous and current marital difficulties
Marital stability
Number and ages of children
Effect of children on patient

SEXUAL
Current sexual status
Sexual preference
Changes in sexual preference
History of previous sexual problems
Current sexual problems
Changes in libido
Extramarital affairs

MEDICAL
History of major hospitalizations
Previous health problems
Previous surgery
Possible history of the following
problems:
Head trauma

Table 12–1 continued

Cerebrovascular disorder
Coronary dysfunction
Hypoglycemia
Anoxia or hypoxia
Toxic or heavy metal exposure
Substance abuse
Alcoholism
Hypertension
Diabetes
Gastrointestinal disorder
Respiratory problems
Genitourinary problems
Headaches
Vertigo

PSYCHIATRIC

History of emotional or psychiatric
  difficulties
History of suicidal behavior
Treatment history
Psychiatric hospitalization history
Psychiatric medication history
Family history of psychiatric difficulties

CURRENT STRESSES

Death or loss of spouse or family member
Divorce or marital separation
Marital difficulties
Job difficulties or termination
Financial difficulties
Sexual difficulties
Loss of friends
Conflicts with others
Academic difficulties
Business difficulties

FAMILY
Parents
  Age and education
  Occupation
  Personality
  Marital status and history
  Substance abuse history
  Psychiatric history
  Criminal history
  Health history
  Relationship with patient
Siblings
  Number and ages of siblings
  Education and occupation
  Personality
  Marital status and history
  Substance abuse history
  Psychiatric history
  Criminal history
  Health history
  Relationship with patient
CLINICAL HISTORY
  Complaints of patient and significant
    others
  History of injury or illness
  Duration of coma
  Duration of posttraumatic amnesia
  Neurologic findings
  Hospitalization history
  Rehabilitation history
  Current residual problems
  Progress within past year
  Effect of injury or illness on patient and
    significant others
  Expectations of patient and significant
    others

Neurologic History

An effort should be made to obtain the patient's neurologic history. Of particular importance are the duration of coma, length of posttraumatic amnesia (PTA), Glasgow Coma Scale scores, type of brain injury (focal versus diffuse), elevated intracranial pressure, presence of intracranial hematoma or infection, brain swelling (edema), posttraumatic seizures, use and duration of a respirator, and medications administered. The author has found that this neurologic data can be helpful in predicting the outcome of cognitive rehabilitation. Table 12–2 presents a list of predictors based on the author's experience.

Table 12–2 Neurologic Predictors of Cognitive Rehabilitation Outcome

Predictor	Good Outcome	Poor Outcome
Coma duration	Less than 6 hours	Greater than 30 days
Posttraumatic amnesia	Less than 24 hours	Greater than 30 days
Glasgow Coma score	Greater than 7	Less than 5
Brain damage	Local	Diffuse
Intracranial pressure	Normal	Elevated
Brain swelling	None	Considerable
Intracranial hematoma	No	Yes
Ventricular size	Normal	Enlarged
Intracranial infection	No	Yes
Posttraumatic seizures	No	Yes
Hypoxia	No	Yes

It is important to determine the patient's and family's perspective on past treatments and prognostic statements. Many patients and their families are told shortly after injury that the prognosis is poor or that most recovery will occur within 6 months, with little further gain after 1 year (Bond, 1975; Bond & Brooks, 1976). Many patients have already exceeded this "magic number" by the time they present for cognitive rehabilitation; their families have given up hope for further improvement and are seeking a simple remedy for the patient's poor motivation or disruptive social behavior.

Medical/Psychiatric History

In addition to exploring the medical and psychiatric factors identified in Table 12–1, the results of the neurologic examination and neurodiagnostic studies should be reviewed. Table 12–3 presents premorbid psychosocial factors that the author has found to be helpful in predicting cognitive rehabilitation outcome. In general, it seems that premorbid intellectual, cognitive, social, and emotional strength confer some degree of immunity to the disruptive effects of brain injury.

Current Problems

It is extremely important to ask patients directly what current problems they feel are a direct consequence of their head injury. The vast majority of patients, particularly during the first year postinjury, tend to deny or minimize their cognitive, emotional, or social problems. The family should be asked to indicate what problems have appeared since injury. Families typically complain of the patient's decreased initiative/ambition, memory difficulties, impatience, loss of libido,

Table 12–3 Premorbid Predictors of Cognitive Rehabilitation Outcome

Predictor	Good Outcome	Poor Outcome
History of achievement	Yes	No
Good social relationships	Yes	No
History of hyperactivity	No	Yes
Learning difficulties	No	Yes
Good academic history	Yes	No
Substance abuse history	No	Yes
Criminal history	No	Yes
Characterological problems	No	Yes
Good relationship with family	Yes	No
Type of family	Warm, supportive	Cold, rejecting
Intact family	Yes	No
Personality	Well-adjusted	History of emotional problems
IQ	Above 120	Below 80
Motivated	Yes	No
Persistent	Yes	No (tended to give up easily)

paranoia, social difficulties, and poor judgment. The author finds the discrepancy between the patient's and families' description of problems to be a rough index of the patient's disability. During the first year, family members may minimize the number and extent of the patient's problems. Asking them to respond "yes" or "no" when specific problems are named can elicit information that is not spontaneously provided.

The author adheres to what he has labeled the "principle of a conditional neurologic lesion," which argues that the cognitive and behavioral manifestations of a neurologic dysfunction vary according to the patient's level of fatigue, emotional state, stress, and metabolic demands. For example, brain injured patients often exhibit a marked decline in cognitive functioning when they become fatigued or stressed. Thus, it is important to ask the patients and their relatives to describe the effects of these factors. One also needs to gain a picture of the patients at their best and to determine salient environmental features for each patient, such as previous activity of each patient, type of environment, time of day, time since last meal, number and identities of people in their area, and the like, that are responsible for fluctuations in each patient's cognitive and behavioral functioning.

It is important to determine how the family is coping with the patient's injury (see Chapter 6). Many families of the traumatically head injured exhibit a calm, rational, and somewhat detached facade, what has been termed the "command performance syndrome" (Sbordone, Kral, Gerard, & Katz, 1984). This behavior often conceals the highly troubled and anxious feelings of the family. Failing to understand the cognitive, intellectual, social, or emotional consequences of brain injury, families are prone to misinterpret the patient's behavior and may develop a hypercritical attitude. Relatives may experience neurotic guilt for the patient's head injury, expressing this through excessive concern for the patient and/or reinforcing the patient's dependency. This often produces a secondary psychological disability for the family that may undermine cognitive rehabilitation.

Recovery from head injury may be conceptualized as undergoing six stages (Table 12–4); however, not all patients may reach the final stages. The author has found it useful to identify the particular patient's location on this scale. For example, for patients in an early intermediate stage of recovery, it is expected that they will deny or minimize their cognitive deficits, but complain of somatic problems. Later in the recovery process, depression and nervousness are anticipated as patients become aware of their cognitive deficits. Thus, the patient's behavior may be "normal" or "nonpathological" for that stage of recovery.

Neuropsychological Testing

The majority of psychologists employ a quantitative approach—that is, the use of psychological tests that produce numerical scores—to assess the traumatic head-injured patient. The chief advantages of this approach are that the patient's scores can be compared to normative data and their own previous performances, and the scores furnish data for research or outcome studies. The primary disadvantage of this approach is that the scores can be misleading and not reflect the head injured patient's cognitive, social, and emotional problems. In addition, the scores themselves may be of limited value in planning cognitive rehabilitation. The advantages of a qualitative approach, which emphasizes assessment of how the patient performs tasks, is that it permits a better understanding of the patient's strengths and deficits and identifies those factors that affect level of performance. Also, information gathered in this way more readily translates into cognitive rehabilitation strategies. Practitioners of this approach, however, must have considerable training and expertise in the neurosciences, rehabilitation, and behavioral neurology. The qualitative approach does not lend itself to simple explanation or reporting, and the results may be influenced by the examiner's particular style of administration (see Chapter 9).

The author strongly recommends that both approaches be used and that great care be taken to describe the manner in which the patient's cognitive deficits are expressed and the conditions under which these deficits can be modified. Emotional and social functioning should also be assessed to determine how the patient is coping with diminished or altered higher cortical functions (Sbordone & Caldwell, 1979). This information can provide the neuropsychologist with crucial data

Table 12–4 Stages of Recovery Following Severe Head Injury

Stages	Characteristics
Early acute	Injury Patient in coma
Late acute	Patient opens eyes Severe agitation-restlessness Severe confusion Disoriented to place and time
Early intermediate	Oriented to place Moderate confusion Denial of cognitive deficits May complain of somatic problems Fatigues very easily Poor judgment Marked to severe attention deficits Severe memory deficits Severe social difficulties Severe problem-solving difficulties
Late intermediate	Oriented to place and time Becoming aware of cognitive deficits Mild confusion Mild to moderate attention difficulties Marked problem-solving difficulties Moderate to marked memory deficits Early onset of depression-nervousness Unsuccessful attempts to return to work or school May appear relatively normal Moderate to marked social difficulties
Early late	Significant depression-nervousness Mild to moderate memory deficits Mild to moderate problem-solving difficulties Frequent comparison to premorbid self Generally mild residual cognitive deficits Little hope of further recovery Has returned to work or school Mild to moderate social difficulties
Late late	Mild memory impairment Mild problem-solving difficulties Acceptance of residual deficits Improving social relationships Return of most of premorbid responsibilities Generally positive self-image

for cognitive rehabilitation planning. Table 12–5 lists neuropsychological tests that are generally used by the author to assess the head injured patient.

The patient's emotional functioning and adjustment to diminished cognitive functioning are assessed by either the MMPI or OBD-168 (Sbordone & Caldwell, 1979), in addition to careful observations of the patient's behavior during testing. The patient's social functioning is assessed informally by observing the patient in the presence of family and others and in familiar and unfamiliar social settings. (The author has found that taking the patient and family out to lunch often provides

Table 12–5 Neuropsychological Tests Generally Used by Author to Assess the Head-Injured Patient

Function	Tests Administered
Attention	Sbordone Attention Battery Stroop Symbol-Digit Modalities Test Trail Making (A & B)
Memory	Logical Memory (immediate and delayed recall) Rey-Osterrieth Complex Figure Sbordone-Hall Memory Battery
Motor	Grip Strength Grooved Pegboard Finger Tapping Luria's Neuropsychological Investigation
Sensory-perceptual	Luria's Neuropsychological Investigation Reitan-Klove Sensory-Perceptual Exam Hooper Visual Organization Test
Problem solving	Luria's Neuropsychological Investigation Raven Progressive Matrices Wisconsin Card Sorting
Language	Controlled Word Association Test Boston Naming Test Luria's Neuropsychological Investigation Token Test
Intellectual	Raven Progressive Matrices Wechsler Adult Intelligence Scale
Constructional skills	Block Design (WAIS) Draw a Clock Draw a Bicycle Object Assembly (WAIS) Rey-Osterrieth Complex Figure

this information.) The author has identified certain features of patient behavior during neuropsychological testing that appear to predict cognitive rehabilitation outcome (Table 12–6).

Assessment of Physical and Social Environment

The physical and social environment of the brain injured patient should also be assessed in terms of the demands or the burden it places on the patient's present level of functioning (Diller & Gordon, 1981). Neuropsychological test data, which outline the patient's strengths and deficits, when combined with a careful assessment of the demand characteristics of the patient's environment, can be used to determine the quality of life that the patient would most likely be expected to have. This is represented in Figure 12–1 by the area of intersection between the patient's strengths and deficits and the demand characteristics of the environment. It has been the experience of the author that this interaction is most commonly determined by the emotional functioning of the patient. For example, patients who exhibit marked anxiety, depression, paranoia, or fearfulness are most likely to interact with that aspect of their environment that places a heavy demand on their deficits and little demand on their strengths. Conversely, patients who do not exhibit marked anxiety, depression, and fearfulness are most likely to interact with those aspects of their environment that place few demands on their deficits and many demands on their strengths. Thus, the task of the neuropsychologist is concurrently to reduce the patient's deficits through cognitive rehabilitation and

Table 12–6 Postinjury Behavioral Predictors of Cognitive Rehabilitation Outcome

Predictor	Good Outcome	Poor Outcome
Motivation	High	Low
Ability to recognize errors	Good	Poor
Persistence	High	Low
Ambulatory	Yes	No
Medications	No	Yes
Judgment	Intact	Poor
Mental flexibility	Good	Poor
Perceptual skills	Intact	Poor
Self-care	Independent	Dependent
Awareness of deficits	Yes	No
Initiation of tasks	Yes	No
Concern for others	Yes	No

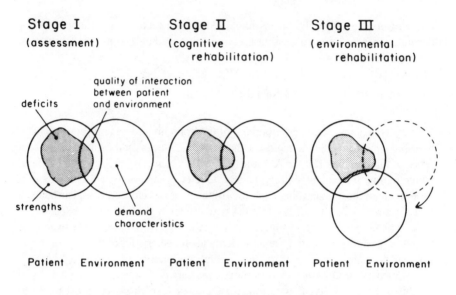

Stage I
(assessment)

Stage II
(cognitive
rehabilitation)

Stage III
(environmental
rehabilitation)

quality of interaction
between patient
and environment

deficits

strengths

demand
characteristics

Patient   Environment   Patient   Environment   Patient   Environment

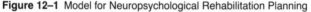

Figure 12–1 Model for Neuropsychological Rehabilitation Planning

Source: From "Rehabilitative Neuropsychological Approach for Severe Traumatic Brain-injured Patients" by R.J. Sbordone, 1984, *Professional Psychology: Research and Practice, 15,* pp. 165–175. Copyright 1984 by American Psychological Association. Reprinted by permission.

modify the environment (by closely working with significant others) so that it interacts with the patient's strengths as much as possible.

Assessment of Secondary Problems

The author has found that the severity of the patient's emotional problems tends to increase over time since injury. Consistent with the principle of a conditional neurologic lesion as discussed above, the patient's maximum level of functioning is rarely achieved and is generally inhibited by secondary emotional problems and social difficulties. Exhibit 12–1 lists some of these secondary problems that can inhibit cognitive functioning in head injured patients. The vast majority of brain injured patients at 1 or more years postinjury generally have a poor understanding of their brain injury, but are painfully aware of many of their shortcomings. They experience a loss of control and mastery over their environment, yet set unrealistically high expectations for themselves. They have a history of major failure, little or no contact with rehabilitation professionals, and have very limited access to community resources. They have numerous financial difficulties and tend to be

Exhibit 12–1 Secondary Problems that Inhibit Cognitive Functioning

Alcohol	Litigation
Comparison to premorbid level of functioning	Loss of hope
Condemnation by family	Loss of mastery over environment
Dependency on others	Loss of social contacts
Depression	Nervousness
Drugs	Pessimistic predictions of recovery
Failure	Poor self-image
Familial pressure	Psychotropic medications
Fatigue	Social difficulties
Guilt	Stress
Impaired awareness of deficits	Suicidal ideation
Infantilization by others	Unable to work
Lack of positive experiences	

overdependent on their family, having lost most, if not all, of their preinjury friends. Finally, they are given little hope by professionals for any further recovery. It is the strong conviction of this author that cognitive rehabilitation will be unsuccessful unless a concerted effort is made to alleviate these secondary problems. The author has found that the behavioral functioning of a head injured patient can be enhanced if the secondary problems of the patient can be minimized through a combination of family counseling, individual psychotherapy (if the patient has only mild memory problems), and structural modification of the environment.

COGNITIVE REHABILITATION

Therapist Directed

The first step in the cognitive rehabilitation process usually is to restore hope to the patient and family. This task can often be accomplished by training the patient to perform a relatively simple but meaningful task or series of tasks, that demonstrates the preserved ability to learn. A series of successes, of course, is highly reinforcing to the patient and family, improves the patient's self-image and sense of mastery, and establishes motivation for further self-initiated activities. Eventually the patient's image within the family improves. The author has found that, as the emotional stresses are gradually alleviated, the patient's cognitive potential will begin to be realized.

Based on the results of the history and neuropsychological assessment, the neuropsychologist devises a specific cognitive rehabilitation program for the patient. Even for patients with similar problems, cognitive rehabilitation programs will vary considerably as they are tailor-made for particular individuals with unique backgrounds and resources who are at different points in the recovery process.

During the early stages of recovery, the major goals of cognitive rehabilitation are to minimize the patient's irritability and the effects of fatigue while trying to improve attention span. The importance of avoiding fatigue in a brain injured patient has been stressed by a number of investigators (e.g., Booth, Doyle, & Malkmus, 1980; Sbordone, 1984). The dysphoric feeling and decreased cognitive functioning that fatigue produces serves to frustrate and punish patients for their cognitive efforts and should be avoided at all costs. The author has found that head injured patients, particularly in the early stages of recovery, can rarely perform a cognitive task for more than 10 minutes. As a rule of thumb, sessions should last approximately 70 to 80 percent of the patient's maximum attention span.

Because most head injured patients have considerable difficulty estimating time, an external timing device or person must provide them with cues to rest. It is unfortunate that many rehabilitative programs throughout the United States subject head injured patients in the early stages of recovery to lengthy therapy sessions. Many of these patients, who show little motivation or initiative, are erroneously labeled as "frontal lobe syndrome." Programs made up of brief modules separated by rest periods would allow such patients to perform up to their potential and perhaps circumvent the development of secondary psychological and emotional problems.

During the intermediate stages of the recovery process, improvement of memory skills is emphasized. Neuropsychological assessment aids the determination of those conditions that permit maximal recall of information, e.g., environmental cues, repeated presentations of material, rehearsal, visual versus verbal presentations, use of imagery, active versus passive encoding, and recognition versus retrieval. Recent studies have suggested that a variety of methods can be effective in improving memory in the head injured patient (e.g., Horton, 1979; Wilson & Moffat, 1984). Patients might be instructed to carry a notebook and pen with them at all times so that they can record their activities and, with the help of a digital calendar watch, the date and time of each entry. This information can be used when they are talking later in the day with family members, who are instructed to praise and encourage the patient's behavior. Patients can also be taught to review the notebooks daily to assist them in planning schedules, shopping excursions, rest periods, meals, and the like.

In the late stages of recovery, patients require training in the areas of problem solving and planning. Once again, neuropsychological assessment is helpful in delineating specific impairments. Some patients may be reluctant to utilize more effective problem-solving strategies due to fear of failure or resistance to change, obstacles that can be addressed by counseling. Many head injured patients are impulsive and allot insufficient time to make decisions. Training that specifically requires a delayed response can be helpful in this regard. In addition, many patients may not adequately understand the requirements or sequence of steps involved in a complex task, such as shopping or cooking, before embarking on it. Thus, training the patient to analyze specific tasks before performing them may be helpful. Some patients exhibit a discrepancy between their verbally stated plans and their actual behavior. For these individuals, management strategies may require the assistance of other family members. For example, a behavior modification approach, in which relatives reinforce increased consistency between verbal and physical behaviors, can be developed.

Regardless of the stage of recovery, it is essential that the neuropsychologist gather careful data demonstrating the amount of progress the patient has made since injury. The author has found it helpful to rely on both neuropsychological test results and environmental competence as reported by significant others. Test results alone often provide an inaccurate gauge of the patient's ability to function effectively in the environment. The author strongly recommends that the data be presented in a chart that can be placed in a conspicuous location in the patient's home. It is helpful for patients to complete the chart, with the help of other family members, so that they become involved in the evaluation process.

Computer-Assisted Cognitive Rehabilitation

During the past few years, neuropsychologists and rehabilitation professionals have become increasingly aware of the possibilities and potential that microcomputers offer for the treatment of brain damaged patients. Advances in computer technology, the growing abundance of computer software, and their decreased cost, have made feasible the widespread application of microcomputer-based cognitive rehabilitation techniques. The microcomputer offers precision, enormous flexibility, and the opportunity to program and control such factors as stimulus duration, display constancy, randomly generated stimuli, and immediate feedback. Programs can be developed or modified that directly address a given patient's deficits, level of abilities, and attention span.

Because cognitive rehabilitation requires lengthy and repetitive drill, not to mention an exceedingly high degree of patience, a microcomputer offers some distinct advantages over a human therapist. A microcomputer frees the therapist's time to treat the patient's emotional and social problems. In addition, the microcomputer offers assessment possibilities that were previously unavailable. It also offers a "second pair of hands," because it can monitor the patient's performance and provide cues to facilitate the patient's performance of a specific task.

Several years ago, the author began to develop computer programs that could interact in a friendly manner with head injured patients to improve their attentional, memory, and problem-solving skills. After over 3 years, the author and his colleagues (Dr. Steven Hall and Mr. Mark Seecof) developed five computer programs: the Sbordone-Hall Memory Battery, the Digit-Digit Test, the Complex Attention Rehabilitation, Problem Solving I, and Problem Solving II computer programs. These programs provide clear and redundant instructions to the patient, monitor performance (in some cases adjusting task difficulty accordingly), offer reinforcement and feedback, allow rest periods, and store and analyze data. Little or no supervision of the patient is needed. Each of the computer programs discussed below is presently being investigated in a carefully controlled study to determine its effectiveness, generalizability, and utility with brain injured subjects. Regardless of these findings, it should be noted that none of these programs has been designed to replace a neuropsychologist or rehabilitation professional. They were intended to provide ancillary cognitive assessment and rehabilitation. Therefore, their use should be carefully monitored and supervised by an experienced neuropsychologist or rehabilitation clinician.

Sbordone-Hall Memory Battery

The Sbordone-Hall Memory Battery has been designed to operate on Apple (II +, IIe, IIc, III) and IBM-PC computer systems. It provides a fully automatic assessment of 18 discrete memory functions, including free recall of alphanumeric stimuli over trials, delayed recall of alphanumeric stimuli, memory loss due to proactive and retroactive interference, recognition memory of alphanumeric stimuli, verbal memory errors, serial position learning, immediate word recognition memory, delayed word recognition memory, picture recognition memory, intentional word recognition memory, incidental word recognition memory, word origin memory, memory loss due to temporal delay or interference, immediate visual recognition memory for single and multiple geometric figures, types of visual memory errors, and storage versus retrieval memory deficits. The program also provides automatic cuing of the subject during testing. Administration requires 45 to 50 minutes. Because the program either generates random stimuli or randomly selects test stimuli from a large pool, it is well suited for serial testing.

A 12-page statistical and clinical analysis of the patient's performance is provided, including a comparison of the patient's performance (in terms of Z scores) to age-matched organic, psychiatric, and normal controls. In addition, the program utilizes powerful statistical techniques, such as signal detection and discriminant function analyses, to evaluate such factors as freedom from distraction, response bias, and test-taking efficiency.

The Digit-Digit Test

The Digit-Digit Test has been designed to operate on Apple (II +, IIe, IIc, III) and IBM-PC computer systems. It is a numerical coding task that requires the patient to select an appropriate stimulus (digit) within a horizontal array, identify a second stimulus (digit) in a vertical array, and rapidly enter the latter digit on the keyboard. The program includes a training paradigm to teach the patient how to take the test. Research has demonstrated that this test is sensitive to the disruptive effects of traumatic brain injury and a variety of subtle neurologic disorders in children and adolescents. This program permits assessment and training of complex attentional skills that are typically impaired following brain injury. The patient's motor and cognitive processing speeds can be separated and compared.

Complex-Attention Rehabilitation Program

The Complex-Attention Rehabilitation Program operates on an Apple (II +, IIe, IIc) computer system using only one disk drive. The program presents the patient with a visual tracking task that can increase in complexity according to the patient's performance. A hand-held joystick is used by the patient to keep a small circle within a constantly moving square, both of which are displayed on a video monitor. At the intermediate level, the task involves simultaneously tracking two squares of different sizes and speeds. At more advanced levels, the program trains the patient to utilize language and problem-solving strategies to perform the task. The program can make decisions such as whether to interpose a rest period, increase or decrease the complexity of the task, provide external cues, or terminate the session. It also contains a speech synthesizer option for vocal presentation to patients with reading problems.

Problem Solving I Rehabilitation Program

The Problem Solving I Rehabilitation Program has been designed to operate on an Apple (II +, IIe, IIc) computer system. It presents the patient with a series of tasks of increasing complexity that require the use of a joystick. The program has been designed to monitor the patient's progress and level of fatigue over many training sessions. The first series of tasks involves moving a small square to a goal box. Initially, the patient is able to see both the goal box and the location of the square. At higher levels, the visual cues are progressively eliminated so that the patient must develop effective problem-solving strategies to solve the task. At the intermediate levels, patients must improve their frustration tolerance and persistence to solve each task, because the program creates invisible barriers and obstacles that obscure the goal box. It makes decisions, based on the patient's performance, to increase or decrease the complexity of the task, provide a variety of different cues, allow short rest periods, or terminate the session. It also "remembers" the patient's performance on previous training sessions, as well as the length of time since the last training session. There is a speech synthesizer option to permit vocal presentation of cues and instructions to patients with reading difficulties. The program also provides an analysis of the patient's problem-solving strategies at each of ten levels of difficulty.

Problem Solving II Rehabilitation

The Problem Solving II Rehabilitation Program has been designed to operate on an Apple IIc or IIe with at least 64K of internal memory. This program trains patients to anticipate the consequences of their actions. It was designed to be of particular use to high-functioning brain-injured patients with residual frontal lobe dysfunction, i.e., problem-solving deficits, poor sequential thinking, impaired self-critical attitude, and cognitive inflexibility. It presents the patient with a series of problems, such as carrying passengers across a river in a boat, of increasing difficulty and complexity that require the patient to consider as many as ten different variables simultaneously. The program critically analyzes the problem-solving approaches utilized by the patient and determines their effectiveness. It also monitors the patient's level of cognitive fatigue. There is a speech synthesizer option for vocal presentation to patients with reading difficulties.

SUMMARY

The author has outlined a neuropsychological approach to cognitive rehabilitation for head injured patients in a private practice setting. The first step of this approach involves gathering a careful detailed developmental, educational, medical, clinical, and social history of the patient in the presence of significant others. Neuropsychological testing should follow, utilizing both quantitative and qualitative data to highlight the patient's relative strengths and weaknesses, as well as to identify conditions that minimize or maximize the patient's cognitive functioning. The patient's physical and social environment should be assessed in terms of the demands or burden it places on the patient. The patient's secondary emotional problems should also be assessed because they may inhibit cognitive functioning. When combined with a careful assessment of the patient's environment, neuropsychological test data can be utilized to establish a cognitive rehabilitation plan for the patient. The first step in the cognitive rehabilitation process usually consists of restoring hope to the patient and family and creating a series of successes for the patient.

A number of premorbid, neurologic, and postmorbid predictors of cognitive rehabilitation outcome and the stages of recovery of severe traumatic head injury were identified and discussed. The need for professionals to provide frequent feedback to the patient and family was emphasized, and the use of computers to assist in the cognitive rehabilitation of head trauma patients was also discussed. In the author's opinion, there will most likely be more treatment of head injured patients within a private practice setting in the future because the costs are generally considerably lower than outpatient hospital settings, and treatment can typically be suited to fit the particular needs and limitations of the individual patient.

REFERENCES

Benton, A.I. (1979). Behavioral consequences of closed head injury. In G.L. Odom (Ed.), *Central nervous system trauma research status report*. Bethesda, MD: National Institutes of Health, pp. 220–231.

Bond, M.R. (1975). Assessment of the psychosocial outcome after severe head injury. *CIBA Foundation Symposium, 34*, 141–157.

Bond, M.R., & Brooks, D.N. (1976). Understanding the process of recovery as a basis for the investigation of rehabilitation for the brain-injured. *Scandinavian Journal of Rehabilitation Medicine, 8*, 127–133.

Booth, P., Doyle, M., & Malkmus, D. (1980). Meeting the challenge of the agitated patient. In *Rehabilitation of the head injured adult: Comprehensive management*. Downey, CA: Professional Staff of Rancho Los Amigos Hospital, pp. 43–46.

Caveness, W.F. (1979). Incidence of craniocerebral trauma in the United States in 1976, and trend from 1970–1975. In R.A. Thompson & J.R. Green (Eds.), *Advances in neurology, Vol 22*. New York: Raven Press, pp. 1–3.

Cooper, P.R. (1982). Epidemiology of head injury. In P.R. Cooper (Ed.), *Head injury*. Baltimore, MD: Williams & Wilkins, pp. 1–14.

Diller, L., & Gordon, W.A. (1981). Rehabilitation and clinical neuropsychology. In S.B. Filskov & T.J. Boll (Eds.) *Handbook of clinical neuropsychology*. New York: Wiley, pp. 702–735.

Geschwind, N. (1975). The borderland of neurology and psychiatry: Some common misconceptions. In D.F. Benson & D. Blumer (Eds.), *Psychiatric aspects of neurological disease*. New York: Grune & Stratton, pp. 1–9.

Hartlage, L.C., & Telzrow, C.F. (1980). The practice of clinical neuropsychology in the U.S. *Clinical Neuropsychology, 2*, 200–202.

Horton, A.M., Jr. (1979). Behavioral neuropsychology: Rationale and research. *Clinical Neuropsychology, 1*, 20–23.

Luria, A.R., & Majovski, L.V. (1977). Basic approaches used in American and Soviet clinical neuropsychology. *American Psychologist, 32*, 959–968.

Meier, M.J. (1981). Education for competency assurance in human neuropsychology: Antecedents, models, and directions. In S.B. Filskov, & T.J. Boll, (Eds.), *Handbook of clinical neuropsychology*. New York: Wiley, pp. 754–782.

Rimel, R.W., Giordani, B., Barth, J.T., Boll, T.J., & Jane, J.A. (1981). Disability caused by minor head injury. *Neurosurgery, 9*, 221–228.

Rothi, L.J., & Horner, J. (1983). Restitution and substitution: Two theories of recovery with application to neurobehavioral treatment. *Journal of Clinical Neuropsychology, 5*, 73–81.

Sbordone, R.J. (1984). Rehabilitation neuropsychological approach for severe traumatic brain-injured patients. *Professional Psychology: Research and Practice, 15*, 165–175.

Sbordone, R.J., & Caldwell, A. (1979). The OBD-168: Assessing the emotional adjustment to cognitive impairment and organic brain damage. *Clinical Neuropsychology, 4*, 36–41.

Sbordone, R.J., & Howard, M. (1985). *Predictors of recovery following head trauma*. Paper presented at Conference on Head Trauma: From Injury to Independence, Kansas City, MO, October 5, 1985.

Sbordone, R.J., Kral, M., Gerard, M., & Katz, J. (1984). Evidence of a "command performance syndrome" in the significant others of the victims of severe traumatic head injury. *The International Journal of Clinical Neuropsychology, 6*, 183–185.

Schneider, A.M., & Tarshis, B. (1975). *An introduction to psychological psychology.* New York: Random House.

Wilson, B.A., & Moffat, N. (Eds.). (1984). *Clinical management of memory problems.* Rockville, MD: Aspen Publishers, Inc.

Part IV

Selected Treatment Techniques

Chapter 13

Social Skills and Rehabilitation

Michael Dunn, Ph.D.

The importance of social rehabilitation of the physically disabled individual was emphasized by many early leaders in the field (Dembo, Leviton, & Wright, 1975; Kahn, 1969; Ladieu-Leviton, Adler and Dembo, 1948), but until recently scant empirical justification had been provided, and suitable assessment procedures and therapeutic techniques were not available. This chapter examines the social consequences of physically disabling illness, presents the theoretical and empirical rationale for including social skills training in rehabilitation, reviews methods of assessment and training of social skills in a rehabilitation context, and provides some practical suggestions for establishing social skills programs.

SOCIAL CONSEQUENCES OF MOTOR AND SENSORY DISABILITY

This section considers four factors that influence the social consequences of disabling illness: (1) attitudes of able-bodied individuals toward the disabled person; (2) conflict and ambiguity in social interaction between disabled and nondisabled individuals and the behavioral results; (3) new, potentially discomforting social situations encountered by the recently disabled person and the coping skills they demand, and (4) the possible impact of poor social skills on rehabilitation and ultimate social adaptation.

Attitudes Toward Disability

The general public's negative attitudes toward the physically disabled individual have been well documented (Albrecht, Harasymiw, & Horne, 1977; Weinberg, 1976; Yuker, Block, & Young, 1966). Interviewing a random sample of middle-aged, middle-class people, Albrecht et al. (1977) found that 76 percent

345

felt that one should not expect as much from handicapped people as from the able-bodied, 43 percent thought that paraplegics are bitter, and 36 percent believed that most handicapped people do not get married. Summarizing much of the early research, Richardson (1963) noted that sex, age, education, and type and amount of contact are important determinants of attitudes toward the disabled individual.

Negative attitudes are thought to be related to such factors as ignorance, anxiety about a similar accident occurring to oneself, fear of embarrassing or offending the disabled person, lack of previous contact with the handicapped, generalized devaluation—the assumption that, because of impaired physical ability, personal qualities are diminished—and the implicit assumption that the handicapped person is being punished for wrongdoing. As Dixon (1977) has shown, people with handicaps also hold many of these same negative attitudes toward people with disabilities, although not with the same intensity as does the general public. She found that the disabled expressed a preference for other individuals with similar handicaps. In a nationwide study, Morgan, Hohmann, and Davis (1974) interviewed 214 veterans with spinal cord injury who were undergoing rehabilitation. When asked about their expectations for the next 5–10 years, 15 percent said that they thought they would be in worse health or dead, 18 percent expected to be in an institution, 13 percent anticipated no social life, and 19 percent expected no or very restricted recreational pleasure. These expectations and attitudes certainly can contribute to and may be the major factor in early depression in newly injured individuals.

However, not all attitudes about the disabled person are negative. Some studies have shown that people with disabilities are perceived as more intelligent, better adjusted, or more considerate than are nondisabled strangers (Asher, 1973; Weinberg, 1976).

The above findings suggest that a disabled individual, when meeting a stranger, is at an immediate disadvantage by virtue of having to confront and counteract a variety of derogatory stereotyped attitudes.

Social Interaction Between Disabled and Nondisabled Individuals

In part because of attitudinal factors, social intercourse between disabled and nondisabled individuals is often filled with ambiguity and conflict (Richardson, 1963). Other factors hindering interaction include cultural values requiring us to be kind, compassionate, and helpful to handicapped people while also treating all people equally and the absence of "rules" defining acceptable interpersonal conduct in these situations. (See Kelley, Hastorf, Jones, Thibaut, & Usdane, 1960 for an excellent theoretical analysis of the social psychological implications of disability; also, see Fusso, 1984 for discussion of the perceived rules for interacting with spinal cord injured people.) Richardson (1963) noted the variety of psychophysiologic and behavioral disruptions to social interaction that may result (Exhibit 13–1).

There is evidence to suggest that disabled persons receive attenuated feedback in social interactions. Hastorf, Northcraft, and Picciotto (1979) found that performance feedback to handicapped persons was determined by the "norm to be kind" custom, rather than by the facts of the situation. Kleck (1966, 1968) and associates (1966) reported that interaction with a disabled individual produced the following responses in able-bodied subjects: motor inhibition, heightened anxiety level (as measured by galvanic skin response), decreased behavioral variability, and a tendency to distort expressed attitudes and opinions so as to make them congruent with those thought to be held by the disabled person. These studies are

Exhibit 13–1 Physiologic and Behavioral Disruptions to Social Interaction with Disabled People

1. Initial reactions toward those who are disabled are less favorable than toward those who are not disabled.
2. There is considerable agreement among subcultures as to which physical disabilities are more or less preferred.
3. Emotional arousal and anxiety occur in varying degrees in an initial encounter with a disabled person.
4. These reactions are present in early childhood.
5. The physical disability initially dominates the attention of the nonhandicapped person. The salience of the handicap leads to inattention to the other attributes of the handicapped person, attributes that normally would be included in initial interpersonal evaluation and used in guiding the initial stages of the interpersonal relationship.
6. The initial interaction frequently includes a feeling of ambivalence on the part of the nondisabled person. For fear of revealing the negative aspects of the ambivalence, the nondisabled person is more formal and controlled in the behavior he or she exhibits.
7. Depending on the experience in the initial social encounter, the ambivalence felt may later be expressed as denigration of the disabled person or as giving overly favorable impressions.
8. There is inhibition of nonverbal behavior, such as gesture, and a tendency to come less close physically.
9. Nonhandicapped people show less variability in their behavior, and they distort their opinions in the directions they feel are more acceptable to the disabled person.
10. Nondisabled people tend to terminate the initial social encounter more quickly with a disabled than with a nondisabled person.
11. The reaction of a parent to the birth of a child with a visible handicap includes some of the characteristics already described; in addition, it includes shock, denial, grieving, social withdrawal, and depression.

Source: From "Some Social Psychological Consequences of Handicapping" by S.A. Richardson, 1963, *Pediatrics, 32,* pp. 291–297. Copyright 1963 by American Academy of Pediatrics. Adapted by permission.

of interest for two reasons. First, they examined behavior in actual situations, rather than responses to questionnaires. Second, they provide experimental support for the contention that, when interacting with disabled people, the behavior of able-bodied subjects may be governed by norms and stereotypes. These findings suggest that disabled individuals experience a diminution of honest social feedback that, if persistent, could produce a panoply of destructive long-term social consequences. Well-developed social skills, although not a panacea, can help the disabled individual minimize these barriers to straightforward dialogue.

General, Disability-General, and Disability-Specific Social Skills

It is helpful to conceive of three broad categories of social skills—those that are of value to all persons, disabled and nondisabled, those that benefit all disabled persons, and those more specific ones that have special applicability to particular groups of disabled individuals (see Table 13–1). Examples of the first type are assertiveness, self-disclosure, and conversational facility. The second category includes refusing unwanted help and acknowledging the handicapping condition.

For people with particular disabilities certain social situations may dictate the need for specific social skills. For example, the person with a spinal cord injury must learn to cope with the possibility of public bowel or bladder accidents. Dealing with waitresses who speak only to one's companions and greeting old friends who are unaware of one's injury have also been found to be difficult situations for the spinal cord injured person (Dunn, 1977; Dunn & Herman, 1982). Some stroke patients with expressive difficulties must learn to ask their listeners to be patient. People with degenerative disorders may need to learn to explain changes in their condition to family and friends (Davis, 1973). Those with disfiguring disabilities may need to learn how to prepare others for an upcoming encounter with them. People who are deaf or blind may also need to acquire special skills (Higgins, 1980; Ruben, 1982).

Age at onset and duration of disability have implications for the kinds of social skills needed by a particular individual. As Battle (1974) has noted, persons with disabilities that are congenital or acquired in childhood often have comparatively little contact with their peers and, consequently, may have inadequate opportunity to develop social graces. Those with adult-onset disabilities are confronted with a radically transformed social environment for which the existing behavioral repertoire is often ill-suited. Newly injured people must learn to manage potentially awkward encounters with old friends. The distinctions among general, disability-general, and disability-specific social skills, although somewhat artificial, do have important implications for the content of training programs.

Effect of Social Skills on Rehabilitation and Social Participation

There is evidence to suggest that socially maladroit disabled persons tend to be "underachievers" in rehabilitation and to be relatively isolated and inactive after

Table 13–1 General Social, General Disability-Related, and Disability-
Specific Social Skills

General Social Skills
  Listening
  Positive and negative assertion
  Self-disclosure
  Receiving compliments
  Confrontation
  Touching
  Conversation
  Maximizing physical attractiveness
  Meeting new people
  Use of humor
  Heterosocial skills

General Disability-Related Social Skills
  Acknowledgment of the disability
  Asking for help
  Acknowledgment of unstated attitudes (making the implicit explicit)
  Refusing undesired help
  Managing unwelcome social advances
  Dealing with staring
  Handling unwanted questions

Disability-Specific Social Skills
  Facilitating communication
  Overcoming early deficits in socialization
  Managing bowel and bladder problems
  Handling reactions to deformity and disfigurement
  Disclosing nonvisible disabilities
  Dealing with reactions to prostheses

---

hospital discharge (Chaiklin & Warfield, 1973; Hyman, 1972; Turem, 1975). Silver and Wortman (1980) and Janis (1983), among others, have noted the importance of social support in adaptation to trauma. Socially skilled individuals are more likely to elicit needed support from their social networks, without which rehabilitation efforts will proceed more slowly and less successfully. The importance of social involvement after discharge from rehabilitation has been discussed by Cogswell (1968) and empirically demonstrated by Norris-Baker (1982), who found that socialization outside the family was the best predictor of imminent medical problems.

Cogswell (1968) has presented a sociological description of the process of resocialization of paraplegic individuals in the community that might be described as ''adventitious'' social skills training. Her subjects sequentially selected social situations based on physical and social accessibility, moving from the easiest and least threatening, such as lower-status friends' homes that were easily accessible, to more difficult settings, such as new, equal-status friends' residences where they required help in entering. Cogswell states that her subjects maintained few relationships with old friends due to their difficulty in establishing a new identity with those who viewed them from a pretrauma frame of reference.

Hahn (1981) and Dunn, Lloyd, and Phelps (1979) have stressed the importance of social skills in sexual adjustment. Phelps et al. (1983) found that the most frequently reported reason for reduced sexual activity among spinal cord injured veterans was decreased opportunity, a problem that improved social skills might alleviate.

In summary, it appears from empirical studies and theoretical analyses (Goffman, 1963; Kelley et al., 1960) that individuals with disabilities exist in an ambiguous and uncertain social environment. Their interactions with able-bodied individuals are constricted by the effects of cultural stereotypes, awkwardness, and indirection. Disabled individuals who are equipped with adequate social skills are better able to counteract the impact of these distorting factors, overcome the artificiality they encounter in social situations, and establish genuine egalitarian relationships with their able-bodied peers.

EVALUATION OF SOCIAL SKILLS WITH REHABILITATION CLIENTS

Evaluation of social skills with rehabilitation clients has three goals: (1) evaluation of social skills training programs, (2) assessment of attitudes and behavior toward people with physical disabilities, and (3) examination of the social behavior of disabled people. This section reviews examples of two common evaluation methods: self-report and behavioral assessment.

Self-Report Techniques

Self-report assertiveness inventories, such as the Rathus Assertiveness Schedule (Rathus, 1973) and the Gambrill Assertion Inventory (Gambrill & Richey, 1975), have been used in two studies (Herman, Van Horn, and Dunn, 1977; Morgan & Leung, 1980) to assess physically disabled individuals' assertiveness and other social skills in non-disability-related situations. These two studies found little difference between the samples of nonhandicapped and handicapped adults in terms of their self-reported assertiveness. If anything, the handicapped respondents displayed a higher level of self-reported comfort than did nonhandicapped college students, although the variance was greater among handicapped respondents.

Two scales have been developed to measure social discomfort in disability-related situations. Ginsburg (1978) designed a 42-item questionnaire by asking adult wheelchair-users to generate difficult social situations. Situations were retained that were rated as (1) the most relevent, (2) requiring an assertive response in order to maximize reinforcement, and (3) able to discriminate among subjects who varied in their abilities and comfort in managing difficult interpersonal situations. Dunn (1977) and Herman et al., (1977) designed the Spinal Cord Injury Assertion Questionnaire (SCIAQ) based on personal and clinical experience. This questionnaire asks respondents to rate on a five-point scale their discomfort and probability of making an assertive response in 26 different situations that may be potentially problematic for people in wheelchairs, e.g., turning down an offer to push the wheelchair. In a study of 81 SCI veterans in four geographic areas, the SCIAQ showed moderate test-retest and odd-even reliability and a significant correlation with the equivalent Gambrill scales (Dunn & Herman, 1982).

The diary method has been used by Mishel (1978) in one of the few studies on assertion training in handicapped persons that has evaluated changes in "real-life" social behaviors as a function of treatment. She found that the subjects who completed the treatment program increased their participation in activities that reflect more freedom of choice.

Behavioral Measures

Self-report measures, of course, do not always reflect actual behavior. Behavioral measures, both obtrusive and unobtrusive, offer the opportunity to evaluate verbal and nonverbal behavior in interpersonal situations. Studies of compliance with a request for assistance (Bull & Stevens, 1980; Piliavin, Piliavin, & Rodin, 1975; Soble & Strickland, 1974) have shown that handicapped persons tend to receive help less frequently than do able-bodied individuals. However, when help is given, it is given in larger measure to a person with a disability. Behavioral measures have also been used as a way of determining which techniques smooth interaction between disabled and nondisabled individuals. Fehr, Dybsky, Wacker, and Kerr (1977) found, for example, that help was more readily given if the disabled subject requested help, with or without eye contact, but that silent struggling produced help half as often. In a study of the efficacy of acknowledgment of the handicap as a social tactic, Hastorf, Wildfogel, and Cassman (1979) used the choice of a co-worker as a behavioral measure. They found that acknowledgment of the disability, even if done anxiously, increased preference for the handicapped person. Behavioral measures have been used as methods of evaluating treatment programs. Pre- and posttreatment simulations of how subjects think they would behave in a particular situation (Dunn, Van Horn, & Herman, 1981; Ginsburg, 1978; Mishel, 1978; Morgan & Leung, 1980) have generally shown more change than the self-report measures.

352 REHABILITATION PSYCHOLOGY DESK REFERENCE

Two multidimensional outcome studies include assessments of social skills. The University of Houston's Longitudinal Functional Assessment System (LFAS) (Alexander, Willems & Halstead, 1980) and New York University's Rehabilitation Indicators Project (RIP) (Brown, Caplan, & Swirsky, 1978; Diller et al. 1983) are attempting to monitor everyday social activities, as well as rehabilitation-relevant behaviors. RIP uses status indicators, activity patterns, and skill indicators, whereas direct observation, diaries, and environmental surveys are employed by the LFAS. Although still in the process of development, these techniques have been shown to be reliable, valid, and useful.

Finally, Lakin et al. (1981) described assessment techniques that permit sampling of specific aspects of a brain damaged person's interpersonal behavior in a staff-patient group. Elaborate scoring procedures for evaluating small group interaction, self-esteem, self-appraisal, interpersonal empathy, and social cooperation have been developed, but results from this procedure are not yet available.

SOCIAL SKILLS TRAINING IN REHABILITATION

Acquisition of social skills can be accomplished by accident or design. It is clear that, although social skills learning does occur in the natural environment, the vagaries of the reinforcement system, as well as the attenuated and unreliable feedback that handicapped persons receive, make reliance on experience alone a risky undertaking.

Peer support groups have been advocated by professionals (Levy, 1978) and consumers (Knight, Wollert, Levy, Frame, & Padgett, 1980) as helpful in the development of social skills. However, there are no controlled studies of the effect of these groups on social skills. Moreover, one might question whether group members provide instructive feedback or merely reinforce maladaptive patterns. Dixon (1981) has also pointed out that the lack of strong group identification on the part of people with nonvisible disabilities may not allow peer support groups to be effective with these populations. However, support groups appear to provide a marginally less haphazard route to the acquisition of social skills than does the "on the job training" of living with a disability.

Any discussion of social skills training must address the question of content. Should a global or situation-specific approach be taken? Should clients be taught specific skills, such as eye contact, "I" messages, and the like? Should they be taught to manage specific situations, such as saying "no" to an insistent salesperson or asking for help ascending stairs? Should they practice dealing with specific types of people, such as doctors, spouses, friends, salespeople, personal service providers, or employers? In rehabilitation, these questions are especially important because specific skills may be required, depending on the disability and the particular situation.

Some of the early literature emphasized the general skills approach (Eisler, Miller, & Hersen, 1973), whereas more recent work has emphasized the acquisition of skills relevant to particular situations and individuals with whom one needs to be socially adept. Specific skills can be taught within the context of specific situations that individuals find to be particularly difficult. (See Heimburg, Montgomery, Madsen, & Heimburg (1977) and Rich & Schroeder (1976) for reviews of this literature and Dunn (1982) and Wilkinson & Canter (1982) for social skills training manuals.) The approach taken is largely a matter of individual clinician's emphasis. Both processes are important. Table 13–1 lists many of the social skills that may be necessary for people with disabilities.

Another question for the clinician is whether training should occur in groups or individually. Most published reports have used groups for the usual advantages of economy, group interaction, modeling, and social facilitation. The reports of Romano (1976) and Wright (1976) were among the first to describe social skills training groups, but no outcome measures were reported. Formally evaluated group training programs in social skills have been reported by Morgan and Leung (1980), Ginsburg (1978), Mishel (1978), Dunn et al. (1981), Gallenberger (1979), and Neal (1983).

Morgan and Leung (1980) compared disabled college students who had participated in ten 90-minute sessions of assertion training, consisting of modeling, behavioral rehearsal, role-playing, coaching, and videotape feedback, with an untrained control group. They found that the trained group improved on measures of acceptance of disability, self-concept/esteem, and social interaction skills. Neal (1983), however, in a study of spinal cord injured veterans, found no differences in outcome measures—reoccurrence of decubitus ulcers, locus of control, self-concept, or social discomfort—among those who participated in a training/ transactional analysis group, those who received peer-directed milieu group therapy, and untreated controls.

Individual social skills training has been used in centers where the number of appropriate candidates is small, where the costs of organizing a group are greater than those of individual training, and/or where specific idiosyncratic situations need to be addressed. Documented descriptions of individual approaches are rare, however. Boham and Selkowitz (1981) presented an individualized treatment program for multihandicapped hearing impaired students that used behavioral analysis and the creation of specific video modeling tapes to be used in the context of a counseling relationship.

Other techniques used in the training of social skills have been exaggerated role-playing—for example, a passive client may attempt to take an aggressive role— use of modeling films (Dunn, Van Horn, & Herman, 1976; Hobart, 1982), instructions, group feedback and role reversal. Hobart (1982) has shown that a training film that allows for covert practice and modeling of appropriate responses and provides instructions produces a significant treatment effect on self-report measures and behavioral simulations of both trained and untrained situations. The remainder of these studies have shown major training effects on behavioral measures of social skillfulness and, in a few cases, statistically significant changes in self-report and observational measures.

The author's current approach to social skills training begins with clinical assessment of problematic situations based on patient self-report, staff observation, upcoming critical events, and the like. Videotape feedback has been found useful for individual clients. Usually, another staff member role plays an antagonist and/or models possible responses for the client. The situation is explained, and clients, except when surprise is part of the problem, such as in an accidental bowel movement, are told to demonstrate the way they normally would deal with the situation. Their role-playing is videotaped, and they are immediately shown the tape. Their opinion of their performance is elicited, and feedback and instructions are based on objective indices of behavior, such as eye contact, loudness of voice, phrasing, and affect. The subject is asked to try again, is revideotaped, and receives more feedback. If the client continues to have difficulty, the response may be modeled by the therapist or shown in a modeling film. Role exaggeration and/or reversal may also be used. Of course, all these techniques may be used in groups as well.

A major issue in social skills training has been the question of generalization of the skills learned in one setting to another setting. Few studies have evaluated whether transfer occurs, but the recent addition of social skills training to the curriculum of predischarge training courses, such as Craig Hospital's Re-entry Program; transitional living facilities, such as the Texas Institute of Rehabilitation and Research's New Options program; and independent living centers, such as the Adult Independence Development Center in San Jose, may provide pertinent data. The New Options program (Cole, Sperry, Board, and Frieden, 1979), for example, integrates social skills training within a community living skills program, addressing such issues as attendant management, consumer affairs, living arrangements, and sexuality. Generalization of the skills learned in classes is facilitated by field trips where the skills are put into practice in real-life situations with immediate feedback from staff and other participants.

Social skills training for people interacting with handicapped persons may also be useful, but until recently, has been unexplored. A social skills program has been described by Badame (1981) for teachers and parents of students with disabilities. Dunn and Lloyd (1981) described a staff training program to deal with sexual questions and comments on an SCI ward, and Dunn (1981) developed a survey to assess staff discomfort in sexually oriented interactions with patients. Staff training programs that teach interpersonal skills to medical students (see Cohen & Fried (1978) for a review) and therapists (Forer & Miller, 1981) have been described. Dunn (1983) has presented a self-report inventory that identifies discomforting rehabilitation situations, thereby enabling inservice training programs to focus on the most difficult situations for staff members. Few other social skills programs have been developed for rehabilitation personnel or families of people with disabilities.

INSTITUTING AND CONDUCTING A SOCIAL SKILLS PROGRAM

This section outlines some techniques for starting a social skills training class, promoting attendance and participation by reticent clients, facilitating group process, and conducting specific classes. These suggestions and techniques are based on experience with SCI patients in Veteran's Administration Medical Centers (acknowledgment is made of the contributions of Elizabeth Van Horn, M.S.W. and Steven H. Herman, Ph.D.). Clinicians working in different settings or with different patients, experience, and/or styles may wish to modify this approach.

Staff and Consumer Group Presentations

Informing influential groups that have contact with patients of the program is an important first step. Officers of local consumer groups, such as the Paralyzed Veterans of America, should be informed of the background, purpose, and general procedures of the training classes. Inservice training for nursing, therapy, and medical staff also facilitates the acceptance of the program. These groups are asked (1) to understand that the classes are not clubs or psychotherapy groups, (2) not to discuss the content of the course, and (3) to support the class leaders in encouraging patients to participate. In addition, the potential benefits to the staff are described, such as reduction of patients' inappropriate attention-getting behavior, angry outbursts, and swearing directed at the staff. Staff members are further warned not to expect instant "cures" and are told that slow, but permanent behavioral change is the goal of the class.

Approaching Potential Class Members

People with visible physical disabilities, especially recently acquired ones, are often unwilling to admit to problems in social and psychological realms, so that asking them to participate in such a training course requires preparation, tact, and skill. The method presented below resulted in a 97 percent acceptance rate and only a 6 percent dropout rate.

- Potential class members are approached individually and asked, "Can you come to my office at ___ o'clock so that we can talk to you for a few minutes about a project we are starting in which we would like your help"?

- If pretesting is used in order to assess the students' specific strengths and weaknesses and the teacher's own effectiveness, then the following presentation may be made: "The medical people here talk a lot about the physical problems of your handicap, but very little is said about the social consequences. You may have already noticed that people sometimes treat you differently than they treat other people, that social situations occasionally come up that are difficult to handle, and that new social difficulties have arisen in connection with your handicap. What we're trying to do is gather information on which kinds of situations lead to the most difficulty for people with your disability. Therefore, we are asking many people with different ages, background, experience with their handicap, and types of injury to participate in a research project. We feel that this information will help others adapt to their handicap and may help you become more aware of these difficult situations. Any information about you specifically will be kept strictly confidential. Are you willing to help us this way?"
- If the patients agree, schedule them for pretesting.
- If they say they do not think they need any help, you may say, "Certainly, but we are trying to obtain information about people with a lot of experience and skill in this area also, so would you agree to participate?"
- If the patients say they do not have the time, you may say, "The staff agree that this is important so they have allowed time to be taken from your therapy schedule so that you can participate. It should only take an hour or so. Are you willing to give it a try?"
- After the pretest, you may ask the patients to return the forms to the office and say, "Did you think that was interesting? We are starting a class in which we are going to be learning how to manage the types of situations that were on the videotape (or self-report measure) by practicing your responses and getting information on how well you're doing. You'll also be able to see how others manage the situations. We would like you to be in the training class so that you and the other class members can benefit. Can we go ahead and include you?"
- Answer any questions the potential class members have, emphasize that this is a "training class" and not a "Group," and describe benefits and success that other patients have gained from the program.

Desirable Equipment and Setting

An effort should be made to gain access to a videotape camera and monitor, preferably the videocassette type. Even though verbal feedback can be given by the instructors and other class members, nothing has the impact of participants being able to see for themselves how they reacted in specific situations. Any props, such as menus, cocktail glasses, table, or a telephone, that can be obtained to make the setting more authentic are desirable, but not necessary. A quiet room where no disruptions can occur is also important.

The videotape "Social Skills for the Spinal Cord Injury Patient" (Dunn, Van Horn, & Herman, 1976), although developed for an SCI population, has been found to be a useful educational tool for staff, families, and people with other physical handicaps, as well as a useful adjunct to the training course. This videotape presents eight situations that spinal cord injured people have found difficult to manage (Dunn, 1977; Dunn & Herman, 1982), along with three possible responses—aggressive, passive, and assertive. Commentary is also provided, but it must be emphasized that group discussion after the videotape or, as Hobart (1982) has shown, cognitive rehearsal is extremely important because of the potential anxiety aroused by the negative consequences of the passive and aggressive responses (see also Dunn et al., 1981).

Preparation for Classes

The following steps should be taken in preparation:

- Decide ahead of time who will be responsible for which segment of the course.
- Share responsibility for reminding patients to come and for setting up the room. Before the first few classes, each participant should be prompted to attend each class.
- Make sure that the "Social Skills Class" is officially listed in the therapy schedule.
- The head nurse and ward secretary should be given a list of participants; because prompt attendance is essential, routine medical tests and diagnostic procedures should be delayed whenever possible.
- During Rounds, make a formal announcement to staff of the time and place of the class.

Process Considerations

The group leader should follow these six guidelines:

1. Do not feed the group solutions or suggestions; try to get them involved in problem solving, e.g., "Who can think of a way to get some assistance in . . ."
2. Make allowances for differences in style—there are no correct or incorrect solutions.

3. Try not to use value judgments ("good" and "bad" ways of relating), but discuss the likely consequences of the various responses.
4. Re-emphasize didactic information if the participant does not understand, e.g., "What is an assertive response; what are its components?"
5. Minimize joking at first; it may be used as a "copout." Do not respond to "hamming it up."
6. Give positive feedback frequently.

Procedures for the First Class

The first class is the most important one in that (1) a fuller explanation of the rationale for the class can be given, (2) patients can see that the procedures are not as threatening as they may have expected, (3) stereotypes of "psychology" or "group therapy" may be dispelled, (4) clients may experience entertainment or diversion, and (5) a fuller understanding of the problems and possible solutions may be gained. Thus it is important to plan and rehearse who will say what and when. The following is an outline for a possible first class:

- Introductory Lecture
  a. Relationship between social skills and rehabilitation
  b. Review background of the issues
  c. Definition of aggression, passivity, and assertion
  d. Basic human rights (Smith, 1975)
  e. Seven components of assertion—eye contact, affect, loudness of voice, latency, compliance, speech disturbances, and requests for new behavior (Eisler et al., 1973); it is recommended that these seven components be written on a blackboard or large sheet of paper.
- First Situation—Refusing Unwanted Help
  a. Introduction—why the situation is difficult
  b. The two co-leaders of the class should model the procedure, with one setting the scene and being the helper while the other is the recipient (who may assert "no", but make no eye contact and use a soft voice). Have class members critique the response by reviewing each component of assertion.
  c. Select the class member who is the most outgoing and will be the most assertive for the first attempt at the situation. "_____, we would like you to try it first."
  d. After the class member's response, if there is videotape feedback equipment available, say "OK, good. Let's play it back and see what you think."
  e. Play back the class member's response.
  f. "OK, in terms of what we said about the components of assertiveness, how do you think you did?"

1) If there is no response, try "What are the components of assertiveness?" If there is still no response, ask the other class members to name a component; ask the first class member how he thought he did on that component. If the class is too critical, support the first class member.

2) If the first class member says, "I think I did great," say "OK, what are the ways you think you did well. In terms of the assertiveness components, let's talk about it in terms of eye contact. What do you think? . . . What does the class think?" Keep reviewing the response according to the components.

3) If the class member says, "Gee, I think I should go to Hollywood. I don't need this training," or some similar joke or evasive remark, ignore the comment and go on to elements of assertion.

g. Ask the class member, "Was that as difficult as you thought it would be? You may be surprised that you may have looked different than you thought you would. Sometimes it can be very beneficial to see yourself as others see you. You'll find that you'll get used to it and may see some things that you want to change." (We found, for example, that the inpatients showed up for the next session in street clothes and were better groomed.)

h. Give each of the other class members a turn at role-playing and being videotaped.

- Postrehearsal Discussion and Summary

a. Use an example from the class member who showed the most change to reinforce compliance with instructions and change and also to point out again the components of assertion.

b. Ask if there are any questions about assertiveness or about the procedure.

c. Discuss discriminating between ignorant and/or genuine offers of help from those offered out of pity or condescension.

d. Discussion of confidentiality of class: "Remember, as we've talked about this with you individually, that the results of the original assessments and the tapes we'll make in the class are completely confidential, as should be the specifics of this class. You wouldn't want others to discuss your performance here, so please don't talk about others. Can you agree to that?

e. If you think of any questions, don't hesitate to ask us. The next class meeting will be at _____.

CONCLUSIONS AND SUGGESTIONS FOR FUTURE WORK

This chapter has described the complexity and ambiguity of the social world of disabled people and surveyed some of the methods of assessing and training the skills required to cope with this world. The conflicting attitudes and emotions about people with disabilities held by the nondisabled population create awkward social encounters and may produce deficits in honest feedback for people with disabilities. Rehabilitation psychologists have adapted assessment and intervention techniques used with other populations in order to prepare disabled people to adapt to their social environment more adequately. Much work remains to be accomplished, however.

The major deficit in the rehabilitative social skills literature today is the lack of outcome studies. Experimental, laboratory-derived assessment techniques have shown improvements in self-report measures and behavioral assertiveness tests, but the effects of social skills training on long-term, functional, objective measures of life change have not been studied. Such studies could be conducted in Independent Living Centers and Transitional Living Facilities that teach social skills. The Rehabilitation Indicators Project and Longitudinal Functional Assessment System might provide suitable outcome measures.

Only two studies reviewed (Hobart, 1982; Morgan & Leung, 1980) reported changes in self-reported assertiveness. Further research is indicated to investigate whether these results are due to the populations studied, content of the training courses, expectations of the trainers, length of treatment, or other variables. Cognitive assessment and therapy (Kendall & Hollon, 1979; Meichenbaum, 1977) have been successfully integrated into general social skills training (Lange & Jakubowski, 1976), but have not yet been reported in the social skills and disability literature. (See Rosensteil and Roth, 1981 for a measure of anticipatory cognitive activity and its relationship to adjustment in SCI.)

Another development in the general assertiveness literature as yet unapplied to the rehabilitation setting is heterosocial skills assessment and training (Curran, 1977). Meeting members of the opposite sex, dating, and maintaining heterosocial relationships may be difficult for individuals no matter what their physical condition. Physical disability can complicate this process, but specific assessment and training in heterosocial skills may alleviate these difficulties.

A final needed development is the creation of more audiovisual aids. The videotape "Social Skills for the Spinal Cord Injured Patient" (Dunn et al., 1976), has been used successfully with people with a number of disabilities, but films that illustrate effective coping responses of people with other disabilities in problematic situations are necessary. Personal experience with videotapes suggests that high technical quality is less important than the depiction of a variety of approaches and the discussion of what has been demonstrated. A good start is the videotape developed at Spain Rehabilitation Center by Susan Hobart (1982). This tape shows competent responses to such situations as refusing help from a relative, dealing with inappropriate sexual questions, and negotiating with an usher. Additionally, home videocameras and recorders make it possible for individual clinicians to make their own modeling films and use videotape feedback for practice in specific problematic areas.

With continued research, development, and application of the techniques presented in this chapter, rehabilitation psychology can make a unique, positive contribution to the overall rehabilitation and quality of life of disabled individuals.

REFERENCES

Albrecht, G., Harasymiw, S.J., & Horne, M. (1977). *Social perceptions of disability.* Paper presented at the meeting of the American Sociological Association, Chicago.

Alexander, J.O., Willems, E.P., & Halstead, L. (1980). *Clinical application of longitudinal functional assessment.* Annual Report, Texas Institute of Rehabilitation & Research, Houston.

Asher, N.W. (1973). Manipulating attraction toward the disabled: An application of the similarity-attraction model. *Rehabilitation Psychology, 20,* 156–164.

Badame, R. (1981). Social skills: The process of learning to take risks. In D.G. Bullard & S.E. Knight (Eds.), *Sexuality and physical disability: Personal perspectives.* St. Louis: C.V. Mosby, pp. 243–248.

Battle, C.V. (1974). Disruptions in the socialization of a young, severely handicapped child. *Rehabilitation Literature, 35,* 130–140.

Boham, B.E., & Selkowitz, S. (1981). Video-counseling for multi-handicapped hearing-impaired students. *American Annals of the Deaf,* 587–590.

Brown, M., Caplan, J., & Swirsky, J. (1978). *Rehabilitation indicators: An overview.* Paper presented at the meeting of the American Psychological Association, Toronto.

Bull, R., & Stevens, J. (1980). Effect of unsightly teeth on helping behavior. *Perceptual and Motor Skills, 51,* 438.

Chaiklin, H., & Warfield, M. (1973). Stigma management and amputee rehabilitation. *Rehabilitation Literature, 34,* 162–172.

Cogswell, B.D. (1968). Self socialization: Readjustment of paraplegics in the community. *Journal of Rehabilitation, 34,* 11–13.

Cohen, B.F., & Fried, T.W. (1978). *Teaching interpersonal skills to health professionals: Resource document I.* (Available from Carkhuff Associates, Amherst, MA).

Cole, J.A., Sperry, J.C., Board, M., & Frieden, L. (1979). *New options training manual.* Houston: Institute for Rehabilitation and Research.

Curran, J.P. (1977). Skills training as an approach to the treatment of heterosexual-social anxiety: A review. *Psychological Bulletin, 84,* 140–157.

Davis, M. (1973). *Living with multiple sclerosis.* Springfield, IL: Charles C Thomas.

Dembo, T., Leviton, G., & Wright, B. (1975). Adjustment to misfortune—a problem of social-psychological rehabilitation. *Rehabilitation Psychology, 22,* 1–100.

Diller, L., Fordyce, W., Jacobs, D., Brown, M., Gordon, W., Simmens, S., Orazem, J., & Barrett, L. (1983). *Final report. Rehabilitation Indicators Project.* New York: New York University Medical Center.

Dixon, J.K. (1977). Coping with prejudice: Attitudes of handicapped persons towards the handicapped. *Journal of Chronic Diseases, 30,* 307–322.

Dixon, J.K. (1981). Group-self identification and physical handicap: Implication for patient support groups. *Research in Nursing and Health, 4,* 299–308.

Dunn, M. (1977). Social discomfort in the patient with spinal cord injury. *Archives of Physical Medicine and Rehabilitation, 58,* 257–260.

Dunn, M. (1981). *Sexual questions and comments on a spinal cord injury service: A sexual interaction survey.* Paper presented at the meeting of the American Congress of Rehabilitation Medicine, San Diego.

Dunn, M. (1982). *Social relationships and interpersonal skills: A guide for people with sensory and physical limitations.* Falls Church, VA: Institute for Information Studies.

Dunn, M. (1983). *The rehabilitation situations inventory: An instrument to assess discomfort in rehabilitation staff.* Paper presented at the meeting of the American Congress of Rehabilitation Medicine, Los Angeles.

Dunn, M., & Herman, S.H. (1982). Social skills and physical disability. In D.M. Doleys, R.L. Meredith, & A.R. Ciminero (Eds.), *Behavioral medicine: Assessment and treatment strategies.* New York: Plenum Press, pp. 117–144.

Dunn, M., & Lloyd, E.E. (1981). *Short term training in staff sex education and spinal cord injury.* Paper presented at the meeting of the American Congress of Rehabilitation Medicine, San Diego, CA.

Dunn, M., Lloyd, E., & Phelps, G. (1979). Sexual assertiveness in spinal cord injury. *Sexuality and Disability, 2,* 293–300.

Dunn, M., Van Horn, E., & Herman, S.H. (1976). *Social skills and the spinal cord injured patient.* (Videotape No. NAC004–179). Washington, DC: National Audio Visual Center.

Dunn, M., Van Horn, E., & Herman, S.H. (1981). Social skills and spinal cord injury: A comparison of three training procedures. *Behavior Therapy, 12,* 153–164.

Eisler, R., Miller, P., & Hersen, M. (1973). Components of assertive behavior. *Journal of Clinical Psychology, 29,* 295–299.

Fehr, M.J., Dybsky, A., Wacker, D., & Kerr, J. (1977). *Eye contact in the social skills of obtaining help.* Paper presented at the meeting of the American Psychological Association, San Francisco.

Forer, S.K., & Miller, L.S. (1981). Role playing: Inservice education for occupational and physical therapists. *Archives of Physical Medicine and Rehabilitation, 62,* 535.

Fusso, T. (1984). *A situational analysis of social interactions involving spinal cord injured people.* Unpublished doctoral dissertation, University of Nevada, Reno.

Gallenberger, C. (1979). *Self-monitoring versus group therapy in assertiveness training.* Unpublished doctoral dissertation, Memphis State University, Memphis.

Gambrill, E.D., & Richey, C.A. (1975). An assertion inventory for use in assessment and research. *Behavior Therapy, 6,* 350–362.

Ginsburg, M.L. (1978). *Assertion with the wheelchair-bound: Measurement and training.* Unpublished doctoral dissertation, University of Connecticut, Storrs, CT.

Goffman, E. (1963). *Stigma: Notes on the management of spoiled identity.* Englewood, NJ: Prentice-Hall.

Hahn, H. (1981). The social component of sexuality and disability: Some problems and proposals. *Sexuality and Disability, 4,* 220–233.

Hastorf, A.H., Northcraft, G.B., & Picciotto, S.R. (1979). Helping the handicapped: How realistic is the performance feedback received by the physically handicapped? *Personality and Social Psychology Bulletin, 5,* 373–376.

Hastorf, A.H., Wildfogel, J., & Cassman, T. (1979). Acknowledgment of handicap as a tactic in social interaction. *Journal of Personality and Social Psychology, 37,* 1790–1797.

Heimberg, R.G., Montgomery, D., Madsen, C., & Heimberg, J.S. (1977). Assertion training: A review of the literature. *Behavior Therapy, 8,* 953–971.

Herman, S.H., Van Horn, E., & Dunn, M. (1977). *Behavioral assessment of general and disability-specific social skills.* Paper presented at the meeting of the American Psychological Association, San Francisco.

Higgins, P. (1980). *Outsiders in a hearing world.* Beverly Hills, CA: Sage.

Hobart, S.C. (1982). *Improving disability-specific social skills: The effects of training and locus of control.* Unpublished doctoral dissertation, University of Alabama, University, AL.

Hyman, M.D. (1972). Social isolation and performance in rehabilitation. *Journal of Chronic Diseases, 25,* 85–97.

Janis, I.L. (1983). The role of social support in adherence to stressful decisions. *American Psychologist, 38,* 143–160.

Kahn, E. (1969). Social functioning of the patient with spinal cord injury. *Journal of the American Physical Therapy Association, 9,* 757–762.

Kelley, H.H., Hastorf, A.H., Jones, E.E., Thibaut, J.W., & Usdane, W.M. (1960). Some implications of social psychological theory for research on the handicapped. In L.H. Lofquist (Ed.), *Psychological research and rehabilitation,* Miami: American Psychological Association, pp. 172–204.

Kendall, P.C., & Hollon, S.D. (Eds.). (1979). *Cognitive-behavioral interventions: Theory, research, and procedures.* New York: Academic Press.

Kleck, R. (1966). Emotional arousal in interactions with stigmatized persons. *Psychological Reports, 21,* 12–26.

Kleck, R. (1968). Physical stigma and nonverbal cues emitted in face-to-face interactions. *Human Relations, 21,* 19–28.

Kleck, R., Ono, H., & Hastorf, A. (1966). The effects of physical deviance upon face-to-face interaction. *Human Relations, 19,* 425–436.

Knight, B., Wollert, R.W., Levy, L.H., Frame, C.L., & Padgett, V.P. (1980). Self-help groups: The members' perspectives. *American Journal of Community Psychology, 8,* 53–65.

Ladieu-Leviton, G., Adler, D.L., & Dembo, T. (1948). Studies in adjustment to visible injury: Social acceptance of the injured. *Journal of Social Issues, 4,* 55–61.

Lakin, P., Ben-Yishay, Y., Rattock, J., Ross, S., Silver, S., Thomas, J.L., Hofien, D., Fawzi, E.M., Hamza, M.H., & Diller, L. (1981). Special procedures for assessing aspects of interpersonal skills of head trauma patients undergoing rehabilitation. *Working approaches to remediation of cognitive deficits in brain damaged persons* (Rehabilitation Monograph No. 62). New York: New York University Medical Center, Institute of Rehabilitation Medicine.

Lange, A.J., & Jakubowski, P. (1976). *Responsible assertive behavior.* Champaign, IL: Research Press.

Levy, L.H. (1978). Self-help groups viewed by mental health professionals: A survey and comments. *American Journal of Community Psychology, 6,* 305–313.

Meichenbaum, D. (1977). *Cognitive-behavior modification: An integrative approach.* New York: Plenum Press.

Mishel, M.H. (1978). Assertion training with handicapped persons. *Journal of Counseling Psychology, 25,* 238–241.

Morgan, E., Hohmann, G., & Davis, J. (1974). Psychological rehabilitation in Veterans Administration spinal cord injury centers. *Rehabilitation Psychology, 21,* 3–33.

Morgan, B., & Leung, P. (1980). Effects of assertion training on acceptance of disability by physically disabled university students. *Journal of Counseling Psychology, 27,* 209–212.

Neal, P.J. (1983). *A psychological treatment program for prevention of decubitus ulcers in spinal cord injured patients.* Unpublished doctoral dissertation, Memphis State University, Memphis.

Norris-Baker, C. (1982). *Behavioral discriminators of health outcomes in spinal cord injury.* Paper presented at the meeting of the American Congress of Rehabilitation Medicine, Houston.

Phelps, G., Brown, M., Chen, J., Dunn, M., Lloyd, E., Stefanick, M., Davidson, J., & Perkash, I. (1983). Sexual experience and plasma testosterone levels in male veterans after spinal cord injury. *Archives of Physical Medicine and Rehabilitation, 64,* 47–52.

Piliavin, I., Piliavin, J., & Rodin, J. (1975). Costs, diffusion, and the stigmatized victim. *Journal of Personality and Social Psychology, 32,* 429–438.

Rathus, S.A. (1973). A thirty item schedule for assessing assertive behavior. *Behavior Therapy, 4,* 398–406.

Rich, A.R., & Schroeder, H.E. (1976). Research issues in assertiveness training. *Psychological Bulletin, 83,* 1081–1096.

Richardson, S.A. (1963). Some social psychological consequences of handicapping. *Pediatrics, 32,* 291–297.

Romano, M.D. (1976). Social skills training with the newly handicapped. *Archives of Physical Medicine and Rehabilitation, 57,* 302–303.

Rosenstiel, A.K., & Roth, S. (1981). Relationship between cognitive activity and adjustment in four spinal cord injured individuals: A longitudinal investigation. *Journal of Human Stress, 7,* 35–43.

Ruben, D. (1982). *Methodological and philosophical adaptations in assertiveness training programs designed for the blind.* Paper presented at the meeting of the Association for Behavior Analysis, Milwaukee.

Silver, R.L., & Wortman, C.B. (1980). Coping with undesirable life events. In J. Garber & M.E.P. Seligman (Eds.), *Human helplessness.* New York: Academic Press, pp. 279–375.

Smith, M.J. (1975). *When I say no I feel guilty.* New York: Dial Press.

Soble, S., & Strickland, L. (1974). Physical stigma, interaction and compliance. *Bulletin of the Psychonomic Society, 4,* 130–132.

Turem, R. (1975). *Comprehensive service needs study.* Washington, DC: Urban Institute.

Weinberg, N. (1976). Social stereotyping of the physically handicapped. *Rehabilitation Psychology, 23,* 115–124.

Wilkinson, J., & Canter, S. (1982). *Social skills training manual.* New York: Wiley.

Wright, T.J. (1976). *The effects of training in the identification of facial expressions of emotion upon selected deaf and hard-of-hearing client/trainees in a rehabilitation facility.* Unpublished doctoral dissertation, University of Georgia, Athens, GA.

Yuker, H.E., Block, J.R., & Young, J.H. (1966). *The measurement of attitudes towards disabled persons.* Albertson, NY: Human Resources Center.

Chapter 14

Computer-Augmented Feedback Displays: Treatment of Hemiplegic Motor Deficits as a Paradigm

John G. Gianutsos, Ph.D., and Arthur Eberstein, Ph.D.

The family of techniques known as biofeedback has gained increasing acceptance within rehabilitation as uncritical acclaim of their efficacy has mounted. Biofeedback treatments have been reported to be useful in the management of a variety of disorders that are commonly found in rehabilitation patients: foot-drop, postural disalignment, spastic hypertonicity, restricted joint mobility, flaccidity, unsteady balance, faulty ambulation, incontinence, hypotension, and compromised endurance. Although the published reports have generally favored the incorporation of biofeedback within a rehabilitation package, few controlled studies have even been attempted. Much of the evidence is based on case histories or anecdotal reports.

Typically, biofeedback involves (1) electronic monitoring of an ongoing physiologic process or activity and (2) providing substitutive sensory feedback to the individual being monitored in order to enable voluntary influence of the process or activity in question.

Several excellent reviews of the clinical uses of biofeedback are already available (Basmajian, 1981, 1982; Blanchard & Epstein, 1977; Blanchard & Young, 1974; Cleeland, 1981; De Weerdt & Harrison, 1986a, & 1986b; Engel-Sittenfeld, 1977; Fernando & Basmajian, 1978; Hatch, Gatchel, & Harrington, 1982; Hume, 1976; Inglis, Campbell, & Donald, 1976; Keefe & Surwit, 1978; Ray, Raczynski, Rogers, & Kimball, 1979; Wolf, 1983; Yates, 1980). Therefore,

Development of the studies and techniques described in this paper were supported by Grant No. G008300071 and Grant No. G008300039 from the National Institute of Handicapped Research, U.S. Department of Education, Washington, D.C.

We acknowledge the efforts of Theodore Wolff, B.S., and Bernard L. Bollettieri, B.A., for their programming expertise and efforts in construction of the various devices. We are grateful to Rosamond Gianutsos, Ph.D., Leslie Packer, Ph.D., Joseph M. Notterman, Ph.D., and Megan P. Willis, M.A., for critically reviewing the manuscript. The invaluable guidance, encouragement, and editorial support provided by Bruce Caplan, Ph.D., throughout its preparation are appreciated.

this chapter illustrates the application of biofeedback principles through the description of a state-of-the-art program of computer-based interventions in the treatment of hemiplegic motor deficits.

Damage to the brain, whether traumatic or vascular in origin, is the prime cause of motor difficulties experienced by several million people in the United States (Neurological and Communicative Disorders, 1976). These individuals are unable to control movements effectively of the involved portion of the body. Although traditional therapy does significantly ameliorate these deficits, these results can be improved (Kottke, 1974).

The need to supplement traditional intervention with other modalities has been acknowledged for decades (Herman, 1973; Moskowitz, Lightbody, & Freitag, 1972; Taft, Delagi, Wilkie, & Abramson, 1962). Although computer-based supplemental therapeutics existed in the 1960s, the cost and esoterica of hardware and software limited their application to large institutional settings. However, technological advances that have occurred in the past two decades have led to a vast reduction in cost. Computer-based biofeedback and biophysical monitoring systems are now within the budgetary means of virtually every health care professional. Used in conjunction with sophisticated behavioral techniques, the by-products of this technology have heralded a new era in physical medicine and rehabilitation. As a result of these developments, renewed interest has also been generated in such therapeutic supplements as myoelectric (EMG) biofeedback, functional electrical stimulation (FES), and functional vibratory stimulation (FVS).

The authors' approach emphasizes computer-augmented visual feedback displays. The goals of intervention are to improve the mobility and coordination patterns of the upper and lower extremities and to restore postural stability, along with the ability to perform weight shift maneuvers essential for ambulation. The programs have been devised, developed, and are currently employed at the Howard A. Rusk Institute of Rehabilitation Medicine, New York University Medical Center. The tactics and procedures employed in the program provide a sound basis for improving functional ability and are described as each goal is considered in turn. The role of feedback in biological activity in general and in motor function in particular is first discussed.

ROLE OF FEEDBACK IN BIOLOGICAL ACTIVITIES

Feedback is essential to survival (Horrobin, 1970). It maintains the environments of cells and organs within limits required for their proper functioning. A feedback mechanism is involved whenever the output of a system is rechanneled into the system in such a way as to alter the system's functioning. In the nervous system, certain entities feed back commands to continue activity (positive feedback mechanism), whereas others feed back commands to stop ongoing activity (negative feedback mechanism).

The motor performance of healthy individuals is influenced by feedback. In particular, coordinated activities, such as playing a stringed instrument or performing gymnastics, are highly dependent on feedback. Even seemingly simple acts that one takes for granted, such as picking up a drinking glass or climbing a flight of stairs, are influenced by feedback arising from within one's own body.

The execution of various motor activities, such as flexing (bending) or extending (straightening) a joint, requires that opposite effects be produced concurrently in a muscle pair the actions of which are mechanically opposed. Thus, extending the elbow requires that the primary agonists of this action (triceps) contract (shorten) while simultaneously the antagonists (biceps) relax (lengthen). Sherrington (1897) referred to this mechanism as "reciprocal inhibition" or "reciprocal innervation." However, the workings of feedback are not restricted to primitive levels of organization responsible for the regulation of simple movements; they also play a crucial role in the acquisition, planning, execution, and elaboration of complex motor skills.

Relevance of Feedback to Motor Skill Acquisition

Feedback mechanisms play an important role in the acquisition of complex motor skills. Consider the process of learning to throw darts. A novice acquires the skill through a series of motoric adjustments. Improvement occurs through the use of such tactics as remembering how previous throws were executed, taking the outcome into account, and then regulating the force and direction of future attempts accordingly. If a weight is attached to the throwing arm or if the player wears a blindfold, accuracy will suffer because the feedback will differ from that by which prior motor activity was regulated. In contrast, the imposition of such conditions may ensure that proprioceptive cues are more closely heeded, and if the initial conditions are reinstated, performance may exceed the original level.

In skill training of this kind, feedback can be utilized either on a continuous or discrete basis. The dart thrower may focus on internal feedback based on changes in muscle tension, joint position, and movement velocity and may also focus on projectile velocity by visually tracking the dart on its way to the target. Yet, the player may be distracted by attending to so much information and may then decide that it is sufficient to focus on the target along with the rhythm with which the dart is thrown. In either case, future motor strategies will be influenced by outcome. If a bull's-eye is scored, the strategy employed may be considered adequate. In order for the individual to decide, however, knowledge of results is needed.

The most effective means of providing feedback about performance is a matter of controversy. Harrison (1977) has proposed that discrete feedback concerning outcome, presented *following an action*, is preferable to continuous feedback. In her opinion, the latter is unduly complex and serves to distract the performer from ongoing internal cues.

Others have advocated providing continuous feedback or augmented information *during an action*, (Adams, 1971, 1984; Adams, Goetz, & Marshall, 1972; Brudny, Korein, Grynbaum, Belandres, & Gianutsos, 1979; Carroll & Bandura, 1982; Herman, 1973; Smith, 1966; Smith & Henry, 1967).

There are intermediate positions as well. DeBacher (1979) subscribes to the view that both methods are equally important, as do the present authors who have found that both methods can be used to advantage, depending on the situation.

Acquisition and maintenance of a complex motor skill operate through subtle cues and have not yet been adequately explained. Often, once external and internal feedback are integrated and the entire motor sequence is automatized, the focus shifts to knowledge of results, with less attention paid to certain aspects of continual feedback. For example, the skilled dart thrower may rely on knowledge of results until there is a noticeable decline in performance. When this occurs the player may change strategy and try to analyze how internal components of prior successful efforts differed from current efforts. Athletic coaches are continually analyzing motor skills in this manner: dissecting a skill into its component parts so that they may instruct an athlete who is encountering difficulty or one whose performance is impeded due to "faulty mechanics." In such cases it is assumed that the player's motor system is healthy, that somatic feedback processes are intact and functioning, but that feedback regarding certain aspects of the activity is going unheeded or being wrongly interpreted. The situation is markedly different when performance has declined due to disease. In these situations where the motor system is malfunctioning, with the result that the body's own feedback processes are faulty, more sophisticated training procedures must be employed.

Motor Deterioration in Hemiplegia

Destruction of cerebral tissue frequently results in motoric deficits partly because feedback from motor action is either compromised or improperly utilized. For example, lateral brain damage, such as from stroke, may cause loss of motor control on the opposite side of the body. Chronic consequences of hemiplegia include decreased extremity function on the involved side as exemplified by flexed fingers and foot-drop. Even following a subtle lesion there is evidence of motoric dysfunction. In the upper extremity there is a tendency of flexors to dominate extensors. Movements are not confined or isolated to the appropriate parts; the limb is usually moved in synergistic fashion as an undifferentiated entity, making fine finger movements and opposition of the thumb difficult to accomplish.

Brunnstrom (1970) described several stages of motor recovery subsequent to the onset of hemiplegia. Initially, there is a paralysis of the flaccid type (diminished muscle tone) that is more pronounced in the limbs distally than proximally.

This is followed by the appearance of spasticity (heightened muscle tone), flexion or extension synergies, and occasionally gross movement initiation. Progress is more evident in the lower extremity than in the upper. Movements are more pronounced in proximal than distal regions of the limbs. In the following stage, the patient can voluntarily initiate synergistic patterns. Spasticity is temporarily more pronounced, declining somewhat in the next stage when the patient may begin to display initiation of individual finger movements. For the majority of patients, recovery does not proceed beyond this point.

Participants in the authors' program typically lack the spatial patterning and temporal sequencing of activity in the musculature controlling the axial, proximal, and distal joints—pelvic, knee, and ankle—that able-bodied individuals take for granted. It is essential to emphasize that, although the musculature of the trunk and extremities is functionally impaired, the nerves and muscles serving these parts are intact and operational. This point is easily illustrated by direct electrical stimulation of the muscles that evokes functional movements. This peripheral procedure involves intervention at the neuromusculature level along the "final common path" (Sherrington, 1906). It has gained notoriety from the work of Petrofsky and others (Benton, Baker, Bowman, & Waters, 1981; Glaser, Gruner, Feinberg, & Collins, 1983; Kralj, Bajd, Turk, Krajnik, and Benko, 1983; Kralj & Vodovnik, 1977; Petrofsky & Phillips, 1984; Phillips, Petrofsky, Hendershot, & Stafford, 1984) who have applied it to ameliorate the effects of spinal cord injury in humans. However, in contrast to spinal cord injury, in which the brain has been effectively disconnected from the rest of the nervous system, the problem in hemiplegia is that portions of the brain itself have been damaged. It is the intricate control of movements previously orchestrated by the brain that is lacking.

A common therapeutic obstacle is that, although there is some residual control of the limb apparatus by the brain, the effects of this control are so slight as to go unnoticed. In traditional therapeutic settings, the impact of such voluntary effort remains undetected and therefore unenhanced; in the face of slow progress or none at all, patients become frustrated and discouraged. However, computer technology allows instant detection and display of the effects of a patient's effort on muscle activity and is the vehicle by which motivation is maintained until movement emerges.

Biopotentials and Motor Activity

Whenever a muscle contracts, the event is accompanied by a change in bioelectric potential. This change in potential occurs along the motoneurone, as well as the muscle fibers, and forms the basis of the electromyographic (EMG) signal. EMG signals are easily monitored with modern electronic instruments. The presence of bioelectric potentials can be detected by means of either needle electrodes or surface electrodes. Needle electrodes are inserted into the muscle through the skin. Very fine ones are used when the activity of a single motor unit is being studied. Surface electrodes do not penetrate the skin, but are placed on it and are used to detect and monitor the sum of the activity of motor units within their proximity. In the authors' program only surface electrodes are used.

Training Normal Subjects to Control Single Motor Units

Early reports of healthy subjects established that feedback could aid in the acquisition of control of muscle activity, even at the level of individual motor units (Basmajian, 1963; Basmajian, Baeza, & Fabrigar, 1965; Harrison & Mortensen, 1962; Wagman, Pierce, & Burger, 1965). The technique involved inserting needle electrodes in the muscle being studied and presenting the amplified signal to the subject by means of a cathode ray tube (visual feedback) and/or a loudspeaker (auditory feedback).

The work of Basmajian and his collaborators is typical (Basmajian, 1963; Basmajian, 1972; Basmajian & Simard, 1967). This group found that subjects could attain precise control over single motor unit activity after only a few hours of training. When provided with visual and auditory feedback, subjects easily learned to control the firing activity of the individual motor units arising from covert and unfelt muscle contractions. Furthermore, a small proportion of these subjects maintained this control in the absence of feedback (Basmajian et al., 1965). More importantly, the subjects could produce a variety of firing patterns in the motoneurone of a single motor unit while the activity of neighboring motoneurones remained silent. The existence of such selectivity seemed extraordinary in view of the millions of cells available to be ''chosen'' and the fact that a number of motor units are generally recruited when a muscle contracts.

However, another explanation may account for the results. Subjects may have learned to gauge the level of tension required to trigger the feedback signal. Motor units are normally activated in a predictable and orderly fashion. Some begin to fire at low-force levels, whereas others do not begin firing until larger tensions are generated. Thus, if a person has learned to produce a level of tension sufficient to fire the particular motor unit being monitored, this may be mistaken for the ability to isolate that unit.

Although the actual mechanism remains controversial, these findings emphasize the importance of feedback for the acquisition and maintenance of fine motor control.

Training Patients to Control Hemiplegic Limbs

The therapeutic relevance of the minute bioelectric events that accompany muscle activity is that their detection and presentation indicate to the patient that volitional effort has produced an effect. Indeed, they are often the only proof of success. Moreover, they provide an objective anchor on which to base therapeutic instruction.

Basmajian (1982) has stated that early workers in the field of clinical electromyography recognized the therapeutic value of the instant feedback provided by EMG signals:

> Even in the infancy of electromyography we used the sound of motor unit potentials to grade the desired strengths and contractions and often recruited the help of the patient. No one thought to give this phenomenon a name. Certainly it was not used as an intensive therapeutic tool. (p. 202)

The process employed by the authors involves transducing myoelectric potentials by means of surface electrodes filled with conductive gel (skin lotion containing salt) and attached to the skin overlying each muscle being monitored. The electrodes are placed in the vicinity of the muscle belly and in alignment with its longitudinal axis. Because the EMG signal is very faint it must be amplified in order to be useful. However, because the signal may contain artifacts arising from other biological processes, such as a heartbeat, or from an environmental source, such as 60 Hz electrical interference, the incoming signal is *filtered* in order to eliminate such influences. The filter rejects all incoming frequencies except those that fall within a specified range known as the bandpass. However, such a "raw" EMG signal is extremely difficult to interpret due to its rapid fluctuations and must be represented in a manner that is intelligible to both patient and therapist. This is accomplished by *rectification* (electronically inverting all negative portions of the waveform and combining them with the positive portions) and *integration* (averaging the energy present in the waveform each one-tenth of a second). All the processing occurs at electronic speed, and the signal is immediately displayed as a continuous waveform on a video monitor.

The visual displays provide patients with immediate feedback concerning the character and degree of myoelectric activity produced as a result of their effort. This feedback is relevant, precise, consistent, and linked to the dynamics of performance. The information is available continually, displayed without perceptible delay, and fulfills a dual role. It informs both patient and therapist of the extent to which the patient's effort has affected the targeted muscle. It supplements or substitutes for somatosensory information that has been distorted, diminished, or eliminated as a result of stroke (Brudny et. al, 1979; Gianutsos, Eberstein, Krasilovsky, Ragnarsson, & Goodgold, 1986).

Displays Employing a Single Waveform for Each Muscle

The authors' approach entails concurrent monitoring of voltages generated by an opponent pair of muscles that control movement about a joint. The voltages are represented on a video monitor as two distinct continuous waveforms, each with a different color. The patient attempts to control and modify the waveforms in keeping with the goals of therapy. The waveforms can be supplemented by including additional features in the display. For example, if increased contraction in a muscle is desired, a horizontal line can be displayed at any level of the screen to serve as a target level. When the output of the motor units recruited during an effort is sufficient to elevate the waveform to or beyond the goal, the patient is rewarded by an audible tone.

Displays Employing One Waveform for a Pair of Muscles

The fundamental goal is to train patients to maximize the difference in myo-electric output generated by the agonist muscle relative to the antagonist until isolated movement emerges. In this regard, a display developed in collaboration with Dr. Joseph M. Notterman has also proven very useful. A single waveform, derived from the instantaneous difference in integrated myoelectric output produced by the muscle pair, is plotted in relation to a horizontal null line at the mid-height of the screen. The waveform traces over the line when the output of the two muscles is equal. It deviates upward from the null line whenever the output of the agonist exceeds that of the antagonist and downward when the opposite occurs. Following each sweep, knowledge of results is provided to the patient by displaying waveforms derived from the agonist and antagonist muscles during the sweep; this information is stored in computer memory.

THERAPEUTIC VIDEO GAMES

Although most practitioners proceed on the assumption that feedback has inherent reinforcing properties, this contention remains to be validated empirically. In many instances feedback itself may be essentially neutral, and its effectiveness may be potentiated if combined with other incentives. Santee, Keister, and Kleinman (1980) compared the effectiveness of EMG biofeedback with and without the addition of monetary incentives. EMG activity of the tibialis anterior muscle of five stroke patients, trained to perform foot dorsiflexion, was significantly greater with biofeedback plus monetary rewards than with biofeed-back alone. Still earlier, Garcia and Rusiniak (1977) proposed that feedback signals having greater hedonic value may serve to improve the magnitude and duration of change. The authors endorse this suggestion on the basis of their work described below.

Visual feedback need not be a continuous waveform. It suffices that the properties or position of an element are programmed to vary systematically with changes in myoelectric activity. Even an arcade-game-type video element can serve as a source of feedback or knowledge of results. This technique capitalizes on the enjoyable and competitive aspects of video games that are inherently engaging and reinforcing for many people. Moreover, the pleasurable act of controlling the game element also has therapeutic consequences—a point to be kept in mind where pediatric clients are concerned.

Biofeedback training using video games is used in a relatively late phase of training. In the early stages of therapy, it may prove advantageous or even necessary for a patient to perform a movement by deliberately "thinking it out" for each joint or through each step of its sequence. The game situation, however, places a premium on speed and smoothness of execution. It necessitates consigning the regulation of movements to mechanisms in the brainstem and cerebellum. "Sugar-coating" therapy by embedding it within a recreational or entertaining context helps circumvent the inevitable problem of boredom created by monotonous, but necessary, repetitive exercises.

The games have several criteria in common. Each game must be designed so that successful play requires patients to perform responses intended to ameliorate their specific motor deficits. In addition, each game must have several degrees of difficulty so that it may be used by patients with varying degrees of deficit and patients may progress within the same game. Because the effects of intervention must be gauged, it is essential that each game contain a routine for record keeping and assessment. Moreover, the measure must reflect progress, not only with regard to the game in question but also relative to other measures related to the patient's motor status.

The great flexibility afforded by the computer has enabled it to address many therapeutic needs. Video elements can be controlled by a variety of inputs. Force transducers can be coupled to these displays for the purpose of training patients to attain postural stability and to perform weight shift maneuvers needed for proper ambulation or to increase their strength. Goniometers can be used to control the video elements for the purpose of increasing active range of motion.

The elements of these games may respond to myoelectric potentials, force, or positional changes. Which of these inputs is used for a particular client depends on the therapeutic requirements and on the goals of the session. Whatever the output, it is effective only when the patient produces responses that satisfy pre-established criteria. All games have been designed to permit accommodation to different levels of ability. Such variables as speed, element size, and complexity of pattern are specified by the therapist before running each program. Several games currently in use are described below.

"Vehicle-Guide" requires the subject to guide a vehicle-shaped element traveling up the screen at a constant speed so that it is maintained on a vertical line bisecting the screen. In the EMG version, the element is displaced left or right as a function of the instantaneous difference in amplitude of the muscle pair. Its therapeutic usefulness is that it requires the player to equalize and regulate differences between a pair of muscles controlling a joint. Hence, if one member of the pair is more spastic than the other, inhibition of this muscle in relation to its counterpart is required.

In "Gran-Prix" the subject is required to keep a vehicle-shaped element on a road, the direction of which is changing in quasirandom fashion. Performance is scored by the percentage of time spent on the road and the number of crashes avoided. In the EMG version, the element is displaced left or right as a function of the instantaneous difference in EMG amplitude of an opponent pair of muscles. In the joint position version, the element moves left or right depending on the angle of the joint being monitored; this has been useful in training subjects to perform reciprocal movements, such as flexion and extension of the wrist. In both versions, vehicle speed may be preselected, or it may be varied *during* the run.

In "Basket-Catch" the subject attempts to position a cursor, resembling a basket, in order to catch a vertically falling element in the shape of a ball. Each ball falls perpendicular to the horizontal at a speed preselected by the therapist. The therapist also selects one of three basket widths. Each run consists of 20 trials, and during each trial the ball descends from one of 200 possible positions along the horizontal axis with position of descent determined in quasirandom order. Performance is measured by the number of catches. In the EMG version, basket position depends on the degree of output from a single muscle or, when a pair of muscles is being monitored, on the difference in output between the two muscles. In the case of a single muscle, the basket moves to an extreme of the field when the output arising from the monitored muscle is low and to the other extreme when the muscle is producing maximum output—the output level is individually determined before each session. Moderate output positions the basket at the halfway mark.

When two muscles are being monitored, the basket is located at the horizontal midpoint when the output of the pair is equal. The basket moves laterally whenever the output of one muscle exceeds that of its opponent by a prescribed proportion. The patient must not only maximize or minimize differences in myoelectric output from the pair but must also *sustain* their relative output once the basket is positioned until the ball arrives. Sustaining the output is not an easy task. If the ball is descending rapidly there is less time to position the basket. If it is descending slowly, there is more time to position the basket, but the position must be sustained longer. In the joint position version, the basket moves left or right, depending on the angle of the joint being monitored.

In "Video-Pong" the subject controls the position of a paddle that travels along the base of the court. The objective of the game is to bring the paddle into contact with the ball, which ricochets off the other three sides of the court, before it strikes the base. Play starts with five balls, with one being deducted each time it makes contact with the base. A point is earned for each volley, and performance is scored by the number of points accumulated during each game. Paddle size and ball velocity may be varied as needed.

Paddle position may be a function of several outputs: force generated, degree of joint displacement, or amount of EMG produced, depending on the modality being trained. All versions of the game require the subject to produce the necessary output so as to synchronize proper positioning of the paddle with the arrival of the ball at the base.

COMBINING FEEDBACK WITH OTHER MODALITIES

Frequently a patient learns to produce increased EMG output as training progresses, but not of sufficient magnitude to cause movement about the joint. In this case, the patient has reached progressively higher target levels, but then many sessions are conducted without apparent progress. At that point, additional modalities can be introduced to augment the biofeedback. Such flexibility is possible because the computer enables the displays to be controlled by a variety of transduced inputs, i.e., myoelectricity, force, or joint position. When myoelectric activity has been reliably produced but has not increased sufficiently to produce overt movement, the authors have supplemented the feedback procedures with functional electrical stimulation. In this procedure, when the waveform representing the muscle being trained attains a designated amplitude, electrical stimulation is delivered to the very muscle being monitored. In most instances, the long finger extensor (extensor digitorum communis) that produces extension at the knuckles (metacarpophalangeal joint) is the muscle involved. The electricity serves to exercise the muscle and may act as a source of somatic feedback. The feedback may be derived both from the point of stimulation and, because muscle contraction as well as joint movement is being produced, from the activated joints, muscles, and tendons as well.

The authors have used a similar procedure in treating foot-drop. If the patient is able to stand, the hamstrings (knee flexors) and quadriceps (knee extensors) are monitored. The goal is to relax the quadriceps while activating the hamstrings to the target level. This is done as the patient stands between parallel bars and begins to flex the hip at the start of the swing phase. When the hamstring level equals or exceeds the target, the stimulator is triggered, resulting in dorsiflexion of the ankle. The patient then follows through to complete the swing phase with the ankle flexed, lands on the heel, and bears weight on the foot. In this procedure, the stimulating electrodes can either be placed over the tibialis anterior (ankle dorsiflexor muscle) or over the peroneal nerve. An advantage of using the latter placement is that both eversion and dorsiflexion result.

Therefore, in addition to the seemingly endless variety of visual feedback displays, the flexibility afforded by the computer permits combined application of many modalities hitherto employed singly. The effects obtained when each of these modalities is applied alone may be potentiated when used in combination.

Nor need treatment be limited to a single level, e.g., voluntary production of myo-electricity in an individual muscle. Depending on the needs of the patient, treatment can encompass a variety of levels, ranging from the training of voluntary movement about a single joint to the training of voluntary control of posture and weight shift maneuvers involving the entire body.

VISUAL DISPLAYS IN EQUILIBRIUM AND WEIGHT SHIFT TRAINING

Some patients are hesitant about participating in therapy because of boredom and fear. Boredom can be decreased substantially by varying the context within which a necessarily repetitive response is performed. Fear, stemming from a perceived vulnerability to mishaps, can be substantially reduced by initially training the patient in a guarded environment.

The authors are currently perfecting a training instrument that provides immediate feedback, as well as knowledge of results regarding symmetry of weight distribution to the legs, the amount of postural sway, and the smoothness of weight transfer within and between feet. The training instrument minimizes the risk of accidents. A parallel bar runs along each side of the apparatus, and a therapist always stands alongside the patient. The platform is an isometric device sensitive to force and does not move. The sensitivity of the instrument is adjustable over a broad continuous range. The components of the instrument are all adjustable and can be tailored to meet individual needs. Under all conditions, visual feedback is provided to the patient on a monitor positioned at eye level.

Both patient and therapist are instantly alerted to abnormal postural movements. Thus, identification and correction of improper weight distribution occur very quickly. An advantage of this platform is that training can begin even before a patient has sufficient endurance to engage in standard ambulation therapy.

Each patient is trained during several phases of increasing complexity. The following are characteristic of all phases: (1) the platform is calibrated while the therapist checks to see that the patient is standing correctly with proper joint and axial alignment; (2) the desired position and forces required to achieve the session's criteria are adjusted; (3) the visual display informs the patient of the magnitude and direction of error, as well as the degree of success; (4) over a number of sessions the desired behavior is progressively shaped to fulfill the necessary prerequisites for advancing to the next phase.

In the initial phase, the patient must distribute weight uniformly along the lateral axis so that significant weightbearing occurs on the involved side (Fig. 14–1). The patient begins with a broad-based stance that is then narrowed as equilibrium improves.

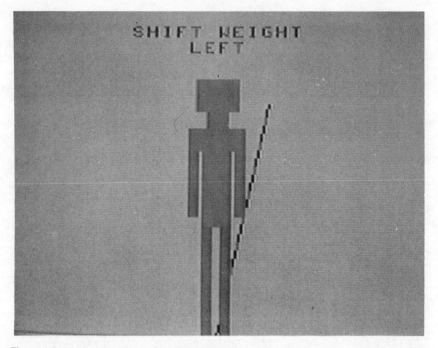

Figure 14–1 Left-right training. Subject attempts to align the vector along the lateral axis. The display illustrates the feedback the subject receives when excess weight is distributed on the left leg.

During the next phase, the patient learns to distribute weight uniformly forward and backward (Fig. 14–2). Procedures similar to those employed during the initial phase are followed.

Then the patient is trained to attain postural alignment and equilibrium along the lateral and anteroposterior (AP) axes simultaneously. This phase continues until the patient can maintain simultaneous alignment on both axes for 10 seconds on two consecutive sessions.

The next phase involves weight shift training. The video screen contains a grid pattern, the origin of which represents the intersection of the lateral/AP axes. When the patient's weight is uniformly distributed on both dimensions, the cursor is superimposed over the origin. A shift in weight distribution displaces the cursor off center. The patient then learns to perform weight shift maneuvers that position the cursor over target points distributed on the grid. Having moved the cursor to a target, the patient must reposition it over the origin, then move it to the next target, etc.

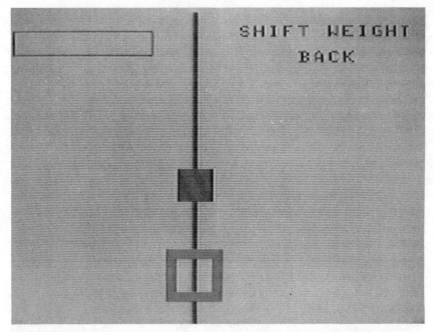

Figure 14–2 Front-back training. By shifting weight along the A/P axis, the subject attempts to fill the large box with the small one. In this display, the subject is being instructed to shift weight backward.

In the remaining phases, the patient is required to perform weight shift maneuvers that move the cursor so as to trace over a pattern displayed on the screen. At first, patients move the cursor along the pattern at their own pace. Later, they are paced by an element tracing the outline of the pattern. These predictable tracking exercises are followed by a phase in which the patient must perform weight shifting so as to track a moving target over an unpredictable path. In both of these phases the tracking tasks are scaled in difficulty, and the patient is trained on tasks that are progressively more challenging.

In the final phases, individuals learn to perform weight shift maneuvers between and within legs to model events that occur during walking. To date, the instrument has been useful in shaping postural and equilibrium control in hemiplegic patients. In addition, several patients with damage to the brainstem and cerebellum have shown dramatic improvement with this method.

SUMMARY

The procedures described in this chapter are based on the fact that feedback—either presented continuously or on a discrete basis in the form of knowledge of results—contributes significantly to the efficient acquisition of skills. Subjects can be trained to control processes or activities that are not routinely associated with volition or to regain control over functions compromised due to disease or trauma.

The principles and techniques that constitute the foundation of the authors' program are neither new nor unique; the essentials have been known for some time. Likewise, tracking procedures are hardly novel. As stated at the outset, physiologic monitoring devices capable of displaying specific bodily processes have been available and used in research for several decades. What is new and exciting is the promise that, through the refinement and joint application of these procedures, rehabilitation specialists will become better able to help their patients achieve meaningful functional improvements.

REFERENCES

Adams, J.A. (1971). A closed-loop theory of motor learning. *Journal of Motor Behavior, 3*, 111–150.

Adams, J.A. (1984). Learning of movement sequences. *Psychological Bulletin, 96*, 3–28.

Adams, J.A., Goetz, E., & Marshall, P.H. (1972). Response feedback and motor learning. *Journal of Experimental Psychology, 92*, 391–397.

Basmajian, J.V. (1963). Control and training of individual motor units. *Science, 141*, 440–441.

Basmajian, J.V. (1972). Electromyography comes of age. *Science, 176*, 603–609.

Basmajian, J.V. (1981). Biofeedback in rehabilitation: A review of principles and practices. *Archives of Physical Medicine and Rehabilitation, 62*, 469–475.

Basmajian, J.V. (1982). EMG feedback in neuromuscular control. In R.S. Surwit, R.B. Williams, Jr., A. Steptoe, & R. Biersner (Eds.), *Behavioral treatment of disease* (pp. 201–213). New York: Plenum Press.

Basmajian, J.V., Baeza, M., & Fabrigar, C. (1965). Conscious control and training of individual spinal motor neurons in normal human subjects. *Journal of New Drugs, 5*, 78–85.

Basmajian, J.V., & Mortensen, O.A. (1962). Identification and voluntary control of single motor unit activity in the tibialis anterior muscle. *Anatomical Record, 144*, 109–116.

Basmajian, J.V., & Simard, T.G. (1967). Effects of distracting movements on the control of trained motor units. *American Journal of Physical Medicine, 46*, 1427–1449.

Benton, L.A., Baker, L.L., Bowman, B.R., & Waters, R.L. (1981). *Functional electrical stimulation: A practical clinical guide*. Downey, CA.: Professional Staff Association of the Rancho Los Amigos Hospital.

Blanchard, E.B., & Epstein, L.H. (1977). The clinical usefulness of biofeedback. In M. Hersen, R.M. Eisler, & P.M. Miller (Eds.), *Progress in Behavior Modification* (pp. 163–249). New York: Academic Press.

Blanchard, E.B., & Young, L.D. (1974). Clinical application of biofeedback training: A review of evidence. *Archives of General Psychiatry, 30*, 573–589.

Brudny, J., Korein, J., Grynbaum, B.B., Belandres, P.V., & Gianutsos, J.G. (1979). Helping hemiparetics to help themselves: Sensory feedback therapy. *Journal of the American Medical Association, 241*, 814–818.

Brunnstrom, S. (1970). *Movement therapy in hemiplegia: A neurophysiological approach*. New York: Harper & Row.

Carroll, W.R., & Bandura, A. (1982). The role of visual monitoring in observational learning of action patterns: Making the unobservable observable. *Journal of Motor Behavior, 14*, 153–167.

Cleeland, C.S. (1981). Biofeedback as a clinical tool: Its use with the neurologically impaired patient. In S.B. Filskov & T.J. Boll (Eds.), *Handbook of Clinical Neuropsychology* (pp. 734–753). New York: Wiley-Interscience.

DeBacher, G. (1979). Biofeedback in spasticity control. In J.V. Basmajian (Ed.), *Biofeedback: Principles and practice for clinicians* (pp. 61–80). Baltimore: Williams & Wilkins.

De Weerdt, W., & Harrison, M.A. (1986a). Electromyographic biofeedback for stroke patients: Some practical considerations. *Physiotherapy, 72*, 106–108.

De Weerdt, W., & Harrison, M.A. (1986b). The efficacy of electromyographic feedback for stroke patients: A critical review of the main literature. *Physiotherapy, 72*, 108–118.

Engel-Sittenfeld, P. (1977). Biofeedback in the treatment of neuromuscular disorders. In J. Beatty & H. Legewie (Eds.), *Biofeedback and Behavior* (pp. 427–438). New York: Plenum Press.

Fernando, C.K., & Basmajian, J.B. (1978). Biofeedback in physical medicine and rehabilitation. *Biofeedback and Self Regulation, 3*, 435–454.

Garcia, J., & Rusiniak, K.W. (1977). Visceral feedback and the taste signal. In J. Beatty & H. Legewie (Eds.), *Biofeedback and behavior* (pp. 59–71). New York: Plenum Press.

Gianutsos, J.G., & Notterman, J.M. (1984, May). *Rehabilitative use of limb-generated EMG voltages*. Paper presented to the 10th Annual Meeting of the Association for Behavior Analysis, Nashville, TN.

Gianutsos, J.G., Eberstein, A., Krasilovsky, G., Ragnarsson, K.T., & Goodgold, J. (1986). Visually displayed EMG Feedback: Single case studies of hemiplegic upper extremity rehabilitation. *Central Nervous System Trauma, 3*, 63–76.

Glaser, R.M., Gruner, J.A., Feinberg, S.D., & Collins, S.R. (1983). Locomotion via paralyzed leg muscles: Feasibility study for a leg-propelled vehicle. *Journal of Rehabilitation Research and Development, 20*, 87–92.

Harrison, A. (1977). Augmented feedback training of motor control in cerebral palsy. *Developmental Medicine and Child Neurology, (London), 19*, 75–78.

Harrison, V.F., & Mortensen, O.A. (1962). Identification and voluntary control of single motor unit activity in the tibialis anterior muscle. *Anatomical Record, 144*, 109–116.

Hatch, J.P., Gatchel, R.J., & Harrington, R. (1982). Biofeedback: Clinical applications in medicine. In R. Satchel, A. Baum, & J. Singer (Eds.), *Handbook of psychology and health* Vol. 1 (pp. 37–73). Hillsdale, NJ: Lawrence Erlbaum Associates.

Herman, R. (1973). Augmented sensory feedback in the control of limb movement. In W.S. Fields & L.A. Leavitt (Eds.), *Neural organization and its relevance to prosthetics* (pp. 197–212). New York: Intercontinental Medical Books.

Horrobin, D.F. (1970). *Principles of biological control*. Aylesbury, Great Britain: Medical and Technical Publishing.

Hume, W.I. (1976). *Biofeedback: Research and therapy*. Montreal: Eden Press.

Inglis, J., Campbell, G., & Donald, M.W. (1976). Electromyographic biofeedback and neuromuscular reeducation. *Canadian Journal of Behavioral Science, 8*, 299–323.

Keefe, F.J. & Surwit, R.S. (1978). Electromyographic biofeedback: Behavioral treatment of neuromuscular disorders. *Journal of Behavioral Medicine, 1*, 13–24.

Kottke, F.J. (1974). Historia obscura Hemiplegiae. *Archives of Physical Medicine and Rehabilitation, 55*, 4–13.

Kralj, A., Bajd, T., Turk, R., Krajnik, J., & Benko, H. (1983). Gait restoration in paraplegic patients: A feasibility study using multi-channel surface electrode FES. *Journal of Rehabilitation Research and Development, (Washington), 20*, 3–20.

Kralj, A., & Vodovnik, L. (1977). Functional electrical stimulation of the extremities. *Journal of Medical Engineering and Technology, (London), 1*, 12–15.

Leiper, C.I., Miller, A., Lang, L., & Herman, R. (1981). Sensory feedback for head control in cerebral palsy. *Physical Therapy, 61*, 512–518.

Moskowitz, E., Lightbody, F.E., & Freitag, N.S. (1972). Long-term follow-up of the poststroke patient. *Archives of Physical Medicine and Rehabilitation, 53*, 167–172.

Office of Scientific and Health Reports. (1976). *Neurological and communicative disorders* (NIH Publication No. 77-152). Washington, DC: Office of Scientific and Health Reports, U.S. Department of Health, Education, and Welfare.

Petrofsky, J.S., & Phillips, C.A. (1984). The use of functional electrical stimulation for rehabilitation of spinal cord injured patients. *Central Nervous System Trauma, 1*, 29–45.

Phillips, C.A., Petrofsky, J.S., Hendershot, D.M., & Stafford, D. (1984). Functional electrical exercise: A comprehensive approach for physical conditioning of the spinal cord injured patient. *Orthopedics, 7*, 1112–1123.

Ray, W.J., Raczynski, J.M., Rogers, T., & Kimball, W.H. (1979). *Evaluation of clinical biofeedback*. New York: Plenum Press.

Santee, J.L., Keister, M.E., & Kleinman, K.M. (1980). Incentives to enhance the effects of electromyographic feedback training in stroke patients. *Biofeedback and Self-Regulation, 5*, 51–56.

Sherrington, C.S. (1897). On reciprocal innervation of antagonistic muscles. Third note. *Proceedings of the Royal Society, 60*, 414–417.

Sherrington, C.S. (1906). *The integrative action of the nervous system*. New Haven: Yale University Press.

Smith, K.U. (1966). Cybernetic theory and analysis of learning. In E.A. Bilodeau (Ed.), *Acquisition of skill* (pp. 425–488). New York: Academic Press.

Smith, K.U., & Henry, J.P. (1967). Cybernetic foundations for rehabilitation. *American Journal of Physical Medicine, 46*, 379–467.

Taft, L.T., Delagi, E.F., Wilkie, O.L., & Abramson, A.S. (1962). Critique of rehabilitative technics in treatment of cerebral palsy. *Archives of Physical Medicine and Rehabilitation, 43*, 238–243.

Wagman, I.H., Pierce, D.S., & Burger, R.E. (1965). Proprioceptive influence in volitional control of individual motor units. *Nature, (London), 207*, 957–958.

Wolf, S.L. (1983). Electromyographic biofeedback application to stroke patients: A critical review. *Physical Therapy, 63*, 1448–1459.

Yates, A.J. (1980). *Biofeedback and the modification of behavior*. New York: Plenum Press.

Chapter 15

Behavior Modification in Rehabilitation: Principles and Clinical Strategies

Jeffrey C. Levenkron, Ph.D.

A fundamental objective for the patient who enters a program of medical rehabilitation is to achieve behavioral change. This holds true for patients with virtually all types of physical and medical disability. Patients with neurologic deficits, neuromuscular dysfunction, orthopedic limitations, cardiac impairments, or any form of stable, life-altering chronic disease state are expected to change to varying degrees the performance of everyday life responsibilities. New life patterns of personal hygiene, self-care, employment, and social functioning must be established and durably maintained. Conversely, highly rehearsed and routine habits may need to be modulated or entirely abandoned. Furthermore, the social networks in which the patient lives—family, friends, and other social contacts— are also challenged by the task of change. Thus, the entire personal and social ecology of the patient entering a program of rehabilitation must be reshaped (Fordyce, 1981).

This chapter examines the set of clinical methods commonly referred to as behavior modification that can aid rehabilitation professionals in helping patients to meet successfully the challenge of behavior change. In its simplest meaning, the term "behavior modification" is understood to refer to a methodology for specifying the current forces that seem to influence parameters of human performance. It denotes a deliberate effort to vary these controlling factors in a systematic fashion in order to achieve change in a specified direction and magnitude (Bandura, 1969; Kanfer & Philips, 1970). Since the popularization of the term in the early 1960s, the principles upon which methods of behavior modification rest have broadened considerably. No longer does this term refer to the relatively narrow laboratory-based model from which it was derived. Its melding with concepts drawn from other spheres of applied psychology (Meichenbaum, 1977) paved the way for more widespread application. Although useful as a category of clinical methods, the term "behavior modification" itself has fallen somewhat out of fashion in recent years (Krasner, 1976). One reason why the term has lost some value is that many users of this clinical methodology, especially in applications to problems of health and disease, have misconstrued it as a fixed set of techniques, rather than a process of *clinical reasoning*.

Behavior modification reflects a way to conceptualize and identify treatment options that can foster the behavior change objectives of rehabilitation. This chapter discusses its underlying concepts, theoretical principles, and specific clinical strategies separately in order to make clear the utility of this method of clinical reasoning and intervention. At the *conceptual level*, it is important to consider that behavior modification is a clinical method that is compatible with other concepts in applied psychology and psychotherapy (Fensterheim & Glazer, 1983; Wachtel, 1977). The effective use of behavioral methods requires an appreciation of how these other concepts, such as personality, relate to clinical applications. Moreover, the *theoretical principles* from which behavioral methods can be derived must be understood in their human dimension. Caregivers in rehabilitation settings treat people, not "organisms." Understanding these principles in a language that is clinically meaningful can only facilitate the effective use of behavioral methods. Finally, the challenge of *strategically employing clinical methods* of behavior modification is to meet numerous practical constraints that operate in medical rehabilitation settings.

Behavior modification is a fundamental component of the rehabilitation process. Despite the need to promote change systematically among rehabilitation patients, the methods of behavior modification are most frequently discussed in theoretical terms (Fordyce, 1982). Typically, only the theory of behavior modification is included in programs in professional preparation for physicians, nurses, occupational therapists, and physical therapists, and many rehabilitation workers continue to have limited familiarity with the practical use and application of the methods of behavior modification. Unfortunately, abstract or theoretical understanding is an inadequate substitute for knowledge of clinical implementation procedures. The supervision of clinical methods for behavior modification remains the responsibility of the psychologist for the rehabilitation team.

A second obstacle that limits the use of behavior modification methods is the negative connotation of the term. Many health professionals hold the view that providing relief of suffering and gratifying the immediate needs of patients with serious medical illnesses should be conducted in an unconditional manner. The mistaken notion that behavior modification requires sacrificing "the caring posture" has dampened enthusiasm for its use by many health care providers.

A third and related obstacle to the use of behavior modification arises from the terminology that is used by many of its practitioners. Behavior modification was initially derived from experimental or laboratory-based models and to this day retains this legacy of a highly technical, mechanistic sounding terminology. One consequence of these historical roots has been to foster an image of clinical practice that is devoid of compassion for the patient. Indeed, this terminology is seen as antithetical to the fundamental precepts upon which humanistic medical care has been established. This problem in language often leads health care providers who ultimately are responsible for implementing behavioral treatments to reject them as incompatible with acceptable clinical practices.

A fourth obstacle arises from the unrealistic expectations of behavior modification's effectiveness. If immediate and dramatic results are not forthcoming following a planned intervention, staff members may conclude that "behavior modification has failed." Thus, the entire intervention methodology is considered to have failed when in fact only one particular application has not produced a therapeutic benefit. This failure indicates the need to revise the intervention.

This chapter examines the practical use of behavior modification in rehabilitation settings. Particular attention is paid to the objections and obstacles that have curtailed the effective use of this form of clinical intervention. First, certain factors that typically operate within medical settings are discussed. These factors impose important constraints, as well as opportunities, that require behavioral interventions to be carefully tailored and distinguished from their use in other (e.g., psychiatric) settings. Second, the principles that are central to the development of a behavioral approach in rehabilitation are discussed in terms that illustrate their suitability for clinical application by nonbehaviorally trained health care providers. The last section of this chapter describes clinical strategies for behavior modification that must be considered for any and all applications.

MEDICAL APPLICATIONS

Many clinical methods of behavior modification were originally developed for use in inpatient mental health settings and to be applied to chronic psychiatric problems (cf. Hersen & Bellack, 1978; Paul & Lentz, 1977). The medical setting, by contrast, imposes a different set of constraints. For example, within psychiatric settings it is commonplace to elicit from the patient the goals and objectives of therapy; as the patient comes having already identified some specific behavioral problem, one can readily establish a therapeutic contract with the patient's active participation. Alternatively, the medical setting typically puts the onus of responsibility for "treatment" on the health care provider. The caregiver has an implied dominance in authority and responsibility that renders the patient subordinate. Treatment provided by the rehabilitation team is something that is *done to* the patient; therapy in a psychiatric setting is something that is *done with* the patient. This subtle distinction has profound implications for sharing and owning responsibility for therapeutic progress.

Several additional features of the medical setting influence the practice of behavior modification. First, in medicine there is a substantial emphasis on treating problems, either involving behavior or health. The elimination of problems or removal of symptoms is the goal. In contrast, the behavioral approach emphasizes not so much what is to be removed, but instead what is to be established. This is more than a semantic distinction. When asked what a patient should be doing with respect to a particular performance requirement, it is necessary, within a behavioral approach, to specify the precise activity. It is more common in medical settings to find out from staff members what the patient *has not* been doing. Unfortunately, the focus on negative behaviors often does not provide a satisfactory basis for developing a behavioral treatment program.

A feature related to the focus on eliminating problems is the tendency for the medical system within rehabilitation medicine to ignore indications of therapeutic success. For example, the nonproblem patient is often seen as "unremarkable." This, of course, runs contrary to a fundamental principle of behavior modification. For example, verbal expressions or motor behaviors suggesting weakness or fatigue may lead to a particular kind of "reinforcing" response on the part of the medical team. In contrast, successful performance may be ignored by the staff, which is contrary to the arrangement of environmental contingencies derived from the behavioral perspective, i.e., ignoring undesirable behaviors ("weakness and fatigue") and reinforcing desirable ones ("vigorous or successful performance").

A final constraint imposed by the medical care system is that certain medical practices take priority and thereby make a behavioral intervention less practicable. For example, certain potentially dangerous behaviors, such as pain behaviors, falling, failure to eat, and the like, cannot be easily ignored and can capture the rehabilitation team's attention in a way that may only serve to reinforce a continuing problem. Medical conditions determine what behavior change is necessary, but may also obstruct the type of intervention that can be used.

CONCEPTUAL ORIENTATION

Behavior modification reflects a conceptual approach to the process of behavioral influence. This conceptual analysis of the rehabilitation process is best described by Fordyce (1982). He identifies four general problem areas that can be understood in behavioral teams: behavioral deficits, behavioral excesses, naturalistic punishment, and reinforcement of behavior.

Behavior modification is *not* merely a set of procedures or techniques. Rather, the procedures and techniques are directly derived from the way in which rehabilitation tasks can be conceptualized in behavioral terms. Once a clear behavioral conceptualization is established, the actual methods are limited only by the creativity of the therapist involved. For example, reinforcement is not a thing, but a process; that is, it is something you "do," rather than something you "have." If a physical therapist chooses to reinforce the performance of an individual patient by varying the level of attention and praise (Trotter & Inman, 1968), this is experienced by some patients as "reinforcing," whereas others may find the response "punishing." Some patients feel embarrassed, undeserving, or simply oppositional when praised by a therapist. Thus, some individuals may perform better when left alone, rather than when closely monitored. For one patient, praise is a reinforcer; for another, being left alone while performing a physical therapy task may be a reinforcer.

No professional discipline or treatment team member is solely responsible for a behavior modification program. That is, behavioral methods can be fully integrated into virtually all rehabilitation tasks. The psychologist, as an expert in this area, could provide consultation and help generate alternative ideas about a behavioral program.

Finally, if behavior change is to be maintained, those individuals who influence the behavior of the patient need to be enlisted in this systematic process. That is, behavior modification does not "fix" the patient. Instead, the interaction of that patient's social environment is strategically and systematically designed, which may include rearranging naturally occurring events in a new contingent manner. Or, an entirely new set of consequences may be established within that patient's environment.

PRINCIPLES

Since its inception, the clinical use of behavior modification has been closely tied to principles of learning theory. Several classic texts are organized according to different theories of learning and conditioning (Bandura 1969; Kanfer & Phillips 1970). This section reviews the principles from which clinical strategies of behavior modification can be derived. A deliberate effort is made to avoid tying any particular principle to a particular problem. Others have reviewed the problem-focused application of behavioral methods in rehabilitation medicine (Ince, 1976, 1980), and there is an extensive body of literature that specifically concerns the application of behavior modification to patients with cognitive deficits arising from neurologic trauma and/or disease (Eames & Wood, 1985; Powell, 1981); a review of this area is deliberately omitted from the present chapter. Instead, the thesis presented earlier in this chapter emphasizes that principles of behavior modification can be flexibly employed to develop clinical interventions spanning the entire range of rehabilitation problems.

Applied Operant Methods

Historically, behavior modification has been dominated by the use of operant conditioning methods (Kazdin, 1984). An operant behavior is a function of its consequences; operant methods emphasize procedures that alter behavior by manipulating or controlling a consequence. Cues that signal these behaviors are important only insofar as they set the stage for a particular behavior that in turn leads to its controlling consequence. This classical formulation offers a powerful scheme to view the development and maintenance of behaviors that are required as part of the process of rehabilitation. The principles for developing or creating a behavior modification intervention utilizing operant methods are described below.

Specifying the Target

A behavioral intervention always begins with the precise specification of a focus or *target* of treatment. A number of characteristics seem to be essential in selecting rehabilitation targets. First, the behavior must be observable. For example, a paraplegic patient who must develop the skill of transfer to and from a wheelchair needs to learn a precise and identifiable set of motor behaviors about which agreement can be easily reached. Similarly, wheelchair "push-ups," a critical hygienic activity, must be incorporated into the ongoing daily life activities (Malament, Dunn, & Davis, 1975). Each of these behaviors is not only observable but can also be counted and monitored when a criterion frequency must be reached. The typical parameters important in specifying a target behavior permit observing or monitoring the (1) frequency, (2) intensity, and/or (3) duration of the behavior. That is, each target should be quantified along one or more of these parameters. Moreover, this must be done in an unambiguous way so that agreement between the patient and the staff member involved can be achieved.

Having specified a target behavior, a range of questions must be explored. Does this behavior lie within the repertoire of the patient? That is, does the patient know how to perform this behavior at all, or will the patient need to learn an entirely new set of skills? The critical distinction between targets that require new learning or "acquisition" and targets that necessitate altering the shape or topography of existing behavior has implications for selecting treatment methods. For example, a paraplegic patient who needs to learn to perform a wheelchair transfer will in all likelihood be developing a new set of motor skills. The acquisition itself may be the target of a behavior modification intervention. A rather discrete pattern of movements may be linked together in steps that can be rehearsed until they are performed smoothly according to some criterion. An entirely separate question may concern the frequency with which an already acquired behavior must be performed. For example, the motor act of wheelchair push-ups can be fairly readily acquired. Yet, the frequency with which this important activity is performed may easily be the target of a behavior modification program. The frequency of push-ups might be increased by associating the behavior with a specific cue that becomes a *signal*. Common cues, such as talking on the telephone, or special cues, such as a timer, can be employed. Different intervention methods are indicated, depending upon whether the aim is to have the patient acquire complex new behaviors or increase performance frequency.

Functional Analysis

Functional analysis refers to understanding or identifying the relation between a specific target behavior and the consequence(s) that maintains or influences this behavior. For any clinical intervention, a functional analysis may be conducted for both current behaviors—already within the patient's repertoire—as well as those behaviors to be acquired. Separate functional analyses for target behaviors that require acquisition or performance often reveal entirely distinct behavior-consequence relationships that may form the basis of a behavior modification program.

At the heart of the functional analysis is understanding how specific consequences alter behaviors. Figure 15–1 illustrates a system for understanding the relation between behaviors and consequences that leads to change in a predicted direction. Four sets of consequences exist, which are defined within the cells of this figure. The types of consequence for particular behaviors are noted in the two columns. As indicated in the top margin, for any given behavior, a consequence is either delivered or removed in a contingent fashion. The effect of these consequences on the target behavior is specified in the rows of this matrix. The measurable parameters of a target behavior either increase or decrease. For any given intervention, the nature of the consequence—either delivered or removed—can be paired with the planned or intended direction of behavior change, i.e., the target behavior increases or decreases.

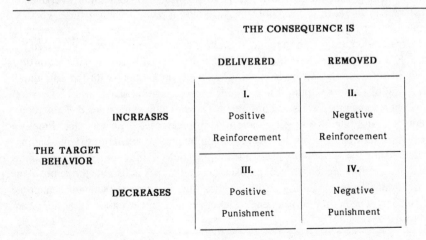

THE CONSEQUENCE IS

	DELIVERED	REMOVED
INCREASES	I. Positive Reinforcement	II. Negative Reinforcement
DECREASES	III. Positive Punishment	IV. Negative Punishment

THE TARGET BEHAVIOR

Figure 15–1 Matrix for the Functional Analysis of Behavior; each cell is defined according to the direction of change observed in a target behavior and the manner in which a consequence is operationalized.

In cell I, a specific consequence is delivered that leads to an increase in the frequency, intensity, or duration of the behavioral parameter. This is the typical definition of positive reinforcement. In cell II, the nature of the consequence is to "lose something" that, in turn, leads to an increase in behavior. This is the definition of negative reinforcement and most typically operates in situations that motivate avoidance behavior. For example, a behavior that is sustained by removing something unpleasant operates under the principle of negative reinforcement.

Cell III identifies a consequence that is delivered, which, in turn, results in a reduction in behavioral parameters. This is most typically thought of as punishment or, in its technical form, positive punishment. That is, the consequence given to the patient is intended to reduce the likelihood of a behavior. Finally, cell IV also refers to a reduction in behavior parameters, one associated with the removal of a consequence. This too is punishment and is considered negative punishment or "time-out from positive reinforcement." When a consequence is labeled as "positive," it refers to the delivery of some contingent event; the term "positive" is used in a technical sense *without* any implied value judgment, i.e., desirable or good. Similarly, negative consequences do not denote undesirable events, but instead refer to some type of contingent removal.

This diagram is surprisingly complex, yet surprisingly complete in the analysis of behavior-consequence relationships. It is helpful to consider this set of relationships in an alternative, less behavioristic language. For example, cell I typically involves delivering a reward or positive reinforcer, such as praise, physical contact, or any other set of consequences that provides some personal, emotional, or physical gratification. Cell II refers to taking away something aversive to instigate an *increase* in behavior. Thus, avoiding pain through action, whether emotional or physical, is typically under the control of negative reinforcement. Procrastination, escape, or a range of everyday life experiences are motivated by people's efforts to reduce the likelihood that they will feel some discomfort. Cell III refers to delivering something aversive, in keeping with the colloquial meaning of the term "punishment." For example, being scolded, criticized, or receiving some other aversive consequence is quite punishing indeed. Those consequences are intended to get people to stop (decrease) their behavior. Finally, punishment often involves the loss of something pleasurable or gratifying. Paying a fine, losing the opportunity to engage in some pleasurable activity, or some other loss of a gratifier are all forms of punishment in that they constitute the removal or "time-out" from something positive. Thus, the direction of behavior change is defined by whether the consequence delivers or takes away either a gratifier or an aversive experience.

Defining the Consequence

Some experiences seem both intuitively and universally to be gratifying. For example, praise, encouragement, and other socially conveyed support are, for most people, reinforcers. There are, of course, exceptions to this observation. Some individuals are assaulted by a compliment, and in response to praise, they may feel uncomfortable and withdraw. For such a person, praise is unlikely to function effectively as a reinforcer.

Aversive consequences may follow the same pattern. Some patients find that closely supervised and physically intrusive assistance is unpleasant and aversive. Such individuals might be motivated to learn new skills that permit them to regain independence and self-reliance. Thus, a particular individual may want to "escape" the physical assistance necessary for self-care by learning selected independent living skills. Another patient may, however, experience close monitoring or supervision as gratification, which would reinforce and sustain dependence and functional limitation.

Determining the likely effect of a particular consequence upon behavior frequently requires inference based upon personality assessment. More powerfully, the effect of a consequence can be determined by observing its existing behavior-consequence relation. For example, a nurse may notice that the more she helps a particular patient, the less the patient seems to do. Conversely, another patient may fight to do more things independently and reject nursing assistance. Thus, the identical degree of physical assistance has entirely opposite effects, depending on the personalities of the two patients. Consequences can be altered subtly on a trial-and-error basis to determine if a particular behavior increases or decreases. Further observation can be used to determine if the correct consequence has been selected.

Selecting the consequence to be used in a behavioral intervention can be guided by the Premack principles (Premack, 1965): Any high frequency behavior can be used to reinforce a lower frequency behavior by establishing a contingent relationship between the two. That is, in an unrestrained setting, those behaviors for which the frequency is relatively higher can be made contingent upon behaviors of lower frequency if the intention is to increase the latter. To take an example, if getting dressed and out of bed is a low frequency behavior and listening to music is a high frequency behavior, a contingency can be established; if the patient gets dressed (the target behavior), then he can listen to the radio (positive reinforcement). This contingency should lead to an increase in the frequency of getting dressed.

By the same token, a low frequency behavior that is made contingent upon a high frequency behavior will, in effect, serve as a *relative* punishing consequence. That is, a low frequency behavior is one that is not freely selected or chosen to be performed when unrestricted. Behaviors that are low in frequency, presumably because they are aversive, can serve as "punishing" consequences when imposed in a contingent fashion. This arrangement forms the obverse of the positive reinforcement arrangement noted above. Keeping in mind that punishment is intended to reduce the likelihood of a behavior, consequences of this variety tend to be utilized in a relatively limited way. For example, a patient, in a burst of temper and frustration, smashes objects on the floor. This behavior may be "punished" by restricting the patient for a defined period of time and requiring the patient to clean up the mess (positive punishment). Alternatively, the patient may lose the opportunity to engage in enjoyable recreational activities (negative punishment or "time-out"). The generalizable Premack principle presents one particularly useful way to define consequences to be used in behavioral interventions. It suggests that one can identify likely reinforcers and punishers by observing which behaviors are *more* or *less* frequent. High frequency behaviors are potential reinforcers; low frequency behaviors are potential punishers. As an alternative to observation, obtaining a careful and complete history often permits identification of those high and low frequency behaviors that may be targeted to produce a therapeutic effect.

Creating Behavioral Programs

Behavioral interventions are usually organized around a specific behavioral program. This program identifies the specific target behaviors, the particular skills or complex responses needed to establish this target behavior, and the consequences that may follow performance of either the skill training component or the target behavior. Figure 15–2 is an example of a form that can be used in creating a behavioral treatment program.

The column on the left of Figure 15–2 identifies the target behaviors that are specified as the goals or objectives of the behavior modification program. The middle section can be used to describe in detail the specific therapeutic tasks, exercises, rehearsals, or new responses that are required in order to achieve the target behavior. Finally, the column on the right identifies the potential consequences that are tied to either the skill training requirements or performance of the target behavior. Using this system of program organization, a clear consensus can be reached for the goals of a behavioral program—that is, the target behavior—the skill training or response requirements, and the nature of the specific consequences to be employed.

Specifying the Target

Target behaviors represent the primary performance objectives of a behavioral program. In its most basic form, the target behavior describes a discrete performance requirement that can be observed and measured. This performance may be a response already within the patient's repertoire; for example, "John will request assistance from his nurse by using the call button placed at the bedside," or "Mary will practice independent ambulation for three laps per day between 8:00 and 10:00 A.M." These highly concrete, explicit, and easily verifiable target behaviors may represent an important part of the patient care management and/or

Figure 15–2 A Treatment Contract Used to Document a Behavior Modification Program

BEHAVIORAL CONTRACT

Page One

DATE _____

Treatment Team:

PATIENT _____

Clinical Psychologist: _____

Primary Nurse: _____

Associate Nurse: _____

Occupational/
Physical Therapist: _____

Attending Physician: _____

Social Worker: _____

TARGET BEHAVIORS   SKILL TRAINING PROGRAM   CONTINGENCY BEHAVIORS

(continued on back)

rehabilitation program. Alternatively, a target behavior may reflect a future goal for which new learning is required, e.g., "Jane will dress herself independently every morning." This requires learning specific skills that permit attainment of the target behavior objective and may follow from a set of exercises or therapeutic activities. Finally, a third type of target behavior is more intangible, but helps orient the staff's efforts with a particular patient. For example, "Mary will feel that members of her treatment team are responsive to her goals," or "Bill will be an active participant on his treatment team."

The target behavior is intentionally written in a way that emphasizes an increase in some behavioral parameter, i.e., the behavior will occur with greater frequency, intensity, or duration. The most successful behavioral programs seek to establish an increase in behavior. When confronted with the need to decrease behavior, an initial strategy is to create the incompatible response. That is, an excess behavior that is seen as undesirable or disruptive to the treatment process can be handled by creating and reinforcing those behaviors with which it is incompatible. One example noted above might be the patient who calls his nurse by shouting from his hospital bed. Instead of "punishing" shouting behavior, the nurse can reinforce the method of communication that is identified as the target behavior: calling the nurse by using the bedside call button. In this way, only desirable behaviors are the focus of treatment. This approach may be successful for two reasons. First, stating the behavior that is to be established clearly defines the performance expectation that is desired. If one were to simply punish the shouting behavior, it is not entirely clear what the patient should be doing instead of shouting. Second, telling the patient *not* to do something creates a kind of behavioral vacuum, a state of affairs that can be expected to be short-lived. More importantly, it can provoke an oppositional response from the patient that is avoided when the positive behaviors are the focus.

A handy rule of thumb is that a target behavior should contain an explicit description of the active and positive behavior as its objective. If the specified target behavior reflects the negative behavior that will elicit aversive control, the behavioral program is less likely to succeed.

New and Complex Behaviors

A behavioral program often establishes a novel response as the goal of intervention. This may require substantial rehearsal and shaping, for the aim is acquisition of new skills. Even if the components of these behaviors are initially within the response capacity of a patient, rote practice is necessary to create a smoothly functioning behavioral pattern.

One must also determine how to set the entire pattern in motion. Cue control represents a way in which the behavior is triggered. The task that faces rehabilitation patients is to "remember" to utilize new skills. Identifying a salient cue to which the new response patterns can be connected offers one way to instigate and solidify this behavior change. The cue may be a tangible object, a particular routine or pattern, or a specific activity. In each case, the new behavior becomes associated with a reliable stimulus that serves as a trigger. Alternatively, the cue may trigger a specific self-instruction that in turn leads to the execution of a behavior.

Artificial cues are occasionally helpful. For example, signals produced by timers or programmable buzzers can be used by the patient as "prompts," e.g., a reminder to do push-ups. If the patient seems to forget to execute certain acts, other reminders, such as notes, colored dots, hand appliances, or any visual prompt, may increase the likelihood of the desired performance.

Managing Consequences

The second avenue to explore in any behavioral treatment program involves creating the motivating set of consequences that can be used to alter a pattern of behavior. As noted earlier, if an effort is made to increase the frequency of a particular behavior, the nature of this consequence involves both positive and negative reinforcement. Most behavioral treatment programs rely heavily on the use of positive reinforcing events or activities as a source of motivation for performance of a particular behavior. These reinforcers can be negotiated and contracted with the patient. Discussing a negotiated agreement with the patient often leads to the explicit contract that identifies how a particular consequence will follow a particular behavior. In some instances, the reinforcer is entirely under the control of a staff member. The best example of this is social reinforcement. A patient who eats independently might receive greater social attention during mealtime than during those times when assistance is required. That is, the nurse strategically starts a conversation with the patient when the latter is eating with the necessary appliance. However, when the nurse must physically assist the process, conversation is limited. In a similar manner, performing a physical activity task may lead to social interaction and even explicit praise, whereas nonperformance does not produce this same social consequence.

In some instances, the reinforcers are under the control of the patient. At such times, a staff member requests that the patient relinquish possession of the reinforcer in order to make it contingent upon execution of a particular behavior. Obviously, it takes considerable persuasion, along with a clear and sincere rationale, to make this type of therapeutic arrangement possible. The patient must be persuaded that arranging for contingent access to a personal possession—for example, a favorite book that otherwise is available on a noncontingent basis—can be a powerful way to "motivate oneself" to change. Thus, the attribution of control and "choice" must reside within the patient. In doing so, it is important to emphasize that patients really make contracts with themselves. A patient who gives a radio to a staff member and regains it in exchange for performance of a particular behavior has made a considerable commitment to a process of change that must always remain the focal objective.

Contingencies that employ negative reinforcement are more difficult to implement in a clinical setting, as one must arrange for a relatively aversive experience that can be terminated upon execution of a particular behavior. In isolation, this strategy rarely works. However, when paired with a positive event that replaces the aversive state, this strategy of differential reinforcement becomes quite powerful. That is, a particular behavior may be instigated because it terminates an unpleasant state. However, following escape from discomfort, continuing the behavior can also lead to additional positive consequences. Thus, the behavior might be initiated because it is negatively reinforced, but it is continued because it is positively reinforced. This may be one of the more powerful uses of differential reinforcement. A commonplace and naturally occurring negative reinforcer may involve therapeutic leave out of the hospital. For many patients, a hospital stay is a boring or confining experience, especially on the weekends. Therapeutic leave ("escape") that is made contingent upon achieving some specified performance goal, such as in the physical therapy gym, may provide an incentive for increasing exercise participation. Moreover, while out on a pass, the natural positive consequences—having fun, feeling successful or independent, and receiving gratification from others who witness the newly acquired physical skills—further strengthen the target behavior, i.e., physical therapy performance. Such an arrangement illustrates how positive and negative reinforcers can operate simultaneously on a single target behavior. Additional examples of naturally occurring states include relative social isolation, activity restriction, or, on the contrary, an intrusive and closely supervised activity.

Classical Conditioning Methods

The second major theory of learning from which behavioral modification principles have been derived is classical conditioning. Clinical strategies based upon classical conditioning tend to be less commonly employed in rehabilitation settings. Unlike the operant methods, which reflect a theory of motivation for acquiring new habits, the classical conditioning strategies seem best suited for altering behaviors that are obstructed by some autonomic-based response, such as anxiety.

Anxiety, fear, and tension can drastically hinder new learning and lead to avoidance. In the rehabilitation setting, these emotional responses can severely hamper progress in therapy. Procedures of behavior change that address these problems almost always focus on weakening the strength of the autonomic or anxious response and reversing the inclination of avoidance.

Weakening Anxiety

Methods of direct intervention to weaken the response of anxiety have been the focus of a large literature in behavior therapy. Treatment of anxiety through relaxation training and its associated therapeutic tactics has been found to be especially effective. One way of conducting relaxation therapy that seems particularly effective is to present it as a technique of self-control, as described by Goldfried (1971).

A related strategy involves biofeedback training, which trains the patient to control physiologic events (see Chapter 14). Rather than directly targeting anxiety, biofeedback is most often used (1) to modify musculoskeletal responses that accompany anxiety or (2) to increase the patient's awareness and control over the subtle variations of the sensory experience. Although overlap between relaxation training and biofeedback clearly exists, the use of biofeedback is especially helpful when there is a need for some new perception of sensory experience that may be tied to a neuromuscular response. The use of biofeedback in rehabilitation has focused on bladder control, heart rate training, and neuromuscular retraining.

Confronting Avoidance Behavior

Anxiety-related problems typically prompt an attempt to escape or avoid the fear-provoking situation. If rehabilitation tasks are anxiety-provoking and elicit avoidance behavior, then therapeutic progress will be hampered. The behavioral strategies for anxiety-based avoidance emphasize exposure and direct confrontation of the anxiety-provoking situation. Theoretically, a reduction in anxiety will follow as a consequence of habituation. However, the tendency to avoid becomes, in itself, habitual. Therefore, considerable effort is required to arrange for direct exposure to those situations that have come to produce avoidance.

CLINICAL STRATEGIES

A common limitation of the literature on behavior modification in rehabilitation medicine is the wide gap that exists between theory and clinical practice; most discussion is generally given either to the learning theory rationale or to data-based demonstration of clinical effectiveness. This section describes several vital elements involved in the implementation of a behavior modification program, elements that are often entirely ignored or overlooked in written descriptions about behavioral methods.

The effective implementation of behavior modification with an individual patient requires a number of clinical skills, including the following: (1) negotiating the behavior modification program with the patient to formulate a contract; (2) presenting the program to the patient in a way that ensures maximum participation and establishes realistic expectations on the part of the patient, as well as the treatment team; (3) for programs employing fixed consequences, imposing these consequences in a manner that ensures consistency and effectiveness; and (4) revising the behavioral program contract. These practical issues are discussed below, and their application is illustrated through presentation of several case studies.

Implementing the Program

Negotiation

As noted earlier, negotiation is central in the development of behavior modification goals or deciding on the use of specific reinforcers. Indeed, the entire process often culminates in a written contract between the patient and the staff that makes explicit the agreed plan. How is this negotiation to proceed?

The first step is for the staff member and patient to agree upon a behavior change goal. This process may begin when a problem has been identified by the staff and discussed with the patient. It is important that the problem be reframed as a positive goal. The patient might have certain goals not shared by the staff, and vice versa. Thus, it may be useful to give the patient an assignment to develop a set of behavioral goals in response to the staff's perception of a problem. This crucial first step must proceed in a give-and-take fashion. Negotiation means compromise on both sides.

One useful tactic is to set aside special contact time between the patient and a staff member for the sole purpose of negotiating some behavior change goal and/or a behavioral contract. This should not take place at the same time as other nursing care, physical therapy activities, etc. are being conducted. A series of such meetings, perhaps at the bedside, that involve this kind of open-ended discussion helps build the alliance that is needed for a contractual therapeutic intervention.

Even more important is the active participation of the patient in developing a behavioral program. Giving the patient a homework assignment, for example, to generate a written list of goals, suggestions for change, or even a list of possible incentives that can be used as reinforcers makes the patient a true participant in this process of treatment. Similarly, jointly preparing a written draft of the treatment contract can facilitate active participation and promote a shared sense of responsibility for the treatment.

Negotiation provides an avenue to "short-circuit" the patient's resistance to behavior change. The patient who is a party to the development of a behavior modification contract has a greater stake in its success and has less motivation to sabotage the process. Negotiation helps avoid development of an adversarial relationship; instead, patients and staff become allies in the treatment process.

Presenting the Contract

The behavior modification program should be an official element of the patient's overall treatment plan. It needs both an introduction to the treatment process, as well as endorsement by all treatment team members, including the patient. After a contract has been negotiated, it should be reviewed by the staff at a treatment team meeting. It may also be useful to have the patient in attendance at such team meetings, if that is an acceptable practice for the facility. For example, team meetings can be scheduled as a conference or conducted as patient rounds. This creates an important collaborative atmosphere and enhances the patient's commitment.

Treatment contracts, as official components of a hospital record, should be formally written out, perhaps typed, and shared among all members of the team. The patient should retain a copy, a copy should appear in the hospital chart record, and additional copies may be given to other treatment team or family members. As a symbol of commitment and endorsement, the contract can be signed or initialed.

The treatment team setting is a particularly useful place to review the expectations and rationale for the behavior modification program. It is important that the consequences be portrayed as logically consistent with the overall objectives. Doing so decreases patient resistance and generates more enthusiasm for the process of change. For example, a therapeutic pass may be used as a consequence to reinforce achievement by a patient of a particular independent living skill by meeting some requisite performance criterion. Similarly, a nursing staff member can devote more time to a patient and thereby provide social reinforcement when the patient's behavior does not divert time and energy for some other caregiving activities. Finally, making certain reinforcers available on a contingent basis can be presented as a luxury, so that it does not undermine continued progress. For example, listening to the radio after having practiced certain self-care skills is analogous to watching television after one finishes assigned homework.

When presenting a treatment contract, it is important to convey to the staff and the patient an expectation that is neither overly optimistic nor pessimistic. Behavior modification is not a "quick fix" for a problem. By observing that change is "hard work," or "takes tremendous effort," a two-fold message is conveyed: first, that energy and commitment on the part of the patient will be necessary for it to be successful; and second, that the staff understands and empathizes with this needed energy output, but nevertheless, expects that behavior change will occur. This strategy, sometimes described as paradoxical pessimism (Weeks & L'Abate, 1982), is often highly motivating.

Imposing Consequences

Staff often feel uncomfortable when it is necessary to impose a consequence for behavior, especially when a patient fails to exhibit a behavior for which positive reinforcement would be provided. When punishment consequences are used, as in the case of time-out from reinforcement, the consequence needs to be imposed sensitively. Patients often question, argue, or respond emotionally in a way that tempts the staff member to alter the agreed-upon contingency. Sometimes the staff member becomes overly rigid and harsh, failing to recognize and acknowledge the distress of the patient. A balance between these two extremes must be found. It is never helpful to engage in a power struggle with the patient. Referring to the written behavioral contract helps to avoid this type of conflict. The document can be examined jointly with the simple observation that "this is our agreement." Patients may engage in a variety of persuasive maneuvers, but maintenance of consistency and mutual respect for this contract is important. Frequently it is useful to observe that staff failure to abide by the agreed-upon consequence would do the patient a disservice, if not a disrespect.

When a patient is upset by imposition of a particular consequence, it is essential that the clinician reflect in an empathic tone an awareness of that distress. That is, commenting on how difficult, effortful, frustrating, or challenging the program must be for the patient communicates a sense of understanding. However, this understanding does not invalidate the agreed-upon behavioral program. The tone that conveys a "yes it's hard, but you can do it" attitude is sometimes helpful. Consequences are never interpreted as a sign of failure or success. Instead, consequences merely serve as incentives. Thus, when patients do not exhibit behavior that would normally earn a particular reinforcer, they have not failed, and negative attributions must be avoided. Ths clinician's posture should be firm, but supportive.

Another response of patients to behavioral programs sometime leads them to split staff members, perhaps by portraying contradictory interpretations of the same event. This kind of staff splitting can dramatically disrupt the consistent imposition of a particular consequence. When changes are made in a program, they should come about through agreement among the entire treatment team in a "public" setting (see below). Finally, unpredictable events often require that a change be made on a temporary basis. For example, extenuating circumstances that seem legitimate may temorarily preclude a particular requirement of a program. A patient who develops an acute illness may be unable to perform targeted self-care skills in order to earn a specified reinforcer. During this temporary state, a contingency may be suspended. Other events that may require the temporary suspension of a contingency program may include changes in physical condition, emotional state, or family support or a revision in the need to provide staff supervision to ensure patient safety. Thus, a particular requirement may be altered in view of new or unexpected mitigating circumstances.

Revising the Contract

Behavioral contracts require continued review and revision. The events that signal a need for revision include both the failure of a contract to produce the desired effect and the power of a program to lead to change. When a treatment program fails to produce some effect, a new analysis needs to be performed. Does the problem lie within the response repertoire of the patient, the potency of the consequences, or the implementation of the overall program itself? Is the patient a nonparticipant in the program and therefore actively resisting any planned effort to instigate behavior change? A successful program also needs revision. For example, when a contingency plan that employs concrete or externally imposed reinforcers has been successful, can the program be revised to use more intrinsically rewarding consequences with equal effectiveness? Revisions of the behavioral program should be renegotiated with the patient as described above.

Case Illustrations

This section describes three cases in which a formal behavior modification program was found to be useful. Before presenting the cases, however, a few important features merit comment. Many publications concerned with behavioral treatments focus on the design and outcome measurement of some experimental manipulation. In contrast, the following cases deliberately avoid presenting data in an experimental-like fashion. Instead, greatest consideration is given to the specifics of clinical implementation and the behavioral principles on which the program rests. The clinical outcome is reported in global terms, as it might appear in a hospital chart or discharge summary. The purpose of presenting these cases is not to persuade anyone that ''behavior modification worked.'' Rather, this section attempts to elucidate meaningful clinical strategies that rehabilitation specialists can put into practice.

A second issue concerns the setting in which these cases were treated. Each case report is taken from the files of a specialty Behavioral Medicine Inpatient Unit that is staffed by an interdisciplinary team, including a psychiatrist, a psychologist, an internist, nursing staff, occupational or activities therapists, and a social worker. The unit staff as a whole possess specialized clinical skills in behavior modification. Although treatment was rendered by a specially trained staff in a unique setting, the methodology is nonetheless generalizable to a variety of inpatient medical settings so long as they are receptive environments in which staff members have some expertise in this area. Each of these patients could have been treated in any general rehabilitation service where the staff had an interest in utilizing the principles and methods of behavior modification.

Finally, for each case, behavior modification was part of an overall treatment plan and therefore represents only one facet of the patient's clinical care. Although only the behavioral approach is discussed, the patient's recovery is surely the result of the entire mixture of therapeutic modalities. In this regard, these cases are not unlike those of patients who are seen in traditional rehabilitation settings. The behavioral approach provided structure and organization to ensure the successful performance and administration of other critical forms of therapy. A patient does not come to an inpatient setting in order to receive a focal or isolated method of treatment. Patients who come for surgery require physical therapy in order to effect a functional rehabilitation. Patients who receive behavior modification do so not to replace, but to augment, the impact of other therapeutic modalities. Thus, the behavioral approach transcends any single therapeutic modality or experience. It is applicable to the total process of patient care.

Case #1

Mrs. H. was admitted for an emergency craniotomy with evacuation of a right subdural hematoma that was apparently sustained when she fell down a flight of stairs during a fight with her husband. Both she and her husband were reportedly intoxicated at the time of her fall. Her postoperative course was complicated initially by hypertension, hypotension, and a urinary tract infection, all of which resolved with medical therapy. However, during a 12-week period of recovery on the inpatient neurology service, she became increasingly verbally belligerent, striking out at staff members, throwing objects during emotional outbursts, and exhibiting periodic episodes of bowel and bladder incontinence. Most problematic was her tendency to fall down while ambulating. Although a physical examination revealed minimal residual neurologic deficits, her apparent anxiety, physical help-lessness, dramatic displays of emotion, listing and unstable gait, and frequent falling episodes led the staff on the neurology service to impose increasing restrictions. This, in turn, appeared to elicit greater levels of functional disability. The patient was then transferred to the Behavioral Medicine Unit where a program of rehabilitation was devised.

Assessment of the patient's functional capacities and difficulties led to identifi-cation of three general problem areas. During her hospital stay, she had grown increasingly unable to maintain personal grooming and hygiene. She failed to bathe, dress, or attend to her physical appearance in any independent fashion. Instead, she invited nursing staff members to perform these activities of daily living, all the while adopting a noncompliant and even belligerent response to nursing assistance. When left to her own devices, she remained in a bathrobe, lying in bed where she was periodically incontinent. A second problem area involved this patient's labile affect and dramatic displays of distress. Observation of this behavior revealed that it probably had two causes; it was in part an emotional response to long-standing marital distress, as well as having some element of organically induced affective lability. Notable was the observation that the patient could regain composure when instructed to "calm down," and this would permit her to express her feelings in a more acceptable fashion. The third problem area involved the patient's inability to ambulate safely throughout the inpatient unit. While on the neurology service, she increasingly reported fatigue, associated with repeated episodes of "falling." As a result, the staff required that she employ first a cane and then a two-handed walker. With these interventions, her ambulation appeared to be more unstable and labored, ultimately leading her to require nursing assistance when moving from a bedside chair to the bathroom. She spent virtually all of her waking hours seated and required close supervision during any transport from place to place on the inpatient unit. A thorough neurologic and orthopedic assessment found only minimal deficits that at most contributed only slightly to this functional disability.

A behavioral treatment program was devised to address each of these problem areas. The initial assessment suggested that the highly regressed behaviors in each problem area were, in part, a function of reinforcing consequences that became associated with those behaviors over the course of hospitalization. Therefore, it was important to identify the desirable behaviors, discuss these targets explicitly with the patient, and link new reinforcing consequences to their performance. By the same token, reinforcement that had unwittingly been provided for functional regression was eliminated.

A facsimile of the behavior modification program developed for this patient appears in Figure 15–3. Three global target behaviors are listed, with each requiring the execution of specific skill training components. The consequences are tied in a specific way to the different skill training elements. Note that the first global target addresses the problem of personal hygiene and is phrased in a pro-active fashion. The requirements of this target include showering, dressing, and personal grooming. Deliberate social reinforcement served as an especially potent consequence. Moreover, the patient relinquished her access to cigarettes; this would be regained only when certain requisite behaviors were executed. This consequence was justified in two ways: She required supervision when smoking because she was a danger to herself and others, and she was persuaded that this would be a fair arrangement that could provide an effective and needed incentive.

The second target behavior was addressed through a series of skill training interventions that had the objectives of refocusing the patient away from symptoms of disability and limiting her exposure to consequences that reinforced helplessness. In particular, appropriate expression of emotional distress was responded to directly, attentively, and supportively. In contrast, when she was belligerent, demanding, and hysterically screamed, "I need my husband right now," there was a removal of reinforcement, i.e., time-out. This consequence could be delivered by averting eye contact or by requesting that the patient place herself in a formal time-out procedure (alone in her room) for a specified interval (5 minutes). Thus, a punishment intervention and a positive reinforcement intervention were balanced to shape more effective and appropriate expression of feelings.

Finally, the third target behavior—difficulty with ambulation—led to an intervention that balanced social reinforcement and nonreinforcement. The patient was

Figure 15–3 Behavior Modification Program for Case #1, Mrs. H.

BEHAVIORAL CONTRACT

Page One

DATE _____

Treatment Team:

PATIENT   Mrs. H.

Clinical Psychologist: JL.

Primary Nurse: TH.

Associate Nurse: BN.

Occupational/Physical Therapist: CM.

Attending Physician: A.O.

Social Worker: A.A.

TARGET BEHAVIORS	SKILL TRAINING PROGRAM	CONTINGENCY BEHAVIORS
#1. Mrs. H. will be responsible for appearing clean and neat while on the inpatient unit.	(a) Mrs. H. will take a shower and wash her hair before breakfast every day. (Assigned nurse on rounds will supervise this.)	• Mrs. H. will remain in her room until she has taken shower and is properly dressed.
	(b) Mrs. H. will dress wearing clean clothes every day, including clean underwear (nurse to √ after completion.).	
	(c) After breakfast, Mrs. H. will brush her teeth (supervised by assigned nurse). After dinner, Mrs. H. will brush teeth (supervised.)	• Mrs. H. may have access to cigarettes in the solarium or conversation alone after bed is made and teeth are brushed.
#1a. Mrs. H. will keep track of her clothing.	(a) Mrs. H. will wash her clothes with supervision of assigned nurse only on: 1) day shift – Tues.; 2) eve shift – Thurs.	• Mrs. H. may wash clothing only with a nurse to decrease chance of losing clothes.
	(b) Mrs. H. will keep her room neat. She will make her bed every morning before attending the 1st therapeutic activity.	• Mrs. H.'s assigned nurse will √ that sheets are clean and offer assistance as needed.
	(c) At bedtime: Mrs. H. will sleep in pajamas.	• Staff will prompt Mrs. H. to change

(continued on back)

(continues)

DATE _____

PATIENT Mrs. H.

Page 2 of 3

TARGET BEHAVIORS	SKILL TRAINING PROGRAM	CONTINGENCY BEHAVIORS
		into pajamas if found sleeping in her clothes.
#2. Mrs. H. will be able to express feelings to others without crying.	(a) Mrs. H. is free to go to her room and cry if she is feeling upset. (b) Mrs. H. may spend the first 5 minutes of her 1:1 contacts with nurses telling about how she is feeling. (c) If Mrs. H. begins to cry on the unit or during 1:1, staff will say, "Mrs. H., I cannot talk to you while you are crying." The staff member will look away until Mrs. H. regains control and stops crying.	Uncontrolled crying is not helpful during 1:1 contact in the halls or when in therapeutic meetings with doctors and nurses. Important notes: (a) The 5 minutes 1:1 time includes all time spent crying. (b) If Mrs. H. is out of her room crying for more than 1 minute, she should be escorted to her room to regain control.
#2a. Mrs. H. will feel proud of herself and her accomplishments.	(a) During 1:1 with evening nurse, Mrs. H. will discuss her day and positive things she has done. This may be done during a walk off the unit. (b) Staff may ask Mrs. H. to lead the way back to the unit following walks off the floor, offering gentle prompting.	Staff will offer prompting and much verbal reinforcement for tasks completed.

Figure 15–3 continued

DATE _____

PATIENT _Mrs. H._

Page _3_ of _3_

TARGET BEHAVIORS	SKILL TRAINING PROGRAM	CONTINGENCY BEHAVIORS
	① Mrs. H. and her nurse will schedule 1:1 appointments for both day and eve. shifts. ② Mrs. H. will attend all activities and therapeutic groups.	
*3. Mrs. H. will maintain safe behavior on the unit. *3a. Mrs. H. will smoke cigarettes safely.	① Mrs. H. will use an ashtray when smoking (not the floor).	· If a staff member sees Mrs. H. doing anything unsafe with her cigarettes, staff will label that behavior as "unsafe" and Mrs. H. will lose cigarette privileges for 24°.
*3b. Mrs. H. will walk safely without falling, or walking into things or people.	① During day shift 1:1, staff will assist Mrs. H. with physical orientation to the inpatient unit. ② Staff will walk with Mrs. H., encouraging her to keep her head up and scanning to the left to compensate for left-sided visual defect.	· All staff to prompt the patient to keep and turn head as necessary. · Staff to give verbal praise when patient is walking safely. If Mrs. H. falls, staff will allow the patient to regain standing on her own. Should she remain immobile on the floor, staff may leave and return when she has resumed standing on her own.

cued to walk with a more upright posture, which became a focus of frequent commentary, e.g., "you look terrific walking like that." More importantly, nine episodes when the patient gently, but dramatically, fell to the floor were entirely ignored. The staff members stepped aside until she stood up, at which time attention in the form of interpersonal contact was delivered. Within the hospital setting, this staff behavior had a number of administrative ramifications. For example, incident reports needed to be filed for each falling episode, and the entire treatment plan was submitted for a quality assurance review. However, following seven incidents in 3 days, the patient never again fell during the remaining 7 weeks of hospitalization.

A number of principles of behavior modification are illustrated in this case. First, the reinforcers were, for the most part, under the control of the staff. Because of this patient's intellectual and functional limitations, the staff felt justified in designing and controlling a number of consequences, an approach that might be more difficult to implement with a higher functioning individual. Second, the behavioral program specified only in general terms the target requirements and the consequences. The individual staff member working with this patient was responsible for deciding whether the required behavior that merited the specific consequence had been exhibited. Finally, it is important to note that the behavioral program did not "cure" this patient. Use of this system of specifying target problems and arranging for motivating incentives facilitated her adaptation and development of compensatory skills. For example, she learned to compensate for her vision deficit by developing a scanning strategy and questioning skills. She did continue to display occasional confusion and poor judgment in several social situations. Nevertheless, her ambulating, cigarette smoking, and activities of daily living all reached a level sufficient to permit transfer to a residential placement.

Case #2

The problem of negotiation and shared responsibility for a behavioral program is illustrated in a second case. Mr. K. is a 23-year-old man with an 18-year history of juvenile onset diabetes. One year before admission, he developed severe peripheral neuropathy in both feet, leading him to quit his job at a bookstore and severely curtailing his ambulation. Other medical problems developed, including repeated retinal hemorrhages that produced significantly impaired vision. Finally, acute peripheral adenoma and hypertension were ascribed to diabetic nephrotomy that was treated medically. Within this context of medical difficulty, the patient ended a close emotional relationship, in response to which he became suicidal. The patient was admitted to the hospital following a suicide attempt by insulin overdose. After stabilization, he was transferred to the Behavioral Medicine Unit where he was to receive a program of rehabilitation intended to help him achieve a higher level of self-care for his current medical conditions and to develop a plan to resume independent living and employment.

Two immediate problems became the targets of assessment and treatment. First, Mr. K.'s uncontrolled diabetes appeared to be a direct result of poor adherence to required dietary and medication regimens. Although some new skills in glucose monitoring were required, the overwhelming factors contributing to his difficulties were motivational. Therefore, a program intended to lower serum glucose levels would emphasize a more prudent balance of food intake, energy expenditure, and insulin utilization. Upon admission, Mr. K. portrayed a history of going days without eating, manipulating his serum glucose ineffectively through changes in insulin dose, and failing to contact physicians for evaluation of a range of physical symptoms of pain. These actions suggested a tendency to behave in a potentially self-destructive manner, something he openly acknowledged. Second, the patient appeared to be oppositional and resistant to efforts to provide him physical and emotional support. He actively rejected direction and prescription with regard to a variety of therapeutic tasks and activities. He would, in his own words, "go on strike" and fail to perform any health-maintaining or therapeutic responsibility. For example, he refused to eat breakfast, attend physical therapy, or even leave his room. All of these difficulties made it difficult for Mr. K. to engage in any meaningful or productive negotiation with the staff. Nonetheless, the staff members pursued a negotiated, occasionally one-sided agreement on targets of behavior change.

A facsimile of Mr. K.'s behavior modification program appears in Figure 15-4. The first target emphasized a clear expectation for maintaining health. It was primarily defined in terms of diabetes management. In collaboration with the patient, a self-care protocol was prepared to include responsibility for attending meals, administering insulin, and performing glucose self-monitoring via finger stick, with a report to be given by the patient to his primary nurse. For example, following a 7:00 A.M. finger stick Mr. K. was expected to eat breakfast at 8:00 A.M., administer insulin at 9:00 A.M., and perform a urinary sugar and acetone (S & A) test and finger stick at 11:30 A.M. Similarly, an afternoon (3:30 P.M.) S & A and finger stick would be required. Finally, insulin would follow dinner at 6:30 P.M., and another finger stick and S & A would be performed at 10:00 P.M. This patient did not happily perform these repeated finger sticks and S & A assays. Therefore, the contract specified that, when he chose to eat his meals, administer insulin, and perform the early A.M. finger stick and S & A assay, he would not be required to perform 11:30 A.M. finger stick. Similarly, by eating lunch he could eliminate the 3:30 P.M. finger stick. Finally, he could avoid the 10:00 P.M. finger stick also by choosing to eat dinner and self-administer his insulin.

It is important to note that the finger stick procedures were experienced as relatively unpleasant by the patient. His refusal to eat at mealtime, which had been

Figure 15–4 Behavior Modification Program for Case #2, Mr. K.

BEHAVIORAL CONTRACT

Page One

DATE _____

Treatment Team:

PATIENT Mrs. K.

Clinical Psychologist: J. L.
Primary Nurse: M. H.
Associate Nurse: Q. P. / J. P.

Occupational/
Physical Therapist: M. C.
Attending Physician: E. Q.
Social Worker: A. M.

TARGET BEHAVIORS

1. Mrs. K. will be responsible for maintaining her physical health.

2. Mrs. K. will use hospitalization productively.

SKILL TRAINING PROGRAM

1. Mrs. K. will follow the diabetic protocol as per schedule. Mrs. K. will initiate contact with staff for all finger sticks and medications. Insulin is to be requested at 9:30 a.m. or within 30 minutes of arrival of breakfast.

2. Mrs. K. will:
(a) Attend all group meetings on her personal schedule;

(continued on back)

CONTINGENCY BEHAVIORS

If Mrs. K. is unwilling to adhere to diabetic control, he will be considered to be in physical jeopardy. This involves:

(a) suspension of grounds privileges through the following shift;

(b) if a 4 hour finger stick with diet glucose reappearance if finger stick is 7–400;

(c) Physical therapy to be cancelled for the day

Mrs. K. will retain the option of planning alternative activities for himself by

Figure 15–4 continued

Page 2 of 2

DATE _____

PATIENT _Mrs. K._

TARGET BEHAVIORS	SKILL TRAINING PROGRAM	CONTINGENCY BEHAVIORS
	(b) Attend treatment team meeting as scheduled;	(a) Complying with program expectations;
	(c) Set up individual appointments with staff by 9:30 a.m. (day shift) and 1:00 p.m. (eve shift);	(b) Informing staff in advance of whereabouts when off-unit plans include;
	(d) Attend daily activities as planned;	By complying with skill training goals, Mrs. K. can schedule an additional 10 minutes of contact time with staff
	(e) Keep appointments for special medical treatments and consultations;	

a pervasive problem, became a target in a contingency that employed a finger stick as a negative reinforcer. That is, an increase in eating behavior would lead to the termination of the unpleasant experience of finger sticks. Moreover, when the glucose level rose above 400, additional venopunctures with stat laboratory-measured results would be required every 4 hours until the level returned to a lower range. This procedure, too, was relatively unpleasant and was used as negative reinforcement.

A second target behavior grew from the observation of this patient's active resistance to participating in treatment. This target was phrased in a positive way, emphasizing that participation in scheduled therapeutic activities would define a beneficial and productive use of this hospitalization. The contingencies for this target behavior involved the free use of off-the-ward privileges during unscheduled times. That is, by following the scheduled component of his program, this patient was permitted to leave the inpatient setting to go anywhere within the medical center complex during his free time. Failure to follow the schedule caused this privilege to be revoked for one 8-hour shift. Thus, grounds privileges were used as a contingent positive reinforcer for program compliance. A variety of cognitive-behavioral therapeutic techniques were employed to address problems of emotional distress, depression, and suppression of feelings.

A major obstacle in the implementation of this program concerned the challenge of negotiation. At various points in the patient's hospitalization, he became belligerent, argumentative, and totally noncompliant. Each time he displayed this behavior, the staff dispassionately adhered to an agreed-upon consequence, whether this was restriction to the inpatient floor, repeated venopuncture, or any other possible consequence that had been specified. Consistency in imposing consequences is the most difficult challenge when dealing with an articulate, logical, and highly emotional patient. It causes the staff member to doubt his or her sensitivity when a patient voices the accusation, "If you really cared about me, you would see that this is unfair." The staff members need to believe and even articulate to the patient that imposing a particular consequence *is* the most helpful and compassionate intervention available.

One especially important factor in administering this particular behavioral modification program was to communicate to the patient the staff's respect for his ability to make his own choices. With choices come responsibilities. A staff member "understood" when the patient was unable to eat a meal, but by so doing, he required an additional finger stick or venopuncture. He was never blamed; instead, he was told that other steps would be taken to ensure his health if he was unable to assist himself. Moreover, when he asked to suspend an agreed-upon consequence, he was told that staff members would be doing him a disservice were they not to stand by their agreement. Thus, consequences must always be portrayed as a way to reaffirm respect, caring, and assistance. The clinical skill needed to convey this message can be difficult to summon amid tense verbal interactions. However, casting consequences in a positive and helpful light, even when it involves limiting privileges or other reinforcing events, is essential to effective behavior modification in the rehabilitation medicine setting.

Case #3

For each of the patients described above, the behavior modification program focused on targets of behavior change that were central to the reasons for hospitalization. In contrast, this spinal cord injured patient entered the hospital for a secondary reason. He had previously completed a rehabilitation program involving physical and occupational therapies, but a major problem with motivation remained a treatment obstacle. This more typical problem characterizes the third case.

Mr. W. was a 31-year-old technical supervisor who sustained a C4-5 extension injury in a diving accident 4 years before admission. Following his injury he was hospitalized for a 5-month inpatient rehabilitation program during which he clung to unrealistic expectations for recovery. However, a subsequent spinal fusion and long postoperative period eventually forced the patient to confront the reality of his permanent disability. Three years after his injury, his marital relationship began to deteriorate. The patient grew increasingly depressed and even more firmly rejected any vocational rehabilitation efforts.

The patient was admitted in an acute crisis. During the 4 months before admission he had displayed increasingly violent verbal outbursts at home and voiced suicidal intent. Having grown more deeply depressed, Mr. W. failed to attend to any routine personal care, abandoning many of the skills he had previously developed, e.g., washing his hair and partial dressing. He poorly practiced his bowel program and had developed several small skin lesions and a urinary tract infection. The hospital admission was arranged as a crisis intervention that would permit Mr. W. to resume some of his previously established independent living skills.

A comprehensive treatment plan was developed that included a bowel training program, occupational therapy to increase personal hygiene and grooming habits, physical therapy to retain muscular tone, and a treatment plan for depression to include individual psychotherapy, marital/family therapy, and pharmacotherapy. Nevertheless, motivational deficits continued to obstruct the patient's participation in each of these intervention plans. Therefore, a behavior modification program was developed that focused more broadly on the problem of participation and treatment. Figure 15–5 presents in global terms the target behaviors that emphasized explicit expectations for daily activity. For example, tooth brushing, setting up a schedule of one-to-one meetings with nursing staff each shift, and participation in a variety of group-oriented activities became expectations. Similarly, the patient was made to be responsible for initiating requests for scheduled

Figure 15–5 Behavior Modification Program for Case #3, Mr. W.

DATE _____

Treatment Team:

BEHAVIORAL CONTRACT

Page One

PATIENT *Mr. W.*

Clinical Psychologist: *JL*

Primary Nurse: *AG*

Associate Nurse: *JMF*

Occupational/
Physical Therapist: *FS.*

Attending Physician: *RY.*

Social Worker: *C.O.*

TARGET BEHAVIORS	SKILL TRAINING PROGRAM	CONTINGENCY BEHAVIORS
1. Mr. W. will feel capable of following a daily schedule to achieve greater independence.	1. Mr. W. will perform the following activities of daily living, assisted where necessary by staff. (1) Brush teeth daily. (a) Use eating utensils at meal-time. (b) be set up by staff when food tray is presented. (i) Attend scheduled therapeutic activities and group meetings. (a) Request control medications at scheduled intervals.	By following this schedule of daily tasks and activities, Mr. W. will grow confident in his ability to meet day-to-day demands.
2. Mr. W. will learn to express his needs, both emotional and physical, more easily and directly.	2a. During the day-shift contact with staff, Mr. W. will: (a) Complete the communication skills exercise focusing on assertiveness. (continued on back)	For completion of target behavior/skill training each, Mr. W. will earn access to off-the-ward privileges.

Figure 15-5 continued

DATE _____

PATIENT _Mr. W_

Page _2_ of _2_

TARGET BEHAVIORS	SKILL TRAINING PROGRAM	CONTINGENCY BEHAVIORS
	(iii) Rehearse and direct expressive statement of wants and/or needs.	during that shift. Failure to complete these tasks will indicate Mr. W's need to
	2b. Mr. W. will participate in the social skills group.	remain more closely supervised by staff.
	2c. Mr. & Mrs. W. will meet with Dr. L. one time per week to discuss methods of conflict resolution.	Weekend therapeutic passes will be planned during weekly couples meetings.

and PRN medications. A second target behavior focused on selected social skills and request making. For example, an effort was made to enumerate specific strategies for making requests or offering complaints. Expression of feelings of distress was identified as an important method of ventilating that could help avoid explosive outbursts.

In this behavior modification program, the targets of behavior change were selected to augment the more medically oriented treatment goals. Specific problem areas within the global objectives for hospitalization were selected as target behaviors. For example, the personal hygiene tasks, such as tooth brushing, became symbolic of an expectation of independent functioning that could be achieved by this patient. Conversely, the regressed behavior that developed appeared to represent, in part, a component of Mr. W.'s depressive state, as well as a response to his marital conflicts. One method of expressing his anger toward his wife was to become increasingly helpless, which necessitated that she, in turn, assume more responsibility. A modest return of independent functioning seemed to follow when care was provided by individuals other than his wife, e.g., the nursing staff. By shifting the caregiving responsibilities to others, there was no longer the extra reinforcement for remaining functionally limited. Thus, the behavioral program had symbolic value, in addition to specifying a system of incentives for behavior change.

CONCLUSION

This chapter describes clinical principles and strategies of behavior modification that are especially pertinent to rehabilitation medicine. These behavioral interventions reflect a process of case formulation and clinical reasoning, rather than a set of techniques to be mechanically applied. Intervention methods are derived on a case-by-case basis and are not necessarily restricted to existing or prescribed procedural steps. A virtue of this conceptual view of behavior modification is its potentially limitless application to the tasks of rehabilitation medicine. However, this approach to clinical reasoning demands careful and detailed analyses of individual cases.

Rather than reviewing documented clinical applications (cf. Ince, 1980), three cases were presented to illustrate both the contributions and limitations of behavior modification. Successful rehabilitation ultimately requires behavior change—whether this involves either the acquisition of new skills of personal hygiene and self-care or maintenance strategies for sustaining a life of maximum independence. When adopted by the entire rehabilitation team, the principles and procedures of behavior modification can assist patients in overcoming behavioral barriers to rehabilitation.

REFERENCES

Bandura, A. (1969). *Principles of behavior modification.* New York: Rinehart & Winston.

Eames, P., & Wood, R. (1985). Rehabilitation after severe brain injury: A follow-up study of a behavior modification approach. *Journal of Neurology, Neurosurgery, & Psychiatry, 48,* 613–619.

Fensterheim, H., & Glazer, H.I. (Eds.). (1983). *Behavioral psychotherapy: Basic principles and case studies in an integrative clinical model.* New York: Brunner/Mazel.

Fordyce, W.E. (1981). Behavioral methods in medical rehabilitation. *Neuroscience & Biobehavioral Reviews, 5,* 391–396.

Fordyce, W.E. (1982). Psychological assessment and management. In F.J. Kottke, G.K. Stillwell, & J.F. Lehmann (Eds.), *Krusen's handbook of physical medicine and rehabilitation.* Philadelphia: W.B. Saunders, Co., pp. 124–150.

Goldfried, M.R. (1971). Systematic desensitization as training in self-control. *Journal of Consulting and Clinical Psychology, 37,* 228–234.

Hersen, M., & Bellack, A.S. (Eds.). (1978). *Behavior therapy in the psychiatric setting.* Baltimore: Williams & Wilkins.

Ince, L.P. (1976). Behavior modification in rehabilitation medicine. Springfield, IL: Charles C Thomas.

Ince, L.P. (Ed.). (1980). *Behavioral psychology in rehabilitation medicine.* Baltimore: Williams & Wilkins.

Kanfer, F.H., & Phillips, J.S. (1970). *Learning foundations of behavior therapy.* New York: John Wiley & Sons, Inc.

Kazdin, A.E. (1984). *Behavior modification in applied settings.* New York: Dorsey.

Krasner, L. (1976). On the death of behavior modification: Some comments from a mourner. *American Psychologist, 31,* 387–388.

Malament, I., Dunn, M., & Davis, R. (1975). Pressure scores: An operant conditioning approach to prevention. *Archives of Physical Medicine and Rehabilitation, 56,* 161–165.

Meichenbaum, D. (1977). *Cognitive behavior modification: An integrative approach.* New York: Plenum Press.

Paul, G.L., Lentz, R.J. (1977). *Psychosocial treatment of chronic mental patients: Milieu social-learning programs.* Cambridge, MA: Harvard University Press.

Powell, G. (1981). *Brain function therapy.* Aldershot, UK: Gower.

Premack, D. (1965). Reinforcement theory. In D. Levine (Ed.), *Nebraska symposium on motivation.* Nebraska: University of Nebraska Press.

Trotter, A., & Inman, D. (1968). The use of positive reinforcement in physical therapy. *Physical Therapy, 48,* 347–352.

Wachtel, P. (1977). *Psychoanalysis and behavior therapy.* New York: Basic Books.

Weeks, G.R., & L'Abate, L. (1982). *Paradoxical psychotherapy: Theory and practice with individuals, couples, and families.* New York: Brunner/Mazel.

Part V

Special Topics

Chapter 16

Sexuality and Physical Disability

Stanley Ducharme, Ph.D.

Most disabling illnesses have implications for sexual functioning. In addition to certain physical changes that are determined by the nature of the disability, major psychological effects occur that are no less powerful (Griffith & Trieschmann, 1983). An important, but often difficult, responsibility of the rehabilitation team is to provide patients with adequate services in this domain. These services include education, individual counseling, couples counseling, and participation in staff training programs, such as the Sexual Attitude Reassessment seminar. This chapter examines the sexual consequences associated with the physical disabilities most often encountered on a rehabilitation unit. (For discussion of the effects of less common neurologic disorders on sexual function, see Boller & Frank, 1982.) In addition, an approach to sexual counseling of the disabled is outlined, and the role of rehabilitation professionals is discussed.

Traumatic physical disability creates an intense narcissistic wound that involves a major mobilization of defenses. Typically there is an initial period of regression that reawakens early separation-individuation phenomena, as well as earlier struggles concerning sexual identity (Ducharme & Ducharme, 1984). A significant number of rehabilitation patients are adolescents and young adults in the process of disengaging from their families and asserting their independence. For these individuals, emotional rehabilitation, and sexual adjustment in particular, is complicated by both pre- and postinjury psychosocial factors.

With time, defenses attenuate and the disabled individual begins the task, necessary for long-term psychosocial well-being, of incorporating a new body image into one's self-concept. To achieve this task, issues of sexual identity, sexual function, and intimate relationships must be specifically addressed.

Although concerns about sexuality may be repressed, they are, in fact, a source of anxiety and self-doubt. Patients frequently perceive themselves as disfigured, helpless, and isolated. Sexual counseling provides disabled individuals an opportunity to acquire pertinent information about sexual functioning, discuss their fears and apprehensions concerning psychosexual issues, and gain reassurance that their physical condition does not preclude successful relationships, intimacy, or an active sex life. Although it is not necessary that all members of the rehabilitation team be skilled sexual counselors, they all should be acquainted with the psychological and functional aspects of sexuality in disabling conditions. Furthermore, they must recognize that, through their interactions, they significantly affect the development of a patient's sexual self-image. The emotional support and information that staff members can provide offer a means of reality testing and reassurance at a time when the patient's ego is extraordinarily fragile.

In 1976, Bregman and Hadley reported that only 50 percent of rehabilitation patients received any information on sexuality during their acute hospitalization. Several factors contribute to this unfortunate omission. Sexuality is often an anxiety-provoking topic for staff members, and therefore discussion of it may be avoided. Also, staff members may unconsciously succumb to the stereotype that disabled individuals are asexual beings. Finally, there are prevalent myths that the disabled person should be protected from such discussions because further emotional turmoil or sexual acting out may result from them. Such notions are not only destructive to the patient's adjustment but also perpetuate societal prejudice against individuals with physical handicaps.

TRAUMATIC HEAD INJURY

Approximately 7,000,000 head injuries are estimated to occur each year in the United States, ranging in severity from minor concussions to severe trauma producing lengthy coma (Caveness, 1979). Males, especially those in the adolescent and young adult ranges, are two to four times more likely to be affected than are females (Rimel & Jane, 1983) because this group is often involved in high-risk behavior that may result in traumatic injury. Clearly, for adolescents, sexuality is a salient subject. It is therefore surprising to find so few formal studies and such slight (or absent) consideration of sexuality in recent texts on head injury (Brooks, 1984; Levin, Benton & Grossman, 1982; Rosenthal, Griffith, Bond, & Miller, 1983).

Brain damage resulting from closed head injury may be either primary (immediate impact) or secondary (delayed) in nature. Contained within the former category are contusions, which have a predilection for the frontal and temporal lobes, and diffuse axonal injuries in the white matter of the brain. The later-developing secondary lesions, resulting from edema or hypoxia, also tend to produce diffuse effects. Teasdale and Mendelow (1984) note that recent studies have stressed the significance of diffuse damage and de-emphasized focal syndromes. However, in view of the selective vulnerability of the frontal and temporal lobes to contusion, it is not surprising to find parallels between the sexual behavior of closed head-injury patients and that of individuals who have undergone frontal or temporal lobec-tomies, as well as those with temporal lobe seizures (see Boller & Frank, 1982). Hyposexuality is the most commonly reported characteristic. If the limbic or hypothalamic regions, which are associated with expression of emotions and primitive drives, are affected, sexual difficulties may well arise. Brainstem involvement may produce impaired arousal or other changes in level of con-sciousness, which may disturb sexual expression.

The literature on sexuality and head injury is sparse, scattered, and occasionally contradictory. Anecdotal reports are more common than group studies. Bond (1984) noted that sex drive may increase (frank disinhibition is frequently described), decrease, or disappear. A decade earlier Weinstein (1974) remarked on this variability, stating that brain damage affects the way in which sexuality is expressed in social contexts. Weinstein argued that the sexual behavior of brain injured individuals is not inherently abnormal, but only seems so by virtue of the situations in which it occurs. Berrol (1981) asserted that the most common sexual consequences of head injury are loss of libido, distractibility, and an impoverished fantasy life. He stated that impotence in the head injured male rarely has a physical cause. Rosenbaum and Najenson (1976) studied ten patients with severe brain injury and their spouses 1 year after onset. They found that sexual difficulties had an interpersonal basis; spouses shrank from intimacy with their partners who no longer resembled the men they had married. McKinlay, Brooks, Bond, Mar-tinage, and Marshall (1981) found that nearly half of the spouses of severely injured patients described alterations in their partner's sexual behavior at 3, 6, and 12 months after injury. Fifty percent of the married patients studied by Mikula and Rudin (1983) reported sexual difficulties.

Although residual physical disabilities may impose some limitations upon sexual activity, it is the cognitive and behavioral sequelae—impulsivity, irri-tability, self-centeredness, lability, rigidity, impaired social judgment, concrete thinking, memory loss, and attentional deficits—that generally have the more profound effects (Lezak, 1978). The following case report illustrates the impact of emotional and cognitive factors on postinjury sexual behavior.

Mr. R.P. is a 34-year-old single male who was evaluated 10 years after he sustained a closed head injury. His mother complained of her son's preoccupation with sex and his relentless sexual drive; she feared that he would be arrested. His obsession frightened and disturbed members of the opposite sex. He approached strange women who would inevitably reject him. He became increasingly depressed from these blows to his masculinity, yet was unable to change his self-defeating behavior. His incontinence was a constant reminder of his sexual difficulties. Urination was a source of sexual stimulation and frustra-tion.

Ultimately, a combination of social skills training with videotape feedback (see Chapter 13), counseling, education, and closer medical management helped R.P. control his sexual drive to some extent; permission to discuss these topics was reassuring and helpful in relieving his depression and anxiety.

Information derived from a neuropsychological evaluation (see Chapter 9) may offer insight into the patient's information-processing skills and style and provide guidelines for the diagnosis and treatment of sexual dysfunction.

If, as the literature seems to suggest, sexual dysfunction following head injury rarely has a physical basis, supportive counseling for both patient and partner would seem indispensable. Partners must understand the effect of neuropsychological deficits on emotional and sexual behavior. They must learn, for example, that the patient's inattentive behavior does not signal rejection of them, but rather organic distractability that may ultimately be resistant to treatment.

Wood (1984) notes that much of the disinhibited sexuality found in the head injured individual is linked to frontal lobe involvement. Lesions in this region typically produce impulsivity, loss of insight, and impaired social judgment, and these deficits compel a poor prognosis. It is difficult to help truly impulsive patients learn to control their behavior through instruction or punishment; when an impulse occurs, such as to fondle a nurse or to expose themselves, they do not pause to reflect on what they have been told—that it is not acceptable behavior—or the aversive consequences that are likely to follow (reprimand, "time-out"). Despite this generally pessimistic outlook, Wood (1984) suggests two specific strategies for managing disinhibited sexual behavior in the head injured patient. The first involves what Wood terms "over learning." For example, in the case of patients who persistently touch staff members in a sexual way, one could institute a "time-out" program for all touching, both sexually tinged and innocuous. With this approach, patients learn to monitor *all* bodily contact. They may then learn to distinguish between contact that is tolerated and that which is not. The second procedure suggested by Wood, which is quite simple, involves punishment in response to the targeted undesirable behavior. Although this method carries the connotation of desperation, Wood claims that the immediate administration of an aversive stimulus (ammonia vapor) is effective in eliminating undesirable behavior. This approach may, however, raise certain ethical concerns.

In summary, the head trauma patient's postinjury sexual adjustment is determined by many factors. Physical factors are less critical than neuropsychological and emotional ones. Distractible, cognitively impaired, and/or impulsive individuals are rarely able to maintain the mechanical or affective aspects of a mature sexual relationship. Their lack of libidinal control and indifference to the consequences of unrestrained expression of desire cause marital chaos. The prognosis becomes even more guarded as the spouse of a head trauma patient comes to recognize personality changes. The burdens of caring for a child-like and dependent adult may produce depression, guilt, and an increased incidence of physical illness in the spouse (see Bond, 1983 for a review). The injured partner may be apathetic and indifferent, disinhibited and demanding, less agile and/or attractive than premorbidly, and insensitive (both physically and emotionally); in addition, the intact partner may be too fatigued by the burdens of providing physical care or repelled by the patient's cosmetic or behavioral changes to initiate sexual contact.

The few reports on marital stability following head injury are contradictory. One long term follow-up study (Panting & Merry, 1972) found a 40 percent divorce rate, whereas another (Walker, 1972) reported a figure of only 11 percent, less than half the prevailing rate for males in the United States. Mikula and Rudin (1984) found a divorce rate of 15 percent among their group of head injured patients studied at least 6 months after onset. These authors noted a tendency for marital difficulties to be more common in the later years after injury. Among their married patients, 75 percent reported experiencing marital difficulties. It is important to keep in mind that the head injured population contains a disproportionate number of individuals with premorbid histories of social maladjustment, drug abuse, and the like (Rimel & Jane, 1983). Within this group an elevated incidence of divorce might be obtained, even in the absence of head injury. Further study of this issue is needed.

Staff members working with the head injured often view these patients as hypersexual because of their disinhibition. As a result, the topic of sexuality is avoided because of the misconception that such discussion will increase their sexual drives. Failure to address this area explicitly, however, cannot be justified; the potential adverse consequences for long-term adjustment are too serious. Families and patients need facts and guidance from informed professionals in the area of sexuality.

STROKE

As with head injury, the sexual consequences of stroke reflect the interaction of physiologic, cognitive, and emotional factors. The sparse data suggest that frequency of sexual activity decreases after stroke, although a recent report described several cases of hypersexuality (Monga, Monga, Raina, and Hardjasudarma, 1986). Physiologic changes are also commonplace.

Bray, DeFrank, and Wolfe (1981) investigated sexual interest, function, and attitudes of 35 stroke patients. They found that, in general, patients continued to have the desire for sexual activity and that libido remained consistent with prestroke levels. An excellent predictor of poststroke activity is the premorbid sexual history and level of activity. Patients who were inactive before the stroke tend to remain so, particularly considering the additional limitations imposed on them from the disability (Goddess, Wagner, & Silverman, 1979).

Bray et al. (1981) also pointed out that a significant number of men experience physiologic changes affecting erection and ejaculation. Many had similar problems before the stroke, but for others these changes were specific sequelae. As erections tended to be incomplete and inconsistent, intercourse was frequently not possible. Ejaculation was even more vulnerable, although some men reported ejaculations without erection.

Hawton (1984) studied a group of relatively young stroke survivors (mean age = 49 years) approximately 6 months after the event. He found that erectile capacity usually returned after approximately 7 weeks. Of those subjects who had been living with a partner and had been sexually active before the stroke, more than half had resumed sexual activity, including intercourse, by the time of the interview. Average time to resumption of intercourse was 11 weeks after stroke. Hawton states that male sexual response, including ejaculatory capacity, is not usually chronically impaired after a stroke. The comparatively young age of his sample was certainly a factor in his conclusions.

For women, the research findings are unclear. However, because lubrication is the physiologic counterpart to the male erection, one would suspect similar changes. Unfortunately, lubrication is difficult to measure. Orgasm appears to be rare for women following stroke; Bray et al. (1981) reported that only one of their female subjects was able to reach orgasm.

Kinsella and Duffy (1979) reported cessation of sexual relations in 83 percent of couples in which one partner experienced a stroke. Sjögren and Fugl-Meyer (1981) reported that stroke survivors engaged in shorter foreplay time and had reduced coital frequency, which approached cessation in many instances. Female subjects reported fewer changes in sexual patterns and less dissatisfaction with changes after stroke than did male subjects, confirming an earlier report by Kalliomaki, Markkanen, and Mustonen (1961).

Decreased motor function can significantly affect poststroke sexuality. Couples may find it necessary to adopt novel positions to accommodate the disabled partner's loss of agility.

Neuropsychological consequences of stroke—poor memory, cognitive deficit, and impaired judgment—may affect sexual expression. Sjögren and Fugl-Meyer (1982) suggest that patients with unilateral neglect, especially when it is associated with hypoarousal and indifference (Heilman, Schwartz, & Watson, 1978), are at particular risk for sexual maladjustment. Sjögren and Fugl-Meyer found that the presence of aphasia did not affect sexual adjustment; this contrasts with reports of other authors (e.g., Kinsella & Duffy, 1979). Elementary sensory loss and dependence in activities of daily living predicted poor sexual functioning.

Clinical depression frequently is observed following a stroke (e.g., Robinson & Price, 1982). This may result from the numerous losses that accompany a stroke, lowered self-esteem, fear of relapse, increased dependency, and the like. Because depression has been associated with decreased libido and impotence in the able-bodied population (Costello-Smith 1981), it is reasonable to suppose that depression can cause secondary impotence in stroke survivors, which would further disrupt attempts to resume sexual activities. Renshaw (1975) notes that depression decreases all appetites, including that for sex. Antidepressant medications may alleviate the mood disorder, but they can themselves cause impotence, as do certain antihypertensive drugs that may be prescribed for the stroke patient.

Bladder or bowel incontinence can certainly dampen enthusiasm for sexual activity. The couple should be advised regarding this possibility, and appropriate timing of voiding or catheterization should be encouraged.

Many stroke patients blame themselves for their condition. They may feel that the stroke was a punishment for some decision or behavior and, therefore, not feel "entitled" to sexual activity following recovery. Helping the patient resolve such guilt may be a lengthy process requiring sensitive supportive counseling.

Guilt may also play a role in the partner's reaction to the patient. Feeling responsible for the stroke may cause the spouse to withdraw or else overcompensate by encouraging the patient's dependency and becoming overly protective. The able-bodied spouse who provides a great deal of physical care may find it difficult to view the patient as an object of desire.

Partners also may fear the disability and feel awkward when the opportunity for intimacy arises. Perceiving the patient as fragile, they may worry about causing further damage or another stroke. This increases the emotional distance between the couple. Without the ability to communicate openly about their apprehensions, the relationship will be in severe jeopardy.

Realignment of sex roles, dependency, and financial stress are especially common among younger stroke survivors, and these produce problems with intimacy and strain the marriage. In general, early sexual activity following stroke promotes self-esteem and is beneficial to the long-term adjustment of patient and partner.

For many stroke patients sexual counseling consists largely of dispelling myths, such as that sexual arousal will trigger another stroke; dispensing information; and providing encouragement to experiment. The potential impact of psychological factors should be discussed as well. Sjögren, Damber, and Liliequist (1983) concluded that sexual dysfunction following stroke was most often attributable to poor coping, rather than to physiologic problems. Supportive counseling, therefore, is likely to be necessary in many cases.

SPINAL CORD INJURY

A welcome contrast to the paucity of literature on sexuality following head injury or stroke is the comparative plethora of writings on the sexual consequences of spinal cord injury (Sha'ked, 1981). The great majority of this literature concerns the problems encountered by males; far less is known or documented about the effects of spinal injury on female sexuality. However, as with head injury, the preponderance of injuries occur to adolescent males, for whom psychosexual adjustment is critical to successful long-term outcome.

Sensation

Sensory disturbances are a prominent symptom of spinal cord injury. Genital numbness is common. For example, a man may be capable of a psychogenic or reflexogenic erection (see below) but be unable to feel his penis in his partner's vagina. Loss of sensation in the vagina or clitoris is common.

Other patients experience some sparing of genital sensation ("sacral sparing"). Although the sensation may not be as complete as it was premorbidly, patients can differentiate between hot and cold temperatures or between soft and hard touching.

Areas of intact sensation, usually just above the level of injury, are reported to be a source of erotic pleasure. These areas may lie along the nipple line or in the vicinity of the neck and ears. Hypersensitivity in the genitals may cause sexual activity to be unpleasant or painful. In such cases, a topical anesthetic lotion or cream should be used before intercourse. The couple's ability to communicate their needs is of primary importance, particularly when sensation is impaired.

Erections

The capacity for erections in men and lubrication in women is either partially or completely lost in most individuals with a spinal cord injury. As with other disabilities, however, this inability does not preclude the possibility for a wide range of sexual activities.

The range of sexual responses varies according to the level of spinal cord injury, as well as the completeness of the lesion. For purposes of discussion, lesions (generally T12 or higher) that preserve the sacral cord are called upper motor neuron lesions. Patients with such injuries have external anal sphincter tone and a bulbocavernosus reflex. Patients with lower motor neuron lesions, which are usually below T12, have a lax anal sphincter and no bulbocavernosus reflex. Roughly 90 percent of men with complete upper motor neuron lesions and 98 percent with incomplete upper motor neuron lesions can sustain erections (Comarr, 1978). Approximately 25% of men with complete lower motor neuron lesions and up to 80% with incomplete lower motor neuron lesions experience erections (Comarr, 1971).

Reflexogenic Erections

Patients with intact sacral cords may achieve a reflexogenic erection. In such cases, stimulation of the genitals, perineum, or bladder is mediated through the S2, S3, and S4 nerve roots via the parasympathetic system. This may produce at least a partial reflexogenic erection, often sufficient for intercourse. However, once stimulation has been removed, the erection tends to recede fairly quickly. Thus, ongoing manual stimulation during intercourse helps maintain the erection. Nevertheless, penetration or intercourse may not always be possible.

Because there is no voluntary control over reflexogenic erections, patients frequently describe them as a source of embarrassment in nonsexual situations. The rubbing of the penis on clothing or even a full bladder may cause an untimely erection. The resulting shame can lead to social isolation if a solution is not found.

Psychogenic Erections

Psychogenic erections in able-bodied men and men with incomplete upper motor neuron lesions are mediated from the cerebral cortex through the thoracolumbar or sacral cord centers. In the spinal cord injured man with lower motor neuron injury, erection is thought to be possible on a psychogenic basis via the thoracolumbar sympathetic outflow (Bors & Comarr, 1960). Such erections are frequently incomplete, causing the patient to feel dissatisfied or inadequate. Anxiety and other psychological reactions may further hinder the patient's ability to achieve erections. Performance anxiety is common following hospital discharge.

Stuffing Technique

Because the quality of erections in spinal cord injured men tends to be so variable, a technique that involves "stuffing" the flaccid penis into the vagina is often used. Using this technique may cause sufficient stimulation to produce an erection. Even without erection, however, many couples find the technique pleasurable and exciting. It allows the couple to engage in intercourse and to participate in what they may perceive as "normal sexual behavior." Vibrators and penis rings are also used by some patients in conjunction with manual stimulation.

Fertility in Males with Spinal Cord Injury

Questions about fertility can be expected early in rehabilitation and typically re-emerge after hospital discharge. This is especially true for those who sustain traumatic injury, because these tend to occur in individuals under 30 years of age.

Because of the nature of the lesion and the period of spinal shock, it may be difficult to predict sexual functioning soon after the injury. However, the outlook for fertility in spinal cord injured men is generally very poor. Although, as previously mentioned, upper motor neuron lesions carry a better prognosis for erections, ejaculation and orgasm occur less frequently. Spinal cord injured men who are unable to ejaculate are, for all practical purposes, infertile.

Those spinal cord injured men who can ejaculate often do so in a retrograde fashion. That is, semen tends to collect in the bladder and to be expelled during subsequent urination. Furthermore, lesions and testicular damage may occur as a result of prolonged intermittent or continuous catheterization. Elevations of testicular temperature, a frequent consequence of spinal cord injury, are not compatible with spermatogenesis (Morales & Harden, 1958).

Brindley (1984) describes some success in obtaining semen using a vibrator or electroejaculation techniques, although the quality of the semen is often poor. Brindley reports 11 pregnancies using artificial insemination with semen obtained by his methods from paraplegic males. These findings are provocative, but replication is required.

For those rare spinal cord injured men who can ejaculate and who have good semen quality, consideration should be given to freeze-preservation of semen obtained as soon as possible after injury. For the great majority of spinal injured males desiring children, however, donor insemination or adoption are chosen to resolve this issue.

Penile Implants

Some men who do not have an intact sacral cord or who are impotent from an organic etiology are candidates for a penile prosthesis. In traumatic injuries, a penile prosthesis should not be considered in the first 6 months following injury. Often such a device is mistakenly regarded as a cure-all and may be implanted before the patient has had an opportunity to adjust psychologically to the changes in his body. When such surgery is performed, it should always be accompanied by counseling for the patient and, if feasible, his partner.

Presently, the most popular prosthetic consists of two sponge-filled silicone rods that are implanted in the perineum or on the underside of the penis. There are relatively few medical complications, and most men using the device experience little pain or infection. The primary disadvantage of such a device is that the penis is permanently semierect, which can be a source of embarrassment.

The inflatable prosthesis consists of a hollow cylinder implanted in the penis, and a fluid reservoir located in the abdomen with a bulb in one scrotal sac. These components are connected with silicone tubes. To achieve erection the patient presses the bulb, forcing the fluid from the reservoir into the hollow chamber. A one-way valve keeps the fluid in the cylinder until the patient compresses a release valve in the bulb, allowing the fluid to return to the reservoir.

Although many patients prefer the inflatable prosthesis, mechanical failures are common, and these must be corrected by surgical replacement of the defective equipment. Another consideration in the choice of a prosthesis is the patient's upper extremity function. Operation of the inflatable prosthesis requires fine manual motor dexterity, which may exceed the capability of many quadriplegic males.

The Spinal Cord Injured Woman

Health care providers often minimize or ignore the sexual concerns of females (Zwerner, 1982). Because society tends to view female sexual behavior as passive, the problems of sexual adaptation in women are incorrectly considered to be less traumatic. From a psychological perspective, the female with a spinal cord injury is burdened with concerns about her attractiveness, her ability to satisfy her partner, and her role as a woman in society. Fears of rejection emerge, affecting current or potential relationships.

Physiologically, there may be problems with lubrication, sensation, and birth control. Because lubrication may be reduced as a result of spinal cord injury, many disabled women experience painful sensations during intercourse. Although these may be alleviated with lubricating jelly, doing so does not affect the psychological ramifications of this physiologic change. Again, sexual adjustment goes beyond a question of simple techniques. It is also a matter of maintaining a healthy sex role identity.

Following spinal cord injury, menses are often interrupted, but resume within approximately 6 months. Full-term pregnancies and deliveries occur. However, they may be complicated by urinary tract infections, autonomic dysreflexia, anemia, and the risk of premature labor that may progress unnoticed due to loss of sensation.

The disabled woman needs to consider contraceptive choices and their potential hazards. Oral contraceptives pose a greater risk of thrombophlebitis for the disabled woman who lacks mobility. The diaphragm demands physical dexterity for correct insertion. The intrauterine device may perforate the uterus and not be felt if the female has lost sensation; thus, it would require regular monitoring. The joint use of spermicidal foam and male condoms may be the method of choice.

Bladder and Bowel

Fears of involuntary urination or defecation and subsequent rejection are major issues to be confronted. Bladder accidents can result as a medical complication of spinal cord injury. Urinary tract infection may also cause chronic urgency and loss of bladder control during sexual intercourse.

Social stereotypes associate incontinence with embarrassment and humiliation. Thus, the fear of a bladder accident creates anxiety and is often regarded as a major reason for social isolation or the termination of relationships. When the possibility of a bladder accident is not discussed with a partner before sexual activity, its occurrence can be a devastating experience for the disabled person. However, when it has been prepared for, it can be treated as a temporary inconvenience.

Emptying the bladder before sexual activity reduces the likelihood of an accident. Persons on an intermittent catheterization schedule, should perform the catheterization prior to sex. Indwelling catheters can be taped to the side of the penis and a condom placed over the catheter.

Females can engage in intercourse despite the presence of a catheter, by taping the tube to the abdomen. For either sex, fluids should be limited during the hours preceding sexual activity, with towels being available should problems arise.

As most patients establish some sort of regular bowel program with predictable results, the possibility of bowel accidents is minimized.

STAFF CONSIDERATIONS

The newly disabled patient's concerns regarding sexuality may be voiced at any time. It is not unusual for patients in the intensive care unit to ask questions about the sexual consequences of their conditions. Other patients, however, avoid the topic entirely, silently drawing their own, often erroneous conclusions. The staff's receptiveness to questions about sexuality can serve as a cue to the patient that it is a legitimate domain of concern in rehabilitation.

If patients themselves do not raise the topic of sexuality, staff members can and should let them know that there are professionals available to discuss this area. Merely stating that most people have questions about sexuality can open the door to further discussion and education. In so doing, staff members counter the misconception that disabled people are asexual beings. It is advisable to broach this subject before the patient's first overnight pass, because this is usually their first opportunity since the onset of the disability to engage in sexual activity.

Sexuality is not the exclusive province of physicians or mental health workers, although in practice these groups often have primary responsibility. Ideally, all rehabilitation staff should be able to discuss, at least to a limited extent, the area of sexuality and disability. It could be argued that the appropriate staff member to discuss sexuality with any given patient is that person whom the patient identifies as the one with whom they feel most comfortable talking about this sensitive subject. Thus, all staff members need to be equipped to handle initial inquiries and to dispel myths.

Of course, sexual education and counseling must be offered with the patient's background, attitudes, and current emotional state in mind. Otherwise, the process may cause undue anxiety, perhaps foreclosing the possibility that the patient will pursue the subject at a later time. Many patients cannot tolerate discussion about sexuality at an early phase; the purpose of initial conversations, therefore, may be simply to sanction later inquiries.

The PLISSIT model, developed by Annon (1974), provides a useful framework for discussing the various phases of intervention. Four successively more sophisticated levels of intervention are postulated—Permission, Limited Information, Specific Suggestions, and Intensive Therapy. Using this model, clinicians can readily identify their own level of competence and determine whether they possess the requisite intervention skills in particular cases.

The first level of intervention—giving permission—may require no more than raising the topic of sexuality in order to let the patient know that this is a legitimate area of interest. Professional sanction alone may relieve some anxiety and encourage patients to think, experiment, and inquire. At the second level of intervention, patients are given specific facts regarding the sexual consequences of their conditions. Doing so corrects misconceptions and prevents future problems. For example, spinal cord injured males should be informed about the effects of cord injury on erectile ability and fertility. In cases of head injury, discussion might center on changes in level of desire. It is usually advisable to include the patient's partner in teaching sessions.

All members of the rehabilitation team should be able to provide these two levels of intervention. At succeeding levels, however, the staff member comes to function more as a counselor than an educator. Thus, more sophisticated interventions should be conducted by those with specific training and/or expertise.

At the next level, specific technical suggestions are offered to the patient and partner. A necessary prologue is the taking of a sexual history to determine the patient's premorbid sexual practices and beliefs. Of course, one must also be familiar with the disability itself and its impact on sexual functioning. Finally, it is vital that the staff member be aware of the patient's emotional status and the psychological significance of the subject of sex. Examples of specific suggestions include advice on positioning, contraceptive measures, bowel and bladder management, and techniques for sustaining erection. Suggestions may also be provided concerning social skills (see Chapter 13) that are related to sexuality, such as ways of meeting new people, effective communication, and assertiveness.

Patients with more complex sexual dysfunctions may require the fourth level of intervention—intensive therapy, which should be provided by professionals with advanced training in the various modalities of sexual counseling. Rehabilitation staff members are obligated to assist in the referral of such patients to suitable therapists. Certainly, rehabilitation professionals with appropriate training may assume this role. Appendix 16–A lists seven institutions that house sexuality and disability training centers from which interested individuals (staff, patients, and families) can obtain information.

SEXUAL ATTITUDE REASSESSMENT PROGRAMS

During the past decade, the Sexual Attitude Reassessment (SAR) seminar has gained widespread acceptance as a means of educating both rehabilitation staff members and the physically disabled themselves. This program was developed by the National Sex Forum in San Francisco, and was modified by Cole (1973) for use in rehabilitation centers. Today, these programs, conducted throughout North America, are operated under the auspices of the National Task Force on Sex and Disability of the American Congress of Rehabilitation Medicine (see Appendix 16–A). The seminar uses explicit sexual material to demythologize and desensationalize sexual behavior and attitudes. In doing so, the program accomplishes its goals of aiding professionals to better understand and accept their own sexuality, as well as the sexuality of others. This is a first step toward acquiring the skills needed to provide sexual counseling to the disabled.

The 2-day program uses a multimedia presentation to cover a variety of topics, such as masturbation, fantasy, homosexuality, and relationships. At strategic points throughout the workshop, participants, usually a mix of disabled individuals and rehabilitation staff, meet in small groups to examine and share their attitudes and feelings about the material presented. Although the SAR seminars have made important contributions, additional programs are needed to train sex counselors of the disabled.

CONCLUSION

The last decade has seen vast changes in the field of sexuality and disability. Most importantly, professionals have come to recognize the prevalence of sexual concerns among their patients and their own obligation to address this area, despite the difficulties involved. There is a growing consensus that sexual teaching and sexual counseling are vital components in the rehabilitation of disabled individuals. Further research, however, must demonstrate their efficacy. The availability of written material on sexuality has facilitated the process and encouraged rehabilitation staff to demand these services for their patients. The development of a network of training centers has also provided support and education to interested staff.

All individuals, regardless of their physical condition, have the capacity for sexual expression. It is the responsibility of rehabilitation professionals to teach, advise, and encourage their patients in the development and growth of this critical aspect of human identity.

REFERENCES

Annon, J.S. (1974). *The behavioral treatment of sexual problems* (Vol 1). Honolulu: Enabling Systems, Inc.

Berrol, S. (1981). Issues of sexuality in head-injured adults. *Medical Aspects of Human Sexuality, 15,* 15–16.

Boller, F., & Frank, E. (1982). *Sexual dysfunction in neurological disorders: Diagnosis, management, and rehabilitation.* New York: Raven Press.

Bond, M. (1983). Effects on the family system. In M. Rosenthal, E.R. Griffith, M.R. Bond, & J.D. Miller (Eds.), *Rehabilitation of the head-injured adult.* Philadelphia: F.A. Davis Co., pp. 209–217.

Bond, M. (1984). The psychiatry of closed head injury. In Neil Brooks (Ed.), *Closed head injury: Psychological, social, and family consequences.* Oxford: Oxford University Press, pp. 148–178.

Bors, E., & Comarr, A.E. (1960). Neurological disturbances of sexual function with special reference to 529 patients with spinal cord injury. *Urology Survey, 10,* 191–197.

Bray, G.P., DeFrank, R.S., & Wolfe, T.L. (1981). Sexual functioning in stroke survivors. *Archives of Physical Medicine and Rehabilitation, 62,* 286–288.

Bregman, S., & Hadley R. (1976). Sexual adjustment and feminine attractiveness among spinal cord-injured women. *Archives of Physical Medicine and Rehabilitation, 57,* 448–450.

Brindley, G.S. (1984). The fertility of men with spinal injuries. *Paraplegia, 22,* 337–348.

Brooks, N. (Ed.). (1984). *Closed head injury: Psychological, social, and family consequences.* Oxford: Oxford University Press.

Caveness, W.F. (1979). Incidence of craniocerebral trauma in the United States in 1976 with trend from 1970 to 1975. *Advances in Neurology, 22,* 1–3.

Cole, T. (1973). A new programme of sex education and counseling for spinal cord injured adults and health professionals. *Paraplegia, 2,* 111–124.

Comarr, A.E. (1971). Sexual concepts in traumatic cord and cauda equina lesions. *Journal of Urology, 106,* 375–379.

Comarr, A.E. (1978). Sex classification and expectations among quadriplegics and paraplegics. *Sexuality and Disability, 1,* 10.

Costello-Smith, P. (1981). Sexual recovery of the stroke patient. *Sexual Medicine Today, 5,* 6–11.

Ducharme, S.H., & Ducharme, J. (1984). Psychological adjustment to spinal cord injury. In D.W. Krueger (Ed.), *Emotional rehabilitation of physical trauma and disability.* New York: Spectrum Publications, pp. 149–156.

Goddess, E.D., Wagner, N.N., & Silverman, D.R. (1979). Poststroke sexual activity of CVA patients. *Medical Aspects of Human Sexuality, 13,* 16–30.

Griffith, E.R., & Trieschmann, R.B. (1983). Sexual dysfunction in the physically ill and disabled. In C. Nadelson & D. Marcotte (Eds.), *Treatment interventions in human sexuality.* New York: Plenum Press, pp. 241–277.

Hawton, K. (1984). Sexual adjustment of men who have had strokes. *Journal of Psychosomatic Research, 28,* 243–249.

Heilman, K.M., Schwartz, H.D., & Watson, R.T. (1978). Hypoarousal in patients with the neglect syndrome and emotional indifference. *Neurology, 28,* 229.

Kalliomaki, J.L., Markkanen, T.K., & Mustonen, V.A. (1961). Sexual behaviour after cerebral vascular accident. *Fertility and Sterility, 12,* 156–158.

Kinsella, G.J., & Duffy, F.D. (1979). Psychosocial readjustment in the spouses of aphasic patients: A comparative survey of 79 subjects. *Scandinavian Journal of Rehabilitation Medicine, 11,* 129–132.

Levin, H.S., Benton, A.L., & Grossman, R.G. (1982). *Neurobehavioral consequences of closed head injury.* New York: Oxford University Press.

Lezak, M.D. (1978). Living with the characterologically altered brain-injured patient. *Journal of Clinical Psychiatry, 39,* 592–598.

McKinlay, W.W., Brooks, D.N., Bond, M.R., Martinage, D., & Marshall, M. (1981). The short-term outcome of severe blunt head injury as reported by relatives of the head-injured person. *Journal of Neurology, Neurosurgery and Psychiatry, 46,* 527–533.

Mikula, J.A., & Rudin, J. (1983, November). *Outcome of severe head injury patients after head injury rehabilitation.* Paper presented at American Congress of Rehabilitation Medicine and American Academy of Physical Medicine and Rehabilitation, San Diego.

Monga, T.N., Monga, M., Raina, M., & Hardjasudarma, M. (1986). Hypersexuality in stroke. *Archives of Physical Medicine and Rehabilitation, 67,* 415–417.

Morales, P.A., & Harden, J. (1958). Scrotal and testicular temperature studies in paraplegics. *Journal of Urology, 27,* 972–981.

Panting, A., & Merry, P.H. (1972). The long-term rehabilitation of severe head injuries with particular reference to need for social and medical support for the patient's family. *Rehabilitation, 38,* 33.

Renshaw, D.C. (1975). Sexual problems in stroke patients. *Medical Aspects of Human Sexuality, 9,* 68–74.

Rimel, R.W., & Jane, J.A. (1983). Characteristics of the head-injured patient. In M. Rosenthal, E.R. Griffith, M.R. Bond, & J.D. Miller (Eds.), *Rehabilitation of the head-injured adult.* Philadelphia: F.A. Davis Co, pp. 9–21.

Robinson, R.G., & Price, T.R. (1982). Post-stroke depressive disorders: A follow-up study of 103 patients. *Stroke, 13,* 635–640.

Rosenthal, M., Griffith, E.R., Bond, M.R., & Miller, J.D. (Eds.). (1983). *Rehabilitation of the head-injured adult.* Philadelphia: F.A. Davis Co.

Rosenbaum, M., & Najenson, T. (1976). Changes in life patterns and symptoms of low mood as reported by wives of severely brain-injured soldiers. *Journal of Consulting and Clinical Psychology, 44,* 881–888.

Sha'ked, A. (Ed.). (1981). *Human sexuality and rehabilitation medicine: Sexual functioning following spinal cord injury.* Baltimore: Williams & Wilkins.

Sjögren, K., Damber, J.E., & Liliequist, B. (1983). Sexuality after stroke with hemiplegia. I. Aspects of sexual function. *Scandinavian Journal of Rehabilitation Medicine, 15,* 55–61.

Sjögren, K., & Fugl-Meyer, A.R. (1981). Sexual problems in hemiplegia. *International Rehabilitation Medicine, 3,* 26–31.

Sjögren, K., & Fugl-Meyer, A.R. (1982). Adjustment to life after stroke with special reference to sexual intercourse and leisure. *Journal of Psychosomatic Research, 26,* 409–417.

Teasdale, G., & Mendelow, D. (1984). Pathophysiology of head injuries. In N. Brooks (Ed.), *Closed head injury: Psychological, social, and family consequences.* Oxford: Oxford University Press, pp. 4–36.

Walker, A.E. (1972). Long-term evaluation of the social and family adjustment to head injuries. *Scandinavian Journal of Rehabilitation Medicine, 4,* 5–8.

Weinstein, E.A. (1974). Sexual disturbances after brain injury. *Medical Aspects of Human Sexuality, 8,* 10–31.

Wood, R.L. (1984). Behavior disorders following severe brain injury: Their presentation and psychological management. In N. Brooks (Ed.), *Closed head injury: Psychological, social, and family consequences*. Oxford: Oxford University Press, pp. 195–219.

Zwerner, J. (1982). Yes we have troubles but nobody's listening: Sexual issues of women with spinal cord injury. *Sexuality and Disability, 5*, 158–171.

SUGGESTED READINGS

Comfort, A. (1978). *Sexual consequences of disability*. Philadelphia: George F. Stickley.

Cornelius, D., Chipouras, S., Makas, E., & Daniels, S. (1982). *Who cares: A handbook on sex education and counseling services for disabled people*. Baltimore: University Park Press.

Eisenberg, M., & Rustad, L. (1980). *Sex and the spinal cord injured*. Washington, DC: U.S. Government Printing Office.

Freedman-Becker, E. (1978). *Female sexuality following spinal cord injury*. Bloomington, IN: Cheever Publishing Inc.

Mooney, T., Cole, T., & Chilgren, R. (1975). *Sexual options for paraplegics and quadriplegics*. Boston: Little, Brown and Co.

Appendix 16–A

Sexuality and Disability Training Centers

Alberta Institute of Human Sexuality
244 Westridge Road
Edmonton, Alberta, Canada T5T1C1

Boston University School of Medicine
New England Regional Spinal Cord Injury Center
75 East Newton Street
Boston, Massachusetts 02118

Moss Rehabilitation Hospital
12th Street and Tabor Road
Philadelphia, Pennsylvania 19141

Rehabilitation Institute of Chicago
345 East Superior - 16th Floor
Chicago, Illinois 60611

Schoitz Medical Center
Kimball and Ridgeway
Waterloo, Iowa 50702

Sunnyview Hospital and Rehabilitation Center
1270 Belmont Avenue
Schenectady, New York 12308

University of Michigan
Department of Physical Medicine and Rehabilitation
1405 East Ann Street
Ann Arbor, Michigan 48109

Chapter 17

A New Perspective on Paraprofessionals in Rehabilitation Counseling

Jack R. Crisler, Ed.D.
Mary Ellen Young, Ph.D.

Paraprofessional, volunteer, peer counselor, aide, technician, lay helper, nonprofessional, indigenous counselor, support personnel—all of these terms have been used to describe the individual who provides a range of services to clients of social service programs, but who does not possess the credentials of a fully accredited professional. In the late 1960s and early 1970s, mental health workers were optimistic that less qualified persons could provide selected services to persons who could not be served by the limited number of available professionals. In community mental health agencies, psychiatric hospitals, and rehabilitation facilities, the hiring of such individuals provided an expanded range of services and more one-to-one helping relationships (Sobey, 1970). It is now time to examine the results of these practices, evaluate their effectiveness, and make recommendations for the future role of paraprofessionals in the provision of services to rehabilitation clients.

This chapter (1) identifies the dimensions of professionals and paraprofessionals in counseling, (2) presents a historical overview of the paraprofessional movement in rehabilitation counseling, (3) describes the current status of paraprofessionals, (4) examines the research on the use of paraprofessionals, (5) discusses pertinent ethical and professional issues, and (6) offers recommendations for future practice. Although a variety of descriptive terms may be used, service providers who have met accepted credentialing standards are called *professionals* and those with lesser credentials are called *paraprofessionals*.

DIMENSIONS OF PROFESSIONALS AND PARAPROFESSIONALS

Paraprofessionals may differ from their professional counterparts on four dimensions—credentials, compensation, level of responsibility, and demographics. Each dimension actually represents a continuum of characteristics that can be used to describe service providers.

On the credential dimension, service providers range from those with minimal education and no license or certification to those whose professional status stems from graduate degrees, licensure from government agencies, or certification by professional organizations.

On the compensation dimension, service providers may be volunteers or may receive payment from minimum wage to a full professional salary. Paraprofessionals are usually at the lower end of the compensation continuum.

Service providers may perform activities that range from tasks calling for little discriminating judgment to complex decisions based on the analysis, synthesis, and interpretation of information about clients. Professionals are assumed to have greater responsibility for providing services than are paraprofessionals, with the latter supposedly managing more of the routine tasks, thereby allowing professionals to focus on the more complex areas.

The final dimension used for separating professional from paraprofessional service providers is demographics. Paraprofessionals are more likely to share a particular demographic characteristic with the client than are professionals. If the service is based on that characteristic, such as race, gender, or disabling condition, then paraprofessionals are called "peer counselors." The literature contains a number of descriptions of peer counseling programs: individuals with disabilities (McCarthy, 1981; Vash, 1981), ex-drug abusers (Snowden & Cotler, 1974), prison inmates (George, Hosford, & Moss, 1978), blacks (Buck, 1977), students (Rockwell & Dustin, 1979; Tucker & Cantor, 1975; Zwibelman & Hinrichsen, 1977), and veterans (Hippolitus, 1981). The assumption is that a peer counselor has "walked in the client's shoes," has a particular sensitivity to and understanding of the client's problems and feelings, and can translate this sensitivity and understanding into a helpful relationship (Jacques, 1972; Mitra, Fitzgerald, Hilliard, & Baker, 1974). Some clinicians have argued, however, that peer counselors may be attracted to this line of work because of unresolved conflicts that may be counterproductive, if not actually destructive (Feild & Gatewood, 1976).

The assumptions that accompany each of these dimensions may not be valid for any given paraprofessional or professional. A person with professional credentials, for example, may be working as a paraprofessional simply because a professional position is not available. A paraprofessional, in contrast, may be responsible for the same complex tasks as a professional worker. In one instance, a clinical psychologist, who also happened to fill the definition of a peer because of his disabling condition, was working as a volunteer with a particular organization (McCarthy, 1981). Boundaries that appear to be clear-cut are often transcended, particularly on the peer dimension.

HISTORICAL OVERVIEW OF PARAPROFESSIONALS IN COUNSELING

1900–1959, Early Evolution

The first treatment programs established in the United States in the early 1900s, such as Hull House and the Henry Street settlements, were developed by individuals with no training in rehabilitation methodology who would not be considered professionals by today's standards (Benjamin, 1975; Hobbs, 1964; Obermann, 1965). Similarly, those persons involved in designing, planning, and implementing the rehabilitation programs established by the Soldiers Rehabilitation Act of 1918 and the Civilian Rehabilitation Act of 1920 were teachers, administrators, and physicians with no formal training in rehabilitation (Obermann, 1965).

During the Depression, social welfare legislation significantly increased the use of paraprofessionals. To curtail the unemployment rate, such programs as the Works Progress Administration and the National Youth Administration trained and placed out-of-school youth, potential school dropouts, and unemployed persons in a variety of human service programs. By 1940, approximately 13,000 persons had been employed through these efforts. In the 1950s, a number of programs, including the New York State Youth Boards Club Project and health education programs serving Indians, Eskimos, and migrant workers, began using peer workers from among the population being served. Most social service programs, however, recruited and employed paraprofessionals from middle-class backgrounds (Benjamin, 1975).

1960–1967, Need Established

In the early 1960s, the manpower need was acute in all of the helping professions (DiMichael, 1968; Patterson, 1966; Savino & Schlamp, 1968; Smits, 1964; Truax, 1968). This need was certainly acute in vocational rehabilitation programs, which were rapidly expanding for several reasons: their success in returning handicapped persons to productive lives, the enactment of legislation extending services to a wider range of disabled persons, and the subsequent increase in funding for those programs (Rubin & Roessler, 1978). Professional rehabilitation counselor training programs were not yet well established, however, and the shortage of professionally trained rehabilitation personnel and the lack of funding to pay them were well documented (Auvenshine, 1971; Crisler, Porter, & Megathlin, 1969; Jacques, 1972; McMahon & Fraser, 1978; Patterson, 1966; Peth, 1971; Porter, Crisler, & Megathlin, 1967; Smits, 1964; Thoreson, 1972; *Use of Support Personnel*, 1968).

To complicate the situation further, some educators charged that much of the professional rehabilitation counselor's time was spent on tasks that did not require master's level training (Crisler, Porter, & Jones, 1971; Jacques, 1972). Also, because most professionally trained personnel had middle-class backgrounds and values, it was felt that they often did not communicate and interact effectively with clients—alcoholics, drug addicts, convicted offenders, and disadvantaged persons—whose values and lifestyles were so different from their own (Jacques, 1972). Because there simply was not sufficient professional manpower to meet the needs of handicapped clients and because the advantages of using personnel from diverse backgrounds were recognized, it was clear that new sources of manpower needed to be identified (Crisler et al., 1969; *Use of Support Personnel*, 1968).

In response to this need, the Rehabilitation Services Administration (RSA) appointed a committee to explore the possibility of using what it called "support personnel" to assist in the delivery of rehabilitation services. In 1967, the committee conducted a survey of 91 agencies. Of these, only 13 had formal programs using paraprofessionals, and most of those had only recently been established. Nonetheless, the study concluded that rehabilitation aides could be a valuable asset in providing rehabilitation services to handicapped persons (*Use of Support Personnel*, 1968).

1968–1975, Expansion

The period from 1968 to 1975 was characterized by rapid growth and expansion of programs and personnel in vocational rehabilitation agencies. In contrast to the 14 percent of agencies using paraprofessionals reported in the 1967 RSA study, later studies reported rates of 60 percent (Crisler et al., 1969), 48 percent (Crisler et al., 1971), and 53 percent (Jones, Babcock, & Dolecki, 1973). McMahon and Fraser (1978) found that 72 percent of the state rehabilitation agencies hired paraprofessionals during this period.

One cannot accurately compare these studies and establish trends in the use of paraprofessionals because of methodological differences across studies. It is evident, however, that a dramatic increase occurred in the number of agencies employing paraprofessionals and the actual number of paraprofessionals between 1967 and 1975.

1976–Present, Decline

Literature discussing the paraprofessional movement in rehabilitation is almost nonexistent from 1976 to the present. McMahon and Fraser (1978) offered several reasons for the decline in the literature: the threat to the professional counselor, inconsistencies in the classification of positions, and disagreement about the role of the paraprofessional. Decreased funding for social programs is another obvious factor (Delworth, 1974; Gartner & Riessman, 1974). Delworth pointed out that "retrenchment has predictably hit the most vulnerable worker group: the paraprofessionals" (p. 135).

In summary, the use of paraprofessionals in rehabilitation settings increased from the beginning of this century until the middle 1970s. Since then, paraprofessionals have received little attention as a resource in the rehabilitation of disabled clients.

STATUS OF PARAPROFESSIONALS IN REHABILITATION

Despite the declining use of paraprofessionals, it is still worthwhile to examine the literature on the roles, models, selection, and training of these workers.

Roles

Auvenshine (1971) differentiated the role of the professional from that of the paraprofessional as follows: The professional provides counseling services, synthesizes and integrates data about a client, and evaluates the effectiveness of interventions based on relevant theory; in contrast, the paraprofessional performs specific tasks of a technical nature, such as transporting clients, intake interviewing, and community public relations, under the direction of the professional counselor. Auvenshine's position was entirely consistent with that of the RSA study, which unequivocally defined the paraprofessional as "supportive to and under the supervision of the counselor" and the paraprofessional function as "technical in nature rather than professional" (*Use of Support Personnel*), 1968, p. 19). Although some authors called for a clearer definition of the role of paraprofessionals (Crisler, 1973; Peth, 1971), others warned that overdefinition could restrict their effectiveness (Galloway & Kelso, 1966; Thoreson, 1972). Wright and Fraser's (1976) Rehabilitation Task Performance Evaluation Scale facilitates the definition and assignment of tasks that are commensurate with the educational and experiential qualifications of both professionals and paraprofessionals. Using such a system, the paraprofessional is assigned specific tasks, whereas the professional focuses on synthesizing and integrating client data.

In actual practice, the role of the paraprofessional varies according to the needs of a particular agency at a particular time. Agencies assign their paraprofessional workers a wide range of responsibilities, including coordination of client services, intake interviewing, and client follow-up. Paraprofessionals may also provide counseling, job placement, case management, coordination of services, and client evaluations, which are functions usually performed by professional staff (Crisler, 1977; Crisler et al., 1971). Jones et al. (1973) identified the seven most frequently reported tasks of paraprofessionals and the percentage of state agencies using paraprofessionals for these tasks: transportation of clients (98 percent), intake interviews (80 percent), public relations (73 percent), placement activity (68 percent), counseling services (44 percent), client evaluation (44 percent), and caseload management (29 percent). Thoreson (1972) concluded that paraprofessionals served as both a complement to and a substitute for the rehabilitation counselor.

Models

Jacques (1972) summarized several organizational models for the use of paraprofessionals in the rehabilitation process:

- *Counselor unit:* The counselor provides the traditional continuity for the client during the entire rehabilitation process, whereas the paraprofessional performs specific functions under the supervision of the counselor.
- *Supervisory unit:* The paraprofessional serves several counselors and is under the direction of one supervisor. The supervisor coordinates the activities of both the counselors and the paraprofessionals, with the individual counselors having the responsibility for maintaining continuity of services for the clients.
- *Vertical specialization:* The rehabilitation process is divided into functions, such as evaluation, counseling, training, and placement. Counselors specialize in and are responsible for a specific area, and paraprofessionals are assigned to the counselors to perform specified tasks or duties within that area.
- *Support personnel unit:* Paraprofessionals manage a caseload and carry out all related counseling functions under the supervision of a counselor.

Selection

Employment requirements for the paraprofessional in rehabilitation agencies vary considerably according to the job title and type of agency. Educational requirements range from none to a bachelor's degree (Crisler, 1977; *Use of Support Personnel*, 1968), with 62 percent of the rehabilitation agencies studied requiring a high school equivalency or less and the remainder requiring some college work or a degree. The establishment of undergraduate degree programs in rehabilitation education supports the movement to increase the educational requirements of the paraprofessional worker.

Other selection criteria considered by agencies include ethnic background, experience as a client in the rehabilitation system, and previous vocational history (*Use of Support Personnel*, 1968). In one survey, Crisler and Crandell (1977) noted that, of 687 paraprofessionals employed, 17 percent were handicapped, 11 percent were at the entry-level counselor position, and 10 percent held the highest-level counselor position. Experience requirements ranged from no requirement to 5 years of work experience specifically in rehabilitation (Crisler, 1977; McMahon & Fraser, 1978). The most commonly used screening procedure was the personal interview, along with recommendation by a current agency employee (*Use of Support Personnel*, 1968).

Training

The professional literature confirms the need for and the effectiveness of training for the paraprofessional (Brown, 1974; Carkhuff, 1969; Carkhuff & Truax, 1965; Danish & Brock, 1974; Delworth, 1974). A deficit consistently documented in the literature is the lack of programs to teach administrators, professionals, and paraprofessionals effective methods of working together within the organizational structure of the agency (Delworth, 1974; Feild & Gatewood, 1976; Sobey, 1970; *Use of Support Personnel*, 1968).

Two studies found that over 60 percent of rehabilitation agencies offered systematic training programs, usually provided by agency staff (Crisler et al., 1971; Jones et al., 1973). The content of training programs varied, but communication skills training, orientation to agency policies and procedures, and sensitivity training were common foci (*Use of Support Personnel*, 1968).

RESEARCH ON PARAPROFESSIONALS

Much of the literature supports the utility of paraprofessionals in human services programs. Jacques (1972) contended that paraprofessionals perform functions that graduate-level counselors cannot, provide new experiential dimensions and coping models, increase the personnel supply, and allow efficient use of professional counselors. Thoreson (1972) stressed the advantages of utilizing paraprofessionals with special populations and programs. Mitra et al. (1974) described the effectiveness of paraprofessionals with the poor and culturally disadvantaged client. They advocated well-defined roles and a career ladder concept for paraprofessionals. Other research demonstrated that paraprofessionals were effective in rehabilitation programs for the mentally ill (Benjamin, 1975; Savino & Schlamp, 1968; Sobey, 1970).

Two reviewers (Brown, 1974; Peth, 1971) concluded that the bulk of the evidence from a wide variety of sources demonstrated the effectiveness of paraprofessionals. Brown (1974) noted, however, that many research studies were characterized by inadequate research designs and that conclusions were often made on the basis of subjective rather than objective data. Peth (1971) also concluded that much more objective research was needed.

Evidence supporting the positive impact of paraprofessionals on client outcome is sparse. However, Truax (1968) reported significantly better outcomes for clients working with paraprofessionals, compared with outcomes achieved by professionals or professionals and paraprofessionals working together. Most substantive research pertains only to the ability of paraprofessionals to develop appropriate human relations skills (Carkhuff, 1968, 1969; Carkhuff & Truax, 1965; Truax & Carkhuff, 1967; Truax & Lister, 1970).

Hoffman and Warner (1976) reviewed the literature on paraprofessionals and found that some studies demonstrated effectiveness, whereas others with the same populations did not. They concluded that the training of paraprofessionals was well documented, particularly communication training, but they questioned how effective paraprofessionals were with specific tasks in work settings. DiMichael (1968) suggested that, because of the large number of variables, research on this topic could not be conclusive. Durlak (1973), however, proposed:

> Let both the critics and supporters of the non-professional use controlled experimental studies as the criteria to settle their differences. Only by carefully examining the adequacies and deficiencies of clinical experimentation can the blind spots, prejudices, and biases of both camps be exposed and the distorted and unfounded claims of treatment success or failure be dispelled. (p. 304)

Sobey (1970) reported the results of a survey of 185 National Institute of Mental Health programs employing over 10,000 paraprofessionals. Over 50 percent of the directors of these programs favored using paraprofessionals to provide a wide variety of services, including counseling, to clients. Muthard and Salomone (1969) reported that rehabilitation counselors felt that only the most routine and repetitive tasks—interviews, placement assistance, and screening procedures—should be delegated to paraprofessionals. Counselors generally felt more confident in the ability of college-trained personnel to carry out some of their functions. Other studies demonstrated the effectiveness of paraprofessionals in specific settings and with specific functions (Allen & Cohen, 1980; Matthias, 1981; Mitra et al., 1974; Ottomanelli, 1978; Riggs & Meyer, 1981; Wehr & Wittmer, 1973).

Several articles indicated that the use of paraprofessionals improved service delivery to clients (Auvenshine, 1971; Mitra et al., 1974; Taylor, 1972; Thoreson, 1972). Increased referrals, more client contact, and enhanced client participation were cited as benefits from the use of paraprofessionals. According to Mitra et al. (1974), the use of paraprofessionals made the rehabilitation process more acceptable to the client, decreased the time lag between services, and allowed a greater number of eligible clients to be served.

Durlak (1979) analyzed the results of 42 studies comparing the effectiveness of professional and paraprofessional helpers across a broad spectrum of settings. He concluded that the evidence supported the effectiveness of paraprofessionals as service providers, regardless of the sophistication of the research design of the studies. He cautioned, however, that there were still many problems with the research designs being used. Nietzel and Fisher (1981) challenged Durlak's conclusions on the basis of inadequate internal validity of the studies, problems with defining professionals and paraprofessionals, and possible misinterpretation of studies that found no significant differences between the two groups. Durlak (1981) answered that, despite their criticisms, their conclusions were not substantially different from his.

Hattie, Sharpley, and Rogers (1984) tried to resolve this debate by applying meta-analysis procedures. Examining effect sizes from 39 of the studies, they concluded that "paraprofessionals are at least as effective, and in many instances more effective, than professional counselors" (p. 540). Experience levels and length of training were significant variables in paraprofessional effectiveness.

Although research documenting the effectiveness of paraprofessionals in rehabilitation settings is far from conclusive, the evidence appears to favor their use in human service fields. Hattie, Sharpley, and Rogers (1984) reported that "884 effects favoring professionals need to be in someone's file drawer before the overall conclusion will be changed in favor of professionals. Only 34 more effects in favor of paraprofessionals are needed" (p. 540).

ETHICAL AND PROFESSIONAL ISSUES

Allen (1973) delineated seven areas of responsibility professionals have for and to the paraprofessionals who work in human services:

1. Professionals are responsible for the overall success or failure of community service programs to which paraprofessionals contribute.
2. Professionals must clearly define the role of the paraprofessional worker, including specific tasks, expectations, and limitations.
3. Professionals must assume responsibility for training, teaching, and supervising paraprofessionals, avoiding the tendency to instill in the paraprofessional—especially the peer counselor—a stronger identification with the professional group than with the group being served.
4. Professionals should assist in the development and maintenance of a job market for the paraprofessionals who are trained.
5. Professionals should contribute to the development of avenues of career advancement for paraprofessionals to ensure that they are not indefinitely restricted to unskilled positions. Along with career mobility, paraprofessionals should also have geographic mobility, with job functions and training requirements consistent across programs.

6. Paraprofessionals who show evidence of performance comparable to professionals must receive comparable financial compensation. The concept of the paraprofessional as "cheap labor" must be eliminated in favor of adequate pay for the level of services performed.
7. Professionals must be aware of their legal liability for the provision of services and the legal implications of the use of paraprofessionals.

Although Allen made these recommendations at the 50th annual meeting of the American Mental Health Association in 1972, they are still relevant after 15 years.

Professional organizations (American Personnel and Guidance Association, 1967; *Use of Support Personnel*, 1968) have clearly identified the counseling role as belonging to the professional, with more technical and supportive tasks assigned to the paraprofessional under supervision. However, there is still confusion over the definition of a professional (Crisler, 1977; Jones et al., 1973; Porter et al., 1967). Educational and supervision requirements for employment as a rehabilitation counselor vary, as do state licensure requirements. Although there is a clear consensus in favor of careful selection, role definitions, training, supervision, and evaluation of both professionals *and* paraprofessionals, considerable disagreement persists over many operational specifics. Despite repeated calls to address these concerns systematically (Auvenshine, 1971; Crisler, 1973, 1977; Jacques, 1972), little has been accomplished.

RECOMMENDATIONS

Rehabilitation agencies, both private and public, have used paraprofessionals to provide services to disabled clients. Although there have been some successful programs, in many cases problems arose because of (1) inadequate definition of the purpose for which paraprofessionals were hired and the roles they were to play; (2) insufficient training and supervision; (3) the tendency of professionals either to assign excessive counseling responsibility to paraprofessionals or to assign them only routine, repetitive tasks; and (4) inadequate opportunity for advancement by the paraprofessional. The paraprofessional has been essentially on a dead-end street, working at low pay with inadequate training and supervision and without much possibility for climbing a career ladder. Ironically, rehabilitation and other social service agencies have advocated, via their own affirmative action programs and sensitivity to the populations they serve, the hiring of workers whose characteristics closely match those of their clients.

The attempt to use paraprofessionals and peer counselors has taught rehabilitation professionals a number of lessons. Persons without graduate degrees, given adequate training and supervision, can perform tasks that have traditionally been assigned to rehabilitation professionals. There is now a better understanding of the functions that can be performed by both the professional and paraprofessional worker. We know that a middle-class professional staff may exhibit a lack of sensitivity to the problems of minority or disabled clients. We have learned that persons working in jobs with little or no possibility for advancement soon become disenchanted and move on to other positions.

Two recent trends may also have had an impact on the use of paraprofessionals in rehabilitation—the movement for licensure and certification of rehabilitation counselors and the increasing need for more counselors to meet the mandates of the Rehabilitation Act of 1973.

The movement toward licensure and certification for rehabilitation counselors has created considerable debate concerning adequate professional criteria (Wolf, 1979). Because this movement has addressed only professional requirements, the issue of paraprofessional qualifications is still not resolved. Agencies may be reluctant to hire paraprofessionals until the issue is settled.

The Rehabilitation Act of 1973 places priority on providing services to the severely handicapped population, those individuals having "severe functional limitations . . . requiring multiple services over an extended period of time" (Wood & Crisler, 1982, p. 16). Data from the state-federal vocational rehabilitation programs consistently indicate that rehabilitation counselors provide services to more than 100 clients per year (Rubin & Roessler, 1978). The complexity of the needs of severely handicapped clients and the multiple services necessary to achieve rehabilitation goals, combined with the number of clients to be served by decreasing resources, may be overwhelming to the practicing rehabilitation counselor. It is imperative that the potential contribution of paraprofessionals be re-examined.

Now is an opportune time to reflect on what we have learned from our experiences with paraprofessionals and to determine future directions. Professionals, along with policy makers and program administrators, are ultimately responsible for decisions affecting the use of paraprofessionals, and should assume leadership in addressing the issues involved. Considering the trends in licensure and certification, the legislative mandates, and the information now available, we must approach the problems in a systematic and formal way by taking the following steps:

- Documenting the unique contributions of paraprofessionals to the mental health and rehabilitation fields. This is particularly pertinent to the potential of peer counselors to contribute to the rehabilitation counseling process.
- Identifying clearly the functions of professional and paraprofessional workers. The delineation of functions may be based on a continuum of responsibility from information gathering to information analysis, synthesis, and interpretation to assist clients in achieving their goals. Beginning paraprofes-

sionals may be assigned less complex tasks but may assume responsibility for more complex tasks as they gain experience and training.

- Urging national organizations and administrative agencies to adopt a consistent attitude and systematic approach toward the use of paraprofessionals in rehabilitation.
- Adopting the concept of a *pre*professional, rather than a *para*professional, worker. The movement of the preprofessional to professional status would be based on the achievement of professional credentials and levels of job performance.

The authors recommend a program that would encourage the recruitment and training of minority and disabled workers as preprofessionals, with the expectation that they would work toward obtaining professional status. Such a program must begin at the administrative level where the role of the preprofessional must be clearly defined and appropriate training programs instituted. Candidates would be selected and trained based on the following three criteria:

1. Preprofessionals should complete 2 years of college work. Sufficient community-based junior college programs are available to enable a reasonable number of minority and disabled students to achieve this level of education. In this way, persons with the potential eventually to work on a professional level are more likely to be hired.
2. Preprofessionals should be evaluated on their capacity to relate to others in a sensitive manner and their commitment to working with others in a helping capacity. They should be willing to learn the skills needed to work on a professional level.
3. Once preprofessional candidates are selected, they should enter a well-defined sequence of educational and work experiences, including periodic evaluations, that provide them with the skills and credentials of a rehabilitation professional. They should receive financial compensation commensurate with the services they are providing.

The work-study component of the Rehabilitation Counselor Training Program at the University of Georgia provides an example of how the preprofessional concept can be applied in rehabilitation. In this program, state and private agency employees attend classes in rehabilitation at the university for 1 week out of every month. Their academic work eventually leads to a master's degree in rehabilitation counseling. The advantage of this system is that the employee can immediately apply classroom learning to work situations, which can be used in turn as educational examples. The combination of work and education integrates theory and practice. The work-study format is by nature sequential and systematic, with clear evaluation criteria. In the authors' opinion, the work-study concept, with appropriate modifications, can be applied to elevate the preprofessional to a professional status in a systematic, organized way to benefit the employee, the agency, and the client.

Such a system would provide the personnel to increase the effectiveness of rehabilitation programs as they now exist and to expand rehabilitation services to other populations not being served. It would also permit the research necessary to document the effectiveness of the programs in fulfilling the national mandate to serve handicapped individuals.

REFERENCES

Allen, D.A. (1973). Peer counseling and professional responsibility. *The Journal of the American College Health Association, 21*, 339–342.

Allen, H.A., Jr., & Cohen, M.S. (1980). Client preference for a disabled counselor. *Rehabilitation Counseling Bulletin, 23*, 165–168.

American Personnel and Guidance Association (1967). Support personnel for the rehabilitation counselor: Their technical and non-technical roles and preparation. *The Personnel and Guidance Journal, 45*, 858–861.

Auvenshine, C.D. (1971). Support personnel and counseling in vocational rehabilitation. *Rehabilitation Counseling Bulletin, 15*, 116–125.

Benjamin, L. (1975). *Paraprofessionals in human services. An ERIC/CAPS perspective on the preparation, training and future of the paraprofessional counselor.* Ann Arbor, MI: University of Michigan. (ERIC Document Reproduction Service No. ED 096 600)

Brown, W.F. (1974). Effectiveness of paraprofessionals: The evidence. *The Personnel and Guidance Journal, 53*, 257–263.

Buck, M.R. (1977). Peer counseling from a black perspective. *The Journal of Black Psychology, 3*(2), 107–113.

Carkhuff, R.R. (1968). Differential functioning of lay and professional helpers. *Journal of Counseling Psychology, 15*, 117–126.

Carkhuff, R.R. (1969). *Helping and human relations* (Vols. 1 & 2). New York: Holt, Rinehart, & Winston.

Carkhuff, R.R., & Truax, C.B. (1965). Lay mental health counseling: The effects of lay group counseling. *Journal of Counseling Psychology, 29*, 426–431.

Crisler, J.R. (1973). Effective paraprofessional utilization—Myth or reality. *The Journal of Applied Rehabilitation Counseling, 4*, 41–47.

Crisler, J.R. (1977). Results of the career ladder survey in state vocational rehabilitation agencies. *The Journal of Applied Rehabilitation Counseling, 8*, 218–227.

Crisler, J.R., & Crandell, E.O. (1977). Employment criteria and salaries for rehabilitation personnel in state DVR agencies having career ladders. *The Journal of Applied Rehabilitation Counseling, 8*, 150–163.

Crisler, J.R., Porter, T.L., & Jones, R.D. (1971). Rehabilitation counselor salaries and benefits: 1971. *The Journal of Applied Rehabilitation Counseling, 3*, 152–166.

Crisler, J.R., Porter, T.L., & Megathlin, W.L. (1969). Rehabilitation counselor salaries and benefits. *NRCA Professional Bulletin, 9*(6), 1–12.

Danish, S.J., & Brock, G. (1974). The current status of paraprofessional training. *The Personnel and Guidance Journal, 53*, 299–303.

Delworth, U. (1974). Paraprofessionals as guerillas: Recommendations for system change. *The Personnel and Guidance Journal, 53*, 335–338.

DiMichael, S.G. (1968). Preparation of rehabilitation technicians in community colleges. *Rehabilitation Counseling Bulletin, 12*, 76–83.

Durlak, J.A. (1973). Myths concerning the nonprofessional therapist. *Professional Psychology, 4*, 300–304.

Durlak, J.A. (1979). Comparative effectiveness of paraprofessional and professional helpers. *Psychological Bulletin, 86*, 80–92.

Durlak, J.A. (1981). Evaluating comparative studies of paraprofessional and professional helpers: A reply to Nietzel and Fisher. *Psychological Bulletin, 89*, 566–569.

Feild, H.S., & Gatewood, R. (1976). The paraprofessional and the organization: Some problems of mutual adjustment. *The Personnel and Guidance Journal, 55*, 181–185.

Galloway, J.R., & Kelso, R.R. (1966). Don't handcuff the aide. *Rehabilitation Record, 7*, 1–3.

Gartner, A., & Riessman, F. (1974). The paraprofessional movement in perspective. *The Personnel and Guidance Journal, 53*, 253–256.

George, G.O., Hosford, R.E., & Moss, C.S. (1978). Using videotape programs for training inmates in peer counseling techniques. *Teaching of Psychology, 5*, 205–207.

Hattie, J.A., Sharpley, C.F., & Rogers, H.J. (1984). Comparative effectiveness of professional and paraprofessional helpers. *Psychological Bulletin, 95*, 534–541.

Hippolitus, P. (1981). Help without hassles: Understanding the emotional wounds of war. *Disabled USA, 6*(4), 5–7.

Hobbs, N. (1964). Mental health's third revolution. *The American Journal of Orthopsychiatry, 36*, 822–833.

Hoffman, A.M., & Warner, R.W., Jr. (1976). Paraprofessional effectiveness. *The Personnel and Guidance Journal, 54*, 494–497.

Jacques, M.E. (1972). Rehabilitation counseling and support personnel. *Rehabilitation Counseling Bulletin, 15*, 160–171.

Jones, R.D., Babcock, R.B., & Dolecki, L.S. (1973). Rehabilitation counselor salaries and benefits: 1973. *The Journal of Applied Rehabilitation Counseling, 4*, 133–148.

Matthias, V. (1981). Baltimore's job squad for the handicapped. *Rehabilitation Counseling Bulletin, 24*, 304–307.

McCarthy, H. (1981). Magnum opus: Self-help in Organization of People Undaunted by Stroke. *American Rehabilitation, 7*(1), 7–9.

McMahon, B.T., & Fraser, R.T. (1978). The future of subprofessionals: A time for evaluation. *Rehabilitation Counseling Bulletin, 22*, 30–37.

Mitra, S.B., Fitzgerald, L., Hilliard, H.S., & Baker, R.N. (1974). Effectiveness of paraprofessionals in the rehabilitation process. *Rehabilitation Counseling Bulletin, 18*, 112–116.

Muthard, J.E., & Salomone, P.R. (1969). The roles and functions of rehabilitation counselors [Special issue]. *Rehabilitation Counseling Bulletin, 13*.

Nietzel, M.T., & Fisher, S.G. (1981). Effectiveness of professional and paraprofessional helpers: A comment on Durlak. *Psychological Bulletin, 89*, 555–565.

Obermann, C.E. (1965). *A history of vocational rehabilitation in America*. Minneapolis, MN: T.S. Denison.

Ottomanelli, G.A. (1978). Patient improvement, measured by the MMPI and PYP, related to paraprofessional and professional counselor assignment. *International Journal of the Addictions, 13*, 503–507.

Patterson, C.H. (1966). The rehabilitation counselor: A projection. *Journal of Rehabilitation, 32*(1), 31–49.

Peth, P.R. (1971). A critical examination of the role and function of the nonprofessional in rehabilitation. *Rehabilitation Counseling Bulletin, 14*, 141–152.

Porter, T.L., Crisler, J.R., & Megathlin, W.L. (1967). Rehabilitation counselor salaries and benefits: 1967. *NRCA Professional Bulletin, 7*(5), 1–8.

Riggs, R.C., & Meyer, R.L. (1981). Training paraprofessional group counseling leaders in the federal prison system. *Journal for Specialists in Group Work, 6*, 96–99.

Rockwell, L.K., & Dustin, R. (1979). Building a model for training peer counselors. *The School Counselor, 26*, 311–316.

Rubin, S.E., & Roessler, R.T. (1978). *Foundations of the vocational rehabilitation process.* Baltimore: University Park Press.

Savino, M.T., & Schlamp, F.T. (1968). The use of the nonprofessional rehabilitation aides in decreasing rehospitalization. *Journal of Rehabilitation, 34*, 28–30.

Smits, S.J. (1964). *National Rehabilitation Association: Rehabilitation counselor recruitment study: Final report.* Washington, DC: Department of Health, Education, and Welfare.

Snowden, L., Jr., & Cotler, S. (1974). The effectiveness of paraprofessional ex-addict counselors in a methadone treatment program. *Psychotherapy: Theory, Research and Practice, 11*, 331–338.

Sobey, F. (1970). *The nonprofessional revolution in mental health.* New York: Columbia University Press.

Taylor, R.D. (1972). Similarity of attitudes: An assumption in the use of support personnel in the rehabilitation of the disadvantaged. *Rehabilitation Counseling Bulletin, 15*, 185–191.

Thoreson, R.W. (1972). Use of support personnel: Necessary change or passing fancy in rehabilitation counseling practice. *Rehabilitation Counseling Bulletin, 15*, 201–210.

Truax, C.B. (1968). The effects of supportive personnel and counselor aides in vocational rehabilitation. *NRCA Professional Bulletin, 8*(4).

Truax, C.B., & Carkhuff, R.R. (1967). *Toward effective counseling and psychotherapy: Training and practice.* Chicago: Aldine.

Truax, C.B., & Lister, J.L. (1970). Effectiveness of counselors and counselor aides. *Journal of Counseling Psychology, 17*, 331–334.

Tucker, S.J., & Cantor, P.C. (1975). Personality and status profiles of peer counselors and suicide attempters. *Journal of Counseling Psychology, 22*, 423–430.

Use of support personnel in vocational rehabilitation (Report of The Committee on Effective Utilization of the Rehabilitation Counselor and Supporting Staff, H. Lucas, Chairman). (1968). Washington: Rehabilitation Services Administration. (Rehabilitation Services Series No. 63–13).

Vash, C.L. (1981). *The psychology of disability.* New York: Springer Publishing.

Wehr, M., & Wittmer, J. (1973). Paraprofessional trainees and counselor education students: A comparison of personality and predicted counseling effectiveness. *Counselor Education and Supervision, 12*, 255–261.

Wolf, A. (1979, April). Legal implications that interface with state certification and the rehabilitation counseling profession. *Professional Report.* (Available from the National Rehabilitation Counseling Association, 1522 Kay Street NW, Washington, DC 20005.)

Wood, T., & Crisler, J. (1982). *Current status of the order of selection process in state vocational rehabilitation general agencies.* Unpublished manuscript.

Wright, G.N., & Fraser, R.T. (1976). *Improving manpower utilization: The "Rehabilitation Task Performance Evaluation Scale."* Madison, WI: University of Wisconsin, Rehabilitation Research Institute.

Zwibelman, B.B., & Hinrichsen, J.J. (1977). Effects of training on peer counselor responses to human sexuality problems. *Journal of Counseling Psychology, 24*, 359–364.

Chapter 18

Single-Case Experimental Approaches to the Assessment of Interventions in Rehabilitation

Rosamond Gianutsos, Ph.D.
John Gianutsos, Ph.D.

Group-oriented experimental designs predominate in behavioral research, and it is assumed that readers are only too familiar with them and their analysis. There are many texts on these topics, such as McGuigan's (1968) classic on experimental design and Welkowitz, Ewen, and Cohen's (1976) work on statistical analysis. This chapter describes an alternative approach that is especially well suited to many research questions of concern to rehabilitation specialists. This approach is called the "single-case experimental design" (Hersen & Barlow, 1976; Kazdin, 1982) or the "small N design" (Robinson & Foster, 1979).

Before outlining the critical features of this experimental design, its distinction from case studies should be emphasized. Case studies appeal to rehabilitation clinicians because rehabilitation ultimately requires attention to the unique needs of individuals, and this approach is sensitive to the specifics of the individual case. This orientation to the individual is preserved in single-case experimental designs, which have the added dimension of scientific control.

Single-case experimental design strategies must also be distinguished from the "quasi-experimental design" (Campbell & Stanley, 1963) in which a baseline period is followed by an intervention phase. This design, which could be designated an "AB" design, lacks sufficient control to qualify as conclusive research; hence it is quasi-experimental. Further, it is not necessarily an individually based design; for instance, one could use it to study the effect of decriminalization on marijuana smoking among college students on a particular campus or the institution of strict enforcement of the 55 miles-per-hour speed limit on traffic fatalities. Nevertheless, there is some overlap between the two methods, as single-case experimental designs frequently contain quasi-experimental elements and can use similar approaches to statistical analysis, e.g., the interrupted time series (see McCain & McCleary, 1979).

Finally, single-case experimental designs developed and still are most often encountered in operant behavior studies, although this philosophical framework is not a necessary component of the methodology (Kazdin, 1982).

The single-case experimental method is very well suited to many needs of rehabilitation clinicians. The method focuses on the analysis of individuals, which is to say that data are typically presented separately for each person, even though several individuals may be included in a single study. Repeated measurements are taken so that data are almost always presented as a function of sessions, trials, or time; this allows evaluation of the effectiveness of a treatment for each individual, over and above spontaneous recovery effects. Characteristically, one assesses the course of recovery by collecting a series of baseline measures and introducing treatment only after a clear trend is established.

In single-case experimental designs, the generalizability of the treatment is addressed explicitly through two kinds of replication studies, which can yield clinically useful information on the differential effectiveness of the treatment for a variety of patients and situations. *Direct replication* is the exact repetition of a study in all aspects that may be reasonably expected to be relevant. *Systematic replication* involves repetition of a study with controlled changes in variables across which generalization may be expected. Examples of such variables are age and educational level of the patient, training materials, therapists, and locations. The idea is to demonstrate that the treatment works, despite variations in these factors. Through this systematic process, the limits of generalizability are established.

In short, it is these features of the single-case experimental approach—they are individually based, they involve repeated measurement, and they are followed by direct tests of generalizability—that are significant for the rehabilitation clinician. (See Coltheart (1983) and Shallice (1979) for further discussion of this method's utility.)

It is important to counter the view that scientific rigor is only associated with group designs and complex inferential statistical procedures. Rigorous control is possible in the systematic use of single-case experimental designs; for those who crave inferential statistics, such procedures are available (Kazdin, 1976; McCain & McCleary, 1979).

Further, it is a misconception to assume that general conclusions must be based on group designs. Perhaps insurance companies, program evaluators, and the government may be able to afford the statistical error of the group-oriented research design; however, the members of a treatment team concerned with the restoration of specific individuals cannot. It is those individuals, after all, who risk becoming stuck in the tails of the distribution. Moreover, the actuarial approach of the group design does not guarantee generalizability. Although clinicians may wish to know the percentage of cases benefiting from a given intervention, they also require information on which individuals will benefit and under what circumstances. As described earlier, these are the issues that are addressed in the replication phase of single-case experimental designs.

Although single-case experimental designs are very useful for rehabilitation clinicians, one cannot be blind to those situations and experimental issues for which group designs are indicated. For example, group-oriented designs are best for situations where an intervention must be used for all members of a group! Would an increase in the drinking age substantially reduce traffic fatalities? Does a law mandating the wearing of seatbelts significantly reduce the incidence of severe head trauma? Does a daily dose of aspirin reduce the incidence of cerebrovascular accident? However, it is difficult to devise a compelling example in rehabilitation, unless one has administrative concerns, where one can only afford to implement one type of treatment and needs to know which is most generally effective.

To compare incompatible treatment packages, one of the group designs is likely to be best, although Kazdin (1982) does describe a single-case experimental design ("Simultaneous-Treatment design") that permits the comparison of two treatments if certain conditions are met—that there is no carryover between conditions and that the conditions are readily distinguishable. If there is a multiplicity of conditions—many levels of one variable, or several variables—a group design is probably required, especially for simultaneous evaluation.

A group design is also appropriate when one seeks to understand the interrelationships, redundancies, and distinct underlying factors of a large number of measures. An example is a study of visual imperception in a large group of brain-injured and nonbrain-injured rehabilitation inpatients (Gianutsos, Glosser, Vroman, & Elbaum, 1983). A variety of perceptual measures were given to each subject, and the data were then factor analyzed. The result was the discovery, based on the identification of redundancies among measures, of distinct syndromes of imperception, including spatial hemi-imperception, foveal hemi-imperception, and lateral scanning disorder. Ironically, this elaborate group design yielded information that will foster the individualization of treatment.

These situations notwithstanding, it is the authors' position that single-case experimental design strategies should be prominent among the options for the assessment of interventions in rehabilitation. Generally speaking, the single-case experimental approach proceeds in well-defined stages, starting with a demonstration in an individual, proceeding to direct replication on similar cases, and concluding with systematic replication, in which the effects of secondary variables are examined. The principal advantage of single-case methods is that they permit one to dissociate treatment effects from other recovery factors, i.e., from "spontaneous recovery." The basic strategy is to determine a baseline sufficient to permit one to predict the "natural" course of recovery, i.e., without treatment. The intervention is then introduced, and any difference from the projected course may be attributed to the treatment. The length of the baseline period, which determines the length of the later phases, should be adequate to establish a stable initial trend and to reveal new trends in subsequent stages. Four sessions (points) is an absolute minimum. Phase lengths should be kept constant both for esthetic considerations and to avoid the temptation to change conditions only when results favor the hypothesis.

Characteristically, the approach is longitudinal, more intensive, and less complex than group-oriented approaches. Having concluded such a study, the converted group-oriented researcher feels more confident about and "in touch" with the findings, but also feels that fewer questions have been addressed. If the study involved retraining (see example below), important information will have been gained about the course of skill reacquisition, which would not have been otherwise available.

SPECIFIC DESIGN STRATEGIES

The two major classes of single-case experimental design are the multiple baseline design and the sequential introduction and withdrawal (ABAB) design. A third class, the simultaneous-treatment design, recently introduced by Kazdin (1982), is discussed briefly.

Sequential Introduction and Withdrawal

The simplest design conceptually, the sequential introduction and withdrawal design, involves the successive alternation of blocks of sessions of "A" and "B" conditions. Typically, one is a baseline or control condition, such as no specific reward for attending treatment sessions, and one is an intervention, e.g., points applicable toward a chosen reward for attendance. Alternatively, one condition may be a conventional therapy and the other an enhanced therapy, such as physical therapy without (A) or with (B) electromyographic feedback.

The return to control (baseline) conditions is critical to the logic of this strategy. If one observes a gain at the time of the introduction of treatment, it is always possible that the introduction of treatment coincided with the effect of some other variable that was actually responsible for the gain. If upon return to baseline conditions, one finds that performance returns to the baseline level, the argument is strengthened that it was the treatment that produced the effect.

A major limitation to this design is the requirement that each condition be independent of the others; that is, each condition ceases its effect when withdrawn and one condition does not influence another. These requirements are often difficult, undesirable or, sometimes, impossible (as with the impact of brain surgery) to meet. The impact of some treatments persists, and this carryover of effects, which is desirable for a training intervention, subverts the logic of this design. A patient with memory difficulty, for example, who has learned to use mnemonic strategies is not likely to abandon them simply because the design of the experiment so dictates.

Simultaneous Treatment Design

In the simultaneous treatment design, the relative power of two or more conditions is evaluated by alternating their administration in a kind of split-session schedule. For example, electromyographic feedback might be employed with graphic results (A) during part of the session and in video game format (B) for the remainder. In this design, each condition must be clearly distinguishable, and again, carryover effects are not anticipated. One examines the comparative effects of the treatments. If no differences are found, however, one cannot tell if the conditions were equally effective or equally ineffective.

Multiple Baseline Designs

In the multiple baseline approach several behaviors or subjects are evaluated at the same (logical) time. This design has the advantage of permitting conditions with effects that may endure or are irreversible. For this reason, it is especially useful for evaluating the effects of rehabilitative training where persistence of treatment effects is desired.

Furthermore, controlled studies may be designed in which no person must be assigned to an untreated control group or is removed from treatment. Instead, control is accomplished by staggering the introduction of treatment. Three kinds of multiple baseline designs are cited by Hersen and Barlow (1976); multiple baseline across behaviors, subjects, and settings.

Multiple Baseline Across Behaviors

A study directed by one of the authors used a multiple baseline across behaviors design to evaluate the effects of electromyographic feedback in the restoration of motor function in hemiparetic upper extremities. Responses to treatment of three muscle groups—shoulder, elbow, and wrist—were monitored. Treatment was introduced after a series of baseline sessions to one muscle group. After further trials, feedback was added for a second group, and later still, to the last muscle group (Gianutsos, Eberstein, Krasilovsky, Ragnarsson, & Goodgold, 1986).

In this design, the behaviors must be independent of each other. In this example, as in most such situations, this assumption is not completely valid as the development of control of the elbow, for example, might influence the recovery of the shoulder. However, the results for two subjects, shown in Figures 18–1 and 18–2, show gains only when treatment was introduced to each muscle group.

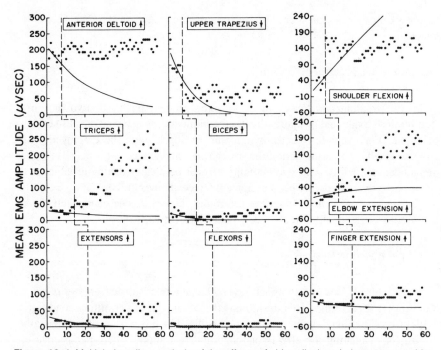

Figure 18–1 Multiple baseline analysis of the effects of video-displayed electromyographic feedback on mean electromyographic amplitude recorded from protagonist/antagonist muscle pairs of the hemiparetic upper extremity. The patient was a 73-year-old man who had suffered a left-hemispheric infarction 3 years earlier. Introduction of the electromyographic feedback to different muscle pairs was staggered. The *broken vertical lines* indicate the session during which feedback was initiated to that group. For each muscle group, data points on the left of the vertical line were obtained during the baseline phase, whereas those on the line or to its right were obtained during the feedback phase. The baseline data points were used to generate a projected trend curve indicated by the *solid curves*. Each session's data point represents the peak electromyograph of six responses without the benefit of feedback about the electromyographic response. The right column of graphs represents the combined score of the protagonist/antagonist pair obtained by subtracting the electromyographic values of each muscle in the middle column from its counterpart in the left column. *Arrow orientation* indicates the therapeutically desired direction of electromyographic change.

Multiple Baseline Across Subjects

The basic strategy in this design is to introduce treatment at different times for each patient in hopes of showing an effect when and only when treatment is introduced. In an early study of mnemonic elaboration training for patients with memory deficits, Gianutsos and Gianutsos (1979) used the multiple baseline across subjects strategy (Figure 18–3). Four brain injured people participated in a series of 18 sessions. Two of them received treatment early, after 6 baseline sessions, whereas the other two began treatment after 12 sessions. Improvements

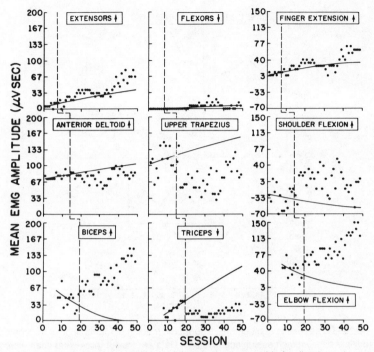

Figure 18–2 The results of a replication of the electromyographic feedback study on a 59-year-old man who had a right-hemispheric infarction 7 months earlier.

were associated with the introduction of treatment, regardless of when it was initiated.

Multiple Baseline Across Settings

These designs apply a strategy similar to the other multiple baseline designs. With it one might evaluate setting effects or their absence—generalizability outside the clinic. The authors know of no examples of this design's use in rehabilitation, however, and refer the reader to Hersen and Barlow (1976) for illustrations.

DETAILED EXAMPLES

Sequential Introduction and Withdrawal Design to Assess the Effect of a Memory-Enhancing Drug

This study was conducted by R. Gianutsos in collaboration with Drs. Clark Randt and Thomas Tartaro of the Department of Neurology, New York University Medical Center.

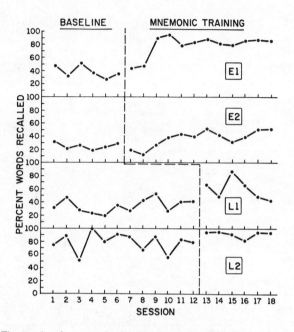

Figure 18-3 The results of mnemonic elaboration training of four brain injured people using the multiple baseline across subjects strategy. Data are from a three-word interpolated task condition. E1, E2, L1, and L2 are different "early" and "late" subjects.

Source: From "Rehabilitating the Verbal Recall of Brain-injured Patients by Mnemonic Training: An Experimental Demonstration Using Single-case Methodology" by R. Gianutsos and J. Gianutsos, 1979, *Journal of Clinical Neuropsychology, 1,* pp. 117–135. Copyright 1979 by Swets Publishing Service. Reprinted by permission.

Peters and Levin (1977) used a double-blind randomized series of sessions of the drug physostigmine and control injections to demonstrate the memory-enhancing effects of the former in a postencephalitic (herpes simplex type) amnesic patient. In the Cognitive Rehabilitation Unit at Bellevue Hospital, the researchers were treating a college professor with the same etiology who experienced an enduring deficit in the registration and retention of new information for more than a few seconds. The patient and aspects of his rehabilitation are described elsewhere (Gianutsos, 1981; Gianutsos & Grynbaum, 1983); data from the initial phases of his treatment are discussed in the second example. The patient had shown some gains in memory function with training, but had stabilized at a level far below his probable premorbid status.

The researchers decided to replicate, in a systematic fashion, Peters' and Levin's (1977) approach by using the single-case experimental methodology. Treatment sessions were arranged in blocks; thus, drug effects could build up over several days, if need be, and conversely, treatment differences would not be diluted by persistence of the drug effects. Also, the course of the drug's effect (immediate or gradual) would be apparent.

The design can be summarized schematically as:

A A' B A' B

Each letter represents a four-session phase: A—a "no drug" baseline, A'—a saline control injection, and B—an injection of physostigmine, 0.8 mg (.017 mg/ kg). There were a total of 20 sessions, the first four of which were baseline testing of memory. The remaining 16 sessions were organized into four alternating blocks. In order to ensure that neither subject nor examiner (R.G.) was aware of the nature of the injection at any given time, the physicians (C.R. and T.T.) who gave the injections were provided an alternate scheme:

A B A' B A'

and asked to utilize one or the other for the study. Measures of short- and long-term storage, as well as retrieval, were derived from two word list retention procedures: (1) Free Recall (see Gianutsos, 1981) and (2) Buschke and Fuld's (1974) Selective Reminding procedure, as used by Peters and Levin (1977). It is important to note that Peters and Levin found that physostigmine enhanced item recall from lists using the Selective Reminding technique, but not on other memory measures, e.g., Benton Visual Retention Test, Supraspan Digit Storage. The present study incorporated those conditions—tests and dosages—that Peters and Levin found to exhibit the greatest effects.

Notwithstanding these precautions, this study was unable to find any evidence that physostigmine improved the memory of our subject, as clearly shown in Figures 18–4 and 18–5. Free recall findings are shown in Figure 18–4. The same pattern holds for all measures derived from the selective reminding procedure, some of which are shown in Figure 18–5.

It is ironic that in one single case this study proved the null hypothesis, albeit only for the one case. The irony arises from the fact that, in group designs, strictly speaking, one needs large sample sizes to retain the null hypothesis convincingly. Yet through simple inspection of the graphic display, one can say with confidence that this dose of physostigmine had no consistent effect on the professor's memory. Whether any dose would have helped and whether this dose would have worked with another patient are questions that remain to be addressed in systematic replications.

Visual inspection of results was sufficient in this study and is customary in the analysis of single case experimental designs. This tradition undoubtedly is attributable to the historic association of these designs with operant methodology.

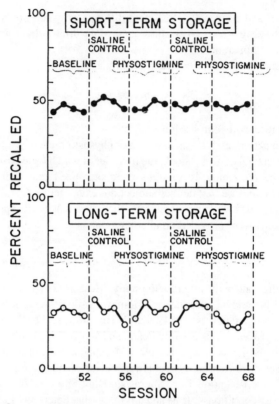

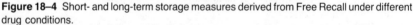

Figure 18–4 Short- and long-term storage measures derived from Free Recall under different drug conditions.

In Skinner's (1950) classic article, "Are Theories of Learning Necessary?" he asserts that if effects are not large and consistent enough to be revealed by visual inspection, they are probably not large enough to matter.

Formal statistical methods are available, including time series analysis (Kazdin in Hersen & Barlow, 1976; McCain & McCleary, 1979; Wallace & Elder, 1980). However, this technique usually requires a lengthy baseline period, which, in clinical situations, is tantamount to withholding treatment. The authors' preference, illustrated in Figures 18–1, 18–2 and 18–6, involves a projected regression line. A detailed description of this approach follows.

Multiple Baseline Across Behaviors

The initial phases of the memory rehabilitation of the professor employed a multiple baseline across behaviors strategy. Because a full report of this study has been published (Gianutsos, 1981), the focus here is on the design aspects.

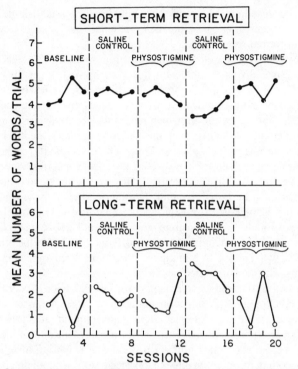

Figure 18–5 Short- and long-term retrieval measures derived from the Buschke and Fuld Selective Reminding task, under different drug conditions.

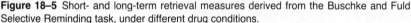

The first step is to define valid target measures to serve as indicators of progress. The task was Free Recall, and the measures were indices of short-term storage (STS) and long-term storage (LTS) derived from distinct lists—those without and with postlist interference—that therefore were independent of each other.

A baseline is then established by conducting a series of sessions during which no other training tasks were scheduled. This phase is critical to the logic of the design because it is here that one determines the projected course of recovery without intervention. It is important to resist the temptation to abbreviate the baseline and initiate treatment. The authors avoid this temptation in several ways. The planned yardstick task(s) is begun early in the evaluation sessions and is administered together with other tasks. In this way, the baseline is partially established before one even contemplates beginning remedial procedures. Also, the authors present this phase as the "do your best" phase, not as the "no treatment" phase. The patient is told, "We want to see how well you can do on your own. Maybe you won't even need our help. If you get stuck, we've got some ideas of ways to help."

Incidentally, the authors take this approach whether the study is defined as "research" or as "treatment." Good clinical practice ought to meet the standards of research, because in clinical work one should seek to establish the efficacy of interventions. By this logic, baseline measurement is just as necessary in clinical practice as in formal research.

In this instance, the baseline lasted only four sessions. A clear trend was established, especially in the indicator that was the first target for treatment—short-term storage. In retrospect, it seems that this length was just barely adequate, and more sessions are recommended. A major determinant is the consistency of scores from session to session, in which regard the professor was remarkable. If there is considerable variability, as in the electromyographic feedback examples, baselines must be longer. It is a good idea to graph the scores after each session and to ask oneself if one is confident in projecting the course of performance. The basic rule is that one must establish a clear trend. However, if the trend is not flat, other considerations must be borne in mind. On the one hand, if the trend is in the direction of the desired effect, it is probably wise to extend the baseline. It will, after all, be difficult to demonstrate gain over and above natural recovery. Furthermore, if improvement is occurring, why intervene? On the other hand, if the patient is worsening—from fatigue, boredom, discouragement, or actual deterioration—change is in order.

The third step is to introduce treatment to the first behavior. According to strict scientific methodology, the selection of the first target behavior ought to be random. However, in this example, as in many clinical situations, there was reason to choose a particular sequence. Here, it made sense to strengthen short-term storage before addressing long-term storage. It is hard to imagine a person successfully coding information into the long-term store without first being able to maintain information in the short-term store.

In this example, the treatment for increasing short-term storage was a verbal Memory Span exercise on which the professor's scores (not shown) also increased. In each session the Memory Span exercise preceded Free Recall. This schedule was maintained for four sessions, which was the phase length. As mentioned earlier in this chapter, the phase length should be at least the same length as the baseline phase and, if longer, a multiple of the length of the baseline phase.

The results (Figure 18–6) showed that introduction of the Memory Span exercise increased the short-term storage index, whereas the long-term storage measure remained the same.

The next step is to introduce treatment targeted toward the second behavior, in this case the long-term storage index of Free Recall. The treatment—Mnemonic Elaboration Training, in which triplets of to-be-recalled words are related in a sentence or image—was added to the sessions using the Memory Span exercise. The result was a small, but distinct, increase in the long-term storage component of free recall.

Statistical evaluation of results using the projected regression technique is the next step. This evaluation confirmed the impression that the increase in the long-

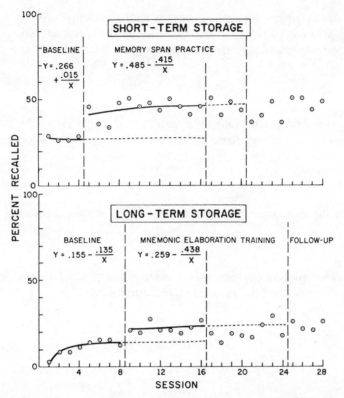

Figure 18–6 Short- and long-term storage measures derived from the patient's Free Recall performance. *Dotted circles* represent observed data points, and *solid lines* represent best-fitting curves, based on the use of a hyperbolic function. *Dotted lines* represent projections of natural recovery derived from baseline performance.

Source: From "Training the Short- and Long-term Recall of a Post-encephalitic Amnesic" by R. Gianutsos, 1981, *Journal of Clinical Neuropsychology, 3,* 143–153. Copyright 1981 by Swets Publishing Service. Reprinted by permission.

term store was "distinct." The first part of the solution involved fitting the baseline data using traditional curve-fitting procedures, specifically deriving a least squares regression line (or curve, if a nonlinear model is used). Below is an example of the projected regression line technique:

The regression equation is computed from pairs of session numbers (x) and the scores (y). The best fitting line is then extended into the subsequent treatment phase. If the new phase represents no change, then the projected line will divide the actual data points approximately evenly.

The long-term storage baseline was not linear across sessions, but rather rose initially and leveled off. This pattern is characteristic of a hyperbolic function, which is expressed by the equation

$$y = b \left(\frac{1}{x} \right) + a$$

In this example, the values of x are the session numbers, and the y are the long-term storage scores. If one takes the reciprocal of x, or

$$x' = \frac{1}{x}$$

then the above equation can be put in the form of a linear equation:

$$y = b x' + a$$

In other words, a conventional linear regression of y and 1/x will yield coefficients a and b. This solution is illustrated below:

x	1/x	y
1	1.00	.0278
2	.50	.0833
3	.33	.0833
4	.25	.1111
5	.20	.1389
6	.17	.1528
7	.14	.1528
8	.12	.1250

The coefficients, a = .155 and b = −.135, can then be put into the hyperbolic equation, together with subsequent values of x, to predict new scores, viz.:

$$y = -.135 \left(\frac{1}{x} \right) + .155$$

The new values of y are the projected values of recall for sessions following the baseline. These have been graphed as solid curves in Figure 18–6. The solid curves in Figures 18–1 and 18–2 are also projections for the electromyographic feedback study using this technique.

At this point one could draw conclusions by comparing, through visual inspection, the projected line and the actual scores in the treatment phase.

Alternatively, one can use a statistical test, such as the binomial test, to evaluate the reliability of the difference between projected and actual scores. The binomial test begins with the null hypothesis that, if the actual scores represent a continuation of the baseline level, then they will be as likely to fall below as above the projected points. In this example, 8 out of 8 actual scores were above the projected line. The likelihood of this outcome was, by the binomial test, sufficiently low (less than .05) that the null hypothesis—that the treatment was not effective— could be rejected.

The choice of the hyperbolic function was based on the assumption that the underlying process was one of initial adjustment followed by leveling off. The coefficients themselves have some meaning. The asymptotic value of the function—the value of y when x becomes very large—is measured by the coefficient a. In this example, a is the limit of improvement of the LTS curve without intervention. In session 1, the value of y is a + b, which means that b must be negative for a function that rises to an asymptotic value. So, b is the difference between the starting point and the limiting value. This hyperbolic function seems to have widespread usefulness for modeling the types of baseline processes involved in rehabilitation. It works just as well when the process involves a settling down, as in an adjustment to novelty.

The choice of function can be a Pandora's box in the use of this technique. It is therefore advisable to determine the function on a priori grounds or, at least, without being influenced by the postbaseline scores.

There are also situations where the binomial test would not work. For example, as illustrated in the shoulder flexion curve of Figure 18–1, when treatment began, there was an immediate increment that was maintained. Because there had been some increase in the baseline, the projected curve rose up to and crossed the actual data. Although the binomial test would suggest the opposite, there was a clear initial treatment effect.

Direct and systematic replications are the next logical steps in this line of research.

ADVANTAGES OF SINGLE-CASE EXPERIMENTAL DESIGNS

This approach is useful for studying rare or unusual cases. Some of the designs—ABAB and multiple baseline across behaviors—are logically complete within each case, which makes them especially useful in these situations.

Single-case experimental designs allow one to discover the course of an effect. Was it sudden or gradual? In the case of the professor, the rapidity of effects suggests that the treatment helped him reactivate an existing skill, not to learn a new one.

These designs allow one to discover a change in the consistency of performance. Frequently, for example, the memory of a head injured person varies greatly at different times. After treatment it might become more predictable, if not better.

Unlike group designs, single-case experimental designs do not confound the number of subjects affected with the magnitude of gain in each. This is an important distinction for the clinician. That is, if there is an average gain of 20 percent in a group design, one cannot tell without looking at the raw data whether 20 percent of the subjects gained a great deal or all subjects gained 20 percent.

Single-case experimental designs rarely conflict with the goals and ethics of clinical practice. It is usually the timing of onset of treatment, not the provision of treatment, which is varied. No one need be denied treatment, nor must effective treatments be withdrawn. In clinical work with group designs, control subjects may withdraw from the experiment once it becomes apparent that treatment is being withheld.

With single-case experimental designs one is more likely to be studying clinically significant effects, as changes must be of a sufficient magnitude to be seen in data on individuals. The researcher observes effects and changes firsthand. Further, with group designs, one often has no sense of the findings until the data are processed statistically. With the single subject approach, one knows immediately whether treatment is having an effect.

In single-case experimental designs, the researcher-subject relationship is quite different—more pleasant and more informative (therapeutic)—than what can develop in the brief formal contact of group designs. There is ample opportunity for subjects to contribute their own perspectives. Where the subject is also a patient, these features are, of course, more consonant with therapeutic goals. Subjects often draw attention to matters that otherwise might have been overlooked.

Philosophically, the individual orientation of single-case experimental designs offers a certain compatibility with the individual nature of the processes one seeks to rehabilitate. For example, memory is not a collective phenomenon, but rather a function of the individual.

CONCLUSION

Single-case experimental designs have great potential for scientifically rigorous, individually meaningful research into the effects of rehabilitative interventions. These strategies may be adapted to specific situations so that one never has to deny or withdraw a potential treatment. They are therefore compatible with the goals of clinical practice, although they do require discipline and a systematic step-by-step approach.

Although there remain circumstances for which group designs are best, the application of single-case experimental approaches, particularly the multiple baseline strategy, will enhance the scientific basis of clinical practice in rehabilitation.

REFERENCES

Buschke, H., & Fuld, P.A. (1974). Evaluating storage, retention, and retrieval in disordered memory and learning. *Neurology, 24,* 1019–1025.

Campbell, D.T., & Stanley, J.C. (1963). *Experimental and quasi-experimental designs for research.* Chicago: Rand McNally.

Coltheart, M. (1983). Aphasia therapy research: A single-case study approach. In Code, C., & Muller, D. (Eds.) *Aphasia therapy.* London: Edward Arnold.

Gianutsos, J.G., Eberstein, A., Krasilovsky, G., Ragnarsson, K.T., & Goodgold, J. (1986). Visually displayed EMG feedback: Single case studies of hemiplegic upper extremity rehabilitation. *Central Nervous System Trauma, 3,* 63–76.

Gianutsos, R. (1981). Training the short- and long-term recall of a post-encephalitic amnesic. *Journal of Clinical Neuropsychology, 3,* 143–153.

Gianutsos, R., & Gianutsos, J. (1979). Rehabilitating the verbal recall of brain-injured patients by mnemonic training: An experimental demonstration using single-case methodology. *Journal of Clinical Neuropsychology, 1,* 117–135.

Gianutsos, R., Glosser, D., Vroman, G., & Elbaum, J. (1983). Multi-faceted measures of visual hemi-imperception in brain-injured adults. *Archives of Physical Medicine and Rehabilitation, 64,* 457–462.

Gianutsos, R., & Grynbaum, B.B. (1983). Helping brain-injured people to contend with hidden cognitive deficits. *International Rehabilitation Medicine, 5,* 37–40.

Hersen, M., & Barlow, D.H. (Eds.) (1976). *Single-case experimental designs: Strategies for studying behavior change.* New York: Pergamon Press.

Kazdin, A.E. (1976). Statistical analyses for single-case experimental designs. In M. Hersen & D.H. Barlow (Eds.), *Single-case experimental designs: Strategies for studying behavior change* (pp. 265–316). New York: Pergamon Press.

Kazdin, A.E. (1982). Single-case experimental designs. In P.C. Kendall & J.N. Butcher (Eds.), *Handbook of research methods in clinical psychology* (pp. 461–490). New York: Wiley.

McCain, L.J., & McCleary, R. (1979). The statistical analysis of the simple interrupted time-series quasi-experiment. In T.D. Cook & D.T. Campbell (Eds.), *Quasi-experimentation: Design and analysis issues for field settings* (pp. 233–293). Chicago: Rand McNally.

McGuigan, F.J. (1968). *Experimental psychology: A methodological approach* (2nd ed.). Englewood Cliffs, NJ: Prentice-Hall, Inc.

Peters, B.H., & Levin, H.S. (1977). Memory enhancement after physostigmine treatment in the amnesic syndrome. *Archives of Neurology, 34,* 215–219.

Peters, B.H., & Levin, H.S. (1979). Effects of physostigmine and lecithin on memory in Alzheimer disease. *Annals of Neurology, 6,* 219–221.

Robinson, P.W., & Foster, D.F. (1979). *Experimental psychology: A small-n approach.* New York: Harper & Row.

Shallice, T. (1979). Case study approach in neuropsychology. *Journal of Clinical Neuropsychology, 1,* 183–211.

Skinner, B.F. (1950). Are theories of learning necessary? *Psychological Review, 57,* 193–216.

Tulving, E., & Arbuckle, T.Y. (1963). Sources of intratrial interference in immediate recall of paired associates. *Journal of Verbal Learning and Verbal Behavior, 1,* 321–334.

Wallace, C.J., & Elder, J.P. (1980). Statistics to evaluate measurement accuracy and treatment effects in single-subject research designs. In *Progress in Behavior Modification, Vol. 10,* (pp. 39–79). New York: Academic Press.

Welkowitz, J., Ewen, R.B., & Cohen, J. (1976). *Introductory statistics for the behavioral sciences (2nd ed.).* New York: Academic Press.

Preparation of this paper was supported in part by Grant No. G008300071 and Grant No. G008300039 from the National Institute of Handicapped Research, U.S. Department of Education, Washington, DC.

Part VI

Medical Aspects

Chapter 19

The Medical Aspects of Disabling Conditions: An Overview

Jean Muller-Rohland, M.D.

This chapter provides an overview of medical aspects of the disabling illnesses most commonly encountered on a rehabilitation unit. The various conditions are discussed with respect to etiology, clinical presentation (symptom complexes), functional deficits, management problems, and possible complications. This chapter is not intended to be exhaustive. The interested reader should consult the references at the end of the chapter for further information (see especially Kottke, Stillwell, & Lehmann, 1982).

Until recently, most injuries and acute medical problems that can produce lasting physical disability were fatal. Thus, chronic conditions were uncommon. In the past 30 years, however, advances in medical knowledge and technology have vastly increased the number of patients with disabling conditions who survive the acute phase. Concurrently, the proliferation of rehabilitation centers has provided places where disabled persons can learn the techniques necessary for independent living. As a result, an ever-greater portion of the population at large can be characterized as chronically disabled.

Although the types of patients seen in rehabilitation settings vary, they usually have physically handicapping features, such as weakness, paralysis, or sensory deficits. Common causes of chronic acquired physical disability are spinal cord injury, cerebrovascular accident (stroke), amputation, traumatic head injury, multiple sclerosis, arthritis, and various neurologic diseases. Because some of these problems are prevalent in the geriatric population (Libow & Sherman, 1981), the rehabilitation team must also treat medical conditions associated with normal aging, such as diabetes mellitus, hypertension, peripheral vascular disease, cardiac conditions, gastrointestinal disorders, and pulmonary problems. These coexisting conditions are not considered in this chapter.

SPINAL CORD INJURY

Epidemiology

Before World War II, spinal cord injury (SCI) was essentially a lethal condition. In the two succeeding decades, methods of management of every affected body system were dramatically improved, substantially reducing immediate mortality and permitting the prospect of a significantly enhanced quality of life for the SCI patient.

Because SCI is not routinely reported to any single central agency, estimates of its incidence are imprecise. One study estimated that roughly 100,000 persons with traumatic SCI live in the United States, and 10,000 new injuries occur each year; approximately 40 percent of these persons have complete paralysis in the affected extremities, and the remainder have varying degrees of function preserved (Yashow, 1978). The annual incidence of traumatic SCI is 3 per 100,000 in industrialized countries, with men being affected five times as often as women (Kraus, Franti, Riggins, Richard, & Borhani, 1975).

Approximately 50 percent of injuries result from motor vehicle accidents, 20 percent from falls, and 15 percent from sports or recreational activities, such as diving accidents. The remaining cases are produced by gunshot wounds, penetrating injuries, such as stabbing, agricultural and industrial accidents, infection, neoplasm (tumor), and interruption of the blood supply because of spontaneous hematoma, cardiac arrest, or aortic aneurysm. According to one large-scale study, 70 percent of all SCIs are sustained by persons between 15 and 34 years of age. At the time of injury, about 60 percent are employed, and one-fourth are students (National SCI Data Research Center, 1978). The death rate from isolated SCI is about 1.4 per 100,000; however, it is higher in patients with multiple trauma (Kalsbeek, McLaurin, Harris, & Miller, 1980).

Because of modern methods of management, the life expectancy of spinal cord injured patients approximates that of the general population; however, quadriplegics have a somewhat reduced life-span.

There is suggestive evidence that SCI patients were premorbidly inclined toward high-risk living (Fordyce, 1964), although this is controversial (Ditunno, McCauley, & Marquette, 1985).

Anatomy and Pathophysiology

The spine is usually composed of 33 vertebrae. There are 7 cervical, 12 thoracic, 5 lumbar, 5 sacral and 3, 4, or 5 fused coccygeal vertebrae. Although there are variations in size, shape, and thickness of bone in the groups of each region, the basic anatomy is the same throughout. The typical vertebra consists of an anterior plate of bone separated from its superior and inferior neighbors by thick cartilaginous pads—the intervertebral disks. Behind this plate (the vertebral body) is a space encircled by a bony ring, consisting of the posterior surface of the body and the vertebral processes connected to it. The processes serve as attachments for muscles and tendons and provide special surfaces for joints with the superior and inferior vertebral processes. In the thoracic region, the ribs attach to transverse projections of the processes, whereas in the sacral and coccygeal regions, the vertebrae are densely fused. The firm ring thus produced provides a protective casing for the spinal cord after it exits the cranium through the foramen magnum. The inferior portion of the spinal cord is the conus medullaris, which lies at the level of the first or second lumbar vertebra.

Pairs of nerve roots, known as *spinal roots,* exit the spinal cord. The roots are named according to the level at which they leave the cord; therefore, the C1 root exits above the first cervical vertebra, and so forth. At the seventh cervical vertebra, the C7 root runs above the C7 vertebra and the C8 root below the same vertebra, thus giving eight cervical spinal root pairs, although there are only seven vertebrae. Below this point all roots lie below the vertebrae for which they are named.

Below the conus medullaris—at L1 or L2: first or second lumbar vertebra—the spinal roots course downward within the spinal canal to leave at their respective levels. The grouped nerve roots look much like a horse's tail at this level, which gives rise to their name—the *cauda equina.* Because the spinal cord is much shorter than the vertebral column, the level of the cord does not correspond to the adjacent vertebra.

Within the spinal cord, the gray matter is arranged in a central "H" pattern. This region is composed largely of connections for neurons entering and leaving the cord at that level. The surrounding white matter contains groups of neurons specifically arranged in bundles or tracts leading to and from the brain. Sensory functions are located primarily in the dorsal and a small part of the lateral and anterior columns, whereas the largest part of the lateral and anterior columns sub-serves motor functions.

Injury to the spinal cord or spinal roots is necessary to produce the symptoms seen in paraplegia and quadriplegia. Usually SCI results from fracture or disloca-tion of the vertebral column, with damage to the cord arising from impingement by bony fragments, herniated disks, etc. or from stretching, bruising, or laceration at the time of the fracture. Edema (swelling) and hematoma (clot) formation from vertebral injury can cause cord damage through direct compression or by reducing the blood supply to the cord (Riggins & Kraus, 1977).

Trauma to the spinal cord or roots produces specific motor and sensory changes depending on the areas of damage (see Figure 19–1). If only part of the cord is affected, the patient has an incomplete injury and will retain some degree of motor or sensory function or both below the level of injury. If the entire cross-section of the spinal cord is damaged in the cervical or first thoracic level, the individual will have symptoms in all extremities and will therefore have quadriplegia. Below T1 only the lower extremities are affected, and the patient has paraplegia.

Signs and Symptoms

The most common initial symptoms (patient's complaints) of SCI are loss of sensation—pain, light touch, temperature, vibration, and position—and move-

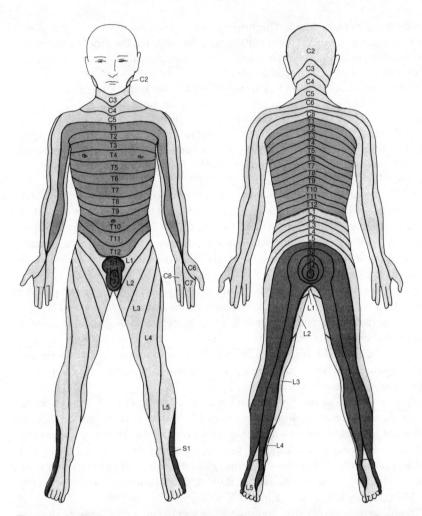

Figure 19–1 Main areas of skin sensation served by the sensory components of each spinal nerve. Some overlap into neighboring segments also exists. (*A*) Front view. (*B*) Back view.

Source: From *Handbook of Severe Disabilities* (p. 68) by Walter C. Stolov and Michael R. Clowers (Eds.), 1981, Washington, D.C.: U.S. Department of Education, Rehabilitation Services Administration.

ment in one or more extremities, as well as pain at the site of vertebral injury. Frequently encountered signs (observations made by the examiner) of injury include abnormalities in the alignment of the vertebrae, especially in the cervical spine; loss of ability to move or feel the involved extremities; and loss of muscle tone. In cervical injuries the patient may also experience respiratory distress.

Other symptoms include inability to control the bowel and bladder, loss of sexual function (see Chapter 16), and changes in the ability to regulate body temperature automatically, which lead to sweats and chills.

MANAGEMENT OF SPINAL INJURY

Improper transport of the injured individual can have destructive consequences. Early studies found that a high percentage of patients showed worsening of symptoms between diagnosis at the scene of the accident and the beginning of hospital treatment, thus indicating aggravation of the injury during transport. This unfortunate and unnecessary occurrence is now far less common, due primarily to improved training of rescue crews. Once a vertebral or spinal cord injury is suspected, the patient must be moved en bloc, preferably on a board or immobilization device, without causing movement of the spine. When the patient arrives in an emergency facility, spinal care must continue while measures are taken to ensure adequate respiration and to establish diagnosis of spinal and other injuries. The patient with multiple trauma, such as head or chest injury, obvious long bone or pelvic fractures, or compromise of the cardiovascular system, in addition to the SCI requires more complicated care at this time. X-rays are the simplest means of diagnosing vertebral fracture, but CT scans or polytomography (x-rays of various levels of the bones) may be indicated.

If a cervical fracture is found, the patient is placed in traction on a flat turning frame (Stryker frame). A metal halo is affixed to the head with pins placed through the outer table of the skull; tong traction may be applied in a similar manner, although this procedure has largely been replaced by halo treatment. Sufficient weight is then used to achieve and maintain alignment of the fracture fragments.

If halo traction is used, the patient may wear a plastic vest or body cast with metal posts attaching to the halo to ensure continued stability. If tong traction is used, the patient must stay on the Stryker frame for about 12 weeks. If the fracture fragments cannot be kept in good alignment by traction, internal stabilization is achieved with wire, and bone fusion can be accomplished using a graft from the pelvis.

Many fractures of the thoracic and lumbar spine require open reduction and internal fixation of the fracture, which are achieved by surgery to realign the fragments and wire or plate them in place. Laminectomy—removal of the posterior elements of the vertebral arch—may be performed to relieve pressure on the spinal cord; bone fusion is often done concurrently in order to ensure permanent stability. Postoperatively, the patient stays on the turning frame until a body cast or molded plastic vest can be fabricated. These devices, which serve to provide additional support, must be worn for 6 to 8 months.

Other organ systems may require attention during this phase of acute care. Patients with cervical and high thoracic lesions may have difficulty breathing because injuries in this region can damage the nerves to the intercostal and abdominal muscles. Such devices as incentive respirometers are used to encourage deep breathing; some patients require tracheostomy or ventilatory support with a mechanical respirator. Lung collapse must be prevented, and any sign of infection—pneumonia or upper respiratory problems, such as colds—must be treated promptly.

Voluntary control of voiding is interrupted following SCI. An indwelling Foley catheter may be inserted to provide continuous drainage of the bladder so that the patient's level of hydration (fluid balance) may be closely monitored. Current practice dictates early removal of the Foley catheter and initiation of an intermittent catheterization program (ICP) in which a straight catheter is used to drain the bladder at regular intervals, usually every 4 to 6 hours. As male patients begin to empty automatically, but not under volitional control, they are usually fitted with external collecting devices, such as condom drainage into a legbag, and ICP is discontinued. Females, however, must use either (1) tapping or facilitation techniques to initiate the stream, (2) medication to relax the bladder so that ICP can be continued without spontaneous emptying, or (3) an indwelling catheter. In patients with low cord injuries, ICP may be continued indefinitely.

Feeding, digestion, and elimination continue in SCI patients, but voluntary control of defecation is interrupted and the bowel can easily become impacted with hard stool. Bowel programs using softening agents and suppositories are begun to induce elimination on a predictable basis. Once the program is well established, the likelihood of accidents or impaction is quite low.

Complications

Urinary tract infections are common in SCI patients and must be treated promptly. For patients who have indwelling Foley catheters, however, a special approach is taken: The presence of a low-grade infection is presumed, due to the contaminating presence of a foreign body (the catheter) and is treated only if the patient becomes symptomatic. The formation of bladder stones—deposits of calcium and other materials—occurs fairly frequently; kidney stones are less common, but are more serious. Both must be treated to prevent the development of more serious complications. All SCI patients should have regular evaluation of the urinary tract.

The potential for skin breakdown—decubitus ulcer—exists in all patients who are unable to shift their weight to relieve pressure and/or lack the sensation of discomfort that alerts them to move. If prolonged pressure is applied, especially over a bony prominence, the blood supply to the area is decreased, and soft tissues may suffer necrosis (tissue death) due to lack of oxygen. The first sign of a decubitus ulcer is an area of redness that does not blanch quickly; this rapidly progresses to either a superficial area of blackened skin or a deeper area of pus covered by blackened scar tissue. Gradually increasing sitting time, frequent turning in bed, and instruction in methods of shifting weight are common preventive measures. If a large decubitus does develop, surgical removal of dead tissue (debridement) and cosmetic plastic surgery may be necessary.

Prevention of thrombophlebitis (blood clots) with subsequent edema formation in the lower extremities is vital. SCI patients are unable to contract the muscles of the lower extremities and are therefore at risk for this problem. The chief danger is the embolization of clots—breaking off and traveling in the bloodstream—to the lungs, but the presence of swelling in the lower extremities can also lead to other complications, such as difficulty with transfers or stasis ulcer formation.

Stabilization and prevention of complications are the primary functions of the medical and nursing staff in the first postinjury weeks (Pierce & Nickel, 1977). A central purpose of the rehabilitation program is to educate patients about the medical aspects of their disabilities so that they can prevent the complications themselves, a necessary skill if they wish to live independently after discharge.

Functional Significance of Level of Injury

Ultimate functional ability is largely determined by the level of injury to the spinal cord. This usually corresponds to the level of vertebral injury within one or two segments, but greater disparity may be present, especially in lumbar and low thoracic injuries. The neurologic level is classified according to the lowest fully functional segment; therefore, "C7 quadriplegia" indicates that the C7 root level is the most distal functioning segment.

C2–C3 Levels

Spontaneous ventilation is not possible in patients with very high lesions because the diaphragm is enervated by fibers from C3, C4 and C5. Until recently, injuries at these levels were almost invariably fatal, but with the advent of ventilatory support systems, patients may survive. Respiratory complications, such as infections, are common, however, and require prompt treatment. Electrophrenic stimulation may be considered in some cases. These patients have limited ability to use a mouthstick or environmental control unit, and they require complete care.

C4 Level

This is the highest level of injury that permits independent respiration. Higher injuries are usually fatal unless artificial respiration is started immediately because the muscles of respiration are denervated; the few survivors require respiratory support. C4-level patients have no voluntary movement of the shoulders or arms and are therefore dependent for all self-care activities and mobility. They do have head and neck movement and can propel an electric wheelchair with tongue or chin controls. Many use a mouthstick to manipulate small objects. Environmental control units can allow these patients to operate appliances or machinery, such as a television, radio, or fan, in their immediate surroundings.

C5 Level

These patients have partial control of shoulder muscles and elbow flexion through the biceps. They are largely dependent for self-care and mobility, although with extensive splinting and overhead pulleys, they can feed themselves to some extent. Electric wheelchairs and mouthsticks are useful for these patients.

C6 Level

Wrist extension and pronation of the hand can be performed; therefore, limited gross hand closure is possible. These patients can feed themselves, assist in their bathing and dressing, roll in bed, rise from a lying to sitting position, and propel a standard wheelchair. Some patients can execute certain transfers, such as from bed to chair, without assistance. C6 patients can drive a car equipped with hand controls.

C7 Level

These patients do not have independent finger and hand control; nonetheless, they can be largely independent in self-care and transfers. They are able to live independently, but usually require an attendant for assistance with tasks requiring fine manual dexterity, such as changing catheters, and with strenuous housekeeping chores.

C8–T1 Level

These patients have varying degrees of control over finger and hand musculature, depending on individual variation in enervation. They are independent in all aspects of self-care and wheelchair mobility, but generally do not attempt ambulation because of the cumbersome bracing equipment and the extensive energy consumption required.

Thoracic and Upper Lumbar Levels

Patients with injuries in the lower thoracic region have some trunk control and improved pulmonary function. Ambulation still requires considerable bracing, and the energy expenditure is usually too great to permit functional ambulation.

Lower Lumbar Levels

Injury at or below L4 usually means that the patient has good control of the hips and at least one knee. With the use of leg braces, patients can ambulate safely with crutches. The effort required is tolerated by most patients.

Patients with injuries below the lumbar levels usually have incomplete injuries involving few roots; significant recovery often occurs.

Incomplete Injuries

Many patients have incomplete injuries to the spinal cord; in these cases, the cord is only partially damaged, and the remaining intact fibers permit some degree of sensory and motor function below the level of injury. Each case is unique, and functional capabilities are dependent on the degree of enervation. Individuals with incomplete lesions may have severe spasticity that is difficult to control. These patients may not walk, despite adequate muscle strength and motor ability. Some common syndromes of incomplete injuries are the Brown-Sequard syndrome (loss of pain and temperature sensation on the same side as the lesion, with loss of movement and joint position sense on the opposite side); anterior cord syndrome (paralysis with preservation of joint position and vibratory and touch sensation below the lesion); and central cord syndromes (more severe paralysis in the upper than the lower extremities). Bladder and bowel programs must be developed for each individual according to the degree of sensation and motor control present. (See Chapter 1 for discussion of the psychological consequences of SCI.)

CEREBROVASCULAR ACCIDENT

Cerebrovascular accident (CVA) or stroke refers to the sudden onset of a focal neurologic deficit caused by a cerebral vascular disorder (problem with the blood supply). Stroke is often fatal, but when it is not, it may deprive the individual of the pleasures of independence and the dignity of self-sufficiency.

Epidemiology

In the United States, stroke is the third most common cause of death, following heart disease and cancer, in persons under the age of 75 and second, following heart disease, in those over 75. It is estimated that about 500,000 strokes occur each year in the United States and that there are 2½ million stroke survivors. Between 30 and 50 percent of stroke patients die within 1 month of onset. Ten percent of survivors recover completely, 40 percent have mild residual dysfunction, 40 percent are more severely disabled and require special care, and 10 percent require total care, either at home or in an institution (National Association of

Rehabilitation Facilities, 1981). Overall, approximately 30 percent of stroke patients are destined for institutional living. Approximately 86 percent of the Framingham CVA patients had one CVA, another 9 percent had two CVAs, and 3 percent had more than two (Gresham et al., 1979).

Etiology

There are two main types of intracranial cerebrovascular pathology that result in stroke—infarction of thrombotic or embolic origin and hemorrhage. Cerebral infarction is the more common cause of both CVA (about 75 percent of strokes in the Framingham study) and permanent disability, as 60 to 75 percent of these patients survive. Intracranial hemorrhage usually produces more severe deficits, but approximately 80 percent of these patients succumb within the first few weeks after onset (Merritt, 1979).

Cerebral infarction usually results from the atherosclerotic process, in which the accumulation of fatty deposits in the arteries progressively causes narrowing and eventual blockage of blood flow. Acute deprivation of blood and the nutrients it carries to the brain is followed by softening and death of brain tissue. The most common sites of infarction are (1) the carotid arteries just distal to the bifurcation, (2) the parasellar region near the circle of Willis, and (3) the posterior circulation in the vertebral or basilar arteries.

Thrombi (blood clots) form easily during episodes of hypotension (lowered blood pressure) that may occur secondary to cardiac disease with arrhythmias and/ or myocardial infarction (heart attack) or during sleep when blood pressure often is lower. The effects of this type of stroke are often noted by the patient upon awakening; symptoms and signs frequently become more severe as the stroke evolves during the subsequent hours or days.

The second main cause of cerebral infarction is embolism of fragments of thrombus from the heart or great vessels. In these cases, bits of the deposit (embolus) break off and are carried through the bloodstream, eventually lodging in a small vessel and blocking the flow of blood beyond that point. The onset of symptoms is usually abrupt in these cases, and there are no warning signs. Deficits often resolve considerably in the first few hours, and the prognosis for recovery of function after such strokes is good.

Intracranial hemorrhage (bleeding) is less common than infarction. The two types of bleeds are named according to their location. They are intracerebral and subarachnoid hemorrhage and were seen in 15 percent and 10 percent of the Framingham study patients, respectively (Gresham et al., 1975). Intracerebral hemorrhage is almost always associated with hypertension and disease of the small arteries in the brain. Rupture of the vessel with acute bleeding into brain tissue leads to acute onset of stroke, often in association with severe headache and vomiting; mental confusion and loss of consciousness frequently follow. The intracerebral hematoma that forms may be large enough to cause a shift of the brain or herniation (squeezing of the brain) through the tentorium. As stated earlier, this type of stroke has a high rate of early mortality; survivors usually have severe neurologic and functional deficits.

Subarachnoid hemorrhage usually begins in the subarachnoid space as the result of an underlying anomaly, such as an aneurysm. The peak age of vulnerability is 30 to 60 years, which is younger than that for other types of strokes. The onset is sudden and often associated with loss of consciousness. Signs localizing the damage to one specific area are not seen unless infarction results from compression or tearing of arteries with hematoma formation or invasion of the cerebral hemisphere by the hemorrhage. Mortality is high, and residual deficits are often severe.

Risk Factors

Hypertension is the single most important precursor of stroke because of the changes it produces in blood vessels, such as microaneurysms and thickening of the walls of arteries and arterioles. Also, most patients with widespread atheroma are also hypertensive; in fact, only 15 percent are completely normotensive (Wolf et al., 1977). In hypertensive patients, the risk for thrombotic infarction is proportional to the height of systolic and diastolic blood pressure.

Diabetes mellitus predisposes to thrombotic infarction in both sexes and in all age groups. The mechanism is unclear, but there appears to be a direct relation with both diabetes and *hyperlipidemia* (increased serum lipids).

Heart disease, especially myocardial infarction, congestive heart failure, and left ventricular hypertrophy, is often present in stroke patients. There is a clear relation between atherosclerotic changes in the coronary vessels and those in the cerebral vessels; furthermore, the incidence of all types of strokes is three times greater among patients who have had a previous myocardial infarction.

Patients who have documented transient ischemic attacks (TIAs) are at increased risk for CVA. TIAs are brief, episodic attacks of symptoms similar to those seen in a CVA. Weakness, numbness, paresthesias, loss of vision, and aphasias may occur, but all symptoms resolve within 24 hours. These episodes result from reduction of blood flow that is sufficient to produce symptoms but not so substantial as to cause infarction. Usually the cause is repeated embolization of very small thrombi, bits of cholesterol, or collection of platelets from the atheromatous plaques. Either the carotid or the vertebrobasilar territory can be involved. Surgical correction by endarterectomy—"cleaning out" the atheroma from the artery—is successful in many cases, although the procedure carries a risk of morbidity of up to 6.6 percent. (Easton & Sherman, 1977).

The association of cigarette smoking with stroke is unproven, as is the use of large amounts of caffeine.

Clinical Syndromes

The various types of stroke share several features. Usually there are no pre-monitory signs, although headache, dizziness, drowsiness, and confusion may be noted. Stupor or coma usually indicate hemorrhage or a large infarction. Mental status changes, such as confusion, disorientation, reduced attention span, and poor memory, are common consequences. The occurrence of focal deficits, such as aphasia and perceptual impairment, depends primarily on the size and location of the affected cortical area, which is largely a function of the point of hemorrhage or obstruction. Individual differences in cerebral organization of function, the pattern of collateral circulation to the lesioned area, and the impact (swelling or reduction of blood flow) on surrounding areas all affect the clinical presentation and may be important determinants of recovery.

Because of the crossed connections between the brain and the periphery, sensory and motor functions of the right side of the body are controlled by the left hemisphere and vice versa. Language is predominantly located in the left hemisphere in 90–95 percent of the population; visual-perceptual functions tend to be associated with the right hemisphere (Kertesz, 1983). The clinical picture—side of hemiplegia, presence of aphasia—thus offers some clues to the location of the involved cortical sites (Fig. 19–2).

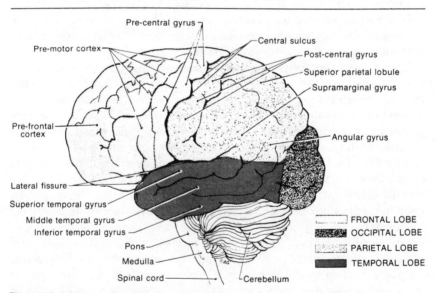

Figure 19–2 Lateral view of the brain

Regardless of the pathophysiologic mechanism involved, localized disruption of the blood supply to the brain is frequently associated with certain signs and symptoms (Holtzman, Panin, & Ebel, 1959). An understanding of the main cerebral circulatory pathways is therefore quite helpful. The brain is supplied with blood by two main arterial systems, the internal carotid and the vertebral basilar. Vessels that link the two systems at the base of the brain form the circle of Willis, from which arise the anterior and middle cerebral arteries. The former feeds much of the frontal lobes, whereas the latter artery supplies massive areas of the cortex, as well as certain subcortical structures. The basilar artery bifurcates into the two posterior cerebral arteries that nourish parts of the temporal and occipital lobes and the thalamus. The posterior cerebral arteries and carotid arteries are connected by the posterior communicating arteries; the two anterior cerebral arteries are connected by the anterior communicating artery (Fig. 19–3).

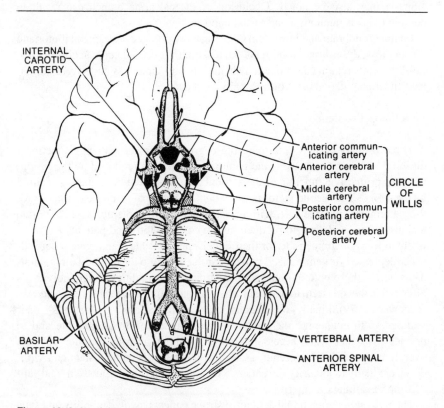

Figure 19–3 Arterial blood supply of the brain

Source: From *Neurorehabilitation* (p. 7) by S. Farber, 1982, Philadelphia: W.B. Saunders Company. Copyright 1982 by W.B. Saunders Company. Reprinted by permission.

Occlusion of the common or internal carotid artery produces no signs or symptoms unless the usual extensive collateral circulation is also compromised. Involvement of the anterior cerebral artery frequently causes contralateral hemiplegia and mild sensory deficits primarily affecting the lower extremity. Clouded consciousness (confusion) or expressive aphasia may also result (Jones & Millikan, 1976).

A variety of deficits may be observed following occlusion of the middle cerebral artery—contralateral hemiplegia and hemianesthesia (more severe in the upper extremity and face), homonymous hemianopsia (unilateral loss of vision), aphasia (with left-sided lesions), and spatial-perceptual deficits (with right-sided lesions). Occlusion of the main trunk of the posterior cerebral artery produces the thalamic syndrome—contralateral transient hemiplegia, permanent hemianesthesia, and spontaneous severe burning dysesthesia (pain). Ataxia, tremor, aphasia, or amnesia may also be noted. Occlusion of the calcarine branch can result in homonymous hemianopsia and visual agnosia.

Pontine, midbrain and brainstem CVAs usually produce widespread motor and sensory loss, dysarthria, vertigo, ataxia, and multiple cranial nerve abnormalities. Strokes in this region cause marked changes in consciousness and severe permanent functional deficits and occasionally are fatal.

Functional Problems

Three primary factors determine the degree of a given patient's functional disability. The first of these is the nature of the deficits produced by the lesion, which is primarily a function of the amount and location of brain damage caused by the stroke. The second factor is the patient's emotional response to illness, for this determines, in large part, willingness to cooperate in therapies that are often tedious, tiring, and slow to produce improvement. Motivated patients are more likely to learn to compensate for their deficits and to achieve maximal independence; depressed or demoralized patients are generally poor rehabilitation candidates, as are those with diminished insight into their condition. Such individuals often fail in the long term to maintain whatever gains they have achieved (Andrews & Stewart, 1979). Finally, the response of the patient's family and friends—their willingness to encourage the patient to be as independent as possible and to provide assistance when necessary—plays an important role. Families that are overprotective and domineering, as well as those that become distant and withdraw, are likely to intensify the patient's deficits, exacerbate depression, and subvert the rehabilitation enterprise.

The most salient functional deficits of stroke patients involve mobility and self-care. Because of weakness or incoordination, patients may have difficulty maneuvering in bed, sitting up, transferring—moving from bed to chair, chair to commode, etc.—ambulating, and climbing stairs. Affected domains of self-care include feeding (cutting meat, failing to notice the food on one side of the plate because of a visual field cut, difficulty with swallowing due to pharyngeal weakness); bathing (inability to bathe the back and functional upper extremity due to hemiplegia); dressing (because of right-left or inside-outside confusion, difficulty with two-handed skills, such as buttoning or shoe tying); and grooming (brushing teeth and hair or shaving). A hemisensory deficit may intensify these problems by reducing the patient's awareness of an extremity. Anesthesia increases susceptibility to injury from hot or sharp objects. Because of aphasia patients may be unable to comprehend directions or communicate their needs.

Complications

Several medical complications can hamper the stroke patient's recovery. The first, and perhaps most important, is concurrent cardiac disease. Approximately 12 percent of stroke patients suffer a myocardial infarction around the time of the CVA, and another 23 percent have arteriosclerotic cardiac disease manifested by congestive heart failure, left ventricular hypertrophy (enlargement), or arrhythmias (disturbances in the cardiac rhythm) (Wolf et al., 1977). Cardiac disease decreases exercise tolerance in any individual; in a stroke patient, the added burden of the inefficient use of the paretic side of the body makes recovery through rehabilitation more difficult and may preclude any meaningful therapy program.

Decubitus ulcers identical to those seen in spinal cord injury patients may occur in CVA patients. The routine care and surgical treatment are the same.

Joint contractures, which result if the patient does not receive daily range of motion activities, force the muscles to work less efficiently. Contractures of the shoulder and upper extremity may impair execution of hygiene tasks or dressing.

Shoulder pain is a frequent complaint among stroke patients. It may be caused or exacerbated by a variety of factors, such as aggravation of pre-existing degenerative changes, repeated minor trauma during therapy or transfers, excessive pulling on the shoulder joint by the weight of a paralyzed arm, or unrecognized fracture or contracture. The shoulder-hand syndrome is a disorder of the sympathetic nervous system that produces pain, changes in the small blood vessels of the hand, and contractures in the involved extremity. The common result of shoulder pain is resistance to exercise of the extremity, which sets in motion a self-perpetuating cycle of pain, decreased use, worsened contractures, and more pain.

Other barriers to recovery include premorbid psychiatric problems; dementia, which may result from multiple small strokes; and emotional lability.

Any patient with a history of stroke has a poorer prognosis for recovery of independence, as subsequent events unmask deficits from previous CVAs for which the patient had learned to compensate. Continuing bowel incontinence without an obvious cause, such as fecal impaction, is a sign of widespread (often bilateral) damage; although this can be managed with suppositories, most such patients become institutionalized because of societal intolerance. Increasing age dictates a less favorable prognosis, if only because older patients often bear the burden of multiple chronic diseases.

Prognosis for recovery, and hence criteria for admission to many active inpatient rehabilitation units, is based upon a combination of factors, including age, history of CVA, presence of bowel incontinence, ability to cooperate and follow directions, availability of support systems for discharge from rehabilitation, concomitant medical problems, and the course of recovery since the CVA. Most neurologic recovery takes place within the first 12 weeks; if this time passes without definite improvement, it becomes less likely that significant neurologic and functional recovery will occur. (See Chapter 3 for discussion of the psychological and neuropsychological sequelae of stroke.)

AMPUTATION

Epidemiology

Amputations are performed for a variety of reasons, including congenital limb deficiency, elective amputation for vascular insufficiency, and emergency completion of a traumatic injury. It is estimated that 75 percent of amputations are performed in persons over the age of 65 (Vitali, Robinson, Andrews, & Harris, 1978). Eight-five percent of these procedures are required because of arteriosclerotic ischemia of the limb, and in more than 45 percent diabetes mellitus is a contributing factor. Less common causes are embolism, vasculitis, trauma, neoplasm, and infection. In recent surveys, 11–13 percent of patients were under the age of 31; 75 percent of their amputations were performed because of congenital deformity, the large part of the remainder resulting from trauma (Davis, Friz, & Clippinger, 1970). In all age groups, lower extremity amputations outnumber those of the upper extremity. Because upper extremity amputees do not usually require inpatient rehabilitation therapy, this condition is not discussed in this chapter.

Levels of Amputation and Appropriate Prosthetic Components

In both traumatic and ischemia-related conditions, the level of amputation is determined by the viability of the soft tissues and the adequacy of blood supply. In general, the greatest possible length is retained in order to make the prosthesis as manageable as possible (Mital & Pierce, 1971).

Amputations at the toe and transmetatarsal levels usually cause little disability and require no prosthesis except for a shoe filler. However, amputations at other levels in the foot are very disabling because they cause painful foot deformities. Syme's amputation involves cutting through the ankle, retaining most of the leg length. It is a rare procedure because the blood supply to the lower leg is usually impaired as well, and a higher site of amputation is necessary for healing to occur.

Before World War II, above-knee amputation (AKA) was the more common procedure, but there has been an encouraging recent shift to below-knee amputations (BKA). This trend has been made possible by the improved accuracy of estimation of blood supply, better surgical techniques, enhanced postoperative management, and the use of antibiotics. By preserving the patient's own knee joint, a BKA allows greater ease of ambulating with a prosthesis. The use of a prosthetic knee joint involves a significant amount of energy; with the knee joint preserved, the patient has better control over the prosthesis and can transfer more easily.

The ideal site for the BKA is 6 inches below the tibial tuberosity, the prominent bony protuberance on the anterior lower leg, just below the knee. The prosthesis consists of a plastic liner that is pulled over the stump before insertion into the plastic laminate socket. This provides total contact between the stump and prosthesis and distributes the load across the entire stump, thereby decreasing the likelihood of skin breakdown. The plastic shank is shaped and colored to look much like the normal leg. Although several designs of ankle and foot components are available, the solid-ankle cushion-heel (SACH) foot is the most commonly used. As the name suggests, the solid ankle and soft heel have no moving parts, yet they permit a fairly normal gait pattern.

The above description applies to the permanent prosthesis that is constructed when the stump has matured and edema has subsided. During the earlier stages, a temporary prosthesis, in which the shank is replaced by a metal pipe, may be used. This provides for easier realignment and adjustment while the patient accommodates to the prosthesis. It also involves less time and expense to fabricate than does the permanent unit.

In AK amputations, the stump should be long enough to ensure adequate length of muscles crossing the hip, yet it should be short enough for easy insertion of the prosthetic knee. The best level tends to be about the middle third of the thigh. Shorter stumps make suspension of the prosthesis more difficult, and the patient cannot easily effect "swing-through" of the leg.

The socket for the AK prosthesis has a quadrilateral shape at the brim, which allows total contact of the stump and the distribution of pressure onto more tolerant areas. Earlier prostheses were "plug fit" sockets shaped exactly like the stump with areas that did not touch the stump where edema could develop. The type of knee joint employed depends on the age and agility of the patient. Hydraulic knees afford a smooth gait pattern at all cadences, but are expensive, require more frequent repair, and are more difficult to control. The locked knee is the most stable variety, especially for older patients or those with poor balance; these units lock automatically when the patient stands up and may be unlocked for sitting. Friction locks are commonly used in permanent prostheses after the patient has learned to ambulate; these allow knee flexion when the limb is swinging through, but are stable when weight is placed on the prostheses. The foot and ankle units are similar to the BK prosthesis.

There are other types of amputations, such as knee disarticulation (amputation through the knee joint), hip disarticulation, and hemipelvectomy (removal of the entire leg and half of the pelvis on the same side); each has its own prosthetic prescription and training requirements.

Prosthetic Training

In general, prosthetic fitting and training have three main purposes: (1) to permit bipedal amputation, (2) to permit or facilitate transfers, and (3) to enhance psychological and social adaptation. Amputees with the following conditions should not be provided with a prosthesis: (1) chronic dementia, which renders the patient unable to manage the device safely; (2) bedridden and terminally ill patients, who cannot realistically use the device; and (3) patients who have already been successfully rehabilitated without a prosthesis and who are independent in transfers, mobility, and self-care. Such patients generally find the prosthesis more of a hindrance than a help.

In most cases, patients can learn to ambulate with a prosthesis through outpatient therapy. Those requiring inpatient rehabilitation usually have bilateral amputations or complicating medical problems. Also, patients with mild confusion or memory deficits may require the more intensive training provided in an inpatient stay.

The prognosis for achieving ambulation for functional distances is very good for the large majority of mentally intact geriatric amputees. Approximately 70–80 percent of unilateral and 50 percent of bilateral BK amputees can ambulate, whereas somewhat less than 50 percent of unilateral and very few bilateral AK amputees can ambulate with a prosthesis. The disparities are attributable to the amount of energy necessary to manage bilateral BK or a single AK prosthesis (Stoner, 1982).

HEAD INJURY

Epidemiology

The epidemiology of head injury is difficult to study comprehensively for several reasons (Klauber, Barrett-Connor, Marshall, & Bowers, 1981). Extremely severe head injuries are usually accompanied by other forms of major trauma, and about 60 percent of these patients die before reaching medical facilities (Field, 1976; Levin, Benton, & Grossman, 1982). Many mild head injuries go unreported. In addition, statistics are unreliable because the various components of a head injury, such as skull fracture, subdural or intracerebral hematoma, or facial injury, are difficult to classify under the existing systems (Levin et al., 1982). All of these factors contribute to a somewhat muddled epidemiological picture.

Because of the lack of reliable U.S. statistics, the National Institute of Neurological and Communicative Disorders and Stroke initiated the National Head and Spinal Cord Injury Survey. This survey is based on hospital admissions from 1970 to 1974. It excludes both minor trauma evaluated only in emergency departments and major trauma victims who died before receiving treatment; however, it is a comprehensive national survey that provides considerable information. This survey reports an estimated incidence of 200 per 100,000 population, and the estimated occurrence in 1974 of 422,000 cases (Kalsbeek et al., 1980). The interested reader is directed to the *Journal of Neurosurgery*, November, 1980 Supplement for the details of the survey, as well as comparisons with other recent studies.

Etiology and Pathology

In general, blunt trauma to the head is more common than gunshot or missile ("penetrating") injuries. Motor vehicle accidents accounted for 49 percent of all cases in 1974, and most of these involved the 15- to 24-year age group; males outnumber females by a 4:1 ratio (Kalsbeek et al., 1980). The use of alcohol is a significant factor in many (Kerr, Kay, & Lassman, 1971). Assaults, falls, and sports accidents are other common causes.

Missile injuries with penetration by a foreign body, hemorrhage, and brain laceration are known as open injuries, as are depressed or compound fractures (those associated with a scalp laceration). Closed injuries are those in which no penetration or fracture of the cranium occurs. Concussion resulting from blunt trauma is due to the acceleration/deceleration forces acting on the brain. Widespread lesions occur from (1) contusion and hematoma formation in the gray matter, (2) skull fracture with or without depression of fragments into brain tissue, (3) brain laceration, and (4) damage to white matter that may not become evident until weeks after the injury. Brain damage may also occur secondarily from a decrease in the supply of oxygen and/or blood to the brain or from a rise in the intracranial pressure causing cerebral edema, compression of the brain against the cranium, and eventual herniation (Cartlidge & Shaw, 1981).

The actual brain damage caused by head injury falls into two categories. Impact or primary damage refers to the immediate effects, such as skull fracture, contusions, and brain laceration. Contusions under the point of impact are termed "coup contusions." They are often associated with impairment of distant areas of the brain known as "contrecoup contusions"; this damage arises from relative movement of the brain across bony irregularities during impact and usually is found on the inferior surfaces of the frontal and temporal lobes (Gurdjian & Gurdjian, 1976). Secondary brain damage, resulting from subsequent processes, such as increased intracranial pressure, intracranial hematoma, ischemia, and infection (e.g., meningitis or abscess formation), may be prevented or reduced by prompt medical management.

Management

Careful monitoring of such factors as state of consciousness, language, amnesia, and motor ability must begin immediately (Jennett & Teasdale, 1981). The extent of impact damage must be delineated and the patient monitored carefully for signs of secondary damage. Examination usually includes skull x-rays to rule out skull fracture and to look for abnormal intracranial air signaling the presence of a hidden fracture. At least 30 percent of head injury patients have another bodily injury; all patients involved in motor vehicle accidents or falls must be screened for other fractures, abdominal injury, and chest trauma. Vertebral fracture, especially of the cervical spine, must be ruled out in any patient with decreased consciousness or with motor or sensory abnormalities. More sophisticated diagnostic measures, such as computed tomography (CT scanning), cerebral angiography, and ultrasound, may be indicated to define the extent of intracranial trauma. Patients with skull fractures and altered consciousness are usually admitted for observation.

The most consistent consequence of traumatic brain damage is a change in consciousness. Although some patients are awake and alert, many are variably attentive, lethargic, stuporous, or comatose. Coma is difficult to define, but it implies the absence of motor or verbal functions. The Glasgow Coma Scale provides a reliable quantified system that can be used by any of the patient's caregivers (Teasdale & Jennett, 1974). Three functions are assessed: eye opening (1 to 4 points), motor response (1 to 6 points), and verbal performance (1 to 5 points). Scores range from 3 (least responsive) to 15 (most responsive). According to Bond (1983), 90 percent of patients with scores of 8 or less are in coma. The scores can be plotted on graphs at intervals (usually every 2 to 4 hours) and the patient's progress visualized quite clearly.

Syndromes

In the head injured as in the stroke patient, the observed constellation of symptoms varies according to the amount and location of injured brain. Statistics concerning the frequency of physical deficits are not reliable because they are usually based on series of patients with persisting complaints or with very severe injuries. Thus, the incidence of lasting neurologic impairment after minor or even moderate trauma is not well studied. Recent research of Rimel, Giordani, Barth, Boll, and Jane (1981) and Barth et al. (1983) suggests that cognitive and attentional dysfunctions are often overlooked in milder cases.* Persistent deficits are quite common after severe head injury (Roberts, 1976). In the Glasgow series, the most common problems were related to cerebral hemisphere dysfunction (hemiparesis, aphasia) or cranial nerve dysfunction. These findings are to be expected on the basis of pathologic findings that show severe disruption in the white matter at a microscopic level (Strich, 1970).

The occurrence of mental changes is extremely common after head injury (Brooks, 1984a; Lezak, 1978). Even with mild concussion, attention span may be reduced, and information processing may be sluggish for some time (Gronwall & Wrightson, 1974). Other components of the postconcussional syndrome are headache, dizziness, poor concentration, memory and other intellectual deficits, fatigue, disordered consciousness (especially common after prolonged coma), and personality changes (Fahy, Irving, & Millac, 1967). Personality changes include loss of initiative, altered affect (lability or blunting), disinhibition, elation, and, occasionally, frank psychosis. These characterological changes are often more difficult for the patient's family and associates to deal with than are the more apparent physical disabilities (Brooks, 1984b).

The residual functional and neurologic impairments may be the result of primary or secondary damage or may arise from scarring (adhesions) at a later time.

The "punch-drunk syndrome" of boxers and football players deserves mention. In these individuals, repeated concussions with consequent cumulative brain damage produce memory impairment and generalized intellectual loss. Such physical signs as ataxia, dysarthria, and tremor may also develop.

The most common delayed complications of head injury are hydrocephalus and epilepsy. The former may be caused either by wasting of the white matter or by formation of posthemorrhagic adhesions. Only 5 percent of patients with blunt trauma develop late seizures, in contrast to 30–45 percent of missile injury patients. Among blunt trauma patients, the incidence of late seizures is increased among those with depressed fractures, dural tears, or hematoma, as well as in those with early seizure activity or posttraumatic amnesia exceeding 24 hours.

Prognosis

Early prediction of outcome for any given patient is difficult. Certainly, accurate diagnosis, adequate initial management, and prevention of complications improve the prognosis.

---

*See the entire issue of *Journal of Head Trauma Rehabilitation*, 1986, vol. 1, no. 2 for a review of the consequences of mild head trauma.

The Glasgow Outcome Scale (Jennett & Bond, 1975) is composed of five categories used to assess degree of persisting disability. The authors suggest that length of time since injury be specified because patients do change categories, especially during the first few months. The categories are: (1) *death*; (2) *persistent vegetative state* (eyes open in response to sleep/wake cycles); (3) *severe disability* (conscious and responsive, but completely dependent); (4) *moderate disability* (independent in self-care and mobility and able to work in a sheltered environment, but with residual problems, such as hemiparesis, aphasia, ataxia, or memory, personality, or intellectual change); and (5) *good recovery* (resumption of normal life, even though minor neurologic or psychological deficits may be present).

Levin et al. (1982) summarize the results of six studies of survivors of severe head injury that employed the Glasgow Outcome Scale. Ranges for the various categories were as follows: good recovery (28–66 percent), moderate disability (16–44 percent), severe disability (10–35 percent), and persisent vegetative state (0–9 percent). VanZomeren and Vandenburg (1985) reported an incidence of 84 percent for "impairment complaints" (forgetfulness, slowness, attention/concentration disturbance) in a group of severe head injury survivors 2 years after onset. (See Chapter 2 for a detailed discussion of the neurobehavioral consequences of head injury.)

MULTIPLE SCLEROSIS

Multiple sclerosis (MS) is characterized by destruction of the myelin sheaths that insulate nerve fibers. Loss of this coating causes a variety of signs and symptoms depending on the size of the affected area and the tracts involved. Symptoms typically vary with time, and early in the disease they tend to remit completely. Indeed, a few patients have complete permanent remissions after only one or two attacks. In most cases, however, there is a gradual deteriorating course, with exacerbations involving other areas of the central nervous system. Following these later attacks, remissions are incomplete, and the condition worsens gradually over several decades. Some patients suffer a rapid downhill course leading to death within a few months of onset (Porterfield, 1977).

The incidence and prevalence of MS are difficult to determine because of the variety of presentations and the absence of a definitive laboratory test. However, there are certain geographic areas, usually in the higher latitudes, where the disease is more prevalent. In the United States, the incidence varies from 6–14 cases per 100,000 in the South to 40–60 per 100,000 in the North, with the Great Lakes region having an especially high rate. There is no evidence for genetic transmission of the disease, although relatives of MS patients are at greater risk. In the United States, more women than men are affected, but this pattern is not found in other countries. In general, MS is a disease of young adults, with the vast majority of patients developing symptoms between 20 and 40 years of age. In many instances, the first signs are bizarre and transient, and precise diagnosis may take years, during which time many different symptoms will have been observed (Poser, 1972).

Because multiple sclerosis can affect any myelinated area of the nervous system, the symptoms and signs are diverse. The most common symptoms are muscle weakness, visual disturbances, problems with urinary control, ataxia of gait, paresthesias, and dysarthria. Mental disturbances, primarily euphoria, mood lability, and intellectual deterioration, are common in more advanced cases. Complaints of pain are rare. Frequently observed signs are spasticity and/or increased reflexes, other abnormal or absent reflexes, intention tremor, nystagmus, and decreased or abnormal sensation.

Two major theories of pathogenesis are currently popular. One indicts an infection—probably a virus—with a long incubation period and modification by environmental factors. The other theory proposes alterations in the immune system whereby the body develops antibodies to its own myelin. The two hypotheses are not mutually exclusive, and there is evidence to support both.

Just as there is no single proven cause, there is no standard treatment. Steroids are beneficial for some patients. In most cases, however, the course of the disease is not significantly altered.

Rehabilitation of MS patients aims at preventing such complications as contractures and decubitus ulcers and enabling the patient to remain active as long as possible. Many patients require placement in institutions as they become progressively weaker and less able to care for themselves, especially if bladder or bowel incontinence develops (Schneitzer, 1978).

GUILLAIN-BARRÉ SYNDROME

The Guillain-Barré syndrome (infectious polyneuritis) results from inflammation of the peripheral and cranial nerves (Hogg, Kobrin, & Schoenberg, 1979). In about 60 percent of cases, the onset of symptoms follows a repiratory or gastrointestinal infection; however, it is not thought that the illness has a bacterial or viral etiology, but rather results from an allergic reaction (Kennedy, Danielson, Mulder, & Kurland, 1978).

In most cases, the mild upper respiratory illness subsides, and after 1 to 2 weeks, the patient notices either paresthesia—numbness or tingling in the hands or feet—or weakness in the lower extremities. Within 2 or 3 days, lower extremity weakness increases and extends to the facial and upper extremity musculature. Maximal weakness is usually present within a few days, although some cases deteriorate over 3 to 4 weeks. Facial weakness occurs in up to 85 percent of patients, dysarthria and dysphagia occur in 50 percent, and spinal accessory nerve involvement is found in 20 percent. The trunk and proximal extremities are usually most severely affected. Respiratory muscles are frequently involved, with about 25 percent of patients requiring temporary respiratory support. Flaccid quadriplegia, with total dependence for self-care and mobility, is not unusual.

Sensory symptoms are frequent but not prominent. Sensation may be increased or decreased, with changes in perception of light touch, vibration, and position sense being the most common. Occasionally, sensory loss is profound, and muscle tenderness is pronounced.

Rate and degree of recovery tend to be directly correlated with speed of onset. Most patients recover completely or have only slight, nondisabling residual weakness, although recovery may take months. A few patients are permanently disabled. Mortality rates of 15–60 percent have been reported, with death usually resulting from respiratory failure or intercurrent infection (Ravn, 1967).

There is no standard treatment other than respiratory support and good nursing care that is necessary to prevent the complications of malnutrition, decubitus formation, and pressure neuropathy. Physical rehabilitation is useful for patients with more severe forms of the disease, but exercise must not be exhausting.

ARTHRITIS

Arthritis, defined as inflammation of a joint, may result from or be associated with numerous disorders (Swezey, 1982). Over 10 million Americans have some form of arthritis, and many are disabled by its effects, primarily pain and restriction of movement. The most common varieties are rheumatoid arthritis (a chronic systemic condition characterized by inflammation of the connective tissue surrounding a joint, often the knuckles or wrists), the arthritis that accompanies rheumatic fever, degenerative joint disease (osteoarthritis), traumatic and infectious arthritis, and the arthritis of gout. The treatments, prognoses, and sequelae of the various types differ; full consideration exceeds the scope of the present discussion. Therapy focuses on preservation of the involved joints and their ranges of motion, muscle strengthening, relief of pain, and conservation of energy. Surgical replacement of severely degenerated joints has become increasingly common.

Arthritic patients referred for inpatient rehabilitation usually have newly replaced joints, require intensive stretching of joints before resuming ambulation, or have severe joint disease and need to learn new techniques for mobility and self-care because of poor upper extremity function.

REFERENCES

Andrews, K., & Stewart, J. (1979). Stroke recovery: He can but does he? *Rheumatology and Rehabilitation, 18,* 43–48.

Barth, J.T., Macciocchi, S., Giordani, B., Rimel, R., Jane, J., & Boll, T. (1983). Neuropsychological sequelae of minor head injury. *Neurosurgery, 13,* 529–533.

Bond, M.R. (1983). Standardized methods of assessing and predicting outcome. In M. Rosenthal, E.R. Griffith, M.R. Bond, & J.D. Miller (Eds.), *Rehabilitation of the head-injured adult,* Philadelphia: F.A. Davis Co., pp. 97–113.

Brooks, N. (1984a). Cognitive deficits after head injury. In N. Brooks (Ed), *Closed head injury.* New York: Oxford University Press, pp. 44–73.

Brooks N. (1984b). Head injury and the family. In N. Brooks (Ed.), *Closed head injury.* New York: Oxford University Press, pp. 123–147.

Cartlidge, N.E.F., & Shaw, D.A. (1981). *Head injury.* London: W.B. Saunders Co. Ltd.

Davis, E.J., Friz, B.R., & Clippinger, F.W. (1970). Amputees and their prostheses. *Artificial Limbs, 14,* 19–48.

Ditunno, P., McCauley, C., & Marquette, C. (1985). Sensation-seeking behavior and the incidence of spinal cord injury. *Archives of Physical Medicine and Rehabilitation, 66,* 152–155.

Easton, J.D., & Sherman, D.G. (1977). Stroke and mortality rate in carotid endarterectomy: 228 consecutive operations. *Stroke, 8,* 565–568.

Fahy, T.J., Irving, M.H., & Millac, P. (1967). Severe head injuries: A six year follow-up. *Lancet, 2,* 475–479.

Field, J.H. (1976). *Epidemiology of head injuries in England and Wales.* London: HMSO.

Fordyce, W.E. (1964). Personality characteristics in men with spinal cord injury as related to manner of onset of disability. *Archives of Physical Medicine and Rehabilitation, 45,* 321–325.

Gresham, G.E., Fitzpatrick, T.E., Wolf, P.A., McNamera, P.M., Kannel, W.B., & Dawber, T.R. (1975). Residual disability in survivors of stroke: The Framingham study. *New England Journal of Medicine, 293,* 954–956.

Gresham, G.E., Phillips, T.F., Wolf, P.A., McNamara, P.M., Kannel, W.B., & Dawber, T.R. (1979). Epidemiologic profile of long-term stroke disability: The Framingham study. *Archives of Physical Medicine and Rehabilitation, 60,* 487–491.

Gronwall, D., & Wrightson, P. (1974). Delayed recovery of intellectual function after minor head injury. *Lancet, 2,* 605–609.

Gurdjian, E.S., & Gurdjian, E.S. (1976). Cerebral contusions: Reevaluation of the mechanism of their development. *Journal of Trauma, 16,* 35–51.

Hogg, J.E., Kobrin, D.E., & Schoenberg, B.S. (1979). The Guillain-Barré syndrome—epidemiologic and clinical features. *Journal of Chronic Disease, 32,* 227–231.

Holtzman, M., Panin, N., & Ebel, A. (1959). Anatomical localization of common vascular brain syndromes. *American Journal of Physiology, 38,* 133–135.

Jennett, B., & Bond, M. (1975). Assessment of outcome after severe brain damage. *Lancet, 1,* 480–484.

Jennett, B., & Teasdale, G. (1981). *Management of head injuries.* Philadelphia: F.A. Davis Co.

Jones, H.R., & Millikan, C.H. (1976). Temporal profile (clinical course) of acute carotid system cerebral infarction. *Stroke, 7,* 64–71.

Kalsbeek, W.D., McLaurin, R.L., Harris, B.S.H., & Miller, J.D. (1980). The National Head and Spinal Cord Injury Survey: Major findings. *Journal of Neurosurgery (Suppl.), 53,* 19–31.

Kennedy, R.H., Danielson, M.A., Mulder, D.W., & Kurland, L.T. (1978). Guillain-Barré syndrome—a forty-two year epidemiologic and clinical study. *Mayo Clinic Proceedings, 53,* 93–99.

Kerr, T.A., Kay, D.W.K., & Lassman, L.P. (1971). Characteristics of patients, type of accident, and mortality in a consecutive series of head injuries admitted to a neurosurgical unit. *British Journal of Preventive Socialized Medicine, 25,* 179–185.

Kertesz, A. (Ed.). (1983). *Localization in neuropsychology.* New York: Academic Press.

Klauber, M.R., Barrett-Connor, E., Marshall, L.F., & Bowers, S.A. (1981). The epidemiology of head injury. *American Journal of Epidemiology, 113,* 500–509.

Kottke, F.J., Stillwell, G.K., & Lehmann, J.F. (Eds.). (1982). *Krusen's handbook of physical medicine and rehabilitation.* Philadelphia: W.B. Saunders Co.

Kraus, J.F., Franti, C.E., Riggins, R.S., Richards, D., & Borhani, N.O. (1975). Incidence of traumatic spinal cord lesions. *Journal of Chronic Disease, 28,* 471–492.

Levin, H.S., Benton, A.L., & Grossman, R.G. (1982). *The neurobehavioral consequences of closed head injury.* New York: Oxford University Press.

Lezak, M.D. (1978). Subtle sequelae of brain damage. *American Journal of Physical Medicine, 57,* 9–15.

Libow, L.S., & Sherman, F.T. (1981). *The core of geriatric medicine.* St. Louis: C.V. Mosby Company.

Merritt, H.H. (1979). *A textbook of neurology.* Philadelphia: Lea and Febiger.

Mital, M.A., & Pierce, D.S. (1971). *Amputees and their prostheses.* Boston: Little, Brown, and Company.

National Association of Rehabilitation Facilities. (NARF). (1981). *The cost benefits of stroke rehabilitation.* Washington, DC: Author.

National Spinal Cord Injury Data Research Center. (1978). *National Spinal Cord Injury Model Systems Conference: Proceedings.* Arizona: Author.

Pierce, D.S., & Nickel, V.H. (1977). *The total care of spinal cord injuries.* Boston: Little, Brown, and Company.

Porterfield, J.S. (Ed.). (1977). Multiple sclerosis. *British Medical Bulletin, 33,* 1–83.

Poser, C.M. (1972). Recent advances in multiple sclerosis. *Medical Clinics of North America, 56,* 1343–1362.

Ravn, H. (1967). The Landry Guillain-Barré syndrome. *Acta Neurochirurgica Scandinavica (Suppl. 30), 43,* 7–64.

Riggins, R.S., & Kraus, J.F. (1977). The risk of neurologic damage with fractures of the vertebrae. *Journal of Trauma, 17,* 126–133.

Rimel, R.W., Giordani, B., Barth, J., Boll, T., & Jane, J. (1981). Disability caused by minor head injury. *Neurosurgery, 9,* 221–228.

Roberts, A.H. (1976). Long-term prognosis of severe accidental head injury. *Proceedings of the Royal Society of Medicine, 69,* 137–140.

Schneitzer, L. (1978). Rehabilitation of patients with multiple sclerosis. *Archives of Physical Medicine and Rehabilitation, 59,* 430–437.

Stoner, E.K. (1982). Management of the lower extremity amputee. In F.J. Kottle, G.K. Stillwell, & J.F. Lehmann (Eds.), *Krusen's handbook of physical medicine and rehabilitation.* Philadelphia: W.B. Saunders Co.

Strich, S.J. (1970). Lesions in the cerebral hemispheres after blunt head injury. In S. Sevitt & H.B. Stoner (Eds.), *The pathology of trauma.* London: BMA House, pp. 166–171.

Swezey, R.L. (1982). Rehabilitation in arthritis and allied conditions. In F.J. Kottle, G.K. Stillwell, & J.F. Lehmann (Eds), *Krusen's handbook of physical medicine and rehabilitation.* Philadelphia: W.B. Saunders Co., pp. 604–642.

Teasdale, G., & Jennett, B. (1974). Assessment of coma and impaired consciousness. *Lancet, 2,* 81–84.

VanZomeren, A., & Vandenberg, W. (1985). Residual complaints of patients two years after severe head injury. *Journal of Neurology, Neurosurgery and Psychiatry, 48,* 21–28.

Vitali, M., Robinson, K.P., Andrews, B.G., & Harris, E.F. (1978). *Amputations and prostheses.* London: Baillier-Tindall.

Walton, J.N. (1977). *Brain's diseases of the nervous system.* Oxford: Oxford University Press.

Wolf, P.A., Dawber, T.R., Thomas, H.E., Colton, T., & Kannel W.B. (1977). Epidemiology of stroke. In R. Thompson & J. Green (Eds.), *Advances in neurology, 16.* New York: Raven Press, pp. 5–19.

Yashow, D. (1978). *Spinal injury.* New York: Appleton-Century-Crofts.

Chapter 20

Clinical Pharmacology in Rehabilitation

Patrick K. Murray, M.D.

Pharmacology is a basic science that examines and describes the interactions of chemicals and living systems: Medical pharmacology confines itself to chemicals or drugs that are useful in prevention, treatment, and diagnosis of illness and to chemicals that are abused by people for recreational purposes.

This chapter focuses on the basic concepts of pharmacology and on specific drugs that are commonly used on a rehabilitation service. Antibiotics are not discussed as they are prescribed only for brief intervals (7–10 days) and only rarely affect a patient's neuropsychiatric status. They are, however, frequently used for the treatment of infections in many rehabilitation patients.

Each drug is discussed under the heading of its most common use. Cognitive and psychological side effects are emphasized. A reference table of all drugs discussed is located at the end of the chapter.

PHARMACOLOGICAL PRINCIPLES

The most common mechanism of drug function is the binding of a drug to a living cell, by which it affects the operation of that cell. Most drugs alter cell operation by binding to receptors that regulate normal cell functions. Other drugs act more generally on all cell membranes, altering permeability or electrical charge.

One is rarely able to observe the actual cellular effect of a drug. Rather, clinical pharmacology assesses drug function by observing the concentration of drugs in the blood and/or the patient's response to the drug. The first section of the chapter discusses the determinants of the concentration of drugs in the blood. Drug concentration is normally expressed as plasma drug level in grams per liter of blood fluid. The second section of the chapter describes specific drugs effects in patients.

The concentration of a drug is generally assumed to have a uniform and predictable effect on cell function. There are two major limitations to this assumption. First, chronic administration of a drug may desensitize the receptor, decreasing the drug's effectiveness over time. More drug, and thus higher plasma levels, will then be required to obtain the desired effect. The model's second limitation is that the effects of some drugs are not clinically apparent for some time, despite seemingly adequate plasma levels. This is especially true of antidepressants; therapeutic plasma levels are usually obtained weeks before the clinical effect is observed. With these two limitations in mind, a basic knowledge of pharmacological principles can aid one's understanding of drug use.

Absorption

Plasma drug levels are determined by the interaction of several factors—completeness of drug absorption, distribution of the substance in the body, biotransformation of drugs, and the excretion of drugs by the body. This dynamic balance is depicted in Figure 20–1.

Drug absorption is the process of getting the drug into the plasma. Intravenous drug administration is the most rapid and complete method of drug absorption. Oral, topical (on the skin), and sublingual (under the tongue) routes allow easy self-administration by the patient. However, absorption by these routes is generally slower and less complete than intravenous administration. Slower absorption is sometimes a desired attribute of a medication and occasionally this quality is manufactured into a drug in the form of sustained release tablets or capsules.

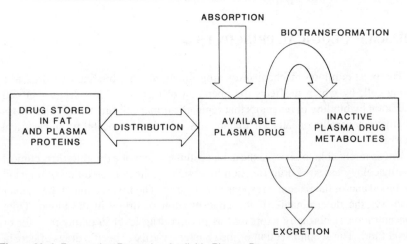

Figure 20–1 Factors that Determine Available Plasma Drug

The other common route of administration is by injection into the skin or muscle. Absorption depends on the drug's solubility in skin or muscle and the blood flow in the tissue. Some drugs are extremely insoluble in muscle and are poorly and erratically absorbed—for example, phenytoin (Dilantin) and diazepam (Valium). Blood flow is also critical in the absorption of injected (parenteral) drugs. In exercising muscle, blood flow is high and absorption rapid. In contrast, when the skin is cooled or the individual is inactive, blood flow is dramatically decreased, and drugs are absorbed slowly.

Bioavailability refers to the fraction of drug absorbed compared to the amount of drug given. It is usually expressed as a percentage and summarizes absorption efficiency.

Drug Distribution

After the drug is absorbed and reaches the plasma, it is distributed throughout the body. It is this distribution that determines how much drug reaches the site of drug action. Large quantities of some drugs are stored in the body, leaving little drug for activity. Some drugs, because of their physical or chemical characteristics, cannot penetrate certain parts of the body. The most important example of an impenetrable feature is the blood-brain barrier created by tight junctions between cells surrounding the blood vessels in the brain. This barrier protects the brain from some potential side effects, but limits the utility of other drugs for central nervous system use.

Excretion

Drugs are excreted or removed from the body primarily by the kidneys. Other less important routes of excretion are feces, sweat, expired air, and saliva. The plasma is continuously filtered by the kidney, and circulating drug is removed in this process.

The excretion rate of most drugs depends on plasma drug concentration. This is called an exponential decay rate and is normally described as the time for half of the drug in the plasma to be eliminated—the *drug half-life*. Figure 20-2 demonstrates the method for determining drug half-life. After four half-lives following drug administration, only 6 percent of the drug remains in the plasma.

When drugs are given at regular intervals, the plasma level can be determined by knowing the single dose level of the drug and the drug half-life. Many drugs are given approximately once per half-life and thus reach 94 percent of their eventual steady state concentration after four doses. When drugs have very long half-lives, a loading dose that is much larger than the eventual maintenance dose is given to shorten the time before a steady state is obtained.

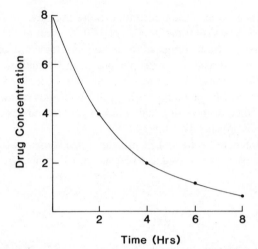

Figure 20–2 Exponential Decay Curve. In this example the time for drug concentration to decline from four units to two units is 2 hours. The drug half-life is thus 2 hours.

A few drugs in regular doses do not decay exponentially, but are removed at a fixed rate of drug per unit time. Example of drugs eliminated in this fashion are aspirin and phenytoin (Dilantin).

Biotransformation

Some drugs are poorly excreted in their native forms. These drugs require conversion in the liver to a form compatible with excretion by the kidney. This process is called *biotransformation*.

Drug biotransformation varies, depending on genetic factors, drug interactions, or liver disease. There are individual differences in the concentration of metabolic pathways in the liver. A dose that is therapeutic for a patient with a slow metabolism may be ineffective for a patient with a fast metabolism. When the liver, the major site of biotransformation, is diseased or malfunctioning as in cirrhosis or severe heart failure, drug doses that would normally be well tolerated can result in toxic levels.

Drugs themselves can stimulate or retard the biotransformation of other drugs; these drug-drug interactions are a major source of therapeutic problems. For example, ethanol, the alcohol in liquors and wines, stimulates the biotransformation of diazepam (Valium), decreasing its plasma level and therapeutic effect.

When evaluating the use of a drug in any given situation, all of the above determinants of drug action must be considered. As these factors vary greatly from patient to patient, and even at different times in the same patient, they are often responsible for the failure of a particular drug to work as expected.

Side Effects

Side effects, or unwanted drug actions, are an important consideration in the prescription and evaluation of drug therapy. Side effects take one of three forms—expected effects, idiosyncratic toxicity, and allergy.

Expected side effects are predictable problems that occur when a drug level becomes too high. Sometimes these high doses are necessary in order to achieve the desired drug effect. For example, diarrhea or hair loss must be tolerated to produce an antitumor effect with cancer drugs. This kind of side effect also occurs when excretion or biotransformation rates are slowed and drug levels rise above those expected with standard dosing regimens.

Idiosyncratic toxicities are poorly understood drug effects that occur randomly in rare individuals. They cannot be anticipated and are unrelated to drug allergy. Prescribers of a drug must be aware of these special side effects in the drugs they use.

Drug allergy is a response that is produced by the immunologic system of the body. Reactions range from rapid and dramatic responses that cause sudden death if not treated promptly to very delayed and mild reactions. Skin rashes are the most common drug allergy. Usually the drug must be discontinued to stop the allergic response.

Adherence

The prescriber of a medication must have knowledge of the patient's cooperation with the drug therapy in order to evaluate drug performance (Sackett & Haynes, 1976). *Adherence* is generally expressed as a ratio of the amount of drug taken by the patient to the amount prescribed. Although this measure is simple and easily understood, it fails to account for problems in dosing intervals that are also important. Patients may take all their medication but at intervals that lessen drug effectiveness or increase toxicity, e.g., taking four tablets once a day rather than one tablet four times per day. No universally accepted measure of adherence is available. In inpatient settings, adherence approaches 100 percent because of the controlled environment and careful monitoring of drug therapy. More than half of all patients in outpatient settings, however, fail to take drugs as prescribed.

It is difficult to predict which patients will be noncompliant. Socioeconomic factors have been shown to be poor predictors. Factors associated with poor compliance include poor understanding of drug effects and side effects, the use of multiple drugs and multiple daily dosing, the expense of drugs, and the quality of the relationship between prescriber and patient (Masur, 1981).

Special Considerations

In rehabilitation settings special consideration must be given to drug therapy with two groups of patients—the spinal cord injured patient and the elderly.

The spinal cord injured patient is especially susceptible to side effects from drugs that affect autonomic function—antidepressants, cardiac and respiratory drugs, and the phenothiazines—because the brain has been disconnected from control of the sympathetic nervous system. Functions of the sympathetic nervous system, such as blood pressure maintenance, bowel motility, and heart rate regulation, lack control from higher brain centers and hence are very vulnerable to circulating drugs that directly affect the system. Bowel and bladder programs and blood pressure control are often dramatically affected by drugs that have autonomic activity.

Psychotropic medications and cardiac drugs can cause marked mental status changes in the elderly, especially when they are used in combination. Elderly patients have four times more adverse drug reactions than do younger patients. The factors that contribute to these toxic problems include loss of lean body mass, a decline in liver and kidney function with age, and an age-related alteration in receptor sensitivity to drug effects. The common use of multiple medications in the elderly certainly contributes to the problems of adverse drug effects.

Drug Abuse

Drug abuse is a common problem in rehabilitation settings where inpatients who are hospitalized for long periods of time may seek pharmacologic relief from boredom. Drug abuse is largely culturally defined. It generally refers to self-administration of a drug that deviates from approved medical or cultural patterns. It may occur sporadically or in a regular compulsive fashion.

Compulsive drug use refers to the regular ingestion of drugs to maintain a subjective state of well-being. If this has a psychological basis, it is called *habituation*. If there is a physiologic basis, abstinence from the drug causes characteristic physical effects, such as gooseflesh or hallucinations, that can be eliminated by resuming drug use. This is described as *physical dependence* and is associated with the development of tolerance or a decreasing drug effect with repeated administration.

Addiction is a behavioral phenomenon characterized by overwhelming preoccupation with obtaining, using, and securing the supply of the drug and a high tendency to relapse after *withdrawal*. Addiction, habituation, and physical dependence are not synonyms, and the dangers and therapy of each need to be differentiated. Physical dependence on narcotic analgesics, for example, exceeds 50 percent among patients who have received a 10-day course of meperidine (Demerol) for pain; however, the symptoms of withdrawal are generally mild, and the incidence of addiction is less than 1 percent.

Opiates, barbiturates, alcohol, and nicotine are the drugs in regular use that have the greatest risk of physical dependence. Cocaine, amphetamines, marijuana, and the psychedelic agents are commonly associated with habituation and regular use on a psychological basis.

The severe symptoms of withdrawal from physical dependence can be avoided by controlled and gradually diminished intake of the drug. If addiction is a component of the dependent state, a behavioral approach is critical to the success of the overall program; drug withdrawal alone is not sufficient.

This classification of drug abuse corresponds to World Health Organization (1973) criteria. It differs from the classification in the *Diagnostic and Statistical Manual of Mental Disorders* (DSM-III). The DSM-III classifies drug abuse as either substance abuse or substance dependence. *Substance abuse* is characterized by a pattern of pathologic use and impairment in social or occupational functioning lasting at least 1 month. *Substance dependence* is characterized by physiologic dependence, i.e., tolerance or withdrawal.

The drugs often used in rehabilitation settings and their most common side effects are discussed below.

CENTRAL NERVOUS SYSTEM DRUGS

This section discusses drugs that have the primary function of affecting the central nervous system (CNS). Many of these drugs have important neuropsychological side effects of which health professionals should be aware.

Hypnotics and Anxiolytics

These drugs are used to decrease symptoms of anxiety and induce sleep. Larger doses are required when the drug is used as an hypnotic than as an anxiolytic. Other considerations are the rapidity of onset of the effects and the duration of action. To induce sleep, a fast-acting drug with an effective duration of about 6–8 hours would be most desirable. For treatment of anxiety, a drug with long-lasting effects would be preferred to obviate the need for frequent dosing.

The most frequently prescribed drugs in this class are the benzodiazepines, the best known of which is diazepam (Valium). These drugs are widely used and are relatively safe; they rarely depress respiration, even in extremely high doses. The longer-acting drugs in this class—diazepam, flurazepam (Dalmane) and chlordiazepoxide (Librium)—frequently accumulate in elderly patients and can cause a depressed state simulating dementia. They should be used with much caution in the older population.

The antihistamines are often used to treat anxiety and induce sleep, but their effectiveness has never been clearly documented. Diphenhydramine (Benadryl) and hydroxyzine (Vistaril) are the most frequently used drugs in this class. Their advantage is their short duration of action and minimal side effects.

A major disadvantage of all the anxiolytics is that tolerance quickly develops to them, making them useless for the symptoms for which they were prescribed unless the dose is increased. They should be used only for short-term problems with anxiety or insomnia. Unfortunately, many people take these medications on a chronic basis and are probably habituated to the drug effects.

Many other drugs are occasionally prescribed for sedation, such as the barbiturates and chloral hydrate, but in general, these drugs cause more problems than the benzodiazepines. The sedative effects of all these drugs is enhanced by ethanol, causing more profound sedation than would be otherwise expected.

Table 20–1 lists the commonly used anxiolytics and sedatives.

Ethanol

Ethanol is a nonprescription CNS depressant. It is widely used by lay people as a hypnotic, analgesic, and euphoriant. It is effective for all of these purposes, but obviously has the disadvantages of physical dependence and addiction. It interacts with many prescription medications; in a rehabilitation setting, therefore, one must know which patients are drinking and prescribe medications with this in mind.

Table 20–1 Anxiolytics and Sedatives

Drug	Half-Life (hours)	Speed of Absorption
Benzodiazepines		
flurazepam (Dalmane)	120	Intermediate
clorazepate (Tranxene)	75	Fast
diazepam (Valium)	32	Fast
lorazepam (Ativan)	15	Intermediate
temazepam (Restoril)	15	Slow
oxazepam (Serax)	10	Slow
chlordiazepoxide (Librium)	10	Intermediate
triazolom (Halcion)	3	Fast
Barbiturates		
phenobarbital	80	Slow
amobarbital (Amytal)	25	Intermediate
pentobarbital (Nembutal)	35	Intermediate
secobarbital (Seconal)	28	Intermediate
Others		
hydroxyzine (Vistaril)	4	
chloral hydrate	7	

Antidepressants

The antidepressants are used to treat patients with moderate to severe depressions. They are most effective when the depression is endogenous and with vegetative signs, but they are also useful in treating reactive depressions. In patients with depression of an uncertain type, such as the elderly patient with possible pseudodementia, a 2-week trial of an antidepressant is frequently indicated. All classes of antidepressants require 10–14 days before a clinical effect can be observed, although side effects can begin with the first dose. Table 20–2 lists the most commonly used antidepressants.

There are three classes of antidepressants—the tricyclics, the tetracyclics, and the monoamine oxidase inhibitors. The tricyclic antidepressants are the most widely used.

The tricyclics are highly effective, but they have a myriad of side effects because of their anticholinergic activity. They routinely cause dry mouth and frequently affect the blood pressure and bladder function. Excessive sedation, confusion, and anxiety are other possible side effects. Imipramine (Tofranil) and protryptiline (Vivactil) can cause insomnia. The more sedating preparations, such as amitryptiline, are generally given at bedtime. All of these drugs must be used with extreme caution in the elderly and in those with heart disease.

Nontricyclic antidepressants are a new class of drugs developed to avoid the anticholinergic effects caused by the tricyclics. They appear to avoid these

Table 20–2 Antidepressants

Drug	Sedation	Anticholinergic Effects
Tricyclics		
amitryptiline (Elavil)	+ + +	+ + +
doxepin (Sinequan)	+ + +	+ + +
nortryptiline (Aventyl)	+ +	+
protryptiline (Vivactil)	+	+ +
imipramine (Tofranil)	+ +	+ +
desipramine (Norpramin)	+	+
New nontricyclics		
maprotiline (Ludiomil)	+ +	+ +
trazadone (Desyrel)	+ +	+
nomifensine (Merital)	+	+
amoxapine (Asendin)	+ +	+
Monoamine oxidase inhibitors (Parnate)	0	0

problems, but have other idiosyncratic toxicities that make their present role unclear. Their efficacy seems to be very comparable to that of the tricyclics.

The monoamine oxidase inhibitors are effective antidepressants, but are rarely used because of their extremely dangerous interactions with some foods and drugs. They have no advantages over the tricyclics.

Antipsychotics/Neuroleptics

These drugs are used for the therapy of a wide variety of acute and chronic psychiatric disorders, including acute mania, paranoia, severe personality disorders, and the agitation associated with head injury. They are also used to prevent vomiting, to relieve chronic hiccoughs, and as an adjunct to analgesics.

Many side effects accompany the use of these drugs. Acutely these drugs can cause severe dystonic reactions characterized by prolonged posturing of the neck, jaw, mouth, and tongue and accompanied by extreme anxiety. Such reactions are easily treated with antihistamines or anticholinergic drugs and reduction of the dose of the antipsychotic medication. On a more chronic basis, either a restless pacing and agitation or parkinsonian signs with rigidity of the trunk and limbs may occur. Problems with low blood pressure and occasional suppression of blood production can arise. Menstrual irregularity and loss of libido are to be expected with chronic use. A late complication in 10–20 percent of patients is tardive dyskinesia—uncontrolled movements of the body, especially the tongue, face, jaw, and trunk. This problem is more common in women and the elderly. It has no treatment, does not generally resolve, and in fact may worsen with withdrawal of the drug.

Table 20–3 lists the more commonly used neuroleptics and their relative strengths, sedative properties, and extrapyramidal (dystonic and parkinsonian) side effects.

Anticonvulsants

Epilepsy is a common problem in rehabilitation units, especially in patients with head injury and in some patients following strokes. Therapy for seizure prevention is dictated by four principles.

1. Different types of seizures require different anticonvulsant medications. Accurate diagnosis of seizure type is thus very important.
2. It is best to give only one anticonvulsant and to titrate it to control the seizures. Seizures frequently can be controlled by what appear to be subtherapeutic amounts of drug.

Table 20–3 Neuroleptics (Antipsychotics)

Drug	Relative Strength	Sedation	Extrapyramidal Effects
Thioridazine (Mellaril)	1	+ + +	+
Chlorpromazine (Thorazine)	1	+ + +	+ +
Prochlorperazine (Compazine)	6	+ +	+ + +
Loxapine (Loxitane)	10	+ +	+ +
Perphenazine (Trilafon)	12	+	+ + +
Trifluoperazine (Stelazine)	20	+ +	+ + +
Thiothixene (Navane)	25	+	+ + +
Fluphenazine (Prolixin)	50	+	+ + +
Haloperidol (Haldol)	50	+	+ + +

3. Patients must be educated regarding the adverse effects of the drugs and the importance of compliance to the regimen. These factors are critical to adherence to the medication regimen and hence the success of the therapy.
4. It is essential to monitor the outcome of the program, the side effects, and the serum levels of the drug.

There are four anticonvulsants used in the therapy of most adult forms of epilepsy. Carbamazepine (Tegretol) is a well-tolerated drug that causes little sedation and is highly effective in controlling most seizures. Phenytoin (Dilantin) is the most commonly prescribed anticonvulsant. Although it is very effective, it causes many predictable side effects, such as hirsutism, gum hypertrophy, coarsening of the facial features, tremulousness, and sedation. Children born of mothers taking phenytoin have an increased incidence of cleft palate and congenital heart disease. Valproic acid (Depakene) has little sedative effect, but it is only rarely useful in adult-onset epilepsy and can cause hepatitis. Phenobarbital, the oldest of the anticonvulsants, is an effective drug for most adult epilepsy, but it invariably causes sedation and generalized mental slowing.

The decision to terminate anticonvulsant therapy is a difficult and complex one. The implications of a recurrent seizure for the patient's vocational prospects, license to drive, and the like, often argue against a trial off the anticonvulsant.

However, half of all patients who have had recurrent seizures can safely stop anticonvulsants. Determining the timing of a trial off anticonvulsants can be difficult because of the above-mentioned concerns.

Analgesics

Analgesics can be divided into three classes—those that work at the opioid receptor, those with analgesic effects unrelated to the opioid receptor, and those useful in the treatment of chronic pain. The last group includes such medications as the tricyclic antidepressants and carbamazepine that are used for chronic pain conditions not amenable to other medical or surgical approaches. The antidepressants may help alleviate pain by improving the depression often associated with the chronic pain syndrome. These drugs are frequently used for the treatment of phantom pain syndromes found in spinal cord injury and amputation. They are described in other portions of this chapter.

The opiate analgesics can be divided into two groups—the pure opiates (agonists) and drugs that have both opiate and opiate antagonism within the same medication (agonist-antagonists). The latter group is considerably less likely to cause dependence. All opiates are effective analgesics, although their relative potency varies greatly. All can depress respiration and cause drowsiness if given in large enough doses. Most cause both constipation and nausea when given at their proper dosage. Tolerance to these drugs is not a major problem in the treatment of acute pain. Excessive concern about addictive potential has led to undertreatment of many patients suffering severe acute pain. Their use for chronic pain is to be discouraged, however, except when the pain is malignant in etiology. In this situation, a long-acting opiate, such as methadone, is probably the drug of choice.

One final consideration is the relative effectiveness of parenteral and oral opiates. If given orally many of these drugs require five-fold increases to maintain their analgesic effectiveness. When this fact is not appreciated, many patients are inadequately medicated. Table 20–4 details the appropriate dosing interval, the oral to parenteral ratio (bioavailability), and the opiate analgesic's strength relative to morphine in treating pain.

The nonopiate analgesics are a very diverse group of drugs that have an uncertain mechanism of action. They all seem to be active within the prostaglandin systems of the body (prostaglandins are cellular hormones responsible for regulation of many cell functions), but how this activity relates to their role as analgesics is still a matter of speculation. Aspirin, acetaminophen (Tylenol), and diflusinal (Dolobid) are the most commonly used drugs in this class, although the nonsteroidal anti-inflammatories (see section on antirheumatic medications) are used with increasing frequency. None of these three drugs has significant cognitive or psychiatric side effects. Diflusinal is a new analgesic with properties and side effects similar to aspirin, such as gastric irritation, but it is effective when given

Table 20–4 Opiate Analgesics

Drug	Dosing Interval (hours)	Oral Bioavailibility (percent)	Relative Strength
Agonists			
morphine	4–6	20	1
hydromorphone (Dilaudid)	4–6	20	8
meperidine (Demerol)	2–3	25	.12
dolophine (Methadone)	24–36 varies	50	1
codeine	4–6	67	.08
propoxyphene (Darvon)	6–8	100	.04
Agonist-Antagonists			
pentazocine (Talwin)	3–4	33	.20
butorphanol (Stadol)	3–4	—	5

only two or three times per day. These drugs are effective for mild to moderate acute pain. They are often given with the less potent opiate analgesics, e.g., codeine and propoxyphene. The value of this combination of low potency opiates and nonopiate analgesics is poorly supported by biomedical research, yet they remain among the most commonly prescribed drugs.

Analgesics alone are not useful for the treatment of chronic pain conditions. Treatment for these patients must involve a multidisciplinary approach, including physical treatments, behavior modification, and relaxation techniques in addition to appropriate analgesics (see Chapter 4).

Antiparkinsonism Agents

Parkinson's disease is characterized by a deficiency of dopamine in certain parts of the brain. Pharmacotherapy attempts either to increase these levels or suppress the antagonists of dopamine.

L-dopa, the most effective drug for moderate to severe Parkinson's disease, increases dopamine levels in the brain. It is usually given with another drug (carbidopa) to prevent some of its gastrointestinal side effects. L-dopa can cause a mild euphoria in some patients and hyperactivity and anxiety in others. In rare instances, a severe psychosis or depression may result. It usually decreases the rigidity of these patients, but the effect wanes in about 3–5 years. At that point, a new drug, bromocriptine (Parlodel), is sometimes effective in maintaining the antiparkinson effects. This drug has side effects similar to those of L-dopa and often causes very vivid and disturbing dreams.

Because the effect of L-dopa is time limited, there has been renewed interest in the use of anticholinergics for early therapy of mild Parkinson's disease. These drugs, such as trihexphenidyl (Artane) and benztropine (Cogentin), suppress the major antagonist of dopamine in the brain. They invariably cause a dry mouth and can produce urinary retention. Confusion and excitement are common in elderly persons taking these medications, which limits their overall usefulness.

Amantadine (Symmetrel), developed for the treatment of viral infections, is used in the treatment of Parkinson's disease, typically in combination with other drugs. Decreased mental alertness, confusion, and lightheadedness may occur with its use.

RESPIRATORY MEDICATIONS

Many patients seen on rehabilitation units suffer from respiratory difficulty because of pre-existing respiratory disorders or as a result of the neurologic impairments responsible for their rehabilitation admission. Most drugs used to treat respiratory problems act by dilating the airways of the lung. There are two basic groups of drugs in this category—the theophyllines and the adrenergic stimulators. Both groups of drugs have uses in acute and chronic respiratory problems. In acute asthmatic attacks, when the problem is sudden constriction of the airway, rapidly acting inhaled or injected preparations are used. In chronic respiratory problems, oral and long-acting inhaled drugs are used to decrease chronic bronchial constriction. The long-acting drugs are also believed to stimulate the respiratory centers in the brain and thus are useful for patients who have neurologic causes for poor breathing function, e.g., high quadraplegics.

The major side effects of these drugs—CNS stimulation with nervousness, insomnia, and tremors—are predictable from their pharmacological effects. Seizures can occur with the theophyllines if the dose exceeds the therapeutic range. Cardiac stimulation causing a fast heart rate is expected with these drugs and can precipitate symptoms of underlying cardiac illness.

Newer noncatecholamine adrenergic stimulators have fewer cardiac and CNS side effects, but tremor is more common with these drugs. The tremor often resolves with continued use. Table 20–5 lists common preparations in each of these classes of drugs.

Two other less commonly used respiratory drugs are beclamethasone (Vanceril) and cromolyn (Intal). Beclamethasone is an inhaled corticosteroid with the actions and side effects of other corticosteroids; it yields positive respiratory

Table 20–5 Respiratory Drugs

Theophyllines	Elixophyllin, aminophylline, theodur, choledyl, aminodur
Catecholamines	Epinephrine (Adrenalin) Isoproterenol (Isuprel) Isoetharine (Bronkometer)
Noncatecholamines	Metaproterenol (Metaprel, Alupent) Terbutaline (Brethine, Bricanyl) Albuterol (Proventil, Ventolin)

effects with very low doses, but can cause thrush, a yeast infection of the mouth. Cromolyn can prevent asthma attacks, but has no use in chronic lung disease or acute illnesses. Its side effects are minimal.

CARDIOVASCULAR MEDICATIONS

The predominant uses for cardiovascular drugs are to reduce high blood pressure, to improve heart contractility, to slow and/or regulate heart rhythm, and to treat or prevent angina, the chest pain produced by the narrowing of cardiac blood vessels. Most drugs with cardiovascular effects can be used for multiple clinical purposes; frequently, a drug has multiple cardiovascular effects in a given patient.

Diuretics

These drugs increase the excretion of salt (sodium) and water by the kidneys and are used for the initial treatment of most patients with high blood pressure. Diuretics are also the mainstay in the treatment of fluid and sodium overload states, such as heart and kidney failure. Thiazide diuretics are generally used for high blood pressure, and furosemide (Lasix) is most commonly used for fluid and sodium overload. Two other types of diuretics—spironolactone (Aldactone) and triamterene (Dyrenium)—are used occasionally with the thiazide diuretics to control potassium loss.

The major side effects of furosemide and the thiazide diuretics are excessive fluid loss causing low blood pressure on standing and the depletion of potassium. The latter problem, which is characterized by generalized lassitude, can be treated by either dietary supplements of potassium—bananas, oranges, tomatoes—or by direct potassium supplementation. Thiazide diuretics also frequently cause impotence.

Antihypertensives

In addition to diuretic therapy, many different drugs are used to lower blood pressure. These drugs act on the peripheral nerves, the brain, or directly on the blood vessels. Those that affect the peripheral nerves, decreasing vascular tone and thus blood pressure, include the beta-blockers—propranalol (Inderal), metoprolol (Lopressor), naldolol (Corgard)—reserpine, and prazosin (Minipress). All can cause low blood pressure, depressed mood, and sexual dysfunction. Prazosin is occasionally given to spinal cord injured patients to prevent autonomic hyperreflexia.

Drugs that decrease vascular tone by direct action on the brain include clonidine (Catapres) and methyldopa (Aldomet). These drugs cause problems with low blood pressure less often than other nondiuretic antihypertensives, but cause sedation and lethargy more frequently. Sexual dysfunction can occur.

The direct blood vessel dilators are hydralazine (Apresoline) and minoxidil (Loniten). Because they speed the heart in a reflex manner, they are generally used with a beta-blocker that controls the heart rate. Hydralazine can cause arthritis and a skin rash, and minoxidil causes excessive hair growth. They have little effect on cognitive or sexual functions.

Captopril (Capoten) is a relatively new drug that affects an enzyme system in the kidney to lower blood pressure. It can occasionally cause serious kidney and bone marrow dysfunction. It affects taste sensation in about 10 percent of patients.

Most hypertensive patients are treated initially with a diuretic; if this is ineffective, a centrally or peripherally acting drug is added. When control remains poor, hydralazine is usually added to the regimen.

Digitalis

Digitalis is a very old drug for congestive heart failure, a condition of inadequate heart pumping action and fluid accumulation. It is also used to slow the heart rate in some situations. Digoxin (Lanoxin) is the most commonly used preparation, although there are many different forms of digitalis.

Therapeutic problems with digitalis are common because it has a very long half-life, and the toxic level is close to the range of therapeutic effect. Side effects can range from a poor appetite and nausea to frank delirium. These effects are commonly seen in the elderly.

Antiarrhythmics

These drugs regularize and slow the heart beat. Some abnormalities of heart rhythm cause impaired pumping action or allow clots to form in the heart and predispose to strokes. Other rhythm problems can cause sudden death. Therapy is tailored to the type of problem.

Digitalis and propranalol (see above) are frequently used to slow the heart. Verapamil (Isoptin) is a relatively new drug used to reduce the heart rate and to prevent recurrent episodes of rapid heart action. It can cause headache and fatigue.

Procainamide (Pronestyl), disopyramide (Norpace), and quinidine are chemically unrelated drugs with similar actions. In a rehabilitation setting, they are most commonly used to prevent life-threatening arrhythmias. Their efficacy for this purpose is unproven. These drugs can also cause a marked fall in blood pressure. Quinidine frequently causes diarrhea and nausea, disopyramide can aggravate congestive heart failure, and procainamide can cause a skin rash and arthritis. Neurobehavioral side effects are rare.

Antianginal Agents

Angina is chest pain that is caused by inadequate blood supply to the heart muscle. Drugs used to treat angina either increase this blood flow or decrease how hard the heart works, thus decreasing the required blood supply.

Nitroglycerin has been used for many years to treat angina. It can be given as a tablet under the tongue (sublingually) to stop an attack or prophylactically as an ointment on the skin. Its nearly universal side effect is headache; severely reduced blood pressure can also occur. Isosorbide (Isordil), a chemical relative of nitroglycerin, taken orally, can prevent angina.

The beta-blockers are another class of potent drugs used to prevent angina.

Nifedipine (Procardia), verapamil, and diltiazem (Cardizem) are relatively new drugs that dilate blood vessels and relax smooth muscle to prevent angina. They have few neuropsychiatric side effects, but may disturb heart rhythm and cause hypotension. Many antianginal agents are also useful in the treatment of autonomic hyperreflexia in spinal cord injured patients.

ANTIRHEUMATIC DRUGS

Therapy for arthritis and other rheumatic disorders usually has two components; one medication is used for short-term anti-inflammatory purposes, and another is directed at the remission of the overall disease process.

Nonsteroidal Anti-Inflammatory Drugs

The nonsteroidal antiinflammatory drugs (NSAID), of which aspirin is the prototype, are most commonly used for short-term relief of inflammation. There is a wide variety of NSAIDs (Table 20–6), all of which are quite useful, and none of

Table 20–6 Nonsteroidal Anti-Inflammatory Drugs

Aspirin
Sodium salicylate
Choline salicylate (Arthropan)
Choline magnesium salicylate (Trisilate)
Diflusinal (Dolobid)
Fenoprofen (Nalfon)
Indomethacin (Indocin)
Meclofenamate (Meclomen)
Naprosyn (Naproxen)
Phenylbutazone (Butazolidin)
Piroxican (Feldene)
Sulindac (Clinoril)
Tolmetin (Tolectin)

which has distinct advantages over the rest. The most common side effect of these drugs is gastric irritation. Indomethacin occasionally causes an unusual hallucination, described by some patients as a dissociation of the body and an ill-characterized floating sensation.

It is best to use one of these drugs at a time, giving each medication sufficient time (usually 1–2 weeks) to have an effect. As one drug often works where other drugs have failed, changing drugs is very common. Objective measures of efficacy, such as joint counts, walking speed, or grip strength—should be employed wherever possible.

Slow-Acting Anti-Inflammatory Agents

The drugs used to induce remission of the disease are slow acting, often requiring 3–6 months before clinical effect is apparent. All these drugs have serious toxic effects; they should only be used when their effectiveness can be clearly shown and their potential toxicities carefully monitored.

Gold salts and penicillamine, used almost exclusively in rheumatoid arthritis, are the two most frequently used drugs in this class. Both are effective in about 70 percent of patients, but almost 50 percent of patients encounter side effects that make it impossible for them to continue the drug. The most frequent side effects are skin rashes, problems with blood production, and kidney abnormalities. The occurrence of side effects with one drug does not necessarily guarantee problems with the other. Chloroquine is effective in about 50 percent of patients with rheumatoid arthritis. Its major side effect is an impairment of vision. Patients using the drug require regular ophthalmological follow-up.

Methotrexate is useful in a wide range of rheumatological illnesses and is generally effective in a relatively low dose. It is well tolerated except for nausea and diarrhea, which affect one-third of patients. These side effects are relieved with a decrease in dose. Methotrexate rarely causes hepatitis. None of these drugs causes significant neurobehavioral effects.

Corticosteroids

Corticosteroids are frequently useful in the treatment of rheumatologic conditions. Their role in the treatment of rheumatoid arthritis remains controversial because they do not alter the course of the disease, despite their beneficial effect on pain and stiffness.

These drugs are potent suppressors of the body's inflammatory processes and are, therefore, effective in the treatment of inflammatory conditions, such as multiple sclerosis, a variety of CNS disorders associated with swelling of the brain, and chronic diseases of the kidney and liver. They are under active investigation for many additional disorders. Their use in acute situations is generally felt to be safe, but a course of more than 10 days may produce serious problems, including thinning of the bones and skin, diabetes, acne, facial swelling, and the development of a peculiar buffalo hump on the back. These drugs frequently cause acute euphoria and an energized state. Some people, especially the elderly, can develop a frank psychosis early in the course of therapy; this is reversed with withdrawal of the drug. The drugs also suppress the body's defenses against infection and stress. Because of these serious side effects, corticosteroids should be used on a chronic basis only with great caution and after a careful weighing of the risks and benefits from treatment.

ANTICOAGULANTS

Anticoagulants are used for the treatment and prevention of blood clots in the veins and arteries, which are quite common in patients with paralysis. The most frequently used drugs are coumadin and heparin. Coumadin is an oral drug that interferes with vitamin K metabolism and thus the ability of the body to clot blood. The major side effect of coumadin stems from an overdose that may cause serious bleeding complications. Because other medications can interact with coumadin and cause elevation of the coumadin level, the clotting ability of the blood must be carefully monitored whenever medications are changed in patients who are taking coumadin.

Heparin is an injected anticoagulant. It causes significantly fewer bleeding complications than coumadin, but it is used less often because it requires an injection at least twice daily. It is primarily used in the early treatment of blood clots through continuous intravenous therapy and in small doses subcutaneously to prevent blood clots. Neither anticoagulant causes significant cognitive problems.

SPINAL CORD INJURY

There are a few drugs that are used almost exclusively in patients with spinal cord injury (SCI). Antispastic agents are used to treat the hypertonic musculature below the level of the SCI. The most widely used compounds are baclofen (Lioresal), dantrolene (Dantrium), and diazepam (Valium) (see anxiolytics). All effectively reduce spasticity, but each has its own drawbacks. Baclofen causes some sedation in many patients, but this usually resolves with continuance of the drug. Depression can also result. The major hazard with baclofen, however, is the occurrence of nightmares and hallucinations if the drug is abruptly withdrawn. All patients should be made aware of this possibility. Because dantrolene can occasionally cause serious hepatitis, careful monitoring of liver toxicity is a requirement for chronic therapy. The drug also causes some weakening in nonspastic muscles. No neuropsychiatric problems with the drug have been reported. The use of diazepam is limited by its tendency to cause sedation in the doses required to treat spasticity.

Mecamylamine (Inversine) is used to treat the excessive sweating that occurs in SCI patients. Because it acts by blocking the autonomic nervous system, it can disrupt bowel and bladder routines and may cause low blood pressure and fainting. On occasion it causes profound CNS effects, including tremor, confusion, mania, or depression.

Etidronate (Didronel) is used to prevent bony deposits about the hip and knee that can occur in patients with SCI and head injury. It probably achieves this effect by decreasing the tendency for calcium crystals to form. It has no known significant side effects.

Anticholinergic medications are frequently used to treat bladder overactivity in patients with SCI. Oxybutynin (Ditropan) and propantheline (Probanthine) are the most frequently prescribed. All such drugs occasionally cause sedation and invariably a drying of the oral mucosa. The latter symptom is poorly tolerated by many patients.

GASTROINTESTINAL DRUGS

Antacids, such as Mylanta and Maalox, are widely used for the symptoms of ulcers and heartburn. They are safe and cause few systemic effects other than diarrhea, but must be taken very frequently to be effective in curing ulcers.

Cimetidine (Tagamet) and ranitidine (Zantac) reduce the acid secretion of the stomach and have been shown to be as effective as antacids in ulcer therapy. They are frequently used to prevent stress-induced gastrointestinal bleeding in severely injured patients. They may produce a pseudodementia in the elderly that is reversed by cessation of the drug. They can cause prolonged impotence in an

Table 20–7: Drug Index

Trade Name	Generic Name	Where Discussed
Adrenalin	Epinephrine	Respiratory
Aldactone	Spironolactone	Diuretics
Aldomet	Methyldopa	Antihypertensive
Alupent	Metaproterenol	Respiratory
Aminophylline	Aminophylline	Respiratory
Amytal	Amobarbital	Hypnotics
Apresoline	Hydralazine	Antihypertensive
Artane	Trihexphenidyl	Antiparkinson
Arthropan	Choline salicylate	Antirheumatic
Asendin	Amoxapine	Antidepressants
Aspirin	Aspirin	Analgesics
Ativan	Lorazepam	Hypnotics
Aventyl	Nortryptiline	Antidepressants
Benadryl	Diphenhydramine	Hypnotics
Brethine	Terbutaline	Respiratory
Butazolidin	Phenylbutazone	Antirheumatic
Capoten	Captopril	Antihypertensive
Carafate	Sucralfate	Gastrointestinal
Cardizem	Diltiazem	Antianginal
Catapres	Clonidine	Antihypertensive
Chloral hydrate	Chloralhydrate	Hypnotics
Chloroquine	Chloroquine	Antirheumatic
Clinoril	Sulindac	Antirheumatic
Codeine	Codeine	Analgesics
Cogentin	Benztropine	Antiparkinson
Compazine	Prochloroperazine	Neuroleptics
Corgard	Naldolol	Antihypertensive
Coumadin	Coumadin	Anticoagulant
Dalmane	Flurazepam	Hypnotics
Dantrium	Dantrolene	SCI
Darvon	Propoxyphene	Analgesics
Demerol	Meperidine	Analgesics
Depakene	Valproic Acid	Anticonvulsants
Desyrel	Trazadone	Antidepressant
Didronel	Etidronate	SCI
Dilantin	Phenytoin	Anticonvulsants
Dilaudid	Hydromorphone	Analgesics
Dolobid	Diflusinal	Analgesics

Table 20–7 continued

Trade Name	Generic Name	Where Discussed
Dyrenium	Triamterene	Diuretics
Elavil	Amitryptiline	Antidepressants
Feldene	Piroxicam	Antirheumatic
Gold salts	Gold Salts	Antirheumatic
Halcion	Triazolon	Hypnotics
Haldol	Haloperidol	Neuroleptics
Heparin	Heparin	Anticoagulant
Inderal	Propranalol	Antihypertensive
Indocin	Indomethacin	Antirheumatic
Intal	Cromolyn	Respiratory
Inversine	Mecamylamine	SCI
Isoptin	Verapamil	Antiarrhythmics
Isordil	Isosorbide	Antianginal
Isuprel	Isoproterenol	Respiratory
L-dopa	L-dopa	Antiparkinson
Lanoxin	Digoxin	Digitalis
Lasix	Furosemide	Diuretics
Librium	Chlordiazepoxide	Hypnotics
Lioresal	Baclofen	SCI
Loniten	Minoxidil	Antihypertensive
Lopressor	Metoprolol	Antihypertensive
Loxitane	Loxapine	Neuroleptics
Ludiomil	Maprotiline	Antidepressants
Maalox		Gastrointestinal
Meclomen	Meclofenamate	Antirheumatic
Mellaril	Thioridazine	Neuroleptics
Merital	Nomifensine	Antidepressants
Methadone	Dolophine	Analgesics
Methotrexate	Methotrexate	Antirheumatic
Minipress	Prazosin	Antihypertensive
Morphine	Morphine	Analgesics
Mylanta		Gastrointestinal
Nalfon	Fenoprofen	Antirheumatic
Naproxen	Naprosyn	Antirheumatic
Navane	Thiothixene	Neuroleptics
Nembutal	Pentobarbital	Hypnotics
Nitroglycerin	Nitroglycerin	Antianginal
Norpace	Disopyramide	Antiarrhythmics
Norpramin	Desirpramine	Antidepressants

Table 20–7 continued

Trade Name	Generic Name	Where Discussed
Oxybutynin	Ditropan	SCI
Parlodel	Bromocriptine	Antiparkinson
Parnate	Tranylcypromine	Antidepressants
Penicillamine	Penicillamine	Antirheumatic
Phenobarbital	Phenobarbital	Hypnotics
Prednisone	Prednisone	Corticosteroids
Probanthine	Propantheline	SCI
Procardia	Nifedipine	Antianginal
Prolixin	Fluphenazine	Neuroleptics
Pronestyl	Procainamide	Antiarrhythmics
Proventil	Albuterol	Respiratory
Quinidine	Quinidine	Antiarrythmics
Reglan	Metoclopropamide	Gastrointestinal
Reserpine	Reserpine	Antihypertensive
Restoril	Temazepam	Hypnotics
Seconal	Secobarbital	Hypnotics
Serax	Oxazepam	Hypnotics
Sinemet	Carbidopa/L-dopa	Antiparkinson
Sinequan	Doxepim	Antidepressants
Stadol	Butorphanol	Analgesics
Stelazine	Trifluoperazine	Neuroleptics
Symmetrel	Amantadine	Antiparkinson
Tagamet	Cimetidine	Gastrointestinal
Talwin	Pentazocine	Analgesics
Tegretol	Carbamazepine	Anticonvulsants
Theophylline	Theophylline	Respiratory
Thiazides	Thiazides	Diuretics
Thorazine	Chlorpromazine	Neuroleptics
Tofranil	Imipramine	Antidepressants
Tolectin	Tolmetin	Antirheumatic
Tranxene	Clorazepate	Hypnotics
Trilafon	Perphenazine	Neuroleptics
Trisilate	Chol mg salicylate	Antirheumatic
Tylenol	Acetaminophen	Analgesics
Valium	Diazepam	Hypnotics
Vanceril	Beclamethasone	Respiratory
Vistaril	Hyroxyzine	Hypnotics
Vivactil	Protryptiline	Antidepressants
Zantac	Ranitidine	Gastrointestinal

occasional patient. Ranitidine seems to cause fewer adverse reactions than cimetidine.

Sucralfate (Carafate), a new drug for the treatment of ulcers, coats the ulcer crater and promotes healing. Because it is not absorbed, it has no systemic side effects and is comparable in effectiveness to the other antiulcer agents.

Metoclopropamide (Reglan) is frequently used to decrease vomiting, treat heartburn and reflux of food into the esophagus, and to speed the transit time of food in the bowel. It is similar chemically to the phenothiazines and has many of the same side effects, e.g., decrease in libido, menstrual irregularities, somnolence, extrapyramidal effects, parkinsonism, and tardive dyskinesia.

CONCLUSION

This chapter describes the drugs (and their side effects) that are most commonly used in a rehabilitation setting. Table 20–7 lists all the drugs discussed in the chapter and the heading under which their basic description can be found. The neurobehavioral effects of medications were emphasized. Many drugs are useful for many purposes. It is critical that all members of an interdisciplinary service understand the implications of drug therapy and the limitations and problems of such therapy.

REFERENCES

Masur, F.T. (1981). Adherence to health care regimens. In L. Bradley & C. Prokop (Eds.), *Medical Psychology; Contributions to behavioral medicine*. (pp. 441–469). New York: Academic Press.

Sackett, D.L., & Haynes, R.B. (Eds.). (1976). *Compliance with therapeutic regimens*. Baltimore: Johns Hopkins University Press.

World Health Organization. (1973). *Youth and drugs*. (Technical Report No. 516). Author.

SUGGESTED READINGS

AMA Division of Drugs. (1983). *AMA drug evaluations (1983)*. Philadelphia: W.B. Saunders.

Blackwell, B. (1973). Patient compliance. *New England Journal of Medicine, 289,* 249–252.

Drugs for asthma. (1982). *The Medical Letter, 24,* 83–86.

Drugs for hypertension. (1982). *The Medical Letter, 23,* 45–48.

Eddy, N.B., Halbach, H., Isbell, H., & Seevers, M. (1965). Drug dependence: Its significance and characteristics. *Bulletin World Health Organization, 32,* 721–733.

Goodman, L.S., & Gilman, A. (1985). *The pharmacological basis of therapeutics*. New York: Macmillan Publishing Co.

Goth, A. (1981). *Medical pharmacology: Principles and concepts*. St. Louis: C.V. Mosby.

Halstead, L.S., & Claus-Walker, J. (1980). *Neuroactive drugs of choice in spinal cord injury*. New York: Raven Press.

Marks, R.M., & Sachar, E.J. (1973). Undertreatment of medical inpatients with narcotic analgesics. *Annuals of Internal Medicine, 78,* 173–181.

Ouslander, J.G. (1981). Drug therapy in the elderly. *Annals of Internal Medicine, 95,* 711–722.

Treatment of cardiac arrhythmias (1983). *The Medical Letter, 25,* 21–28.

Index

Aadalen, S., 136
Aalberg, V., 53
Abrams, K., 17
Absorption (pharmacology), 502–503
Achte, K. A., 53
Acker, M., 5
Activities of daily living (ADL)
    SCI and, 7
    stroke and, 79, 84, 90
    testing and, 260
Activity curtailment, pain and, 104, 108, 113
Activity Pattern Indicators, 21–22
Adherence (pharmacology), 505
Adjustment stages. *See* Stage theories of adjustment
Admission criteria (Palo Alto program), 301
Adult Independence Development Center, 354
Age
    head injury and, 37
    social skill rehabilitation and, 348
    spinal cord injury and, 24
        goals and, 11
        pain and, 7
    staff vulnerabilities and 230–33
    stroke and, 66, 72
    TAPI subjects and, 191
Aggressive behavior, 28
Ajax, E. T., 261
Albert, H., 79
Albert, M. S., 253
Albrecht, G., 146, 345
Alcohol abuse
    head injury and, 56
    in rehabilitation setting, 506–507
    SCI and, 17, 28–29, 158

Aldomet (methyldopa), 516
Allen, D. A., 445, 446
Amantadine (Symmetrel), 514
Ambulatory aids, pain and, 109
American Heart Association, 85, 180
Amnesia
    head injury and, 41
        memory disorders and, 45–46
        single-case design example and, 460–61
Amputation
    epidemiology of, 488
    prosthetic components and levels of, 488–90
    prosthetic training and, 490
Analgesics, 512–13
Andberg, M. M., 158
Anderson, D., 117
Anderson, T., 115
Anderson, T. P., 158
Anderten, A., 137, 138
Aneurysms, stroke and, 66, 68–69
Anger
    family adaptation system and, 178–79
    staff/patient conflict and, 200, 205, 231
    stroke and, 86, 88
    temporal lobe disturbances and, 295
Annon, J. S., 431
Anomia, 258
Anosognosia, 137
Antacids, 520
Anterior cerebral artery occlusion (stroke), 70, 71–72
Antianginal agents, 517
Antiarrhythmics, 516–17
Antibiotics, 501. *See also* Pharmacology
Anticholinergics, 514
    SCI and, 520
Anticoagulants, 519–20

Antidepressant medication, 14, 88, 121, 154, 425, 508–509
Antihypertensives, 516
Antiparkinsonian agents, 513–14
Antipsychotics, 510
Antirheumatic drugs, 517–19
Antispastic agents, 520
Anxiety, 28, 88, 105, 155
    conditioning and weakening of, 396, 397
    denial and, 140
    sexual functioning and, 419, 427, 430
    staff distress and, 227, 229, 235
Anxiolytics (pharmacology), 507–508
Aphasic syndromes. *See also* Language disorders
    head injury and, 44
    stroke and, 70, 72, 76–78, 79, 82, 85, 484
    tests and, 257–59, 263
Apraxia
    neuropsychological testing and, 256
    stroke and, 77, 79
    limb, 80–81
Apresoline (hydralazine), 516
Aprosodias
    depression
        and brain damage and, 147
        and stroke and, 153
"Are Theories of Learning Necessary?" (Skinner), 462
Arthritis, 496
    antirheumatic drugs and, 517–19
Ashenhurst, E. M., 139
Assertiveness training, 314
Assessment. *See also* Neuropsychological assessment
    behaviorial changes and SCI and, 21
    behavior modification and personality, 391
    chronic pain and, 110–12
    emotional adjustment and SCI and, 24–25
    social skill, 350–52, 354
    stroke and behavioral deficits and, 81
        depression and, 82
        initiative and, 74
Assessment of intervention (single-case experimental design)
    advantages of, 467–68
    analysis and development of, 453–56
    design strategies for
        multiple baseline, 457–59, 462–67

sequential introduction and withdrawal, 456–57, 459–62
    simultaneous treatment, 457
Assigning meaning to experiences (with disabled patient), 226
Athelstan, G., 8, 12, 18, 23, 26
Atherosclerotic heart disease, cerebral embolism and, 68
Athletes, "punch-drunk syndrome" and, 493
Attentional deficits, head injury and, 45
Aubenshine, C. D., 441
Audiologic consultation (Palo Alto program), 303
Audiovisual aids, 360
Avella, J., 114
Aversive consequences, 391
Avoidance behavior, 397
    pain analysis and, 108–109
Ayllon, T., 54
Azrin, N. H., 54

Baade, L. E., 257
Badame, R., 354
Baker, G., 283
Baretz, R. M., 138, 141, 143
Bargaining (family adaptation system), 177–78
Barlow, D. H., 457, 459
Barry, M. J., 55
Barth, J. T., 493
Basmajian, J. V., 370, 371
Battle, C. V., 348
Bauer, M., 153
Bear, D. M., 140
Beck Depression Inventory, 82, 155, 156
Beck, L., 256
Behavioral aspects of pain, 106–109, 110, 111
Behavioral assessment (social skills program), 351–52, 354
Behavioral deficits
    head injury and, 38–39, 49–53
    intervention and, 53–55
    SCI and, 21–22, 27–30
    stroke and, 72–81
Behavioral disruptions (between disabled and nondisabled), 347–48
Behavioral scientist, 220
    and staff distress
        attitude toward and roles of, 236–37
        educational activity and, 238–40

methods and, 237–38
Behavioral studies, single-case
experimental design and, 453
Behavior Medicine Inpatient Unit, 401
Behavior modification
as aid to rehabilitation, 383–85
case illustrations of, 401–415
clinical strategies (program
implementation)
contract presentation and, 399
contract revision and, 400–401
imposing consequences and 399–400
negotiation and, 398, 407
conceptual orientation and, 386–87
medical application of, 385–86
new and complex behaviors and, 394–95
principles of
applied operant methods, 387–92
classical conditioning methods and,
396–97
creating behavioral programs and,
392–96
target behavior and, 392–94
Bellile, S., 158
Bemporad, B., 147, 152
Benadryl (diphenhydramine), 507
Benson, D., 44, 77, 152, 258, 259, 263
Benton, A., 254
Benton, A. L., 81, 255, 260, 268
Benton Visual Retention Test (BVRT),
266, 268
Ben-Yishay, 48, 283
Bernstein, M., 12
Berrol, S., 421
Beta-blockers, 516
Billings, A., 146
Binder, L. 150
Bioavailability, 503
Biofeedback, 114, 119
behavior modification program and, 397
biological activities and role of, 366–72
combining with other modalities, 375–76
equilibrium and weight shifting training
and, 376–78
rehabilitiation programs and, 365–66,
378–79
single-case experimental design and, 458
videogame therapy and, 372–75
Biopsychosocial data, 189
Biotransformation (pharmacology), 504
Black, F. W., 148, 269
Bladder control, SCI and, 478, 481. *See
also* Incontinence

Blanchard, E., 119
Blashfield, R., 133
Blass, J., 247
Bleeding, anticoagulants and, 519
Bloomer, H. H., 265
Blumer, D., 263
Body image, SCI and, 6–7
Bogdonoff, M., 171
Boham, B. E., 353
Bolger, J., 57
Bolla-Wilson, K., 251
Boll, T., 254, 493
Bond, J., 271
Bond, M., 42, 43, 44, 53, 149, 421
Bond, M. R., 492
Border-zone infarction (stroke), 69–70
Bors, E., 6, 15, 158
Boston Diagnostic Aphasia Examination,
257, 258
Boston Veterans Administration Hospital,
262, 268
Botwinick, J., 264
Bourestom, N., 13
Bowel program. *See also* Incontinence
SCI and, 478, 481
stroke and, 487–88
Boyd, J. L., 260
Bracey, O. L., 49
Bracken, M., 12
Bracken, M. B., 134, 135, 141
Bradford, D. C., 261
Bradley, L. S., 141
Brain damage. *See also* Head injury;
Stroke
depression following, 147–48
employment and, 281
head injury and, 37–38, 47–48, 50, 51,
52, 491–92
sexual functioning and, 420
motor difficulties and, 41–42, 366
neuropsychological assessment and, 247,
248, 252, 259
postconcussion syndrome (minor brain
injury) and, 57–58
psychotherapy and, 283–84, 288
SCI and, 5, 29
stroke and, 484–86
Brain electrical activity mapping (BEAM),
304
Brain injury rehabilitation in private
practice. *See* Private practice cognitive
rehabilitation programs

Brain injury Rehabilitation Unit program
 (Palo Alto Veterans Hospital)
 family and, 304, 317
 historical background of, 299–300
 microcomputer use and, 315–16, 317–19,
  320
 patient population and, 301
 principal elements of, 301–304
 special procedures in
  goal attainment follow-up and, 311–12
  independence rating and, 305–307
  standard problem list and, 307–310
 staffing and, 300
 treatment outcome data and, 317
 treatment stages of
  orientation, 312–14
  three phase process, 314–17
Bransome, E., 256
Bray, G. P., 423, 424
Bregman, S., 420
Breznitz, S., 137, 138, 140, 143
Brindley, G. S., 428
Brooks, D. N., 44, 149, 421
Brooks, N., 149
Brouwer, W. H., 45
Brown, B., 119
Brown, C., 114
Brown, E. R., 267
Brown, G., 265
Brown, M., 21
Brown-Sequard syndrome, 481
Brown, W. F., 443
Brunnstrom, S., 368
Buchtel, H., 271
Buck, F., 18
Bugen, L., 172
Bulman, R., 12
Burish, T. G., 141
Burke, D., 7
Burnout (staff), 223–24
Buschke, H., 264, 265, 461

Cameron, M., 15
Canter, S., 353
Caplan, B., 145, 255, 300
Capoten (captopril), 516
Carafate (sucralfate), 524
Cardiac arrest, 65, 70
Cardiac disease (concurrent with stroke), 487
Cardiovascular medication. See also
 Medication; Pharmacology
 antianginal agents, 517

antihypertensives, 516
antiarrhythmics, 516–17
digitalis, 516
diuretics, 515
Cartlidge, N. E. F., 148
Case studies, 453
Cassem, N. H., 136, 137, 138
Cassileth, B. R., 134
Cassman, S. R., 351
Catapres (clonidine), 516
Catastrophic illness and caregiver distress
 anxiety and, 227, 229, 235
 assigning meaning to experiences and,
  226
 avoidance of distress and, 224–25
 behavioral scientist and, 220
  attitude toward and roles of, 236–37
  educational activity and, 238–40
  methods and, 237–38
 burnout and, 223–24
 conflicting aims and, 228
 counteridentification and, 232
 dynamic unconscious and, 226
 educational solutions to, 234–36
 emotional distress and, 227
 empathy and, 224
 ethical issues and, 232–33
 evidence of, 221–25
 exposure, self-esteem, and performance
  anxiety and, 229
 hidden vulnerabilities and, 230–33
 inferences of, 225–33
 narcissistic vulnerability and, 231–32
 overview of, 219–20
 outcome and effectiveness of program
  for, 240–41
 patient complaints and, 222–23
 patient tranference and, 230
 personality behavioral areas and, 224
 poor defenses and, 227–28
 psychic trauma and, 225–26
 psychological learning (resistance to)
  and, 227
 repression of distress and, 224–25
 staff complaints about patients and,
  221–22
 staff complaints about staff and, 222
 trauma and, 228
 uncertainty and, 229
Catchlove, R., 117
Category Test, 270, 271
Cavanaugh, S., 145

Cayner, J., 117
Cerebral artery occlusion (stroke), 70, 71–72
Cerebral embolism (stroke), 68
Cerebral hemispheres, poststroke depression and, 152–53
Cerebral infarction, 482
Cerebral thrombosis (stroke), 66–67
Cerebrovascular accident. *See* Stroke (cerebrovascular accident)
Charatan, F. B., 154
Chemical dependency. *See* Alcohol abuse; Drug abuse
Chesney, M. A., 119
Children, disabled parents and, 18
Chodoff, P., 137
Chronic illness
    family adaptation system phases
        bargaining, 177–78
        denial, 176–77
        depression, 178–79
        fear (fight or flight), 174–76
        mourning, 179–80
        rapprochement, 180
    family intervention goal and, 171–74
    family role in rehabilitation and, 171
Chronic pain. *See* Pain (chronic)
Cigarette smoking, 483
Cimetidine (Tagamet), 520
Ciolino, C. P., 152, 153
Civilian Rehabilitation Act of 1920, 439
Cleveland, M., 18
Clonidine (Catapres), 516
Cobb, W., 153
Cognition
    computer-assisted program and, 315–16
    head injury and, 38, 41, 42, 48–49, 52
        depression and, 149
        medication and, 55
    pain and deficits in, 122
    Palo Alto program and, 299
    SCI and, 5
        brain injury and, 29
    stroke and, 71, 74, 86, 89, 93
Cognitive-behavioral intervention, pain and, 114, 119
Cognitive functioning tests, 269–71
Cognitive rehabilitation programs in private setting. *See* Private practice cognitive rehabilitiation programs
Cognitive Rehabilitation Unit (Bellevue Hospital), 460

Cognitive retraining program. *See* Brain Injury Rehabilitation Unit program (Palo Alto Veterans Hospital)
Cognitive therapy (Presbyterian Hospital), 285, 286–89, 291
Cogswell, B., 22, 349, 350
Cohen, J., 453
Cohen, K., 117
Cole, T., 115, 432
Coma
    head injury and, 492
    stroke and, 484
Comarr, A., 158
"Coming Back from Stroke" (videocassette), 85
Communication skills training, 314
Community
    head injury neurobehavioral consequences and, 55–56
    SCI and reentry into, 22, 30
    stroke and reentry into, 83
        counseling and, 86
        treatment after, 91
Competence, head injury and legal concept of, 48
Complex-Attention Rehabilitation Program, 339
Complex Figure Test, 259, 266
Computed tomography (CT) scans, 304
Computers
    biofeedback treatment and, 366, 378–79
        augmenting feedback and, 375–76
        equilibrium and weight shift training and, 376–78
        videogames and, 372–75
    muscle activity and, 369
    Palo Alto program and, 315–16, 317–19, 320
    private practice environment and, 337–40
Conditioning (behavior modification), 387
    classical, 396–97
Conflict between staff and patient. *See* Staff/patient interaction
Conflicting aims of staff, 228
Congestive heart failure, digitalis and, 516
Conomy, J., 6
Consciousness
    head injury measures and, 39–41, 492
    stroke and, 69, 91, 92
Consequences (behavior modification)
    defining, 390–92
    imposing, 399–400

managing, 395–96
"Conservation-withdrawal," 146
Constructional ability testing, 268–69
Consultants (medical), 293
Consumer groups (social skills programs),
   355
Contraceptives, 429
Control. See Locus of control
Controlled Word Association test, 258
Cook, D., 11, 140–41, 155
Cope, D., 5
Coping techniques, 133
   denial and, 136, 141
Corley, M., 121
Corsi, P., 266
Cortical lesions, 251
   depression and, 147
Corticosteroids, 519
Costa, L., 257, 262, 269
Costs (Presbyterian Hospital program), 295
Counseling
   family adaptation system and, 178
   head injury and family, 56
   pain treatment and vocational, 113
   Palo Alto program and family, 304
   peer, 438
   sexual functioning, 87, 419, 425, 431, 432
   spinal cord injury and, 26–27, 29
   stroke and, 81, 85–87, 90–91, 153
Counteridentification, 232
Cox, D. J., 119
Craig Hospital re-entry program, 354
Craig, K., 109
Crandell, E. O., 442
Crewe, N., 8, 12, 18
Crisler, J. R., 442
Cue control (behavior modification),
   394–95
Cultural background, SCI and, 19–20
Curry, H. B., 67
Cutting, J., 139

Daly, D. A., 265
Damber, J. E., 425
Darley, F. L., 259
Darnton, S. W., 265
Davidson, R., 148
Davis, J., 346
Dean, A., 171
DeBacher, G., 368
Decision-making deficit, stroke and, 72–74
Deckel, A. W., 136, 140, 150

Decubitus ulcer
   SCI and, 478–79
   stroke and, 487
Deelman, B. G., 45
Defense mechanism, 194
   staff distress and, 227–28
   educational solutions for, 235–36
Defensive retreat, adjustment stage in SCI,
   25–26
DeFilippis, N. A., 270
DeFrank, R. S., 423
Degenerative disorders, 200
   social skills and, 348
DeJong, G., 20
Delirium, head injury and, 41
Dell Orto, A., 171, 172
Dementia, stroke and, 68, 74–75
Denial, 205, 284
   adjustment stage in SCI and, 25–26
   costs and benefits of, 141–42
   defined populations and, 139–41
   definitions and determinants of, 136–39
   family adaptation system and, 176–77
   head injury behavioral deficits and, 51,
      52–53
   management of, 142–44
   staff and, 133–34, 136, 138, 142, 143, 144
   stage theories of adjustment and, 133–35
Dependence (support)
   head injury and, 42
   stroke and, 89
Depression
   behavior modification in SCI patients
      and, 412
   brain injury and, 147–48
   family adaptation system and, 178–79
   head injury and, 53, 56, 148–50
   medication and, 14, 88, 121, 154, 425,
      508–509
   pain and, 105, 121
   SCI and, 9, 12–15, 17, 25, 27, 28, 154–60
   staff and, 133–34, 159, 160
   stage theories of adjustment and, 133–35
   stroke and, 82–83, 87–88, 150–54
   views on, 144–47
Depression Adjective Checklist, 82
DeRenzi, E., 262, 266
Derogatis, L., 114
Developmental maturity, staff vulnerabilities
   and, 230–31
Dew, M., 10
Diabetes mellitus, 483

Diagnostic and Statistical Manual of Mental Disorders, drug abuse definition and, 507
Didronel (etidronate), 520
Diehl, L., 56
Digitalis, 516
Digit-Digit Test, 338–39
Digit Span test, 46
Dikman, S., 149
Diller, L., 48, 137, 269, 283, 352
DiMichael, S. G., 444
Dimsdale, J., 136
Diphenhydramine (Benadryl), 507
Disability. *See also* Catastrophic illness and caregiver distress
  denial and, 141
  head injury and
    behavioral, 49–53
    neuropsychological, 43–47
    physical, 38–39
  medical aspects of (an overview)
    amputation, 488–90
    arthritis, 496
    cerebrovascular accident (stroke), 481–88
  Guillain-Barre syndrome, 495–96
  head injury, 490–94
  multiple sclerosis, 494–95
  SCI and
    behavioral, 21–22, 27–29
    emotional, 12–17, 23–26
    physical, 4–8
  social consequences of, 345–50
  spinal cord injury
    acute care period and, 477–78
    anatomy and pathophysiology of 474–75
    complications and, 478–79
    epidemiology of, 473
    functional significance of level of injury, 479–81
    improper transport and, 477
    signs and symptoms of, 475–77
    staff/patient conflict and nature of, 197–203
Disability-appropriate behaviors, acquisition of, 142
Disability payments (Social Security), 102
Disinhibition, 52
Dislocation, SCI and, 475
Disorientation, 254–56
Distribution (pharmacology), 503
Ditropan (oxybutynin), 520

Diuretics, 515
Divorce, SCI and, 18. *See also* Marital relationships
Dixon, J. K., 346, 352
Driving, stroke and impaired, 73
Drug abuse
  head injury and, 56
  pain and, 104, 108, 111, 117, 121
    detoxification and deconditioning and, 112–13
  SCI and, 17, 28–29, 158
Drugs. *See* Medication, Pharmacology; *names of specific drugs*
Dunn, M., 350, 351, 353, 354
Durlak, J. A., 444, 445
Dybsku, A., 351
Dynamic unconscious, 226
Dyparthria, 258

Eberly, C., 14
Eckhardt, L. O., 134, 142
Edinger, J., 14
Educational activity, staff distress and, 234–26, 238–40
Eisenberg, M., 10–11
Elderly, drug therapy and, 505–506, 519
Electroconvulsive therapy, 154
Electromyographic (EMG) signals
  muscle contraction and, 369
  pain treatment and, 114, 119
  therapeutic value of, 371, 372, 375
  videogames and, 373–74
El Ghatit, A., 18
Elithorn, A., 262
Emotional adjustment to SCI. *See* Psychological adjustment to SCI
Emotional distress (staff), 227
Emotional expression deficit, head injury and, 51
Emotional problems of disabled, conventional psychiatric nomenclature and, 145–46
Emotional surveillance, denial and impaired, 140
Empathy, 224
Employment
  brain injury and, 281, 294, 295
    Palo Alto program and, 316
  head injury and, 42, 54, 55, 56–57
  pain and, 105–106, 108, 112, 119
    employers and, 124, 125
    occupational therapy and, 113

return-to-work and, 117–18
workers' compensation claims and,
    112, 123
paraprofessional selection and, 442–43
SCI and, 4, 21, 22–23
Encephalopathy, 65–69
Epilepsy
    drugs and seizure prevention and, 510–11
    head injury and, 493
Epperson, M., 177
Equilibrium training, 376
Erections (sexual functioning)
    disability and, 426–27
    penile implants and, 428–29
Erickson, R. C., 263
Ernst, J., 10
Ethanol (pharmacologic analysis), 508
Ethical issues
    paraprofessionals and, 445–46
    single-case experimental design and, 468
    staff and complexity of, 232–33
Etidronate (Didronel), 520
Ettlin, T., 6
Evaluation. See Assessment
Ewen, R. B., 453
Excretion of drugs, 503–504
Exposure (scrutiny of staff), 229

Faglioni, P., 262, 266
Family, 3. See also Marital relationships
    head injury and, 42, 49, 50, 55–56, 284
    pain and, 113, 117, 122, 123
    Palo Alto program and, 304, 317
    "partializing" and, 137
    pre-existing conflicts in, 186–87, 203
    Presbyterian Hospital program and,
        291, 292–93
    private practice programs and, 325,
        328–29, 329–30, 335, 340
    SCI and, 17–19
        counseling and, 26
        and education and support for, 29
    stroke and, 73, 83, 84, 85, 86–87, 90–91,
        92, 486
Family adaptation system (for chronic
    illness)
    family intervention goals and, 171–74
    family role in rehabilitation and, 171
    phases of
        bargaining, 177–78
        denial, 176–177
        depression, 178–79

fear, 174–76
    mourning, 179–80
    rapprochement, 180
Fantasy (staff/patient relationship), 201,
    206
Farberow, N. L., 159
Farber, W., 257
Fear (fight or flight), family adaptation
    system and, 174–76
Feedback. See Biofeedback
Fehr, M. J., 351
Feibel, J., 153
Fertility, spinal cord injury and, 427–28
Fey, S. G., 105, 117
Filskov, F. B., 254
Financial difficulties (of patient), 334–35
Fine, B. D., 227
Finger Oscillation Test, 256
Finklestein, S., 150
Fink, S., 7
Fisher, C. M., 67
Fisher, S. G., 445
Fisk, A., 154
Flora, J., 121
Fogel, M. L., 255
Folkman, S., 136
Follow-up
    chronic pain and, 115, 120
    head injury and, 42–43
    Palo Alto program and, 311–12
    stroke patient and, 91
Folstein, M. F., 151, 152
Foot amputations, 488–89
Foot-drop, feedback and, 375
Fordyce, W., 8, 28, 107, 108, 115, 116, 122,
    139, 146, 148, 176, 386
Fractures
    head injury and, 492
    SCI and, 475, 477
Framingham study, 83
Frangione, R. M., 117
Franklin, M., 8
Fraser, A., 154
Fraser, R. T., 440, 441
Free Recall procedure, 461, 463
Freundlich, A., 119
Fromm, A., 13
Frontal lobe lesions, sexual functioning
    and, 422
Frontal lobe syndrome, 336
Fugl-Meyer, A. R., 424
Fuld, P. A., 264, 265, 461

Fullerton, D., 15
Funding (for rehabilitation in private
practice), 325
Furosemide (Lasix), 515

Gainotti, G., 137, 139, 152
Gait distortion, pain and, 109
Gallenberger, C., 353
Gambrill Assertion Inventory, 350
Games, neuropsychological testing and,
271. *See also* Videogames
Gans, J., 14, 133, 139, 145, 153, 159, 171,
231
Garcia, C., 247
Garcia, J., 372
Garlington, B. E., 116
Gastrointestinal drugs, 520-24
Gates-MacGinitie Reading Tests, 258
Geisler, W., 15
Geist, C. S., 143
Geller, B., 134
Gestalt Completion Test, 261
Gianutsos, J., 458
Gianutsos, R., 49, 458, 459
Ginsburg, M. L., 350, 353
Giordani, B., 493
Giurgea, D., 109
Glasgow Coma Scale, 39, 57, 327, 492
Glasgow Outcome Scale, 42, 494
Glenn, R. L., 148
Goal-directed behavior, head injury and,
51-52
Golden, G., 136, 138
Goldiamond, I., 19, 134
Goldstein, G., 257
Goldstein, K., 152, 283
Gollin, E. S., 261
Golper, L. A. C., 73
Goodglass, H., 77
Goodstein, R., 81
Gordon, W., 21, 269
Gordon, W. A., 158
Gottschaldt, K., 260
Graduate Record Examination, 271
Green, B., 10-11
Grief, E., 88
Greydanus, D. E., 134
Griffin, P., 119
Griffith, V. E., 154
Grigsby, T., 10-11
Gronwall, D., 58, 255
Groot, H., 15, 16, 158

Grossman, R. G., 43, 281
Group discussion, staff distress and,
238-39
Group-oriented research design, 454-55
Group psychotherapy
head injury and denial and, 52-53
Presbyterian Hospital and, 289-91
Gruen, A., 139
Guillain-Barre syndrome, 199, 495-96
Gullickson, G., 155
Gunshot wounds, 474
Gunther, M. S., 160

Hackett, T. P., 136, 138, 143
Hackler, R., 15, 157
Hadley, R., 420
Hahn, H., 350
Hakmiller, K., 6
Hall, K., 5, 42
Hallucinations, head injury and, 41
Hamilton Rating Scale, 148, 151
Hamsher, K., 81, 254
Handicapped Problems Inventory, 156
Hanson, R., 8, 18
Harasymiw, S., 158
Harley, J., 153
Harrison, A., 367
Hart, R. P., 148
Harvey, R., 15, 117
Hastorf, A. H., 347, 351
Hattie, J. A., 445
Hawton, K., 424
Haynes, S., 119
Headaches, relief of migraine, 119-20
Head injury
complications of, 492-93
denial and, 135, 139
depression and, 53, 56, 148-50
epidemiology of, 490-91
etiology and pathology of, 491-92
management of, 492
mental change and, 493
neurobehavioral consequences of
background on problem of, 37-38, 58
behavioral deficits and, 38-39, 49-51
denial, 52-53
depression, 43
emotional expression, 51
impulsivity and disinhibition, 52
initiative increase or goal-directed
behavior, 51-52
behavioral intervention and, 52-55

cognitive problems and, 38
cognitive remediation and, 48–49
community (social) and family and,
    55–56
disability spheres and, 38–39
employment rehabilitation and, 56–57
mental competence and, 47–48
minor brain injury and, 57–58
neuropsychological assessment and, 247,
    271
neuropsychological deficits
    attention, 45
    general intellectual function, 43–44
    memory disorders, 45–46
    problem-solving skills, 47
    speech and language disorders, 44
    visuospatial and perceptuomotor
        dysfunction, 46–47
neuropsychological program and, 284,
    288
prognosis for, 493–94
recovery and, 39–43
sexual functioning and, 52, 420–23
staff and, 230
types of, 37–38
Heartburn, medication and, 520
Heaton, R. H., 257, 270
Hecaen, M. S., 79
Heilman, K. M., 75, 140
Heinemann, A., 143
Hemianopsia, 78
Hemiplegia
    motor control training and, 370–72
    motor deterioration and, 368–69
    stroke and, 484
Hemispheric involvement in poststroke
    depression, 152–53
Hemorrhagic stroke. See also Stroke
    intracerebral, 66, 69, 91
    intracranial, 482–83
    subarachnoid, 68–69, 91, 483
Hendler, N., 114
Henry Street Settlement, 439
Heparin, 519
Herman, S. H., 351, 355
Hersen, M., 457, 459
Higgins, P. C., 146
Hilbom, E., 53
Hilgard, E. R., 119
Hobart, S. C., 353, 357, 360
Hoffman, A. M., 444
Hohmann, G., 6, 18, 346

Hohmann, G. W., 143, 159
Holroyd, K. A., 119
Home care, 171
    stroke and, 86–87
        depression and, 87–89
        family therapy and, 90–91
        rehabilitation outcome and, 92
Home environment
    Presbyterian Hospital program and, 293
    private practice programs and, 333–34
    stroke and, 87
Home visits to stroke patients, 154
Hooper, H. E., 260
Hooper Visual Organization Test, 260,
    261
Hope, 335
    importance of, 142–43, 144
Horowitz, M. J., 134
Howard, M., 13
Howell, T., 15, 155
Hudgens, A., 115
Hull House, 439
Human service program, paraprofessionals
    in, 443
Hurwitz, L. J., 139
Hydralazine (Apresoline), 516
Hydrocephalus, head injury and, 493
Hydroxyzine (Vistaril), 507
Hypertension
    antihypertensives and, 516
    diuretics and, 515
    stroke and, 65, 69, 483
Hypnosis, pain control and, 114, 119
Hypnotics (pharmacology), 507–508
Hypoglycemia, 65
Hypotension, 70, 482

Identification with patient, 232
Illness (catastrophic). See Catastrophic
    illness and caregiver distress
"Illness conviction," pain and, 122
Illness and family adaptation to. See
    Family adaptation system (to chronic
    illness)
Impotence, 428–29
Impulsivity, 52
Inactivity, pain and, 104, 108, 113
Inattentiveness, 254–56
Incontinence, 70
    bowel training (behavior modification
        case example) and, 412
    sexual functioning and, 425, 429–30

stroke and bowel, 487–88
Independent living, 72, 391
  NRP and, 292
  Palo Alto program and, 305–307
  SCI and, 20
  stroke and, 73
Inflammation, drugs and, 517–18
Initiation deficit, stroke and, 74
Initiative, 51–52
Insight deficits, stroke and, 72–74
Intellectual function, head injury and,
  43–44
Intervention assessment. *See* Assessment
  of intervention (single-case experimental
  design)
Interview (psychological). *See* Team
  Attended Psychological Interview (TAPI)
Intravenous drug administration, 502–503
Inversine (mecamylamine), 520

Jackson, D. R., 142
Jacobsen, R., 260
Jacques, M. E., 442, 443
Jaffe, D., 171
James, M., 261
Jane, J., 493
Janis, I., 137
Jasnos, T., 6
Jeffrey, J., 260
Jenik, F., 19
Jennett, B., 42
Johnson, K. L, 257
Joint contractures, stroke and, 487
Jonassen, S. A., 265
Jones, D., 262
Jouse, A., 15
Judd, C., 10
Judgment deficit, stroke and, 72–74

Kaeser, H., 6
Kahn, R. I., 137
Kalliomaki, J. L., 424
Kalthoff, R. J., 234
Kaplan, E., 77, 250, 268
Karp, S. A., 260
Kathol, R. G., 145
Kazdin, A. E., 456
Keefe, F. J., 114
Keister, M. E., 372
Kelley, H. H., 350
Kemp, B., 11
Kendall, P., 14

Kerns, R., 152, 171
Kerns, R. D., 141, 146
Kerr, J., 351
Kerr, M., 262
Kerr, W., 157
Kertesz, A., 259
Khella, L., 17
Kidneys
  antihypertensives and, 516
  drug excretion and, 503, 504
Kinsbourne, M., 147, 152, 250
Kinsella, G. J., 424
Kleck, R., 347
Klein, M., 15
Kleinman, K. M., 372
Klein, R., 171
Klerman, G. L., 146
Kornstein, S., 148
Korsakoff's syndrome, 263
Krantz, D. S., 136, 140, 150
Kraus, J. F., 57
Krauss, I., 251
Krumberger, J., 18
Krystal, H., 225
Kubler-Ross, E., 144
Kwentus, J. A., 148

LeBaw, W. L., 139
Lacunar infarction (stroke), 67–68
Lakin, P., 352
Langer, K. G., 152
Language disorders. *See also* Aphasic
  syndromes
  head injury and, 41, 44
  stroke and, 72, 76, 93, 484
Language tests, neuropsychological
  assessment and, 257–59
Language therapy (Palo Alto program),
  303, 315
Lasix (furosemide), 515
Latow, J. F., 154
Lawrence, C., 263
Lawson, N., 14, 156
Lazarus, R., 136, 138
L-dopa, Parkinson's disease and, 513–14
"Learning About Stroke" (videocassette),
  85
LeBaron, S., 134
Lee, D., 262
Leftoff, S., 89
Legal aspects of neuropsychological
  assessment, 48, 253

Lehman, L., 21, 158
Lehman, R. A. W., 270
Leung, P., 353
Levels of Cognitive Functioning Scale, 39–40
Leventhal, B., 269
Levine, J., 140
Levin, H. S., 43, 281, 460, 461, 494
Levita, M., 257
Lezak, M., 50, 171, 175, 251, 254, 257, 258, 265
Liliequist, B., 425
Limb apraxia, stroke and, 80–81
Limbs, amputation and, 488–89
Lipowski, Z., 146, 176
Lipsey, J. R., 147, 150, 151, 153
Lishman, W., 149
Lloyd, E., 350, 354
Lloyd, G. G., 145
Locus of control, SCI psychological adjustment and, 11–12, 27
Long Beach Veterans Administration Hospital, 15, 16
Long, C. J., 149
Long, D., 114
Longitudinal Functional Assessment System (University of Houston), 352
Loniten (minoxidil), 516
Lovitt, R., 146
Low back pain, 103, 124
Lung cancer, denial and, 140
Luria, A. R., 283
Lynch, K., 10
Lynch, W., 300

Maalox, 520
McCampbell, E., 270
McCauley, R., 253
MacDonald, M., 15
McGuigan, F. J., 453
McHugh, P. R., 151
McKinlay, W. W., 149, 421
McMahon, B. T., 440
Magiearo-Plansy, R., 143
Magnetic resonance imaging (MRI), 304
Maiburger, R., 151
Malec, J., 117
Mandelberg, I. A., 44
Margolis, R., 267
Marital relationships. See also Family
    head injury and, 55
    pain and, 107, 110, 111, 112, 113

Presbyterian Hospital program and, 291
SCI and, 17–19
sexual functioning and, 423, 425
stroke
    and family therapy and, 90
    and sexuality and, 84–85
Markkanen, T. K., 424
Marquette, C., 24
Marshall, J. C., 265
Marshall, M., 421
Marshall, M. M., 149
Marshall, R. C., 73
Martinage, D. P., 149, 421
Massive counteridentification, 232
Matarazzo, R. G., 88
Matas, M., 105
Matching Familiar Figures Test, 259, 263
Mattis, S., 43
Mauss-Clum, N., 175
Mayer, J., 10–11
Mecamylamine (Inversine), 520
Mechanie, D., 171
Medical consultants, 293
Medical history, 328
Medical system, behavior modification and, 385–86
Medication, 415. See also Pharmacology
    amnesia case and, 460–61
    cerebral embolism and, 68
    chronic pain and, 104, 108, 111–12, 115, 116, 117
        antidepressants and, 121
        detoxification and deconditioning and, 112–13
        physicians and, 124
    head injury behavioral management and, 54–55.
    memory-enhancing, 459–62
    and SCI
        for depression, 14
        for pain, 28
    sexual functioning and depression and, 425
    and stroke
        and antidepressants, 88, 154
        and sexuality, 84
Memory
    head injury and, 41, 45–46, 57–58
    pain and, 104
    Palo Alto program and deficits of, 315
    private practice rehabilitation programs and improvement of, 336

single-case design example and, 460–63
stroke and, 73, 76, 78, 89
testing and, 250, 263–68
Mendelow, D., 420
Menstruation
drug use and, 510
spinal cord injury and, 429
stroke and, 84
Mental competence, head injury and, 47–48
Merskey, H., 102–103
Methotrexate, 518
Methyldopa (Aldomet), 516
Metoclopropamide (Reglan), 524
Meyer, R. G., 119
Middle cerebral artery occlusion (stroke),
70, 486
Mikula, J. A., 148, 421
Mikulic, M., 19
Mill Hill Vocabulary Test, 43
Mini-Mental State examination, 255
Minnesota Multiphasic Personality
Inventory (MMPI), 8, 13–14, 105, 116,
140, 149, 155, 285, 302, 304, 332
Minoxidil (Loniten), 516
Mirsky, A., 256
Mishel, M. H., 351, 353
Missel, J., 16–17, 27
Mitchell, D. M., 119
Mitchell, D. R., 119
Mitchell, K. R., 120
Mitra, S. B., 443, 444
Monoamine oxidase inhibitors, 510
Montebello Center Spinal Cord Unit
(Baltimore), 17
Mooney, D., 119
Moore, B. E., 227
Moos, R., 146
Morgan, B., 353
Morgan, E., 346
Mortality rate
head injury, 37, 491
MS and, 494
SCI, 157–58
stroke, 65, 70, 91–92, 481, 483
Motor activity
biopotentials and, 369–70
motor control training and, 370–72
videogame therapy and, 372–75
weight shift and equilibrium training
and, 376–78
feedback and, 367
head injury and, 41–42, 366

stroke
and left hand deficit in, 72
limb apraxia and, 80–81
middle cerebral artery occlusion
and, 70
vertebrobasilar stroke and, 71
Motor deterioration in hemiplegia, 368–69
Motor skill acquisition, feedback and,
367–68
Motor vehicle accidents
head injury and, 491
SCI and, 474
Mourning (family adaptation system),
179–80
Mueller, A., 8
Multilingual Aphasia Examination, 265
Multiple baseline single-case design
(intervention assessment), 457–59, 462–67
Multiple sclerosis, 199, 494–95
denial and, 141
Muscle relaxation techniques, pain
treatment and, 113–14
Mustonen, V. A., 424
Muthard, J. E., 444
Mylanta, 520
Myocardial infarction, denial and, 135

Nagler, B., 13
Najenson, T., 421
Narcissistic patients, 204
Narcissistic vulnerability, staff and, 231–32
Nathanson, M., 139
National Head Injury Foundation, 56
National Head and Spinal Cord Injury
Survey, 491
National Institute of Mental Health, 444
National Institute of Neurological and
Communicative Disorders and Stroke
(NINCDS), 101, 102
National Sex Forum (in San Francisco),
432
National Task Force on Sex and Disability
(of the American Congress of
Rehabilitation Medicine), 432
Neal, P. J., 353
Neglect (unilateral), 75–76
Negotiation (behavior modification
program), 398
Nehemkis, A., 15, 16, 158
Neurobehavioral consequences of head
injury. *See* Head injury, neurobehavioral
consequences of

Neuroleptics, 510
Neurological deficits
  denial and, 138, 139
  stroke and, 67, 71-72, 74, 92
Neurological lesions, depression and, 148
Neurologic history, 327-28
Neurology (Palo Alto program), 302-303
Neuromuscular disability, depression and,
  151
Neuropsychological assessment. See also
  Assessment; names of specific programs
  approaches to, 249-50
  insights gained from, 247-49
  nonstandard procedures and, 250-52
  private practice programs and, 330-33,
    340
  reassessment indications and, 253-54
  sexuality and, 422
  tests for
    attention/concentration, 254-56
    constructional ability, 268-69
    higher cognitive functions, 269-71
    language, 257-59
    memory, 263-68
    perception, 259-63
    psychomotor functions, 256-57
    scores and, 252-53
Neuropsychological rehabilitation program
  of the Brain Injury Rehabilitation Unit
  (BIRU) at the Veterans Administration
  Medical Center. See Brain Injury
  Rehabilitation Unit program (Palo
  Alto Veterans Hospital)
Neuropsychological rehabilitation program
  (Oklahoma City Presbyterian Hospital)
  medical consultants and, 293
  methods of intervention in
    cognitive group therapy, 287-89
    cognitive retraining, 286-87
    group psychotherapy, 289-91
    independent supervised therapy, 292
    individual therapy, 291-92
    milieu meeting, 292
    relative groups, 292-93
    staff meeting, 292
  outcome measure improvements and,
    294-96
  overview of, 281-82
  patient selection, 284-86
  staff development and, 293-94
  treatment rationale and philosophy and,
    282-84

Neuropsychologist, 248, 249-50
  Palo Alto program and, 299-300
  private practice and, 323-24
Neuropsychology (Palo Alto program), 302
Neuroradiology (Palo Alto program), 304
Neurosensory Center Comprehensive
  Examination for Aphasia, 257, 265
Newcombe, F., 259, 265
Newman, R., 116
New Options program (social skills
  training), 354
Newton, N., 265
New York University Institute of
  Rehabilitation Medicine, 44, 48-49, 52,
    93, 352, 366
Nichelli, P., 266
Niederland, W. G., 225
Nietzel, M. T., 445
Nielson, W., 15
Nigeria, SCI study of paraplegics and
  quadriplegics in, 19-20
Nonsteroidal anti-inflammatory drugs
  (NSAID), 517-18
Northcraft, G. B., 347
Nortriptyline, 154
Notterman, Joseph M., 372
Novack, T. A., 149
Nursing home, stroke patient and, 91, 92
Nwuga, V., 19
Nyquist, R., 15, 158

Occupational therapy
  brain-based deficits and, 249
  pain treatment program and, 113, 122
  Palo Alto program and, 303
  paraprofessionals and, 439-40
O'Donnell, J., 17
Oltman, P. K., 260
Operant pain concept. See also Pain
  avoidance and, 108-109
  modeling of pain behavior and, 109
  pain behavior and, 106-107
  positive reinforcement and, 108
  treatment and, 109-110
    behavior analysis and, 110-111
Orientation (Palo Alto program), 312
Ornstein, P. H., 234
Orthopedic disabilities, depression and, 151
Osborne, D. P., 267
Osterrieth, H., 259-60
Ostreicher, H., 265
Oxybutynin (Ditropan), 520

Paced Auditory Serial Addition Test, 255
Pain
 chronic
  analgesics and, 513
  characteristics of, 102–106
  defined, 101, 102–103
  effective treatment components and,
   120–23
  medication and, 104, 108, 111–112,
   115, 116, 117, 121
   detoxification and, 112–113
  multidisciplinary treatment concept
   and, 109–115, 118
  new directions in treatment of, 123–25
  operant pain concept
   avoidance and, 108–109
   modeling of pain behavior and, 109
   pain behavior and, 106–107
   positive reinforcement and, 108
  overview of, 101–102
  physical examination and, 103–104
  prevention and, 124
  treatment outcome studies and, 115–20
 counterprojection and, 215
 head injury and, 40
 spinal cord injury and, 7, 28
Painter, J. R., 116, 117
Palo Alto Veterans Administration Medical
 Center program. *See* Brain Injury
 Rehabilitation Unit program (Palo
 Alto Veterans Hospital)
Paralysis. *See* Hemiplegia, Paraplegics;
 Quadriplegics
Paraplegics
 resocialization of, 349–50
 SCI and, 4, 6, 8, 15, 18, 19–20, 22
 stroke and spastic, 70
Paraprofessionals
 compared with professionals, 437–38
 ethical issues and, 445–46
 historical overview on, 439–41
 organizational model and, 442
 recommendations for rehabilitative
  agencies and, 446–49
 research on, 443–445
 roles of, 441–42
 selection of, 442–43
 status of, 441–43
 training and, 443
Parise, M., 119
Parkinson's disease, drug use and, 513–14,
 524

Patients
 complaints about staff and, 222–23
 guilty, obsessional, 206–208
 hyperindependent, 204–205
 identification with, 232
 the "likeable," 209–210
 moral masochist, 205–206
 narcissistic, 204
 Palo Alto Veterans Hospital program
  and, 301
 Presbyterian Hospital program and
  choice of, 284–86
 private practice and history of, 322–30
 schizoid, 208–209
 types of, 473
Patient's past, importance of, 192–96
Patient's projections, staff avoiding
 becoming object of, 196–97
Patient/staff interaction. *See* Staff/patient
 interaction
Patient transferences, staff distress and,
 230
Peabody Picture Vocabulary Test, 258
Pearlson, G. D., 150, 153
Peck, E. T., 148
Peer counseling, 438
Peer support groups (social skills program),
 352
Penile implant, 428–29
Perception tests, 259–63
Perceptuomotor dysfunction, head injury
 and, 46–47
Permission, Limited Information Specific
 Suggestions, and Intensive Therapy
 (PLISSIT), 431
Personality
 behavior modification and assessment
  of, 391
 disability and changes in, 281, 290, 294
 premorbid SCI, 8–9, 24
 SCI and disorders of, 27–28
Peters, B. H., 460, 461
Peth, P. R., 443
Petty, F., 145
Phantom sensations, 137
 SCI and, 7
Pharmacology. *See also* Medication
 antibiotics, 501
 anticoagulants, 519–20
 antirheumatic drugs, 517–19
 cardiovascular medications
  antianginal agents, 517

antiarrhythmics, 516–17
antihypertensives, 516
digitalis, 516
diuretics, 515
central nervous system drugs
analgesics, 512–13
anticonvulsants, 510–12
antidepressants, 14, 88, 121, 154, 425,
508–509
antiparkinsonian agents, 513–14
antipsychotics/neuroleptics, 510
ethanol, 508
hypnotics and anxiolytics, 507–508
defined, 501
gastrointestinal drugs, 520–24
principles of
absorption, 502–503
adherence, 505
biotransformation, 504
concentration of drugs and, 501–502
distribution and, 503
drug abuse and, 506–507
drug function and, 501
excretion and, 503–504
side effects and, 505
special considerations, 505–506
respiratory medications, 514–15
spinal cord injury and, 520
Phelps, G., 350
Physiatrist, pain treatment and, 110
Physical environment assessment, 333–34
Physical examination, pain and, 103–104
Physical problems
with head injury, 38–39
with SCI, 4–8
Physical reconditioning, pain treatment
and, 122
Physical therapy (Palo Alto program), 303
Piasetsky, E., 269
Picciotto, S. R., 347
Plasma drug levels, 502, 503
Popkin, S., 251
Porch Index of Communicative Abilities,
257
Positron emission tomographic (PET)
scanning, 304
Potassium, 515
Power, P., 171, 172, 176
Pratt, C., 10–11
Premorbid level of function, 252
Premorbid personality characteristics. See
also Personality

disability superimposed on, 203–210
SCI and, 8–9
staff/patient conflict and, 192–96
Presbyterian Hospital rehabilitation
program. See Neuropsychological
rehabilitation program (Oklahoma
City Presbyterian Hospital)
Pressure sores, SCI patients and, 158, 159
Previdi, P., 266
Price, M., 158
Price, T., 251
Price, T. R., 147, 150, 151, 153
Prigatano, G. P., 49, 57, 139, 143, 149, 267
Primary Mental Abilities test, 251
Private practice cognitive rehabilitation
programs
assessment process
and patient history
of current problems, 328–30
of medical/psychiatric background,
328
of neurologic background, 322–28
and physical and social environment,
333–34
and secondary problems, 334–35
and testing, 330–33
computer-assisted procedures and,
337–40
overview of, 323–24
private practice environment and, 324–25
therapist-directed procedures and, 335–37
Problem Solving Rehabilitation Program
(I and II), 339–40
Problem-solving skills, 287
head injury and deficits in, 47
private practice therapy and, 336–37
Propantheline, 520
Prosthetic devices and training, 488–90
Prugh, D. G., 134, 142
Pseudobulbar affect, 83
Psychiatric history, 328
Psychiatric staffing, staff distress and,
239–40
Psychiatry (Palo Alto program), 303
Psychic trauma, staff and, 225–26
Psychological adjustment to SCI
adjustment theories and concepts and,
8–12
behavioral changes and, 21–22
depression and, 9, 12–15, 17, 25, 27, 28,
154–60
mental health professionals and, 3–4

physical problems and, 4–8
problems following, 12–17
sensory changes and, 5–6
services and, 23–27
social and interpersonal factors and, 17–21
special problems involved in, 27–30
work and, 22–23
Psychological change, pain and, 105, 110, 111
Psychological factors, denial of, 138, 139
Psychological intervention, staff/patient conflict and, 187–88
Psychological interview. *See* Team Attended Psychological Interview (TAPI)
Psychological learning, staff and resistance to, 227
Psychological status (staff), 230–31
Psychologist
behavior modification and, 387
SCI and, 3–4
Psychomotor functions tests, 256–57
Psychophysiologic disruptions (between disabled and nondisabled), 347
Psychosocial consequences of stroke
depression, 82–83, 148, 150–54
emotional reactions and, 81–82
sexuality and, 84–85
social factors and, 83–84
Psychosocial history (Palo Alto program), 304
Psychostimulants, behavioral management in head injury and, 54
Psychotherapy group (Presbyterian Hospital program), 289
"Punch-drunk syndrome," 493
Punishment, behavior modification and, 391–92, 400
Purdue Pegboard Test, 256–57

Quadriplegics, 137, 196, 209
SCI and, 6, 14, 15, 16, 20, 22

Rabbitt, P., 251
Randt, Clark, 459
Randt, C. T., 267
Randt Memory Battery, 265
Ranitidine (Zantac), 520
Rao, K., 147, 150, 153
Rap group (Palo Alto program), 314
Rappaport, M., 42

Rapprochement (family adaptation system), 180
Raskin, E., 260
Rathus Assertiveness Schedule, 350
Rau, M. T., 73
Raven Progressive Matrices (standard or colored) test, 43, 251, 261, 262, 269
Ravenscroft, K., 147
Raymond, P. M., 152
Reality orientation, head injury and, 41
Redden, J., 142
Reding, M., 153
Reglan (metoclopramide), 524
Regression, 198–99
Rehabilitation. *See names of specific disabilities and programs, i.e.,* Brain Injury Rehabilitation Unit program (Palo Alto Veterans Hospital); Private practice cognitive rehabilitation programs, *etc.*
Rehabilitation Act of 1973, 447
Rehabilitation Counselor Training Program (University of Georgia), 448
Rehabilitation Indicators Project (New York University), 352
Rehabilitation Services Administration (RSA), 440, 441
Reinforcement, behavior modification and social, 395, 396
Reinforcement (pain behavior), 108, 113
Reinhardt, L., 116, 118, 120
Reitan, R. M., 149
Relaxation techniques
pain treatment and, 113–114
Palo Alto program and, 314
Religious dogma, 200–202
Renshaw, D. C., 425
Research
brain damage, 147
head injury and, 38
pain outcome, 115–20
paraprofessionals and, 443–45
SCI and, 4, 5, 14
adjustment and, 10
depression and, 25
sexual functioning and, 7–8
single-case experimental design, 453–56, 467–68
design strategies and, 456–59
detailed examples and, 459–67
social skills for disabled and, 360–61
stroke, 88, 89

Research Diagnostic Criteria (RDC), 155
Respiratory complications in SCI, 477–78, 479
Respiratory pharmacology, 514–15
Responsibility
    paraprofessionals and, 445–46
    staff accepting limited, 236
Rey, A., 259
Rey Auditory Verbal Learning Test, 265
Rheumatic heart disease, cerebral embolism and, 68
Richards, J., 7, 155
Richardson, S. A., 346
Rimel, R., 57, 493
Risk factors (cerebrovascular accident), 483
Roberts, A., 115, 116, 118, 120
Robins, A. H., 151
Robinson, A. L., 270
Robinson, R., 251
Robinson, R. G., 147, 148, 150, 151, 152, 153
Rodin, G., 144
Rogers, H. J., 445
Rogers, P., 270
Rohe, D., 23, 26
Role-playing
    Presbyterian Hospital program, 288
    social skills program, 353
Romano, M. D., 353
Rose, J. E., 43
Rosenbaum, A. H., 55
Rosenbaum, M., 421
Rosenthal, M., 54, 56, 148
Rosenthal, R., 10
Ross, E. D., 148, 153, 263
Rosse, R. B., 152, 153
Rosvold, H., 256
Roueche, J. R., 139, 149
Roy, R., 105
Ruckdeschel-Hibbard, M., 152
Rudin, J., 148, 421
Rudy, T. E., 141, 146
Rush, A., 148, 153
Rusiniak, K. M., 372
Rusk Institute of Rehabilitation Medicine (New York University Medical Center), 366
Russell, E. W., 267
Ryan, M., 175

Safilios-Rothschild, C., 10
Sakinofsky, I., 15

Salomone, P. R., 444
Santee, J. L., 372
Sarason, I., 256
Sarno, M. T., 44
Sbordone-Hall Memory Battery, 338
Schachter, S., 5
Schaie, K., 251
Schapira, B., 114
Schedule For Affective Disorders and Schizophrenia (SADS/L), 155
Schenkenberg, T., 261
Schwartz, M. F., 257
Schwartz, R., 140
SCI. See Spinal cord injury (SCI)
Scialfa, C., 267
Scotti, G., 262
Scott, M. L., 263
Seiler, W., 6
Seizure, drug use and, 510–11
Seixas, E., 17
Selective disavowal, staff and conscious, 235–36
Selective Reminding procedure, 461
Self-care, stroke and, 486–87
Self-Concept Inventory, 11
Self-destructive behavior, 408. See also Suicide
    SCI and, 15–17, 27, 158–59
Self-esteem
    NRP and, 290
    patient/staff relations and, 186
    SCI, psychological adjustment and, 10–11
    staff distress and, 229
Self-knowledge, 235
Self-neglect, 202
Self-report technique (social skills program), 350–51
Seligman, M., 25
Selkowitz, B. E., 353
Sensory changes
    disability and sexual functioning and, 426
    Guillain-Barre syndrome and, 496
    SCI and, 5–6, 475
    stroke and, 70, 71
Sequential introduction and withdrawal single-case design (invervention assessment), 456–57, 459–62
Seres, J., 116
Serial Digit Learning Test, 264
Sexual functioning
    counseling and, 87, 419, 425, 431, 432
    head injury and, 52, 420–23

pain and, 107
pre- and postinjury psychosocial factors
    and, 419–20
reassessment of attitude and, 419, 432
spinal cord injury and, 7–8, 27, 425–30
staff and, 423, 430–32
stroke and, 84–85, 423–25
    counseling and, 87
training centers and, 436
Shankweiler, D., 257
Sharpley, C.F., 445
Shaw, D. A., 148
Shelley, C., 257
Shelton, J. L., 119
Shepard, M. J., 134, 135, 141
Sherman, B., 158
Sherrington, C. S., 367
Shinar, D., 150
Shipley-Hartford test, 253
Shipley Institute of Living Scale, 258, 269
Shontz, F., 7, 135
"Sickness" role, pain and, 107
Side effects (drug), 505
Siller, J., 12–13
Silver, B., 119
Silverman, J., 28
Simultaneous treatment single-case
    design (intervention assessment), 457
Singer, J., 5
Single-case experiment design. *See*
    Assessment of intervention (single-case
    experimental design)
Sinyor, D., 151, 152
Sjogren, K., 424, 425
Skinner, B. F., 462
Sleep problems
    central nervous system drugs and, 507–508
    pain and, 104, 111
    SCI and, 17, 28
Smirni, P., 266
Smith, A., 254
Sobey, F., 444
Social environment assessment, 333–34
Social factors
    change and, 383
    head injury and, 39, 41, 55–56
    NRP and, 288
    pain behavior analysis and, 107
    private practice programs and, 328, 333–34
    SCI and, 17–21
    stroke and, 83–84
        family and, 91

Social reinforcement, 395, 396
Social Security Administration, 102
Social skills program
    evaluation methods
        behavioral measures and, 351–52
        self-report techniques and, 350–51
        outcome studies and research and, 352,
            360–61
    program for
        approaching potential class members
            and, 355–56
        consumer groups and staff and, 355
        equipment and setting of, 356–57
        preparation for classes in, 357
            first class and, 358–59
        process considerations and, 357–58
    social consequences of disability
        attitude toward disability and, 345–46
        nondisabled individuals and, 346–48
        rehabilitation and, 348–50
        social skill categorization and, 348
    training in, 352–55
"Social Skills for the Spinal Cord Injury
    Patient" (videotape), 357
Soldiers Rehabilitation Act of 1918, 439
Spain Rehabilitation Center, 360
Spasticity, 369
    antispastic agents and, 520
Spectacular and impulsive confabulations,
    stroke and, 73
Speech disorders, 44. *See also* Aphasic
    syndromes
Speech therapy (Palo Alto program), 303
Spinal Cord Injury Assertion Questionnaire
    (SCIAQ), 351
Spinal cord injury (SCI)
    acute care period and, 477–78
    anatomy and pathophysiology and, 474–75
    behavioral changes and, 21–22
    behavior modification and, 412
    complications and, 478–79
    denial and, 135, 140–41
    depression and 9, 12–15, 17, 25, 27, 28,
        154–60
    drug considerations, 505–506, 520
    emotional problems following
        adjustment to disability, 23–26
        alcohol and drug abuse, 17
        depression, 12–15
        suicide and self-destructive behavior,
            15–17
    epidemiology of, 473

fertility and, 427–28
functional significance of level of injury
    and, 479–81
hope and, 143
mental health professionals and
    rehabilitation and, 3–4
psychological adjustment to, 8–12
psychological services (adjustment to
    disability) and, 23–27
psychophysiologic consequences of, 4–8
sexual functioning and, 7–8, 27, 425–30
signs and symptoms of, 475–77
social and interpersonal factors
    cultural context, 19–20
    independent living, 20
    marital and family relationships and,
        17–19
    medical and rehabilitation services
        and, 19
    societal attitudes and, 20–21
social skills and, 346, 354, 355, 357
special problems of
    brain injury, 29
    chemical dependency, 28–29
    community re-entry, 30
    education and support for family
        and, 29
    pain and, 7, 28
    personality disorders, 27–29
    self-destructive behavior, 15–17, 27
    treatment program structure and, 29–30
staff and, 230
stage theory and, 9–10, 155
transport problems and, 477
vocational impact of 22–23
Splinting, SCI and, 480
Spreen, O., 254, 260
Springer, C., 153
Sprock, J., 133
Squires, N., 251
Stabbing, 474
Staff distress and catastrophic illness. See
    Catastrophic illness and caregiver distress
Staff/patient interaction
    denial and, 133–34, 136, 138, 142, 143,
        144
    depression and, 133–34, 159, 160
    family adaptation system and, 174–75,
        176, 177, 178, 179, 180, 181
Team Attended Psychological Interview
    (TAPI)
    goals in, 187–88

procedures in, 188–90
reasons requested, 191–92
staff patient difficulties
    disability-related, 197–203
    non-disability related, 192–97
    premorbid character pathology,
        203–210
teaching concepts
    counterprojection and, 214–16
    projective identification and, 212–14
    time framework and, 210–12
Staff transference, 231
Stage theories of adjustment
    SCI and, 9–10, 155
    staff and patients with painful
        psychologic states and, 133–34
Standard Problem List (BIRU of Palo
    Alto), 308–310
Starr, L., 151
Starr, L. B., 147
State/Trait Anxiety Inventory, 155
Stauffer, E., 158
Stephenson, G. R., 138, 141, 143
Sternback, R. A., 106
Steroids, multiple sclerosis and, 495
Stick Test (Parietal Lobe Battery), 268
Stilson, D. W., 270
Stoner, E., 17
Storandt, M., 264
Stress
    denial and, 140
    pain treatment and reduction of, 113–14,
        119
    staff distress and, 219
    stroke and, 85
Strobel-Kahn, F., 136
Stroke (cerebrovascular accident)
    assessment for neuropsychological
        consequences and, 247
    behavioral deficits associated with
        aphasia, 76–78
        assessment of, 81
        dementia, 74–75
        initiation lack, 74
        insight, decisions, and judgment
            deficits, 72–74
        limb apraxia, 80–81
        memory and, 78
        unilateral neglect, 75–76
        visual deficits and, 78–80
    clinical syndromes and, 484–86
    complications and, 487–88

defined, 65–66
denial and, 135, 139, 140
depression and, 82–83, 87–88, 148, 150–54
epidemiology of, 481–82
etiology of, 482–83
functional problems with, 486–87
incidence of, 65
left-brain damage and, 72–73, 75, 76, 78, 79, 80, 81, 82
neuropsychological and neurological deficits and, 67, 71–72, 271
outcome and, 89
  mortality as, 91–92
  rehabilitation and, 92–93
psychological consequences of
  depression, 82–83
  other common emotional problems, 83
  sexuality and, 84–85
  social factors and, 83–84
  treatment of
    after discharge, 91
    educational counseling and, 85–87
    family therapy and, 90–91
    individual, 87–89
regional (brain) syndromes, 65
  anterior cerebral artery occlusion, 70
  border-zone infarction, 69–70
  middle cerebral artery occlusion, 70
  vertebrobasilar stroke, 71
right-brain damage and, 72–74, 75, 78, 79–80, 81, 82, 91, 93, 263
risk factors and, 483
sexual functioning and, 84–85, 87, 423–25
somatosensory diminution and, 371
staff and, 230
types of
  cerebral embolism, 68
  cerebral thrombosis, 66–67
  hemorrhagic, 68–69, 91
  lacunar infarction, 67–68
A Stroke Family Guide and Resource (Bray and Clarke), 85
"Strokes: A Guide for the Family" (American Heart Association), 85
Strong Vocational Interest Inventory, 23
Strub, R. L., 148, 269
Studdert-Kennedy, M., 257
Stuss, D. T., 44
Substance abuse. *See* Alcohol abuse; Drug abuse
Sucralfate (Carafate), 524

Suicide, 407
  head injury and, 53, 149–150
  SCI and, 15–17, 27, 157–58
  stroke and, 83
Surgery
  pain and unnecessary, 105
  penile implant, 428–29
Surwit, R., 114
Susset, V., 152
Swisher, L., 253
Swiss Paraplegic Center (Basle), 19
Symbol Digit Modalities Test, 255
Symmetrel (amantadine), 514
Syringomyelia, 200
Szetela, B., 148, 152

Tabbador, K., 43
Tagamet (cimetidine), 520
Tamkin, A. S., 260
Tardive dyskinesia, 510, 524
Tartaro, Thomas, 459
Taylor, C. B., 121
Taylor, G., 13–14
Taylor, S. E., 244
Team Attended Psychological Interview (TAPI), 185
  goals in, 187–88
  procedures in, 188–90
  reasons requested, 191–92
  staff/patient difficulties
    disability-related, 197–203
    non-disability-related, 192–97
    premorbid character pathology and, 203–210
  subjects in, 191
  teaching concept analysis and, 210–16
Teasdale, G., 43, 420
Tennessee Self-Concept Inventory, 11
Tests for neuropsychological assessment. *See* Neuropsychological assessment, tests for; *names of specific tests*
Teuber, H., 262
Texas Institute of Rehabilitation and Research, 354
Theobald, D., 119
Thiazide diurectics, 515
Thomas, M., 105
Thom, D., 13
Thompson, M., 157
Thoreson, R. W., 442, 443
Three-Dimensional Constructional Praxis, 268

Thrombi (blood clots), 482
Thrombophlebitis, SCI and, 479
Thrombotic infarction, 483
Thurstone, L., 260
Tiffin, J., 257
Timming, R., 117
Todress, I. D., 137, 138
Token Test, 257
Traction, SCI and, 477
Trail-Making Test, 255, 257
Tranquilizers. *See also* Medication;
  Pharmacology
  chronic pain and, 104, 116
  head injury behavioral management
    and, 54
Transference
  induced, 240
  patient, 230
  staff, 231
Transient ischemic attacks (TIAs), 483
Transport, SCI and improper, 477–78
Trauma, staff and continuous, 228
Traumatic head injury. *See* Head injury
Treatment. *See also names of specific
  disabilities*
  of chronic pain
    effective components of, 120–23
    evaluation and, 110–12
    follow-up and, 115
    new directions in, 123–25
    outcome and, 115–20
    treatment phase and, 112–14
  cognitive-behavioral approach to
    counseling and, 26
  denial management and, 142–44
  Guillain-Barre syndrome and, 496
  head injury
    behavioral intervention and, 53–55
    cognitive remediation and, 48–49
    medical aspects of, 492
    recovery progression and, 39–43
  MS and, 495
  rehabilitation staff and, 229
  single-case experimental design and,
    453–56, 467–68
    design strategies and, 456–59
    detailed examples of, 459–67
  spinal cord injury
    depression and, 156–57
    pain and, 28
    sexual activity and, 7
    structure of, 29–30

stroke
  depression and, 153–54
  outcomes and, 91–93
  of psychological consequences,
    85–91
Treatment contracts, behavior management
  and, 399, 400–401
Tricyclics, 508
Trieschmann, R., 4, 8, 10, 19, 23, 135,
  145, 157, 159, 160
Truax, C. B., 444
Turk, D., 141, 146, 171
Tweedy, J., 247
Tyre, T., 117

Ulcers, gastrointestinal drugs and, 520–24
Ullman, M., 139
Uncertainty, staff distress and, 229
Unconsciousness
  head injury and, 39–41, 492
  stroke and, 69, 91, 92
Unemployment, chronic pain and, 105, 123
Unilateral neglect, stroke and, 75–76
University of Minnesota, 115–16
Urinary tract infections, SCI and, 478

Van Allen, M. W., 255
Vandenburg, W., 494
Van Horn, Elizabeth, 355
VanZomeren, A., 45, 494
Varney, N., 81, 254
Vash, C., 9, 11
Vaughan, H. G., 257
Vauhkonen, V., 53, 149
Verbal Concept Attainment Test (VCAT),
  270
Vertebrobasilar stroke, 71
Veteran's Administration Medical Centers
  social skills programs, 355
Videogames
  Palo Alto program and, 317–19
  single-case experimental design and, 457
  therapeutic feedback, 372–75
Videotapes
  Presbyterian Hospital program and, 289
  social skills program and, 354, 356–57,
    360
Villardita, C., 266
Viney, L. L, 136
Violon, A., 109
Virginia Mason Medical Center Pain
  Program, 102, 105

Vistaril (hydroxyzine), 507
Visual cancellation tasks, 255
Visual constructional deficits, 81
Visual Form Discrimination test, 259
Visual neglect
    stroke patient and, 86–87
    testing and, 250
Visuospatial dysfunction
    head injury and, 46–47
    stroke and, 78–80
Vocational counseling, pain treatment
    and, 113
Vocational rehabilitation. *See* Employment
Von Salzer, C., 13
Voshart, K., 144
Vulnerabilities (staff hidden), 230–33

Wacker, D., 351
Waller, D. A., 137, 138, 144
Waller, J. A., 73
Walsh, K. W., 254
Warner, R. W., 444
Warrington, E. K., 261
Watson, R. T., 140
Wechsler Adult Intelligence Scale-Revised
    test, 250, 251, 252, 253, 255, 258, 260,
    261, 264, 268, 269–70, 285, 302
Wechsler, D., 252
Wechsler Memory Scale, 265, 267, 302
Weight shift training, 376–78
Weinberg, J., 255, 261, 269
Weiner, M. F., 146
Weinstein, E. A., 137, 421
Weisman, A. D., 138, 143
Welkowitz, J., 453
Wepman, J. M., 143
Westbrook, M. T., 136
Western Aphasia Battery, 265
Wheelchairs
    electric, 480
    societal attitudes toward disability
        and, 21
White, R. G., 120

Wiggins Hostility Scale, 156
Wilcox, N., 158
Wildfogel, G. B., 351
Wilkinson, J., 353
Willems, R., 114
Williamson, D., 119
Williamson-Kirkland, T. E., 117
Wilmot, C., 5
Wilson, R., 252
Winnick, H. Z., 225
Wisconsin Card Sorting Test (WCST), 270,
    271
Withdrawal
    drug use and, 507
    pain and detoxification schedule and,
        112–13
Witkin, H. A., 260
Wittkower, E., 13
Wood, F., 149
Woodforde, J. M., 58
Wood, R. L., 54, 422
Work. *See* Employment
World Health Organization (WHO),
    drug abuse and, 507
Wolfe, T. L., 423
Wortman, C., 12
Wright, B., 8, 10
Wright, G. N., 441
Wrightson, P., 58
Wright, T. J., 353
Wynne-Jones, M., 15

Yospe, L., 116
Young J., 5

Zager, R., 24
Zangwill, O. L., 283, 294
Zantac (ranitidine), 520
Zappala, G., 266
Zazula, M. A., 43
Ziegler, E., 140
Zlutnick, S. I., 121